k mg
10/83

£2.50

Penguin Education
Introducing Social Psychology

D0414562

Introducing Social Psychology

Edited by Henri Tajfel
and Colin Fraser

Penguin Books

Penguin Books Ltd, Harmondsworth,
Middlesex, England
Penguin Books, 625 Madison Avenue,
New York, New York 10022, U.S.A.
Penguin Books Australia Ltd, Ringwood,
Victoria, Australia
Penguin Books Canada Ltd, 2801 John Street,
Markham, Ontario, Canada L3R 1B4
Penguin Books (N.Z.) Ltd, 182–190 Wairau Road,
Auckland 10, New Zealand

First published 1978
Copyright © Henri Tajfel and Colin Fraser, 1978
All rights reserved

The acknowledgements on page 10 constitute an extension of this copyright page.

Made and printed in Great Britain by
Hazell Watson & Viney Ltd,
Aylesbury, Bucks
Set in Monotype Times

Contents

6 Contents

Part Three **Representations of the Social World**

8 Contents

Acknowledgements

The editors and publishers wish to thank the following for permission to use copyright material:
Academic Press, Dr E. E. Jones and Dr K. E. Davis for Figure 11, from *Advances in Experimental Psychology*, vol. 2, 1965, edited by L. Berkowitz; Academic Press and Dr Gary Yukl for Figure 16, from *Organizational Behaviour and Human Performance*, 6, 1972; International Universities Press, Inc., for Figure 3, from *Journal of the American Academy of Child Psychiatry*, 9, 1, January 1970; McGraw-Hill Book Company for Figure 10, from *Individual in Society*, by D. Krech and others, 1962, and Figure 13, from *Psychology, a Study of a Science*, vol. 6, 1963, edited by S. Koch; and the Society for Research in Child Development, Inc., for Figure 4, from *Child Development*, 40, 1969.

Parts of Chapter 15, 'Language in Society', are a modified version of a paper by J. A. Fishman which appeared in *Revista Interamericana de Psicologia*, 2, 1973. The material is used with the permission of the publishers.

Preface

Like many other social and human sciences, social psychology has been in turmoil in recent years. The 'identity crisis' and soul searching which are now so prominent are the result of recent social changes and the intellectual questioning that went with them. The easy optimism of the years of 'growth' and relative affluence has gone. During the last decade or so, there were many good reasons for questioning not only the achievements of technology but perhaps even more so the achievements and promises of social analysis which always lagged far behind technology. The students in many countries were amongst the first – in the late sixties – to start upsetting the apple-cart and to ask of their teachers a large number of highly un-. comfortable questions.

In the social and human sciences this had led to many new developments, some of them – in our view – 'good' and some 'bad'. One must place in the first category an increasing awareness amongst social psychologists (and others) that they should have something meaningful to say about social reality rather than remain confined to what has been called the 'rat-infested ivory towers'. But these new urges, desires, requests and demands also had some negative effects on the development of social psychology. Prominent amongst these was the rapid flux of fads and fashions, some of them come and gone at bewildering speed. Common to many of them was (and still is) an insistent demand that social psychology – or any other kind of psychology – should be concerned with the 'whole human individual'; anything less than that is seen as a waste of time and effort. These requests have rarely been accompanied by articulate suggestions as to how this undoubtedly desirable synthesis could be achieved; or by useful indications as to what might be the rational procedures which would guide our steps in the march towards the promised land of 'wholeness'. 'Social relevance' cannot be achieved by abandoning systematic theoretical analysis. As Kurt Lewin once said, there is nothing as practical as a good theory. 'Human relevance', in turn, cannot be achieved if all we do is to state the unquestionable truths that each human individual is unique, that this uniqueness is our most valued asset, and that, when we describe or analyse some selected parts of it, we are bound to neglect some others. Despite all these truths, nothing very useful can ever come from attempts to construct a social psychology based on the suggestion that the most suitable sub-title for a book on the subject would be something like 'life in general'.

This book could not claim to live up to such a subtitle. On the other hand, it does try to take into account, both in the selection of its themes and in their treatment, some of the justified criticisms of the wilder irrelevancies of social psychology. Many of these criticisms have been rightly directed at the predominant use of experimental methods in the study of social behaviour. Our view of these criticisms is a simplistic one: some experiments are bad and some are good. Which of the two they are does not depend upon the use of experimental methods *as such*. The major advantages of experiments are in the relative simplicity of their logic and results; these are also their major disadvantages, since only too often simplicity turns into blatant over-simplification (see the last part of chapter 1). Experiments can be useful in our attempts to understand social behaviour, or they can end up as a useless travesty of it. Success or failure depend largely upon the quality of ideas (or theories) from which an experiment derives. Good ideas (or interesting theories) often lead to experiments which expand our knowledge and provide new *hints* about the texture of our social life; trivial ideas (or theories) lead to trivial or silly experiments. This simple truth applies with equal force to other methods of research in social psychology – be they field studies, naturalistic observations, or 'accounts' taken from social 'actors'. In themselves, considered just as methods, they are not a panacea for our ills; nor need they be considered, as they often are by purists, as examples of a sad disintegration of lofty 'scientific' standards of research. It is, as in the case of experiments, the quality of the ideas on which they are based which decides in the end whether they are valuable or largely devoid of interest.

It will be clear from what has just been said why we adopted in this book an eclectic approach to methods of social psychology. We have been less eclectic in our choice of themes. After a presentation, in Part One, of the social, biological and cross-cultural perspectives on the subject, we go on, in Part Two, to a discussion of the major aspects of human social behaviour as it is displayed in direct ('face-to-face') interactions between individuals. We start with an account of the early development of these interactions, followed by a description of the processes of communication, verbal or not, which are involved in all human transactions. When human beings meet or co-exist, a crucial feature of their relationship is whether they compete or cooperate as individuals. A chapter on this subject is followed by two chapters which discuss the next stage of face-to-face human interactions: small groups, their structure and leadership, their 'processes and products'.

Human social behaviour is what it is because we are thinking animals, even if 'thinking' is by no means co-terminous with 'rational'. Human social activities are guided by our attempts to understand the social environment and by the 'models' of it that we create inside our heads. This modelling is the subject of Part Three of this book which, in its four chapters, progresses from images we form about other individuals to the general processes of the formation and change of attitudes, to our 'models' about the society at large. These wider conceptions about social reality are reflected and displayed in behaviour in large-scale social settings which is discussed in Part Four.

We have tried to adopt a *social* perspective on social psychology. This is reflected in three features of the book. The first of these derived from a decision that, in a subject which is as wide and unwieldy as social psychology, something had to give, to be left out. We feel that, although individual differences between people and the development and functioning of their personalities are fundamentally important subjects in their own right, they are not the main focus of interest for the study of social behaviour and experience. Our main interest as social psychologists is not in what makes *individuals* differ from each other. It is rather in those aspects of the interaction between people and their social environments, small or large, which contribute to the social *sharing* of behaviour and experience, and of the meaning of both.

We have thus devoted a large part of the book to social interaction between individuals. A good deal of understanding about these interactions has been achieved with the help of traditional theories and methods of social psychology. Our second decision was not to seek novelty at all costs. We have included in the book many of the 'traditional' theories and findings which appear to us to retain their validity and interest.

Our third decision was based on our wish to achieve a sensible balance in presenting the subject. Most of social psychology, both 'traditional' and 'new', is still today almost entirely devoted to inter-actions between individuals. Very little of it is concerned with the relationships that exist between individual or inter-individual be-haviour on the one hand, and its large-scale social settings on the other. We explain in the Introduction to Part Four why we feel that this is a narrow and one-sided approach to the subject. In this book we try to redress the balance by devoting a large section (Part Four) to general discussions about various crucial aspects of the 'interface' between social behaviour in inter–individual or small group settings and society at large.

This book is a common enterprise of its several authors, and – as its editors – we owe a very large debt of gratitude to our contributors for their patience, tolerance and willingness to write, re-write, expand and delete. One important and unacknowledged contributor to the book is the University of Bristol which decided, in the mid sixties, to foster and encourage the development of social psychology within its department of psychology. Of the seventeen chapters in this book, eleven and a half were written by people who are working, or have worked, as social psychologists in Bristol University in the last eight or nine years.

Lesley Singleton and Barbara Firth typed and retyped the in-creasingly unwieldy manuscripts and increasingly endless (or so they seemed) lists of references. Let them find here not only our ac-knowledgement of the work they have done, but also our apprecia-tion of their cheerfulness and patience in doing it.

HT
CF
February 1977

Part One
Perspectives

Introduction

As the aim of social psychology is to analyse and understand human social behaviour, it is difficult to think of any 'perspective' which is not, in some ways, relevant to it. Literature, history, the arts, social, moral and political philosophy, various conceptions of human 'nature' – from Man as an 'actor' to Man as a 'responding mechanism' – all contribute to our views about social behaviour. Therefore, in a book aiming to introduce social psychology, a selection of perspectives must be made. Our selection is reflected in two ways in this book. The three chapters of Part One reflect one set of criteria; the remainder of the book develops, in the main, *one* of these perspectives.

The three approaches to the understanding of social behaviour represented in Part One are: social psychology seen as a social science (chapter 1); social behaviour as it relates to the evolutionary history of the species (chapter 2); and social behaviour considered across the diversity of its cultural settings (chapter 3). There is a simple reason why we have chosen these three perspectives. In the short history of the attempts to create a disciplined and systematic study of human social behaviour, most of the theories and data which seem to stand up to critical inquiry, instead of emerging and submerging unpredictably in a rapid flux of fads and fashions, derive from the approaches represented in these three chapters.

Chapter 1 consists of two parts: a discussion of some of the basic problems of social psychology is followed by a critical description of the main methods used to study these problems. Social psychology is here conceived as a discipline which aims at an integration of the psychological functioning of individuals with the social settings, small and large, in which this functioning takes place. We look therefore at individual behaviour as it interacts with its social context and as it, more often than not, *derives* from that context. Most of human action is social interaction. Much of it is *created* by social interaction which shapes and modifies even those of our activities which often appear to us as individually determined. This is as true of our face-to-face interactions with others as it is of the uniformities of social behaviour displayed in the wider settings of societies at large. A description of the advantages and shortcomings of the major methods employed to study social behaviour forms the concluding part of the chapter.

The second perspective (chapter 2) considers the contribution of the evolutionary history of our species to its contemporary social behaviour. A human social being is distinctively human but he is also a social *animal*. As John Crook writes (page 54), 'very few today still consider Man closer to angels than to animals'. He discusses certain continuities of social behaviour from animals to Man, but also warns against some of the attempts at facile 'explanations' of the complexities of human social behaviour based on direct parallels with animal behaviour. The Darwinian tradition, combined with the new methods developed by the ethologists, of studying animal societies in their natural surroundings, have already provided us with important new insights into animal social behaviour. These methods have also been used to great advantage in studying some aspects of social interactions in our own species. The major questions which the ethologists ask about these interactions concern their psychological causation, their development in an individual, their function and the particular way in which this function is fulfilled. Some of the examples of the ethological analysis given in the chapter deal with crowding and population dispersion, non-verbal communication, competition and cooperation in social groups, and certain evolutionary aspects of the development of human social organization.

Chapter 3 is concerned with the understanding of human social behaviour that we can gain by considering similarities and differences between cultures. Is there a 'universal human nature', and if so, what are the features and the limitations of this universality across different cultures? Some of the data relevant to these questions come from psychological studies, but most of the information originates from field studies undertaken all over the world by social anthropologists. Gustav Jahoda tries in this chapter to establish a balance between the 'universals' (some of which relate directly to the issues discussed in chapter 2) and the impact of specific and diverse cultures. Social behaviour, as we observe it, is the product of this balance between the 'universal' and the 'culture-specific'; this is true both of individual behaviour and of certain features of social organization which affect masses of people sharing a common cultural setting of their lives.

Of the three major perspectives discussed in Part One of the book, one only is developed in its remaining parts: the integration of individual psychological functioning with its social settings. Parts Two, Three and Four are concerned, in their various ways, with several aspects of this integration. The two comparative perspectives – the evolutionary and the cross-cultural – provide a reminder that at some future time a synthesis will have to be achieved of the present studies of social behaviour with studies of its evolutionary roots and its cultural diversity. The achievement of this future synthesis is vital, both for practical and for theoretical reasons. But the aim of this book is not to present an image of social psychology as it might ideally become in the future. It sets out to present the subject as it stands at present, with its many achievements and limitations. One of the major limitations is precisely in the lack of an explicit common framework with ethology and social anthropology. A good deal of work is being done at present to build the first foundations of such a framework. But a description of this work would have to go well beyond 'introducing social psychology' as a subject in its own right. The interested reader will find in the lists of further reading at the end of each chapter in Part One many suggestions for exploring these new directions.

Chapter 1
Social Psychology as Social Science

Henri Tajfel and Colin Fraser

Looking at the 'obvious'

We are all social psychologists. The subtleties of social interaction would not be possible if we were not able to monitor, skilfully and continuously, the effects of our own and others' social actions. Throughout our lives we swiftly interpret our social surroundings and just as swiftly react to these interpretations. (Chapters 5 and 9 of this book describe some of the processes underlying these various adaptations.) But a question must inevitably arise in the mind of anyone leafing through these pages. As most of us seem to be doing so well in dealing with the complexities of our social environment, what is social psychology for and what is it about? We have all learned to handle most of the incredible variety of 'face-to-face' relationships and encounters which confront us daily. We have also acquired opinions and beliefs, likes and dislikes, attitudes of approval or disapproval concerning the wider social contexts of our lives. We have general loyalties and affiliations and general ideas about human nature, religion, justice and injustice, social stability and social change; and ideas also about the large-scale social events which affect us, such as wars, revolutions, inflation, unemployment, various systems of government, etc. On the whole, we react to these events (or sometimes contribute to creating new ones) to the best of our ability, according to our interests as we perceive them and in accordance, as far as possible, with our value judgements. We are able to be social, to survive in our social environments, because we know how to do it. What then is the need for a social psychology which, on the face of it, could only restate what we know already by making more explicit the knowledge and accumulated experience shown in our daily social behaviour?

It would not be too difficult to find examples of these 'restatements of the obvious' in the research and writings of social psychologists. This is inescapable in view of the nature of the questions they ask about social behaviour and social experience, the principal aims of social psychology being to study, as systematically as possible, various aspects of the interaction between individuals, between and within social groups, and between individuals and social systems, small or large, of which they are a part. It may be necessary to point out that much of what superficially appears obvious becomes less so on closer inspection.

Let us take an example from a well-researched area of social psychology, studies of conformity, some of which are discussed in chapter 7. People tend to be influenced to varying extents by the judgements of the overwhelming majority of a group to which they belong, even if they sometimes have good reasons for initially disagreeing with the majority's views. Some experiments have shown that an inverse relationship exists between an individual's degree of confidence in his own judgement and the extent of his 'yielding' to the majority. Many factors combine to create this degree of confidence, and one of them is the clarity of the information that an individual receives about the events or the stimuli he is asked to judge. An 'obvious' relationship can be formulated: the clearer the information, the greater will be the confidence in one's own judgement, and therefore the less 'yielding' there will be. However, we can also formulate another possible and equally obvious relationship: the *less* clear the information, the more an individual may feel that his judgement is as good as anyone else's, and therefore, the less he will 'yield' to the majority. Both the above statements are common sense, and there is no doubt that each of them is valid in *some* conditions.

It is not, however, the detailed specification of these conditions which is the real theoretical problem. The fundamental question concerns the social factors which determine whether an individual will interpret information as being 'clear' or not; to what extent, and in what circumstances, can overwhelming social consensus lead to certainties which may replace the search by individuals for their own independent information about various aspects of the world in which they live? In other words, to what extent is the very notion of 'clarity' inescapably social? The problem is not only 'theoretical'; individual, cultural, political and historical differences are often of great importance in the course of human relations and communication between individuals or between human groups. So, there are many differing social and individual versions of the 'obvious'. (See chapter 12 for a further discussion of this issue.)

Much of our behaviour can be ascribed to the exercise of our individual choices in the face of changes continuously presented to us by our environment, and in ourselves. One way to view the subject-matter of social psychology is perhaps to describe it as the study of this interaction between change and choice (cf. Tajfel, 1972). Choices and decisions we make appear to us self-determined, and indeed many of them are. It is just as true, however, that much of our behaviour derives from its social background and context, although very often we are hardly aware of this. And thus, the subjectively 'obvious' reasons or causes for doing one thing or another are like the tip of an iceberg; a great deal of what is submerged can only be properly understood if our individual choices are set against the background of their social causation.

The difficulty of doing social psychology is therefore the difficulty one has in questioning what is taken for granted, the difficulty of adopting the stance of a visitor from Mars. And yet, this is only one aspect of a two-sided dilemma. A Martian visitor would understand nothing about human social behaviour unless, in addition to his ability to ask awkward questions about the 'obvious', he also managed to have some understanding of the meaning of that behaviour to those who participate in it. Thus, a social psychologist cannot do his job properly if he relies solely on an alienated 'objective' stance; nor can he do it properly if he relies on an analysis of social behaviour consisting of simply a re-description and systematization of the accounts of their actions given him by the participants. In the first case, we would have an over-deterministic push-button image of social Man; in the second, we would deny ourselves the possibility of searching for explanations which are not accessible to subjective individual experience. The dilemma is a real one, and it is vividly illustrated in the present-day controversies about what might be the most fruitful way to undertake the analysis of human social behaviour (e.g. Berger and Luckmann, 1967; Harré and Secord, 1972; Israel and Tajfel, 1972).

Needless to say, the social psychologist cannot miraculously combine objectivity and empathy in a uniquely wise conceptual system. Like everybody else, he needs intellectual crutches. His crutches are his methods of research, which will be described in more detail later in this chapter. Social psychology is at present in a state of flux and change, and of exciting controversy. There is some argument about research methods, but even more controversial are the criteria for deciding which are the really important questions in research on human social behaviour. So let us consider the nature and selection of problems which are, have been, or should be, the major problems of social psychology.

The perspective of social psychology

Popular conceptions of human nature abound. In some of them the complexities of human social behaviour are reduced to one or another 'basic' principle, the key which will enable us to unlock the mysteries of our great achievements and great failures. In recent years we have had a rich choice of these 'basic' principles: the territorial Man, the dominant Man, the imperial Man, the aggressive Man, the hierarchical Man, the hunting Man, the carnivorous Man, and a number of other variations which all have in common the selection of one theme in human 'nature' as the explanation for much of our social behaviour. The popularity of some of these over-simplified (and strangely masculine) accounts will undoubtedly provide impetus for more to come.

Although none of these images deserves to be taken seriously, they cannot be too lightly dismissed. There are two reasons for this. The first is the popular success that some of them have enjoyed. This easy diffusion of certain ideas about human nature together with the authors' views about their presumed social 'consequences' present in themselves an interesting and important social psychological problem. Simple and unitary ideas about social and psychological causation have always been easily accepted and diffused – but this still does not explain why certain *kinds* of simple ideas catch on more widely than others: an important question.

The second and more immediately relevant reason is that Man is a creature both of his biological evolution *and* of his social and cultural development. Human social behaviour cannot be understood if its study is based predominantly on inferences from the species' evolutionary past; but neither can it be properly understood if it is assumed that this past can be forgotten (see chapter 2).

The interaction of our biological past with our cultural and social past and present is a very complex affair. The first reason for this complexity is that it is very difficult to offer a neat definition of 'social behaviour'. So a discipline such as social psychology cannot be neatly defined nowadays in terms of its *subject-matter*, which it often shares with many other disciplines. It finds its identity more clearly in concentrating on the study of particular *aspects* of a common knot of problems in which other disciplines are also interested. For example, in the field of intergroup relations, social psychologists are mainly interested: in establishing links between an individual's interpretation or perception of social situations and his behaviour and attitudes towards the groups to which he belongs and other groups; in the ways in which various kinds of intergroup situations may affect an individual's motives concerning 'ingroups' and 'outgroups', and in the ways in which certain motives may affect, in turn, the nature of these intergroup relations; in analysing the processes of communication which help or hinder the diffusion of certain modes of behaviour and attitudes towards ingroups and outgroups. There is obviously a considerable overlap between these interests and those of the other disciplines. But despite this overlap, the perspective is different in various ways from that found in sociology, anthropology or political science. The social psychologist is interested in information about how the various social structures, social systems or groups affect an individual's ways of viewing the world in which he lives and of acting in it; and about how his 'nature' (i.e., his motives, emotions, perceptions and interpretations) will in turn affect his functioning in groups and the relations between groups. Put very simply, social psychology is concerned with many of the relations between the individual and society, in particular those relations which are mediated through face-to-face interaction with others. It is also, however, concerned with the background of these interactions – their wider social and cultural context. We have referred above to human social behaviour as being the result of an interaction between 'human nature' and the social environment. One aspect of this is the effect of the social environment on certain 'basic' psychological processes such as motivation, perception, learning, thinking, memory, etc. The study of this is at the borderline between general and social psychology, and therefore will not form a major focus of interest in this book.* It will be briefly mentioned here, however, in order to highlight one of the major choices that social psychologists have to make in their study of social behaviour and experience. The question is: should we be concerned with psychological 'universals' or should we gear our theories and research towards the *specific* settings of social behaviour?

Bartlett's (1932) early work on selective remembering, in which he was able to show how the selection and modification of what is remembered may depend upon the cultural setting of the remembered material, is an early and classic example of the study of the interaction between psychological processes assumed to be 'basic' and their social setting. Another example is Witkin's (1962) work on 'psychological differentiation', followed by many studies since, which related individual modes of perceiving and interpreting certain aspects of the environment to ecological and social variables in a culture. Still in the study of perception, much work has been done to see how some marginal differences in perception (such as in the perception of geometric illusions) relate to differences in the visual environment of various human groups (e.g. Segall, Campbell and Herskovits, 1966). In the field of motivation, McClelland (e.g., 1961) initiated some twenty years ago a long series of studies on the socially determined differences between individuals or social groups in their 'achievement motivation', i.e. in the 'needs' which lead them to seek certain forms of competitive success.

The interest of much of this work has been in the comparative data it yielded; that is, comparisons between people living in different social, cultural or ecological milieux helped to assess the effects on Man's psychological functioning of his environment. It has some-

---

* Much of this material can be found in some of the earlier textbooks of social psychology, such as Secord and Backman, 1st ed., 1964; Krech, Crutchfield and Ballachey, 1st ed., 1962.

times been found that these effects are marginal, and that the basic *processes* of visual perception remain the same while the different types of information people receive about the environment may lead to different *interpretations* of what they perceive (cf. Tajfel, 1969a). The same can be said about cultural differences in the kind of material that is remembered, or even about some of the cultural or social differences in motivation. But these cautious conclusions about the marginal effects of culture or society on certain 'basic' mechanisms of Man's psychological functioning raise a number of difficult problems when we consider the more central aspects of human social behaviour. For example, it is undoubtedly true that perceptual constancies (such as our ability to perceive the size of objects as constant despite the variations in their retinal size at different distances) are not affected by our social experience or environment. Or that, although people living in different circumstances may acquire different goals, the processes underlying the learning of these goals will be roughly the same, whether they are basically social or not. However, when we are concerned with the study of social behaviour and experience, the questions we must ask will often be different. Admitting the general basic characteristics of certain psychological and physiological processes, how can we undertake a useful analysis of what people actually *do* in the social settings in which most of their lives are spent? The problem is that we shall not find appropriate answers to questions about actual social behaviour if we confine our study to these basic processes. Or rather, we shall obtain answers which are so general and so *similar* in a great variety of social situations that they will teach us very little about social behaviour.

The major problem for social psychology is therefore to chart a suitable course between two extremes. On one side lie the dangers of restricting our interests to 'fundamental' psychological processes as these are 'affected' by Man's social environment. As has just been mentioned, the outcome would be a bland and dull generality of 'laws' largely insensitive to the richness and complexity of the social settings of social behaviour. On the other hand, an emphasis on the specificity and uniqueness of each social situation presents the danger of reducing the subject to little more than a collection of detailed descriptions of unique cases. Undoubtedly, these case descriptions are often necessary and they become of paramount importance in applied social psychology, when the task is to understand, for practical purposes, the functioning of a particular social setting, such as a factory, a hospital, or a community. But this 'understanding' can be achieved only if the special cases can be related to some general principles.

The major problems of social psychology are therefore confined in an intermediate area between two extremes: too much generality and too much specificity. Parts Two, Three and Four of this book attempt to cover much of this area. Here we shall consider, in very general terms, the *kinds* of preoccupations which they represent.

Social behaviour and mutual expectations

The basic principle of human social behaviour is the convergence of mutual expectations. The development of expectations about the behaviour of others begins almost as soon as life itself (see chapter 4). It does not take long before, in a complicated symbolic ballet, I expect you to expect me to expect you (and one could go on) to do one thing or another. Reciprocity of expectations is the very stuff of social behaviour. Their development from birth to maturity in an individual, their validation or invalidation in the course of interaction with others, powerfully determines most of what we do. The ability to react in a reciprocating manner develops through interaction with others. Unless we are recluses, most of our actions are interactions; they occur in situations where we must take account of the expectations of those with whom we are interacting. Through interaction we learn about the society we live in, how to relate to it and, occasionally, how to change it. The individual rarely encounters society directly, as a disembodied abstraction; he encounters it through other people. These are some of the reasons why Part Two of this book is concerned with the diverse aspects of face-to-face interaction, though the study of face-to-face interaction does not by any means cover all of social psychology.

Let us take as an example the topic of competition and cooperation between individuals. There is no doubt that a great deal can be learned and inferred about human competition and cooperation from the study of lower evolutionary orders; also from considering in detail the learning of new skills as it is affected by the consequences following each of the responses we make. But this is not all. In the normal course of events, any act of competition or cooperation between two or more human beings is part of a long-term pattern, explicit or implicit. This pattern cannot exist without some kind of a representation or an 'image' of what the other person is like, is doing, and is likely to do; and this is as true of competition as it is of cooperation. Our 'strategies' also depend upon the image we have of the other person's image of ourselves; and so it goes on.

These sets of mutual expectations can be, and have been, subjected to systematic study. They also form the background of social behaviour in various kinds of small groups and organizations (chapters 7, 8 and 13); and also of successful communication, verbal or non-verbal, between individuals (chapter 5). The development of expectations needs to be studied with two major questions in mind. The first concerns their building up in the child as a combined function of the innate potentialities of the human organism and of its early social experience. The second question concerns the detail of the social and cognitive processes which enable us to *attribute* to others, with whom we interact, various characteristics which are relevant to their behaviour towards ourselves and our behaviour towards them. Without these attributions, our social world would remain forever unstable and unpredictable; they represent therefore one of the major forms of the individual's adaptation to his social environment. These two questions are dealt with in chapters 4 and 9.

But this is only one part of the story. We are social beings not only when we engage in face-to-face interaction with others, be it with individuals, in small groups, or in organizations. Just as we breathe whether we are alone or in company, so we remain social when we are left to ourselves. The multiple strategies of face-to-face social interaction are only possible because they are based simultaneously on two major principles which have to be combined and re-combined in every social encounter. One of these principles is that there is a predictable range of *similarity* in the social behaviour of *all* the people with whom we come in contact. In other words, assumptions about others' behaviour are based not only on their presumed individual characteristics, but also to a large extent upon the expectation that many features of social behaviour are shared within a culture, a society or a community, or even across cultures, societies or communities. In part, we act on the basis of 'implicit' theories about a common human social 'nature' based on our past experience. The other principle concerns the expectation of *differences* in the social behaviour of other people. These are of two kinds: they may be attributed to the individual characteristics of people we have come to know well; and there may also be differences attributable to the 'kind' of people they are, or we think they are.

Therefore, the course of any social encounter is affected by an interplay of three implicit 'theories' each of us has about the others who are involved: (i) the general range of social behaviour expected of everyone; (ii) the range of social behaviour expected from those in certain social categories – whether national, racial, social, professional, religious, sex or age; or in a combination of these; and (iii) the range of social behaviour we expect from a person on the basis of our specific knowledge about him as an individual. The 'specific knowledge' about an individual is of course affected by the general range of socially shared expectations, as in (i) above, and by the 'categorial' range mentioned in (ii).

Thus one of the fundamental points of departure for the study of social behaviour is that we always carry in our heads a highly complex symbolic representation of our social environment. This determines to a large extent the general nature of our expectations about the behaviour of others, and provides a continuity to our social behaviour which transcends by far the variation in innumerable face-to-face encounters. It also provides us with 'theories' of various kinds, on which we often act, about the causes and the sequences of social behaviour of other people. This applies not only to those we meet or know directly, but also to humanity at large. These 'theories' are used as a background for understanding and reacting to the large-scale social events which affect our lives, such as social conflicts of various kinds, whether war, unemployment or violence. This symbolic background to social behaviour is much more intangible than the details of face-to-face social interaction which can be directly observed. Its analysis and understanding are, however, at least as crucial for the purpose of providing a coherent account of human 'social nature' as are these intimate and minute 'surface' details. (Parts Three and Four of this book are concerned with this symbolic background of social behaviour and its reflection in wider social settings.)

Social psychology and wider social processes

In its search for a level of inquiry, neither too general nor too specific, social psychology must be concerned with understanding social behaviour both through 'basic' psychological processes and through the social systems within which this behaviour is manifested. We shall consider in this section the consequences of this interaction for the study of social behaviour.

In order to do this, we must consider once again the questions about social behaviour that are asked by various other disciplines. On the biological level, the questions tend to be about the genetic and physiological determinants of human adaptation to, and transformation of, the social environment; answers are often sought in terms of evolution and ecology, their effects on the structure of the human organism, and the effect of this structure on behaviour (see chapter 2). An example of this is the work of the ethologists on the instinctive aspects of human aggression in their relation to various forms of intraspecific aggression in other species.

The 'purely' psychological questions about the determination of social behaviour are generally of two kinds. They may be concerned with basic processes showing a clear evolutionary continuity such as conditioning, the simpler forms of human learning or the physiology of motivation. Alternatively, they may focus on those characteristics of the human species that are very different from those displayed by other species: language and other forms of symbolic communication, cognitive development, the role of inference in perception, etc. It is likely, however, that these 'higher' forms of human behaviour are possible only *because* they operate within universally human contexts of face-to-face social interaction (see chapters 4 and 5). Whether these forms of behaviour are considered as 'purely' psychological or as social psychological from the outset, they are often studied in terms of general laws of functioning, sometimes closely interacting with the biological level, and sometimes taking this level for granted as providing the range of what is *possible* in human behaviour, but not necessarily predicting the detail of what actually happens. One example is the relationship between what is known about human neurophysiological functioning, and the detailed account of the development of logical thought in the child. Although the studies of the development of logical structures must take into account what is known in neurophysiology, their results cannot be *predicted* from this knowledge. Perhaps one day such predictions will be possible, but this seems at present a very remote contingency. Meanwhile, it is obviously much more economical to gain knowledge directly through asking questions which are specific to the problems of cognitive development, and devising methods of research which are directly suitable for answering these questions (see, for example, Bruner *et al.*, 1966; Piaget, 1965).

Sociological questions about human behaviour are concerned with its determination by social, economic and political structures. The answers often include direct predictions: for example the extent of discrimination against certain social groups, such as racial minorities, is related to the economic situation of a country. Durkheim's early work on the social factors underlying the rates of suicide provides another classic example. Suicide 'was, on the face of it, the most private of acts. Explaining it, or, more precisely explaining differential suicide rates sociologically, would be (for Durkheim) a singular triumph' (Lukes, 1973, p.194).

The biological, psychological and sociological questions about human behaviour provide a background against which the kind of questions asked by social psychologists can be described. Some of them, relating to interaction between individuals, have already been discussed in the section of this chapter on reciprocity and are also exemplified in various chapters of Part Two. We shall now try to exemplify the other major preoccupations of social psychology – the symbolic representations of the social world (Part Three) and behaviour in wider social settings (Part Four).

The study of attitudes, to which chapters 10 and 11 of this book are devoted, provides a good example both of the dilemma of choice between the general and the particular and of the differences between the kind of questions asked by social psychologists and those asked by the practitioners of other disciplines. As will be seen in chapter 10, there have been many definitions of 'attitude' in social psychology. There is however general agreement about two points. The first is that attitudes can be conceived as an individual's summing up in various ways of his experience and that this summing up helps in his adaptation to the social events which he encounters; were it not for this summing up, we would have to start from scratch in deciding what to do about each new event or individual confronting us. The second point of general agreement is that, despite the many methods which have been devised to study and measure attitudes, we are often not in a position to predict *directly* an individual's social behaviour from our knowledge of his social attitudes. This is due in part to the complex relations which exist between an underlying attitude towards a person or an issue and all kinds of constraints which exist in many social situations, and which will often prevent the attitude being directly expressed in behaviour.

A distinction has already been made between three kinds of expectations: the 'general', the 'categorial' and the 'individual' (see p. 30). In the same way, the study of an individual's attitudes may be conceived as combining an understanding of: (i) the general principles – arising from the interaction between the human organism and the information it receives – which guide our gathering of information about the outside world, (ii) the *kind* of people we are dealing with and the nature of the social interactions in which they are engaged; and (iii) individual idiosyncrasies. General theories of attitude formation and attitude change are concerned, in their own way, with (i) above. If we were interested in the attitudinal differences between people of, for example, different ages, or differing cultures, or socioeconomic status, we would have to explore their special characteristics, situations, and the special kind of information they may be receiving as in (ii); and we would have to undertake a special study of individual cases if we were interested in (iii).

Let us now look at the different approaches to the study of attitudes, comparing the social psychology approach with that of 'pure' psychology or sociology. In psychology, the study of attitudes is an applied subsection of the more general principles of human learning or perhaps human processing of information. To the social psychologist such information is vital. But even in considering the first category of problems mentioned above, i.e. the general functioning of attitudes, more is needed for a *social* psychological understanding. We cannot begin to understand the functioning of attitudes in any of their social settings without knowing something about the system of values and norms in which they are embedded. Social psychology also differs from sociology; if we take human groups as defined by socio-economic status, age, or occupation, etc, it is in principle possible to relate directly many aspects of their social behaviour *as a social entity* to their position in the social, political and economic structures of which they are a part. But this is not enough. The 'objective' aspects of social situations do not function in a psychological vacuum any more than general psychological principles operate in a social void. Attitudes and values intervene between large-scale social processes and the social actions undertaken by masses of people. As will be seen in Part Three of this book, changes in attitudes are far from being a simple reflection of 'objective' events and of the information received about these events. It is not only that information is often deliberately manipulated in one way or another. The manner in which it is selected, distorted, misunderstood, invented or ignored may be crucially important in establishing links between what has 'actually' happened in the social world and the social behaviour manifested as a result. For example, inflation is primarily a socio-economic phenomenon. At the same time, there is no doubt that some of the reasons why inflation breeds more inflation can be found in its powerful psychological effect on the attitudes of millions of people. Or, to put the point more generally: some modifications in social attitudes and social behaviour may well be caused *in the first place* by processes of 'objective' social change. But once these psychological modifications are triggered off, they acquire their own momentum and, in turn, contribute to further social changes.

Part Four – social behaviour in wider settings – introduces four major topics: social behaviour in organizations; the wider psychological functions of language in society; the psychological aspects of intergroup relations; and the psychological aspects of some contemporary environmental problems.

The common denominator of these four topics is that organizations, language, group affiliations and hostilities, and environmental problems have to do with people who belong to definable social *entities*. The psychological implications of this 'sharing' of wider social settings could not be encompassed by a social psychology restricted to the study of face-to-face interaction. Indeed much of the interaction between individuals is itself powerfully affected by these wider contexts in which all social encounters are set.

It is true, of course, that the influence of these wider social contexts is to a very large extent observed, mediated, expressed and reflected in face-to-face encounters. But this does not mean that social behaviour can be understood solely on the basis of an analysis of these encounters, however detailed and minute such analysis may become – no more than one could understand the functioning of the human brain through an analysis, however complete, of the interactions between its individual cells. 'Reduction' of the study of human social behaviour to an interplay of motives, skills, strategies and cognitions displayed in face-to-face interaction would leave us with a curiously deflated image of Man as a social being. It is not that these interactions amongst individuals are unimportant or can be ignored. The point is that if we went no further in the analysis of social behaviour, we would leave out some of the most crucial aspects of its *organization*.

Our hope is to gain an understanding of certain *regularities* in social behaviour *as it actually occurs*. To pursue knowledge of regularities means that we cannot, like the novelist, rest content with insights into individual cases or situations. The results of the research which are communicated must, as far as possible, avoid or at least reduce, the idiosyncrasy of the point of view from which they originate. In the social sciences this is not always easy – some would say that it is not even possible. One can still assert that this is at least desirable and should remain one of our aims. In turn, the contents of what is communicated should be, in principle, as widely applicable as possible and as clearly predictive of future social events as they can be made to be.

The requirement of wide application must be complemented by the understanding of social behaviour as it *actually* occurs. Here again, a distinction must be made between the range of what is possible and the options' open to a person within this range. This concerns the relation between the study of general *psychological* processes and the study of social behaviour. Social behaviour is an end-product of biological, psychological and social chains of causation. The general studies of perception, learning, memory or motivation provide us with essential information about the underlying framework within which social behaviour and experience must remain; but by themselves they do not clarify what actually happens. This has been aptly expressed by Martin Richards (1974):

... biological endowment does not determine outcomes – it provides means and not ends. Human development would not be possible without a social world. This is something that is missed by theorists who argue that the infant is a social being and that his behaviour patterns such as crying or smiling constitute social behaviour. Implicit in this view is the idea that the behaviour pattern determines its own social meaning . . . In contrast to this, I would argue that the infant's behaviour pattern is of biological origin but it is made social by its recognition and interpretation by adults. Its meaning is negotiated by those who interact with the infant.

This argument about the biological origins of behaviour is valid in the case of the psychological endowment of the human organism considered outside its social context. For example, Piaget's conceptions about the moral development of the child or the later work on the same subject by Kohlberg (cf. Piaget, 1932; Kohlberg, 1964; Graham, 1972) must take into account the limits of what is possible given the development of certain cognitive structures, certain forms of learning, and certain stages of motivational functioning. But the relation of children's observed social behaviour or attitudes to moral principles and moral judgement can only be considered against the background of the *contents* of morality characteristic of a society. A moral act has no meaning, and cannot guide behaviour, outside of the real or symbolic presence of others. We can, however, go one step further; the 'others' who are actually or symbolically present are to a large extent *interchangeable*. Despite individual differences in moral judgement and behaviour, there is a basic common fund of principles without which social communication about morality would not be possible. The *general* process whereby the child progressively attains the capacity to judge his own and other people's actions in terms of principles which transcend self-interest cannot be studied, as we have already said, without the knowledge of the cognitive structures which makes this 'decentration' (see chapter 3) possible and which themselves could not have been formed without social interaction. But equally, this development cannot be studied without the knowledge (often implicit, but nonetheless always present) of the nature and structure of the general principles which are being assimilated. In one sense, individuals are no more than dispensable and replaceable channels of communication used by a culture or a society.

The important implication of this interchangeability of individuals is that it takes social psychology beyond the study of face-to-face interaction. The *social* environment of a human being consists in fact not only of other people with whom direct contacts are established. Many symbolic features of this environment remain constant despite the randomness of direct contacts. Together they amount to certain rules about the functioning of the social environment which are crucially important for individual adaptation to it. If we tried to understand human social behaviour solely on the basis of a detailed analysis of the structure of its social environment, we would end up with a social psychology of an empty organism. If we tried to understand it solely on the basis of the psychological structure of the human organism, we would be in serious danger of ending up with a social psychology of an organism functioning in an empty environment.

This is why none of the four major themes which make their appearance in Part Four are concerned with random *collections* of individuals behaving in a similar manner in similar circumstances simply because they are, in some basic ways, psychologically similar. The social psychological analysis of their behaviour takes into account the fact that those individuals are largely affected by their interaction within a wider social entity – often an 'organization' (chapter 13) – which is itself a part of an even wider social environment.

Quite obviously, language is *the* means of communication and diffusion of ideas in the society at large. Important as it may be to study non-verbal communication along with language in face-to-face interaction (see chapter 5), the wider social psychological aspects of communication must be concerned above all with 'language in society' (chapter 15), with the common social psychological functions it serves and the uses to which it is put. As will be seen in chapter 15, one of these functions relates to the division of mankind into different linguistic groups. But it would be exceedingly naïve to consider relations between human groups only in terms of similarities amongst individuals who belong to one and the same group, and their differences from individuals who belong to other groups. Any two or more human groups which are in contact within the same environment, physical or social, develop various kinds of relations – of power, competition, cooperation, superior status, inferior status, etc. It is perhaps not an exaggeration to say that the kind of relations which develop between large-scale groups (e.g. social, ethnic, religious, cultural) *define* the structure of a society. Therefore, just as in the case of face-to-face interaction we must look at the processes of inter-individual cooperation and competition (chapter 6), so in considering individuals *in* society, we must consider the psychological aspects of relations between social groups. The study of intergroup behaviour viewed in this perspective must take into account both the similarities and the differences that exist between inter-individual cooperation and competition on the one hand, and, on the other, cooperation and competition as they are manifested in intergroup behaviour (chapters 16 and 17).

The fourth major theme in Part Four also goes back, but in a very different form, to one of the issues raised in Part Two on face-to-face interaction. The discussion of small groups in terms of 'processes and products' (chapter 8) is principally concerned with what happens *inside* a face-to-face small social group. Each group has its social environment which consists of other groups and very often many of these groups must function together in a common physical environment. This interaction and some of the social psychological aspects of the ensuing 'environmental' problems are examined in chapter 14, which deals with problems posed to social entities by changes in their *physical* environment just as chapters 15, 16, 17 are concerned with the dynamics of the wider *social* environment.

*

Some alternative methods

Thus far we have attempted to characterize the nature of the social psychological individual and to draw some limits to the domain of social psychology; we have highlighted two major foci, the study of reciprocity and a concern with larger scale social processes; we have related those major problems to the organization and contents of this book. We now have some idea of the major questions which social psychology should be asking. The remainder of this chapter will consider, in general terms, some of the problems involved. What are the intellectual crutches, or methods of research, potentially available to us, and what are their strengths and weaknesses?

In attempting to find answers, the professional social psychologist will not proceed exactly as does the lay social psychologist, the man in the street with whom we started this chapter. The former will accept constraints which the latter is much less concerned about. For one thing, the social psychologist assumes his answers should be clear, consistent and comprehensive. He will aim to explain phenomena which interest him by means of theories which are explicitly formulated rather than vague or ambiguous, which avoid explaining similar events by means of contradictory principles, and which try to cover at least a moderately wide range of phenomena, rather than relying on different, *ad hoc* explanations in each slightly different situation. A second constraint is that the evidence used by the social psychologist must be open to public inspection, replicable and verifiable. It is certainly true that important new questions may be raised by personal introspection and intuition or by casual observations or second-hand reports from others, and that at various stages of inquiry when more systematic and replicable data are not available resort can usefully be made to such sources of evidence. These should not be thought of as 'last resorts', but rather as first ones. The social psychologist accepts that if arguments are to be clearly resolved and his discipline is to build cumulatively on firm foundations – in short, if he is to justify his self-description as a 'social scientist' – then, in addition to developing explicit theory he must use verifiable evidence. It is this second requirement which will concern us in the next few pages.

As a 'scientist', the social psychologist might use evidence derived from *experiments*. Notice, however, that every attempt to study behaviour in a systematic fashion is not an experiment. If we simply make careful observations of how often people crossing main roads make use of zebra crossings, we are not conducting an experiment. Similarly, if we interview one hundred people to find out their attitudes towards unemployment, we are not experimenting. We are using systematic empirical methods; but 'experiments' are not synonymous with 'empirical research', they are only a sub-class of it.

In order to carry out a piece of research which can justifiably be called an experiment, an investigator must be in a position to control what is happening. The traditional account of an experiment is that the experimenter holds constant all potentially relevant features of a situation apart from one, which he systematically varies or manipulates, and he then records the effects of this systematic variation on some likely measure. The feature of the situation which is systematically varied is called the 'independent variable' and the thing measured to detect the effects of the manipulation is called the 'dependent variable'. In fact, experiments on social behaviour can be considerably more complex than this description would suggest. If an experiment is designed in an appropriately systematic fashion, several independent variables can be manipulated in the same experiment and the effects of the different variables, together with the interactions amongst them, can be disentangled by sophisticated statistical analyses. In addition, the effects may be assessed by a number of dependent variables. (A relatively simple introduction to the design of experiments is given in chapter 2 of Crano and Brewer, 1973.)

In many studies the investigator may not wish to exert such control over the phenomena he is observing. Alternatively, for ethical or practical reasons, it may not be possible for him to do so. Thus, we can distinguish between experimental and non-experimental studies in social psychology, the latter often being called 'observational studies'. In doing so, however, it should not be thought that we are distinguishing between extreme control by the investigator in the experiment and no control at all in observational studies. Rather, we should recognize degrees of control. In experiments, independent variables may be manipulated with varying precision. In observational studies, when such manipulations are not being attempted, the investigator can impose more or less control on what he observes, when he observes, and how he observes it. In fact an array of alternative methods available to the social psychologist can usefully be thought of as lying along a dimension or continuum of control, rather than as falling into two and only two mutually exclusive categories. As is apparent from Figure 1, the high control end may be represented by the fully fledged experiment conducted in a highly controlled laboratory setting, and the low end by relatively unstructured obser-

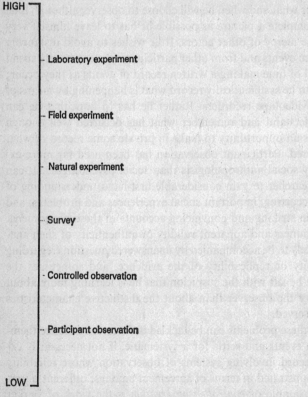

Figure 1   Alternative methods, on a dimension of control exerted by investigator

vation, with a number of additional methods variously positioned between the extremes. Let us look briefly at the distinctive features of each of the six methods in turn.

When W. F. Whyte (1955) studied American street gangs and more recently James Patrick (1973) studied gangs in Glasgow they made use of *participant observation*. Although not full gang members, these researchers observed at first hand, and took part in some of the everyday activities of the gangs. They did not aim to vary or change the phenomena they observed but simply to learn as much as they could about the activities and life-styles of the particular gangs they had access to. In participant observation, the researcher may exert some control over what and when he will choose to observe, although if he wants as complete a picture as possible he has to leave himself very much at the mercy of other actors. If he wishes to avoid distancing himself from events and from other participants, he can hardly spend a great deal of time making a written record of events as they occur; even less can he systematically record what is happening by means of audio- or videotape recorders. Rather he has to hope that he can notice, understand and remember what has occurred well enough until he has an opportunity to make in private some record of what has transpired. Participant observation has been used far more extensively by social anthropologists than social psychologists. It can allow a researcher to gain considerable first-hand understanding of naturally occurring, important social experiences and problems, and can result in striking and convincing accounts of these phenomena. But the vividness and apparent validity or authenticity of such analyses are likely to be accompanied by unanswered questions regarding the reliability or replicability of the evidence, and sometimes the reader may be left with the suspicion that he is learning more about the biases of the observer than about the distinctive characteristics of those observed.

Some of these problems can be tackled if observers distance themselves from events and settle for a systematic, if not necessarily exhaustive, record involving systems of observation whose reliability can be demonstrated in terms of agreement amongst different observers. One example of *controlled observation* is the work of Barker and Wright (1955), referred to in chapter 10, in which trained observers kept detailed records of the activities of selected children throughout an entire day.

Many of the best loved tools of the social scientist are, in fact, particular techniques for controlled observation, for example the interview, the questionnaire, and the standardized test and attitude scale. Each of those permits an investigator to make controlled observations leading to data which are likely to be at least moderately reliable, in the sense that they could be replicated, for example on another occasion by another investigator. But if people know they are being observed will they be as ready to reveal as much as they might to a participant observer? Will controlled observation provide much evidence about intimacy or idealism or illegality? And in addition to failing to detect certain types of behaviour, may the act of observing not run the risk of changing the phenomena being observed, so that self-consciousness or exhibitionism, for example, are encouraged? These are questions to which we shall return.

Further control can be exerted by systematically determining in advance the nature of the people to be observed. Thus, a researcher may decide to observe and compare similar numbers of men and women, or people of different ages or from different social backgrounds. Notice that the researcher cannot be said to have manipulated an independent variable; he is not in a position to create and vary the sex, age or social class of his respondents. But by taking advantage of pre-existing bases for social categorization he can attempt to ask and answer finer questions than, 'What does some notional average person think or do about—?' He can increase his control over the study by increasing the care he takes in attempting to ensure that differences associated with, say, different sexes or age groups really tell us about sex or age, rather than about some other naturally confounded factor which has also been allowed to vary across the social categories he has chosen to compare. The combination of controlled observation and the choice of different categories of respondents to permit at least the beginnings of systematic comparisons, can be said to characterize the social *survey*, a technique commonly used by social psychologists in the study of social attitudes, for example.

It can be tempting to think of a survey in terms of independent and dependent variables. Thus, social class or political party allegiance of respondents may seem like independent variables and reported earnings and ethnic group attitudes like dependent variables. But normally one is on very dubious grounds if one attempts to attribute causation rather than simply correlation to such observed relationships. After all, it may well be that reported earnings determine social class positions rather than the reverse, or attitudes to immigrant groups cause the choice of party, rather than party allegiance determining attitudes. Or again, there may be no direct causal relation in either case; the causal agents may be other factors which have not been identified in the surveys in question. But occasionally in settings where an investigator would not dare to set up an experiment, 'nature' may appear to have done his work for him, in that, through events beyond any investigator's control, a potential comparison may exist in which everything save one crucial difference appears comparable. Officialdom may have assigned families in need of rehousing to high rise blocks or traditional council semi-detached houses more or less at random. Or the only obvious difference amongst several very similar schools in similar neighbourhoods may be the extent to which each school streams, or refuses to stream, pupils in terms of attainment. If an alert social scientist succeeds in systematically collecting data in such settings, he can claim to have carried out a *natural experiment*. Thus, when Festinger and his colleagues (Festinger, Riecken and Schachter, 1956) observed an apocalyptic group preparing to meet a predicted cataclysm, they were able to test their ideas about the way in which social support affected people's reactions to the disconfirmation of some of their major beliefs by observing the contrasting reactions of two sub-groups of believers, those who expected to meet their doom in the company of other believers and those who would lack such sympathetic support. Social psychologists could, and should, make even more use than they have of such 'naturally' occurring variations, even although certain inherent difficulties have to be acknowledged. Natural experiments require alertness, ingenuity and resourcefulness on the part of investigators, and even given those qualities a suitable set of circumstances may not present itself. Armageddon is not always conveniently at hand! And other things which are supposed to be equal may turn out to be more unequal than hoped. Festinger's two sub-groups, for example, could be distinguished in terms of other characteristics as well as the presence or absence of co-believers. Nevertheless, the use of a natural experiment is one way in which social psychologists can strive to attain balance between experimental control and the study of real-world phenomena.

An alternative is to move further in the direction of control and create a *field experiment*. Here the investigator does attempt to create experimental manipulation, but he devotes considerable efforts to carrying out his experiment in as natural a setting as he can devise, and if he is successful the participants may not even realize that they are taking part in a research study. Two early and influential studies, by Sherif and Sherif (1953) on intergroup relations and by Lewin and colleagues (Lewin, Lippit and White, 1939) on leadership, provide illustrations of such an approach. Sherif systematically varied, over time, factors intended to promote competition or cooperation between groups of boys taking part in a summer camp (see chapter 17); Lewin established small clubs for boys and then deliberately varied the type of leadership offered by the adult leaders. As a result, in both of those studies it can be argued that the children were observed in familiar and involving contexts, where, in addition, the investigators could have confidence that the systematic variations observed amongst groups were the outcome of the experimental manipulations rather than of some other factors outside their control. Both studies are justifiably 'classics'. Field experiments, however, have been relatively rare in social psychology, in large part because of the combination of time, effort, ingenuity and judgement necessary to get such a study just right. In addition, due to the less than complete control that is normally possible in a field setting, there can often be the risk of an uncontrolled event occurring which might complicate the task of interpreting what happened in the study, or, at worst, ruin what was an expensive and time-consuming piece of research. Furthermore, ethical problems are clearly raised by field experiments in which settings are so natural that participants do not realize they are being studied.

Right at the high control end of our continuum of methods lies the *laboratory experiment*, which was briefly characterized at the beginning of this section. Here, often in a specially designed physical environment, the social psychologist can exclude many irrelevant considerations and can exert sufficient control over the situation to be able to manipulate one or more independent variables.

Before proceeding further, several qualifications are in order regarding our six-way classification. For one thing, as was implied by the notion of an underlying continuum, the dividing lines are by no means hard and fast. For another, the classification is not necessarily exhaustive; other writers might wish to identify additional methods, such as the clinical method or simulation techniques, which are not quite synonymous with any of our six. Furthermore, in practice many studies represent combinations of elements taken from what have been presented as different methods. A laboratory experiment, for example, may derive its dependent variables from the use of controlled observation techniques such as scales or questionnaires or trained observers scoring interaction in the laboratory. Alternatively, as in the work of R. F. Bales and his collaborators (see chapter 7), a laboratory setting can be used for a study which, strictly speaking, is an observational study rather than an experiment. Thus, our classification should not be thought of as an exhaustive listing of mutually exclusive methods, but rather as a simple indication of the range of alternatives open to the empirically minded social psychologist.

Strengths and weaknesses of the laboratory experiment

Despite this variety of available methods, the use of the laboratory experiment has been the most distinctive feature of methodology in social psychology. In all probability, experimental studies represent at least two thirds or even three quarters of all studies in social psychology (see chapter 7, p. 180, for more precise figures in one major area). The use of laboratory experiments most readily distinguishes social psychology from other social sciences such as sociology or social anthropology. For many this has been a sign of social psychology's rigour and sophistication. Those who take this view also tend, explicitly or implicitly, to assume that progress in the most advanced natural sciences should provide a model for progress in the social sciences. The use of laboratory experiments, then, becomes a goal to be striven for whenever possible, because they carry with them certain important strengths.

One general strength is the pressure towards explicitness exerted by experimenting. If an investigator is really hoping to control, in one way or another, all potentially relevant features of the situation, then he must attempt to be very clear about what is, and what is not, relevant, to a degree that may not always hold when using non-experimental methods. Indeed, it can be argued that, even when experiments are not possible or appropriate, an investigator can sharpen his own thinking by attempting to devise hypothetical experiments and thereby forcing himself to confront questions of detail that might otherwise be left vague and unspecified.

A second strength of the experiment lies in its ability to answer questions of cause and effect. If change in a dependent variable can be consistently related to change in an independent variable, and if one can be confident that the only feature of the situation to vary is that carefully manipulated by the investigator, then it is reasonable to claim that the change in outcome *is* caused by the manipulation. Given the complexities of experimenting with human social behaviour, it is sometimes the case that what seemed like simple cause and effect in one study subsequently proves to be a more complex issue. Nonetheless, in an experimental situation claims about causation are likely to be more plausible and much simpler to make than in a non-experimental study.

Furthermore, the precision of an experiment makes it well suited for the testing of refined hypotheses or predictions. In an area of inquiry about which little is known, one may have only the haziest of expectations and a study undertaken simply to delineate 'what goes on' is quite appropriate. But as what occurs becomes clearer, then one can expect more refined attempts to explain the set of phenomena in question. These theories are likely to be capable of generating specific hypotheses about relations amongst variables or about aspects of the phenomena as yet little understood. The testing of such hypotheses can yield new evidence which may help refute, or strengthen, the theory which generated the hypotheses. Particularly in so far as a theory is capable of predicting, not just that, say, x and *y* will be associated, but that there will be a particular one-way causal relation between them, then an experiment is likely to be the most appropriate way of testing the hypothesis.

These are some of the conventional strengths of the experimental methods (see Crano and Brewer 1973: Hyman, 1964). Recently, however, some social psychologists have become very critical of the use of experimental methods (e.g. Harré and Secord, 1972) and others, even if still using experiments themselves, have become uneasy about certain features of them. The heart of this critical view lies in the fact that, unlike the natural sciences, the social sciences are studying thoughtful, self-conscious, reactive human beings for whom the fact that they are being studied may have a crucial effect on how they will behave. The suggestion that the problem would disappear if people did not know how they were being studied is no solution. For one thing, one immediately encounters ethical problems in deciding which, if any, procedures would be acceptable, and many professional and fund-giving bodies, such as the American Psychological Association and the Social Science Research Council, as well as university departments and individual researchers, insist on quite explicit rules being followed on such ethical issues. Certain types of activities, such as behaviour in public places open to public inspection, may be considered legitimate for unannounced research, but these lend themselves more readily to non-experimental investigations than to experimental studies in a laboratory.

What, then, are some of the problems created by a person knowing he is taking part in an experiment? One possibility is that he may decide to be awkward or to mislead the investigator by choosing to act in a bizarre or atypical or dishonest way; that, at least, is one common difficulty often proposed, usually by people other than social psychologists. Experience, however, suggests that, in practice, the exact opposite is a more common problem, namely experimental subjects are, if anything, too cooperative. Martin Orne (1962) became interested in this question when he found it impossible to devise non-painful tasks that subjects in a psychology laboratory would refuse to do or would quickly stop doing. Even when he presented subjects with 2000 sheets of random numbers, asked them to add up on each sheet 224 pairs of numbers, and immediately each sheet was completed tear it into at least thirty-two pieces before tackling the additions on the next sheet, subjects typically would continue working on the task for several hours. As often as not, the experimenter would give up before the subjects. Orne argued that an important feature of many laboratory experiments was their implicit 'demand characteristics'. That is, subjects would interpret the aims (or demands) of an experiment in a particular way and would normally attempt to satisfy those aims, whether they were seen as demanding persistence, or speed, or obedience, or whatever. In so far as demand characteristics are the same across all the different conditions in a study one can say that a constant error or irrelevance has been introduced throughout, and try to argue that this may not be too important. But what if, inadvertently, the experimenter creates demand characteristics in, say, an experimental group which differ from those in a control condition? He might find consistent differences which would be due not to the variable he was explicitly manipulating but to implicit 'demands' of which he himself was unaware. The notion of different demand characteristics operating in different conditions within a single experiment may in turn account for another set of problems relating to experiments, namely those of 'experimenter bias' (Rosenthal, 1966). Robert Rosenthal and his colleagues conducted a series of studies in which different experimenters were led to have different expectations regarding the performance of different sets of subjects who were, in fact, comparable. Instead of obtaining data showing no differences between the comparable groups, the experimenters found differences, generally in line with their expectations. These differences may have been achieved by creating different 'demands', such as subtly demanding that certain subjects try harder than others, or they may have been produced by the experimenter inadvertently giving more information or feedback to subjects whom he expected to do well. The implication of these demonstrations is that when a hypothesis is confirmed it may be due to uncontrolled bias on the part of the experimenter rather than to the variable which is explicitly being manipulated.

Demand characteristics and investigator bias can cause problems for other methods apart from laboratory experiments, but precisely because of the control the investigator can exert in the laboratory, they are generally regarded as being particularly problematic there. Experimental techniques can and have been improved to minimize the risk of demands and biases, and that is one positive feature to have emerged from recent work by social psychologists on 'the social psychology of the psychological experiment' (Miller, 1972; Wrightsman and Brigham, 1973). But increased sophistication and improved techniques are not sufficient in themselves to dispose of the critical view on experimenting.

For demands and biases can be regarded as specific illustrations of the more general point that a laboratory experiment in the social sciences may be a very special type of social situation, which participants with any degree of social sensitivity are likely to react to in an appropriate fashion. For example, it is normally an encounter between strangers, one of whom, the experimenter, knows much more about the situation than do those participating as subjects. Furthermore the encounter takes place in a particular institutional context, namely a scientific-educational one, and as a result the experimenter is invested with considerable legitimate authority. One striking illustration of this point is the work of Stanley Milgram (1974) on obedience to authority. Milgram found that a majority of ordinary, reasonable adults would administer to another person electric shocks which they were led to believe could be highly dangerous or even fatal, if ordered to do so as part of a scientific experiment. One view of Milgram's research is that he demonstrated that horrifying consequences of obedience to authority, which we have come to recognize can occur in armies or total institutions such as prisons, can also be produced in the name of science and education.

Conclusions

Our intention in pointing to some of the problems of laboratory experiments in social psychology is not to argue that experiments are impossible or should not be done, but rather to stress that no single method is likely to resolve all the problems of empirical research. Each of the methods we described earlier has its pros as well as cons. Some of these are specific to specific methods, but in addition, an overall pattern can be detected. In an excellent introduction to the topic of research design, Campbell and Stanley (1966) distinguished the *internal validity* from the *external validity* of experiments. The former refers to the extent to which differences amongst experimental conditions can be unambiguously attributed to the experimental treatments themselves. The latter is concerned with the generality or generalizability of the observed differences; to what extent can they be generalized to other populations, situations, etc.? It is hard to resist the conclusion that the strengths of the experiment are more obvious with regard to problems of internal validity than external validity. But as we move from the high control laboratory experiment towards the low control methods, we sense that increasingly the balance tips in the other direction. To clarify this point, we might invoke a slightly different distinction, that of *reliability* and *validity* of measurement. Reliability is held to refer to the extent to which a researcher succeeds in measuring something consistently, and validity refers to the degree to which the something being measured is actually what should be measured. Methods at the high control end of our continuum appear to emphasize reliability, sometimes to the possible detriment of validity, whereas studies with low control purchase apparent validity by ignoring the need for high reliability. Or, to make the point just once more, with an even more general but crude distinction, we would argue that social psychologists, like all other social scientists, aim at both *rigour* and *relevance* in their work, yet often both cannot be attained simultaneously and either a compromise must be settled for, or a choice emphasizing one or the other. Different methods represent different choices and compromises. If a researcher opts for non-interventionist observational techniques he is deciding to stress potential relevance to the everyday world in the hope that the likely loss of rigour will not be so great as to entirely vitiate his findings; the nearer to the high control pole a preferred method lies, then the more the investigator is emphasizing the need for rigour, at a risk to relevance.

If this analysis is accepted, the optimal research strategy is obviously one involving a number of methods, whose strengths and weaknesses can complement one another. We can have more confidence in compatible conclusions drawn from a variety of different approaches than in similar findings from the repetition of only one technique.

This does not mean that all methods are equally appropriate for all questions or at each point in the development of a programme of research. As was implied earlier, in a relatively unexplored area where there is a need simply to be able to describe what goes on and to identify what the important phenomena and variables seem to be, then non-experimental methods are likely to be particularly appropriate. Once it is possible to move to more precise questions generated by a relatively sophisticated theory, rather than by an *ad hoc* set of working assumptions, and to problems of explanation rather than description, then experimental methods come into their own. In the fairly recent past, an over-emphasis on the use of laboratory experiments has meant that social psychologists have been prone to using over-refined methods to ask too limited questions too soon. In addition, even when justified in taking our problems into the laboratory, we have been reluctant to bring them back out again. In practice, it is very unrealistic to think that a set of major questions will be exhaustively answered by taking just one trip along our dimension of control, from participant observation to laboratory experimenting. The conclusions emanating from the laboratory will require testing in a variety of naturalistic contexts, and new questions will be raised in each part of the research sequence. Thus, research should involve almost cyclical movements from the field to the laboratory and back again to the field. Indeed, there are encouraging signs that such patterns, and a related openness to alternative methods, have recently become somewhat more common (McGuire, 1973: Swingle, 1973).

The methodological strength and sophistication of social psychology lies not with any single method of research, but with the variety of differing methods available for use. We hope this conclusion will be amply justified in the chapters which follow, and that the reader will be able to judge for himself, or herself, the success attained, through the use of those methods, in the search for answers to the major questions of social psychology.

Further Reading

An excellent review of the development of social psychology can be found in:

Allport, G. W. (1969), 'The historical background of modern social psychology', in G. Lindzey and E. Aronson, eds., *The Handbook of Social Psychology*, vol. I, Reading, Mass, Addison-Wesley.

Differing views about what should be the main approaches to social psychology are well represented in the following books:

Berger, P. L., and Luckmann, T. (1967), *The Social Construction of Reality*. London, Allen Lane.

Berkowitz, L. (1975), *A Survey of Social Psychology*, Hinsden, Ill., The Dryden Press.

Harré, R., and Secord, P. F. (1972), *The Explanation of Social Behaviour*, Oxford, Basil Blackwell.

Israel, J., and Tajfel, H. eds. (1972), *The Context of Social Psychology: A critical assessment*, London, Academic Press.

Jones, E. E., and Gerard, H. B. (1967), *Foundations of Social Psychology*, New York, Wiley.

Kelvin, P. (1970), *The Bases of Social Behaviour*, London, Holt, Rinehart & Winston.

The following provide a good background for the study of research methods:

Crano, W. D., and Brewer, M. B. (1973), *Principles of Research in Social Psychology*, New York, McGraw-Hill. A not very complex general treatment of alternative research methods in social psychology.

Campbell, D. T., and Stanley, J. C. (1966), *Experimental and Quasi-experimental Designs for Research*, Chicago, Rand McNally. A sophisticated but very clear introduction to principles and details of research design.

Chapter 2
Evolution and Social Behaviour

John Hurrell Crook

Introduction: Man and beast

Any attempt at a definition of human nature is dependent upon the educational, cultural and professional background of the thinker. Doctors, lawyers, advertising experts, physicists, biologists and sociologists would all select contrasting aspects for emphasis and probably adopt different criteria for determining when 'nature' is human or not. Even so, very few today still consider Man closer to angels than to animals. Yet, even among scientists best equipped to consider the question, there remain exceedingly acrimonious disputes about the relevance of biology to the study of Man. Underlying modern debates one may still detect the grinding of axes representing inherent yet rarely explicit political attitudes. Fortunately, scepticism is a healthy ingredient of many scholars' minds and the wilder implications of certain 'socio-biological' theories are perhaps unlikely to be translated into ideas expressed in action.

Inferences from animal to human behaviour have become popular in exactly this kind of context as the huge sales of books by Robert Ardrey (1967) and Desmond Morris (1967) testify. Such works should be used more as examples of assumptive thinking and its consequences than as texts reflecting the nature of current science. Used in this way their value is assured. Unfortunately, the furore surrounding some of the notions paraded in these works as conclusions drawn from a science which is still developing has tended to place ethology under a cloud at precisely a time when its contributions to social psychology could be considerable. It is the purpose of this chapter to present a case in favour of a more biologically concerned science of social psychology than is currently common.

What then does the study of animal behaviour have to offer in the field of social psychology? The remainder of this chapter will be concerned with the discussion of three key questions. Is an ethological approach distinctive? What contribution does it add to the established methodologies in psychology generally? What additional comprehension of human social life is to be gained from an entry to the field by an ethological route? Relatively few ethologists or social psychologists have attempted to answer these questions, which have much in common with a similar set of questions concerning the relations between ethology and social anthropology. We draw our answers here from a number of attempts to establish the distinctiveness of ethology and to discuss systematically questions of this kind.[*]

History and characteristics of a biological approach to social behaviour

The study of animal behaviour, later to be called ethology, originated within the zoology of the nineteenth century. Major parts of Darwin's work on the origin of species (1859) and the 'descent' of Man (1871) refer repeatedly to questions about the evolution of 'instinctive' behaviour in both animals and Man. The focus of the theory of sexual selection (1871) concerns the effects of the behaviour patterns of one individual of a species on another and the selection of those patterns repeatedly leading to successful mating. Darwin also originated the science now called 'human ethology' in his detailed analyses not only of non-verbal communication in Man but also in careful descriptive studies of the behaviour of babies and children (1872). This work was shot through with constant references to similarities observed in non-human primate and other mammalian or avian behaviour. Darwin's towering achievement, remarkable insight and devoted scholarship remained in many ways unique and isolated. It was not for about another century that knowledge of primate behaviour in the wild expanded sufficiently to allow informed comparisons between human and non-human primate behaviour so that possible lines of evolutionary derivation could be worked out in a manner

* Cf. Crook, 1970; Fox, 1967; Tiger and Fox 1966; Tinbergen, 1972. The following symposia of papers will also be found useful: Ashley Montagu, 1973; Blurton-Jones, 1972; Campbell, 1972; Crook, 1970; Hinde, 1972; Korn, 1973.

other than by sheer guesswork. Likewise, apart from an occasional scholar, the same time elapsed before ethologists (Andrew, 1963; van Hoof, 1962) and social psychologists (e.g. Birdwhistell, 1952; Argyle, 1967) once more studied non-verbal 'kinesic' behaviour in human interaction (see chapter 5). Only in the last decade have the Darwinian initiatives blossomed in the field of child psychology (e.g. Blurton-Jones, 1972).

Similarly an interest in animal societies quite clearly conceived as cybernetic systems (although without the term being used) originated with A. Espinas as long ago as 1878. Espinas, sociologist and philosopher, rather than zoologist, was well aware of the importance of studying the ecological context of a social system if its maintenance and historical development were to be understood. Emile Waxweiler (1906) took the step of considering sociology, the study of human society, as a subsection of a broader science of social ethology, in which social systems throughout the animal kingdom were to be the subject of analysis. These openings died after a brief flowering and the questions raised by these authors were not reconsidered, or in some cases even rediscovered, until a few years ago (Crook and Goss-Custard, 1972).

Following the First World War the science of animal behaviour had eventually to be created afresh. Even the foremost of the new investigators had little knowledge of or interest in the earlier history of the subject (Jaynes, 1969). The new wave was characterized by an immense sense of excitement and intellectual discovery. Konrad Lorenz, with his extraordinary ability for forging challenging hypotheses from detailed studies of birds and animals in open enclosures, created almost single-handed a massive set of theoretical formulations that lie at the groundwork of what Klopfer and Hailman (1967) now term 'classical ethology'. Niko Tinbergen (1953), in a set of brilliantly contrived experiments, not only began the process of evaluating Lorenz's theories but opened up the study of the function of behavioural traits in systems such as the communication processes of gulls. Descriptive field study related to the study of behavioural evolution had been started even earlier by Julian Huxley, who anticipated Lorenz in the formulation of several key concepts, and by naturalists, such as Elliot Howard, who did much work on the problem of territory in birds.

Many characteristics of this classical phase of ethology remain pronounced in modern ethology. First of all there is a concern with the whole range of key questions inherent in evolutionary biology. In relation to a 'piece' of behaviour these questions are: (i) What is its *proximate* causation? The question concerns the physiological mechanisms responsible for its appearance; (ii) How has it developed in the life of an individual? This question is addressed at the manner in which 'nature' and 'nurture' or the genetic and 'experiental' factors have interacted in individual development or ontogeny; (iii) What is the function of the behaviour? In other words, how does the behaviour operate to increase the survival and reproductive potential of an individual, its young and close kin? (iv) Why is this function fulfilled in this particular way? Often the same function could apparently be met in ways other than it is. The question concerns the evolutionary history of the particular species (its phylogeny) and various constraints on the species' adaptability that may have arisen during its history. It requires some understanding of the selection pressures, environmental and social, that may have progressively moulded the genetic background of a species' behaviour.

This set of questions parallels exactly those which are asked about a given bone or other structure in anatomical zoology. They have been posed in this manner since Darwin's time, and form the basis of biological inquiry. The questions are all interconnected. The answer to any one of them has effects on the answers to all the others. It is this interconnection that gives biological theory and philosophy its integral appearance and coherent structure.

Recent work on group, as opposed to individual, behaviour shows that this list of questions now requires some development and amplification (Crook, 1970a). Individual animals live within social structures; these structures have various dispersion patterns and communication systems of varying complexity. They provide the immediate context of an individual's behaviour, much of which concerns adjustments to or modifications of the responses of other individuals of his species. Some of these structures consist of elaborated social devices which facilitate cooperation between the sexes, or even between distantly related individuals, and improve the success of individual reproductive strategies. Other social mechanisms have the function of reducing the probability of antagonism between individuals or of stress caused by differences in status; in this way they facilitate the cohesion of groups. Groups themselves may be of significance as they decrease the probability of an individual member's death through predation when compared to the risks to which an isolated individual could be exposed. Many aspects of individual behaviour are dependent on the presence of others; 'dominance' and 'territory' are two examples. But talk of a dominance 'drive' of an individual or the 'territorialism' of a species is meaningless without an adequate analysis of patterns of population dispersion, group communication and the dynamics of relationships between individuals in groups. Dominance behaviour and territorial defence occur in ways which are often dependent upon particular social and demographic circumstance; therefore, their manifestation and 'strength' are largely contingent upon social context.

We know now that the dispersion patterns of species' populations are in general more variable than are the behavioural elements of communication among their members. For example, the social organization of populations of the same primate species may differ in contrasting ecologies. Thus the proportional occurrence of one-male or multi-male reproductive groups in langurs varies in different parts of India, with often dramatic effects on the interactions of individuals within the groups. Even the same stereotyped signals may be used with contrasting functions in populations of the same species inhabiting forest or open savannah conditions (see review in Crook, 1970a). Likewise, in a number of well-studied ungulate species (e.g. Estes, 1966; Jarman, 1974), the relations between defence of space, mating system, nomadism and ecology differ in contrasting circumstances and are related to similar effects in the carnivore populations that prey upon them. It follows that attributes of social structure must be considered as group characteristics and cannot be treated analytically in quite the same way as behavioural features of individuals. Social organization is not only responsive to direct environmental influence – as when a population adjusts spatially to temporal or topographical contrasts in dispersion of food items; but it is also subject to historical change in locally learnt traditions of exploitation of the environment and in the use of 'innate' signalling patterns. It is therefore clear that answers to the questions concerning the development and the functions of individual behaviour require an under-standing of the social processes operating in groups which constitute the social environment of the individuals.

Thus, individual behaviour evolves not only within a physical but also within a social environment. Animals that fail to adapt to group norms or whose behavioural traits are in some ways too deviant are less likely to reproduce and are more susceptible to ejection from a group than others. Social selection of this kind must have had a major effect in stabilizing the genetic basis of temperamental traits and various motivational characteristics. Complex mammalian societies probably maintain strong selection pressures on the 'pattern-ing' of individual interaction. The analysis of the behaviour of a species must therefore concern itself with the demographic and social structuring of the species' population as well as with the features of the physical environment.

The addition of this social dimension to the ethological analysis of behaviour is relatively recent and its full implications need working out. It is clear that at least two problems are involved – first, the analysis of the relationship between different levels of organization and, second, the differences between systems found at different levels of organization. For example, the information determining behaviour-al performance is derived from several sources of which the main ones are: (i) genetic; (ii) developmental conditions and learning; (iii) local traditions; (iv) group and population organization; (v) the ecology of the species and the composition of the ecological commu-nity in which it lives. In a metaphorical sense each of these sources may be said to belong to one of successive 'environments' which form a series like a set of concentric circles. Not only is group beha-viour an expression of the genetically based responses of individuals, it is also directly affected by ecology.

The density and patchiness of a species' population is both a result of social processes and of abundance and distribution of resources. Both ecological and social factors operate to curtail the overall abundance of a species in a given area (Archer, 1970; Watson and Moss, 1970). Social organization is an adaptation to environment, some of its aspects being more flexible than others. For example, communication and mating systems vary least when different local populations are compared. This suggests that these systems are firmly controlled genetically and include phylogenetic contraints on adaptability. They will not change easily in response to local environmental differences. The actual spacing of a population and the size and composition of groups tend to be more labile and responsive to environmental conditions.

Social factors such as crowding often exert major effects on the behaviour of a population. This is especially true when food resources are in excess supply so that numbers can build up to peak figures which are ultimately controlled by the physiological effects of stress induced by aggression. Aggression increases when crowding cannot be relieved by emigration (Archer, 1970). Socio-demographic systems are regulated by numerous interacting variables, which include the availability and abundance of resources, the degree of social tolerance to crowding, the density of the population and the opportunities for emigration or nomadism. Historical changes in socio-demographic systems are thus dependent on alterations in these key constraints governing the system. They may be driven either environmentally or socio-physiologically or both (Crook 1970b).

The open and adaptive nature of socio-demographic processes and their multiple determination means that social organization is in large measure a 'biotic' adaptation expressing the consequences of the development of particular genotypes in particular environments. One cannot treat group characteristics as simple 'innate' products of neo-Darwinian selection. The same is true of the ecological community as a whole. Both systems 'evolve' through complex shifts in the controlling factors, of which the natural selection of genotypes is but one of many. Similarly, the importance of acquired behaviour traditions and protocultural elements in the flexible social organizations of primates means that their form of change through time is more akin to human history than to the evolutionary processes responsible for, say, the courtship displays of lizards. Nonetheless, it remains true that genetic determinants have a profound effect in specifying what degree of flexibility in a society is possible through constraints on individual adaptability. Likewise complex social attributes such as altruism are now understood to have been naturally selected and many features commonly treated as cultural may be largely specified as to their occurrence rather than as to content by innate programmes (see Alexander, 1974; Wilson, 1975).

Ethological methods in the study of human social behaviour

In recent years a number of workers have begun adopting an etho-logical approach in studying human behaviour. Often such researchers did not begin as zoologists but rather have extended their horizons to adopt a biological and evolutionary perspective on the problems they wished to investigate. Blurton-Jones (1972), following the more orthodox route, commenced research on the behaviour of school-children following detailed studies of motivation in geese and tit-mice. In introducing *Ethological studies of child behaviour*, he pointed out that the contributors to the book had trained in subjects ranging from physics and biology to physical anthropology and psychology and had had postgraduate experience ranging from invertebrate genetics to psychotherapy. What is it that such workers have found attractive in ethology? The answer is method. Ethological methods have a number of relatively distinctive features which include the following:

(i) The habit of relating studies of mechanism, development and function within an integrated perspective; consequently as we have suggested above, results in one area tend to stimulate thinking and hypothesis-making in others.

(ii) The idea that studies of context and of interactions between levels of causation is an important consideration in the analysis of behaviour has echoes in other areas. For example, in Richards and Bernal's (1972) study of mother–infant interaction many factors are analysed and, in addition, different levels are studied. They emphasize the importance of interactions between social context, mother–infant interaction and the physiological factors affecting that inter-action.

(iii) Ethologists commonly begin work with simple descriptive observations as free as possible from *a priori* hypotheses. The same is true in some of the recent child studies and in research on non-verbal communication. The 'sit and watch' phase of investigation is kept as open as possible and hypotheses generated from relations in the collected data themselves.

(iv) While ethologists have sometimes described behaviour in terms of the effects it produces, thereby using a 'functional' description, they more usually describe behaviour simply in terms of the postures, posture components, sounds or sound components that arise in naturally occurring events. While there are many problems involved in an effective description of human social behaviour which often depends on subtle shared assumptions for its meaning, Blurton-Jones (1972) argues that such methods allow better replicability, greater objectivity, reduction in bias and vagueness inevitably involved in using 'mentalistic' terminology, and an easier return to original data for fresh analyses.

(v) Problems faced by ethologists in the analysis of motivation have left them with an entrenched suspicion of any 'blanket' variable in explanation. Hinde's (1959) important analyses of terms such as 'drive', 'stimulus' and 'response' and recent models concerned with the physiological control of behavioural elements rather than with changes in 'motivation' have all stressed this point of view. Transference of this attitude to other areas is most valuable.

Aseptic description and precision in quantitative recording appear obvious. advantages in any account of complex behaviour. The relative simplicity of the ethologists' approach may appear to some social psychologists and other social scientists as limiting the scope of inquiry into social behaviour to its relatively simple aspects, and thus leaving out many of its important complexities. It does, however, seem important to see how far such an objective scientific methodology can take us.

Experimental studies on gaze direction and other non-verbal components of conversation by social psychologists such as Argyle (1967) utilize methods similar, in certain respects, to those of modern ethologists. In his survey of human face-to-face interaction Vine (1970) emphasizes the increase in depth given to such studies by considering the evolution of facial musculature and its role in the communication of affect. Kendon and Ferber (1973) have studied the stereotyped and complex patterning of responses that occur when human beings meet one another on a sociable occasion such as a party and Eibl-Eibesfeldt

(1970) concludes from lengthy surveys of motivational expression among primitive peoples that many such rituals are common to humanity as a whole and imply a strong genetic component in their determination.

Social anthropological studies of certain small-scale societies reveal organizational parallels with non-human higher primates such as chimpanzees or baboons. Tanaka (1973) describes six features characterizing the flexibility with which the Gwi bushmen adapt to seasonal shifts in their nomadic life. Firstly the changes in group size relate to the distribution of plant foods and their density. Cooperation occurs in group hunting. Visiting and interchange of group members (intermarriage) is usual. Isolation of problem persons is balanced against sharing of resources which tends to maintain social equilibrium. Territories are vague and boundaries obscured thus allowing frequent fusion and fission of groups. Fusion often occurs for purely social purposes allowing affiliation. All these characteristics are found in elementary form among chimpanzees and seem to comprise a primordial base for human culture observable, to varying degrees, in the organizations of highly sociable animals.

Such examples not only reveal that ethological methods can be, and are being, applied to complex human social behaviour but also raise the possibility that when they are applied they may reveal universal features of Man's social behaviour as well as important analogies, and even homologies, between Man and non-human species. These latter questions will receive further attention. It is as well to note, however, that important though ethological methods may be, it is undeniably the broader evolutionary perspective, the return to Darwin's approach to the explanation of Man, that is the most powerful source of contemporary interest. It is thus worthwhile concluding this chapter with some evaluative comments on the state of theory and inference in this area.

Contemporary studies on the social evolution of Man

Man knows himself to possess powers which mark him off as unique in the animal kingdom. We also know that we are potentially capable of bringing about our extinction on this planet together with that of much of the other animal life that has evolved here. The problems of warfare, over-population, social disorder and change, over-exploitation of natural resources and pollution engage our attention increasingly and we face them sometimes almost in desperation. Yet we know very little of our precise evolutionary origins. While such knowledge is unlikely to solve these problems directly, it may provide a better perspective from which to view realistically our limitations; it may also evoke an appropriate contrition in the face of a planet groaning under our ecological presumption. Clearer comprehension usually leads to wiser practice.

The argument from animal to Man is perforce indirect and put together from considering a multiplicity of sources. The evolutionary record is broken – our immediate ancestors are as dead as the dodo and their original behaviour difficult to infer. Yet, although 'precise' science is only occasionally applicable in this inquiry, this in no sense makes the inquiry intellectually disrespectable. As Lack (1966) pointed out, both evolutionary theory and the theories of population dynamics were for a long time speculative. Only recent breakthroughs in biochemistry and in the monitoring of populations have made these inquiries more 'precise'.

Ethology can help in several ways to fill the gap and replace speculation by more informed inferences and theory building. Primate ethology allows inference from comparative study that (i) reveals the diversity of social organization and behaviour within the mammalian order to which we belong; (ii) explores the socio-demographic economy of our primate relatives within natural ecosystems; (iii) in conjunction with studies of social carnivores allows suggestions about the probable evolution of hunting and hence perhaps also of warfare in our own species and the morphological and behavioural changes likely to be associated with this; (iv) provides analyses of the communication systems that preceded the evolution of language and which we retain in non-linguistic communication; (v) shows up in broad perspective the unique characteristics evolved by our own species.

In addition, research on group dynamics with wild and captive non-human primates as well as with other mammals and birds reveals the involvement of social behaviour in the regulation of both group size and type and often in the determination of population densities as well. Gender differences in behaviour, based both on contrasts in endocrine mechanisms and on social learning, are reflected in contrasting sex roles in social groups. Male primates are by no means always the dominant thugs some authors would make them out to be. The sex-relation is geared in very complex and poorly understood ways to the adaptation of the total social organization to ecology and functions in maximizing the mating and rearing success of individuals of both sexes. Group cohesion and the inclusion of adult males within social groups composed of females and younger animals is relatively rare in mammals (see Eisenberg, 1966; Orians, 1969; Crook, 1977) and only occurs alongside the emergence of complex systems of communication allowing social control of conflict. Cooperative behaviour arises within systems of social competition and differential ranking (Crook, 1971) and a proportion of group members often endure behavioural constraints and considerable physiological stress. Indeed, we can see here, in part, the source of that which we term neurosis in our own species.

Let us take a look at three topics currently in the forefront of debate; (i) the nature of inference from animals to Man; (ii) the problem of linguistic and cultural universals; and (iii) the theory of social evolution in proto-hominids and early Man based on primatological considerations.

(i) Inference from animals to Man

Many misunderstandings have arisen in this area largely owing to incautious assertions advocated in recent popular books. Ethologists do not consider Man in any sense as 'merely' an animal. Earlier tendencies to project findings from studies of geese, rats, baboons or other animals on to interpretations of human nature are modified by the realization that every animal species is uniquely specialized to a given habitat and has followed its own unique evolutionary pathway. Generalizations from crow to pigeon are as 'dangerous' as vague generalizations to Man from other animal studies. Assertions that certain human or animal traits are homologues of one another have been very damaging because they appear to imply a common 'innate' genetical basis. Where such assertions refer to group characteristics such as territorial behaviour, the causation of which is complex, their naïveté becomes crippling in any attempt at systematic theory building. We know now that the nature–nurture controversy has led many of us repeatedly into logical and heuristic culs-de-sac. There is no such dichotomy, for the inherited genetic constitution is only one of numerous factors, both intrinsic and extrinsic to the organism, affecting development. We know too that the determining factors change with time as the individual develops.

Nonetheless, genetic inheritance undoubtedly plays a crucial role in fostering the emergence of particular neuro-endocrinological mechanisms and predetermines, to degrees that vary with the character concerned, the limitations on the expression of certain traits (e.g. the form of facial expressions) and capacities (e.g. learning abilities). Such conclusions are matters of fact arising from controlled genetic experiments with animals ranging from fruit flies to dogs and from human genetics itself. The use of these traits (i.e. the 'meaning' of facial expressions in different cultures) and capacities may however differ in contrasted social environments due to their programming into cultural levels well above the biological.

In traditional zoology there are clear distinctions between analogy and homology. The former is a feature of one animal or species which has the same function as that in another, while the latter is the same morphology occurring in different animals. Homologues may also have functional equivalence and homology may thus be considered an aspect of analogy. Similar anatomical characters may thus express common origins or they may have arisen independently and have become similar through convergence. Structures with the same function may or may not have common origins, their functional resemblance being due to adaptations of different materials to common needs. Inferences to common structure must always be distinguished from those to common sources in evolutionary time. Homologues are usually analogous characteristics that have been traced to common ancestry and known to be due to the expression of common mechanisms. The necessary evidence in behavioural comparison is usually very difficult to get.

As a primate, Man shares certain anatomical features with other species in the order; there is both genetical continuity and matura-tional repetition. Man also has unique anatomical features, not least those concerning the size and organization of the brain. Behavioural analogies between Man and other primates are many but few pro-bably amount to examples of homology. Man's culture and educa-tional processes ensure that behaviour develops within a highly con-trolling social environment providing most of the information moulding performance. The primary determinant of development, especially that concerning human group characteristics, is cultural. But this is true to some extent of all higher mammals with complex group life. The main difference lies in the progressive nature of changes in human culture itself. Education and the incorporation of new discoveries and of changing systems of symbols into socializa-tion resulted in the steady shift to ever more complex social organi-zations throughout the course of human history. The question asked of ethologists refers to the extent that the influence of genetically based 'deep structures' may have in limiting the range of variation possible in a historical process; for this has an undoubted significance for social and political policies concerning the future of Man. For example, the recent debates on the possible innate character of human aggression and territoriality, grossly oversimplified in popular works, could influence policies concerned with population settlement or resettlement and the location and dispersion of racial minorities. Likewise, an understanding of biological factors, such as hormones, which may affect differentially the attitudes, skills and emotionality of the two sexes, has a bearing on contemporary prob-lems concerning the role of each sex in society.

(ii) Universals of communication in Man

The comparative study of non-verbal communication in Man and other primates indicates that in postural and facial expression there are many features suggesting not only similarity of expressive form, implying common mechanisms of behaviour pattern control, but also common motivational structures underlying 'intent' (to attack, flee, mate, etc.). The expression of motives is important if group cohesion through control of interactions between individuals is to be maintained and regulated. It is clear that complex communication in non-human mammals correlates with advanced social cooperation, social control of affect and complex groups which include members of different ages and sexes. Hunting dogs, elephants and chimpanzees afford good examples.

The facial expressions of man, although containing elements found in other species, are nonetheless unique and, taken together with other features of kinesic communication, often highly variable between cultures (see chapter 5 for a fuller discussion of kinesics). Certain kinesic signals are common to all human cultures so far investigated and also appear in people who are born deaf and blind. In addition certain overall patterns (e.g. anger, greeting, flirting) are similar across a wide range of cultures although still to a degree labile and subject to cultural conditioning. Most of these features are concerned with intimate personal face-to-face interactions which have an emotional content, and it is in this area that the similarities of a more general qualitative kind with non-human primates are found. These cross-cultural resemblances are not necessarily determined independently of experience but may well involve aspects of behaviour acquisition in development common to the species as a whole – and even across species. The diversity between culture patterns more often reflects contrasts in verbal usage or levels of relationship more complex than the face-to-face. For example, group norms expressing collective modes of repressing aggression influence the ways in which people expect to relate to one another. Such norms find their expression in the formalities of common speech.

The presence of phylogenetically acquired motor and receptor mechanisms of facial expression is not improbable but the extent of their influence remains unknown. Certainly expression of motor components may often be culturally repressed – especially where sexual elements are concerned.

Language is unique to Man; Lenneberg (1969, see also in Korn, 1973) considers it to be a biologically based species-specific characteristic. He points out that language occurs throughout the species, in all cultures, its onset is correlated with maturational age and it develops in the same way out of infant 'babbling'. In all languages it appears to have the same formal operating characteristics which seem to have been constant throughout recorded history, and it is functionally dependent on the presence of certain quite specific and unique brain areas (Geschwind, 1970).

The debate remains open. The current studies of chimpanzee 'language' abilities and communicative systems in other animals having design features approaching those of human speech are of interest comparatively, but do not help greatly in understanding the evolution of the biological basis of the particular type of speech communication characteristic of Man. Comparisons between animal and human communication throw light primarily on non-linguistic modes of interpersonal expression. The prerequisites of language imply a level of cognitive complexity wholly unique to Man.

(iii) *Evolution of human social organization*

The nativism in classical ethological theory together with the work of Eibl-Eibesfeldt and Chomsky has led some social anthropologists to look for an innate 'biogrammar' underlying human social organizations at least at the basic level of family, all-male group, etc. (e.g. Tiger, 1969). Earlier in this chapter we argued that such an approach to group characteristics is not always helpful. Social organization is likely to be an open and adaptive system controlled by numerous variables of differing kinds operating at several levels. The 'innate' elements in such systems may be important and the presence of common patterns throughout mankind and analogies in related species suggest some such presence to be inevitable. Yet their significance as determinants and as constraints on development and diversity of forms has in no case been adequately researched. It is here that popular accounts of ethology have most misrepresented the science by overstressing the nativistic approach. Evidence from many fields including palaeontology, physical anthropology, ecology, ethology and primatology, is needed for a theory about human social origins. Scholarly work of a very careful nature is essential if any-thing other than vague speculation is to result (see Crook, 1975).

Jolly (1970) presents a two-phase theory of the differentiation of hominid from cercopithecid ancestral populations. Using a very detailed set of analogical comparisons with baboons, especially the

Gelada (*Therapithecus*), he argues that ancestral hominids became seed-eaters as they gradually emerged from the forest fringe in correlation with climatic and vegetational changes in Africa. The adaptive shift involved changes in oral shape, a reduction of anterior dental apparatus, the freeing of the forelimbs as a consequence of sitting to forage using the hands, and the start of making artefacts as tools. In addition, as Crook and Gartlan (1966) also suggested, the social organization probably shifted from something like the chimpanzees' type of multi-male reproductive unit with a very open organization originally adapted to fruit eating in forests to a one-male 'harem' type of unit that could either consociate with others or disperse in relation to varying degrees of food abundance and patchiness. These features, representing a 'grade' (Huxley, 1959) of correlated adaptations to a particular environment and foraging system, were pre-adaptive to further changes as additional ecological shifts led to the occupation of savannah. In this second phase, meat and vegetables entered the diet, hunting became more extensive and weapons developed from earlier tools. The oral cavity developed together with brain mechanisms for increasingly effective sound communication and control leading to language acquisition. These features comprise a 'grade' of co-adaptations to a new mode of foraging in which high-energy protein foods were obtained by co-operative hunting facilitated by language.

As Washburn and Lancaster (1968) stress, the hunter-gatherer phase of history comprises the longest period of hominid existence during which almost all his unique biological adaptations must have emerged. Agricultural ways of life in contrast have endured for far less than one hundredth of human history. Bipedalism, the development of hunting from its occurrence in ancestral form (see Teleki's (1973) fascinating account of predation in contemporary chimpanzees), weapon development, and a marked division of labour between the sexes must all have emerged in this period. The use of a base or shelter, as with other animals foraging from a den, means that areas near home tend to become most heavily exploited (Hamilton and Watt, 1970) and supplies where possible are accumulated against famine at the primordial 'village'. Cooperation in all-male groups is facilitated, much as happened in pack hunting carnivores, to increase hunting efficiency and the harem unit became stabilized as the 'family', probably increasingly monogamous, based on the home in the village. These early protocultures must have shown considerable variation depending on local ecology – as indeed Maitland Bradfield's (1973) study of later Amerindian populations shows – and population dispersion, village size, duration of village site occupancy, nomadism, foraging range size and so on must have varied.

In some areas the need for large exclusive hunting ranges containing relatively poor supplies doubtless led to intergroup conflict analogous to that shown by rival Hyaena clans (van Lawick, 1970). In such warfare, perhaps occasioned in relation to food shortage, cannibalism may have begun to play a major role. While the one case of cannibalism reported from the chimpanzee may have been accidental, its potential appearance in advanced Hominoidea is clearly not restrained by the submissive posturing available to 'true' carnivores such as cats and dogs when in conflict. This potential for a systematic killing of his own kind is unique to Man. While the use of weapons from a distance makes the process both effective and economic, and language allows the planned attack, there are deeper psychological peculiarities present as well. The 'blood lust' and 'cruelty' of carnivores together with the courage and cunning involved in hunting may get transferred into the disputes that occasion not only war but also extreme interpersonal rivalry and murder. It is perhaps at this point that an understanding of human history may demand a new evaluation of the contributions of psychoanalysis to our problems (e.g. Brown, 1959).

Freud's insightful association of the phenomenon he termed the 'Oedipus complex' with the killing of the father in a primordial cyclopean horde may not be quite such a fantasy as some recent scholars have assumed. Freud was well aware of the compression of the time scale in his study, which was largely inspired by Greek mythology concerning primordial personal relationships. Fox (1967) stresses, rightly in my view, that early Man, in adapting to savannah, probably developed a form of one-male reproductive unit from a chimpanzee type of loose multi-male consociation. In the Gelada (Crook, 1966; Dunbar, 1975), still the best model in this type of comparison, there is extensive rivalry between harem owners and potentially reproductive young adult males. Complex interactions involving both subterfuge and direct fighting resolve the conflict in which young males acquire mates – sometimes including the females of the former harem owner. The latter is not, however, killed but vanquished into a subordinate old age. A comparable but different process occurs in the Hamadryas baboon (Kummer, 1968). The whole story vindicates the Freudian myth in a remarkable way, although of course the extent to which the analogy is valid remains open to debate. The comparable process in Man would have differed much in detail. The point is that in Man the development of hunting and the use of weapons for killing at a distance, without a concomitant evolution of intraspecific signals turning off aggression, seems to have produced a psychology which, in situations of sexual deprivation and rivalry, facilitates the link between sex and murderous aggression that is a basis of so much human evil.

The regulation of human conflict lies at the cultural level through the institution of rules and laws. Fox (1972) traces the way in which alliance and constraint in intergroup relations stem from the exchange of the products of labour and reproduction. Kinship and moiety systems develop from the regulated exchange of women in marriage and together with trading alliances establish complex networks stabilizing potential conflict between groups. The fact that such systems are only partially successful in the control of group aggression, is, however, only too manifest throughout human history.

By means of a yet further analogy with the Gelada baboon, Wickler (1967) proposed that the shift from dorsal to frontal mating was associated with the transfer of posterior sex signals to frontal chest areas associated with the sitting position adopted for seed eating, etc., in Gelada (Crook and Aldrich-Blake, 1968), and Jolly (1970) infers that a related transfer is an element in the first stage of hominid development. The giving of sex signals posteriorly would have little value if posteriors were mostly sat upon, and transfer of displays to other body areas would be selected. Morris (1967), taking these arguments further, suggests that hairlessness, increased skin sensitivity, the loss of oestrus and long-term female receptivity to mating evolved as devices for frequent sex between a mated pair that would tend to facilitate the maintenance of parental bonds of importance in the rearing of children as well as increasing social stability and reducing competition for the possession of women. However, other views on the evolution of hairlessness and skin sensitivity are available (Newman, 1970) and we are clearly entering a highly speculative area. Suffice it to say, primate ethology and modern field studies are greatly increasing the amount of evidence we need in constructing synthetic theories of this kind.

One aspect is of considerable practical importance. Do the gender contrasts in human behaviour and role playing relate to some deep biologically based substructure or are they due to cultural conditioning in a male-dominated world? Current evaluations take a more tolerant view of the role of biology than Kate Millet (1971) would like. While the extreme form of nativism apparent in Tiger's (1969) work is unlikely to be maintained, numerous studies of endocrine function in determining psychological contrasts between the sexes and of the course of behavioural development in boys and girls all suggest a complex interplay of biological and socio-cultural determinants that still need more balanced evaluation (Crook, 1973).

Conclusions and summary

(i) Ethology is a comprehensive approach to the study of behaviour that originated within traditional evolutionary biology. With its parent science, it shares a concern with problems of proximate causation (genetics, physiological mechanisms), ontogenetic development, functional analysis and evolution in terms of natural selection. In addition, since behaviour occurs in social contexts, problems of the relations between communication, social organization, population dynamics and ecology have recently come much to the fore. Social systems cannot be treated as unitary processes produced by simple genetic determinants. They are open and adaptive systems controlled by many factors operating at several levels (e.g. genetic, endocrinological, social, environmental) and with varying time scales. The extent to which the neuro-endocrinological substructures of perceptual, cognitive and motor functions and the possible innate programming of behavioural sequences confine the expression of motivation and the range of social organization within certain limits is in all cases still an open question. Yet this is a real issue – the old dichotomy between nature and nurture is an anachronism to be replaced by modern analysis of processes of development.

(ii) Ethological theory and methods have been through the fire of criticism and re-evaluation for twenty years. Modern ethology has escaped the excessive influence of the motivational theorizing of the 1930s and emerges as a hard pragmatic approach to behaviour analysis. While there are undoubtedly areas of psychological inquiry where the consideration of biological involvement is not directly relevant, these areas appear to be shrinking and we can expect a greater interplay and fusion between ethology and social psychology in the years ahead.

(iii) The methods of ethology are proving of especial value in the study of social psychology of children and in the analysis of human non-verbal communication. Researchers with widely contrasting academic backgrounds have found this to be true. Present psychological methods can be usefully supplemented by more direct observation, greater concern with contexts, more critical evaluation of the meaning of variables suggested for study and the development of new techniques of data reduction and analysis.

(iv) The evolutionary approach to behaviour promotes a widened perspective from which particular problems can be viewed afresh, often leading to striking new insights and lines of attack. The reconstruction of the origins of human social behaviour involves a synthetic utilization of information from several sciences. Field studies in primate social ethology have set off a new phase of evolutionary thinking in anthropology which may prove of great importance to social psychology. We have discussed the problems involved in making inferences from animals to man, and looked briefly at current work on universals of communication in Man and theories of human social evolution.

(v) The popular interest in ethology is not without cause. The human predicament in this century demands a re-evaluation of our view of ourselves. After having behaved like gods for whom everything is possible in an environment of supposedly unlimited resources we are learning that the population problems of animals bear similarities to our own and that our socio-economic behaviour is poorly adapted to the current conditions of our own making. Awareness of the presence of psycho-biological constraints within ourselves, even if the extent and significance of these remains inadequately examined, is likely to promote optimizing rather than maximizing strategies of economic and social exploitation. An attitude of contrition in the face of this despoilt planet is appropriate if the crime of hubris is not to exact its ultimate toll.

Further Reading

Campbell, B., ed. (1972), *Sexual Selection and the Descent of Man*, Chicago, Aldine. Surveys recent research and theory on selection occurring within animal societies with articles on the functions of gregariousness and the origins of mating systems, altruism and cooperation as well as wide ranging discussions of social spacing and aggression.

Crook, J. H., ed. (1970), *Social Behaviour in Birds and Mammals*, London, Academic Press. A collection of research and review articles ranging in topics from socio-ecological studies of stress in rodents, through social studies of primates to the ethology of human facial expressions.

Hinde, R. A. (1974), *Biological Bases of Human Social Behaviour*, New York, McGraw-Hill. An ethologist's view of human behaviour mainly by way of inferences from animal data, strong on developmental studies and processes.

Lerner, I. M. (1968), *Heredity, Evolution and Society*. San Francisco, W. H. Freeman. A good textbook discussing relations between biological and genetical principles and evolutionary change in societies.

Wilson, E. O. (1975), *Sociobiology: The new synthesis*, Harvard, Belknap. A contemporary synthesis of recent developments in natural selection theory and socio-ecology of animals with insights on Man.

Chapter 3
Cross-Cultural Perspectives

Gustav Jahoda

Introduction

From the dawn of human history until the twentieth century, people everywhere saw themselves as radically different from others. Travellers in remote parts of Africa, Asia, the South Seas or South America brought back tales of the strange and exotic modes of life they had encountered. Similarly, the inhabitants of these distant parts had names for themselves which can be roughly rendered as 'the people' (e.g. 'Navaho' or 'Bantu'), seeming to imply thereby that only they were really fully human; the same was true of the ancient Greeks and Chinese. During the last half-century western technology has swept across the globe, carrying in its wake western ideas and beliefs; the latter include both Christianity and Marxism, science and education. The modern air-traveller who goes from the airport to the air-conditioned hotel may therefore be forgiven if he feels that the world has been homogenized and most of the glaring differences wiped out. In fact he would be quite wrong, as he could readily discover by moving out of the urban centres to the villages and settlements in which a large proportion of the world's population continue to live. It is true that hardly any have remained entirely unaffected by change; on the other hand, much of the change has been peripheral and the basic pattern of life, including mode of subsistence, customs and rituals, ideas and beliefs have remained intact. Although it has been defined in many different ways, it is essentially this coherent pattern of behaviour and its products that are described by the term 'culture'.

A purely static and descriptive notion of culture would, however, be inadequate and misleading. Culture is also what the distinguished geneticist Waddington called an 'information-transmitting system', which provides man with an evolutionary system distinct from the biological one governing the animal world. There is no evidence that our Stone Age ancestors were biologically very different from modern man, and most of the vast transformations that have taken place appear to have been the outcome of cultural evolution which is socially rather than genetically transmitted. The manner in which different types of cultural change occurred was, of course, considerably influenced by such factors as habitat and ecology, which limited the range of possible modes of adaptation open to people within a given environment. Thus Aborigines living in extremely arid regions of Australia had fewer options available to them than inhabitants of tropical islands with lush vegetation and an abundant supply of meat and fish. Such circumstances will also influence the nature of a people's social organization, but that is the business of the social anthropologist. The psychologist is primarily concerned with understanding the behaviour of individuals and its determinants, and the study of culture and ecology is a means to that end. While social psychologists are chiefly interested in the social factors affecting behaviour, the cross-cultural approach is not confined to these; in fact both its major problem and the greatest opportunity it offers is that of disentangling the effects of predominantly social from other influences on behaviour.

Since the issue is a complex one, it is best presented schematically (Figure 2). The column on the left represents ecologies, the nature of the physical environments; it should be noted that two of these are represented as being roughly the same, and one as different. In the centre column separate cultures are shown ($C_1 - C_3$) together with what are here somewhat clumsily called their 'transmission mechanisms' (TM). This joint presentation is intended to indicate that cultures are not free-floating entities, but are in most of their aspects embodied in the social structure and the behavioural patterns of the people. The actual referent of the term 'culture' can vary widely, and it must be admitted that there is a considerable element of arbitrariness in the concrete specification of the extent of a culture. Thus the term 'western culture' might encompass the whole of Europe and the US, but could for certain purposes exclude such areas as the extreme south of Italy. Broadly speaking 'culture' can refer to groups

ecologies   cultures, together with their   individuals
transmission mechanisms

Figure 2 Schematic presentation of relationships studied

of nations, or a single one; or it can refer to sub-units such as tribes, social classes or castes. While this vagueness may be somewhat disconcerting, it does not matter a great deal in practice as long as an investigator clearly identifies the unit with which he is concerned.

The key transmission mechanism is of course the family, though it is never the sole one. In western culture the formal educational system and the mass media are important transmission channels; in tribal groups the preparation for initiation, the rite of transition to adult status, is often undertaken by people outside the extended family. In addition, there are in all societies subtle ways in which cultural norms and values are communicated in the course of ordinary everyday social interaction. The process used to be thought of as a kind of casting people within a culture into a particular mould, but this is much too rigid an image. One might think of it more in the way Kepler fancied the stars affect people:

In what manner does the countenance of the sky at the moment of a man's birth determine his character? It acts on the person during his life in the manner of the loops which a peasant ties at random around the pumpkins in his field: they do not cause the pumpkin to grow, but they determine its shape (quoted in Koestler's *The Watershed*, p. 42).

One might then liken culture to a specific length of string tied around a particular part of the pumpkins; when mature they would then exhibit a basic similarity of shape in spite of a wide range of variation. This basic similarity, the joint product of all the influences mentioned, is symbolized by C in the right-hand column of Figure 2; in other words, members of culture C_1 will share certain characteristics which distinguish them from members of C_2. It will be noted that the squares representing individuals contain three further entries, which will now be described in turn.

First of all S refers to features of specific psychological processes, being the outcome of *direct* effects of ecological conditions. Although this is an important sphere of cross-cultural study it usually seems to have little if any bearing on social behaviour and will therefore be only briefly illustrated. A famous case is the work of Segall, Campbell and Herskovits (1966) who postulated that 'terrain permitting unrestricted distance vision like an open plain or a closed-in environment such as a dense forest region would lead to' the learning of contrasting habits of perceptual inference. The arrows leading to S_1 and S_2 represent such effects, which are relatively independent of the salient aspects of a culture.

So far no account has been taken of the fact that individuals at birth are not empty vessels, but are equipped with genetically transmitted characteristics which can again be analytically separated into two parts. One of these is what might be crudely called 'universal human nature' (U) present in all normal humans everywhere; the other consists of genetically determined individual variations around this, labelled G_{x1} to G_{y3}. Since these are not relevant for the present purpose, they will henceforth be ignored as indicated by the broken line surrounding them. Nevertheless, it must be pointed out that their presence greatly increases human variability; and while this is no doubt desirable on biological and aesthetic grounds, it makes the task of isolating the component parts vastly more complicated.

It may have been noted that genetic elements of whole populations, as distinct from those of individuals, have been left out of this scheme. There was a time when differences between peoples were almost invariably put down to 'race', and as John Stuart Mill pointed out long ago this tended to be a pseudo-explanation which saved a lot of trouble in looking for other factors. Nowadays we are often not at all clear in the case of various psychological characteristics whether or not they have a predominantly genetic basis. Hence it is more common to work on the opposite assumption, namely that environmental factors might be responsible; and it is only when extensive research has failed to show the likelihood of such factors operating that one is ready to consider genetic elements.

The conceptual framework offered here represents an ideal towards which cross-cultural psychologists are working, but so far it remains a fairly distant one. Given the limitations of both theory and method, the immediate goals are more modest. Broadly speaking they are twofold: (i) describing varieties of social behaviour encountered in different cultural settings and attempting to analyse their origins; (ii) sorting out what is similar across different cultures and thus likely to be our common human heritage. These will be dealt with separately for convenience, but in practice there is a good deal of overlap in aims and methods. Generally (i) focuses more on complex social aspects of behaviour such as personality and attitudes, while (ii) tends to be more concerned with fundamental psychological processes.

Varieties of character and social behaviour and their origins

There has long been interest in what used to be called 'national characters', and the ideas of David Hume on this are shrewd and in some ways entirely in harmony with current thinking. He wrote as follows:

The vulgar are apt to carry all *national characters* to extremes; and, having once established it as a principle, that any people are knavish, or cowardly, or ignorant, they will admit of no exception, but comprehend every individual under the same censure. Men of sense condemn these un-distinguishing judgements; though, at the same time, they allow that each nation has a peculiar set of manners, and that some particular qualities are more frequently to be met with among one people than among their neighbours. The common people in Switzerland have probably more honesty than those of the same rank in Ireland; and every prudent man will, from that circumstance alone, make a difference in the trust he re-poses in each. We have reason to expect greater wit and gaiety in a French-man than in a Spaniard; though Cervantes was born in Spain (*Of National Characters*).

Translated into contemporary jargon he is saying that although ignorant people take national stereotypes too seriously, they contain a core of truth and therefore should not be altogether neglected as a guide to behaviour (see chapter 1). Hume then went on to speculate about the causes of observable national differences. He thought that 'physical' causes, by which he meant ecology, including climate, were relatively unimportant: he attributed differences to 'moral' causes, what we would call social and economic factors. At the same time he remained at the level of generalities and was unable to say anything about the process whereby differences arose and came to be transmitted. This needed a theory of personality and social beha-viour, and such a theory was provided by Freudian psychoanalysis. Freud postulated that the critical variable influencing adult charac-ter is the mode of child-rearing. It only needed a further step to assume that ways of bringing up children might vary systematically in different cultures, and an attractive and seemingly straightforward explanatory model was at hand. This step was taken by Abram Kardiner, an American psychoanalyst in close touch with anthro-pologists working in a wide range of cultures. Kardiner (1945) pro-posed that each culture has what he described as a set of 'primary institutions', consisting in the main of child-rearing practices, family organization and subsistence techniques. These result in a 'basic personality structure' (BPS) characteristic of the given culture, which in turn generates congruent 'secondary institutions' comprising art, folklore and religion. Since each culture contains, of course, a wide variety of different personalities the BPS must be regarded as merely one element, albeit a key one, of the personalities within that culture. The virtue of this kind of scheme is that it promises to throw light on the relationships between E, TM and C in Figure 2. Thus among the Alorese the mainstay of the diet consisted of vegetable crops, for which women were responsible; this led to maternal neglect, producing a BPS characterized by anxiety, suspicion and mistrust.

How were these conclusions arrived at? The anthropologists returning from the field brought with them (i) ethnographic descriptions, (ii) biographies of informants and (iii) Rorschach protocols. Kardiner studied (i) and formulated an expected BPS with the aid of this material; he then went on to analyse (ii) while a Rorschach expert scored (iii) 'blind' (i.e. without knowing from which society the protocols came, which might have led to bias). Subsequent comparison of the pictures yielded from these different sources were regarded as showing a good fit. This kind of approach which has come to be known as the 'culture-and-personality school' was followed by a series of similar studies. Yet although the material provided was usually rich and fascinating, the weaknesses of the method became increasingly obvious.* First of all this type of inquiry usually started by taking for granted (rather than demonstrating) the universal validity of the bulk of psychoanalytic theory. The claimed empirical verification by means of projective techniques has also undergone critical scrutiny; samples of subjects were usually small, and their nature unspecified. Moreover, the cross-cultural validity of projective techniques remains somewhat debatable. Leaving this aside, it has been noted that even within such small samples considerable heterogeneity of character emerged, throwing doubt on the concept of BPS. In general the theoretical framework had to be very loose so as to

---

*LeVine (1973) has looked at the whole issue afresh and made proposals designed to overcome the problems. However, at present this remains a programme and no empirical research has as yet been conducted along the lines he suggested.

accommodate highly complex data; at the same time, this looseness practically guaranteed some kind of fit between theory and data as viewed after the event. No broad principles have been isolated which would enable us to make predictions about cultures other than those already intensively studied. In sum it was a brave attempt, but an excessively ambitious one in view of the relatively crude tools at our disposal. In spite of this the effort has not been altogether wasted; more recent work of this kind has avoided some of the earlier mistakes, and for instance, Whiting (1963) has made a more solid contribution towards our understanding of the effects of child-rearing in different cultures.

In order to overcome some of the troubles of the 'culture-and-personality' school an entirely different research strategy was devised which is highly ingenious, permitting the testing of psychological hypotheses without any interaction between individuals and psychologists. The tool mostly employed for this purpose is known as the Human Relations Area Files (HRAF), containing ethnographic descriptions of more than 200 cultures in every part of the world. The information is organized into categories covering most major aspects of social life. For instance, those relating to infancy and early childhood include scales dealing with five aspects of the transition from infancy to childhood; they are roughly summarized as follows:

   weaning – from late and gentle to very early and severe;

   motor skills – from strong encouragement to strong discouragement;

   autonomy – from late and gradual to very early and abrupt;

   elimination control – from none during infancy to before six months;

   covering genitals – from naked adults to covering from birth.

Since HRAF also stores a vast range of data about adult behaviour, it is possible in theory to test an enormous variety of hypotheses about the relationships between different aspects of behaviour cross-culturally. In practice the range is somewhat restricted, as the amount of information available for each culture and its quality tend to be rather uneven. Nonetheless, it is usually possible to find a sizeable number of cultures for which adequate data are available.

As an example one might cite one of a series of studies by Whiting (1959), quoting the basis of his hypotheses in his own words:

If a parent in caring for a child and satisfying his needs was frequently absent when he was in a high state of need – that is, hungry, cold, or suffering from some other discomfort – he would be very likely to engage in fantasies which would represent his mother or other caretaker satisfying his needs. Assuming that the mother eventually comes and feeds him or covers him up, this act should reinforce his magical thinking and increase the probability that he will produce fantasy images of his mother when she is absent and he is in need. It is our hypothesis that this type of magical thinking underlies a preoccupation with ghosts and spirits of the dead at the cultural level of abstraction. Specifically then, our hypothesis may be stated as follows: Those societies which are relatively neglectful of infants should be more afraid of ghosts at funerals than those societies in which children are treated indulgently during their infancy (p. 182).

Whiting then analysed material from forty-five cultures for which appropriate information was available in HRAF, which yielded the following distribution:

Degree of	*Fear of Ghosts at Funerals*	
Over Indulgence	*Low*	*High*
HIGH	20	5
LOW	8	12

It will be seen that there is a strong and significant association in the predicted direction. This is consistent with the hypothesis, though it cannot prove it because it is possible that a common factor might underlie both variables. For instance, it is quite conceivable that a harsh environment both forces the parents to be less indulgent and increases the probability of a fear of ghosts. In fact, there is another well-known HRAF study by Barry, Child and Bacon (1959) which suggests that the type of subsistence economy in a culture strongly influences the mode of child-rearing. In terms of Figure 2 this study would link E with both TM and C, while the Whiting study just discussed would be confined to the relation between the TM and C alone. The kind of approach exemplified by HRAF is potentially very fruitful, but it is open to a number of weaknesses among which the adequacy of the raw material is perhaps the major one.* Recognition of this difficulty has led to modifications of research strategy as illustrated by a recent study of the effects of parental deprivation on children. Instead of relying exclusively on pre-coded data in HRAF, Rohner (1974) not only went back to the original ethnographic sources, but combined this method with actual field studies, both intra- and cross-cultural. While it is too early to judge the success of this venture, it seems to have considerable promise.

In the studies so far discussed actual data about both child-rearing and adult characteristics were considered, but this is not always necessary. In some cases particular mechanisms of transmission are put forward on theoretical grounds, and certain consequences predicted. An example of this is the work of LeVine (1966) whose point of departure was the work of McClelland (1961) on achievement motivation (*nAch*). LeVine postulated the existence of specific correspondences between individual motivations and the requirements of social roles within given societies. The social system is viewed as a selective and normative environment which exerts pressures in favour of those personality traits which enhance performance in salient social roles. The pressures operate through socializing agents such as parents or teachers who influence the developing individuals through direct or indirect training methods – the TM in Figure 2. The result is a skew of personality traits in the population towards the socially desirable motives. It should be noted that unlike in Kardiner there is no assumption of any uniformity of basic character structure throughout the population.

Whilst McClelland claimed religious ideology as the key element related to *nAch*, LeVine regarded the status mobility system as crucial. This refers to the manner in which a person can rise within a hierarchy of ranked positions. In some cultures the traditional pattern for moving up the social scale is that of attaching oneself to a high-

* Another is 'Galton's Problem', so called because he raised it in 1889 during the discussion of Tylor's pioneering paper proposing what amounts to cross-cultural survey method. The problem, briefly, is that of distinguishing 'historical' associations due to a common social heritage from 'functional' ones which are assumed in hypothesis testing. Several solutions to this problem have been proposed (cf. Naroll, 1970).

status person and being obedient and loyal towards this person; in others it may be outstanding performance in fulfilling an occupational role that is rewarded by high status. Now in Nigeria where LeVine was working there are two groups, the Hausa and the Ibo, whose status mobility systems emphasize compliance and achievement respectively. The Ibo in particular place high emphasis on skill, enterprise and initiative, which are rewarded by the attainment of a set of ranked titles awarded with great ceremonial display. Hence LeVine predicted that the Ibo would be higher in *nAch* than the Hausa.

In order to test this hypothesis he used a novel method, collecting reports of dreams from samples of members of these two groups and scored them for achievement imagery. Thus a dream of winning a scholarship to study abroad would be scored positive for *nAch*, whilst one of winning a girl at a party would be negative. On this basis the percentage of *nAch* dreamers among the Ibo was forty-three, as compared with only seventeen among the Hausa. This highly significant difference is, of course, consistent with the hypothesis. Studies of this kind may be viewed as being quasi-experimental, the culture being the 'treatment' and particular aspects of the behaviour of individuals the dependent variable. As has already been pointed out, no actual data are collected on *TM* whose nature is merely inferred from general information about the social structure. The characteristics of samples of individuals are then compared in C_1 and C_2; it should also be observed that the aim is no longer to describe the personality as a global entity, but merely to bring out differences in the frequency with which one particular motive is operative.

Although LeVine's work is a model of its kind, it must be said that in general cross-cultural studies of personality and motivation are fraught with difficulties and pitfalls. Therefore there has been a tendency to move away from this risky and somewhat unrewarding sphere, following the cognitive trend prevailing in other areas of psychology. Prominent here is the study of 'subjective culture', pioneered in the main by Triandis. This focuses on comparisons of the ways in which people in different cultures experience their social environment. The aim is primarily that of describing cognitive structures, involving the analysis of what are often highly complex relationships. As an example one might take 'A cross-cultural study of role perceptions' by Triandis (1972), which started with an elaborate theoretical formulation that cannot be presented here. In essence it suggested that a limited number of general factors (solidarity, status, intimacy and hostility) should be able to account for most of the variance in role perceptions both within and across cultures. An instrument called 'the role differential' was constructed after pre-tests of subjects in various cultures which provided information about the kinds of behaviour likely to occur between persons holding the various roles. The outcome was an extensive set of scales involving 100 role pairs such as male–female or father–son. An illustrative item will be given, which also shows that some of the items in the scales may appear somewhat bizarre to the outsider: 'A prostitute would/would not let a client go first through a door.'

At the same time it also indicates that the items are well-defined and relate to specific situations, whether or not the subjects had actually experienced these themselves. This instrument was administered to some 1800 subjects in the US, Greece, India, Peru and Taiwan. Results indicate that role perception is relatively homogeneous within cultures, though there are variations associated with personality, education and social status. There were large variations across cultures, which do not readily lend themselves to a summary; for instance it emerged that the father–son role is quite different in India and Greece. However, it would be misleading to isolate such individual instances, since the main object was to delineate clusters and demonstrate that they can be analysed according to a limited set of dimensions. Triandis suggests that the construction of this kind of cognitive map can be of major importance in understanding various aspects of behaviour, including those related to social change and modernization. In terms of Figure 2 the analysis concentrates on the right-hand column, comparing individuals within and between cultures.

The approaches mentioned so far were mainly of the survey type, employing interviews, projective techniques and other verbal measures. In recent years more experimental procedures have been introduced and one example is the work on cooperative and competitive behaviour, first stimulated by anthropological observations which suggested that the mode of child-rearing in rural communities appears to be more likely to induce cooperative behaviour. Madsen and Shapira (1970) report on a series of studies with children in which this notion was tested, using a game-like task with children where success was dependent on cooperative behaviour. Comparative studies of urban and rural children in several cultures fully supported the hypothesis. There have also been a few field-experiments, such as the cross-national one by Feldman (1968). An experimenter would approach a randomly determined passer-by in a city street with the question 'Excuse me, sir, did you just drop this dollar/5 franc bill?' The dependent variable was the frequency with which people accepted the money (which had, of course, not been dropped). The percentages of subjects cheating their compatriots or foreigners in Boston and Paris respectively are set out below.

	Boston	Paris
fellow-citizen	14%	2½%
foreigner	27%	5%

It will be seen that while in absolute terms people in Paris were more honest than those in Boston (a blow to American self-stereotypes) both similarly favoured their countrymen. Now historically it has always been more reprehensible to harm a member of the ingroup than an outsider. Moreover, what was judged good and evil varied widely in space and time. Thus in Europe it used to be good to torture and burn witches, or in India widows were ritually immolated – the range of permissible or prescribed behaviour is vast. Does this mean that morality is relative to culture, or does it have universal aspects? This leads on to our second theme.

Universals of human behaviour

The problem of moral behaviour is a complex one that cannot adequately be dealt with here. It is possible to make a distinction between the contents of moral judgements and the process of arriving at such judgements, which has a strong cognitive component. While there can be no argument about cultural diversity of content, certain basic principles may well have a biological as well as social basis, being essential to the survival of any human group; for instance, no culture is known where there is freedom to kill, maim, or steal from anybody one dislikes. Given these common elements, one can go on to investigate the process of arriving at moral judgement. Piaget (1932) has suggested that its development follows a sequence of stages, which were subsequently modified by Kohlberg and tested cross-culturally (1969). He used a set of stories like one about a desperately poor man who stole food for his wife, asking whether he should have done it. According to Kohlberg the justifications for their answers offered by children in widely varying cultures followed a closely similar age trend. If this finding is replicated by other investigators, then the process of making moral judgements will have been demonstrated as a pan-human one, independent of specific variations in content. This makes good sense if one considers that the process is primarily a cognitive one. Currently one of the most active fields of research is that focusing on the cross-cultural validity of the Piagetian model of cognitive development, which in general is standing up very well to this stringent test (cf. Berry and Dasel, 1973). However, since this cannot be dealt with here, the quest for universals will be illustrated with something more directly relevant to social interaction, namely the facial expression of emotions.

This problem has a long history, beginning with Darwin, who asked missionaries and travellers to complete a questionnaire about people in various parts of the world:

It seemed to me highly important to ascertain whether the same expressions and gestures prevail ... with all the races of mankind ... Whenever the same movements of the features or body express the same emotions in several distinct races of man, we may infer with much probability, that such expressions are true ones – that is, are innate or instinctive. Conventional expressions or gestures, acquired by the individual during life, would probably have differed in the different races, in the same manner as does their language (quoted in Klineberg, 1935).

Darwin's conclusion was that there are some basic expressions of emotion which are genetically determined, though he was well aware that many aspects are learned. The opposite view, that there is no inherited component, has been put forward recently by such writers as LaBarre (1947) and Birdwhistell (1963). These 'relativists' in the main support their views by descriptions, often anecdotal, of cultural differences; and until recently the 'universalists' did little better. Then Ekman (1972) embarked on an extensive series of careful studies which go a long way towards resolving the problem. He employed two complementary methods, which he calls the 'components' and 'judgement' approaches. In the first, facial expressions are regarded as responses to be measured, and a 'Facial Affect Scoring Technique' (FAST) was devised for this purpose; in the second, facial expressions are treated as stimuli to be judged in terms of the emotions they convey. Thus in one of the experiments American and Japanese subjects sat alone (so as to avoid the influence of culturally governed display rules) watching stressful and neutral films, while at the same time their own facial expressions were being videotaped. Japanese and American judges who viewed these tapes were found to be largely in agreement irrespective of whether they rated members of their own or of the other culture. Moreover, a FAST analysis carried out on the same tapes showed that the facial expressions in response to the stressful films were closely similar for both cultures – no indication of oriental inscrutability!

Although these findings were replicated in several literate cultures, it could be argued that they are all exposed to common mass media and might have learned to 'read' each other's emotional expression. Hence further studies were conducted with illiterate people in remote New Guinea tribes, using specially adapted methods. Subjects were told a story and asked to point to the one out of several photographs which portrayed the emotion described in the story; and they managed to do this with a high degree of success. The other method (using different subjects) was to read the stories and ask them to adopt the appropriate facial expression of the hero of the story, and this was videotaped. Then American college students, who had never seen a New Guinea tribesman, were asked to judge the emotion expressed; and again most of the emotions were correctly judged under these circumstances. In this manner Ekman clearly demonstrated that there is a universal element in the expression of emotion.

Cognitive development and emotional expression are only two examples of areas in which psychologists are working to tease out the universal human from the culture-bound features of behaviour. Others include such processes as perception, memory, categorization and aesthetic judgements. This kind of work has an importance extending well beyond social psychology, in as much as it serves to correct the cultural biases unavoidably inherent in the majority of psychological studies confined to western cultures – and within these often restricted to introductory psychology students! There are indications that some psychological 'laws' may have to be revised in the light of this research.

Cross-cultural research and social change

Although the initial impetus in cross-cultural psychology research came mainly from social psychologists, this was merely a historical accident and its scope now encompasses all aspects of behaviour. It is perhaps because the problems of social behaviour turned out to be more difficult and intractable that the field came to be widened, and this has led to further advances which themselves contributed to our understanding of social behaviour. As has already been hinted earlier, for instance, our knowledge of the process of stereotyping had until fairly recently not progressed very much beyond the general notions put forward long ago by Hume. It is, of course, true that our technology has become more efficient and large amounts of descriptive data have been collected where Hume had to rely on impressions. An increase in our understanding has been achieved when certain theoretical principles derived from general psychology were brought to bear on social behaviour, as in Tajfel's work described in chapter 12. The first really adequate theory of stereotypes was put forward by Campbell (1967) and began to be tested cross-culturally soon afterwards (Brewer, 1968).

The difficulties of establishing the nature of the relationships presented in Figure 2 will have become evident from the earlier discussion of the various attempts to cope with them. The crux of the matter is that one had to deal with exceedingly complex variables such as social and economic structures, modes of child-rearing or subsistence over which the psychologist lacks any control. Since a clear picture of the general cause-and-effect nexus is lacking, and possibly unattainable on an exclusively psychological level, it follows that the contribution of social psychologists towards the problems of cultural and social change cannot be unduly ambitious. A concrete example will help to illustrate this. A new variety of rice (IR 8) has been introduced in the Philippines (as well as other parts of south-east Asia) which has a far higher yield and is more disease resistant than the indigenous variety that remained unchanged for centuries. However, IR 8 requires special treatment; sprays and fertilizers must be used, irrigation water controlled and harvesting adjusted to the different rates of growth. In sum, a whole range of established ways of behaviour have to be substantially changed if the new variety is to be successfully grown; but this is not all. Under the existing share tenancy the farmer may benefit very little, the bulk of the gain accruing to the landlord. Or again, even where the farmer is his own boss, so many of his relatives might wish to help with the harvest and borrow the proceeds of the sale of his rice, that he is little better off in the end. Hence it is not surprising that many farmers gave up and reverted to traditional ways. This example is drawn from a study by Guthrie (1970), and is typical of many parts of the developing world.

In the face of such daunting problems, is there anything cross-cultural psychology can do to help? The answer is that there are several ways in which a modest contribution can be and has been made, and some examples will be given. The most common function has been a diagnostic one, which can be of value to social planners in developing countries. Given that their goal is modernization (though not necessarily westernization), it can be ascertained what proportion and what sections of the population have an outlook receptive to change. Several scales have been developed for this purpose, one of the most widely used being the overall-modernity (OM) scale of Smith and Inkeles (1966) which characterizes the individual responding in the modern direction as follows:

1. He has an active interest in public issues.
2. He wants higher education for his children.
3. He approves of new agricultural techniques.
4. He prefers candidates who have higher education.
5. He believes that hard work is important for his country's future.

6. He approves of science.
7. He approves of family limitation.
8. He is interested in world news.
9. He believes that he can understand the thinking of distant peoples.
10. He agrees that a man can be good without religion.

It is obvious that scales of this kind have a number of assumptions built into them (e.g. the puritan ethic) which may be questionable. The OM scale is fairly crude, but this is probably unavoidable with an instrument designed for comparisons between various countries and cultures; and it has been successfully used for this purpose. Other more refined scales have been specially constructed for specific cultures, taking their particular characteristics into account. Among the most interesting ones of this type are the T-W (Traditional-Western) scales prepared by Dawson for West Africans (1969a), Australian Aborigines (1969b) and Hong Kong Chinese (1971). In the case of the last of these, Dawson conducted an experiment in which he measured the galvanic skin response (GSR) as an index of anxiety and conflict over tradition versus modern values in a context of pressure towards attitude change. This is one of the very few examples of the employment of physiological measurement in this sphere.

Since the objective of the social planner is to change people's behaviour in relation to such areas as agricultural methods, health habits and family limitation, psychology can help in persuasion attempts. There have been some very useful studies of this kind, as for instance, by Spector and others (1971) which tried to identify the optimal communication media for getting people to adopt new practices. However, it turns out (not surprisingly) that it is very much harder to get people to change their way of life than to buy a different brand of toothpaste. A complementary task is that of assessing whether the introduction of a community development or similar scheme does alter motivations in the direction of self – as well as collective improvement. Sinha (1969) carried out an important investigation of this in India. Although some effects of the development programme were discernible 'there was not much evidence that the masses in the villages had shaken off their "placid, pathetic contentment", nor was there much sign that new aspirations and urges for development had begun to pulsate in the rural population' (p. 44). An experiment has also been conducted in urban areas in India with the object of providing direct training in achievement motivation, using procedures with a theoretical rationale; the outcome of this work by McClelland and Winter (1969) was promising, though not conclusive.

It seems likely that in the longer run cross-cultural psychology will make a greater indirect contribution through its influence on education than it has been able to do through the kinds of direct attacks illustrated above. This is because there is evidence that schooling does more to transform people's outlook as well as giving them skills, than any other experience; for instance, 'modernity' as assessed by various scales nearly always correlates most highly with years of schooling. This will not only involve social psychology in a cross-cultural context, on which this chapter has concentrated, but also developmental and experimental cross-cultural work. The boundaries of academic fields are to a large extent arbitrary, and where the problem demands it they must be crossed. Although cross-cultural psychology can trace its ancestry to the end of the nineteenth century it lay fallow for nearly half a century. In view of this, its progress over little more than two decades has been substantial, and it may be safely predicted that in the future, psychology, in general, as well as social psychology in particular, will undergo considerable changes as they become gradually pervaded by a cross-cultural perspective, correcting our present tendency to look at the world through our own cultural prism.

Further Reading

Kaplan, B., ed. (1961), *Studying Personality Cross-Culturally*, Evanston, Row Peterson. An overall survey of the older work in this field, including a presentation and critical assessment of Kardiner's work.

Hsu, F. L. J. (1972), *Psychological Anthropology*, Cambridge, Mass., Schenkman. Similar to the above but somewhat wider and more up-to-date in its coverage, including surveys of work in major world regions.

Price-Williams, D. R., ed. (1969), *Cross-Cultural Studies*, Penguin Books. A collection of readings dealing with cognitive aspects as well as some culture–personality problems.

Munroe, R. L. and R. H. (1975), *Cross-Cultural Human Development*, Monterey, Calif., Brooks/Cole. Contains an account of child development in three different cultures, and is a good general introductory text.

Lloyd, B. B. (1972), *Perception and Cognition: A cross-cultural perspective*, Penguin Books. A concise critical survey of a field which has become the predominant concern of cross-cultural psychologists.

Cole, M. and Scribner, S. (1974), *Culture and Thought*, New York, Wiley. Covers similar ground in more detail, and is written from a distinctive and increasingly important theoretical standpoint.

Brewer, M. B., and Campbell, D. T. (1976), *Ethnocentrism and Intergroup Attitudes*, New York, Wiley. A novel departure, describing an attempt at the cross-cultural testing of social psychological theories.

Berry, J. W. (1976), *Human Ecology and Cognitive Style*, New York, Wiley. Another pioneering work cutting across the usual personality-cognition distinction which links both to ecological variations.

Brislin, R. W., Lonner, W. J., and Thorndike, R. M. (1973), *Cross-Cultural Research Methods*, New York, Wiley. A more advanced text which not only discusses methods, but gives numerous examples of their application.

The two main journals dealing with cross-cultural psychology are the *International Journal of Psychology* and the *Journal of Cross-Cultural Psychology*.

Part Two
Social Interaction

Introduction

The study of social interaction has always been one of the main concerns of social psychology. Such study immediately reveals part of the complexity of the task of the social psychologist, in that the problems of studying and understanding the behaviour and experience of even two people interacting together are much more than twice those of studying just one person. Such study also implies that the appropriate unit of analysis for social behaviour is often the interacting unit – the two-person dyad or the small social group – rather than the individual. It can, in fact, be argued that studies at this level of analysis, which is neither that of the general psychologist nor of the macro-sociologist, have been the most distinctive contribution of social psychologists; indeed for some writers social psychology is synonymous with the study of face-to-face interaction.

We have taken a more ambitious view of our discipline. To be concerned with interaction as *the* goal runs the risk of ending with a social psychology of nods, twitches and interpersonal exchanges, all of which take place in some unspecified limbo land. For us interaction is central, not just for its own intrinsic fascination, but as the most important means whereby individuals and the social systems within which they live come into contact. Whether a creator or a creature of society, a person will bring about change or be changed himself through his contact with others. Thus social interaction provides the mediating link in the three-level analysis – individual: group: society – which should be characteristic of social psychology. That, at any rate, is the goal at which we must aim. Much of the material at hand, however, has been focused on only part of the full picture; in particular, on the dyad or group alone or on the relations between the group and the individuals in it. Since a textbook cannot consist solely of hopes or exhortations, the chapters in this section inevitably represent a compromise between what the authors hope their fields of interest will become and what they have been and are. Part Two, then, is focused particularly on the second unit in the chain, and Parts Three and Four will take a more comprehensive view.

As good a place as any to start our study of interaction is at the beginning, and in chapter 4 H. R. Schaffer suggests that the beginning of interaction lies in the child's very early manifestations of reciprocity in his reactions to those around him. Striking developments in the nature and selectivity of social interaction in the first year of the infant's life appear to be precursors of the elaborate, comprehensive and sophisticated social skills which the individual develops throughout his life-span (cf. Looft, 1972; Stone and Farberman, 1970, Part Nine). An exhaustive treatment of the development of interactional skills in childhood could include the child's acquisition of language, his increasing interaction with peers, his ever-developing sense of self, and the changing nature of interaction and friendship in adolescence. But the territory is too vast and the topics, as yet, too fragmented for that to be possible or sensible here. So Schaffer wisely chooses to follow his analysis of very early social developments with a discussion of the problems involved in the child's attaining full communicative competence. Here the concern is not with the acquisition of the complexities of the language system as a cognitive achievement on the part of the child, but with the properly social question of how the child succeeds in using language to communicate effectively with others, that is, as the basis of his social behaviour.

This theme is continued in chapter 5, where C. Fraser starts by illustrating how a child must learn to relate different communication systems to one another and to the situation or context in which they are being used. Thereafter he attempts to analyse in some detail linguistic and non-linguistic communication in face-to-face interaction. To help organize the disparate materials relevant to this topic, he makes use of a simple framework of four systems and three types of communication. It is strange that for such a central problem in social psychology, much clarification and synthesizing remains to be done. Language and communication play crucial and omnipresent parts in interaction and in man's understanding of his society, yet social psychologists, at least until very recently, have fought shy of the detailed study of communication which is a necessary prerequisite for the full understanding of social behaviour and social systems. It would be wrong to say that social psychology has ignored communication. But in so far as it has been an important concern, for example, in the study of persuasive communications in attitude change (see chapter 11), communication has been studied in terms of concepts and inferences several steps removed from a detailed account of how communication is carried out linguistically and non-linguistically. If the type of description and analysis of interaction outlined in chapters 4 and 5 can be combined with the study of the effects of communication, as discussed in chapter 11, then we would have the basis of a much more powerful and much more detailed account of interaction than hitherto.

Of necessity, more traditional treatments of social behaviour were much more molar and often concentrated on the outcomes of interaction, eschewing the fine details of interaction processes. A major theme within this tradition has been the study of interpersonal co-operation and competition, and, in chapter 6, Eiser presents a balanced appraisal of this area. He devotes the first half of his chapter to one particularly influential tradition of work, namely the experimental study of gaming behaviour, which has assumed the central importance for cooperation and competition of the pay-offs received by participants. The view of human cooperativeness, or lack of it, which emanates from such work is a rather depressing one. But, by questioning some of the major emphases and limitations within that tradition itself, and by examining, in the second half of the chapter, more recent concerns with altruism and with notions of justice, Eiser argues that implacable competitiveness and over-whelming concern with short-term self-interest need not be our lot. There is hope for us after all.

Two deliberate omissions from our account of dyadic interaction merit brief comments. We could have asked 'Why do people interact?' and 'With whom are they likely to interact?' Both questions are important and potentially of considerable interest to the social psychologist. As yet, however, there is little basis for attempting an answer to the first, other than in terms of the material already presented in chapter 4. In so far as social psychologists do touch on the question 'Why interaction?' they usually conclude that it satisfies some general needs or specific goals of individuals, but the conclusions are normally examples of answers which are either too general or too specific to be very informative. (See the discussion of the perspective of social psychology in chapter 1.) They are usually implausibly psychological, completely ignoring sociological constraints and pressures which often ensure that we have little choice but to associate with others, in families or in factories, for example. The position is rather different regarding the second question, 'With whom shall we associate?' A great deal of empirical effort has recently gone into studies of factors that contribute to interpersonal attraction (e.g. Berscheid and Walster, 1969; Huston, 1974). Although this work is alluded to at several points, we have not provided a systematic account of it because, as yet, the a-theoretical, experimental studies which constitute the bulk of these efforts do not, in our view, contribute intellectually convincing answers to the intrinsically interesting questions posed by the development and maintenance of attraction to particular people.

Much of our interaction occurs not with a single other person but in small social groups, of relatives, friends and workmates. Chapter 7 begins with a brief consideration of whether or not it is possible to extrapolate from dyads to groups, and then introduces some of the basic concepts held to characterize groups. In chapters 7 and 8, C. Fraser then presents a selective review of the vast amount of work on small groups, or group dynamics. In chapter 7 he considers different types of structure in groups, and their relations to what happens in group interaction. In addition, there is an analysis of alternative conceptions of leaders and of leadership, in an attempt to answer questions such as 'Can leaders be readily identified?' and 'What constitutes leadership behaviour in groups?'

The two major topics of chapter 8 are the group processes which occur during interaction and the products or outcomes which result from group interaction. In the former the focus is on the processes of mutual influence in groups, especially normative and informational social influence. The operation of social influence processes is also used to explain some distinctive phenomena of group decision-making, which have been described as group polarization effects. The second part of the chapter contains a brief discussion of some of the factors which determine the productiveness of groups and the satisfaction experienced by group members. The latter includes an evaluation of the effects of sensitivity groups. In chapters 7 and 8 use is made of many experimental studies of group interaction. A recurring motif running through both chapters is an attempt to assess the validity of such evidence.

Many issues considered in connection with small groups, such as leadership and effectiveness, reappear on a larger scale in chapter 13, on interaction in organizational settings, which serves as a bridge between the detailed examination of face-to-face interaction and the larger scale questions of Part Four.

Chapter 4
The Development of Interpersonal Behaviour

H. R. Schaffer

Introduction

Interpersonal behaviour is extraordinarily complex, involving the fine dovetailing, with a great deal of precision, of a wide range of responses emitted by the participants. Yet so proficient are we in this task that in the course of everyday life we are rarely conscious of its complexity. It is only under rare and exceptional circumstances that we regard such behaviour as other than automatic – only when, for instance, we encounter disruptive conditions, witness pathological manifestations, or, for that matter, attempt to analyse and study it for the sake of scientific curiosity.

How does such proficiency come about? One way of answering this question is to adopt the developmental approach and ask how the child develops the ability to behave appropriately in interaction situations. In this way we attempt to examine the mature product in terms of the forces in the individual's past history that have brought the relevant behaviour patterns into being. There are two aspects to such an account, the descriptive and the explanatory. On the one hand, we set out to describe the nature of the child's interpersonal behaviour at various stages of development and delineate the special characteristics of each stage, and on the other hand we attempt to understand how the sequential changes we thus find are brought about. It is this approach that we shall adopt in the present chapter, and our special concern will be to examine how the young child learns to interact with other people.

In asking how a child learns to interact with others, we are already in danger of making an unjustified assumption, namely that this process is environmentally induced and can be fitted into conventional learning frameworks. That all-pervasive controversy, the heredity–environment issue, certainly dominated early accounts of the growth of social behaviour, supplying 'explanations' that ranged from William McDougall's (1908) gregarious instinct (which helps to ensure that man, by virtue of his innate endowment, is driven to seek the company of others) to the behaviourists' assertion that sociability develops only because the child learns to associate people with somatic satisfaction. To declare that both heredity and environment play a part is, of course, easy; it is less easy to spell out the nature of their interaction. But perhaps the most basic weakness of such early accounts was that they attempted to provide explanations before a body of descriptive data had been made available. It is only within recent years that systematic descriptions of social behaviour in early childhood have been published, and it is on these that we shall draw.

The beginnings of dyadic reciprocity

As was argued in chapter 1, the hallmark of all interpersonal behaviour is its reciprocity, and yet until quite recently psychology generally neglected this feature. Under the influence of stimulus-response methodology, interpersonal activities were mostly studied as though they were one-way processes; in laboratory studies of mother–child interaction, for example, measures such as the number of times the child made physical contact with the mother would be taken and their sum used as some index of the interaction; nothing would be said about how the mother responded to such contacts, in what way the nature of her response in turn impinged on her child, how this affected his further responsiveness to her, and so forth. Yet any relationship is, after all, an essentially two-way process, a kind of ping-pong game where the move of each partner is to some extent dictated by the previous move of the other, and where a close synchronization of behaviour patterns can thus emerge within the dyad. It is the development of this two-way process which any account of early social development must seek to encompass.

Reciprocal orientation

From birth on, the baby is already equipped with the means of social interaction. He manifests, that is, a variety of responses in the presence of other people to which these individuals react in a more or less predictable manner and which can thus form the beginnings of interaction sequences. These responses may be of a very basic and primitive nature – as may be seen for example, in the baby's capacity for bodily orientation. Blauvelt and McKenna (1961), in an observational study in which they recorded in great detail the behaviour of neonates during feeding, found that these babies were already capable of very precise orientational movements of the head and body. These movements were so well coordinated with those of the mother's that the two partners could fairly readily settle into a positional pattern conducive to further interaction – in particular of course, feeding, to which the mutual orientation formed a preliminary. The point of this observation is that it shows the newborn infant to be far from inert; he responds to stimulation provided by the mother with active movements that may, according to circumstances, be adaptively directed towards her, or away from her. At a later age level a somewhat similar phenomenon has been observed; Stern (1971) found a striking temporal relatedness between infant head movements and the ongoing maternal movements in $3\frac{1}{2}$-month-old babies, in that the infant's head-turns away from the mother occurred predominantly when she was approaching the infant, while head-turns towards the mother occurred with her withdrawals from the infant's visual field. Though the movements involved were so small that they became evident only from frame-by-frame analysis of films, they resulted in a mutual approach–withdrawal pattern that was mostly initiated by the mother but could in fact be initiated by either partner. The pattern showed a synchronicity that was striking in terms of the timing, rhythm, and sequencing of the interactive behaviour – as Stern puts it: 'A waltz serves as an analogy. Certain steps and turns will be cued by one partner – in between those cues both know the programme well enough to move synchronously for short periods' (Stern, 1971, p. 513).

Whatever interpretation one may wish to put on this observation (and one possibility is that the infant is attempting to control the amount of stimulation delivered to him by his mother), it provides us at a descriptive level with an illustration of one of the earliest and most basic forms of reciprocity. The infant, it appears, is biologically adapted for mutual interaction, and such interaction can be initiated and maintained by a broad range of responses that are reciprocal in nature and have signalling value.

Social signalling systems

The sending and receiving of interpersonal signals involves a variety of sensory modalities. As Vine (1970) has pointed out, each distinct system of source-plus-receiver may be regarded as a separate communication channel; for example, the tactual-kinaesthetic channel is involved in the mother's awareness of the baby's shifts of posture while she is holding him close to her, whereas her awareness of his cries refers to the vocal-auditory channel. Such distinctions are discussed in more detail in the next chapter. Though interpersonal behaviour at all age levels generally depends on the integration of a number of source-plus-receiver systems into multi-channel signalling, for the sake of convenience research workers have generally studied each such system in isolation.

Two social signalling systems which deserve special attention for their role in early development are the crying response and the smiling response. The signalling function of crying is particularly obvious, for by its means the young child can alert the mother, summon her to his side, and thus initiate interaction. Help-seeking behaviour using vocal means is found in the young of many species, but is especially important in those where the offspring is initially unable itself to get to the mother's side. This applies in particular to the human baby, where investigations have shown the cry to be not simply an unpleasant noise but to constitute a high frequency microrhythm regulated by apparently endogenous (or built-in) brain mechanisms and arranged as an auditory pattern involving quite complex sequences. Fine-grained analyses have shown the existence of three distinct types of pattern, associated with hunger, anger and pain (Wolff, 1969). Each is marked by the same temporal sequence of cry-rest-inspiration-rest, but the relative length of these components varies from one pattern to another in such a way that mothers generally have no difficulty in distinguishing between them. The pain cry, in particular, has arousing properties that the other two do not have and will ensure that the mother takes prompt action. It seems, therefore, that quite different information is carried by these patterns, that they act as signals to the child's caretakers, and that by their means the baby is already capable of determining to some extent when and how much attention he obtains. There are, moreover, individual differences in the duration of the various sequences and in the intervals between them, so that a mother is likely to respond differently to different babies. This, we may note, is one of the earliest indications of individuality; it helps, moreover, to show up the inadequacy of any view of socializing being entirely a matter of parents determining the behaviour of children. Children, even the very youngest, can determine the behaviour of parents and thereby help to create the atmosphere in which they will be reared. This point is made even more forcefully by the finding that brain-damaged infants may show quite irregular crying patterns, presumably because of injury to the endogenous mechanism which controls this response. Under these circumstances the signalling capacity of the baby will, of course, be adversely affected, with considerable implications for the mother's ability to care for the child. The end-product that we are likely to see then is a disturbed mother–child relationship, which in the past has only too often been ascribed to faulty mothering. If, however, we are willing to concede the point that a child does not start life as a *tabula rasa*, it becomes evident that such a disturbance may well begin with the child rather than the mother.

When a mother answers her child's cries she provides him with a contingency experience. It takes many such experiences and considerable cognitive development before an infant becomes capable of anticipating the outcome of his action and employing signals like the cry in a purposive and intentional manner. Yet mutual adaptation of maternal activity and infant crying occurs much earlier. This is illustrated in a study by Sander *et al.* (1970), in which infants who had been reared in a hospital nursery for the first ten days were transferred on the eleventh day to the individual care of one of two

Figure 3   Cumulative crying counts

nurses, *X* or *Y*. There was continuous automatic recording of activity and crying, and all interactions of nurse and baby were also noted. As shown in Figure 3, there were considerable individual differences even in the first ten days in the amount of crying, even though the nursery environment provided a fairly homogeneous experience for all infants. Subsequently, however, crying scores shifted fairly systematically according to the identity of the caretaker. It is apparent that infants cared for by nurse Y came to cry much less than those cared for by nurse X – a change presumably related to the fact that nurse Y's interactions with her babies were generally much longer, even though she did not respond as promptly to the cries as nurse X.

As far as smiling is concerned, quite a lot is now known about the developmental course of this response. It makes its initial appearance within the first week or two of life, is reliably elicited by certain visual and auditory stimuli from the second month on, reaches a peak of vigour around the fourth month, and becomes increasingly selective throughout the first year of life in terms of the stimuli which evoke it. There has been some disagreement as to whether smiling is indeed a 'social' response, i.e. whether it is elicited only by human-like stimuli or whether it can be observed in relation to other stimuli too. Some of the earlier investigators (Spitz and Wolf, 1964; Ahrens, 1954) considered that the human face was both the necessary and the sufficient stimulus for the smile, and though early on in the first year a mask with nothing but two eye-like dots was found to be just as effective as the full face, the human-like quality of the stimulus was considered to be an essential attribute. This conclusion has been challenged by Piaget (1953), who considered that the smile is essentially a sign of recognition and can thus be called forth by any object, social or inanimate, that is familiar. By experimentally familiarizing infants to initially novel inanimate stimuli (representing both visual and auditory patterns), Zelazo and Komer (1971) were able to confirm such a recognition hypothesis; for one thing, the infants did smile to these non-social stimuli, and for another, there was a tendency for smiling to increase with growing familiarity and then to decrease once again as the stimulus became over-familiar.

It remains true, nevertheless, that the human face is the most powerful elicitor for the baby's smile. In the early weeks of life it is triggered off by a very simple stimulus configuration, consisting principally of a pair of eye-like dots. A mask containing nothing but such dots is at first as effective in eliciting the smile as the mother's face. It is as though the infant is set, by virtue of his biological equipment, to be triggered by certain quite specific yet primitive stimuli – stimuli that are generally (though not necessarily) found in conjunction with other human beings. In so far as these other people, in their turn, find the baby's smile something that is attractive and delightful, and in so far as the child's caretakers in particular are likely to respond by smiling and other signs of attention, an interactive chain is set up and the child's chances of care, protection and survival are thus enhanced. The smile, in other words, has succeeded in its biological function as a signalling device.

Similar 'fixed action patterns' that are released by certain key stimuli have been described by ethologists for a wide range of animal species. Some animals may continue to function in this more or less automatic fashion, whereas the human infant, by virtue of his considerable perceptual learning capacity, soon becomes capable of responding to more differentiated and more individualized stimuli. Thus Ahrens (1954) by taking the human face to pieces, as it were, and observing infants' responses to stimuli containing only one feature at a time, was able to show that after about four months of age responsiveness to the eyes diminishes somewhat and the mouth becomes increasingly effective in eliciting smiling and attention. In time it requires the whole face, rather than certain parts only, to call forth the response, and eventually, at about seven or eight months of age, the infant ceases to smile at just any human being and relates to certain familiar individuals only. It is as though at first the infant's information processing apparatus is inherently set to abstract only certain universal features, but in time, with increasing experience and exposure to other people, the child becomes capable of assimilating more and more of the stimulus event. In due course, therefore, a restriction takes place in the range of eliciting stimuli; the child has learned to smile at mother rather than at eye-like dots.

Mutual gazing

The visual system is one of the most mature sensory systems at birth, and by about three months of age it has reached almost adult standards of efficiency. Because of its on-off character and the consequent ease of both initiating and terminating contact with another person it is particularly well suited to dyadic interchange, and it is thus not surprising to find that the visual–visual channel is one of the earliest means of interpersonal communication.

That the face is a particularly attractive visual stimulus to the baby has already been noted. Thanks largely to the work of Fantz (1961), it is now well-established that from birth on infants have quite definite visual 'preferences', i.e. visual attention tends to be selective rather than indiscriminate. Amongst the environmental attributes which are known to be particularly attractive to the baby are pattern, movement, high contrast, complexity, and three-dimensionality. Now if one were to design an optimal stimulus that combines all these attributes and that would therefore be particularly worthy of attention, one would probably end up with a human face. Taken in conjunction with the fact that the positions naturally assumed by mother and baby in the course of feeding, changing, and other care-taking activities maximize the opportunity of exposure to the face, it is no wonder that this becomes such a significant feature to the baby.

Much of the research on early social looking has involved inanimate stimuli such as photos of faces, masks, or TV images, and has thus of necessity been concerned with uni-directional gazing. Relatively little is known so far about the beginnings of mutual gazing, yet its importance in forming the first social bond has been widely acknowledged. Thus Robson (1967), for example, has suggested that eye-to-eye contact is an innate releaser of maternal caretaking responses; Wolff (1963) has reported how real eye-to-eye contact, beginning at about six weeks of age, has a dramatic effect on mothers by making them feel related to a more responsive person; and Klaus *et al.* (1970), observing mothers' first contact with their newborn baby, were particularly struck by the intense interest of the mothers in seeing the baby's eyes and their tendency always to arrange the infant's position so as to be *en face*.

In one of the first detailed investigations of infant–mother gazing patterns, Stern (1974) was able to demonstrate clearly the interactive nature of this behaviour in a play situation involving three-month-old babies. The mother under these circumstances tends to hold her gaze at the baby a relatively long time, usually until the infant responds by gazing at her. Once mutual gazing is initiated, the mother goes on looking at the baby, while he looks at her, looks away, looks back again, and so on, as though wishing to modulate the arousal obtained by such interaction. It is thus the infant and not the mother who takes the initiative in 'making' and 'breaking' contact. The alternation so produced has, however, a regularity which Stern believes may well be a manifestation of an underlying biological rhythm which the infant brings as a 'given' to the interaction with his mother. The mother herself, during such episodes, tends to produce 'supernormal' stimuli; she leans forward, her voice is extra distinct, her gestures exaggerated and slowed, and her face far more expressive than it would be when interacting with an adult – as though wanting to ensure that the infant's attention on her should be maintained. It may well be that the ability to provide such supernormal stimulation defines the degree of maternal responsiveness – a variable that has been found to be correlated with the intensity of the infant's attachment to the mother, and which may well be expressed by such means as the extent of the mother's animation and the modulation of her facial expression.

It has been suggested (Jaffe *et al.*, 1973) that there may be regularities in the temporal patterning of mother–infant gazing that are similar to those found in adult verbal conversations, and discussed in the following chapter. If this is borne out, it would suggest the existence of rules of reciprocity that are independent of both age and the particular communication channel used. Let it be emphasized that this is as yet only a hypothesis which needs a great deal of work before it can be substantiated. What can be asserted is that from the beginning of life eye-to-eye contact is one of the main vehicles whereby reciprocity is fostered between the child and his caretakers. In view of Harlow's (1958) striking findings on the role of skin-to-skin contact in the growth of mother–infant attachments among rhesus monkeys, there has been a tendency to generalize these observations to human development – quite unjustifiably so, however, for while each species may be equipped with certain mechanisms that bind offspring to their parents, the nature of these mechanisms differs from species to species, and among humans the distance receptors assume prime importance in this respect (Walters and Parke, 1965).

But visual interaction is not only of the direct, eye-to-eye kind; it also assumes indirect forms, i.e. it may take place via features of the environment to which both partners pay simultaneous attention and which therefore come to serve as topics of mutual interest. Collis and Schaffer (1975) have demonstrated a pronounced tendency on the part of mothers to monitor the visual focus of their infants' gaze and then, almost automatically, to follow that gaze. Again we have an illustration of the way in which mutuality is fostered; the infant's spontaneous attention to his environment induces the mother to look towards the same object and, knowing his focus of interest, she is then able to use this as a context for further interaction with him by verbally labelling the object, describing it, demonstrating it, bringing it within the infant's reach, and so on. Mutual attention, in other words, may constitute merely the first step in an interactive sequence based on a joint topic. And in due course the child too will learn the significance of other people's gaze direction and will thus be able to follow as well as lead interactions of this kind. Yet another social skill required for interpersonal reciprocity is then acquired.

Attachment formation

The reciprocity of social behaviour is one primary characteristic, its selectivity another. The adult whose interpersonal relationships are all of an indiscriminate nature is judged to be psychopathic and to have failed in one of the main tasks of early childhood, namely the establishment of social bonds to certain specific individuals. The concept of attachment is used to express such selectivity (Schaffer, 1971). It denotes particular feelings which people have for one another, and behaviourally is expressed in the tendency to seek the proximity of certain other individuals. Though such a tendency may be expressed in many different ways, it occurs almost universally among animals as well as in man, and has a biological utility to those in a condition of infantile helplessness that makes it a clearly adaptive behaviour pattern (Bowlby, 1969).

Developmental course

One way of demonstrating the existence of an attachment in a young child is to separate him from the other person – as happens, for example, on hospitalization. Observations of infants under such conditions have shown (Schaffer, 1958) that, with indices of separation upset such as crying, activity, and responsiveness to nurses, a break occurs at the age of approximately seven months. In those above this age, protest, negativism to hospital staff, and upset in feeding and sleeping are to be found; in those below this age a separation from the mother elicits no protests and strangers are accepted as mother-substitutes without any obvious change in the level of responsiveness. The same has been found by studying the behaviour of children in the first eighteen months of life in a number of everyday separation situations, such as being put down after being held or left alone in the room with a stranger (Schaffer and Emerson, 1964). Under such circumstances the child may protest even in the first half-year, but his protests are evoked by termination of contact and lack of stimulation in general, and it is only in the second half-year that these become focused on specific individuals such as the mother. People, that is, are no longer interchangeable; the child has formed a bond with certain particular individuals whose company he seeks and whose loss of attention he finds upsetting. A crucial milestone in the child's social development is thus reached at this time, as a result of which a change in mother-figure is no longer tolerated.

The change from indiscriminate to specifically directed behaviour is something we have already noted in connection with the smiling response. Why should this occur? The explanation advanced at one time for the source of the infant's tie to the mother was in terms of 'cupboard love'. According to the secondary drive theory of sociability, the child becomes attracted to his mother because he learns to associate her presence with the reduction of hunger tensions, so that in time a secondary social drive emerges whereby the child demands the mother's company for its own sake. However, the work of Harlow (1958) has shown very clearly that this is unlikely to be the case; infant rhesus monkeys, given the choice of mother surrogates constructed of wire mesh or covered in terry cloth attached themselves invariably to the latter – despite the fact that their milk supply came from the former. 'Contact comfort' appeared to be the crucial variable in fostering the attraction, not the satisfaction of somatic needs.

In human infants, it has already been stated, the main perceptual mechanism at work is vision rather than touch, but here too it is in perceptual attraction and not in cupboard love that one should seek the basis of sociability. Through constant contact with such a visually salient object as the face, the infant gradually 'learns' the mother – i.e. he comes to establish a central representation corresponding to her and is thereby enabled to recognize her. Recognition involves differential behaviour, and there are indications that from the third month on the infant is already capable of responding differentially to the mother as compared with unfamiliar people. Yet this alone, it must be emphasized, cannot be taken as a sign of attachment – this, as we have just seen, does not emerge until several months later. Only in the third quarter of the first year will the infant cease to respond positively to strangers, and only then will he show an orientation to the mother in her absence by means of separation upset. Differential responsiveness plus the ability to remain oriented to the absent mother are thus the necessary conditions for the emergence of an attachment. The first of these involves recognition, the second recall – a cognitively more complex skill which appears developmentally somewhat later and which may depend on the same sort of processes that Piaget (1955) has described for the emergence of the object concept (Schaffer, 1971).

Once an attachment has been formed, the child has in the mother a secure base from which he can explore his environment. Attachment, that is, leads paradoxically to detachment. The latter term was used by Rheingold and Eckerman (1971) to describe the tendency of the child to separate himself on his own volition from the mother in order to investigate his surroundings. Such departures depend to some extent on age; the older the child the further the distance he will travel from mother and the longer he will stay away from her. To some extent they also depend on conditions that foster exploration; thus Rheingold and Eckerman, in a simple laboratory setting, were able to demonstrate that time away from mother depends on the number of toys made available, their location, and whether they were present from the start or added later. Such detachment is, however, not necessarily a negation of attachment; it should, rather, be seen as an indication of the child's growing ability to remain oriented to mother over time and distance. He now no longer needs her continuous perceptual presence, for he has, so to speak, internalized her and can carry her with him wherever he goes. And this means that, from the second year on, the relationship to the mother becomes a far more flexible and far more complex phenomenon, for it is now no longer a simple and direct striving for proximity but an orientation that can be combined with a multiplicity of other activities and relationships – an orientation that may remain dormant for long periods but that can still emerge under certain conditions in its original form of a need for close proximity.

Attachment objects

With what specific individuals does the young child form his first social relationships? As long as the secondary drive theory of sociability prevailed, there was never any doubt about the identity of the primary object – namely the mother, who feeds and cares for the child and who, under ordinary circumstances of family life in industrialized societies, spends more time with him than any other individual.

Empirical examination of this question has, however, provided a rather more complex picture (Schaffer and Emerson, 1964). For one thing, from the beginning of the phase of specific attachment formation the child is capable of forming a number of such bonds simultaneously. The number appears to be largely a function of the social setting in which the child is reared; in polymatric families, i.e. where his care is in the hands of a number of caretakers, he is likely to form multiple attachments, whereas in monomatric families one all-exclusive relationship is more probable. Furthermore, the identities of the individuals selected by the child provide useful clues as to the factors which foster attachment formation. Mothers are generally the principal objects of attachment, but such individuals as fathers, grandparents, aunts, and even young siblings have also been frequently found to elicit attachment behaviour. These individuals may only rarely participate in any aspects of the child's physical care (another argument against the secondary drive theory); they tend also to spend only a limited part of the day with the child. What seems to be more important is the readiness with which an individual is prepared to respond to the infant's signals and his general willingness to engage in playful interaction. By responding contingently to the infant's behaviour, he is able to enter into sequential chains of interactive behaviour, and it is thus the people with whom reciprocity can be built up most easily who come to form the salient objects in the child's social world.

In the past, early social development has been almost exclusively examined from the point of view of the relationship with the mother. Without wishing to deny the importance of this relationship, it does appear that a wider focus is required and that the child's capacity for multiple attachments must be recognized. In this connection, the role of the peer group needs particular mention. Thus Freud and Dann (1951) have described a group of six children, aged between three and four years, who had spent their life in a concentration camp and whose only persisting company had been each other. Under these circumstances all their attachment behaviour came to be centred on their own group – 'they cared greatly for each other and not at all for anybody or anything else'. That such a situation need not be so atypical is well illustrated by Bettelheim's (1969) account of development in the Israeli kibbutz system, where the communal method of child-rearing by professional caretakers produces a person whose capacity for individual ties tends to be blunted but whose loyalty to the group takes precedence over all else. And on an even wider scale Bronfenbrenner (1971) has shown how the peer group comes increasingly to influence the behaviour of children in both the USA and the USSR – in the former case, he claims, in opposition to the standards of adult society, with ensuing conflicts and anti-social behaviour; in the latter, by fostering at an early age a concern for others and a feeling of community.

Interaction competence in later childhood

With increasing age a child has normally the opportunity of participating in an ever-widening range of social encounters – within the extended family, in the neighbourhood, at school, and so on. In each he may be assigned a distinctive role and be expected to develop particular kinds of interactive skills, thus increasing the demands made on his communicative competence. Let us look at some aspects of these developments.

The concept of egocentrism

Mature communicative competence involves what Cicourel (1973) has called the 'reciprocity of perspectives principle'. This refers to the ability of the individual to appreciate that another's point of view is not necessarily the same as his own and to know how to make due allowance for the difference. The lack of this ability denotes an orientation which, according to Piaget (1926), constitutes a major characteristic of early childhood, namely egocentrism. The essential meaning of egocentrism is an embeddedness in one's own point of view (Looft, 1972), which in infancy is so absolute that it describes a complete lack of subject–object differentiation; at this time the child has no concept either of the self or of the other person as an independent being. But even after infancy (and most of the empirical work relating to this concept has been done with pre-school children) the child is still so dominated by one point of view (his own) that he has difficulties in allowing for the existence of other points of view which are held simultaneously and yet are equally valid.

As an illustration of egocentrism, Piaget has used the 'three-mountain problem' (Piaget and Inhelder, 1956). A model of a landscape with three mountains is put on a table and the child is asked to indicate (by means of drawing or picking out a picture) how the landscape would look from a number of perspectives. According to Piaget, the pre-school child simply cannot understand how the landscape will appear from another side of the table or even realize that it would look different. Only subsequently, when he gains the facility to deal with two relationships simultaneously, will he become capable of 'decentring', i.e. he will no longer be dominated by the single most salient element that captures his attention, and be able to take into account the possibility that the same object may in fact give rise to different perceptions, depending on one's point of view.

Subsequent work has shown that Piaget's account is somewhat over-simplified and that, under given task conditions, young children do show awareness of another person's viewpoint. And yet, there can be no doubt that in the early years children are much more dominated by their own perceptual view than subsequently. So how does the child grow out of the egocentric phase? The answer, according to Piaget, lies in his repeated interpersonal interactions, which gradually force on to him the realization that a conflict exists between his point of view and that of others. Through play and verbal exchange the child discovers the dissonance between his own information and that which guides the behaviour of other people; the conflicts and arguments with other children in particular make it necessary for him to re-examine his own concepts and assumptions. The only way to rid himself of the resulting contradictions and achieve coherence among his experiences is to abandon egocentrism.

Egocentric and sociocentric speech

The concept of egocentrism has been evoked to explain a wide range of childhood phenomena including, in particular, communication failures. A study by Krauss and Glucksberg (1969) illustrates this well.

Pairs of children in kindergarten, first, third, and fifth grades (i.e. ages 5, 6, 8, and 10 years respectively) sat on opposite sides of a table with a screen between them. One member of the pair was to describe a 'nonsense' shape to the other, so that the latter could correctly pick it out from among a collection of shapes in front of him. The results over a number of trials are given in Figure 4. Although initial performance differed little for the four age groups, there was a marked difference in the rate at which errors were reduced. The younger children tended throughout to give idiosyncratic, non-descriptive accounts of the shapes (e.g. 'this one right here') which could not possibly be used by the listener for identification purposes. Unlike the older children, the five-year-olds were unable to learn in the course of the task that their partner's requirements had to be taken into account if the task was to be solved successfully. Communication failure thus occurred.

As with the spatial perspective-taking illustrated by the three-mountain task, so with verbal communication too Piaget believed that in the early years egocentrism is absolute. This is seen in his

Figure 4 Mean errors over trials for matched-age pairs in the kindergarten and in grades 1, 3 and 5

analysis of children's conversations (Piaget, 1926), in which he found a developmental sequence that he delineated in terms of three stages. In the first stage genuine verbal interchanges do not occur. Children engage in a series of monologues rather than in conversations, using speech as a commentary on their own actions and not as a means of informing others. Remarks are not addressed to another child with the intention that he should reply – there may even be little concern as to whether the other child can hear the remarks. The second stage is an intermediate one in which speech begins to lose its egocentric nature and becomes sociocentric, and it is only in the third stage (not till the age of seven, according to Piaget) that speech becomes truly communicative in function, the child using it with the explicit intention of providing the other person with some information.

Again it appears that Piaget greatly overstated his case. In a study of four-year-old children's language, Shatz and Gelman (1973) found that the manner in which these children talked varied considerably with the age of the person addressed – whether he was a two-year-old, another four-year-old, or an adult. Thus speech to two-year-olds was considerably simplified compared with speech to older listeners, containing shorter and grammatically simpler utterances and accompanied by greater efforts to attract and sustain attention. In this respect at least these children did show awareness of the other person's requirements and were able to adjust their behaviour accordingly.

It becomes apparent that the details of Piaget's formulation of egocentrism need amending. Furth (1969), for instance, has criticized the vagueness of this concept when applied to speech and has insisted that no normal child of any age ever uses language primarily for purposes of self-communication. According to him, the social use of language is always foremost. It may well be that the either-or characterization suggested by Piaget's stage sequence is misleading and that even early on in the pre-school period speech is never entirely egocentric. Nevertheless, that some sort of progression along the egocentric–sociocentric continuum occurs with age is borne out by too many studies to dispense with this notion altogether.

Role-taking skills

The communicative function of speech is related to a wider area that has of late been studied in terms of the development of role-taking skills. This refers to the ability of the individual to infer the covert psychological properties of others, their feelings, dispositions, capabilities, and so on – 'people reading', as Flavell (1970) has described it. (For a related set of concepts, see chapter 9 on attributions.) This cannot, of course, occur while the child is still imprisoned by his egocentrism, for it involves discriminating the role attributes of others and recognizing them as distinct from one's own. One would therefore expect to find with increasing age, development in this capacity; in addition, one can expect such a development to be of considerable aid in making interpersonal communication more effective.

Most of the relevant studies (see Flavell, 1968, on this topic) have required children of various ages to take part in tasks that necessitate the ability to shift perspective. For example, children are familiarized with a story and are then asked to retell it to a *younger* child in such a way that he would understand it. The speaker's version is then scored for the number of simplifications it contains. Or a child is asked to play the role, first of a shy little girl telling her teacher about a visit to the zoo and then of a bold little girl relating the same story. Skill in role enactment is defined in terms of the differences between the two versions. In yet another experiment by Flavell, the child was taught a simple competitive game, which he had to teach to an adult. For half the children, however, the adult was blindfolded and therefore required very different information from that suitable for a sighted person. In all these studies a definite age progression occurred; the capacity to sense the role-taking requirements of the communication situation seemed almost completely absent in the first four years of life, emerged thereafter and gradually increased in middle childhood up to adolescence, when it levelled off.

It is possible, however, that the age at which signs of role-taking skills first become apparent has been somewhat overestimated by such experimental studies. It may have been that the unfamiliar and relatively difficult tasks involved were beyond the capacities of the youngest children. That is the implication of the findings, discussed previously, of Shatz and Gelman (1973) that four-year-olds talked differently to two-year-olds than to adults or to other four-year-olds. Such early signs of role-taking are, however, likely to be fragmentary and partial.

It is not till the end of childhood that interpersonal communication can assume a mature form. Some sort of interactional capacity is, as we have seen, already present at birth, and there is thus little doubt that from the beginning the child is pre-adapted to social life. Even a baby can be a powerful transmitter of signals, affecting the behaviour of those around him, and thereby incidentally, pouring scorn on uni-directional theories of socialization that see the child as a mere recipient of adult pressures. Such early interactions are limited, however, on two major counts. In the first place, the infant's interactive behaviour is not marked by intentionality, for he has not yet acquired the considerable cognitive sophistication required to be able to anticipate the outcome of his actions. And in the second place, for much of the early years it is difficult for the child to consider several points of view simultaneously, as a result of which he will tend to remain unduly dominated by his own particular perspective. These are powerful cognitive constraints on his interpersonal functioning, and it is only the act of social living itself that can free the child from their influence.

Further Reading

Blurton-Jones, N., ed. (1972), *Ethological Studies of Child Behaviour*, Cambridge, Cambridge University Press. Contains a number of descriptive studies of child–child and mother–child interaction, based on ethological techniques of research.

Parke, R. D., ed. (1969), *Readings in Social Development*, New York, Holt, Rinehart & Winston. Contains a wide variety of reports on early social behaviour, including such topics as sociability in infancy, imitation, social reinforcement, dependence and independence, and sex-role development.

Richards, M. P. M., ed. (1974), *The Integration of the Child into a Social World*, Cambridge, Cambridge University Press. A varied collection of papers, a number of which explore in more detail issues raised in this chapter.

Schaffer, H. R. (1971), *The Growth of Sociability*, Penguin Books. A summary of work done on social development in infancy, with particular reference to the establishment of the first social bond.

Schaffer, H. R. (1977), *Mothering*, London, Open Books. A review of the different ways in which the parent–child relationship has been studied by social scientists, with special emphasis on the dyadic nature of the relationship.

Sluckin, W. (1971), *Early Learning and Early Experience*, Penguin Books. A number of representative studies of the nature and effects of early experience in both animals and humans.

Chapter 5
Communication in Interaction

Colin Fraser

Introduction

If a friend told you, 'You're an idiot', but said this with a smile, you might well feel that the assertion was not intended to be as unfriendly as it seems in print. In fact, you might treat it as a joke, in which the positive and negative elements just about cancel each other out. But such a combination coming from a woman would be interpreted by a child as distinctly negative and unfriendly, according to Bugental, Kaswan and Love (1970). They carried out an intricate study in which they used a number of messages each composed of three separable components: (i) a verbal component, e.g. 'You really did a fine job'; (ii) a vocal or 'intonational' component; (iii) a visual or facial component. They were then able to produce messages consisting of all possible combinations of positive and negative (friendly and unfriendly) verbal, vocal and visual components. Their study raises a number of points of interest for us.

It immediately reminds us that language, the most familiar and most studied of the human systems of communication, is not the only form of communication operating in face-to-face interaction. In fact, when we use language we normally use it accompanied by, or embedded in, a rich multi-system context, and it would be surprising if the different systems did not interact in the encoding and decoding of communications. Bugental's study demonstrates that such interactions do occur and that they are not always simple additive or averaging ones. Sometimes, for example, the information potentially available in one system will be completely discounted if contradicted by information in another. Furthermore, the fact that certain combinations of components were interpreted differently by adults and children indicates that one task facing the child in developing the communicative competence discussed in the previous chapter is that of integrating the various communication systems he is mastering.

In addition, Bugental's study raises a number of questions about the description of face-to-face communication. How many systems of communication are there? How are they organized? How do different systems interact? Such questions will be discussed in the next section, where the emphasis will be on 'communication as behaviour'. There we shall be particularly concerned with describing the observable behaviour or the overt forms of the messages that occur during communication. But Bugental's study also implies other questions. Do different systems serve the same or different functions? What information is transmitted by the systems? What is the meaning of the communicative behaviours? These questions focus on 'communication as meaning', which will be the emphasis of the section on three types of communication.

Study of the message form, or surface structure, of communication is necessary but not sufficient in itself for explaining the meanings or understandings that are communicated. This can also be illustrated from Bugental's work. She found that the exact meaning of a combination of components varied with the nature of the participants involved in the encoding or decoding of the message. Thus, the same set of components could mean different things depending on whether an adult or a child decoded the message, and in addition the meaning of the set of components differed for the child depending on whether a man or a woman produced the message. (For the children, a smile from a man 'cancelled out' accompanying negative verbal and vocal components, but a female smile failed to do so.)

Thus, as we found in chapter 4, communication involves relating the overt forms of messages to the participants in the encounter. But it entails much more than this. Hymes (1972) has claimed that we must take into account at least sixteen different 'components of speech' if we are to understand how spoken language is used in communication. These components, which include features of message forms, aspects of social settings, and mixtures of the two, can be condensed into eight major categories which, Hymes ingeniously proposes, can be remembered by the mnemonic SPEAKING. For example, 'S' stands for 'setting', or 'scene', which includes time, place and physical characteristics of the situation, as well as the 'psychological setting' or cultural definition of the occasion; 'P' stands for 'participants', who may be speakers, intended addressees, hearers, members of an audience, and the like; 'E' refers to 'ends', or purposes of interactions, such as whether the aim is to issue an invitation, engage in an argument, or accomplish a cooperative task. But as will become clear by the end of the chapter, perhaps there is even more to communication than that. First, however, let us return to the task of describing the observables of communication.

Four communication systems

In this section we shall introduce a number of basic concepts in the study of linguistic and non-linguistic communication, and, it is hoped, reveal the richness of the behaviour involved in conversation, the prime exemplar of human communication. The descriptions of the different systems that contribute to a conversation will necessarily be brief. Fuller accounts of the structure of language are available in any introductory text in linguistics (e.g. Crystal, 1971; Bolinger, 1975); more detailed descriptions of the non-linguistic systems can be found in Argyle (1969) and Laver and Hutcheson (1972). It is important to realize that language is a very distinctive, very specifically patterned means of communication. All known human societies have been found to possess such means, no non-human species have been shown to; even striking successes in teaching chimpanzees fragments of language-like communication systems (Gardner and Gardner, 1971; Premack, 1970) hardly contradict the latter claim. Although the examples to be given here will be confined to English, many of the general statements will be applicable to all languages. In addition, I suggest it is convenient to analyse language into two major components, the verbal and the intonational, and for simplicity of exposition I shall describe each as a system in its own right.

The verbal system

Let us start with smaller units of analysis and work our way up to the much longer sequences that make up speech. Obviously speech depends on sounds and it is probably the case that no two sounds produced by a speaker are ever completely identical. Normally, however, we ignore many variations in duration, aspiration and the like and treat, for example, all 'b' sounds as if they were the same. All languages appear to operate with a limited number – usually several dozen – such basic classes of sounds, or phonemes. (These are not the smallest possible units of analysis; many linguists regard phonemes as composed of clusters of more microscopic distinctive features.)

Individual phonemes are not meaningful in themselves, but they are lawfully combined into longer segments which do have meaning. The smallest meaningful unit in a language is a 'morpheme' which can be a short word, or part of a word; all words contain at least one morpheme, but all morphemes are not complete words. For example, 'chair' is one morpheme because it cannot be broken into smaller meaningful units, but 'chairman' consists of two morphemes, and 'chairmanship' consists of three.

With the units of 'morpheme' and 'word' we enter the domains of grammar and semantics. Grammar describes the structuring of morphemes into words and words into longer sequences, whereas semantics organizes the content of morphemes and words and relates them to the non-linguistic world about which the verbal system is being used to communicate. A semantic analysis of language *per se* tells us much, but not everything, about the meaning of what is said, because meaning is also derived from the social setting, and from implicit, shared understandings and common backgrounds which are difficult to pin down. Much of the rest of the chapter is about the very wide range of meanings that can be communicated, but for the moment let us focus more on the (grammatical) structure of the verbal system.

Morphemes are combined into words, words into larger phrases and clauses, and these, in turn, into units we shall call 'utterances'. An utterance can be thought of as a sentence-like chunk, which is used to express something approximating one whole idea. Notice, however, that many common types of utterance in conversation do not correspond to conventional notions of a sentence standing in isolation. Depending on what has been said before or on what is self-evident in the situation, sentence fragments can be acceptable utterances. For example, in response to the appropriate question, virtually any word, phrase or clause could constitute an entire utterance.

In the past, it has often been implied that the largest structural unit of language is the single sentence, or utterance, and it is only recently that linguists have felt themselves in a position to start doing justice to the regularities that extend beyond the boundaries of single utterances (e.g. Sinclair and Coulthard, 1975). The analysis of such regularities is called 'discourse analysis' and the structural dependencies from utterance to utterance are often termed 'cohesion'.

Intonation

What has been described so far is not, even schematically, a complete description of spoken language. Rather, it corresponds approximately to those features of speech which are conventionally preserved in written form, primarily the words. But, in speaking, this verbal system is completely combined with, or overlaid by, the systematic use of different pitches, stresses and junctures. It is not the words themselves which tell us whether, 'You think they'll be all right', is to be taken as a declarative or an interrogative, but a drop or rise in pitch at the end of the utterance. Similarly, it is not the words which distinguish a 'black board' from a 'blackboard', or 'lighthouse-keeping' from 'light housekeeping'. The distinctions are dependent primarily on differences in stress patterns.

The intonational system is composed of patterns of pitch and stress, with junctures marking the boundaries of the units over which pitch and stress are interacting. Systematic changes in intonation mark systematic changes in meaning within utterances. Intonation also affects larger units of discourse. Quite a subtle form of cohesion across utterances is the use of emphasis. If you joined a conversation just in time to hear someone say. 'John's car is *blue*', with a marked stress on 'blue', you could assume that previously someone had claimed it was some other colour. (You might try to work out the different implications of having a heavy stress on each of the other words in turn in that same sentence.)

The study of intonation has not been as well developed as that of the verbal system, but it is clear that the two interact very closely, and together they comprise spoken language. To complicate matters, however, there is a further vocal system, which is not generally regarded as linguistic, i.e. as forming part of language *per se*. But before considering this non-linguistic system of paralinguistics, and the other non-linguistic system of kinesics, a few comments are in order regarding the terms 'system' and 'communication'.

Strictly speaking a system is an integrated, coherent whole containing interlocking elements or parts, and thus 'system' seems an appropriate term to describe both the verbal and the intonational components of language. It may be somewhat more questionable to apply it to non-linguistic means of communication. As we shall see, paralinguistics may prove to be a collection of vocal phenomena which it is convenient to lump together under one heading, but which scarcely form an integrated, interdependent whole. Something similar might be said of kinesics, where several potentially distinguishable systems are for present purposes being lumped together under one heading.

In addition to their being less systematic, non-linguistic systems of communication may also be less 'communicative'! Everything that a person does should not be treated as 'communication'. It *is* possible that every feature of a person's behaviour, and for that matter his appearance, could be given some interpretation by some other person, but if every tic, pimple and egg-stained tie becomes a 'communication' then communication becomes an unwieldy and uninformative term. Wiener *et al.* (1972), Lyons (1972) and many others have stressed the need to distinguish between communication and behaviour which may, under certain conditions, act as a sign for an observer or decoder. The former involves a socially shared signal system or code which entails intentional encoding and decoding. This removes from the domain of communication many isolated actions, idiosyncratic acts, and signals which may be interesting in themselves and may be quite informative (or appear to be informative) about the individual concerned, but they will not be treated as communication.

Language in use may contain some unintended elements, but in general clearly merits the label 'communication'. However, we are often not in a position to be certain with nonlinguistic behaviours that what is happening really is communication. In what follows, we shall concentrate on non-linguistic behaviour that does appear to be part of a communication system and which also is likely to accompany language. Using this belt-and-braces approach, we may inadvertently omit some communicative behaviour and include some sign behaviour but we should catch much of the most important non-linguistic communication. It should be noted, however, that terminology in this area is much less settled and agreed upon than in the study of language (see Birdwhistell, 1961; Abercrombie, 1968).

Paralinguistics

When we vocalize we do more than use the verbal and intonational systems of language. We also produce a variety of additional vocalizations, some of which, at least, are culturally determined, shared by members of a given social group and used communicatively. These include 'ums' and 'ahs', coughs, splutters, giggles, and the like. Other paralinguistic phenomena are usually held to be responsible for the ill-defined notion of 'tone of voice'. They include extremes of intensity, pitch and drawl, including yelling and whispering. Laughing and crying, moaning and groaning, whining, yawning and even belching are also paralinguistic elements.

Paralinguistics can also be thought to cover phenomena relating to the timing of speech, and to the use of silence in speech, particularly in the form of pauses or hesitation phenomena. A distinction usually drawn here is between unfilled (or silent) pauses and filled pauses, involving sounds like 'um', 'ah', and 'er'. Various functions have been proposed for hesitation phenomena. They may be used by the speaker to discourage interruptions and to keep the floor. They may permit and indicate planning of speech. Or they may be indices of anxiety. Precisely which phenomena fulfil which functions is still open to dispute (Cook, 1971). Some features of hesitation, timing and speech rate may well be primarily idiosyncratic elements of personal style. Like stable features of voice quality, these can provide what Laver (1968) has called indexical information, i.e. information about supposed characteristics of the speaker, without being, in our sense, part of a system for communication.

Kinesics

This term will be used to describe body and facial movements, many of which have now been shown to occur in culturally standardized forms with clear communicative significance. One investigator (Sheflen, 1964) has argued, for example, that there are only about thirty traditional American gestures and an even smaller number of postural configurations of communicative importance for Americans. The same investigator has claimed that, at least in psychiatric interviews, posture and body movement is used to mark different phases or units of the interaction. Between the relatively small unit of a single verbal utterance and the complete interaction, which he termed a 'presentation', Sheflen identified two intermediate-sized units. Several utterances formed a 'point' whose beginning and end were marked by shifts in head posture. Several successive points constituted a 'position', or phase lasting up to five or six minutes. Beginnings and ends of 'positions' were indicated by gross shifts in posture, such as changing from sitting forward to leaning back in a chair. It would be interesting to know if such kinesic changes are emphasizing features in the interaction which discourse analysis could show are also being conveyed linguistically.

Such seems to be a primary function of hand movements (Argyle, 1969). Although hand movements, in large part, are socially shared and vary from society to society (Efron, 1941) it has proved difficult as yet to provide a useful set of categories to describe the variety and richness of them. Like hand movements, head movements are highly visible, but unlike the former, their variations are limited. Nevertheless, head nods and shakes can convey important information about the listener's attentiveness, agreement, and encouragement for the speaker to continue. The fact that in certain societies nods and shakes mean the reverse of what they mean in English-speaking countries (Leach, 1972) indicates that head movements constitute a learned, socially shared, though simple, system of communication.

Facial movements can be analysed in great detail. According to Vine (1970) one form of traditional Indian theatre makes use of six standard eyebrow positions and twenty-eight eye-positions. A more recent analysis of naturalistic behaviour (Birdwhistell, 1968) described four eyebrow positions, four eyelid positions and seven positions of the mouth. Presumably, it is to configurations of such minute facial movements that people react when they infer emotions from facial expressions, although it seems likely that at least some of the information being used in such inferences is not strictly communicative. One need only think, however, of a smiling face to appreciate that facial expressions can have important communicative significance. Indeed, it can be argued (Argyle, 1969) that the face is second only to the voice in what is called, after all, face-to-face communication.

One particularly interesting set of head and facial movements are those involved in gazing at another person and in mutual eye-contact (Argyle and Cook, 1976). Gaze and eye contact can be important for obtaining the attention of another, perhaps in order to start an interaction and for indicating one's own attentiveness, or inattentiveness, during the interaction. They can also play a part in communicating one type of relationship rather than another, such as an asexual friendship or a much more sexually oriented one. In addition, gaze and eye-contact play an important part in regulating conversation and they will be discussed in more detail below, as part of 'interaction regulation'.

During a conversation, the kinesic, paralinguistic, and linguistic elements are constantly changing and hence can be described as 'dynamic features' of the interaction. They are changing, however, against a more constant background to the conversation, made up of what Argyle and Kendon (1967) have termed 'standing features'. These relatively unchanging aspects of an interaction, such as proximity and appearance of the participants, can themselves be used to communicate. The distance between two people can be a clear, and shared, index of the relationship between them or of the type of communication, public or private, for example, that they are currently engaged in. Much the same can be said of the dress and grooming of the participants. For completeness' sake, it is useful to bear in mind these standing features, but it is as well to be aware of certain differences between them and the systems described above. In addition to their relative lack of change during a conversation, standing features may not seem to be 'behaviour' in the way that the use of the systems is. Furthermore, one may often feel that the standing features are part, not so much of the message form, but of the social setting.

Relations amongst the systems

An analysis of face-to-face communication in terms of the four different systems is a first step in revealing the richness and intricacy of human communication processes. It is also a useful basis for understanding several simpler analyses, which though sometimes used interchangeably, are in fact confusingly different. By now, it should be clear that when communication is divided into the verbal and non-verbal, as social psychologists tend to do, this is not the same as splitting it into linguistic and non-linguistic components. Furthermore, neither of those distinctions corresponds to an analysis in terms of the two major channels of communication defined by the sensory-motor apparatus involved. Figure 5 illustrates these differing distinctions, and reveals that whereas all three of them agree in

Figure 5   The four systems, and some competing distinctions

separating the verbal from the kinesic, they apportion the intonational and the paralinguistic quite differently.

Normally the different systems operate in a compatible and supportive fashion. A person arguing that something is particularly important is likely to use both verbal and intonational means to do so, and it is unlikely that paralinguistic or kinesic cues would indicate boredom or flippancy. It is improbable that a conveyor of sad news will sound or look happy. The non-linguistic systems, particularly head and hand movements, are often used to emphasize or 'punctuate' the linguistic elements. One might in fact be tempted to assume that compared to the linguistic systems, the non-linguistic ones are relatively unimportant, and such a conclusion would appear to receive strong support from a study by Moscovici and Plon (1966).

These investigators had pairs of final-year Parisian *lycée* pupils discuss films together for twenty minutes. A conversation took place in one of four 'speaking situations': (i) face-to-face, (ii) face-to-face but with an opaque screen between the participants, (iii) side-by-side, (iv) back-to-back. For our immediate purpose, the interesting comparison is that between (i) and (ii) which involves only the presence or absence of kinesic elements including the apparently very important one of facial expression. Moscovici and Plon used measures of the syntactic classes of the words in the conversations as indices of the ways in which the conversations were organized for the discussion of the topic. They found clear differences between conversations in situations (iii) and (iv) and those in (i). But no differences were found between situations (i) and (ii). In discussing this study, Moscovici (1967) concluded that in the screen situation, 'the suppression of non-linguistic signals had no marked effect; participants conversed as though gestures, body movement, and facial expressions did not normally play a major role in communication or serve as cues for transmitting information' (p. 259). Although such a sweeping conclusion is hardly justified on the basis of this study alone, given the limited nature of the linguistic indices used, it does correspond to what many linguistically oriented researchers might feel.

But before concluding that language invariably dominates face-to-face communication it is as well to consider what happens when the systems do not appear to be in agreement, as in Bugental's study for example. Other illustrations have been provided by Argyle and his colleagues. Argyle *et al.* (1970) studied the relative effects of verbal and non-verbal messages conveying superiority, neutrality, or inferiority of the speaker. For example, the superior verbal message came from an experimenter who, amongst other things, told potential subjects that the study was too complex for them to understand. The inferior verbal message included apologies, description of the experiments as 'rather silly', and admissions of near incompetence. The non-verbal differences involved differences in 'tones of voice', facial expressions and head-orientations. For example, superiority was conveyed non-verbally by cues including a loud, dominating voice, an unsmiling face and a raised head. All combinations of the three verbal and three non-verbal components were presented on videotape to subjects who rated the communication on a series of scales. From these ratings Argyle *et al.* concluded that the non-verbal cues were much more important than the verbal ones. At best, with compatible components, the verbal components strengthened the perceived nature of the message. When the components were in conflict, the verbal cues were more or less ineffective. Broadly similar conclusions emerged from a subsequent study by Argyle, Alkema and Gilmour (1972) on the communication of variations in friendliness–hostility.

One point to be borne in mind, however, is that it is not obvious how one directly compares the potential 'strength' or effectiveness of message forms in different systems. Does one spoken 'very' equal two downward finger jabs . . . or vice versa? It is just conceivable that in both studies, the investigators hit on convincing non-verbal variations and unconvincing verbal ones. But it must be added that studies by other investigators, similar in general outline but with different message forms, have produced outcomes in general agreement with those of Argyle.

In addition, it is not clear which types of non-verbal cues had marked effects. If tone of voice were dominant and if variations in tone of voice were achieved intonationally rather than paralinguistically, it could be argued that the linguistic system as a whole remained more important than a combination of non-linguistic systems. This conclusion is implausible, however. In studies by Mehrabian and by Bugental, the non-verbal cues have been separated in slightly more detail. Mehrabian and Ferris (1967), for example, estimated that in their work the impact of verbal, tone of voice and facial components could be expressed in percentage terms as 7:38:55. Thus, even if tone of voice were entirely intonational, which is unlikely, the linguistic systems were less influential than facial expression alone, which does not fit with Moscovici's claims.

The resolution of this apparent contradiction concerning the importance of linguistic and non-linguistic systems is not hard to find. When Moscovici claimed that various non-linguistic components had little role to play in communication or in transmitting information, in the context in which he wrote the 'information' being transmitted was information about the topic of discussion, namely films.

The communication in question can be thought of as 'representa-tional' or 'ideational' or 'propositional' communication.

This type of information was not being assessed in the Argyle and Mehrabian studies. They were concerned with the communication to others of the attitudes of the speakers, with what can be called 'inter-personal communication'. Particularly, when systems were in con-flict, they found the non-verbal, and especially the non-linguistic, systems conveyed most information about the superior or inferior, friendly or hostile attitudes of the speaker, but they were not interested in what was being discussed while these attitudes prevailed. The linguistic systems made that clear; it is possible that the non-linguistic cues alone could not have distinguished amongst superiority (or friendliness) manifested in the context of a discussion about the existence of God, the running of an experiment, or the price of sausages.

So communication systems can be used to communicate about the topic or about the attitudes and relations of the participants. A related distinction has, in the past, been conveyed by contrasting language as 'message' and as 'expressive behaviour'. But a third focus of communication can occur, the conversation itself; the speakers are likely to communicate in order to maintain and control the conversation. This third type of communication can be called 'interaction regulation'. A somewhat similar three-way distinction has been drawn by Laver and Hutcheson (1972) who have pointed out that in conversation three types of information are being exchanged, cognitive information, indexical information and information con-cerning interaction management.

Halliday (1970, 1973) has also drawn related distinctions amongst three 'language functions', the ideational, the interpersonal and the textual. The fact that Halliday's discussions were centred on language alone conveniently reminds us that language can be used not just for representational information but for all three types of communication. Think of, 'You're a louse' and 'Let me finish, then you can have your say'. Similarly, non-linguistic systems can convey representa-tional information, as well as play major roles in interpersonal com-munication and interaction regulation. A combination of gestures, head and eye movements could make quite clear, for example, who is to move which piece of furniture into which room. So, to some extent, different communication systems are substitutable for one another, and can be used for each of the three types of communication.

Nevertheless, there do seem to be clear differences in emphasis regarding what type of communication is normally carried out by the different systems. Representational communication is largely the province of language, with its systematic structure and semantic mapping on to the non-linguistic world. On the other hand, a great deal of interaction regulation is non-linguistic, and all systems can readily be demonstrated to convey interpersonal information. The remainder of this chapter will provide brief accounts of illuminating studies on each of the three types of communication.

Three types of communication

In order for either representational or interpersonal communication to occur in face-to-face interaction it is obviously necessary for the interaction to be initiated and maintained. Therefore interaction regulation will be considered first. Interpersonal communication will then be discussed and illustrated before we examine what, in the writer's view, remains the primary function of conversation and communication, the exchange of representational information.

Interaction regulation

The form a conversation takes is determined, in part, before the conversation itself begins. The potential participants are almost certain to share some assumptions, norms, or rules about conversing, particularly if their cultural and social backgrounds are similar. Very basically, they are likely to take for granted that a two-person conversation will consist of alternate contributions from each person, that only one person will speak at a time and, if through inadequate interaction regulation, both speakers talk simultaneously, then one or the other should stop very quickly. They may operate with more specific rules of conversation, related, for example, to the social relations between the participants and/or the situation they are interacting in. They may both accept, for instance, that as strangers meeting for the first time, they will participate roughly equally in short alternative contributions, or as interviewer and interviewee, the latter will do most of the talking, or as customer and salesgirl the former will take the initiative in determining the topic of conversation. Such taken-for-granted bases of interaction, usually left implicit rather than made explicit, are amongst the prerequisites for conversation being explored and explicated by micro-sociologists usually dubbed 'ethnomethodologists' (see Douglas, 1970).

But such rules for conversation hardly dictate the very fine-grained 'meshing' that goes on in interaction, and as interaction regulators they are supplemented by communication occurring during the interaction itself. Argyle and Kendon (1967) and Argyle (1969) give accounts of the form that such communication takes, at least in western societies.

The conversation may be initiated by mutual eye-contact, indicating that the participants are ready and willing to interact. Once the conversation has started, each person looks at the other intermittently. These looks or glances are directed around the other's eyes, last between 1 and 10 seconds each or between 25 and 75 per cent of each person's total time. The amount of time that each spends gazing at the other is considerably more than that spent in mutual eye-contact.

The listener is likely to spend more time looking at the speaker than the speaker at the listener. When the speaker, while in full flow, does look at the listener the latter is likely to nod or give an encouraging vocalization. The speaker, when he starts, probably looks away. When he comes to clear grammatical breaks in what he has to say, the speaker is likely to glance briefly at the listener. When he approaches the end of his contribution he will look longer at the listener. If, however, the speaker hesitates or pauses because he is stuck for a word, or an idea, he is not likely to look at the listener.

Such cues appear to aid conversation regulation in a number of ways. The speaker checks that the listener is in fact still listening, and that he is understanding. A puzzled expression or slight head shake can be enough to tell the speaker to repeat or paraphrase what he has just said. The averting of gaze by the speaker when he stumbles or pauses decreases the likelihood of interruption and mutual talking. The looking up by the speaker just prior to the end of his contribution, signals to the listener that it is almost his turn. Duncan (1972) published a very detailed account of signals and rules for taking turns at speaking, in which he demonstrated that turn-taking signals were given in all of the communication systems he studied, linguistic, paralinguistic and kinesic.

If the above claims about interaction regulation are justified, several things follow. If, for example, visual information is denied interactors, then conversation should be less smooth and more difficult to maintain. Some support for this comes from Argyle, Lallgee and Cook (1968). Someone learning to use a telephone or talking, for the first time, to a blind person, should find this difficult, or at least different from a normal conversation. And although we doubtless learn rules for talking on the telephone, or, if necessary for conversing with the blind, a fine enough analysis should indicate that the 'meshing' of speakers in such situations differs, in certain respects, from what occurs in face-to-face conversation between sighted individuals.

Interpersonal communication

During an encounter a great deal of information is made available regarding the participants and their relations to each other. This information can be organized around three broad topics: (i) social and personal identities; (ii) temporary states and current attitudes; (iii) social relationships.

(i) *Social and personal identities.* If he wishes, a listener, or observer, can make very many inferences concerning a speaker's background and the social groups to which he belongs, as well as inferences about supposed personality characteristics. The speaker's accent, dress and even hairstyle might lead to confident assumptions regarding his social class membership and education. Apparently distinctive aspects of the speaker's voice quality, movements and posture might lead to inferences regarding personality dimensions.

One difficult problem is that of deciding how much of the available evidence is really communication and how much is merely sign behaviour which can be used for inference making. To take one example, the relatively permanent quality of a person's voice is a product of two main sets of factors (Laver, 1968), the anatomy and physiology of his vocal equipment, and his habitual muscular adjustments or 'settings'. It is most unlikely that cues deriving primarily from the former, over which the speaker would have no control, would be thought of as 'communication', whereas information conveyed via habitual settings might or might not be depending on how precise one's criteria were.

Suffice it to say that, in addition to inadvertently providing sign behaviour, speakers do communicate information about their social backgrounds and stable personal characteristics via a number of systems of communication. Readers interested in a fuller presentation of material on this topic should read Robinson (1972) or Argyle (1969).

(ii) *Temporary states and current attitudes.* In addition to inferring or attributing (see chapter 9) stable characteristics, people also make inferences about temporary states. 'Is the person on the other side of the desk really angry with what I've just said?' 'Why should Joe, sitting here drinking beer, seem so anxious?' Such inferences could be based on sign behaviour but, clearly, emotional states can be explicitly communicated. Your boss might tell you that he's angry, or communicate the fact by quite deliberate hand movements or facial expressions.

The distinction between emotional states and currently salient attitudes is far from a decisive one, but can perhaps be best conveyed, in the way Robinson (1972) does, by, in the former case, focusing attention on a state *per se* (e.g. 'happy', 'angry'), which could, however, have implications for behaviour and, in the second case, focusing on behaviour and attitude to others (e.g. 'friendly', 'hostile') which, nevertheless, could imply an accompanying emotional state. The discussions above of studies by Bugental, Argyle and others have indicated how attitudes towards another person can be conveyed in a variety of ways and how non-verbal systems appear to be particularly powerful in this respect.

A less commonly discussed question is that of conveying attitudes towards the topic of discussion rather than towards the other participants. Interest and involvement or distaste and displeasure regarding what is being discussed can be conveyed in a variety of non-linguistic ways, including postures, facial expression and paralinguistics. Wiener and Mehrabian (1968) have shown that they are also consistently communicated by the way one uses language itself.

On several occasions, while watching television, I have been intrigued by politicians and public figures who, while ostensibly expressing concern for disadvantaged groups, have kept referring to 'those people' or 'that sort of person'. These usages struck me as indicating a distancing from or even distaste for the persons supposedly close to the politicians' hearts.

Wiener and Mehrabian (1968) have systematically shown how in the choice of certain key words or phrases a person can communicate 'immediacy' or 'non-immediacy', that is a positive or negative attitude towards the object or topic of his communication. According to these investigators, the two examples just quoted would be instances of non-immediacy conveyed by the use of 'spatial' demonstratives, such as 'that' or 'those' rather than 'this' or 'these'. Another common indicator of non-immediacy is 'temporal' distancing, whereby the relationship between the speaker and the topic of his communication is displaced from the present to either the past or the future.

(iii) *Social relationships.* Interpersonal communication includes not only information about one participant or another but also information regarding the relationship between participants. This can be conveyed non-linguistically. Smiling, or even more, bodily contact (Jourard, 1966) can, in western societies, indicate very effectively an intimate relationship. In addition, a number of interesting studies have been carried out on the language of social relationships.

In America, Brown and Ford (1961) explored the choice of forms of address in face-to-face interaction using a variety of types of data, including actual usage in a Boston business firm, usage recorded in a Midwestern town, usage in both current and older American plays, and reported usage of business executives from a number of American cities. As would be the case in Britain, they found the most common address forms were first name alone (FN) and title plus last name (TLN). In thinking of when you would call someone Bill rather than Mr Jones, you probably feel it could have something to do with how well you know each other, or again it might be connected with your relative statuses. Brown and Ford showed that, in fact, usage of those address forms, as well as less common ones like last name alone and multiple names, can in large part be predicted from a knowledge of the solidarity or intimacy and the status or power relations of interactors. The difference between the mutual use of TLN and the mutual use of FN is a function of intimacy; the non-reciprocal pattern of one person using TLN and the other FN is a function of status differences, with the higher status person receiving the form that is also the more formal, less intimate one. Furthermore, in so far as a dyad progresses from mutual TLN through non-reciprocal usage to mutual FN, it is the higher status person who normally initiates changes.

In English, a person who is not sure of his status or intimacy relations with another can avoid having to code them by addressing the other as 'you', provided he already has gained the attention of the other person. But speakers of many other languages do not have this option. Even if he does not use FNs or TLNs, a Frenchman has always to choose between using *tu* or *vous*. Brown (1965) presents impressive evidence that very similar relations hold amongst status, intimacy and pronoun forms in a large number of the world's languages as were found with American FN and TLN. Furthermore, the message forms that play a part in the language of social relationships are not restricted to forms of address and pronoun use. Brown (1965) and Geertz (1960) amongst others have pointed to the elaborate system of linguistic honorifics that characterize many Far Eastern societies and which also can be shown to vary systematically with status and intimacy relations. And there are probably more aspects of English which systematically correlate with social relations than we sometimes acknowledge. Consider greetings, such as 'hello' as opposed to 'good morning' (see Brown and Ford, 1961) or the use of imperative forms. To whom do you use imperative forms (e.g. Shut the door!) rather than command with interrogatives (e.g.

Could you shut the door?) or even declaratives (e.g. There's a draught coming in)? Certainly, I frequently use imperatives to my youngest child but rarely to my wife. And I find that I require a few meetings with someone else's children before I will order them about or threaten them with dire fates in the way I do my own.

Thus, as far as message forms are concerned, the language of social relations can be very rich. But are status and intimacy the only relevant aspects of the social settings? Somehow, that seems too simple and too tidy. In fact, an obvious question to ask is, what are the bases of status and intimacy? Relative status can be based on a variety of aspects of the relations between two people, as can intimacy. Need status differences based on one's job be coded in exactly the same way as those related to age? Friedrich (1972) has presented a detailed analysis of pronoun usage in nineteenth century Russia, in which he demonstrated that at least ten components of the social setting could be related to pronominal use. These were: the topic of discourse: the context of the speech event: the age, generation, sex and kinship status of the participants: dialect: group membership: relative legal and political authority: emotional solidarity. In other words, conclusions expressed solely in terms of status and solidarity are broad generalizations, largely justifiable, which ignore many fascinating nuances and fine details.

In conclusion, Friedrich also drew attention to the use of non-linguistic message forms, such as eye-gaze, which may suggest more intimate relations than the verbal forms proclaim. And Brown and Ford (1961) demonstrated that an aspect of kinesics, namely putting one's hand on someone's shoulder, operated as an index of relationships much as did address forms. Thus, what at first may have seemed like a peculiarity of American FNs and TLNs turns out to be just one manifestation of intricately patterned correspondences between the linguistic (and non-linguistic) forms used by speakers and the social relations between them.

Armed with the concepts 'interaction regulation' and 'interpersonal communication' we are still some way from being able to describe a normal conversation, although, at first thought, these two types of communication may seem sufficient to characterize exchanges which the social anthropologist Malinowski (1923) described as 'phatic communion'. With this phrase, he was referring to exchanges of politeness, inquiries about health, comments on the weather, and the like, which he claimed, fulfilled the primary functions of cementing social relationships and for which the exact meaning of the words was largely irrelevant. A very clear instance of this was the claim, once made to me by the father of the groom at a wedding reception, that in the receiving line, as he smiled and shook hands, he had said to each guest in turn 'Kippers and jam', and no one appeared to have noticed. Normally, however, the meaning and appropriateness of what was said would have a bearing even on such social exchanges. A cheerful extolling of the merits of the weather on a miserable, wet day, or a fervent thank you and good-bye on arrival would most probably divert attention from interpersonal matters to the topic of the conversation. Even phatic communion usually involves communication about something over and above social relations.

Representational communication

Representational or referential communication is what we normally think of when we talk simply of the 'meaning' of what was said. It is the core of linguistic communication, the most complex of the three types of communication and, in certain respects, the least understood.

A major contribution to understanding it would be the development of an adequate account of the semantics of language (and perhaps of the other systems of communication). 'Semantics', like 'meaning', has been used in a number of different ways, and Lyons (1968) provides a useful introduction to the area. Here the term is being used to refer to the relations between linguistic forms and the extra-linguistic world that they are being applied to. Such an account would entail an analysis of how speakers of a language organize the world around them, an analysis of how they organize the linguistic forms they use, and an account of how the two are related. Think for example of what is involved in the differences between breakfast: dinner: tea, and breakfast: lunch: dinner as accounts of social class differences in eating habits. In terms of referents, one is indicating in both cases the three major meals of the day, and, to simplify, let us claim that the three referents or events are relatively similar for both classes. However, both classes use only two identical terms, 'breakfast' and 'dinner', and in only one case, 'breakfast', is the same meal labelled in the same way by both classes.

Obviously, understanding an invitation to dinner should be simpler for two people operating with the same semantic structures than for two people with differences in semantic structures (particularly, in the latter case, if one assumes mutual insensitivity to the differences in each other's backgrounds). More elaborate demonstrations of the importance for communication of similarities and differences in semantic structures have been provided by a number of social psychological studies of cognitive similarity and communication effectiveness (see Mehrabian and Reed, 1968). For example, Triandis (1960), as part of his study, found that pairs of undergraduates who, individually, had used similar words in describing sets of pictures, were more successful than dissimilar pairs in a communication task where they had to identify which picture they both held in common. There is a need for further explorations of the role in communication success and failure of completely shared semantics, as opposed to similarities in non-linguistic categories but with linguistic dissimilarities, and shared linguistic forms with differing underlying categories. Such studies should have clear relevance for some of the cross-cultural and intergroup questions discussed in chapter 15.

It must be stressed that, contrary to what might have been implied by the simple example above, a semantic analysis involves a great deal more than specifying concrete referents for individual words. It involves, for instance, the specification of much more complex semantic relations between sets of persons, objects and activities and longer linguistic strings (cf. Fillmore, 1968). But even if two individuals had identical semantic systems, would effective representational communication then be guaranteed? It seems improbable. The mapping of language on to the non-linguistic world is only part of an analysis of representational communication. At least as important would be an understanding of what parts of his semantic system a speaker chooses to use in a particular situation. What does he bother to say? What does he take for granted?

When we talk, we say surprisingly little, at least compared to what we could say to make the same point or compared to what potentially might be relevant. Osgood (1971) has illustrated this very concretely. If a father said to his son, 'Please shut the door', it is most likely (at least in textbook families) that the door would be shut without further ado. Yet if the referential information were to be made completely explicit it could be argued that the father would have to say something like, 'We both know that you are able to shut doors. There is a door in the far corner of this room. That door is open. I, as your father, desire that that door should be closed by you'. Fortunately, the father, like everyone else, would presuppose a great deal and thus would manage with four words rather than thirty-nine.

The systematic study of presuppositions in communication will be an extremely complex task. A first, simple step has been taken by Osgood (1971) in an attempt to discover what is involved in 'simply describing' something to another person. Osgood arranged a sequence of short 'scenes'. Observers had to describe each scene in a single sentence for the benefit of a hypothetical six-year-old boy behind a hypothetical screen. The observers first saw the investigator holding a black ball. Then they saw the ball on the table. Next, the ball was rolling on the table. Then, it was rolling more slowly. And so on, with changes in colour and size of balls, different objects being introduced, and the like. Thus, knowing what could and could not be presupposed by both speaker and listener from the preceding scenes, Osgood was able to examine the relations between a limited set of presuppositions, or segment of shared reality, and linguistic forms. To take only one example, he noted that 'usage of adjectives and adverbs clearly reflects presuppositions on the part of the speaker as to the amount of information possessed by the listener about the entity being referred to' (p. 512). The more that could be presupposed, the less need for adjectives and adverbs to qualify and elaborate.

If representational communication is to be explained as a mixture of semantics and presuppositions, the above example could give the impression that all that is required is the analysis of the overt message plus the immediate social setting or context. But a further, and final, complication has to be pointed out. Presuppositions can depend on factors nowhere represented in either the current social setting or the discourse itself. To take an illustration from Garfinkel (1972, p. 316):

HUSBAND: Dana succeeded in putting a penny in a parking meter today without being picked up.

WIFE: Did you take him to the record store?

The meaning of that exchange to the participants involved, amongst other things, presuppositions regarding their four-year-old son being brought home from nursery school, his height in relation to parking meters, the husband's having bought a record, the possibility that the son may or may not have been with him when he did. And subtler and subtler common background and shared assumptions could be invoked if one wished.

As Rommetveit (1972a, 1972b) has argued, to understand representational communication one must understand the extent to which two people can build up a shared view of reality, or intersubjectivity. New information is only comprehensible if it can be tied or related to a shared understanding of other information. The presupposed shared reality may be represented in the overt form of an utterance but often only in a cryptic, minimal way. Thus, to understand what has or has not been communicated, it can be more informative to know what was left unsaid than to know what was actually made explicit. Detailed directions can result in thoroughly lost travellers, yet, in the oft-quoted case of Kitty and Levin in Tolstoy's novel *Anna Karenina*, an exchange of the initial letters of words was sufficient for complete understanding.

Clearly, the appropriateness of the presuppositions made by speaker and listener will prove crucial for representational communication, and this suggests that an analysis of representational communication in terms of presuppositions should not be carried out separately from an analysis of interpersonal communication. What one knows about another person and about one's relation to him or her is crucial in deciding what to discuss and in determining what is presupposed in discussing it. If social psychology could throw light on the interweaving of social relations and presuppositions it would be much nearer to the heart of communication than it has ever been before.

Conclusion

Some of what has gone before can be summarized by indicating what remains to be done. Knowledge of the linguistic and non-linguistic systems, and their interrelations, can be used to fill out, in much more detail than hitherto attempted, an account of how interactional processes such as attribution, persuasion, cooperation and consensus operate in the everyday world. In doing this, a more systematic explanation will have to be given of how message and social setting interact. This will not complete the study of communication, which depends on a great deal that is shared by participants yet not easily recovered from either behaviour or situation. We shall, paradoxically, have to spend a great deal of time studying what is not said or signalled at all.

Further Reading

Danziger, K. (1976), *Interpersonal Communication*, New York, Academic Press. A readable introduction to communication in face-to-face interaction.

Robinson, W. P. (1972), *Language and Social Behaviour*, Penguin Books. A sound, critical introduction to a variety of topics in the social psychology of language and communication.

Bolinger, D. (1975), *Aspects of Language*, 2nd. ed., New York, Harcourt Brace Jovanovich. A wide-ranging and up-to-date introduction to linguistics.

Gumperz, J. J., and Hymes, D., eds. (1972), *Directions in Sociolinguistics*, New York, Holt, Rinehart & Winston. A good collection of recent papers on the topic of language and its social context.

Giglioli, P. P., ed. (1972), *Language and Social Context*, Penguin Books. Another good set of papers in sociolinguistics.

Argyle, M. (1969), *Social Interaction*, London, Methuen. Contains considerable material on non-verbal communication.

Laver, J., and Hutcheson, S., eds. (1972), *Communication in Face-to-Face Interaction*, Penguin Books. An interesting collection of papers emphasizing non-verbal communication and indexical information.

Chapter 6
Cooperation and Competition between Individuals

J. Richard Eiser

Cooperation and competition: the state of the game

There can be few areas of social psychology that are simultaneously as fascinating and as frustrating as that of interpersonal cooperation and competition. The importance of understanding why individuals come into conflict with one another, and of discovering means whereby such conflict may be reduced, are all too obvious. Yet, for this very reason, many social psychologists have acted as though the general importance of the problem was sufficient justification for their own particular theoretical preconceptions and choice of experimental methodology, and, working on the apparent assumption that any empirical knowledge is better than none, have frequently confused the replicability of their results with their relevance to real-life interactions.

The basic assumption of most research in this area has been that an understanding of interpersonal conflict and cooperation must start from a specification of the 'pay-offs', that is, the harmful or beneficial outcomes that accrue to each individual in an interaction as a function of his behaviour. In the simplest terms, it is assumed that individuals will be more likely to cooperate with one another when it is in their interests to do so than when it is not. Yet, as we shall see from experimental studies, the mere presence of a common interest does not guarantee cooperation if either participant can achieve a short-term gain by acting in his own self-interest against the common good. An unusual illustration of this problem is provided in a paper by Hardin (1968), who compares the present world population crisis with 'the tragedy of the commons' in medieval England. When villagers were given the right to graze their animals on common land, each individual villager could make a greater personal profit by increasing the number of animals he grazed there, but as more and more villagers followed suit, the grass disappeared, and the villagers ended up with a collective loss rather than a gain. Similarly, each family may find greater individual pleasure in larger numbers of children, but each new child places an additional demand on already dwindling world resources.

To look at conflict and cooperation from the point of view of the pay-offs of the participants had, it must be admitted, a number of attractions. If one could discover the pay-offs involved in an interaction, one could attempt to quantify them, and make reasonably precise calculations of the relative pressures towards competition or cooperation, and hence predict the behaviour of the participants. What is more, one could try to simulate such interactions by creating the same pay-off combinations in an experimental situation, and so put one's predictions to the test in the controlled atmosphere of the psychological laboratory. Hence the two-person 'experimental game' was born, and was greeted by experimental social psychologists with understandable enthusiasm. Here at last was a means of carrying out controlled observation and experimentation on an important social problem. But now, many journal issues, and many button-pressing, gate-shutting, rocket-firing generations of student subjects later, a more pessimistic and sceptical mood has emerged (Nemeth, 1972; Plon, 1974).

It is now very much in vogue among some critics of this research tradition to point to the undeniably restrictive and 'artificial' conditions under which such studies have typically been conducted, and to take it as self-evident that the way in which subjects have been found to behave in such experimental games can have no relevance for an understanding of real-life conflict and cooperation. This argument, in the form in which it is often presented, is conceptually inadequate. Psychology, not to say science generally, has typically made good use of artificial and restricted conditions to enable controlled observation of particular phenomena. Artificiality *per se* need not render the results of experimental research invalid, *provided the crucial variables have been adequately represented and operationalized*. At the other extreme, supporters of this research tradition have generally adopted one of two radically different lines of defence. On the one hand, there are those who retain a touchingly fundamentalist faith that these games are in fact direct analogues of typical real-life conflicts. On the other hand, there are those who profess that they are not concerned with the generalizability of their research, but are simply interested in gaming behaviour for its own sake. This latter defence seems rather like listening to an old prospector, who has spent the best years of his life panning for gold beside the same creek without success, claim that he likes prospecting there because of the scenery. We might commend him for his doggedness, but would direct our own search elsewhere.

The study of interpersonal conflict and cooperation, then, is at present facing an identity crisis, but though there may be ample room for scepticism regarding the hopeful promises of earlier research, there is no reason for pessimism concerning the future if the real lessons of past work are recognized and appreciated.

It will be argued that the weaknesses of previous research have been primarily conceptual, not methodological. The problem has been not with experimental games as such, but with the basic assumption that cooperation and competition can be adequately understood in terms of the quasi-economic pay-offs contingent on each participant's behaviour. It was this assumption that led to the selection of such games as a methodological tool, but as we shall see, it does not offer an adequate account *even of behaviour in the games themselves*. By the end of this chapter we shall have looked at more recent approaches to questions of cooperation and its absence and we shall have a much richer view of the prospects for interpersonal cooperation. But first let us look at some of the games that dominated work in this area for a decade or so.

Examples of experimental games

(i) *Coordination games*

The essential feature of these games is that the different players have to take it in turns to act for their greatest individual advantage if they are to end up with a profit, or to avoid ending up with a loss. The players have to decide among themselves how they are going to take turns. Just as it would be a pretty chaotic state of affairs if motorists at crossroads had always to get out of their cars and discuss who should cross first, so time is at a premium in the coordination games and the sooner the players can work out a mutually satisfactory rule of procedure, the better for everyone it will be.

The most widely used coordination game has been the 'trucking game' developed by Deutsch and Krauss (1960, 1962). This involves two players, each of whom is supposed to operate a trucking firm, referred to as 'Acme' or 'Bolt'. Each player gets paid a fixed sum, minus a variable cost which is a function of the length of time he takes for each load of merchandise he delivers to his destination. Each player has two possible routes to his destination, either a short main route including a section of one-lane road, or a long alternative route which would involve a small loss (see Figure 6). The danger is that both players will attempt to use the shorter route at the same time, and meet head-on in the one-lane road. Unless one of the players then

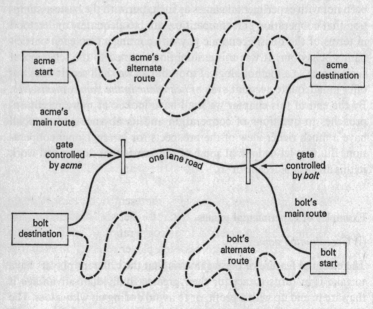

Figure 6   Road map for the Deutsch and Krauss trucking game

backs out, deadlock and mutual loss will ensue. The obvious co-operative solution is for the two players to take turns at using the shorter route, but whether or not they achieve this solution can be dependent on a number of factors.

The primary concern of the Deutsch and Krauss studies was with the effect of threat on the emergence of cooperation. The capacity of either player to threaten the other was achieved by giving him control over a gate situated at the end of the one-lane road nearest his own starting position. When this was closed, the other player's exit from the one-lane road would be blocked. Depending on the condition, both, one or neither of the players had control of a gate. Cooperation, and with it joint profit, was highest in the 'no-gate' condition, when neither player could threaten the other, and lowest in the 'two-gate' condition.

(ii) *The Prisoner's Dilemma game*

By far the most frequently used of all experimental games was the Prisoner's Dilemma (PD). It owes its name to an imaginary situation in which two accomplices are awaiting trial, and each has the option of informing on the other, with the hope of receiving a lighter sentence for himself. If neither of them informs on the other, both their sentences are likely to be moderate; if one informs but the other does not, the informer receives only a light sentence, but the other receives a severe one; but if both inform, they will both receive moderately severe sentences, and so be worse off than if they had both kept quiet. Since they have to make their decisions independently, the dilemma for each of them is whether they can trust the other not to inform.

In the laboratory this dilemma is represented by a two-person game in which each player has a choice between two alternative responses on each trial, referred to as cooperation (*C*) and defection or competition (*D*). The outcomes each player receives on each trial depends *both* on his own behaviour and on the behaviour of the other player. These outcomes can be represented in terms of the following matrix, where the first figure in each cell of the matrix represents the outcomes of person *A* and the second the outcomes of person *B*.

Person B's choices

		C	D
		x_1, x_1	x_2, x_3
Person A's choices	C		
	D	x_3, x_2	x_4, x_4

Thus, if A and B both choose C, both receive x_1; if both choose D, both receive x_4; if one chooses C and the other D, the one who chooses C receives x_2, and the other receives x_3. The PD game is distinguished from other games of a similar format by the following rules concerning the relative sizes of the respective pay-offs: (i) $x_3 > x_1$, $x_4 > x_2$; and (ii) $2x_1 > x_2 + x_3 > 2x_4$. Thus, a typical PD matrix might look like this:

Person B's choices

		C	D
		C	D
Person A's choices	C	3, 3	$-1, 5$
	D	5, -1	1, 1

Subjects would typically be shown the matrix, and the extent of their mutual interdependence would be fully explained.

In the jargon of gaming research, this is an example of a 'non-zero-sum mixed-motive game'. 'Non-zero-sum' refers to the fact that there is at least one cell of the matrix in which the sum of the outcomes of the different players does not equal zero. This distinguishes it from 'zero-sum-games', such as poker, in which what one person wins, another person loses, so the total winnings and losses for the different players add up to zero. 'Mixed-motive' refers to the fact that the game could motivate players either to be competitive or to be cooperative. From the point of view of person A's *individual* outcomes, on any given trial he will receive more points for himself if he chooses D rather than C, whatever person B chooses. Thus, in our example, if person B chooses C, person A will get 5 if he chooses D as against 3 if he chooses C; if person B chooses D, it will still be better for him to choose D and get 1, rather than C and get -1. The problem is that if person B thinks the same way, they both are likely to choose D and receive relatively low pay-offs. From the point of view of the maximum *joint* outcomes, they should each choose C, but by choosing C they each leave themselves open to exploitation if the other switches to D. A choice of D by person A, therefore might either represent an attempt at exploitation, if he expected person B to choose C, in the hope of gaining the highest individual pay-off of 5, or, if he expected person B to choose D, an attempt at self-defence, so as to ensure that he did not receive the minimum pay-off of -1.

An important variant of the PD is the game of Chicken, which differs from the PD in that $x_2 > x_4$; in other words, the worst possible individual pay-off for either player occurs when both choose D, although the highest individual pay-off is still obtained by choosing D when the other player chooses C (Rapoport and Chammah, 1966). If, in our example, x_4, i.e. the outcome of a joint choice of D, was changed from 1 to, say, -5, the game would be one of Chicken rather than a PD. The game owes its name to the situation when two motor-cyclists ride head-on towards each other down the centre of the road; whoever turns off first to let the other pass (C) is 'chicken', but if neither turns off (DD), both get killed. Because of the extra risk attached to the DD outcome, the best defence against an opponent who is going to play D is to play C. The move D in Chicken is thus clearly competitive, and cannot be construed as an attempt at self-defence as it can in the PD.

Factors influencing the level of cooperation

If taken at face value, the typical behaviour of subjects in experimental games presents a rather depressing picture. The low levels of cooperation commonly found in coordination games are, if anything, an improvement over the PD, where the proportion of C moves in any interaction can easily drop to around 30 per cent, even though the mutual benefit of cooperation is made quite clear. With it having been clearly established that subjects do not readily adopt a simple reinforcement strategy of 'win-stay, lose-change', or any other similar rubric which would allow stable cooperation to emerge after a handful of trials (Sidowski, 1957: Kelley *et al*, 1962), research on experimental games has attempted to identify factors that may make subjects less competitive, and has become increasingly concerned with the possibility that features of the experimental paradigm itself might artificially inhibit the development of cooperation. Unless otherwise stated, the PD is the game used in the studies to be mentioned.

(i) *The other player's strategy*

Although subjects in the PD are made aware of the relationship between their own outcomes and the choices of the other player, the 'other player' is often simulated, or is a confederate of the experimenter playing according to a predetermined strategy. Two extreme strategies are when the confederate unconditionally cooperates (100 per cent C), or alternatively unconditionally competes on every trial irrespective of the subject's own choice (100 per cent D). In the PD, a 100-per-cent-C strategy produces higher levels of cooperation from the subject, on average, than does the 100-per-cent-D strategy, which forces the subject to respond D in self-defence. This difference is reversed in Chicken, where the structure of the game forces the subject to choose C when faced by a consistently competitive opponent (Sermat, 1967). The higher average level of cooperation in the PD produced by the 100-per-cent-C strategy, however, disguises a bimodal distribution in the pattern of subjects' responses; whereas some subjects reciprocate by consistently cooperating in return, other subjects take advantage of the situation to gain the maximum individual pay-off by choosing D. This tendency to exploit another player whose behaviour is unconditionally cooperative is particularly marked when the standard PD matrix is changed to one in which the subject sees the other player as more powerful than himself (Swingle, 1970).

When the other player's response pattern is less consistent, higher overall levels of cooperation are not necessarily reciprocated by greater cooperation on the part of the subject. What becomes more important is whether the confederate's behaviour is at all determined by the subject's own responses. One of the most commonly used pre-programmed strategies is the 'tit-for-tat' (TFT) strategy, in which the confederate chooses, on each trial, the response chosen by the subject on the *previous* trial (the confederate's choice on the first trial being decided arbitrarily or randomly). This has the result of rewarding the subject for cooperation and punishing him for defec-

tion, and is one of the more effective strategies for raising cooperation – more effective, at any rate, than a strategy containing the same
proportion of C responses but in a random order unrelated to the
subject's actual behaviour. For a fuller discussion of these and other
strategy variables, the reader is referred to the comprehensive review
by Oskamp (1971).

(ii) *The nature of the rewards*

One of the commonest general criticisms against gaming research is
that subjects might not take their task as seriously as experimenters
have supposed; they might, in fact, see the task as 'just a game', and
thus be less concerned with the actual rewards or punishments they
receive. This argument gains a certain measure of plausibility from
the fact that the stakes in such games have generally been very low.
The actual pay-offs are often in the form of points which have no
significance outside the experiment, or are the equivalent of minimal
real money amounts (e.g. 1 point = 1 cent). Since mutual cooperation is the means by which highest *joint* profit can be achieved, by
giving subjects only negligible rewards one may effectively be re-
moving any incentive for cooperation.

The support for this argument is generally inconclusive. One study
which shows clear improvement in cooperation as a function of
increased reward level is that of Gallo (1966). Using a modified
version of the Deutsch and Krauss trucking game, he found that subjects playing for real money won an average of nearly $5 each over
20 trials, whereas those playing for imaginary rewards ended up with
imaginary losses of nearly $20 each. McClintock and McNeel (1966)
also found more cooperation in a high reward condition than in a
low reward condition.

However, both these studies used games which present subjects
with a qualitatively different kind of choice from that involved in the
PD. In the PD, increasing the real money equivalents of the pay-offs
does not only increase the motivation to cooperate, it also increases
the temptation to compete. For this reason, it is perhaps not too
surprising that manipulations of absolute reward level in the PD
have not yielded any very clear or consistent effects on level of co-

operation (Oskamp and Kleinke, 1970). Where differences are found, they tend to be in the direction of increased cooperation for real as compared with imaginary pay-offs (e.g. Radlow, Weidner and Hurst, 1968). These effects, however, are not of sufficient magnitude to justify the assumption that the use of imaginary pay-offs seriously inhibits the emergence of cooperation in the PD.

A more powerful manipulation is to vary the *relative* sizes of the different pay-offs, regardless of their real money equivalents. Rapoport and Chammah (1965) proposed that the tendency to cooperate in a PD should be related to the ratio $(x_1 - x_4)/(x_3 - x_2)$, which is termed the 'Cooperation Index'. Terhune (1968) found more mutual cooperation when the Cooperation Index was increased, particularly among individuals scoring highly on the personality trait of need for affiliation. The *structure* of the pay-offs in the PD and other games thus appears to be generally a more important factor than the absolute level of the rewards.

(iii) *The opportunity to communicate*

An obviously 'artificial' feature of experimental games is the fact that the players typically cannot communicate with one another. Often this restriction is imposed with no more sinister motive in mind than to maintain the experimental deception of a simulated partner. Nonetheless, there is reason to suppose that this may be an important factor contributing to low levels of cooperation in some circumstances.

Since uncertainty concerning the other player's intentions, and the consequent risk associated with the cooperative move, constitute the basic dilemma of the PD and similar games, it can reasonably be expected that the opportunity to communicate may clear up some of this uncertainty and hence lead to greater cooperation. A free discussion period half-way through the game has been found to lead to greater subsequent cooperation in the PD (Scodel, Minas, Ratoosh and Lipetz, 1959) and in a modification of the PD for six-person groups (Bixenstine, Levitt and Wilson, 1966). Voissem and Sistrunk (1971) found that subjects who could pass notes of a standard form, expressing their intentions and/or expectations, before each trial of a 100 trial PD became progressively more cooperative as compared with a no-communication group, who became more competitive as the game progressed; two other conditions with partial communication opportunities showed intermediate levels of cooperation. In coordination games, Mintz (1951), in an early simulation of a panic situation, found that subjects could remove cones more efficiently from a narrow-necked bottle when discussion was permitted. On the other hand, Deutsch and Krauss (1962) established that simply providing subjects with the opportunity to communicate if they wish is no guarantee that they will in fact make use of this opportunity. Subjects talked to each other most in the 'no-gate' condition and least in the 'two-gate' condition, but even in the 'no-gate' condition most subjects did not communicate, possibly because communication took time, and time cost money.

One of the more important factors limiting the facilitating effects of communication on cooperation was brought to light by Deutsch (1958). In a *cooperative* condition, each subject was made to feel concerned with the other player's outcomes as well as his own; in an *individualistic* condition each subject was told that his only concern should be with his own outcomes; and in a *competitive* condition each subject was told to make as much money for himself as possible, and also to do better than the other player. In each condition, subjects felt that the other player shared their orientation. When subjects were allowed to exchange written notes beforehand the percentage of cooperative responses in the individualistic condition jumped to 70·6 per cent as compared with 35·9 per cent when communication was not permitted. The corresponding increases were from 89·1 per cent to 96·9 per cent and from 12·5 per cent to 29·2 per cent in the cooperative and competitive conditions respectively. Deutsch concluded that,

When subjects are competitively oriented, there is little commitment to what one communicates and hence little basis for trust as a result of the communication one receives. It would seem that the situation has to be ambiguous as to whether the individuals will interrelate themselves cooperatively or competitively, rather than clearly competitively, before an individual will assume that communications are informative rather than misleading (p. 275).

Restricting the opportunity to communicate, however, may do more than just make it difficult for the players to discern each other's wishes and intentions. The very fact of being isolated from one another may make the players see their interaction as more of a mechanical than an interpersonal affair, to which the norm of reciprocity (Nemeth, 1970) and other codes of conduct which operate in everyday encounters are somehow less applicable. Wichman (1970) had women play seventy-eight trials of a PD under an isolation condition, in which they could neither hear nor see each other, a condition in which they could see but not hear each other, a condition in which they could hear but not see each other, and a condition in which they could both see and hear each other. The median levels of cooperation over the first seventy trials in each condition were 40·7 per cent, 47·7 per cent, 72·1 per cent and 87·0 per cent respectively. The overall conclusion is manifestly clear: the more freely and naturally subjects can communicate, the more they cooperate.

Attributions of intention in mixed-motive situations

Of the three factors influencing the level of cooperation which we have just been considering, the two which have a direct effect on the subject's outcomes are the strategy of the other player, and the level of reward. If the subject's own behaviour is simply a function of the outcomes he receives, then these should be the factors which have most influence on his level of cooperation. The most dramatic increases in cooperation, however, have been produced by giving subjects the opportunity to communicate with one another, even though the strength of these effects may vary across different conditions, and even though permitting communication does not guarantee its occurence. These findings suggest that an understanding of interaction in mixed-motive situations is likely to depend as much upon an understanding of how individuals attribute intentions to one another as upon a consideration of their overall gains and losses. In chapter 9 we shall examine interpersonal attributions in some detail. Here we shall briefly illustrate how they might operate in gaming situations.

Kelley and Stahelski (1970b) have proposed that the extent to which a player in the PD or any similar game will see his partner as having cooperative or competitive intentions will be affected by his *own* intentions in the interaction. In what they refer to as the 'triangle hypothesis', they propose that, whereas cooperative individuals may see their partner as likely to be either cooperative or competitive, competitive individuals will predominantly interpret their partner's intentions as competitive. If one were to test a group of subjects, and then plot their own intentions against their expectations of their partners' intentions, a triangular shape should result (see Figure 7).

expectations as to other's orientations

	cooperative			competitive
cooperative	X	X	X	X
		X	X	X
own orientation			X	X
competitive				X

Figure 7 The triangle hypothesis

The most crucial aspect of this relationship concerns the attributions made by subjects when the other player chooses *D*. Because of the structure of the PD, such a choice might represent either an attempt at exploitation (if the other player felt the subject would choose *C*) or an attempt at self-defence (if he felt the subject would choose *D*). Thus even if the other's original intentions were cooperative, he might be forced to choose *D* if the subject's own behaviour was competitive. Kelly and Stahelski argue that competitive individuals make an 'attributional error' in taking insufficient account of the causal influence of their *own* behaviour in making the other act competitively. Thus, by attributing competitive intentions to their partner, they force him to act competitively, with the result that their attributions become self-fulfilling.

In support of this hypothesis, Kelley and Stahelski (1970a) show that, whilst the intentions of a competitive player in the PD tend to be accurately perceived, a player whose original intentions are co-operative tends to be seen as cooperative by a cooperative partner and competitive by a competitive partner, largely because, against a competitive partner, he is forced to *behave* competitively. Kelley and Stahelski see the differences in the kinds of attributions made by cooperators and competitors as evidence that they 'have different views of their worlds' (1970b, p.66) which reflect differences in personality, particularly in authoritarianism, generalizable to other interactions, and not specific to their behaviour in mixed-motive games. It should be noted, however, that Sermat (1970) found only slight evidence for individual consistencies in competitiveness across different kinds of situation, and Miller and Holmes (1975) have questioned the generalizability of the 'triangle hypothesis' beyond the PD situation.

There is also evidence that a person's intentions can affect the *kind* of information he will look for in a situation where his partner's intentions are unclear. In a study by Eiser and Tajfel (1972), each subject could 'buy' from the experimenter information about the value to his partner of each message his partner received and the cost to the partner of each message the partner sent. Subjects asked for much more information concerning the value to the other of their own messages, rather than the cost to the other of those they received from the partner, but this difference was significantly smaller among subjects whose declared intentions were less competitive. If one considers that information concerning the other's costs would provide information concerning the extent to which the other was merely trying to minimize his own costs, then it would appear that the more cooperative subjects showed relatively more interest in information which would enable them to infer the reasons for their partner's apparent behaviour, and less interest in information that would enable them to control their partner's outcomes, than did the less cooperative subjects.

Self-presentation and subjects' definition of the situation

As important as the attributions subjects make about each other's intentions are their expectations as to how their own behaviour will appear to others – such 'others' including not only the partner with whom they are interacting, but also the experimenter and anyone else who may witness their behaviour. In many situations, the *symbolic* value of a person's behaviour – what it may be taken to represent – is likely to be as important to that person as the pay-offs which his behaviour produces. This is true even with regard to the effects of a variable which directly affects the subject's monetary outcomes, namely the size of the real money equivalents of the points in the pay-off matrix. Messé, Dawson and Lane (1973) have shown that subjects' motivation to earn substantial rewards by mutual cooperation is affected by what they consider an equitable rate of pay for their participation in the experiment. When playing a PD for high monetary rewards, subjects who had previously spent one hour and forty minutes completing questionnaires for the experimenter were more cooperative than subjects who did not have to complete the questionnaires first; this difference disappeared when subjects played for minimal rewards. In the same vein, Gallo (1972) reports anecdotal evidence that, when questioned afterwards as to why they had not cooperated more consistently and so earned more money subjects may often get indignant and reply that they are not greedy. Thus the same subjects who, from the experimenter's perspective may be acting competitively may, from their own point of view, be acting cooperatively *towards the experimenter* by not exploiting their opportunity to obtain inequitably large remunerations for their services.

Clear differences in level of cooperation can also be produced if the format in which the pay-off matrix is presented is altered so as to emphasize different implications of cooperative and competitive play. Evans and Crumbaugh (1966) found that subjects cooperated at a rate of 48 per cent against a TFT ('tit-for-tat') strategy when presented with the PD matrix in standard form, the matrix values being $x_1 = 3$, $x_2 = 0$, $x_3 = 4$ and $x_4 = 1$. However, when subjects had to choose between the responses 'Give him 3' and 'Give me 1', cooperation increased to 63 per cent. The point is that both these procedures are *logically* equivalent (if both players chose 'Give him 3' this would have the same effect as both choosing *C*) but they do not appear to be equivalent *psychologically*. The latter procedure is closely related to what Pruitt (1967) refers to as a 'decomposed' PD. The essential feature of a decomposed PD is that the pay-offs are shown to each player in the following form:

		Your gains	Other's gains
	C	a	b
Your behaviour			
	D	c	d

This would be equivalent to 'Give him 3' and 'Give me 1' if $a = 0$, $b = 3$, $c = 1$ and $d = 0$. Pruitt compared the level of cooperation obtained with a PD presented in standard format, with that obtained with three different decomposed PDs, all of which were mathematically equivalent to each other and, at the same time, to the standard PD. Cooperation on the standard PD was around 50 per cent, but over the last five of a series of twenty trials dropped to around 15 per cent on one decomposed game, whilst climbing to 78 per cent and 82 per cent on the other two. In a later study using the same decomposed PDs, Pruitt (1970) found that the reasons subjects gave for choosing *C* or *D* on the first trial varied markedly in the different games. In all these games the joint outcomes accruing from cooperation and competition are identical, but subjects' own interpretation of the choice before them, and their resultant behaviour, are radically different.

Just as such mathematical sleight of hand can alter the meaning of cooperation and competition for the subject, so can the wider context in terms of which he feels his behaviour will be evaluated. Eiser and Bhavnani (1974) found more cooperation when subjects were led to interpret a PD as a simulation of international negotiations or of 'real-life encounters between different individuals' than when given control instructions, or led to regard it as a simulation of economic bargaining.

The general conclusion to be drawn from the evidence presented in this and in preceding sections is quite clear. To concentrate solely on the economic pay-offs associated with cooperation and competition, and ignore their psychological significance, is to look at barely half the picture.

Altruism and helping behaviour

In the research we have so far considered, cooperation could be broadly defined as behaviour undertaken together with another person for the attainment of mutual benefits. Even though these mutual benefits may involve a sacrifice by each player of aspirations to higher individual outcomes, such aspirations are in fact unattainable by either player if both act competitively. This definition of cooperation in terms of 'working together' (quite apart from its etymological propriety) serves to distinguish cooperation from cases where one individual will act unilaterally to 'do good' to another, often at some cost to himself. Interest in this latter class of behaviour, alternatively called altruism, helping or pro-social behaviour, has mushroomed over the past few years to the point where its popularity as a research area has quickly overtaken that of experimental games. No comprehensive survey will be attempted here of the diversity of topics studied within this general field (see Krebs, 1970; Macaulay and Berkowitz, 1970, for representative reviews). Instead, we shall single out a few of the themes which bear most directly on problems of cooperation and competition between individuals.

Any naïve notion that people will necessarily behave with less apparent selfishness in real life than they do in experimental games receives a nasty jolt from studies, usually conducted in large American cities, concerned with the question of whether bystanders will intervene to help another person in an emergency. There is much evidence that even when people are distressed or shocked at another's fate, they may be extremely reluctant to take the initiative in providing any concrete assistance. When Kitty Genovese was murdered in March 1964 in New York City, thirty-eight witnesses looked on from their windows without anyone coming to her assistance or even telephoning the police during the more than half-an-hour long assault (Rosenthal. 1964). Since then, much research has attempted to discover the factors that may inhibit helping in such situations.

One of the clearest results obtained with simulations of a variety of emergencies, from workmen falling off ladders to smoke seeping through air vents, is that a bystander is more likely to intervene if he is by himself than if he is in the presence of others who could also intervene. Darley and Latané (1968) have suggested that a possible reason for this effect may be that the responsibility for helping becomes 'diffused'. Diffusion of responsibility here means that each person is likely to say to himself something like 'I expect someone else will do something about it' or 'I don't see why I should help if no one else is going to'. Another possible reason is that a bystander may take into account the reactions of other bystanders as a basis for discerning the extent of the emergency and as cues as to how he himself should respond.

An experiment which compares these two possibilities is by Ross and Braband (1973). Subjects were required to work on a card-sorting task alone, or in the presence of either a normally sighted or a supposedly blind confederate. After the experimenter had left the room, one of two emergencies occurred: either the sound of a workman hurting himself and screaming, or the sound of some glass crashing followed by smoke pouring into the experimental room from a part of the laboratory that had supposedly been taken over by the chemistry department, who had advertised their presence with a notice on their door saying 'Dangerous work in progress'. Neither emergency produced any reaction from the confederate. When faced with the 'scream' emergency, 64 per cent of the subjects tested alone reacted within five minutes of its onset by leaving the card-sorting task to go and investigate; when paired with a confederate only 28 per cent reacted if he was blind and 35 per cent if he was sighted. In the 'smoke' condition, the percentages were 50 per cent for subjects working alone, 64 per cent (a non-significant improvement) for those paired with a blind confederate, and 14 per cent for those paired with a sighted confederate.

These results cannot be squared with a diffusion of responsibility interpretation, since in neither emergency could subjects have expected the blind confederate to be capable of helping. In the 'smoke' condition, where the signs of the emergency were primarily visual, the inactivity of the blind confederate provided the subject with no information for inferring what his own response should be, so he responded as though the confederate was not there. In the 'scream' condition, where the signs were auditory, the unresponsiveness of the blind confederate inhibited intervention as effectively as when he was sighted. Related evidence comes from a study by Bickman (1972).

The ambiguity of the emergency is clearly an important factor determining subjects' readiness to intervene, although the variety of situations that have been used makes it difficult to draw direct comparisons between different studies. Clark and Word (1972), for instance, found that *all* subjects intervened in a condition where a maintenance man was heard to fall and cry out in agony, regardless of the size of the group, but if only the fall was heard, and no cries of agony, the percentage of helping dropped to around 30 per cent. Ambiguity about 'what should be done', however, seems generally more important than ambiguity about 'what is happening'. What was happening was clear enough in the Kitty Genovese murder, and in the 'smoke' condition of the Ross and Braband study, the density of smoke in the experimental room was thick enough to force some subjects to get out of their chairs and continue the card-sorting task standing up!

Other research has studied helping in non-emergency situations by seeing how people respond to simple requests for assistance. Darley and Latané (1970) report data obtained when passers-by were approached in the street and asked for a minimal amount of money (10 cents). Even when no explanation was given for the request, 34 per cent handed over the 10 cents; when the person making the request explained that he needed to make a telephone call, 64 per cent of those asked helped him out; whilst 72 per cent did so if he said his wallet had been stolen. Langer and Abelson (1972) found similar differences in reponses to 'legitimate' or 'illegitimate' requests for a passer-by to make a telephone call, or post a bulky envelope. In a particularly imaginative study of bargaining behaviour in a naturalistic setting, Dorris (1972) approached a number of coin dealers with a set of rare coins, saying that he had just inherited them, and knew nothing of their value (thus leaving himself open to possible exploitation), but wanted to sell them. The average initial offer from the dealers was $8.72 in a 'neutral appeal' condition, but if the experimenter made a 'moral appeal', saying that he needed the money to buy textbooks to study for his examinations, the average initial bid was $13.63. According to other coin experts, offer of $12 or more would be reasonably fair for the coins in question.

Darley and Latané (1970) have argued that such variations in level of helping are best understood in terms of the costs which would be incurred by the person giving help. In support of this, they mention that requests for help involving no cost to the giver, e.g. to tell the time, are granted more frequently than requests for even as minimal an amount of money as 10 cents. They also cite a study by Allen, in which travellers on the New York subway heard a conferedate give obviously false directions to another traveller (also a confederate). They were less likely to correct the misinformer if the request for directions had not been directed to them specifically, or if the misinformer had already created the impression of being a dangerous character by looking up from a magazine on muscle-building and shouting threats of physical assault at a fourth traveller (yet another confederate) who tripped over his feet.

Whilst it is clear that helping can be inhibited if it involves costs or danger to the helper, Darley and Latané do not explain how a cost analysis could account for their own findings that help is given more readily to someone who *justifies* his need for help – an effect since confirmed by Dorris (1972), and by Langer and Abelson (1972). Instead, they attempt to discredit what they see as the major alternative to a cost analysis, namely an explanation in terms of the norms involved in different situations. However, their assertion that 'any serious attempt to deal with the various response rates in normative terms must involve the postulation of a proliferation of norms' (p. 99) is merely sophistry. It amounts to saying that there can be no general norms for deciding on the justifiability of any given request, or alternatively that all requests are *equally* obligating from an ethical or normative point of view, and therefore that economic considerations are all that can distinguish situations in which help will be given from situations in which it will not. When one attempts to identify what such general norms may be, however, one is hindered by two preconceptions that have dominated much of the research so far conducted in this area.

The first of these relates to the restricted range of situations in which helping has generally been studied. For all their claims of greater realism, it is questionable whether studies of bystanders' reactions in emergencies, or of people's responses to requests for small favours, provide any firmer basis for theorizing about pro-social behaviour in general than do studies of cooperation and competition in more obviously artifical laboratory conditions. Society as a whole is based upon the institutionalization of social obligations, even though how such obligations are defined varies from culture to culture. A *truly* anti-social person is either an outlaw, an outcast, or an expert dissembler of his intentions; he is not a typical experimental subject. Even the witnesses of the Genovese murder were 'law-abiding citizens'.

The second preconception is the tendency to regard helping and withholding help as products of two diametrically opposed sets of norms or motives, the one essentially pure and selfless, the other evil and selfish. A similar tendency to see cooperation and competition as irreconcilable opposites runs through most of the gaming research reviewed earlier in this chapter. Although the terminology has changed, this is little advance over the medieval notion of angels and devils wrestling for one's soul. An alternative possibility is that people are not particularly motivated *as such* either to be helpful and cooperative or to be unhelpful and competitive, but instead are strongly committed to a norm of fairness and justice. As Lerner (1970, p. 207) has put it, 'We want to believe we live in a world where people get what they deserve or, rather, deserve what they get.'

Justice and self-interest

If, as is suggested, a belief in a just world may be, if anything, more fundamental than a commitment to unconditional self-gratification, then a person's decision to give or withhold help from another is likely to depend less directly on his own costs than on the answers he finds to the questions 'Does this person deserve to be helped?' and 'Would I personally be justified in withholding help?' If the answer to the first of these questions is 'No', a decision *not* to help can be seen as quite consistent with a belief in fairness and justice. Thus, there is the temptation to see certain others as deserving any misfortunes that befall them, particularly if one feels personally unable to provide redress. Michener (1971) mentions the case of a high-school teacher in Kent, Ohio, who asserted that the four students shot dead by Ohio National Guardsmen at Kent State University in 1970 deserved to die, even though two of them were not involved in the demonstration. He claimed that 'Anyone who appears on the streets of a city like Kent with long hair, dirty clothes or barefooted deserves to be shot.' Laboratory studies have also claimed a similar tendency for victims to be rejected or blamed for their own sufferings (e.g. Lerner and Simmons, 1966; see also p. 245).

But what happens to a person who believes in justice, yet sees the sufferings of others as undeserved? He can either withhold help, and thus allow the injustice of the others' suffering to continue, or he can give help, and thus forego benefits which he, as a just person, feels he has earned and deserved. At this point he is likely to look to other 'just people' similar to himself for a definition of how to act justly in this dilemma. He will do as much as the next person; he will pay taxes for welfare programmes, donate money to famine relief organizations, consume less resources in times of shortage, provided he feels that others like him are doing the same. In this way he can feel he is doing 'his bit', whilst continuing to have what he deserves, since what he deserves is what others like him have. If he rejects this criterion of 'what others would do' and attempts to act unilaterally to correct any injustice he comes across, he will never be able to feel entitled to anything he has or wants, since there will always be someone worse off than himself.

With the protection of this criterion, a person is likely to be quite ready to reduce his outcomes in an interaction, and improve the outcomes of another. Adams (1963) found that if workers paid on a piece-work basis felt they were being overpaid, they would voluntarily reduce their rate of output, but attempt to improve the quality of each piece produced, whereas others who felt that they were being overpaid on an hourly basis would increase their rate of output. The Messé et al. (1973) study of equity and reward level in the PD, which was discussed on p. 165, reflects a similar process. This same criterion, however, allows an individual, in certain situations, to pursue his own interests even though by doing so he may impede the chances of others to achieve their goals. These situations are ones which are governed by what Lerner and Lichtman (1968) and Lerner (1971) refer to as norms of *justified self-interest*, which 'imply equal opportunity and risk among the participants as well as the pursuit of self-interest within the rules of what is fair and equal' (Lerner and Lichtman, 1968, p. 226).

Provided a participant in such an interaction observes the rules of 'fair play', he is not censured for capitalizing on any extra luck that comes his way, or on any extra effort he invests to improve his individual outcomes. Lerner and Lichtman, however, point out two kinds of situations in which the behaviour of the other participant can make it no longer justified for the individual to act in this way. The first is when the other participant appeals for help or special consideration and thus puts himself in a dependent rather than equal position in the interaction. The second is when the other deliberately refrains from capitalizing on a fortuitous opportunity to improve his own outcomes to his partner's detriment. When this happens 'the rules of competition have been elevated to a more gentlemanly level' (p. 227) and his partner is obliged to act with similar restraint in return. In the Lerner and Lichtman study, female students were led to believe that they could choose between participating in a learning experiment either in a condition involving negative reinforcements (shocks), or in a control condition involving no shocks, but if they chose the control condition, their partner (another subject) would be assigned to the shock condition. When told that their opportunity to make the choice had been determined on a random basis, most subjects saw this as a situation which justified their acting in their own self-interest, and only 9 per cent chose the shock condition for themselves. On the other hand, if they were told that their partner had asked the experimenter to pass on the message that she was really scared about the shock and would prefer to be in the control condition, 72 per cent chose the shock for themselves. Similarly, when told that their partner had been the one who had initially been given the choice of conditions, but had said 'that she would prefer to let you decide', 88 per cent put themselves in the shock condition.

Results like these cannot be reconciled with any notion that a person's decision to help another is based purely on a consideration of his own tangible costs; nor do they support the picture suggested by a superficial interpretation of the gaming and altruism literature, that human beings are fundamentally self-centred, amoral and cynical in their social interactions. For most people, a very different picture may be nearer the mark, that they are scrupulously concerned with doing what they see as fair in any situation, and expect others to do likewise. This same norm of fairness, however, can allow them to act in their own interests, even to the detriment of others, if the situation is construed as one of fair competition to which the norm of 'justified self-interest' applies.

How individuals define their relationships with one another on the basis of such norms is of far greater importance in determining whether they will cooperate or compete than the pay-offs which their behaviour may produce. Although study after study has attempted to change subjects' behaviour by manipulating their outcomes, few have tried to control directly for whether such outcomes will be seen as fair or justified. This is primarily a criticism of theory, rather than of methodology – a problem of the kind of questions social psychologists have been asking, rather than of how they have tried to answer them.

By giving subjects no clear guidelines on how their behaviour will be evaluated, and little basis for discerning the intentions of other participants, experimenters have created a 'social trap' (Platt, 1973) in which subjects have felt justified in acting to protect their immediate self-interest. Once this happens, and any single participant unilaterally construes the situation as one of fair competition, it becomes even more 'justified' for other participants to do likewise. Just as in the 'tragedy of the commons' with which we started this chapter, the dangers associated with real-life versions of such traps are only too apparent. Such dangers, however, may depend less on the reluctance of individuals to make sacrifices for the common good, than on an inappropriate conception of what is just and fair. By identifying the conditions which may lead people to adopt more enlightened definitions of the relationship between justice and self-interest, social psychology still has a chance to help us find a way in which such traps may be avoided.

Further Reading

Gergen, K. J. (1969), *The Psychology of Behaviour Exchange*, New York, Addison-Wesley. A short paperback giving a simple introduction to aspects of exchange theory.

Wrightsman, L. S. Jr, O'Connor, J., and Baker, N. J., eds. (1972), *Cooperation and Competition: Readings on mixed-motive games*, Monterey, Calif., Brooks/Cole. A wide-ranging but very well-selected collection of journal articles, supported by some very valuable chapters written specifically for the book. It is definitely *not* an introductory text, however.

Swingle, P. G., ed. (1970), *The Structure of Conflict*, New York, Academic Press. This again is not an introductory text. A good book for theoretical critiques, rather than just a source-book for references.

Macaulay, J., and Berkowitz, L., eds. (1970), *Altruism and Helping Behavior*, New York, Academic Press. An important collection of theoretical and review chapters compiled when altruism research was still in its relatively early stages. Although not intended as an introductory text, it is mostly very readable.

Chapter 7
Small Groups
1. Structure and Leadership
Colin Fraser

Introduction

What is a small group?

The German sociologist Georg Simmel (1950) argued that in marriage '. . . the decisive difference is between monogamy and bigamy, whereas the third or twentieth wife is relatively unimportant for the marriage structure'. Similarly, for Simmel, 'a marriage with one child has a character which is completely different from that of a childless marriage, but it is not significantly different from a marriage with two or more children . . .' (pp. 138–9). To justify further a distinction between two-person and larger groupings Simmel pointed out that in larger groups, unlike dyads, the removal of one member does not mean the disappearance of the grouping, coalitions and sub-groups become possible, and complete unity of mood and feeling is exceedingly unlikely to prevail. Simmel's insightful observations have been borne out by subsequent investigations. For example, in a study of dyads and groups discussing and attempting to agree on a problem in human relations, Bales and Borgatta (1955) found that, compared with larger groups, dyads tended to stress supportive acts and avoid disagreements more. And O'Dell (1968), in a study of emotionality expressed in interactions of two, three, four and five persons, reported that almost all the significant differences involved dyads versus the other sized groupings, the major finding being that the dyads produced only three quarters as many interactional acts as triads, quartets or quintets. In addition, dyads expressed relatively less hostility but more tension.

These and other findings justify the social psychologist in modifying an old adage to read, 'two's a dyad, three's a small group'. Although certain similarities can be discerned, behaviour in groups cannot be understood by simple extrapolation from dyadic interaction, described in previous chapters. A four-person group is not simply a dyad multiplied by two.

Three persons make up the smallest small group; the size of the largest one is less clear. A useful guide, though, is the proposal of the American sociologist R. F. Bales (1950) that, provided '... each member receives some impression or perception of each other member distinct enough so that he can ... give some reaction to each of the others as an individual person ...' (p. 33) then a collection of people can be termed 'a small group'. Thus a large lecture room of students would hardly qualify, but a stable school class of thirty or more children would. In practice, we are concerned with groupings of from three to about three dozen persons.

Size alone, however, is far from being a sufficient criterion for accepting a collectivity or aggregate of persons as a 'small group'. Would we wish to regard as a group every bus queue or waiting-room full of people? If not, what are the basic characteristics of a group? Undoubtedly, the principal characteristic is that of sustained *interaction*. The members of a group act and react towards one another so that their behaviour becomes mutually influencing or interdependent. In addition, a number of other recurring features are likely to be found. The members of a group will develop a *perception* of the group as 'real' and of themselves as members. Some of the behavioural consequences of this perception of the group's existence for both group members and for others are discussed in chapters 16 and 17 on intergroup relations. The group will develop shared group *goals*. Even if the group was established in response to an externally imposed purpose, it is likely to interpret and perhaps re-interpret this purpose or aim according to its own lights, and it is almost certain to add additional self-generated goals. Over time, *norms* internal to the group will arise. The members will act and expect each other to act in standard ways, and members disregarding these norms will lay themselves open to disapproval and the possible exercise of sanctions by other group members. In so far as sets of norms come to be organized around certain 'positions' within the group, e.g. mother, chairman, food-preparer, then the group will come to have a set of *roles*. One further feature to be noted is that a distinctive set of *affective relations* is likely to hold. Group members are unlikely to be emotionally neutral or indifferent to one another. Some members will be more liked and more popular than the rest, and, in certain groups, there may be disliked isolates.

Other possible criteria of 'groupness' could be found, but the above six are the criteria most commonly invoked. With these concepts we could, if we wished, decide whether a given set of people waiting for a bus were a group, or merely a queue. We can also give an answer to a question raised from time to time (see Allport, 1924; Campbell, 1958), namely 'are groups "real"?' We would not argue for the extreme reification of the group implied by terms such as 'group mind' or 'collective unconscious'. But we could not accept the individualistic view that groups have no reality and are merely convenient labels for referring to the aggregate of behaviours of sets of individuals. In fact, small-group researchers sometimes deliberately create 'synthetic groups' which are nothing more than the aggregation or summing, by the investigator, of the behaviour and productivity of independent individuals, and these synthetic groups provide a useful baseline for deciding what is distinctive about group performance. In general the performances of groups and of synthetic groups do differ and to explain the differences it is necessary to invoke one or more of the criteria for groups proposed above. In so far as group interaction, perception, goals, norms, roles and affective relations are necessary to predict and explain the functioning of people in groups then we can say that groups are, in fact, real.

Four types of small groups

Very many of our everyday activities are carried out as group members, with our families, friends, work-mates and others. Thus the study of groups is important partly because they are such ubiquitous phenomena, but also partly because much of the contact between individual and society is mediated by groups. To put some meat on the bare conceptual bones outlined above, let us look briefly at three very common types of groups: families, friendship groups, and work groups, each of which is discussed in rather more detail in Argyle (1969). We shall see that, though most of the basic characteristics of groups are readily discernible in each of these three types of groups, the characteristics operate somewhat differently and are of varying importance in the different groups.

(i) *Families*. The family we are born into is the small group to which most of us owe primary allegiance for the first fifteen or twenty years of our life, and, indeed for many people in our society, it remains a focus for allegiance throughout their lives. Clearly there is sustained interaction, though it changes systematically decade by decade. Perception of group membership is sufficiently strong that it may be normally taken for granted, though we are continually reminded of it every time we complete a form or questionnaire. Group goals are numerous, relating both to maintaining good relations within the family itself as well as to more external, instrumental achievements. Affective relations, though complex and perhaps ambivalent, remain very important. The life of any family is regulated by many norms, some externally imposed by wider social structures and accepted by families generally, others internally created by the individual family group to help organize its own way of life. Traditionally many norms have impinged on a clearly articulated role structure, organized particularly in terms of age distinctions – i.e. parents versus children – and sex distinctions. At the moment, particularly in middle-class households, the sex-roles are being modified somewhat, and perhaps differences really are being reduced.

(ii) *Friendship groups*. These probably are most common during adolescence and although they show some similarities to family groups, and appear to take over some of the functions of the family for the older child, they reveal some interesting contrasts with the family. For one thing, although these groups will have evolved their own norms for regulating behaviour and for indicating group membership, these norms may well not be organized around a distinctive set of roles, different members taking over key functions in different situations. Furthermore, the overriding goal, perhaps even more obviously than for a family, is likely to be the maintenance of the group *per se* and the well-being of its members. The function of the friendship group is for its members to meet as a group, and, indeed, simply 'being' in such a group is already 'well-being'. Additional, shorter-term instrumental goals may be created, but if they are not attained it may not be too important provided that some enjoyment has been experienced along the way. In later adolescence, these single-sex groups will disappear as members increasingly prefer dyadic interaction with the opposite sex, before going on to establish small groups of their own!

(iii) *Work groups*. If one thinks of a committee, or a workshop or office group, then ostensibly the major goals are instrumental or task oriented. The well-being of the group *per se* is intended to be secondary, although it is by no means uncommon for a committee, having achieved the aims set it, to create further task goals for itself in order to rationalize its own continuing existence. The work group *is* likely to have a clear role structure, probably of a hierarchical type, with a chairman, manager or foreman supposedly acting as leader. It is important to recognize that this externally imposed structure may not correspond to the leadership or power structure that operates in practice within the group. Indeed, the fact that the work group, unlike the friendship group or family, is likely to be an integral part of a larger formal organization which attempts to exert considerable detailed control over it, raises many questions about small-group functioning which are not so readily apparent in the other two types of grouping. (See chapter 13, on social behaviour in organizations.)

Given the obvious importance of these everyday groups in socializing the individual and regulating his day-to-day work-life, it would be reasonable to assume that after about half a century of small group studies, social psychologists would have a clear and detailed picture of how such groups normally function and hence of the contribution made by them to the meshing of individuals and social systems. Unfortunately, this assumption is not justified. McGrath and Altman (1966) located well over 2000 reports of small-group studies prior to 1960. Of these, 55 per cent had been conducted in laboratory settings, another 30 per cent had more laboratory than field elements in them, and less than 5 per cent had been carried out in natural settings. As the amount of small-group research continued to increase through the 1960s, so did the move into the laboratory. There have been some recent indications that a reversal of this trend may be under way, but it is clear that the majority of small-group studies have been far from optimally designed to tell us about types of groups important in the world around us. The point was made in very succinct, if extreme, form by Barker (1966) when he wrote, 'What we have in a typical small-group experiment, then, is a temporary collection of late adolescent strangers given a puzzle to solve under bizarre conditions in a limited time during their first meeting while being peered at from behind a mirror'. Thus the majority of research reports introduce us to a type of group we have not yet considered.

(iv) *Laboratory groups.* Typically, these consist of five or six first- or second-year American university undergraduates, all of the same sex. They have not known each other prior to the experiment, they meet together for an hour or two, and then their life as a group is over. When we look to see how the defining characteristics of a group operate in this case, we have problems. Sustained interaction lasts for two hours at the most, and it is only for that period that there is much chance of the members having any perception of group membership. Group goals are minimal, as are internally developed norms. Because the members were selected to be as homogeneous as possible, it is very unlikely that role differences will emerge naturally, and because friends, or enemies, were not permitted to be in the same group affective relations are weak. In fact, laboratory groups are hardly groups at all. More charitably we could argue that many small-group studies are, in fact, controlled studies of only the very earliest phases of group development.

This highlights one very interesting, but badly neglected set of problems, namely developmental factors in group functioning (or, for that matter, in relations between groups; see chapter 17 for comments on the value of Sherif's work in this latter respect). As we shall see later in this chapter, Bales and his colleagues have clearly demonstrated that even laboratory groups change over time. The conclusions one could draw about leadership in such a group after several meetings are likely to be systematically different from one's impressions during the first meeting (Bales and Slater, 1955). And one or two studies of more naturalistic groups can be cited to make related points. Newcomb (1961), for example, observed that for males in a student residence the primary basis for attraction and friendship changed over time from proximity of rooms to perceived similarity of attitudes. More generally, Tuckman (1965), on the basis of a review of the limited evidence from natural, laboratory, training and therapeutic groups, attempted a general summary of group development, in terms of four stages: forming, storming, norming and performing. That is, groups start with a period of orientation followed by some interpersonal conflict and polarization. Only after that do they develop cohesiveness, together with their own norms and rules, and this in turn is a prelude to getting down to the ostensible job at hand. Despite these attempts, however, we still lack a detailed picture of group changes over considerable periods of time. Nor have the beginnings and endings of groups received much systematic attention. What are the institutional and interpersonal reasons why groups come into being in the first place, and under what conditions are they likely to disband or, alternatively, disintegrate? What accounts for an individual's joining or leaving an already established group?

Unanswered questions about group development draw attention to one set of limitations on the generality of findings from laboratory groups; Barker's cynical summary, which was quoted earlier, implies a number of others. But we may be in danger of over-emphasizing the limitations of laboratory groups. Shaw (1976) has pointed to striking similarities between laboratory and natural groups with regard to certain features of attraction, brainstorming, conformity, leadership and the setting of group goals, and Swingle's (1973) entire book stresses similarities between laboratory and field studies.

In the remainder of this chapter, and in the next, we shall not prejudge the issue. Having pointed to some of the likely problems with the experimental evidence, we shall recognize the fact that most of our evidence concerning small groups, including the most coherent bodies of findings, comes from experimental studies in the laboratory.

We shall attempt to use this evidence in discussing four of the major foci of concern in this vast field: group structure, leadership, social influence processes and group outcomes or effectiveness. In each of these important areas, the aim will be to convey some impression both of the richness of group phenomena and of the variety of methods that have been used to study them. But we shall not lose sight of the recurring problem of the generality of the findings.

Group structure

If, on casually observing a group for some time, you found it difficult to discern clear-cut patterns in what was happening, you should not be surprised. Group activity can be so rich and can present such a flux of events that a straight description is far from being a simple task. But imagine you could 'freeze' the group at one point in time – by, for example, viewing over and over again a short segment of video-tape – and, a little later, at another point, and at another. Then you might find that the same people were doing the same sort of things or were being reacted to in a similar way by others. In which case you would have discovered at least part of the group's structure. By *structure* we mean the relatively stable relationships among elements in a group, and this can be contrasted with group *process*, which refers to changes in activity over time.

Any distinction between structure and process is an attempt to separate conceptually features of a situation that, in practice, are intertwined. For example, both can be cause and both effect; the formal structure of a newly established committee is likely to deter-mine, at least in part, subsequent processes of interaction; the processes that occur within an initially unstructured group may well lead to the emergence of structure. The distinction between structure and process allows us to use the concept of structure to treat together several interesting sets of phenomena. But a few more qualifications are needed.

First, the elements structured may be either individual members or positions in a group. One test to determine which is operating in a specific case is to observe what happens if changes of personnel occur. If the structure changes markedly, then the elements were likely to have been individuals; if no change occurs, then the structure was probably dependent on positions. Secondly, structures can vary in their formality or explicitness. A new work group in a large organization may well be assigned a very explicit, formal structure, whereas some friendship groups may also be structured, but in much more informal ways. That structures of differing degrees of formality may operate, and conflict, within a single group is illustrated in, for example, Hew Beynon's (1973) very interesting account of work-life in a car factory.

Finally, to talk of *the* structure of a group as if there were one and only one structure involves making some very big assumptions. It is safer to start by allowing the possibility that there may be as many different structures in a group as there are distinguishable dimensions in terms of which relatively stable patterning can occur. We can then ask if similar or different patterning is discernible on the various dimensions. But before taking this question further, let us look at a few of the most intensively studied 'dimensions' of group structure.

(i) *Affective or liking structure.* In mapping the structure of likes and dislikes in a group, the elements mapped are normally individuals rather than positions, and the best-known method for constructing the map is the sociogram. This is one specific technique devised by a somewhat unorthodox psychiatrist, Jacob Moreno (1934), for representing choices, preferences, or patterns of affect in a group, that is for representing *sociometric* data. Group members might be asked to select the members of their group whom they most like. The resulting set of choices can be conveniently represented in a form that looks something like a schematic diagram of the battle of Hastings. The technique has been used particularly with classroom-sized groups, but for simplicity's sake, imagine a six-person group, each member of which has been asked to choose two others. The resulting sociogram is presented as Figure 8. At a glance one can see that D is extremely popular but C is something of an isolate. There are also two incipient sub-groups, $A + B$ and $E + F$, with D having two-way links with both. Obviously, the data, and the possibilities for interpretation, will be much richer with larger groups.

The affective structures of school classes have been established in

Figure 8   A sociogram for a six-person group

order to assist in determining seating arrangements, to detect cliques, and for various other purposes. More generally, given such data it is not hard to see how they might relate to questions of leadership, scapegoating, intragroup cooperation and conflict, and the like. However, at least two important qualifications must be borne in mind. First, sociometric choices normally represent preferences, desires or attitudes and, as is demonstrated in chapter 10, attitudes frequently do not bear a one-to-one relation to overt behaviour. Secondly, different choices are likely to produce different liking structures. Choices concerning leisure activities are frequently different from work choices, as was demonstrated in an early study by Jennings (1950) of friendship and leadership amongst girls in an American correctional institution.

Sociometric choices have also been important in the study of group cohesiveness, which though a somewhat elusive concept, has been considered by many to be a crucial determinant of the productivity of groups, the satisfaction felt by members, and many other things. Cohesiveness has often been defined so broadly – viz. the sum of all the forces acting on all of the members to remain in the group –

that it is hardly surprising that it was felt to relate to a number of features of group functioning. A more restricted, more under-standable and probably more useful definition, however, is the sociometric one of Lott and Lott (1965), that cohesiveness is 'that property which is inferred from the number and strength of mutual positive attitudes among the members of the group' (p. 259).

(ii) *Communication structure.* Communication structures may be laid down for or emerge from a group, and these structures may enhance, limit or determine a number of group phenomena. Most commonly communication structure has been studied by means of imposed networks of communication with positions as elements, although, as we shall see, some of the more interesting findings de-pend on both a positional analysis and an account of what individuals do with the positions. Research with imposed communication net-works has made use of an extremely restricted communication situa-tion, but the volume of research using this has been far from restricted. Shaw (1964) has reviewed in detail the intricate and fre-quently contradictory findings. We shall look at only a few of the earlier studies which appear to tell quite a coherent story.

Bavelas (1950) described a laboratory set-up in which members of a group were seated in individual cubicles, connected by slots in the walls, through which written messages could be passed. Quite dif-ferent nets could then be created by the experimenter opening or closing different slots. Four of the most commonly studied net-works are depicted in Figure 9. They are five-person nets, in which a circle represents a position and the connecting line represents a two-way channel. Using some of these networks Leavitt (1951) examined, amongst other things, the efficiency of five-person groups in solving simple symbol identification problems, i.e., which symbols were common to all the cards which had been distributed to members. He found that more centralized nets, e.g. the wheel, were more efficient than less centralized ones, e.g., the circle. Shaw (1954) demonstrated that, while this held for simple tasks, with more complex ones the reverse was the case, because of the desirability of increased op-portunities for exchange of information. If this is so, it should follow that, on really complex tasks, the all-channel net should be best, and in fact in a number of studies this has proved to be the case.

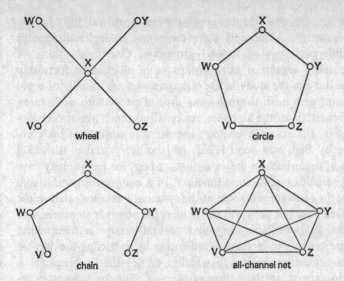

Figure 9   Some frequently studied communication networks

But, note, this need not imply that the full positional structure is utilized throughout the task. It may be that the all-channel net permits an appropriate and quite different individual organization or structure to emerge from within it. The importance of both the imposed, formal, positional communication network and the emergent, informal, individual decision-making network was nicely illustrated by Mulder (1960). He compared wheels with circles, and in addition calculated for each group a Decision Centrality Index, which was, in essence, the discrepancy between the most active and the next most active sender of decision-taking messages, i.e. the greater the discrepancy the more centralized the decision-making was held to be. Mulder found that both the topological structure of the communication net and the centralization of decision-taking were determinants of group effectiveness, in that the most efficient groups were the more centralized wheels, followed in efficiency by the more centralized circles followed in turn by the less centralized wheels, with the less centralized circles being least efficient.

Studies of communication networks have also been concerned with satisfaction of members and questions of leadership. But it is hard to suppress one's doubts about the real-world validity of much of the research. Admittedly there are rough analogies discernible with different types of natural groupings. One might think of hierarchically organized work groups or of all-channel friendship groups. But can the study of five strangers who are initially of equal status and who push through slots slips of paper with nothing on them but letters of the alphabet, really tell us much about decision-making in, for example, complex industrial organizations? A comparison by Blau and Scott (1963) of laboratory studies with field studies of organizations indicates that, at best, the former may have some heuristic or sensitizing function. In a complex organizational setting, they can suggest some of the systematic relations that might be looked for, but they will fail to alert the observer to others. For example, in both laboratory and natural groups a hierarchical structure is likely to increase coordination by restricting the number of communication links, and whether or not this is beneficial is likely to depend on the nature of the task. But the laboratory research will probably fail to point out that a likely consequence of reducing vertical communication is an increase in horizontal communication amongst 'peers', i.e. members of the organization ostensibly of equal status. In such cases, the horizontal communication itself is likely to become differentiated, and some 'peers' will be consulted more often than others. Thus, within the formal network, informal nets will also develop, which will make the organization's communication structure, and communication processes, far more intricate than is implied by the experimental studies.

(iii) *Power structure*. The study of power structure may be in terms of individuals, or positions, or some mixture of the two. Collins and Raven (1969), making use of a classic analysis by French and Raven (1959), define social power 'as the potential influence of some influencing agent, O, over some person, P. Influence is defined as a change in cognition, attitude, behaviour, or emotion of P which can be attributed to O' (p. 160). They suggest that six different types of power should be distinguished, each having its own distinctive basis. From the perspective of P, the person being influenced, these six types can be briefly characterized as follows.

1. Reward power: P perceives that O has power to reward him, as in familiar notions of child and mother.

2. Coercive power: P perceives that O has power to punish him, as in traditional stereotyped conceptions of child and father.

3. Referent power: P wishes to identify with or be like O, as with a fan adopting hairstyle and dress of a pop-star.

4. Expert power: P attributes greater knowledge to O, as in certain aspects of pupil–teacher relationships.

5. Legitimate power: P accepts norms (probably internalized) that O should have influence over him, as when someone accepts a judge's ruling, despite his own views.

Note that each of these five types of power is dependent on the nature of the influencing agent. Some feature or features of O are crucial for the exercise of power; if P made the same demands, they would not necessarily be accepted. But independently of the person who supplies it, information itself can be power.

6. Informational power: based on information which is independent of the social nature of the source, as when one encounters a convincing argument which changes one's plans, but whose source one cannot remember.

The operation of power structures will be apparent in later discussions of leadership and of social influence processes, and will not be elaborated on here. Instead, this is an appropriate point at which to return to questions of the unity or multi-dimensionality of structure within a group. For example, if there are six different types of power, might there not be, in one group, six different power structures? Certainly Collins and Raven (1969) argue that power structures based on different types of power will affect group behaviour differently. And we have already seen that multiple choice structures can exist in the same classroom and that distinguishable formal and informal communication networks can operate simultaneously in the same organization. Thus the claim that there really is *one* structure to a group does not seem very convincing.

Does this mean, however, that 'group structure' consists of any number of unrelated structures? To return to social power, for instance, are the different dimensions likely to be totally independent? Reward, coercive and referent power may well go hand-in-hand in a family, and let us hope that expert power usually bears some positive relation to informational power. Furthermore, on occasion O may have to choose which type of power to use, precisely because he has several conflicting alternatives open to him. A teacher who actually likes his students to identify with him will wield all the referent power he possesses, but cannot afford to invoke too often his expert power. More generally, Cartwright and Zander (1968) have pointed to several lines of evidence which suggest that conceptually separable types of structure may not, in practice, operate independently. A number of writers have proposed that where there are different bases for hierarchical organization, e.g. economic position versus prestige, there are also pressures towards *status congruence*, i.e. agreement amongst potentially differing status rankings. French and Raven (1959) assumed that sociometric structures and power structures would bear some relation to each other; popularity would increase power, and power would lead to increased attractiveness and hence popularity. In a laboratory study, Exline and Ziller (1959) deliberately created two different bases for status within groups, apparent task ability and voting power. Groups with incongruent status relations demonstrated greater instability and, if given the opportunity, tended themselves to try to bring about status congruence.

Thus, although structural aspects of liking, communication and power each merit independent study, and although structure in one area should not be assumed, simply on *a priori* grounds, to apply to another, nonetheless it seems likely that there will be limitations on the number of unrelated or conflicting structures to be found in a group, and that pressures will operate in favour of consistency across potentially separable domains.

(iv) *Additional structures*. Liking, communication and power have been the areas most frequently studied with regard to group structure. But there are other possibilities, such as structure related to other status dimensions or structure defined by the flow of work in an industrial group or organization. One very important type of structure is role structure. Structures based on differentiated roles can be found in traditionally organized family groupings and in many small work groups. They are, however, particularly apparent in larger organizations (see chapter 13).

For the moment, let it suffice for us to note that one common type of role structure is a hierarchical one, which provides a link with our next theme, leadership. Perhaps leadership would be best analysed in terms of leader, lieutenant and follower roles. But, if that were so, would it mean there could be no leadership in the absence of a stable role structure in a group? And do we not tend to think more readily of leaders in terms of individual personality characteristics rather than in terms of roles within a group structure? Such questions obviously require more detailed consideration.

Leaders and leadership

Hollander and Julian (1969) start their helpful review of work on leadership with the words 'The history of leadership research is a fitful one. Certainly as much, and perhaps more than other social phenomena, conceptions and inquiry about leadership have shifted about' (p. 387). This suggests a useful strategy for conveying some of the complexities involved in studying leadership, namely a brief presentation of four rather different approaches that have been adopted in this field at one time or another. Then we shall consider the possibility of a synthesis of these views.

(i) *Personality characteristics of leaders.* Traditionally, political studies were in large part the study of leaders, their social backgrounds and personal characteristics. Such studies of great men predated investigations by social psychologists, but possibly created a set of implicit assumptions which were incorporated into early research. From what may well have been the first empirical study of leaders by a psychologist (Terman, 1904) onwards, great efforts were made to specify personality and social correlates of individuals identified as leaders. And such correlates were discovered in abundance. If anything, too many were discovered, in that different studies tended to produce quite different lists of characteristics. The nadir of this approach came with Bird's (1940) review of twenty studies of the traits of leaders. In all, almost eighty characteristics were reported, of which more than half were reported in only one study, very few indeed were common to four or more investigations, and only one, intelligence, emerged from at least half of the studies.

It is simple, with hindsight, to see how this profusion could have come about. As the number of studies increased, so did the range of tasks and situations, and it is unrealistic to expect the same set of people to be leaders right across the board. Even if there were some common characteristics of captains of football teams these characteristics might not be found in the leaders of groups of Hell's Angels or amongst the directors of research units. Even the de Gaulles and Mao Tse-Tungs of this world are probably happy to pass the initiative to others should they find themselves in situations where limousines will not start or Cabinet Ministers faint.

But although it was clear by about 1950 that measuring the characteristics of people who were leaders was an approach of limited fruitfulness, some weakish generalizations did emerge. Shaw (1976, p. 275) summarizes this literature by claiming that on average group leaders will score higher than other group members on measures of ability – such as intelligence, amount of relevant knowledge and verbal facility; of sociability – such as social participation, cooperativeness and popularity; and of motivation – such as initiative and persistence.

(ii) *Situational factors.* In the light of what has been said, it is not surprising that emphasis switched from attempts to locate recurring personality traits to the study of consistency or inconsistency of leadership across variations in the situation (e.g. Gouldner, 1950). It became clear (Hare, 1960) that the more the investigator changed the situation, the more he reduced consistency in who did the leading. While this was a healthy corrective to the previous undue concern with a very individualistic personality-oriented view of leadership, the situational approach carried its own limitations with it.

For one thing, its proponents over-reacted against notions of personal characteristics, sometimes conveying the impression that no cross-situational consistencies held at all. But more crucially, in taking as its key concept 'situation', this approach was tied to a concept which social psychology has been and still is notoriously unable to cope with adequately. We all have considerable intuitive knowledge of a large number of different situations, but the systematization of such knowledge has made little progress. What dimensions can be used to analyse situational variations? How do we demonstrate that group members are not back in the same situation of two hours ago but are in a different one? Thus when evidence was amassed that the situation was important for the study of leadership, it was an extremely messy truth that was being proclaimed.

By looking for changes in leaders from one situation to another, a situational approach probably still retained assumptions about leaders that may not have been justified. It focused on specific individuals, albeit different ones in different situations. But what if, within one situation, leadership is equally likely to be shown by all members, or at different points in time passes from one to another right round the group? Are they all leaders, or are there no leaders? Indeed, can groups have more than one leader at a time?

(iii) *Leadership functions*. An alternative and very flexible approach is, at least temporarily, to dispense altogether with the concept of *leader* and to look instead for behaviour that would count as *leadership*. Leadership, then, might be defined as any and all behaviour which moves a group towards the attainment of its goals. It might transpire that most of such behaviour in one particular group emanates from one member, in which case he could be dubbed 'leader'. In another group two individuals might predominate, in a third group leadership behaviour might be equally spread throughout the group, and in a fourth one, no leadership behaviour at all might be apparent.

Of course, if leadership turned out to consist of a very large number of unrelated specific acts, then further analysis would be difficult. But superficially different acts might turn out to be correlated, in which case we could say that a large number of leadership behaviours can be organized in terms of a much smaller set of leadership functions. Again, if leadership functions proved to be idiosyncratic from group to group and from situation to situation, we would end up with yet another set of unhelpful lists to file away with the early lists of personality traits. But similar functions might emerge from different studies, in which case we would have at least the beginnings of a coherent picture of leadership.

In fact, leadership functions have been reported in studies using a variety of methods, including direct observations of groups, questionnaire reports by members, and complex statistical techniques, such as factor analysis, as well as intuitive inference. Although specialist functions are frequently observed to hold for specific tasks, in addition a limited number of functions occur again and again. Let us look at a list of labels for pairs of contrasting functions which have been isolated by half-a-dozen different investigators in quite different types of studies, with populations varying from bomber-crews to

Initiating structure-in-interaction	: Consideration
Advance purpose of group	: Make members feel secure
Instrumental	: Affective
External to group	: Internal to group
Goal-oriented activities	: Maintenance of group
Task behaviours	: Social-emotional behaviours

undergraduates in laboratory groups. The argument is that these are not a variety of leadership functions but different labels for the same two leadership functions. Each of the terms on the left appears to be referring to behaviour which advances the instrumental goals of the group, whereas the labels on the right describe activities which help ensure the well-being of the group itself. If at least these two functions, which we shall call task leadership and social–emotional leadership, are accepted as important, recurrent functions, can we say anything about how they are normally distributed within a group? Does one person typically demonstrate both, so that each group does after all have a clear-cut leader, or are they usually spread in an apparently unsystematic fashion throughout the group? While attempting to find evidence that will help in answering these questions, we can describe yet another, slightly different, approach to the study of leadership.

(iv) *Leadership roles.* Roles are treated in much more detail in chapter 13, so here we shall provide only a very brief discussion. The concept of 'role' refers to a position rather than to an individual. Position is a rather static, structural concept; role is a dynamic concept referring to processes and behaviour. Hence a role might be thought of as a position in movement.

If leadership behaviour proved to be exceedingly diffuse in a group, and moved from person to person in an apparently unsystematic fashion, then there would not be grounds for invoking the concept of leadership roles. To be justified, a role analysis of leadership would seem to demand, as a minimum, relative stability in leadership behaviour organized around one or more key persons who produce a predominance of such behaviour. In addition, if these individuals were to leave the group, their positions should remain and, once filled, the leadership structure of the group should be more or less as it was before, although different people might now be performing different functions.

One body of research which has produced evidence satisfying some of these requirements – in fact, those of stability and predominance of key persons, with questions of change of personnel being somewhat ignored – is that derived from the work of Bales and Slater (1955), using Bales's (1950 and 1970) method of interaction process analysis. Amongst other things, this method involves trained observers coding each behavioural act in a small group into one of twelve categories, which currently (Bales, 1970) are labelled as shown:

A	positive actions	1 seems friendly
		2 dramatizes
		3 agrees
B	attempted answers	4 gives suggestion
		5 gives opinion
		6 gives information
C	questions	7 asks for information
		8 asks for opinion
		9 asks for suggestion
D	negative actions	10 disagrees
		11 shows tension
		12 seems unfriendly

This category system has usually been applied to *ad hoc* laboratory groups. Bales himself clearly recognized that, initially, such collectivities were barely groups; what were being observed were early steps in group formation and development. By careful observation of groups over a number of sessions from their inception onwards, Bales and his colleagues were able to study the development of role differentiation and the emergence of leaders.

Using evidence from the above category system as well as group members' responses to questions after each session, as to which member of the group had contributed the best ideas or was best liked or stood out as leader, Bales and Slater (1955) discovered that leadership commonly came to be organized around two differentiated but complementary roles. One person, who was likely to score highest on the 'Attempted answers' categories, was seen as the 'ideas man', and was considered by the others to be the leader. After the first session of a group, the same person was frequently also high on liking, but with successive sessions he became less liked by the others, and a second person emerged who continued to be liked and scored high on 'Positive actions' categories. Why this particular developmental pattern? Bales and Slater proposed that by his very activity the person most active in the ideas or task area deprived others of the chance to produce ideas, or he convinced the group that his ideas were to be preferred. As a result he was seen as a source of tension and a possible focus for resentment, and it became crucial that leadership be manifested in the interpersonal or social–emotional area. Typically, another less active but better liked group member assumed this responsibility. Thus leadership came to be organized around two roles, occupied by two different persons, who are usually described as 'the task specialist' and the 'social–emotional specialist'.

This brief account does not do justice to the Bales–Slater theory of leadership role differentiation, or to possible weaknesses and criticisms. From the original analyses, for example, it was not clear if the two 'leaders' were markedly or merely marginally distinguishable from the other group members, and whether liking by others, rather than social–emotional behaviour *per se*, played a dominant part in the identification of the social–emotional specialist. These and other possible weaknesses were examined in detail by Burke

(1972) and, in general, further support was provided for the Bales–Slater approach, with one interesting qualification which we shall look at shortly.

The analysis in terms of two types of leadership seems to have considerable intuitive appeal. It is not difficult to think of instances of group members quietly reducing overt conflict and 'keeping the group together' until a satisfactory consensus can be reached. The traditional differentiation of the roles of father and mother appears to resemble the distinction between task leader and social-emotional leader, and Grusky (1957) has provided an account of a psychological clinic in which a similar distinction between two types of specialist prevailed.

Yet, though many instances of dual leaders doubtless do occur, need leadership always be organized in that fashion? Verba (1961) suggested that the separation of roles may have been enhanced in laboratory groups of students for a number of reasons, one of the most important of which was that in non-laboratory groups the task leader very frequently has organizational or institutional bases of legitimacy. (One might say he can exercise legitimate power not normally available in laboratory groups; if a person has an organizational basis for his leadership but fails to utilize power, then he is normally said to demonstrate 'headship' rather than leadership.) When a chairman of a committee or head of a department pushes for a solution to an urgent problem, group members may well feel he is doing precisely what he should be doing and far from resenting it may be all the better disposed towards him. In so far as a task specialist can achieve goals important to group members, he may, in addition, create considerable satisfaction amongst members, and thus combine in one person both task and social–emotional leadership. Certainly, Verba's (1961) review of non-laboratory evidence suggested that one person filled both roles more frequently than was implied by the Bales–Slater theory. Burke (1972) provided strong support for Verba's views in studies in which, using laboratory groups and Bales' scoring system, he compared groups for which task activities had high legitimacy or low legitimacy. It was only in the latter that differentiation of task and social–emotional leadership occurred.

Signs of a synthesis

In summary we have seen that leadership in a group may take a variety of forms, but at least two functions are likely to be fulfilled, a task or instrumental function and a maintenance or member satisfaction function. These may be fulfilled primarily by two different leaders, although if institutional legitimacy is the case one person may carry out both. To a limited extent, the leaders who emerge may demonstrate certain recurring personal characteristics, although who will emerge as leader will depend in large part on the nature of the situation. If one attempts to take into account all of these points, plus others, such as the behaviour of followers, and the relation of leaders and groups to larger organizations (see, in particular, the final section of chapter 13), then a realistic view of the intricacy of leadership and leadership theory starts to emerge.

One major attempt to grapple with and synthesize a number of these considerations is the contingency model of leadership effectiveness formulated by Fiedler (1964, 1967), whereby the effectiveness of two contrasting styles of leadership is held to be contingent on the favourability of the situation for the leader. Fiedler restricted his interest to task leaders who could be clearly identified as occupying a leader role in an organization or small group. *Leadership style* was not measured directly but by means of intercorrelating indirect measures, the most frequently cited of which was the 'LPC score'. Leaders were asked to describe on a number of evaluative scales their 'least preferred co-worker' (LPC) from previous working environments. A high LPC score represented a favourable attitude and a low score an unfavourable one; as the theory was originally formulated, it was assumed a high score was characteristic of a friendly, accepting and permissive leader, and a low score typical of aloof, demanding task-oriented leaders.

The favourability of a situation was defined in terms of the ease with which the leader was able to control and direct the behaviour of the members of his group, and this depended, in turn, on three critical variables, or sets of variables. The most important of these was the leader–member relations, the situation being favourable to the extent that the leader had the loyalty and confidence of his group.

The next most crucial was the task structure, whereby the more clearly structured the task, the more favourable the situation. Thirdly, the greater the power of the leader's position, in terms of rewards and sanctions available to him, the more favourable the leader's situation.

Fiedler found that, with regard to effectiveness in achieving group goals, low LPC leaders were more successful than high ones when the situation was very favourable or unfavourable to the leader, whereas high LPC leaders did better when the situation was only moderately favourable. In other words, when things are ideally suited to a leader, he should get on and lead; when things are near chaos, forceful task leadership is better than nothing; when the situation is delicately balanced, then tact, consultation and consideration are likely to pay the best dividends. Although the precise interpretation of the relation between LPC score and favourability is open to debate (see chapter 13 for a recent re-interpretation), the basic relationship itself has been remarkably consistent across a wide range of occupations, from basketball teams to army tank crews and supermarket butchers.

Fiedler's theory is not without flaws. Some have criticized it on methodological and statistical grounds (Graen et al., 1970), others would wish to conceptualize leadership styles differently (Yukl, 1971), and Fiedler (1972) himself has proposed a partial re-interpretation of the earlier work. But the contingency model is an important pointer to the way in which the study of leadership should develop. It attempts to relate personal styles, situational factors, leadership functions and roles. In addition, it represents something of a move towards what Hollander and Julian (1969) insisted on, namely the treatment of leadership as a process of mutual influence between leaders and other participants, rather than as the study of one role in isolation from the system of which it is only a limited part. Those authors also argued that much more attention needs to be focused on the emergence and maintenance of leadership over time, on questions of succession and legitimation of leaders, on followers' expectations and perceptions as they relate to the source of the leaders' authority and to the possibility of identifying with the leader, and on the study of leadership in complex organizational contexts. In each of these cases, it could be argued that experimental studies of laboratory groups would be particularly vulnerable to criticism on the grounds of lack of validity. In future work on leadership, field studies of natural groups may well come into their own.

Further Reading

Cartwright, D., and Zander, A., eds. (1968), *Group Dynamics: Research and theory*, 3rd ed., New York, Harper & Row. A large book of readings, with much helpful editorial material. See especially Parts One, Seven and Five.

Shaw, M. E. (1976), *Group Dynamics: The psychology of small group behaviour*, 2nd ed., New York, McGraw-Hill. A solid, stolid textbook, with a bit about everything.

Smith, P. B., ed. (1970), *Group Processes*, Penguin Books. An inexpensive book of readings, with a number of papers very relevant for this chapter and for chapter 8.

Collins, B. E., and Raven, B. H. (1969), 'Group structure: attraction, coalitions, communication and power', in G. Lindzey and E. Aronson (eds.), *The Handbook of Social Psychology*, vol. 4, 2nd ed., Reading, Mass, Addison-Wesley. A quite complex review of work on group structure.

Gibb, C. A., ed. (1969), *Leadership*, Penguin Books. An inexpensive book of readings, containing many classic papers on leadership.

Chapter 8
Small Groups
II. Processes and Products

Colin Fraser

Social influence processes

Introduction

Having considered the structure of groups and, with the topic of
leadership, having set groups in motion, let us now examine some of
the general processes that occur during group interaction, particularly
processes of social influence. The study of social influence processes
has frequently been described in terms of *conformity* or the formation
and enforcement of *norms*. A first question is, what do we mean by
'norms'?

On the one hand, the term is often used to describe regularities in
behaviour shown by members of a group or larger unit. For example,
a norm for one friendship group may be that it meets twice a week
without fail; and there is a very clear norm in the United Kingdom that
we drive on the left-hand side of the road. On the other hand, 'norm'
is also frequently used to describe, not shared behaviour, but shared
expectations about behaviour. Thus we can say that there are norms
for returning books borrowed from friends, even though we have no
idea of the percentage of borrowed books actually handed back;
sometimes it seems very small. We could argue that there are behavioural or descriptive norms and expectational or prescriptive ones.
Instead, we shall assume that a norm usually – one could say
'normally' – has two components, a behavioural one and an expectational one, which may not always be in perfect agreement. Certainly
social psychologists have sometimes used norm to describe the one,
sometimes the other, sometimes a mixture of the two.

Another distinction worth noting is that between externally derived
and internally derived norms. External norms can be thought of as

norms which operate on a wider scale and which each member carries into the group situation, more or less irrespective of the specific behaviours which occur in that particular group. Many may be general cultural prescriptions, about interpersonal consideration, honesty, and the like. Others may be the sort of 'taken for granted bases of everyday behaviour' studied in ethnomethodology (cf. Garfinkel, 1967; Turner, 1974). Another important source of externally derived norms is the larger organization of which the small group may be a part. Some attention has been paid to external norms in industrial contexts, as will be seen in chapter 13. Otherwise social psychologists have tended to ignore the operation of external norms in their study of influence processes. The internal norms, or what Homans (1961) has termed 'elementary social behaviour', are norms developed by the group members themselves as a result of their own group interaction. Internal norms have been the concern of the majority of small group studies, and it is these that we shall discuss in the following sections.

Some classic studies and recent modifications

As early as 1924 F. H. Allport had reported that inter-individual variance in judgements was reduced if individuals made their judgements, of pleasantness of odours or heaviness of weights for example, in the presence of others working on the same task, and subsequently (1962) he suggested that these results illustrated a desire to belong to the group or to be in agreement with others.

In 1935, Muzafer Sherif produced an even more striking demonstration of influence processes. He took a standard phenomenon in the study of individual perception, the autokinetic effect, and used it to make an important social point. An individual taking part in the control condition in Sherif's study sat in a completely darkened room and attempted to judge the amount of movement shown by a pinpoint of light; after a number of trials, he would settle down to a fairly constant estimate of movement. If, however, two or three individuals sat in the same room announcing their judgements in turn, their initially diverse judgements would converge over trials, even although there was no overt pressure for agreement or compromise from other participants or from the experimenter. Thus an experimentally induced internal group norm was established, and if a group member was subsequently asked to make further judgements on his own he would tend to stick to the previous group norm (Sherif, 1935 and 1936).

The outstanding feature of the autokinetic effect is that the perceived movement is entirely an illusion. The pinpoint of light is in fact stationary, and only appears to move against a completely dark background which removes all cues as to the location of the light. The situation is not merely ambiguous, it is thoroughly misleading. This point was central to a recent re-analysis of the Sherif effect by Alexander *et al.* (1970). They demonstrated that the emergence of the group norm was dependent not just on the internal group features but also on reasonable assumptions about the situation carried into the laboratory by the members. When subjects had the situation explained to them so that they expected the illusion, the Sherif effects were not obtained. Subjects tested individually did not settle on stable responses, and pairs of subjects did not converge on common answers.

Thus, by providing additional information, Alexander *et al.* reduced the misleading and ambiguous nature of the situation for their subjects. A first thought might be that social influence processes will lead to a shared norm only in such ambiguous situations; when individuals can accurately assess a situation for themselves, they will not converge. Although there is some truth in such a notion, it is far from being the whole truth, as the studies of Solomon Asch made clear.

Asch (1951 and 1952) devised a situation in which a subject had to say which of three comparison lines was equal in length to a standard line, all four lines being simultaneously presented for the subject's inspection. If, in a control condition, an individual attempted this task on his own, then he performed with a very high degree of accuracy; the perceptual judgements involved were relatively simple and unambiguous. However, experimental subjects performed in the midst of the experimenter's confederates or stooges, who on selected trials would all announce an erroneous answer. In this situation, the 'naïve' subjects agreed with the manifestly wrong answer approximately one third of the time. This degree of conformity was considerably less than in the Sherif situation, showing that the ambiguity of the situation does play a role, as Asch himself demonstrated with systematic variations of his stimulus materials. But quite detectable conformity occurred even in an apparently unambiguous situation. And Asch's findings have been repeated and extended by many investigators (e.g. Crutchfield, 1955; Milgram, 1961).

Indeed, it may well be, that, striking though they were, Asch's demonstrations have had too much impact. Instead of being accepted as evidence of how, in a minority of cases, a lone individual, confronted with a unanimous majority who disagree with him, will be willing to deny the evidence of his own eyes, these findings have sometimes been over-generalized and unjustified extrapolations made from them. At least, that is what Moscovici and Faucheux (1972) have argued, in a series of studies which have modified the Asch paradigm in an interesting way. Social influence studies have often been cited in support of notions of irresistible group pressures, of the victory of majority thinking over the ideas of a minority, and of conformity to a dominant *status quo*. If these were the inevitable outcomes of social influence, it is hard to see how new ideas would ever become accepted by a group, how individual members could change the views of the group, or how a group could become an agent for innovation and change rather than a bolster for accepted beliefs, yet, as in France in the late 1960s, each of these activities seems very familiar.

Moscovici and Faucheux studied such processes by standing the Asch procedure on its head, and thereby providing a possible link between the topics of leadership and of social influence. Instead of presenting a minority of genuine subjects with a majority of inflexible stooges, they confronted a majority of naïve subjects with one or two committed collaborators. On trial after trial, this committed minority stuck to its position, in some cases an implausible one, and by the end of different studies some group members had changed the type of responses they were giving on a word association test or had conceded that obviously blue-coloured stimuli might be rather more green than they had originally thought. Thus the study of social influence processes can be much richer than the demonstration of submission to majority pressures.

Informational influence and normative influence

Let us explore a little further what may have been happening phenomenologically in the Sherif and Asch situations. In the case of the autokinetic effect, a subject was in an unfamiliar situation about which he knew very little. He probably had less than complete confidence in his perception of the amount of movement shown by the unstable light and in his ability to translate his perception into inches. His feelings towards a fellow subject may well have been, 'Your guess is as good as mine', and this other guess, then, would have conveyed some apparently useful information to the subject. Looked at in this way, the willingness of subjects to move towards one another's judgements appears quite understandable.

The Asch situation seems rather different. There a genuine subject could see quite clearly that the correct answer was, say, line *B*. Then to his surprise, and dismay, he heard all the others present agree it was line *C*. Rechecking the stimulus lines did not help; the obvious answer was still *B*. Clearly something strange was happening. He could stick to his own judgement if he wished and be the odd man out, and this is what the naïve subjects did about two thirds of the time. But he might have felt that he did not really wish to appear an oddball. If he disagreed with all the others it would have been an uncomfortable position to be in, with fellow subjects thinking him strange. So, it might be simplest just to agree, to announce '*C*', when it really looked like *B*. Here, then, the subject is concerned with the best thing to do in the eyes of the others, rather than with using the replies of the others as information about the right answer.

Yet it is conceivable that even in the Asch situation the latter possibility might have been operating. Imagine a baffled subject who, in an attempt to understand what was happening, reasoned that it was extremely unlikely that five other people would make the same silly mistake. There must be a reasonable explanation. Perhaps the subject's position was producing a distorted view of the stimuli, or maybe he had missed something in the instructions that the other subjects had picked up. Therefore, all-in-all, the judgements of five others might be a better guide to reality than his own, probably inadequate, reactions. Hence he would say '*C*' after all. And to complete the possibilities, let us reconsider the Sherif effect and concede that elements of agreeing for agreement's sake, of appearing sensible in the eyes of the others, may have been operating there, in addition to concern for the correct answer.

The conceptual distinction that we have been drawing between normally confounded influence processes has been formulated, in one way or another, by a number of social psychological theorists. Jones and Gerard (1967, pp. 309–15) review a number of formulations. One of these, the Deutsch and Gerard (1955) distinction between normative and informational social influence was formulated specifically in the context of the Sherif and Asch studies: *Normative social influence* was defined by Deutsch and Gerard as 'influence to conform with the positive expectations of another'. In turn, 'positive expectations ... refer to those expectations whose fulfilment by another leads to or reinforces positive rather than negative feelings, and whose non-fulfilment leads to the opposite, to alienation rather than solidarity'. *Informational social influence* was defined as 'influence to accept information obtained from another as evidence about reality' (p. 629). Deutsch and Gerard demonstrated that normative influence can be increased by strengthening the 'groupness' or cohesiveness of a set of individuals, and decreased by creating anonymity for individual responses. Schulman (1967) extended their analysis of experimental situations by demonstrating that influence, especially normative influence, can emanate from the experimenter as well as from group members.

Normative influence and informational influence will often operate simultaneously, and variables – such as amount of interaction–which affect one may well also affect the other. A detailed discussion of the difficulties which are met in attempts to separate them unequivocally is contained in Tajfel (1969a). Nevertheless, the distinction appears to be a helpful one. It reveals that when people talk of 'conformity' with some distaste, it is likely to be normative influence that they have in mind. The notion of informational social influence stresses a rationality in group interaction and influences which is often precluded by discussions exclusively confined to group pressure and conformity (also see chapter 12). The similarity of informational social influence and informational power and the obvious overlap between normative influence and the five source-dependent bases of social power mentioned in the previous chapter suggest links amongst concepts of influence, power and leadership.

In addition, the normative–informational distinction is a useful tool to apply to what has been a most actively investigated area of group processes, that of group decision-making with and without risks. Because this topic provides a fairly typical illustration of experimental research on group processes *and* products, and raises interesting questions of explaining and generalizing certain distinctive group phenomena, we shall examine it in some detail.

Group polarization, including group risk-taking

As was suggested earlier, group influence studies became enmeshed in an implicit (American) ideology which often went beyond the available evidence. As Doise (1971) has argued, group interaction was at the time associated with conformity, which in turn was held to involve the justifiable notion of convergence within a group, and the much less justifiable idea that convergence was normally towards an average or moderate or safe position. Perhaps it was because this second tenet of a widely shared but unexplicated set of assumptions was contradicted in a study by Stoner (1961) that so much attention was quickly paid to 'the risky shift'. Stoner used a set of 'choice dilemmas' to compare the riskiness of decisions made by individuals and by groups. Each dilemma described a hypothetical situation in which a central figure had to choose between a safe but relatively unattractive alternative and a more attractive but riskier one. For example, a young graduate in industry had a choice between remaining in his very safe, well-pensioned, moderately paid job or accepting a more senior, challenging, better-paid post with a small new firm, which might not survive competition. Or again, a low-ranked chess-player in a championship had a choice between eventual but honourable defeat and a very risky move which would result in either unexpected victory for him or a complete collapse. The riskiness of decisions was measured in terms of the lowest odds of the risky alternative being successful that a subject would insist on before recommending that the risky alternative be attempted. So, if someone said he would recommend the risk even if there were only three out of ten chances of its proving successful, he would be acting relatively riskily, whereas an insistence on nine out of ten would be a very cautious decision.

Stoner devised a procedure which became standard for most of the subsequent research on this topic. First, he asked sets of persons to take entirely individual decisions on the questionnaire. Then they were asked to function as groups and come to unanimous decisions on each problem in turn. As a third step, they were asked to think again and indicate final individual decisions on each dilemma. In addition, a number of subjects took individual decisions twice over, without any group interaction, to control for the possibility that any effects which might emerge from the groups might be due simply to taking the same decision more than once rather than to the interaction *per se*. Such individuals normally showed no systematic changes from first decision to second. But the groups functioned in an unexpected fashion. Despite studies of influence processes which were held to predict that there would be no difference between (the average of) individual decisions and group consensus, and despite management 'folklore' concerning bold individuals and cautious committees which was held to predict that individuals would be riskier than groups, what, in fact, emerged was that group decisions were riskier than individual ones. Furthermore, although individuals, once released from the group situation, moved back a little towards their original decisions, they remained, on average, riskier than they had been initially. Thus, an internal norm appeared to develop and to persist even outside the group setting, and this norm was riskier than would have been predicted on the basis of the starting points of individual group members.

This finding was quickly replicated by other investigators, and extended to different subject populations, including middle-level managers and groups in countries other than the United States, and, to a lesser extent, to different types of risky decisions, including gambling situations and a situation with risks of discomfort and injury to participants. Kogan and Wallach (1967) reviewed these early studies in some detail. The riskiness of group decisions was of interest, not only as an apparent exception to the supposed moderateness of group decisions, but also because of possible practical consequences. Perhaps unexpectedly risky decisions were being made all the time by committees, boards and Cabinets. The spectre was even conjured up of members of the American National Security Council one by one walking gravely into a meeting to consider a nuclear alert and then *en masse* skipping gleefully out to proclaim, 'We've pressed the button.' But before deciding that social psychologists had unearthed a hitherto undetected threat to the world's stability, we should examine the phenomena in a little more detail.

The risky shift had emerged most clearly when data were summed over different items, and thus the possibility existed that the shift to risk was an overall trend which concealed exceptions and counter-examples. In fact, from the earliest studies onwards two of the original twelve choice dilemmas had quite consistently produced group shifts to caution, but either had been swamped by the other items, or, in some cases, had even been removed from the questionnaire to make things tidier! Gradually additional items were created which also elicited shifts to caution (Stoner, 1968; Fraser, Gouge and Billig, 1971) and it emerged that, whereas the original risky shift items had elicited relatively risky individual decisions, on cautious shift items individuals initially took relatively cautious positions. Thus, the generalization implied was that groups shifted further in the direction that the individuals were already inclining towards. But need that apply only to risk-related questions? Might it not hold more generally?

In fact, a group of French social psychologists, led by Moscovici, had already started to demonstrate that it did. Using Likert-type rating scales (see chapter 10) Moscovici and Zavalloni (1969) and Doise (1969) had studied attitudes towards General de Gaulle and towards Americans, judgements regarding General de Gaulle, and attitudes towards a school of architecture. In all cases they found that group discussion resulted in shifts towards the extremes of the scales. Thus the *lycée* pupils involved were on average moderately well disposed towards de Gaulle and the group decisions were even more favourable; individually they were mildly anti-American and the groups were more negative. Moscovici and his colleagues described such shifts as *polarization* effects, and they hypothesized that the shift to risk was just one example of more general group polarization phenomena. This suggestion was strongly supported in a study by Fraser, Gouge and Billig (1971), who showed that the great majority of shifts to risk or caution were instances where the average of initial decisions were on one side of a neutral point and the group decisions moved further in the direction of the already preferred pole. Subsequently, polarization effects have been demonstrated with a wide range of non-risk-related problems (Myers and Lamm, 1976). The risky shift appears to have little to do with risk, and the general area is now labelled, by Europeans, as 'group polarization', and, by Americans, as 'choice shifts'. Two further questions deserve attention; how can group polarization be explained, and how extensively does it operate?

Proposed explanations of the original risky shift were numerous, if rather simple-minded. One suggestion was that individuals were afraid of the consequences of failure contained in the risky alternative, but they would be willing to take riskier positions if there could be a sharing or diffusion of responsibility with others. Another proposal was that individuals initially played safe but through further familiarization with the problem (and this could occur through group interaction), they would realize they could afford to take more risks. Yet again, simple leadership notions were invoked. Thus risk-taking people were more influential, or perhaps risk-taking people were also more extroverted and hence more influential. As it became clear that cautious shifts and shifts unrelated to risk-taking also had to be explained, many of these limited (and often implicitly individualistic, non-interactional) explanations lost favour. A systematic review is contained in Dion *et al.* (1970).

The explanation that survived best invoked the idea of shared values, and by now 'value theory' has a number of variants (see Pruitt, 1971). The crucial treatment, however, was that of Roger Brown (1965). He argued that, in America and perhaps elsewhere, there was a widely accepted value for risk, at least for moderate risks, and this underlying value might affect group decisions in two rather different ways. On the one hand, it could operate via social comparisons. People wished to appear at least moderately adventurous but, on first encountering choice dilemmas, were uncertain as to which scores represented their desired position. In discussion, at least some subjects would discover that, compared to others, they were not as adventurous as they had thought, and so would shift to risk. According to this view, the crucial function of interaction was the exchange of positions. An alternative view was that the discussion itself would highlight the underlying value. The arguments and information exchanged would remind people of the social value and they would move in such a way as to implement it. Brown was aware of the possibility of cautious shifts, and he proposed that in certain, unspecified, situations a value for caution would operate and hence, through the same mechanisms which worked with risk, cautious shifts would result.

Value theory survived as an explanation partly because other proposals fell by the wayside and partly because it was held to be compatible with many of the group risk-taking data (see Pruitt, 1971). Yet conceptual shortcomings were always apparent. First, the notion of a value was never spelled out in detail, and perhaps for that reason the theory has not been directly tested in a really adequate way. There have been no independent measures of values which could be shown to correlate with, let alone cause, shifts. Furthermore, it was never clear in anything other than a *post hoc* way when the supposed values of risk and caution would operate. In addition, most of the decisions seemed to be affected by a large number of different values; a discussion of a major career choice, for example, could touch on job-success, the importance of money, personal fulfilment, family security and a number of other 'values', as well as an occasional invoking of the desirability of taking a risk. And, of course, once shifts were detected with non-risk materials, the number of values that had to be postulated increased with each new type of problem.

There is a sense in which the description of group polarization implies that something *is* preferred or chosen or valued and that interaction increases this preference. But every choice or preference that an individual or group makes need not be dependent on widely shared values. If on one occasion I prefer raspberry ripple to chocolate ice-cream, does that mean there has to be a 'raspberry ripple cultural value'? It is more sensible to concede that value theory is an empty explain-all which has outlived its usefulness.

It seems most likely that an adequate explanation will be found in a detailed analysis of the influence processes that occur in a group. Group polarization occurs most markedly on items on which individuals' initial decisions are at least moderately extreme, which means that the distribution of all the subjects on such an item is likely to be skewed, i.e. individuals will be piled up at the generally favoured end of the scale, with a gradual tailing off towards the non-preferred pole, and this in turn means that a majority of the subjects in a typical group formed from this population will, in varying degrees, already favour one alternative, with one or two group members being 'deviant'. (For a discussion of 'skewing' see Vinokur, 1969.) Furthermore, there is evidence (Ellis *et al.*, 1969; Vidmar, 1970) that variance or heterogeneity of initial individual positions is a necessary condition for shifts to occur. Given, then, that 'skewed heterogeneity' characterizes the views and positions of group members, both informational and normative influence processes should operate to produce shifts.

A very reasonable assumption is that the positions argued for and the information transmitted by group members will bear some relation to the positions originally held by the members. Thus, in a group initially inclining towards a risky decision, with, say, three risky, one neutral and one cautious position represented, discussion is likely to be dominated by pro-risk arguments. And it is clear (e.g. Myers and Bishop, 1971) that there is considerable informational imbalance in discussions leading to group polarization. All items of information may not be equally important; relevant arguments should be more effective than irrelevant ones, and novel or unshared arguments may be more crucial than familiar ones. Vinokur and Burnstein (1974) have proposed as an explanation of group shifts a 'partially shared relevant arguments' model of the information in group discussion. Indeed, in a theoretically sophisticated series of papers, Vinokur, Burnstein and colleagues have attempted what, at first sight, might appear to be an explanation solely in terms of informational influence. But it should be noted that their use of the term 'information' is a very broad one, and, it can be argued, confounds informational with normative influence.

It seems unlikely that normative influence plays no role in group polarization. For one thing, in observing group discussions one can see it happening. It is not uncommon to find that the final steps of consensus consist of an agreed majority urging a still mildly recalcitrant individual to accept the majority view and get on to the next problem. The group urges, but does not present new arguments; the deviant screws up his face, shrugs and accepts. The effects of a reduction in normative pressures can be seen in the reduction of the size of shift in the absence of consensus.

Fraser (1971) gave additional examples of how a normative–informational analysis can account for many of the fine details of group polarization findings. The size of shifts and the extent to which they are caused by normative and/or informational influences will depend on the nature of specific situations and the opportunities for the exercise of the two types of influence. Burnstein *et al.* (1973) and Myers *et al.* (1974), using rather different procedures, have attempted comparisons of normative and informational influences. In both studies, both types of influence were found to operate, but in each case the informational effect was larger than the normative one. This is probably a fair reflection of the relative importance of the two sets of influence processes in the experimental situations normally studied.

But what about the external validity of group polarization research? Clearly there are a variety of possible differences between 'real' decisions made by 'real' groups and decisions about choice dilemmas or attitude items taken by experimental groups. To simplify, let us briefly consider two obvious types of differences; one is the *ad hoc* nature of experimental groups as opposed to the shared history, norms and procedures of, say, established committees, and the second is the fact that the latter, unlike the laboratory groups, normally take decisions which will be acted on, with appreciable consequences ensuing perhaps for the committee members themselves as well as for others. In fact, in the experimental literature, there are a few studies relevant to both these points. Although hypothetical decisions were involved, Siegel and Zajonc (1967) and Chandler and Rabow (1969) had used clinical teams and families, respectively, and had obtained the usual shifts. Although using *ad hoc* groups, Wallach, Kogan and Bem (1964) and Clement and Sullivan (1970) had studied decisions with consequences for the decision-makers involving, respectively, risks of physical discomfort and poor college grades. Both sets of investigators had obtained shifts, although Clement and Sullivan simply reported that they had found no risky shifts and ignored the cautious shifts present in their data.

It took a long time, however, before a study appeared in which, with a minimum of intervention by investigators, the usual decisions of established decision-making groups were gathered and analysed for group polarization. In their study of job evaluation by trios of British civil servants, who had first carried out individual evaluations and then met to achieve consensus, Semin and Glendon (1972) reported that consistent averaging, not polarization, had occurred. Celia Gouge and the present writer carried out similar studies. Eventually we obtained data from nine trios of university examiners, one clinical team in child psychiatry and two student union committees taking financial decisions (see Fraser, 1973). None of the three types of decision-making groups polarized; in general, the examiners and the clinical team averaged, and the financial committees actually became less extreme, i.e. the committees gave away slightly less money than the individual members were inclined to do.

As we conducted our studies, numerous differences between the laboratory and the committee decisions became apparent to us, such as the greater structuring and tidiness of the laboratory groups' decisions, the practical constraints that limited many committee decisions, and the existence of major role differences, unrepresented in the laboratory groups, yet obvious in the committees. But, for a relatively parsimonious explanation of the contradictory findings from the two types of studies, let us return to a point stressed early in the previous chapter, namely, that established groups have many shared norms whereas laboratory groups are usually studied only at the very beginning of a developmental process of norm formation. A laboratory group could not have achieved the common view of the group's function that appeared to be true of the financial committees, viz. to provide most of the money requested but to try to make resources last by pruning here and there. Laboratory subjects would not have knowledge of each other's, and of their group's, likely decisions and thus would not be able to take them into account in their own thinking about a problem. (The few real groups involved in experimental studies and cited above would not have had norms to apply specifically to the unfamiliar problems they were confronted with.) In short, the hypothesis is that group polarization is particularly likely to occur prior to a group's possessing a set of norms for taking one particular type of decision. Notice that group polarization could occur in established groups, if they were required to take decisions of a novel or unfamiliar kind or even, perhaps, if forced to take familiar types of decisions in an unfamiliar way. Furthermore, even if group polarization ceases to be apparent in the decisions of established groups, this may be because the polarization, as it were, has already occurred in the initial individual decisions; the group decisions could still be more extreme than the average of half a dozen unacquainted individuals.

But we should be cautious in concluding that group polarization is a phenomenon of limited generality. There is at least one relevant study which did find polarization. Walker and Main (1973) compared records of decisions on civil liberties cases where the hearings had been conducted either by a single US federal judge or by a trio of such judges, and they found that more extreme judgements were given by the trios. There are of course problems in ensuring that the two sets of judges and the two sets of cases were strictly comparable. It may also be that the trios of judges were rather like *ad hoc* groups and that civil liberties cases are so varied in nature that each one presents an unfamiliar problem, hence the Walker and Main findings would be quite in keeping with the proposals in the previous paragraph. Or, perhaps the problems of generalizing research findings on social influence processes are even more complex than proposed.

Some very 'real' groups

The present writer is inclined to conclude, contrary to fears expressed early on in the study of the risky shift, that if the world disappears in the midst of a nuclear holocaust it will be for reasons other than group polarization. Even this assertion, however, can be called into question by an unusual and fascinating book by Irving Janis (1972), which is a study of really major policy-making groups based on published reports and records of their activities. Janis attempted to indicate certain recurring small-group processes involved in major policy 'fiascos'. On the basis of analyses of such pre-Watergate episodes as President Kennedy's invasion of Cuba at the Bay of Pigs, President Johnson's escalation of the Vietnam War, the defenceless-ness of Pearl Harbor, and Neville Chamberlain's policy of appease-ment, Janis concluded that a recurring set of features could be identified as having taken place in the policy-making groups involved. He dubbed these 'groupthink', which was short for 'a mode of thinking that people engage in when they are deeply involved in a cohesive in-group, when the members' strivings for unanimity over-ride their motivation to realistically appraise alternative courses of action' (p.9). This mode of thinking involved a variety of techniques for reducing the expression of dissident views within the group and for avoiding external sources of information which might not fit with the group's restricted analyses of the problems confronting them.

One conclusion might be that the august bodies studied by Janis demonstrated group polarization resulting primarily from internal normative influences. But that is too glib. Whether the complexities of the decision-making contexts being studied can really be boiled down to such a simple concept as 'group polarization' is very debat-able. There is the problem of never being certain that 'the facts' of the case are at hand. And 'explaining' the political events in group polarization terms is dangerously close to espousing a social psycho-logical explanation of history. Although an improvement on a purely psychological account of history, this would still commit the fallacy of ignoring organizational, institutional and economic factors.

But Janis's book provides a set of rich case studies which the in-terested reader can use to further his understanding of social influ-ence processes. He can, if he wishes, distinguish the operation of normative and informational influences. He can attempt to assess the relative importance for the policy-makers of internal and of ex-ternal norms. He can also see in action some of the factors often ignored in experimental studies, such as the operation of leadership and power, and the relationship between the small group and larger organizations. In addition, the book raises many important questions about the effectiveness of groups.

Group effectiveness

Introduction

Effectiveness was one of the earliest questions investigated by small-group research workers. Indeed what is often claimed to have been the first controlled experiment in social psychology, that of Triplett (1898), might be regarded as an example of such work. On a task which involved winding string in on a fishing reel, he compared children working on their own with children working competitively in pairs, and this can be regarded as one variant of a common type of early social psychological study involving the comparison of people working alone and working in the presence of others. The groups in the second condition can be described as side-by-side 'groups' rather than face-to-face, interacting groups, and the question being posed was essentially whether such 'groups' were more effective than individuals. Subsequently, the question of 'groups versus individuals' was examined in other contexts also, and it became apparent that a simple answer favouring one or the other was unlikely to emerge. Depending on the nature of the task, sometimes the individual would appear the more effective. For example, it might be more efficient to hand a problem over to one individual if man-hours spent on the task should be minimal, if it were possible to identify in advance the most capable individual available, and if there were likely to be severe problems in organizing a smooth division of labour. But if a variety of skills would be required for successful completion of the task, if a division of labour appeared to be feasible, and if quality or accuracy of the end product was important then a group would, most probably, be a better bet. Much fuller accounts of the intricacies of comparing individuals and groups are given in Hare (1962) and Davis (1969).

Notice that, so far, we have begged questions of what is meant by 'effectiveness'; effective by what standards, and effective for whom? Imagine two groups of workmen who set out to build two comparable office blocks. One group takes two years to complete their block, but do so relatively uneventfully and then move on, as an experienced and cohesive work-force to tackle more demanding projects. The second group complete their block in only fifteen months, but have to work under such pressure, that two are killed in accidents, five more are seriously injured, and the remainder are so exhausted and disgusted that to a man they subsequently take up market-gardening. Which, then, is the more effective group? The latter's rate of production on the one job was clearly higher, and in terms of short-term profitability to their employer they were extremely effective. Yet judged by a longer term perspective, by the values of the workers themselves, and by the continuity of the group, the former group would appear the more effective. Clearly then a number of alternative criteria of effectiveness can be envisaged. Let us simplify, however, by accepting a very common analysis of effectiveness in terms of two sets of criteria, which should remind us of discussions of leadership in the previous chapter.

Productivity and satisfaction

There are criteria, such as quantity, quality, economy and speed, which measure a group's success on the extrinsic task. Such measures of external task effectiveness are commonly described as assessing *productivity*. In addition, there are criteria internal to the group itself, such as satisfaction with the group and the other members, pleasure at being in the group, willingness to remain in it. Measures of socioemotional effectiveness and group maintenance are usually considered under the heading of *satisfaction*.

This distinction between effectiveness as productivity and effectiveness as satisfaction should be observed in any discussion of the outcomes of small group interaction. Some may cavil at this claim, asserting that surely the two sets of criteria are highly correlated; a happy, contented group must be a productive one, a productive group will be a satisfied one, and similarly with dissatisfaction and poor productivity. Doubtless one could find groups for which these relations do hold. An influential early study of effectiveness, the Hawthorne study, provides an apparently striking instance. In the late twenties a group of investigators began in the Hawthorne plant of the Western Electric Company in America a series of studies extending over a number of years (Roethlisberger and Dickson, 1939). In one sub-set of investigations, 'the test room studies', a small group of experienced female workers were removed from the large department where they assembled telephone relays to a small test room where they were to continue with essentially the same work. This was done to permit the careful investigation of the effects on productivity of a number of changes in the working conditions, including the length of the working day or week, the introduction and patterning of rest periods and the seating arrangements of the women. Over a period of four years productivity increased continually, and more or less independently of any of the deliberate changes in working conditions. Thus, output started to increase even before rest periods were introduced into the daily routine, it continued to rise as rest periods were increased in frequency, it rose further when they were completely removed and further still when they were restored again. The conclusion drawn was that, in this situation, the employees were enjoying the attention they were receiving from management, the relaxed, self-imposed discipline and supervision, and the opportunities to interact with one another. The crucial determinants of changes in output were not the systematic modification of the physical conditions of work but the continually increasing cohesiveness and *esprit de corps* of the small group of women (Turner, 1933).

But notice, it seems likely that the employees were accepting the management's goals regarding output and permitting their interpersonal satisfaction to contribute to increased productivity. (Widespread unemployment and lack of alternative jobs may also have had something to do with the employees' reactions!) Had they developed group cohesiveness and *esprit de corps* as a result of deliberately defying management policy on some issue, then high satisfaction would have gone hand-in-hand with very low productivity. Thus a simple, direct link between productivity and satisfaction should not be thought of as inevitable. For example, in a study of a group of salesmen in the clothing department of a department store, Babchuk and Goode (1951) found that the morale of the salesmen was higher when they worked together in a cooperative system rather than competed with each other for customers and sales. However, when they did compete they sold more suits. Reviews of relevant studies (e.g. Brayfield and Crockett, 1955) suggest that employee attitudes as measured by morale surveys need bear no simple or appreciable relationship to job performance. Although a strong positive relation between group productivity and member satisfaction may remain as a worthwhile ideal to be aimed at by a group, it is safest to assume that these two sets of criteria can operate relatively independently of each other. (See also the second half of chapter 13, especially the section on the question of job satisfaction in work organizations, where a similar assumption is made.)

What factors, then, determine differences amongst small groups in their productivity and satisfaction? One valuable consequence of posing this question is that an answer to it involves virtually a summary of all that is known about small group structure and process. Such a summary was attempted by Krech, Crutchfield and Ballachey (1962) and we shall be guided by their analysis. They first drew attention to a large number of features which exist from or even before the point in time at which a group is established, and these they called the 'independent variables' of group effectiveness. Steiner (1972) in a more recent analysis of group productivity has considered similar factors under the headings of 'demands' placed on the group and 'resources' possessed by the group. We shall regard them as the *givens* of the situation, that is, the features of the group and its context established in advance, whether by management or experimental social psychologists. These givens can themselves be subdivided. One set can be loosely labelled 'structural factors.' These would include the initial or formal status hierarchy in the group and its initial or formal network of communication, as well as its size, and heterogeneity, and the distribution of skills and personality characteristics of the group members. A second set of givens is the characteristics of the task facing the group. Groups may differ in effectiveness because the tasks they tackle vary in their nature, or in their difficulty, or in such demands of the situation as the time available for completion of the task. In addition to structural and task givens, there are also environmental or contextual features which can crucially influence effectiveness. These include features of the physical setting for the group's work, the group's place within a larger organization and its relationships with other groups.

Variations in the givens may directly influence productivity and satisfaction of groups. For example, on occasion size differences alone may determine productivity differences between two groups.

GIVENS

Structural variables	Task variables	Contextual variables
initial status hierarchy	nature of task	physical setting
initital communication network	difficulty of task	group's place in larger organization
size of group	situational constraints	relations with other groups
members' skills and personality characteristics	.	.
heterogeneity of members	.	.
.	.	.
.	.	.

EMERGENT PROCESSES

leadership style
social influence processes
emerging norms
group motivation
distribution of participation and communication
cohesiveness
.
.
.

OUTCOMES

productivity
satisfaction

Figure 10 Simple framework for the understanding of group effectiveness (from *Individual in Society*, by D. Krech and others. Copyright © McGraw-Hill Company, Inc., 1962. Used with permission of Mcgraw-Hill Book Company.)

Very often, however, the givens affect the outcomes through an intermediate class of variables, namely the processes which develop once the group has started to function. The given features of groups' situations interact and lead to variations in *emergent group processes* which in turn result in differences in *outcomes*. Thus, whatever the formal status hierarchy decided on in advance, an actual set of influence processes and a style of leadership will emerge; however the formal communication network was organized, an actual distribution of participation and communication will occur, which may or may not be patterned in a way which corresponds to the formal network. In addition, emergent processes will involve variations in group norms, task motivation and cohesiveness, all of which will help produce differences in outcomes.

Clearly the effects of givens and of emergent processes cannot normally be considered independently of one another. Size and cohesiveness, for example, are likely to interact in determining effectiveness. In addition, it will sometimes be difficult to decide whether a particular variable, such as leadership style, is to be treated as a given, or as an emergent process; and cohesiveness, an emergent process, and satisfaction, an outcome, may sometimes be difficult to distinguish. Furthermore, the accompanying diagram depicts an over-simplified view of the relations amongst the different classes of variables. For instance, the structure, task and contextual variables are unlikely to be established entirely independently of each other; the nature of the task and place of the group in the larger organization, for example, may well determine the initial communication network. Finally, although givens are shown as influencing emergent processes which in turn influence outcomes, the pattern of causes and effects must be enriched by the operation of feedback from later to earlier stages. Thus, the leadership style or group norms which emerge through group interaction could themselves lead to a redefinition of certain of the apparent givens of the situation, and the actual outcomes which result may lead to reappraisal of features of both givens and emergent processes. But despite its over-simplified nature the basic framework presented in Figure 10 has the merit of succinctly conveying some of the richness and complexity of attempts to understand the determinants of group effectiveness.

Satisfaction in experiential groups

The practical consequences of understanding the determinants of productivity are considerable, and Steiner's (1972) systematic analysis of productivity and process is one helpful step towards such an understanding. Yet in the past fifteen years or so, rather less attention has been paid to the systematic study of productivity. Interest in small groups has shifted to the internal concerns of groups and to the social–emotional satisfactions of group members. The most recent boom in group activities has lain with *experiential groups*. This general term will be used to refer to a variety of only partially distinguishable types of groups variously called T-groups, human-relations laboratory groups, sensitivity groups, encounter groups, personal growth groups, sensory awareness groups, and many other things besides. It can be suggested that the most obvious origin of what has become the experiential group movement was the development in the United States in the late 1940s of training (or T) groups. In these, professional or managerial persons met with a relatively non-directive trainer or leader and attempted to improve their human-relations skills by analysing and understanding the group processes occurring in their own T-group. Since then the number and variety of experiential groups has increased dramatically (Back, 1973), and it is probably fair to suggest that there have been some tendencies for their techniques and aims to change over the years. Thus, on the whole, they have tended to become more dramatic in their techniques and have increasingly emphasized non-verbal rather than verbal behaviour and communication; their primary focus has increasingly shifted from the group to the individual; their aims have more frequently been formulated in terms of personal adjustment or therapy, rather than education or training (or a distinction between education and therapy has been denied). Although such changes do provide a rough and ready characterization of differences between, say, the original T-groups and more recent sensory awareness groups, it is important to recognize that there are many different types of groups still operating under the 'experiential' banner, some with their primary focus on the self, others focused on interpersonal relations, some concerned primarily with groups, and yet others geared to organizational and intergroup questions. Although some groups do attempt to increase the self-awareness of their members by continuous sessions of several days in which communication is mainly non-verbal and use is made of nude body massage, there are still many fully clothed managers sitting round tables once a week hoping to understand, and perhaps even change, the organizations they work within.

Nonetheless, despite the considerable variations, the different types of experiential groups do appear to share certain distinctive attributes. For all of them, what are normally internal problems of personal and interpersonal satisfaction actually make up the 'external' task set for the group. In this extreme concern with members' socio-emotional well-being and satisfaction, stress is placed on the desirability of the ready expression of affect (with considerable variations amongst groups regarding the amount of cognitive input regarded as desirable). Generally the group and its direction of development are relatively unstructured, the leader or facilitator being there to help the members rather than to take them through pre-arranged sequences of activities. Finally, these groups seem designed to encourage a self-consciousness about their members and their personal relationships hard to equal in the history, study or practice of group behaviour, apart from the equally recent innovation of group psychotherapy, which can be distinguished from some of the more person-oriented experiential groups only in terms of the history of recruitment of participants to the groups, and the institutional settings within which the groups function. A very sympathetic introduction to what happens in experiential groups is provided by Rogers (1973).

What effects do experiential groups have on their members? Do they, as some enthusiastic proponents argue, function as a major force for personal and interpersonal learning, change and growth, proving of considerable benefit to the majority of people who participate in them? Or, as various critics would have it, do they provide distraction for the self-concerned middle-class, financial 'rip-off' for those who run them, and psychological damage to a not inconsiderable minority of participants? A simple answer is unlikely to be justified. For one thing, more effort has gone into development and exploration than into careful evaluation, although more and better evaluation research is becoming available. But since the intended effects are complex, rich and sometimes almost intangible, and since both aims and techniques can vary considerably, adequate evaluation is no simple matter. This can be illustrated by one important and relatively sophisticated study of a dozen and a half experiential groups of a variety of types carried out by Lieberman *et al.* (1973). Of the two hundred or so students who participated, they concluded that approximately one third still exhibited benefits six months after the groups had terminated, approximately one third showed no lasting effects and rather less than one third either had dropped out of the groups or, in the case of about 8 per cent of the original participants, showed continuing adverse effects. This study does not agree with various evaluations of the effects of older-style T-groups. Although these reviews vary somewhat – some (e.g. Gibb, 1970) being more positive than others (e.g. Campbell and Dunnette, 1968) – the research on T-groups reports in general a higher percentage of beneficiaries than Lieberman *et al.* do, together with a negligible casualty rate.

Might it be that the differences in findings are due to the fact that Lieberman *et al.* carried out a more demanding evaluation than did some of the T-group studies which accepted reports from participants, friends of participants or even leaders, all of whom might have felt subject to social influence pressures to report favourably? Indeed, had Lieberman and colleagues simply accepted the claims of leaders or participants, which they report, they would have concluded that the great majority of members had benefited. But by no means all of the positive T-group conclusions were based on such inadequate evidence, and Lieberman *et al.* can themselves be accused of having used different criteria for assessing casualties in the encounter groups from those used with non-participating controls, thereby overestimating the damage done by the groups. Two alternative possibilities are implied by the findings of Lieberman *et al.* that casualties varied with the nature of the leaders and the participants. First, casualties were highest with 'energizers' i.e. leaders who emphasized emotional arousal and tended to be aggressive, and lowest with 'providers', who emphasized caring for members and the giving of cognitive understanding. It may be, of course, that the typical leader of the relatively undramatic T-group corresponds more to the latter than to the former type. Secondly, casualties were highest amongst members who appeared to be relatively immature and unstable, and low in self-esteem. In many of the earlier T-group studies, participants were older, moderately successful professionals who, thus, may have been unlikely to be adversely affected.

At the risk of oversimplifying a complex set of questions, we can conclude that the evidence suggests that for bona fide, well-run groups with experienced and caring leaders, the probability of benefiting is much higher than that of coming to any harm. The further question, though, of what might be achieved by investing equivalent amounts of effort and money in other forms of social action, raises issues that could be debated indefinitely though probably not resolved.

If less effort has been put into evaluating the effects of experiential groups than into running them, then, not surprisingly, even less effort has been expended on explaining what happens in them. The beginnings of serious theoretical analyses of the group processes involved are only just becoming apparent (Cooper, 1975). Such theory should lead to much better understanding of how experiential groups function and affect their members. But will they readily enlighten us about other small groups? Perhaps not. After all, one of the grounds for being fascinated by experiential groups is their very unfamiliarity, almost uniqueness. Usually they are temporary collections of strangers who agree to ignore many of the conventions of most familiar groups. Their exclusive concern with internal group processes and the well-being of the members marks them off from the typical work-group and, to a lesser extent, family. It might be proposed that they will tell us, albeit in a speeded-up fashion, a great deal about the development of friendship groups. But they carry with them a self-consciousness absent from the latter, and it need not be the case that when an encounter group disbands all its members wish to remain friends.

It seems that psychologists have invented a fifth type of group, to add to the family, the work-group, the friendship group, and the experimental group, with which we started our discussion of small groups. The experiential group shares with the experimental one the advantage that it is very convenient as well as interesting to study, and the disadvantage that what it will tell us about family, work and friendship is not at all clear.

Conclusions

In these two chapters on small groups we have looked at ideas and evidence in four main areas: group structure; leadership; social influence processes; effectiveness; most of the evidence that has been used in our discussions has come from experimental research. In this way, I hope a fair picture has been painted of what the study of small groups has been, and in large part still is. To conclude, a few words would seem in order about predictions and hopes for the future.

Awareness, and a better understanding, of the limitations of findings from both experimental and experiential groups will increase, as work in both areas continues. Studies of experimental groups will become more mathematically sophisticated and thus more theoretically explicit. Some of the faddishness of experiential groups will disappear. In so far as work in that area concentrates on personal and group changes in organizational contexts, it may usefully provide impetus to studies of the sort to be discussed in chapter 13.

But the greatest need is for naturalistic investigations of the groups that contribute so much to our everyday experiences. Such studies will have to be longitudinal in nature, to encompass the phenomena of group formation, change and dissolution. They should attempt, through techniques of multivariate analysis, to grapple with the relations amongst the numerous variables which influence behaviour at work or in the home, rather than examining only one or two variables at a time. And they should be designed, not merely to document effects or outcomes, but to encourage theoretical analyses of the emergent group processes which lead to the observed outcomes. These are all tall orders, but if the study of small social groups is to continue as one of the most important concerns of social psychology, then attempts to satisfy these demands will have to become commonplace.

Further Reading

Janis, I. (1972), *Victims of Groupthink: A psychological study of foreign-policy decisions and fiascoes*, Boston, Houghton Mifflin. A very readable analysis of the decision-making processes of some crucial small groups of this century.

Wheeler, L. (1970), *Interpersonal Influence*, Boston, Allyn & Bacon. A simple introduction to a variety of different lines of work on social influence processes.

Moscovici, S., and Faucheux, C. (1972), 'Social influence, conformity bias, and the study of active minorities', in L. Berkowitz, ed., *Advances in Experimental Social Psychology*, vol. 6, New York, Academic Press. A review of some novel lines of work on social influence processes.

Davis, J. (1969), *Group Performance*, Reading, Mass., Addison-Wesley. An intelligent little book which reviews experimental studies of group performance and productivity.

Steiner, I. D. (1972), *Group Process and Productivity*, New York, Academic Press. A systematic analysis and synthesis of some of the major determinants of group productivity.

Rogers, C. R. (1973), *Encounter Groups*, Penguin Books. A very sympathetic introduction to the phenomena and study of experiential groups.

Part Three
Representations of the
Social World

Introduction

In Part Three we shall be concerned with ways in which people represent to themselves their understanding (or partial understanding) of the social world in which they live. In successive chapters the foci for these social representations increase in scope. In chapter 9, on interpersonal attributions, we examine how an individual represents to himself particular people and their actions. In chapters 10 and 11, we focus on the individual's representations of salient social issues, categories, institutions, i.e. the sorts of social phenomena about which an individual is likely to hold at least a moderately coherent attitude. And in chapter 12, we take a still broader look at how an individual views his social world. Despite differences in focus and scope, however, the different sets of representations have important features in common. Attributes, attitudes and views of the social world are not simply summaries of overt behaviour; rather they comprise an individual's own orientation to his social environment which, sometimes at any rate, may crucially determine his own social behaviour. The necessary reverse side of the coin is that an individual's social representations are also attempts to organize, understand and perhaps even predict the behaviour and experiences of others.

Part Two was concerned with the dyad and group and the individuals in them; in Part Four individuals and their interactions will be placed in a much wider social context. In addition to presenting work in several intrinsically important areas of social psychology, Part Three can be seen as a link between those two other parts because, Janus-faced, it looks in both directions. Donne's truth that 'no man is an island' applies as much to any individual's cognitions as to anything else about him. To begin with, our social representations are built up through interaction with other people (cf. chapters 4 and 5), through family, friends and an increasing number of acquaintances. But the views and behaviour displayed by our family, friendship and work groups are themselves influenced by the social backgrounds, positions and conditions of all those people. In addition, we soon encounter more remote influences and sources of information, although, it is true, they are in large part selected as a function of our background. The social climate of a school, the 'tone' of a neighbourhood, the assumptions, implicit as well as explicit, of the mass media are examples of the numerous important influences on our understanding of the world around us. The face-to-face and the apparently distant and remote are, in practice, virtually inextricable in any complex, pluralistic society; there is no doubt that both play crucial parts in our representations of the social world.

In chapter 9, J. R. Eiser analyses the covert assumptions and interpretations that we make about individual people, and sometimes about ourselves. Social psychology has long been interested in the impressions made by and the assumptions held about persons in interaction, and work in this area was commonly labelled 'person perception' or 'impression formation'. Much of the earlier work was simplistic and piecemeal. But theoretically more sophisticated ideas leading to more systematic inquiries have resulted from the development of theories of attributions. In the first part of chapter 9, Eiser provides an exposition of these theoretical developments in discussing questions such as, 'What sort of intentions do we attribute to others, if we do indeed attribute intent?' and 'How do we decide when a person acts because of some internal state or characteristic, and when because of features of the particular situation?' Later in the chapter, he points to some of the practical and behavioural implications of his analysis, such as the possible operations of self-fulfilling prophecies on the part of schoolteachers.

The study of social attitudes – their stability and change, their relations to social behaviour, and the problems raised in attempting to measure them – has been, for a long time, one of the most central areas of social psychology. That social attitudes comprise an important part of our social representations seems self-evidently true, yet this has proved a complex area for study, often frustrating because of the large number of factors necessarily involved in relating attitudes to what people actually do or in predicting changes in attitudes. In chapters 10 and 11, J. M. Jaspars tackles these issues in a scholarly, honest, yet critical manner. Chapter 10 is a careful analysis of some of the problems encountered in conceptualizing and measuring attitudes, and in his discussion of 'the attitude–behaviour problem', Jaspars reveals many of the issues involved in the pervasive question of the relation between representations and actions. Chapter 11 uses a simple communication model, built around 'source, message, channel and receiver', to present an integrated, but critical, review of some of the most important empirical findings about changes in attitudes. Given the methodological sophistication of much of social psychology, it is not unreasonable that even an introductory text should make use of a few simple equations; nevertheless, the congenitally a-mathematical reader should be able to follow quite closely the argument in the relevant part of the first half of chapter 11 simply by a careful reading of the accompanying text.

In chapter 12, H. Tajfel argues that the major social determinants of an individual's view of his world are: (i) the social or cultural consensus and the changes in it; (ii) social values in their permanent state of conflict and change. These two major determinants of what is sometimes called 'social cognition' interact with the perceptual, categorizing and judgement processes about which a good deal is known; that is, they affect the outcomes of these processes as well as being affected by them.

As we have argued, the internalization of values and social representations is achieved, initially, through interaction with a selected few; but soon an individual's sources of information widen dramatically to include all the 'groups', the smallest and the largest, of which he is a part or aspires to be a part, and all the modes of communication with him that these groups have at their disposal. If it were not for the fact that some basic rules for viewing the world are *common* to all of them, the individual could do no more than move from one narrow 'socio-centrism' to another (cf. Piaget, 1965). The fact that these rules are common to many societies, or sometimes perhaps even universal, does not mean that they can be thought of as being 'biologically determined' independently of social interaction. It only means that social interaction has its own features, some of which may well be common to all human beings at all times, and that these features inevitably affect the 'individual' processes of cognition.

Social interaction is a basic ingredient in the development and maintenance of many forms of human cognition, just as cognition determines many forms of human social interaction. This interdependence is based on the variety of cognitive *demands* and *requirements* that social interaction imposes upon a human individual; and these demands and requirements derive in turn from the conditions of life, both physical and social, which determine not only the needs, modes of action, and the achievements of any organized society but also the selection of its cognitive perspectives or representations. This selection of cognitive perspectives is the subject of chapter 12.

Chapter 9
Interpersonal Attributions

J. Richard Eiser

Persons as causes

Our behaviour towards other people depends to a large extent on the impressions we form of them, our interpretation of their past and present actions, and our predictions of what they will do in the future. It is easy to see, therefore, why social psychologists should be so concerned with the judgements people make about one another, since an understanding of social behaviour must depend, in part at least, on an understanding of social perception. 'Interpersonal attribution' is the term used to refer to the process or processes by which we come to *attribute* various dispositions, motives, intentions, abilities and responsibilities to one another – in short, how we come to describe one another in particular ways.

At first sight, describing other people seems to be something we should be able to do very easily. Language provides us with a rich repertoire of terms to distinguish subtle differences in others' appearance, behaviour and personality. Allport and Odbert (1936) discovered some 18,000 'trait names' in a standard English dictionary, of which 4504 seemed to describe 'consistent and stable modes of an individual's adjustment to his environment' (Allport, 1937, p. 306). Whilst this list naturally included large numbers of synonyms, such a vast vocabulary still testifies, at the very least, to the importance we attach to interpersonal descriptions. We may marvel at the ability of the Hanunoo of the Philippine Islands to find names for ninety-two varieties of rice (Conklin, 1954), and take this as evidence of the central importance of rice in Hanunoo society, but even ninety-two words for rice bear no comparison to 4504 words for people. Yet, it may be questioned whether we can apply many of these terms with a degree of certainty comparable to that of a Hanunoo identifying his varieties of rice. We can, of course, describe someone as 'blue-eyed', 'employed at the bank', 'married for two years', and so on, without getting into any serious epistemological difficulties. These are matters of fact that can be decided on as objectively as the variety of a grain of rice. But when we come to describe the same person as 'generous', 'business-like', or 'scheming', the criteria we are using are far less easy to define. One of the main reasons for this is that there is no simple one-to-one relationship between a particular action and a particular description. If someone donated a large sum of money to charity, it might seem natural to call him 'generous', but if we discovered that he avoided a large income tax liability by doing so, or that he was a candidate in a forthcoming election, we might be more inclined to call him 'business-like' or 'scheming'. Even though the actual behaviour being referred to was the same, we certainly would not regard these acts as having the same meaning.

Why then should such words figure so prominently in our language, and what functions, either logical or psychological, do they perform? One suggestion is that terms like 'generous', etc., are simply shorthand descriptions of consistencies in a person's behaviour. For instance, Ryle (1949, p. 89) has proposed that the sentence 'he boasted from vanity' could be expanded to 'he boasted ... and his doing so satisfied the law-like proposition that whenever he finds a chance of securing the admiration and envy of others, he does whatever he thinks will produce this admiration and envy'. This definition contains the important implication that, when we describe a person's behaviour on any one occasion, we somehow take into account what we know about his behaviour on other occasions, but it still raises certain problems. We may want to say that a person acted out of vanity on one occasion, without wishing to imply that he was typically vain. Ryle's definition implies that to do so would be self-contradictory. An alternative approach is to suggest that what makes a person's behaviour, for example, 'generous' rather than 'business-like' are his motives or intentions. This only helps, however, if we can specify the criteria by which we can decide what a person's motives or intentions are. Often a person's intentions may not be very mysterious. As Anscombe (1963, p. 8) has put it, 'if you want to say at least some true things about a man's intentions, you will have a strong chance of success if you mention what he actually did or was doing'.

Interpersonal attributions of the kind we have been considering, then, are not descriptions of *something other* than behaviour, but neither are they mere descriptions of behaviour (in the sense that an account of which muscles a person moved would be a mere description). Essentially, such attributions categorize behaviour in terms of *why* we suppose it occurred; in effect, they offer an interpretation of the behaviour being described in terms of what we feel we can say about the person's wishes, motives and intentions, his awareness of what he is doing and his ability to do it, and the situational constraints under which he is operating. A theory that proposes to account for such attributions, therefore, cannot simply view 'target persons' as though they are passive objects of perception, possessed of certain traits and characteristics that merely have to be observed and reported. The logic of such attributions itself requires that we should conceive of persons as active agents, at least in principle capable of free and intentional action, and as possible causes of their own behaviour.

When we make an attribution about another person, therefore, we are essentially trying to interpret or explain his behaviour, and in so doing render our social environment that much more predictable and intelligible. The size of the vocabulary at our disposal is evidence of the importance we attach to doing so, but there is still no guarantee that our interpretations will be correct or free of bias. The philosophical question of whether a statement concerning another's intentions or motives can be said to be true or false is a notoriously difficult one (see, e.g. Anscombe, 1963), and will not be our concern here. But there remain the equally important empirical questions of what kind of information people actually take into account in order to make such attributions, what factors may bias the attribution process and what may be their behavioural consequences. It is with these latter questions that this chapter is concerned.

Attribution theory

Attribution theory is the name given to the set of theoretical principles proposed to account for how people draw causal inferences about one another's behaviour. Although social psychologists have been interested in the problem of the perception of social causality for some considerable time, it is only recently that these principles have been drawn together into a cohesive theoretical framework, capable of generating new research questions and of making predictions concerning the effects of different conditions. At the present time, however, the framework proposed is still somewhat global.

The origins of attribution theory (like those of the cognitive consistency theories of attitude organization) are to be found in the work of Heider (1944, 1958) on phenomenal causality. Heider assumed that people are motivated to perceive their social environment as predictable and hence controllable. He also assumed that the means by which we come to be able to predict social events is essentially similar to how we predict physical events; we look for the necessary and sufficient conditions for such events to occur. Central to this endeavour is the distinction between *personal* and *impersonal causality*. As he wrote (1958, p.16):

Of great importance for our picture of the social environment is the attribution of events to causal sources. It makes a real difference, for example, whether a person discovers that the stick that struck him fell from a rotting tree or was hurled by an enemy. Attribution in terms of impersonal and personal causes, and with the latter, in terms of intent, are everyday occurrences that determine much of our understanding of and reaction to our surroundings.

The perception of personal causality depends, in turn, on the perception of intentionality. Heider took as instances of 'true' personal causality only those cases where the person's actions are intentional or purposive. Cases where the outcome of a person's behaviour is unintended 'are more appropriately represented as cases of impersonal causality' (1958, p. 101), and for this reason 'intention is the central factor in personal causality' (1958, p. 102). The extent to which a person will be seen as responsible for a particular action outcome, however, will depend not only on his intentions, but on the extent to which the outcome cannot be attributed to impersonal or environmental factors. Even so, the potential influence of impersonal factors can frequently be underestimated. We are inclined to assume some correspondence between a person's behaviour and his intentions, even when other causal factors are present.

More recent formulations by Jones and Davis (1965) and Kelley (1967, 1971) have built upon and extended these basic notions. Jones and Davis conceive of the process of attributing dispositions to an actor in terms of the model represented diagrammatically in Figure 11, which they explain as follows:

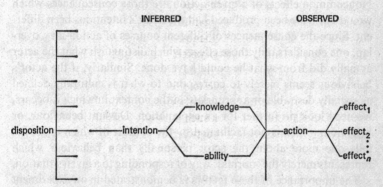

Figure 11   The action–attribute paradigm (from Jones and Davis, 1965, p. 222)

It is assumed that the perceiver typically starts with the overt action of another; this is the grist for his cognitive mill. He then makes certain decisions concerning ability and knowledge which will let him cope with the problem of attributing particular intentions to the actor. The attribution of intentions, in turn, is a necessary step in the assignment of more stable characteristics to the actor (p. 222).

The conditions of knowledge and ability are important, in that, for a perceiver to attribute certain outcomes of actions to the intentions of the actor, he must assume that the actor knew his behaviour could have these outcomes and was also *capable* of producing these outcomes intentionally. When the perceiver infers that the actor's behaviour is 'in character' – or, in other words, when a similar description can be applied both to the behaviour and 'underlying characteristics' of the actor – the perceiver is said to have made a *correspondent inference*. Thus, if an actor is observed to exhibit domineering behaviour, the most 'correspondent' inference would be one that took this domineering behaviour as a direct reflection of his intention to dominate, which in turn reflected a disposition to be dominant. The degree of correspondence of an inference (i.e. the extent to which a person's behaviour is seen to reflect his intentions and dispositions, rather than the influence of external situational constraints) is held to depend upon (i) the number of *noncommon effects* of a given action, and (ii) the *social desirability* of these effects. Noncommon effects of a given action are those consequences which would not have been produced had the actor's intentions been different. Since the consequences of different courses of action may overlap, one considers only those effects which distinguish what the actor actually did from what he could have done. Similarly, if the actor's behaviour seems merely to correspond to what is culturally defined as socially desirable or appropriate in the context in which it occurs, we need look no further for an explanation. Deviant behaviour, or behaviour which is not facilitated by the context in which it occurs, tells one more about the actor personally than behaviour which represents merely the 'normal' way of responding to a given situation.

The importance of these factors is demonstrated in an experiment by Jones, Davis and Gergen (1961). Student subjects listened to one of four tape-recordings of a simulated job interview, in which they heard the interviewee being instructed to play the role of someone applying for a job either as an astronaut, or as a submariner. In the 'astronaut' condition, subjects then heard the interviewer describe the ideal astronaut as someone with inner resources who does not need the company of others – an 'inner-directed' person. In the 'submariner' condition, they heard the ideal submariner being described as 'other-directed', i.e. obedient, cooperative, friendly and gregarious. Half the subjects in each condition then heard the interview proceed with the interviewee responding in a very 'inner-directed' manner, whilst the other half heard him responding in a very 'other-directed' manner. Subjects were then asked to say what they felt the interviewee was '*really* like as a person'. Subjects who had heard the astronaut candidate responding inner-directedly, or the submariner candidate responding other-directedly, rated the interviewee, who was behaving in line with the requirements of the occupational role, as moderately affiliative and moderately independent, and expressed low confidence in their judgements. The other-directed astronaut candidate, however, was confidently rated as very conforming and affiliative, and the inner-directed submariner candidate confidently rated as very independent and non-affiliative. Jones and Davis (1965, p. 237) take these results as indicating that

behaviour which departs from clearly defined role requirements cries for explanation. The fact that the effects of such behaviour are presumably low in cultural desirability makes the behaviour intriguing to the perceiver. The fact that there are few reasons why a person would behave that way (the action leads to a limited number of noncommon effects) provides the basis for a correspondent inference concerning the intentions and dispositions of the actor.

Conceptually the most difficult aspect of the Jones and Davis model is their apparent tendency to regard dispositional inferences merely as an extension of intentional inferences. The case of inferring that a person has a 'domineering disposition' from observing him exhibit domineering behaviour (which is an example provided by Jones and Davis themselves) brings out some of the problems. There might easily be circumstances in which we would describe someone as domineering, even if he insisted that he was not trying to dominate us. We would do so primarily if we felt his behaviour was uncalled for by anything in the situation, and if we had evidence that he behaved in a similar fashion in other situations. On the other hand, if we felt that the person's behaviour was fully justified under the circumstances, we might well say that his behaviour and its consequences corresponded exactly to what he intended, but would not then call him domineering. To say that a person behaved *intentionally*, in the sense that he knew what he was doing and could have acted otherwise, is not the same as saying that he behaved that way *with the intention* of bringing about certain consequences. Nonetheless, Jones and Davis are correct on the more general point that the information value of behaviour is proportionate to its distinctiveness.

Kelley (1967, 1971) has proposed a more tightly knit model to represent the causal schemata implied in interpersonal attributions. The basis of these schemata is a 'naïve version' of J. S. Mill's method of difference; the effect is attributed to that condition which is present when the effect is present and absent when the effect is absent. Thus a perceiver's impression of another person can be thought of as an observation (analogous to a dependent variable in a factorial experiment) which might change as a function of a change in one or more of the following: (i) *stimuli* (target persons) – Who is the other person being observed? Would the perceiver judge others in the same way? (ii) *perceivers* – Who is the perceiver? Would other perceivers judge the same target person in the same way? (iii) *time* – When did the observation take place? Would the perceiver make the same judgement whenever he observed the target person? (iv) *modality* – How did the perceiver observe the target person? If he used a different means of observation, would he form the same judgement? Corresponding to these four factors, Kelley lists four types of criteria which, if violated, will make it less likely that the perceiver will attribute his impression of another person to some 'internal' characteristic of that person. These are referred to as distinctiveness, consensus, consistency over time, and consistency over modality.

Distinctiveness. If the impression one has formed of a stimulus (target person) is caused by characteristics of that stimulus, then changing the stimulus should change the impression. Thus, if a perceiver P_1 describes another person O_1 as 'generous', we need to know that there could be some other person whom P_1 would *not* describe as 'generous', before we can assume that O_1 is really generous, and not just imagined to be so by P_1. This is related to the notion that if O_1 is exhibiting the same behaviour (creating the same impression) as would be exhibited by O_2, O_3, O_4, and so on, in the same situation, we can learn little from this about what O_1 is 'really' like.

Consensus. If P_1's impression of O_1 is due to something about O_1 and not something about P_1, then other perceivers, P_2, P_3, P_4, and so on, should share P_1's impression of O_1. If they do *not* share his impressions, then P_1 should have less faith in his own opinion of O_1.

Consistency over time. If P_1's impression of O_1 reflects what O_1 is 'really' like, this impression should not change with repeated observation. Dispositional inference presumes behavioural stability.

Consistency over modality. P_1's impression of O_1 should not depend on the means by which O_1 was observed. O_1 should not be seen as 'generous' in some respects, and as 'mean' if different kinds of information are taken into account.

To test the hypothesis that different kinds of 'data patterns' would lead to different kinds of attributions, McArthur (1972) presented subjects with a number of statements describing the reaction of a particular person to a particular stimulus (e.g. 'John laughs at the comedian'). These statements were each accompanied by three other statements which gave information concerning consensus ('Almost everyone who hears the comedian laughs at him' v. 'Hardly anyone who hears the comedian laughs at him'), distinctiveness ('John laughs at hardly any other comedians' v. 'John also laughs at almost every other comedian') and consistency over time ('In the past John has almost always laughed at the same comedian' v. 'In the past John has almost never laughed at the same comedian'). For each of these sets of information, subjects were asked to rate the probability that the person's response to the stimulus (John's amusement at the comedian) was due to (i) something about the person whose behaviour or response is being described, i.e. John (*person attribution*), (ii) something about the stimulus or target, i.e. the comedian (*stimulus attribution*), (iii) something about the particular circumstances (*circumstance attribution*), or (iv) some combination of two or more of the factors i, ii and iii. If subjects chose iv, they were asked to specify which combination they had in mind. Since 'i *and* ii' was quite a frequent choice, this was treated separately from the other combinations and referred to as *person-stimulus attribution*.

As predicted by Kelley's model, person attribution was most frequent where there was low consensus, low distinctiveness and high consistency (e.g. 'John laughs at the comedian; hardly anyone who hears the comedian laughs at him; John also laughs at almost every other comedian; in the past John has almost always laughed at the same comedian'), and stimulus attribution was most frequent where there was high consensus, high distinctiveness and low consistency. In addition, circumstance attribution was dependent mainly on consistency, being more frequent in cases of low consistency. Person-stimulus attribution was most frequent in cases of high consensus, low distinctiveness and high consistency, and low consensus, high distinctiveness and high consistency. The readiness of subjects to make person-stimulus attributions is especially interesting in view of the current debate in personality theory between those who conceptualize individual differences in behaviour in terms of enduring dispositions or traits, and those who view them as the product of an interaction between persons and specific stimulus conditions (Mischel, 1968, 1973; Bowers, 1973). Apparently McArthur's subjects allowed for the possibility of just such an interaction in their attributions.

Attribution of responsibility

The distinction between personal and impersonal causality can have important implications for the kinds of moral or evaluative judgements people make of one another. If a person's behaviour produces good or bad outcomes, this makes quite a difference to our view of that person, provided we see him as responsible for the outcomes in question. If a person can be seen to be producing certain outcomes intentionally, the question of his responsibility for those outcomes is unproblematic. A more intriguing question concerns what factors may lead us to regard a person as responsible for outcomes he did not intend. When accidents occur, what determines whether we blame them on the people concerned, or dismiss them as chance events?

An experiment by Walster (1966) tested the hypothesis that the more serious an accident, the greater should be the tendency to assign responsibility for it to a person, rather than to chance. She presented her subjects with a tape-recorded account of how a young man 'Lennie B', out on a drive with his friend, parked his six-year-old car, that he had just bought, at the top of a hill. While they were gone, the handbrake failed, and the car rolled down the hill. Each subject then heard one of four different descriptions of the consequences of this event, ranging from mild (the car ran into a near-by tree stump and was slightly dented) to severe (the car ran all the way down the hill and crashed into a grocer's shop dazing a child and badly injuring the grocer). Walster found, the more severe the consequences, the more subjects tended to see the accident as Lennie's fault. Later research, however, has generally failed to confirm the finding that attribution of responsibility is directly related to severity of consequences (Shaver, 1970a, 1970b; Shaw and Skolnick, 1971; Walster, 1967). As Wortman and Linder (1973) have pointed out, these studies may have confounded severity with the likelihood of certain consequences; they found that a person was seen as having acted more wrongly when the likely consequences of his action were severe, irrespective of whether these consequences actually occurred.

A particularly interesting kind of situation that has also been studied is when the victim, and not just the perpetrator of the behaviour, could conceivably be held responsible for his or her sufferings. The need to believe in a 'just world' in which good and bad outcomes are a function of people's deserts may in certain circumstances lead people either to blame the victim for the accident, or to derogate his general character. In other words, either one says 'It was his own fault', or else 'He's such a nasty kind of person that he deserves to have bad things happen to him.' Since there is an implied 'trade-off function' between these two alternative strategies of restoring one's belief in a just world, one can derive the counter-intuitive prediction that a victim will be held *more* to blame for his own misfortunes, the *less* his misfortunes seem merited by the kind of person he is. Support for this prediction comes from a study by Jones and Aronson (1973), who found that the victim of a rape attack was seen as more to blame for her misfortunes when personally respectable (married or a virgin) than when less respectable (divorced). (The respectability variation is itself interesting from the point of view of the 'just world' hypothesis; divorcees may be derogated – i.e. seen as less respectable – to justify the fact that they are divorced.) However, this did not deter subjects from recommending harsher sentences for the rapist when the victim was more respectable.

A major weakness of the attribution of responsibility research to date, however, has been the ambiguity surrounding the central concept of responsibility itself. As Fishbein and Ajzen (1973) point out, Heider (1958) distinguished five levels at which a person could be said to be 'responsible' for particular outcomes (see also Shaw and Sulzer, 1964). At the first level, a person might be said to be responsible for all effects with which he was associated (*association*); at the next level only for effects he was instrumental in producing (*commission*); at the next level only if he could have foreseen the effects (*foreseeability*); at the next level only for effects he intended (*intentionality*); and finally, only if his intended behaviour was not a function of external factors beyond his control (*justification*). In most studies, subjects have simply been asked to rate the responsibility of the target person without it being explicitly stated at what level they should respond. Thus the same target person might be rated as responsible by one subject, on the grounds that he was clearly instrumental in producing the effects in question, as not at all responsible by another subject, since he equally clearly did not intend the effects, whilst a third subject might not be able to make up his mind because of uncertainty over whether the effects could have been foreseen. In view of this ambiguity, the inconclusiveness of research in this area is not altogether surprising.

Attributions of responsibility, therefore, are not necessarily the same as attributions of personal causality. In most of these studies, there is no implication that the actor or victim *intended* the consequences in question, so for Heider these would not be instances of 'true' personal causality (see p. 238). What seems to be mainly at issue in these studies is whether the consequences could have been foreseen and prevented, i.e. the highest level of responsibility with which they are concerned is that of foreseeability (although this has typically *not* been made explicit to the subjects). In terms of the Jones and Davis (1965) model, what are crucial are the assumptions that can be made about the target person's knowledge and ability. The question of the level of responsibility at which one *ought* to operate when making such attributions, however, is a problem for ethics, not psychology. To hold a person responsible is to make a moral judgement about him, and not necessarily to infer his intentions and dispositions from his behaviour.

Discounting situational constraints: 'internal' v. 'external' attributions

An assumption common to all formulations of attribution theory is that, if a person's behaviour can be seen as merely a response to constraints of the situation, the cause of the behaviour should not be attributed to 'internal' characteristics of the person, but to 'external' characteristics of the situation. This does not necessarily involve the assumption that anyone who responds to situational demands does so unintentionally. The crucial question is, 'Would the person have behaved in this way if the situation had been different?' If the answer is yes, we make an 'internal' attribution to the person, and if it is no, we make an 'external' attribution to the situation. The assumption of personal causation is not, however, easily shed. It was shown by Jones and Harris (1967) that even when a person expressing an opinion is not doing so in conditions of free choice (i.e. he is *assigned* to defend a certain point of view) the subjects tend to attribute to him to some extent the opinion he is defending, although they know that he is doing it as a result of a random assignment of roles. A follow-up study demonstrated the relevance of certain individual differences to this kind of attribution process. According to Rotter (1966), individuals differ in the generalized expectancies which they form with regard to the 'locus of control of reinforcement'. At one extreme, 'internals' attribute the cause of the reinforcements they receive to their own personal attributes or endeavours; at the other extreme 'externals' see such reinforcements as due largely to chance, or forces beyond their own control (see Lefcourt, 1972, for a review). Jones *et al.* (1971) presented, to a group of 'internals' and a group of 'externals', a strongly favourable essay supposedly written under conditions of choice or of no choice, and found the 'internals' were more sensitive to the choice variable than were the 'externals'.

More recently Kruglanski and Cohen (1973) looked at attitude attribution in a situation where the target person's apparent freedom of choice was less clear-cut. Subjects were presented with an essay favouring either cooperation or competition 'in human affairs', which they were told had been written in response to a request by a survey worker so worded as to allow the writer to choose which side to support, but at the same time indicating the side the survey worker would prefer him to choose ('because we are particularly interested in the kinds of arguments people bring up on this side of the issue'). In the *conforming* condition the target person supported the side supposedly requested by the survey worker, and in the *deviant* condition, he supported the side the survey worker had asked him *not* to choose. Background information about the target person also was provided so that subjects would expect either a cooperative or a competitive essay to be 'in character'. The target person was seen as less constrained to take the stand he did and holding an attitude more in line with that which he expressed, when behaving 'in character' than 'out of character'. The conforming v. deviant variable was effectively ignored when subjects made attributions about 'in character' behaviour, but in the 'out of character' condition, greater correspondence between true and expressed attitude was attributed to the target person whose behaviour was deviant.

Self-attribution

Although our concern so far has been with how we form impressions of *other* people, many of the same principles have been applied to the question of how we infer our *own* feelings, attitudes and dispositions. At first sight, this may seem a strange question to ask. Don't we know our own feelings, and so on, without having to infer them? Well, apparently not, at least not always. Instead, self-descriptions seem to involve some kind of observation of our own responses, and an interpretation of them as a function of the situational context in which they occur.

A classic demonstration of this phenomenon is the study by Schachter and Singer (1962; also see chapter 10) who placed subjects either in a situation where they had to fill out a questionnaire containing insulting material in the presence of a stooge who behaved increasingly angrily as the session progressed, or in a situation where they had to wait with a stooge who started fooling around with a number of objects in the room and generally behaved in a very euphoric fashion. Some of the subjects had been injected with epinephrine (adrenalin), a drug which causes physiological arousal, but were not told that the drug would make them feel aroused. Another group received the epinephrine injection, but were forewarned about its effects, and a group of control subjects received a placebo injection. Subjects in the first group tended to behave more emotionally than subjects in the other two groups, expressing anger when paired with the angry stooge and euphoria when paired with the euphoric stooge. In other words, they attributed the arousal symptoms produced by the drug to their own anger at the experimenter or amusement at the stooge. Subjects who had been correctly informed about the drug's effects, on the other hand, were able to attribute their arousal to the drug, and thus could explain their arousal without having to label it as anger or amusement.

Related research by Nisbett and Schachter (1966) and by Storms and Nisbett (1970) leads to similar conclusions. Nisbett and Schachter tested subjects' toleration of a series of electric shocks, increasing in intensity, just after they had been given a placebo pill. One group were told that the pill would produce a number of autonomic arousal symptoms, whilst another group were told that it would produce a number of irrelevant physical symptoms. It was predicted that the first group would be able to attribute the arousal in fact produced by the shocks to the pill, and so would be able to think of the shocks themselves as less painful. In fact, they were able to tolerate shocks four times more intense than those endured by the other subjects. Storms and Nisbett demonstrated that techniques of this kind can have certain practical therapeutic applications (see also, Valins and Nisbett, 1971). They reasoned that, if insomnia is produced by re- hearsal of emotionally arousing cognitions, then subjects who were told that placebo pills would help them relax but in fact still felt aroused might infer, 'if I feel as aroused as I do now, when a drug is operating to lower my arousal, then I must be very aroused indeed' and should thus have greater difficulty in getting to sleep than subjects who were told that the pills would make them feel aroused, and could thus attribute their arousal to an external cause. As predicted, the group who expected to feel more aroused by the pill reported that they fell asleep quicker on nights when they took the pill.

A particularly important aspect of work on self-attribution con- cerns people's perceptions of their own motivations for engaging in certain behaviour. If a person receives large rewards for acting in a certain way, he will not need to make the attribution that the task itself was interesting or enjoyable; the external rewards provide sufficient justification, regardless of any *intrinsic* enjoyment provided by the task itself. An implication of this is that it is possible to undermine a person's 'intrinsic motivation' to engage in a particular activity for its own sake, by giving him excessive *extrinsic* rewards or payment for doing so. Strong support for this notion comes from studies by Deci (1971) and Lepper, Greene and Nisbett (1973). Deci found that college students who were rewarded for an interesting activity during the second of three work periods showed a greater decrease in performance from the first to the third period than a control group who received no payment. Lepper *et al.* gave nursery school children either expected or unexpected rewards for engaging in an intrinsically interesting activity, and then compared their behavioural persistence at the same activity during a free play period two weeks later. The children who had not expected any reward on completion of the task, and therefore could not regard their own behaviour as an attempt to obtain any extrinsic reward, still appeared to find the task as interesting two weeks later as did a control group who had received no reward. However, those who had expected to receive rewards for their earlier activity spent only about half as much time as the other two groups on the same activity in the free play period where no rewards were forthcoming.

A similar kind of reasoning has been applied to problems in the field of attitude change. According to Bem (1967), a person's attitude is not the outcome of any motivational process such as a tendency to reduce dissonance, but instead a description by him of his own overt behaviour, and essentially the *same kind* of description as would be given by an outside observer (see chapter 10). Implied in this approach is the assumption that a person would be more likely to infer his beliefs from his behaviour in contexts where his behaviour could not be attributed to situational constraints. Kiesler, Nisbett and Zanna (1969), for example, found that subjects who had agreed to try to persuade passers-by to sign a petition against air pollution, using arguments prepared by the experimenter, expressed attitudes more strongly against air pollution when the relevance of their own attitudes to such behaviour was emphasized than when led to feel that the scientific value of the study was sufficient justification for their behaviour.

Whilst there seems reasonable evidence that people may often infer their own attitudes and feelings from an observation of their own behaviour, it does not follow that they necessarily make exactly the same kind of inferences as would be made by an outside observer. According to Jones and Nisbett (1971, p. 80) 'there is a pervasive tendency for actors to attribute their actions to situational requirements, whereas observers tend to attribute the same actions to stable personal dispositions'; in other words, actors should make fewer personal or 'internal' attributions about their own behaviour than observers. In support of this, Nisbett *et al.* (1973) report that observers who witnessed the responses of actors to a request to volunteer for a social service task predicted that the actors would respond in the same way to a similar request in the future (thus making a relatively internal attribution), whereas the actors themselves did not predict any general correspondence between their current and future behaviour. They also found that students would ascribe more personality trait descriptions to others than they would to themselves, and that when asked to account for their own, and their best friend's, choice of girl friend and of major course subject, students would make fewer 'entity' attributions (i.e. would offer fewer reasons in terms of attributes of the girl friend or the course), and more 'dispositional' attributions (in terms of their own, or their friend's, personality) when describing their friend's choices than when describing their own.

Storms (1973), however, has convincingly shown that the normal differences between the attributions made by actors and observers can be reversed by the simple device of letting actors observe their own behaviour on videotape. When the actor was given the opportunity of observing his own behaviour in a two-person conversation from what had been the observer's orientation, he became even more 'internal' in his attributions than the observer. Similarly, when the observer viewed the conversation from what had been the actor's orientation, his attributions attached relatively more importance to the situation. This suggests that there may not be anything very special about self-attributions *as such* that leads to the typical actor–observer differences, but rather that an actor quite literally cannot see himself in the same way as he would appear to an observer, whereas an observer cannot see the situation in the same way as it appears to the actor, especially when he himself is interacting with the actor and hence may be influencing how the actor behaves.

Attributions as self-fulfilling prophecies

Person perception is not just a spectator sport. Whenever we are involved in an interaction with another person, our behaviour towards him will depend, to a greater or lesser extent, on the kind of person we think he is, the impressions we have formed concerning his attitudes and abilities, and how we expect him to behave towards us. In a sense, we *need* to make interpersonal attributions if we are to behave appropriately. At the same time, our own behaviour may constrain the way in which this other person can behave towards us; it may define his role in the interaction. If such constraint is sufficiently strong or persistent, we may force him to behave in a manner which confirms our expectations.

A particularly important example of this is when we make attributions of another person's ability. Jones and Goethals (1971) draw attention to the fact that first impressions can have a disproportionate influence on our judgement of a person's ability, or of other attributes that we expect to be relatively stable and consistent over time. Once we categorize someone as 'intelligent', later information about him may be assimilated to this category. 'These categories are like hypotheses about the nature of reality being confronted. Once a categorical decision is made, subsequent information is distorted to fit the category or to confirm the hypothesis – as long as it is not too discrepant from the category's typical instance' (Jones and Goethals, 1971, p. 43).

Such initial categorizations do not only influence the processing of subsequent information; they may also influence the information itself, by shaping the behaviour of the person so categorized. In their book *Pygmalion in the Classroom*, Rosenthal and Jacobson (1968) set out to demonstrate the influence that teachers' expectations could have on the scholastic achievement of their pupils. They claimed that when teachers were told that certain pupils in their class were likely to show especially marked improvement, their favourable expectations could result in those pupils, who were in fact randomly selected, showing quite dramatic gains in measured I Q. Snow (1969), however, has pointed out a number of serious methodological flaws in the research which Rosenthal and Jacobson presented, including the specific measure of ability employed, and the statistical treatment and interpretation of differences in IQ gains between the various groups. Subsequent research, that has concentrated on identifying the mechanisms through which teachers' expectations might have their effect, has provided a more convincing case for the existence of the phenomenon. At the same time such research suggests that its magnitude and universality may be less than at first supposed. (See also the brief discussion in chapter 13, pp. 342–4.)

Meichenbaum, Bowers and Ross (1969) examined the effects of teachers' expectations on the academic and classroom behaviour of fourteen institutionalized teenage girl offenders. Six of the girls who were identified to their teachers as 'late bloomers' showed significant improvement as compared with the remaining eight in their general classroom behaviour, and in their performance on courses assessed by 'objective' test (e.g. mathematics, science). On courses where assessment was more 'subjective', however (e.g. literature, history, English), expectations had no effect. An analysis of the teachers' interactions with the girls indicated that the improvement of the 'late bloomers' was not due to their receiving more total attention; it was rather that the *quality* of teacher–student interaction was more positive and encouraging. A similar conclusion was reached by Rubovits and Maehr (1971), who found that 'gifted' pupils did not receive more total attention than 'non-gifted' pupils, but were called upon and praised more often. Rubovits and Maehr (1973) subsequently studied the behaviour of white female students on a teacher training course towards black and white pupils, some of whom were identified as 'gifted' and some as 'non-gifted'. White pupils received significantly more total attention than black pupils, especially when categorized as 'gifted'. 'Gifted' pupils were called upon more often when they were white, but not when they were black. White pupils received more praise than black pupils overall, and whereas 'gifted' whites received more praise than 'non-gifted' whites, 'gifted' blacks received *less* praise than 'non-gifted' blacks. Findings such as these may well have implications for the continuing debate on race and intelligence.

A further study by Meichenbaum and Smart (1971) shows that

students' own expectations can influence their academic performance in a similar way. First-year university engineering students who were academically borderline showed significant improvement on two out of four required courses, reported greater self-confidence and evaluated their course more positively when given positive assessments concerning their future performance after taking a set of ability interest tests. This result is interesting, in that it shows that the expectations others hold about a person may not only influence his behaviour, but also how he thinks about himself. This directly supports a long tradition of theorizing (see, e.g., Gergen, 1971), that holds that a person's self-concept is, to a large extent, an internalization of how he thinks others see him. As Mead (1925, p. 273) once wrote, 'We are in possession of selves just in so far as we can and do take the attitudes of others towards ourselves and respond to those attitudes.'

The interrelationships between social behaviour, social role, self-concept and interpersonal perception are issues that are ideally suited to an attributional analysis. At the same time, one should not fall into the trap of supposing that all attributions are automatically self-fulfilling. Quite simply, if a change in behaviour cannot produce the effect we expect, our expectations by themselves are impotent. Similarly, how we categorize another person may limit the kind of role he can adopt in interactions with us, but in many situations he may be free to leave the interaction, to force us to reconsider our assessment of him, or if all else fails, to play the role without identifying with it.

Conclusions

Interpersonal attributions, above all else, are descriptions of behaviour. If they were not – if instead they were the product of some kind of telepathic guessing game – many of the findings discussed in this chapter would be quite mysterious. If attributions referred primarily to the 'private' contents of a person's mind, then it would be difficult to understand how we could attribute responsibility to a person without consideration of his intentions, how the attributions we make about our *own* attitudes and emotions should resemble so closely the attributions we would make about another's attitudes and emotions on the basis of similar data, or how a person's behaviour could be moulded by the attributions others make about him. At the same time, however, interpersonal attributions do more than merely reiterate the behavioural data on which they were based. In addition, they evaluate the behaviour in question and offer an interpretation of it in terms of hypotheses concerning the presumed effect of personal and situational factors. Since these hypotheses can be predictive as well as evaluative, their importance for an understanding of social behaviour can scarcely be overestimated.

Further Reading

Shaver, K. G. (1975), *An Introduction to Attribution Processes*, Cambridge, Mass., Winthrop. A well-organized and readable introduction to theory and research in this area. Published in paperback, it provides a good deal of reasonably up-to-date information although it makes no attempt to review many studies that have appeared in the last few years.

Jones, E. E., Kanouse, D. E., Kelley, H. H., Nisbett, R. E., Valins, S., and Weiner, B. (1971), *Attribution: Perceiving the causes of behavior*, Morristown, N. J., General Learning Press. An extremely useful collection of original articles, also available singly, containing most of the theoretical statements with which recent research has been concerned. The style of writing tends to be closer to that of a review article in a journal than to that of an introductory textbook.

Heider, F. (1958), *The Psychology of Interpersonal Relations*, New York, Wiley. The book that started it all. The fact that much of it has been overtaken by more recent research is a credit to the impact it has had. It is still worth reading, though, and not just for 'historical' reasons.

Chapter 10
The Nature and Measurement of Attitudes

J. M. F. Jaspars

The concept of attitude

Although it has been described as one of the key concepts of social psychology or even as the most distinctive and indispensable concept in (American) social psychology, no commonly accepted definition of the concept of attitude exists. In a way this is hardly surprising because the word attitude has more than one meaning in the English language. Derived from the word *aptitudo* in late Latin and influenced in its meaning, through Italian, by another Latin word *actus* (Italian = *atto*) the term attitude has acquired the significance of an aptitude, a fitness or tendency for action. In the field of art, however, a quite different meaning of the word developed, indicating the posture of a figure in a sculpture or painting (Allport, 1935). Both meanings were explicitly recognized in psychology at the end of the nineteenth century and the beginning of this century, when terms like 'mental attitude' and 'motor attitude' were still in vogue.

As a unified concept, belonging exclusively to the domain of social psychology, the concept of attitude was granted an important position in the social sciences by G. W. Allport in his classic review in the first handbook of social psychology (Murchison, 1935). Allport defined an attitude as 'a mental or neural state of readiness, organized through experience, exerting a directive or dynamic influence upon the individual's response to all objects and situations with which it is related'. This is an admirably eclectic definition that manages to combine components of previous definitions in one conception; however, it tends to gloss over various controversies. It does not make a distinction between mental and motor attitudes; it does not say how enduring the state of readiness is; it tells us that attitudes are organized through experience but fails to mention that psychologists at that time were quarrelling about the relative importance of instincts and habits in influencing behaviour; it leaves open the possibility that an attitude has either a dynamic or a directive influence on behaviour; it does not make clear to what extent 'the individual's response' is shared by other people and thereby becomes a common or collective response; nor does it specify the objects to which it is related; and finally, the definition is not clearly related to the procedures for measuring attitudes developed at that time.

It is not surprising therefore that a unified concept of attitude was attacked by McDougall (1933) on the grounds that the term was used to cover a multitude of facts of many kinds including almost every variety of opinion and belief and all the abstract qualities of personality, such as courage, obstinacy, generosity, humility, as well as units of affective organization which were called 'sentiments' by McDougall. There is, however, some unity in diversity, and although Allport's definition may be too eclectic it can be used as a frame of reference to show both the diversity and the unity of opinion that exists with regard to the concept of attitude.

Allport's definition implies that in one way or another an essential feature of an attitude is that it cannot be observed directly but must be considered as a 'state of readiness' for response which has to be inferred from overt behaviour. It is an intervening variable or a hypothetical construct introduced to explain why people react differently to the same stimuli. An intervening variable is usually defined as a process inferred to occur between stimulus and response, which accounts for one response rather than another to the same stimulus. When such a variable is assumed to have its own properties, additional to those required for the explanation of the state-of-readiness connection, it is usually said to be a hypothetical construct. Whereas an intervening variable is, strictly speaking, only a theoretical concept existing in the mind of the observer, a hypothetical construct is thought to exist 'really' in the organisms and allows the investigator, so to speak, to put an electrode into it.

Seen from this point of view, the idea of attitude is neither new nor unique. Whenever some intervening variable or hypothetical construct is postulated between stimuli and responses in psychology, it is very often assumed that the variable or construct corresponds to residues of past experiences which are somehow retained by the person or organism and which guide, bias, or otherwise influence behaviour. This general notion, however, does not allow for a very discriminating terminology. Campbell (1963), who made a careful theoretical study of the concept of attitude, assembled about seventy-five concepts which are currently in use in psychology and which all refer to his idea of an 'acquired behavioural disposition'. A few examples are: belief; cognitive structure; conditioned reflex; conviction; determining tendency; expectancy; habit; intuition; motive; opinion; personality trait; set; value. In addition Campbell points out that the main problem in studying attitudes or acquired behavioural dispositions is that in most cases we do not know the past history of the organism and therefore have to decide what is the residue of experience on the basis of observations of the present behaviour. It is, he writes, as if we were to study, as animal psychologists, a visiting rat from another laboratory without knowing anything about its previous history. We would typically run the animal through a variety of tests and observe its behaviour under different conditions. Hopefully, the co-occurrence of stimuli and responses would give us a clue as to the nature of the residue of its past experiences. But how far are we willing to go in making inferences of this kind on the basis of our observations? That is one of the basic questions that has divided social psychologists in attitude research.

Self-description, probability and latent process conceptions of attitude

Since attitudes are usually measured, as we shall see, by asking people to react to a number of verbal statements about their affinities for, and aversions to, some identifiable aspect of their environment, it is tempting from a behaviouristic point of view to define an attitude as nothing but peoples' self-descriptions of those affinities and aversions. This is the point of view taken by Bem (1965, 1968) who apparently regards himself as an 'unreconstructed behaviourist'. Behaviourism as a school or system of psychology originally defined psychology as the study of behaviour and limited the data of psychology strictly to observable activities. An 'unreconstructed behaviourist' thus refuses to speculate about processes that intervene between stimulus and response. 'Reconstructed' behaviourists allow themselves to speak about internal mediating responses (Fishbein, 1967b; Osgood, Suci and Tannenbaum, 1957; Staats and Staats, 1958).

In Bem's interpretation of the concept of attitude, the notion of an internal state which can be considered as a residue of previous experience that determines behaviour is completely dropped. An attitude is a particular type of verbal behaviour by which a person describes himself. It is suggested moreover by Bem that a person who gives such a self-description is not describing his 'private internal environment', but his public behaviour, which is also accessible to an outside observer.

When a person answers 'yes' to the question 'Do you like brown bread?' he is, according to Bem from whom the example is taken, not describing strongly conditioned internal responses only known to himself, but he is making an attribution or inference from his own overt behaviour, which is exactly what an outside observer would do. His wife might answer the question for him by saying 'He probably does, because he is always eating it.' The self-descriptive parallel inference would be: 'I probably do, because I'm always eating it.' This behaviouristic attitude theory is in fact a new version of a general theory of emotions once proposed by James and Lange (Stern, 1934) which stressed the effects of bodily processes on our subjectively felt emotions. 'We do not cry' William James wrote, 'because we are sad, we are sad because we cry.' As we saw in the previous chapter, there is good evidence from fairly recent research which indicates that the judgement of our own emotional states depends to some extent upon the circumstances in which we experience those emotions. For example, by manipulating the external cues in a situation, Schachter and Singer (1962) were able to evoke self-descriptions of emotional states as disparate as euphoria and anger from persons in whom identical states of physiological arousal had been induced.

The behaviouristic interpretation of the concept of attitude appears at first sight to turn upside down the whole notion of attitude as an important determinant of behaviour. It seems that it is not the attitude which determines behaviour but behaviour which determines the attitude. This is, however, not the case in Bem's conception. According to him, the self-description which we call attitude can in turn become a self-instruction which guides our behaviour. The Russian psychologist Luria (1961) has suggested that children learn to guide their own behaviour by 'internalizing' the directive speech of their parents. Attitudes conceived of in this way can be interpreted as self-instructions which have their origin in the instructions of others. This behaviouristic interpretation remains strictly within the realm of the observable and refrains from making inferences about internal states.

However, in defining the concept of attitude, most social psychologists go at least one step beyond what can be observed. For example, DeFleur and Westie (1963) make a distinction between 'probabilistic' and 'latent process' conceptions of attitudes; the main difference between these two conceptions is in the kinds of inferences which their proponents derive from observable attitudinal responses.

The idea behind the probability conception is that attitudinal responses are more or less consistent; that is, a series of responses towards a given attitudinal stimulus is likely to show some degree of organization, structure or predictability. The attitude thus becomes an inferred property of these responses, namely their consistency. Stated in another way, attitudes are equated with the probability of recurrence of behaviour forms of a given type or direction. The latent process view also begins with the fact of response consistency; but it goes one step beyond this and postulates, as Allport and most social psychologists do, some hidden or hypothetical variable functioning within the individual, which shapes, acts upon or mediates the observable behaviour. Campbell (1963) expressed this idea when he stated that an attitude is 'evidenced' by consistency in response to social objects.

Campbell also proposed that an attitude, in the probabilistic tradition, could be defined as an (enduring) syndrome of response consistency with regard to (a set of) social objects. The advantage of this definition is that it focuses attention on the characteristic of attitudes that is basic to all the techniques of attitude measurement, response co-variation. In one way or another all these techniques are based on that principle. The question is whether one wants to regard an attitude simply as the behaviour (response) syndrome which can be observed or as some latent, hidden, variable creating the syndrome. As we have said, most social psychologists are willing to take this second step, but depending upon their theoretical orientation different conceptions of the intervening process or latent variable are proposed.

Is an attitude a lever or a template?

If one is willing to grant attitudes the status of an intervening variable or hypothetical construct, how does one picture such a variable or construct, since it cannot be observed? Basically there are two conceptions. Learning theorists view an attitude as an implicit response; cognitive theorists are more inclined to conceive attitudes as templates through which we perceive reality. This difference of opinion goes back to the early distinction between motor and mental attitudes, which was ignored by Allport (Jaspars, 1973).

The first attempt to cast the concept of attitude in terms of learning-behaviour theory was made by Doob (1947). He defined an attitude as 'an implicit drive producing response considered socially significant in the individual's society'. This definition states that an

$$S_e \longrightarrow (r_i \longrightarrow s_i) \dashrightarrow R_o$$

where S_e = stimulus or stimulus pattern external to the individual which gives rise to

r_i = implicit response which acts as

s_i = internal stimulus which leads to

R_o = overt response

Figure 12   Simple version of Doob's learning-behaviour theory model of attitudes

attitude is an 'implicit' response which occurs within the individual as a reaction to stimulus patterns and which acts at the same time as a stimulus affecting subsequent overt responses. In elaborating upon this definition Doob indicates that such an implicit response may be conscious or unconscious, distinctly verbal or vaguely proprioceptive, i.e. internal. In its most simple form such a theory can be represented by the diagram presented in Figure 12, although various authors have developed more complicated models of this intervening process (Rhine, 1958; Fishbein, 1967b).

An attitude seen as an implicit response has two important consequences. First, such a conception implies that an attitude is not an enduring disposition because, as Chein (1948) has pointed out, by any ordinary usage of the word, a 'response' occurs and is gone; it does not persist. Secondly, the outgoing, efferent, decoding part of the intervening process is stressed and not the incoming, afferent, perceptual or encoding aspects as most cognitive theorists do. The difference between these two interpretations can best be seen by looking for a moment at the problem of attitude change, to which we will return in chapter 11. When a person changes his attitude towards a particular social stimulus – e.g. the concept of 'politician' – because he hears that his friends have a high opinion of this profession, does it mean that he is only inclined to make new responses to a stimulus which he perceives in the same way as before or does the attitude change imply that he also re-defines the stimulus, and perceives it in a different way? Cognitive theorists like Asch (1948) have argued that such a re-definition indeed occurs and that attitude should be conceived as a 'set' which selectively influences the perception of the attitude object. Campbell (1963) has expressed these different conceptualizations aptly by speaking of the template and lever conceptions of attitudes, and he has represented the two interpretations in a cartoon-like illustration (Figure 13).

Figure 13 Template and lever conceptions of attitudes (from *Psychology, a Study of a Science*, vol. 6, edited by S. Koch. Copyright © McGraw-Hill Company, Inc., 1963. Used with permission of McGraw-Hill Book Company).

Most social psychologists, however, do not regard attitudes exclusively as response levers or as perceptual templates. In many conceptions the structure of the process intervening between stimulus and response is described either in terms of means and ends or in terms of affections, cognitions and conations.

The expectancy-value and the three-component structure of attitudes

For a long time it seemed that attitudes were divided into three related parts, the cognitive, affective and conative. This trichotomy has a venerable philosophical past and it is still in use in other areas of social psychology. It is a distinction that is related to the difference between the template and lever conceptions of attitudes discussed above. The cognitive part or component of attitudes refers to the perception or cognitive representation of the attitude object by the person. The affective or emotional component of attitudes refers to the person's feelings of liking or disliking of the attitude object. The conative or action component has to do with the person's behavioural tendencies regarding the attitude object.

Most theorists who espouse the three-component view of attitudes argue, however, that the three components are organized in a consistent fashion. Positive feelings about the attitude object go together with assigning positively evaluated traits and positive action tendencies to that attitude object. There is good evidence that there does exist at least some cognitive, affective and conative consistency of attitudes (Campbell, 1963; Vidulich and Krevanick, 1966). Most attempts to change people's feelings about certain issues by providing them with new information about the issue are based upon the implicit idea that cognitive and affective components of attitudes are positively related. In an interesting experiment Rosenberg (1960) was able to show that one can also change a person's beliefs or cognitions about an attitude object by changing his or her affections for the attitude object by means of post-hypnotic suggestion.

More recent attitude theories (Rosenberg, 1956; Zajonc, 1960; Fishbein, 1963; Jones and Gerard, 1967) tend to describe the structure of attitudes as a composite of expectations (i.e. perceived instrumentality or 'usefulness' of the attitude object to the person's goals, or the perception that the attitude object has certain attributes) and values (i.e. the evaluation of the goals or attributes related to the attitude object). There is quite clearly an attempt in models or theories, such as for example Fishbein's, to separate the cognitive from the evaluative or affective components of attitudes. Beliefs about an attitude object are defined as the perception of associations between the object of attitude and certain attributes or goals. Thus typical belief statements found in attitude research are expressions like: 'negroes are athletic' or 'having a steady income tends to be achieved by being a member of a trade union'.

The affective or value aspects of an attitude are defined as the evaluation of the associated goals or attributes. Thus the evaluations corresponding to the beliefs just mentioned could imply that the attribute 'athletic' or 'having a steady income' are good, valuable, etc. Fishbein's theory does not assume that evaluations and beliefs are positively related, but simply that the attitude is the sum of the evaluatively weighted beliefs. (There is, in fact, considerable controversy about Fishbein's assumption that an attitude is the weighted sum of the beliefs and not, for example, the weighted average). Fishbein does not regard action tendencies as a component of attitudes but treats these tendencies as behavioural intentions which are in part determined by the attitude of the person towards the act that he intends to perform.

Attitudes and related concepts

Both conceptions of attitudes – the three-component model and the expectancy-value model – point to two important issues about the nature of attitudes. In the first place, there are, as we have seen, alternative views as to what an attitude is. Is it simply a self-description? Is it a response syndrome, an intervening variable, an internal response, a disposition, a perceptual template? All these conceptions exist and it should not surprise us therefore that it is not always easy to distinguish attitudes from related concepts like beliefs, opinions, values, etc. Campbell, who defines an attitude as an acquired behavioural disposition, was able, as we saw before, to come up with approximately seventy-five concepts in psychology which fall more or less under the same definition. Nevertheless some attempts have been made to distinguish between attitudes and related concepts. One such distinction has been discussed already in relation to Fishbein's attitude theory. According to Fishbein, an attitude is an evaluatively weighted sum of beliefs, whereas beliefs are perceptions of association between attitude objects and attributes or goals. Beliefs in Fishbein's terminology are what other social psychologists have called cognitions, knowledge or opinions. The distinction that is usually made between these concepts and the concept of attitude is analogous to the distinction made by Fishbein. In the conception deriving from learning theories (Doob, 1947), attitudes have cue and drive properties whereas knowledge has only cue properties, which is about the same as saying that attitudes have affective (dynamic) and cognitive (directive) properties whereas knowledge has only the latter characteristic. A distinction along similar lines has been proposed for the concepts of attitude and opinion. An opinion according to this view would be similar to a belief in Fishbein's terminology. As a matter of fact Fishbein interchanges the use of both concepts (Fishbein and Ajzen, 1972). Other social psychologists have suggested, however, that opinions are overt expressions of attitudes, or that opinions deal with matters of fact which are potentially verifiable, whereas attitudes refer to matters of taste. It should be realized, however, that these two distinctions are not in contradiction with the definition of opinion given by Fishbein.

Values and attitudes form another pair of related concepts. Sometimes a value is simply seen as a broader attitude but more often values are regarded as components of attitudes. This is especially clear in expectancy-value theories of attitudes. It should be pointed out that values are here defined in a subjective way. Heider (1958) has shown, however, that in common-sense psychology values carry the connotation of being 'objectively' positive. Values in this sense are, like norms, impersonal and have interpersonal validity.

We could go on with this discussion and compare the concept of attitude with the many related concepts which have been proposed in psychology to explain why people react differently to the same situations. But this would be a futile exercise consisting mainly of trying to find distinctions that correspond to existing names rather than dealing with real distinctions for which a discriminating terminology is required.

What appears to transpire from the various conceptions of attitudes is at least the very general notion of a covert process or structure, with cognitive and motivational properties, which determines behaviour. A crucial problem is how successful we are in predicting behaviour from a knowledge of a person's attitude. This is the second basic question which is raised by the various conceptions of attitudes discussed above. But before we can discuss the problems of predicting behaviour from attitudes, the methods used for measuring attitudes need to be briefly presented.

The measurement of attitudes

In his theoretical study of the attitude concept, Campbell (1963) approaches the problem of attitude measurement from a very general and fundamental point of view, in line with his definition of the concept of attitude as a behavioural disposition. In his view such a disposition provides coordinations of behaviour with reference to environmental settings. The presence of a certain attitude, or, more generally, of a disposition can thus be inferred from the co-variation that is observed between stimuli and the responses of a person to these stimuli, as was discussed on p. 258.

A procedure for attitude measurement that is consistent with this notion would therefore seem to be to assign an observer to the person whose attitude we want to know and to follow this person around, writing down the stimuli he encounters and his responses to these stimuli. If the person would show consistently a certain type of behaviour (response) in certain situations (stimuli), and not in other situations, we would be inclined to infer that he has a disposition to behave in a particular way. Needless to say, this is a time-consuming procedure which is seldom adopted by social psychologists for measuring attitudes. A possible model is a study by Barker and Wright (1963) in which an eight-year-old boy was followed around for a whole day. Although the study was not designed for measuring the attitudes of the boy, the observational record of the boy's behaviour in his natural surroundings certainly makes such a study possible. For evaluating the actual current practices of attitude measurement, it is important to keep this 'ideal' procedure in mind as a criterion.

Most attitude measurement procedures introduce a number of restrictions. First of all it is not customary to follow persons around in their natural surroundings and observe all their reactions to a variety of stimuli. Usually we are interested only in a particular type of reaction to a specific class of stimuli. We may want to know for instance whether a person or group of persons are disposed to react positively or negatively to members of a certain minority group. Thus if we are interested in finding out whether a negative attitude exists in the United States towards Chinese people we might travel around the country in the company of a Chinese couple, visit as many restaurants, hotels and camping grounds as we can and observe the reactions of the owners or managers of these places. Are our 'stimulus' couple received courteously or are they refused admittance? That is essentially the procedure which was followed in a well-known study by LaPiere in the thirties (LaPiere, 1935).

Again this is obviously not a very practical procedure for studying attitudes and for that reason we may be tempted instead to telephone or write to a number of restaurants and hotels in order to make reservations for a couple, with a Chinese name, to see whether such reservations are accepted or not. In other words we could substitute for the actual stimulus (the Chinese couple) a symbolic representation of the stimulus (a fictitious name) and we would hope that this symbolic stimulus would elicit a reaction similar to the response to the actual stimulus. This is certainly not always the case, but it is more or less standard procedure in attitude measurement to work with substitute stimuli. These substitute stimuli are moreover usually verbal statements about the attitude object.

In the course of the past fifty years various procedures for measuring attitudes have been developed along these lines and the formulation of an attitude as a disposition relating stimuli and responses allows us to distinguish three broad approaches to attitude measurement. As we have seen, the observations we are likely to collect in studying attitudes are verbal *responses* of a number of *people* or subjects to a particular class of *stimuli*. Consequently some attitude measurement procedures can be described as *subject-centred* approaches, others as *stimulus-centred* approaches and a third group of procedures as *response-centred* approaches (Torgerson, 1958).

Perhaps the most common type of attitude scale has been the subject-centred approach pioneered by Likert (1932). The investigator begins by collecting a large number of statements which he considers relevant to the attitude he wishes to measure. These are then administered to a pilot sample of subjects each of whom is asked to indicate, usually on a five- or seven-point scale, how strongly he approves or disapproves of each statement, and a total score is calculated for each subject. There then follows the most distinctive step in the Likert-type procedure, a very careful item analysis to discover the items which agree amongst themselves and discriminate most effectively amongst the subjects. A major part of this analysis is the calculation, for each item in turn, of the correlation between all the scores on that item or statement and the total scores of all the subjects. As a result, items which do not distinguish amongst subjects, or which are ambiguous or which appear to be measuring something other than the attitude in question are removed, and a more limited number, say from ten to thirty, of intercorrelating and discriminating items are selected to make up the scale to be used in the actual investigation, where the procedure is as described for the subjects in the pilot sample.

An alternative, but equally careful and complex, procedure is that involved in the Thurstone-type stimulus-centred approach (Thurstone and Chave, 1929). This again begins with the collection of a large number of statements representing a wide variety of positions on the issue. But these are then presented to a group of 'judges' who are asked, not to indicate their own attitudes, but, as objectively as possible, to sort all the statements into eleven piles or categories in terms of how favourable or unfavourable an attitude is implied by each statement. A score or scale value can then be calculated for each statement or stimulus by taking account of the judgements of all the judges. Items which appear ambiguous or on which judges disagree markedly amongst themselves are eliminated and the final scale itself consists of a selection of the remaining items which are chosen so that they are distributed at roughly equal intervals across the whole range of scale values. Subjects, to whom the scale is then administered, are asked to select the three (or four) items which best represent their views and a score for each individual is calculated from the scale values of the items he chooses.

A third approach is the response-centred one represented by Guttman-type scaling. Here the hope is, via a very detailed analysis of patterns of responses of pilot subjects, to discover a limited set of statements which are perfectly ordered in terms of favourability – unfavourability of attitude. Thus, if an individual replied 'yes' to the item 'Would you accept West Indians as work-mates?' one should expect him also to say 'Yes' to all items which implied willingness to associate in even less intimate situations; if the same individual said 'No' to 'Would you accept West Indians as neighbours?', unwillingness to associate might then be expected in all more intimate situations. In a perfect Guttman scale, it should be possible just from a knowledge of the total number of items endorsed by an individual to reproduce perfectly the pattern of his responses.

To summarize, in a stimulus-centred approach, such as a Thurstone-type scale, the assignment by 'judges' of scale values to stimuli such as attitude statements is the cardinal part of the procedure. In the response-centred approach, for example the construction of a Guttman scalogram, an analysis of response patterns is the central feature of the procedure. In the subject-centred approach, such as a Likert-type scale, the analysis of the co-variation of the reactions of the subjects is the essential part of the construction of an attitude scale. Technical treatments of these and other attitude measurement procedures can be found in Dawes (1971) and Edwards (1957).

If one conceives of attitudes as behavioural dispositions which can be interpreted as relatively enduring properties of persons which vary in degree, then, according to Scott (1968), an adequate measure of attitudes would:

1. reflect the intended property veridically;
2. be unaffected by irrelevant characteristics either within the subject or within the testing situation;
3. not modify the property in the course of measuring it;
4. make sufficiently fine distinctions among persons to represent gradations along the scales as conceived;

5. yield results substantially equivalent to those produced by another adequate instrument measuring the same property;
6. yield equivalent scores on a retest administered within a time period in which the property can be assumed to remain constant;
7. be relatively easy to construct, administer, score and interpret (p. 251).

These characteristics can be summarized under two main headings which were briefly discussed at the end of chapter 1: *validity* and *reliability* of attitude measures. A measure of an attitude is valid to the extent that the measurement instrument measures what it intends to measure. Extraneous determinants influence the validity of attitude measurements unfavourably. For this reason many attempts have been made to reduce the influence of other characteristics of the respondents, to reduce the influence of irrelevant characteristics of the testing situation, and to prevent the attitude being modified in the course of measuring it.

These various approaches for dealing with aspects of the problem of validity of attitude measurement techniques still leave us with the question of how to determine whether an attitude scale really measures what it intends to measure.

One way of answering this question is by testing the scale against a criterion which the scale is supposed to *predict*. To a certain extent this is the problem of the attitude–behaviour relationship which will be discussed on pp. 271–5. In many cases it is not easy, however, to specify a single unique criterion which a particular attitude is supposed to predict, but to the extent that such criteria are available prediction can be used to determine validity. As we have pointed out, this does not necessarily imply that a positive correlation between attitude scales and criterion behaviour must be found. Criterion behaviour and attitudinal responses should refer to the same latent disposition; that is, test for *predictive validity*.

Another way of determining validity is to test the measurement instrument by correlation with theoretically relevant variables. This procedure is sometimes called *construct validation*. The basic idea is that two different instruments which, on theoretical grounds, are supposed to measure, at least in part, the same construct should show positive intercorrelations. The danger implicit in this procedure is of course that positive intercorrelations may be caused also by such spurious similarities as comparable administration procedures. It is clear, therefore, that a construct validation procedure should rule out such influences. A procedure for doing this to some extent has been proposed by Campbell and Fiske (1959). The main characteristic of this procedure is to measure a variety of attitudes (or more generally 'traits') by various techniques or methods. The approach is therefore known as the multi-trait/multi-method procedure.

The multi-trait/multi-method procedure points in addition to some of the other characteristics of adequate attitude measures formulated by Scott (1968), which we have subsumed under the main heading of *reliability*. The least one can expect of an attitude measurement is that there is agreement between two efforts to measure the same attitude through maximally similar methods. An attitude scale should at least measure something consistently; in other words the scale should be a reliable measurement instrument. Two halves of the same scale, a second administration of the same scale or a parallel scale should produce the same or similar results. In fact, each of the three approaches to measurement discussed above can be used to construct attitude scales of high reliability. It should be remembered, however, that although reliability of measurement is a necessary condition for validity, it is by no means a sufficient condition for it.

Attitudes and behaviour

Do attitudes predict behaviour? To the dismay of many social psychologists a considerable amount of research devoted to this question appears to show that little or no such relation exists. Wicker (1969) who has reviewed most of the work in this area concludes that 'taken as a whole, these studies neglect that it is considerably more likely that attitudes will be unrelated or only slightly related to overt behaviours than that attitudes will be closely related to actions. Product moment correlation coefficients ... are rarely above 0·30 and often are near zero' (p. 65).

Does this mean that we should abandon the concept of attitude in social psychology? Probably not. It is certainly true that a case against attitudes and attitude research can be made (Jaspars, 1973) but one overstates it when one argues that the concept is not necessary (Abelson, 1972) or should be abandoned (Chein, 1948).

A common reaction to the negative findings just mentioned is to solve the problem by denying that it exists. Because attitudes are usually measured by verbal means one can sidestep the problems of the relationship between attitudes and overt behaviour by denying that anything exists beyond the verbal expressions or that such scales measure whatever they measure; so why worry! It is of course true that what people have to say about each other or about various social issues can have some intrinsic value and may be studied in its own right, but such a position certainly overlooks the fact that the concept of attitude was not developed as a *l'art pour l'art* idea, but to explain variable stimulus–response connections.

It is more common, therefore, to point out that behaviour is determined by other factors besides attitudes and that if one wants to predict behaviour accurately these other factors should be taken into account. Wicker (1969) suggests that the following factors may be important:

1. personal factors
    a. other attitudes
    b. competing motives
    c. verbal, intellectual, social abilities
    d. activity levels

2. situational factors
    a. actual or considered presence of certain people
    b. normative prescriptions of proper behaviour
    c. alternative behaviour available
    d. specificity of attitude objects
    e. unforeseen extraneous events
    f. expected and/or actual consequences of various acts.

Although it is very likely that one or more of these factors may interfere with the relationship between attitudes and behaviour and when taken into account might lead to better predictions of behaviour, we do not as yet have much evidence on these issues. The factors suggested by Wicker originate mainly from *a posteriori* explanations given by researchers who failed to find a correlation between attitudes and behaviour. Nevertheless, it seems plausible that a combination of all or some of these factors should make predictions of behaviour possible, since the list of factors given by Wicker contains the components of an almost complete theory of social behaviour.

Fishbein (1967b) has actually developed a relevant theory of behaviour as an extension of his attitude theory. In this theory three kinds of variables that function as the basic determinants of behaviour are identified as: (i) attitudes towards the behaviour; (ii) normative beliefs (both personal and social), and (iii) motivation to comply with the norms. Note that Fishbein does not deal with the general attitude of a person towards a social object but with the attitude towards a particular behaviour in a given situation. The attitude in this restricted sense, according to his definition of attitudes, is composed of the beliefs of the person about the consequences of a certain act in the situation and his evaluation of these consequences. The normative factor of Fishbein's behaviour theory also consists of two components; the belief about what the individual personally feels he should do and the belief about what society says he should do. These normative beliefs are in turn weighted by the person's motivation to comply with the norms.

Symbolically, the central equation of the theory can be expressed as follows:

$$B \approx BI \ [Aact] \ W_0 \ + \ [NB(Mo)] \ W_1$$

where:

B = overt behaviour
BI = behavioural intention
$Aact$ = attitude toward the act
NB = normative belief
Mo = motivation to comply with the normative belief
W_0 and W_1 are empirically determined weights.

Fishbein does not deny that other factors mentioned by Wicker are important but he suggests that they operate indirectly by influencing one or more of the three basic determinants.

We do not have as yet sufficient evidence to conclude whether Fishbein's theory can handle the presumably complex relationship between attitudes and behaviour suggested by Wicker's list of interfering factors. Empirical studies have so far dealt only with fairly trivial problems and avoided the real issue by substituting, as in Fishbein's formula, behavioural intentions for behaviour (e.g. Ajzen and Fishbein, 1972). For a number of reasons, studies of this type do not provide us with the evidence that is necessary to show that in complex real-life situations attitudes are important determinants of behaviour in conjunction with other factors. The general idea and Fishbein's specification of it may still be correct but until we have good evidence, no definite conclusion can be drawn.

Finally it is important to realize that the search for a positive association between attitudes and behaviour may be, in one sense, a misguided effort, because we are not testing and cannot test directly the hypothesis that attitudes are important determinants of behaviour; we can measure an implicit response or disposition only by inferring attitudes on the basis of behavioural indices. In most cases verbal attitude measures are used and the correlation coefficients we have referred to above are in fact measures of association between verbal and other behavioural responses. The relationships we have discussed are associations between what people say and what they do. From the research reported above and, above all, from everyday experience, we know that people do not always do what they say. But that is not really the issue. The real question is whether verbal and other behavioural responses are, in fact, expressions of the same underlying implicit response or disposition. Even assuming that this is the case, it does not follow necessarily that verbal and other behavioural indices of a person's attitude should correlate highly.

The most obvious reason that militates against a strong correlation between the two types of attitude expressions is suggested by Wicker's list of interfering factors. To the extent that these factors are the same in the 'verbal' and the 'other behaviour' situation, a positive association between what people say and what they do can be expected. However, this does not imply that even when those factors are the same or similar a strong association need be found in terms of a traditional coefficient of correlation. A verbal measure may be a much weaker index of an underlying attitude than some other behavioural response. It may require simply a much stronger negative attitude for the owner of a restaurant to refuse entry to a Chinese couple than to cancel a reservation in writing (LaPiere,

1935). It is highly probable that somebody who shows the first type of behaviour will also show the second type of behaviour, but the reverse does not hold. Somebody who takes the high hurdle, to borrow an illustration from Campbell (1963), usually also takes the low hurdle but the reverse is much less likely. This may be the most important intrinsic reason why it is so difficult to predict actual behaviour in a particular situation from a knowledge of a person's verbal response to a questionnaire. If we could develop ways of measuring attitudes that would make the verbal hurdle of the same height as the overt behavioural hurdle, perhaps by taking into account the factors suggested by Wicker, or in the form proposed by Fishbein, we might be able to restore the concept of attitude as an important determinant of social behaviour to its rightful status in social psychology.

Summary

An attitude is usually defined as a residue of past experience which is retained by the individual in the form of a disposition or implicit response and as such affects the behaviour. Opinions about the exact nature of attitudes differ. According to Bem attitudes should merely be considered as self-instructions which can be directly obtained. Most social psychologists argue, however, that attitudes are intervening variables or hypothetical constructs which cannot be observed directly. Learning theorists define this variable or construct as an implicit response stressing the efferent or decoding part of the intervening process, whereas cognitive theorists emphasize the perceptual or encoding part. In other conceptions the process intervening between stimuli and responses is either described in terms of means and ends or in terms of affect, cognition and conation.

Opinions and beliefs lack the affective or dynamic qualities of attitudes. Values are either seen as broader attitudes or as the evaluation component of attitudes.

Over the years, three different approaches to attitude measurement have emerged which can be described as stimulus-centred, response-centred and subject-centred, each of which must be looked at in terms of the validity and reliability of the scales produced.

The correlation between measured attitudes and behaviour is in general rather low. This can be explained by assuming that other factors also influence behaviour and in this way disturb the relationship between what people say and what they do.

Further Reading

McGuire, W. J. (1969), 'The nature of attitudes and attitude change', in G. Lindzey and E. Aronson (eds.), *The Handbook of Social Psychology*, vol. 3, 2nd ed., Reading, Mass., Addison-Wesley. Probably the best overall review of the field.

Jahoda, M., and Warren, N., eds. (1966, 1973), *Attitudes: Selected readings*, 1st and 2nd eds., Penguin Books. Both editions contain useful and only partially overlapping selections of important studies on attitudes.

Fishbein, M., ed. (1967), *Attitude Theory and Measurement*, New York, Wiley. A book of readings which pays special attention to questions of theory and measurement.

Dawes, R. M. (1971), *Fundamentals of Attitude Measurement*, New York, Wiley. The best modern technical treatment of attitude scaling.

Thomas, K., ed. (1971), *Attitudes and Behaviour: Selected readings*, Penguin Books. A useful collection of papers on the relations, and lack of relations, between attitudes and behaviour.

Chapter 11
Determinants of Attitudes and Attitude Change

J. M. F. Jaspars

Introduction

Most studies of attitude change have been guided by common-sense notions about the factors important in determining attitudes and attitude change. In so far as theoretical models have been proposed for describing and explaining attitude change, the connection with empirical research has been fairly loose. This is not to say that empirical studies could not be related to these theoretical notions. On the contrary, in this chapter we will try to show first of all how various models of attitude change proposed in the literature are interrelated, and secondly how results of experimental and field research can be organized using this theoretical frame of reference. For this reason we will not present an exhaustive survey of empirical findings; research in the area of attitude change is very extensive and such surveys have already been published elsewhere (Fishbein and Ajzen, 1972; McGuire, 1969; Kiesler and Munson, 1975). It is still one of the major areas of social psychological research, although research efforts have recently taken a different line of attack (Kiesler and Munson, 1975).

Attitudes are, as we have seen, usually considered as residues of previous experience which influence behaviour either in the form of dispositions or as internal responses. This rules out, by definition, the possibility that attitudes could be determined directly by genetic or physiological factors. Still, one has to consider the possibility that dispositions which are generally seen as determined by the social environment could have genetic or physiological roots. McGuire (1969) points to possible genetic factors involved in ethnocentrism, and to the effects of ageing, illness or certain pharmacological and surgical interventions on social attitudes. One has to admit, however, that the evidence is only indirect. With respect to genetic factors McGuire's argument is mainly based on animal studies; with respect to physiological factors it is obviously very difficult to separate the effect of illness or age *per se* from the effects of altered social roles or accumulated experience.

In practice, social psychologists have paid almost exclusive attention to the social environment as the major determinant of (social) attitudes. In general, attention in attitude research has focused on social communication as *the* determinant of attitude change. The effect of direct experience with the attitude object or the effect of education on attitude formation are usually studied under other headings in social psychology, such as intergroup relations and socialization (see chapters 4, 16 and 17). We will accept this traditional distinction in our discussion of attitude change, but we want also to point out that much of what will be said here can be applied to studies of social influence which are often discussed under a different heading (see chapter 8).

Communication models of attitude change

Attitude change can be seen as a function of the various components constituting the process of transmitting information. The terminology for describing this social process is borrowed from communication engineering. In any communication system one can distinguish the *source* of communication (or *sender*) which emits the information, the information itself which constitutes the *message*, the communication *channel* which mediates the message, and the *receiver*. The source is directly or indirectly a person or group of persons; the message can be considered simply as what is said, whereas the channel refers to how messages are transmitted to the receiver, who, like the source, is a person or group of persons. When the effects of each of these components on attitudes are studied, the components can be varied along numerous dimensions. This is what in fact has been done without much regard to theory and has resulted in a rather heterogeneous collection of research findings. The sort of questions which have been asked include: Is an expert source more effective than a non-expert? What is the effect of similarity between source and receiver? Are emotional messages more effective than rational appeals? What is the effect of ordering various parts of a message in different ways? Are written messages more effective than spoken messages? How effective are the mass media as compared with person-to-person communication? Is active participation of the receiver in the communication process more effective than passive reception? Are some people easier to influence than others?

It should be realized moreover that all these questions can be asked, and to some extent have been asked, with respect to various aspects of the effects of the communication process. Which component of an attitude has been affected by the communication; the affective, the cognitive or the behavioural? If no effect is apparent, is it because the receiver has not paid attention to the message or because he has not understood it? If an effect results, how long will it last?

In order to create some structure in this abundance of questions and findings we will first discuss a general communication model based on various models presented in the literature and then show how research findings from a number of areas of research can be related to this general model.

In a formal sense we have basically a simple situation. The message in a social communication situation usually consists of statements or assertions by the source expressing or explicitly advocating an attitudinal position with respect to the attitude object. Let us call this, the advocated attitude of the source towards the attitude object, *as perceived by the receiver, A_s*. On the other hand, we have also the attitude of the receiver towards the attitude object before the communication between source and receiver takes place. Let us call this, the original attitude of the receiver towards the attitude object, A_r.

The question of attitude change through communication now reduces to the fundamental issue of how the receiver will integrate his original position and the position expressed by the source. General information processing theories suggest that this is done mainly in a simple additive fashion (Rosenberg, 1968). There is some evidence that information processing is more complex than is suggested here, but it appears that complex models and simple additive models have approximately the same predictive power (Slovic and Lichenstein, 1971).

Applied to the attitude change problem a general additive information processing theory would predict that after the communication has taken place

$$A_r' = W_s A_s + W_r A_r \tag{1}$$

where:

A_r' = attitude of the receiver towards the attitude object after the communication

A_r = original attitude of the receiver towards the attitude object

A_s = the attitude towards the attitude object expressed by the source

W_s and W_r = weights assigned to the values of the attitudes expressed or held by source and receiver.

In this general form equation 1 can be interpreted and has been interpreted in two different ways depending upon the interpretation given to the weights. If we simply treat the weights in a straightforward absolute manner, equation 1 suggests that the attitude of the receiver after the communication is the weighted *sum* of the originally held attitude and the attitude advocated by the source. For instance, if the receiver is in favour of, say, legalizing abortion, and the source tries to convince him that abortion should be legalized, a *summative* attitude change model predicts that the attitude of the receiver towards legalized abortion would become even more favourable.

If we interpret the weights in equation 1 in a relative sense by assuming that

$$w_s = \frac{W_s}{W_s + W_r} \quad \text{and} \quad w_r = \frac{W_r}{W_s + W_r} \tag{2}$$

an *averaging* model of information processing would result and equation 1 would become

$$A_r' = \frac{w_s A_s + w_r A_r}{w_s + w_r} \tag{3}$$

Equation 3 indicates that the attitude held by the receiver after the communication will be the weighted average of his original attitude and the attitude expressed by the source. In the example presented above this could mean that if the source expresses a less favourable (but still positive) attitude towards legalized abortion than the attitude held originally by the receiver, the receiver would become (slightly) less positive about this issue. A summative model would predict, as we have seen, a more favourable attitude in this case.

Since the evidence with respect to these two information processing models is equivocal and because the averaging model has been widely applied to attitude change studies we will adopt the second, relative, interpretation of the weights to be assigned to the attitude values of source and receiver. At any rate, in most attitude change situations the positions of the source and receiver are opposite to each other; and therefore, a summative and an averaging model of attitude change will lead to similar predictions in most cases.

So far we have only expressed the attitude of the receiver before and after the communication in relation to the message. We have not yet expressed the attitude change that takes place in the receiver directly. It is easy to see, however, how this could be done by developing equation 3 if attitude change ($\triangle A_r$) is conceived as the difference between A_r' and A_r.

$$\triangle A_r = A_r' - A_r = \frac{w_s A_s + w_r A_r}{w_s + w_r} - A_r \qquad (4)$$

which leads to

$$\triangle A_r = \frac{w_s A_s + w_r A_r - A_r(w_s + w_r)}{w_s + w_r} \qquad (5)$$

which simplifies to

$$\triangle A_r = \frac{w_s A_s - w_s A_r}{w_s + w_r} \qquad (6)$$

or

$$\triangle A_r = \frac{w_s}{w_s + w_r}(A_s - A_r) \qquad (7)$$

Equation 7 indicates that attitude change is a function of the algebraic difference between the attitude expressed by the source and the original attitude of the receiver, multiplied by the relative weight of the source. This is in effect a special case of the so-called proportional change model of Anderson and Hovland (1957) which expresses the relative weight of the source simply as a general change parameter, C. Psychologically the change parameter is interpreted sometimes as the susceptibility of the receiver to the message communicated by the source.

The special case of the proportional change model which we have presented here suggests that both forces in the source and in the receiver contribute to the change parameter. This is essentially the position taken by French (1956) who has applied the proportional change model to social influence processes in small groups. According to a slightly modified restatement of French's formulation, the strength of the *resultant force* which a source A can exert on a receiver B in the direction of A's attitude is proportional to: (i) the strength of the basis of *power of A* over B and (ii) *the size of the discrepancy* between their attitudes. As was discussed in chapter 7, the basis of power of A over B can be, for example, the liking of B for A, the ability of A to mediate rewards or punishments for B, the legal right of A to prescribe a certain behaviour for B, the extent to which A has greater resources (knowledge or information) than B (French and Raven, 1959). Representation of attitude change according to this model is given in diagram form in Figure 14.

Figure 14 illustrates the weighted average model of attitude change in a simple fashion. The slopes of the lines originating from the attitude positions of the source and the receiver indicate the weights or the power S and R have with respect to each other (and potentially with respect to other Rs or Ss) on the attitude continuum. The size of the attitude discrepancy is represented by the distance between A_s and A_r on the attitude continuum. The position of the receiver after the communication (A_r') is the point of intersection (equilibrium) where the power of the source over the receiver equals the power (or resistance) of the receiver with respect to the source. The reader can easily check, by assigning numerical values to w, w_r, A_s and A_r, that this is indeed a diagrammatic representation of equation 7. The basic

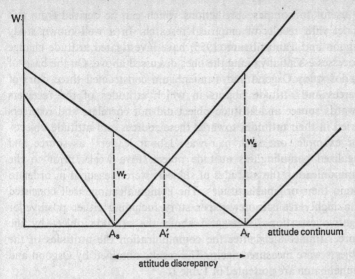

Figure 14   Attitude change according to a weighted averaging model

point of the model is that any factors which influence the process of attitude change can be related either to the slopes of the force lines in Figure 14 or to the discrepancy between the positions of S and R on the attitude continuum. Factors related to characteristics of the *source* can be represented by a change in the slope of the force line originating at A_s. Factors related to the *message* can be incorporated in the model by changing the position of A_s on the attitude continuum. A change of *channel* characteristics can be conceived of as related to either the slopes or the discrepancy between attitude positions. In social communication situations the distinction between channel and message (or even between channel and source or receiver) is sometimes difficult to make and rather arbitrary, because conveying a message in a different way can very often be interpreted as conveying a different message. We will therefore not make a distinction between (formal) message factors and channel factors in the rest of this discussion. *Receiver* characteristics finally can be related to the slope of the resistance line originating from A_r.

Before developing our attitude change model any further it may be useful to compare predictions which can be derived from this model with results of empirical research. In a well-known study Osgood and Tannenbaum (1955) have investigated attitude change processes essentially along the lines discussed above. On the basis of a pilot study Osgood and Tannenbaum constructed three pairs of sources and attitude objects in which attitudes of the receivers towards source and attitude object did not correlate and receivers varied in their attitudes towards these sources and attitude objects. For example, one such pair was 'labour leaders' as source and 'legalized gambling' as attitude object. Five weeks prior to the communication the attitudes of subjects were measured in order to obtain their original attitudes. The communication itself consisted of a highly realistic newspaper story including either positive or negative assertions (messages) about the attitude object by the source. Immediately after the communication the attitudes of the subjects were measured again. The results obtained by Osgood and Tannenbaum are presented in Table 1.

TABLE 1   *Attitude change as a function of message and receiver factors* (re-computed from Osgood and Tannenbaum, 1955)

	Original attitude of receiver toward attitude object		
	positive	*neutral*	*negative*
positive message about attitude object	+0·08	+0·34	+0·18
negative message about attitude object	−0·17	−0·30	−0·07

Attitudes were measured on seven-point scales with extreme values of −3 and +3. The scores in the table represent average direction and amount of change under the different conditions.

If we compare the results obtained by Osgood and Tannenbaum with our expectations based upon equation 7 or Figure 14, it is clear that the major implication of the model is confirmed by the results. A positive message by the source produces a change in a positive direction, a negative message produces a negative change. It is equally obvious that the changes are fairly small. The largest change does not amount to more than a twentieth of the total range. This is typical of most (experimental) attitude change studies.

There is, however, also quite clearly an exception to what one could have expected on the basis of the attitude change model presented above. According to the model, changes should be larger when the discrepancy between the attitude expressed by the source (message) and the original attitude of the receiver is larger. This is not the case, however. The largest changes are found when the initial attitude of the receiver is neutral. Apparently it is more difficult to change an extreme attitude than a neutral attitude. This suggests that the *weight* to be assigned to the *receiver is a function of his original position on the attitude continuum*. In the neutral region of the attitude continuum the slope of his resistance line is smaller and the point of intersection in Figure 14 will be closer to the attitude position expressed by the source. The results of the Osgood and Tannenbaum study thus give us a clue as to how to interpret w_r. If our model is to correspond with the results of the Osgood and Tannenbaum study we would have to assume that w_r is at least a function of the original attitude of the receiver A_r.

What about the weight to be assigned to the source? It seems reasonable to assume that this weight is at least in part determined by the attitude toward the source. If the attitude of the receiver towards the source is positive the power of the source over the receiver is greater according to French and Raven (1959), and consequently the force line of the source in Figure 14 would be steeper, resulting in a larger attitude shift in the direction of the position advocated by the source. Since Osgood and Tannenbaum also measured the attitude of the receivers towards the various sources it is possible to test this interpretation of the model. Table 2 presents the results of the Osgood and Tannenbaum study again, but now separately for receivers with positive, neutral and negative attitudes towards the source.

As can be seen our expectations are confirmed in the sense that a positive source has a greater influence in the direction implied by the sign of the message. It seems reasonable, therefore, to assume that

TABLE 2 *Attitude change as a function of message, source and receiver factors*
(re-computed from Osgood and Tannenbaum, 1955)

	Original attitude of receiver toward attitude object		
	positive	*neutral*	*negative*
positive message			
by positive source	+0·19	+0·90	+0·40
by neutral source	+0·14	+0·30	+0·18
by negative source	−0·09	−0·19	−0·03
negative message			
by positive source	−0·32	−0·67	−0·14
by neutral source	−0·27	−0·29	−0·13
by negative source	+0·07	+0·08	+0·06

Attitudes are measured on seven-point scales with extreme values of +3 and −3. Scores represent average direction and amount of change under the different conditions.

w_s is at least in part a function of the attitude of the receiver toward the source, S_r.

Table 2 shows, however, that the influence of the source goes beyond enhancing the change implied by the message. A negative source making positive statements appears to have a negative effect and a negative source making negative statements has apparently a small positive effect. Apart from assuming that a positive source receives a larger weight, we would have to assume that a negative source obtains a negative weight, which would lead to changes opposite to the direction intended by the source or we could take account of this effect by assuming that the position of the message on the attitude continuum is changed by the nature of the source. The discrepancy between the attitude expressed by the source and the attitude held by the receiver would be perceived as large by the receiver in the case of a positive source, and as small (or even on the other side of his own position) in the case of a negative source. The last solution is the one adopted by Osgood and Tannenbaum in the study to which we have referred. The model they have developed for explaining attitude change is known as the *principle of congruity* and is expressed below, using the notation we have developed here instead of Osgood and Tannenbaum's original notation.

$$\triangle A_r = \frac{|S_r|}{|S_r| + |A_r|}(S_r A_s - A_r) \tag{8}$$

Here $|S_r|$ and $|A_r|$ and the absolute values of S_r and A_r, are utilized to express the fact that more extremely held attitudes should receive larger weights. The 'boomerang effect' of a negative source is taken into account by multiplying A_s by S_r. The congruity model developed by Osgood and Tannenbaum can thus be considered as a special case of the weighted averaging model, which we have proposed in equation 7 and Figure 14. The reverse effect of a negative source can be taken into account by assuming that the source has negative power over the receiver, as was suggested above.

We will therefore propose as a general attitude change model the model expressed by equation 7 and Figure 14, but we have to add now that (i) the weight to be assigned to the receiver is a curvilinear function of his position on the attitude continuum, i.e. the more extreme his position, the higher the weight will be, and (ii) the weight to be assigned to the source is a function of the attitude of the receiver towards the source.

Now that we have formulated our general model of attitude change in terms of source, message and receiver parameters, we have to specify the variables which determine the value of these parameters. These may be different from situation to situation and form a rather heterogeneous collection of determinants, but they are functionally equivalent in their effects on the parameters of our general model. This two-stage approach to the problem of attitude change is important because the variables which we are going to discuss do not influence attitude change simply and directly, since the various parameters interact in their influence on attitudes. Thus it does not make much sense to study, in isolation, the effect of the 'expertness' of a source on a person's attitude, because the effect of the source variable depends also on the source-receiver discrepancy and on the 'resistance' weight to be assigned to the receiver. (Expertness can, however, affect directly the weight of the source in the communication situation.) In discussing research findings we will have to keep this two-stage analysis in mind, because it can help to reconcile some inconsistent results that have been reported.

It should be noted that the attitude change model presented above does not do justice to all the theoretical formulations of attitudes and attitude change which have been proposed. It captures the main points of the learning approach, together with a field theoretical and a cognitive consistency approach to the study of attitude change. However, it does not deal with the cognitive approach in the broader sense, nor with the functional approach (Asch, 1948, 1952; Katz, 1960; Katz and Stotland, 1959).

According to functional theory attitude change depends heavily upon the function of the particular attitude for the individual. First, holding a certain attitude can have a *utilitarian or adaptive function* for the individual. By this Katz (1960) and Katz and Stotland (1959) mean that holding certain attitudes can be instrumental in reaching a particular goal. In the famous study, *The Authoritarian Personality*, Adorno *et al.* (1950) were able to show that 'conventional anti-semites' were hostile towards Jews because this facilitated their acceptance by an anti-semitic environment. Secondly, an attitude can have an *economic or 'knowledge' function* because attitudes involve a simplification, or oversimplification, of the complexity of the real world. As such they provide us with fairly straightforward implications for action in complex situations. Thirdly, attitudes can have an *expressive function* according to Katz (1960). The expression of an attitude can be seen as an opportunity for the *acting out* of tensions or as a means of *self-assertion* or a way of *justifying* one's behaviour after the fact. In all these cases the attitude object itself or the 'content' of the attitude is relatively unimportant. And last but not least, attitudes can have *ego-defensive* functions, because they can help us to deal with our inner conflicts. The classic illustration here is again the study by Adorno *et al.* (1950), in which it was suggested that anti-semitism has little to do with Jews,* but

* Sartre in his essay on anti-semitism (Sartre, 1947) had independently come to the same conclusion. According to Sartre, Jews are nothing but a pretext to the anti-semite; if the Jews did not exist, the anti-semite would have to invent them (see chapter 17).

should be seen as the displaced expression of latent aggressive tendencies against a substitute or scapegoat, because these tendencies cannot be expressed against the source of frustration or aggression which, according to the theory, is originally the person's father.

If the functional distinctions made by Katz, Stotland and others are correct, it is not too difficult to see what the consequences are for the study of attitude change. It is to be expected that quite different variables will be related to attitude change when the functions which are served by particular attitudes are different. If an attitude has mainly an adaptive function, it is most likely to be changed by an appeal to the usefulness of the change for reaching a valued goal. On the other hand if the attitude serves mainly a knowledge function, it may be expected that new information is effective in changing it. Expressive attitudes can possibly be changed by providing the person with other means for expressing himself or for self-realization or justification. And finally, attitudes which have mainly an ego-defensive function might be changed by providing the person with insight into the real causes of his behaviour.

Although there is no strong evidence to support these views, the functional theory makes clear that our model of attitude change is only a 'surface' model. It deals with the attitude as expressed by the receiver and measured on an attitude continuum, but it does not ask why the receiver holds a certain attitude. Nevertheless, it is very probable that, depending upon the answer to this question, the weights of the receiver in our model (or even some of the other parameters) will vary. There are in fact two different answers to this question which can be found in the literature. The first is a motivational answer as presented by functional theory. The second is a cognitive answer; a person may hold a certain attitude because he perceives reality in a particular way. Or stated differently, we understand why a person holds a certain attitude once we know how he perceives or experiences social reality. This cognitive answer is of course related to the distinction made in the previous chapter between attitudes as levers and attitudes as templates of reality. What we are suggesting here is that an attitude change as represented by our model comes close to identifying attitude change with a change in overt responses without asking the question whether that change implies only the selection of another lever or also a change of the underlying template of reality. Just as the functional or motivational basis of an attitude may affect the parameters of our attitude change model, the cognitive basis can do so as well. If we do not deal with these effects in the following discussion of source, message and receiver determinants of attitude change it is because research on attitude change has hardly gone below the surface level of overt attitudinal responses.

The power of the source

Source variables which have been studied in relation to attitude change can be readily organized according to various forms of power the source has over the receiver: expert power, attraction power and reward or coercive power (French and Raven, 1959).

It has usually been found that *expert* sources are more effective than sources which are perceived as less expert, less intelligent, etc. This is true especially in experimental studies. Research of this type was carried out at Yale University in the USA as part of a larger communications research programme under the direction of Carl Hovland (Hovland, Janis and Kelley, 1953). In one of these experiments, students heard a tape-recorded speech in favour of a more humane treatment of juvenile delinquents. In one condition the speech was attributed to a judge, in another condition to a member of the audience, and in a third condition to an ex-delinquent. After the communication the students who were told that the speech was given by a judge showed the most favourable attitude towards a lenient treatment of juvenile delinquents (Kelman and Hovland, 1953). This type of experiment can be repeated with slight variations *ad infinitum* without telling us very much more. The essential point is whether expertness affects the power of the source over the receiver, for example by causing the receiver to develop a more favourable attitude towards the source. One might suspect that this is usually the case when an expert communicates information of an instrumental nature but not when he makes assertions about values (Jones and Gerard, 1967). But even when experts stay clearly within the boundaries of their competence they may not be the most effective sources, as research on diffusion of innovation in developing countries has shown. To the extent that the adoption of new ideas and practices is influenced by other persons, the attitude of a local opinion leader may be much more important than the activities of a foreign expert (Rogers and Shoemaker, 1971). Clearly other characteristics of the source, apart from expertness, affect his power over the receiver.

Two interesting secondary findings related to expertness should perhaps be mentioned. First, the effects of source-expertness on attitude change appear to suggest that the receiver pays a lot of attention to the arguments brought forward by the source in support of his assertions and that these arguments are instrumental in changing the attitude of the receiver. This is, however, not necessarily the case. It was found by Hovland, Janis and Kelley (1953) that a credible source had an effect on attitudes but not on the learning of arguments. Bauer (1965) has argued that this can be explained by assuming that the receiver does not pay too much attention to the arguments once he is convinced that the source is credible. However, when the credibility of the source has not been ascertained, arguments play an important role.

The second side effect concerns the so-called objectivity of the source, the subject of a vast amount of research. Intuitively one would expect that if the receiver perceives the source as disinterested, unbiased and as clearly stating his intentions, he will be influenced more by the source. Research evidence does not provide strong support for this assumption and even appears to suggest that, if anything, the opposite is true (McGuire, 1969).

Attraction appears to have, in general, an effect on attitude change in line with intuitive expectations. Consistency theories, like Osgood's congruity model, are explicitly based upon the idea that liking between persons will bring about similarity (of attitudes). It is to be expected that similarity in other respects may provide a similarity of attitudes. We also find that familiarity (which may lead to the discovery of similarity which in turn may lead to liking) has an effect on attitude change. Although the obvious appears to be the case in these instances, this does not mean that no questions remain. It is one thing to state that similarity between source and receiver affects attitude change, but it is quite something else to know in what respect similarity must exist in order to affect a person's attitudes. For example, it seems obvious that similarity in superficial characteristics is less important than ideological similarity, but is similarity in social class between source and receiver more or less important than ideological similarity? In fact, we are not in a position to answer such questions in an unequivocal way, as research by Rokeach (1960) and Triandis (1961) has shown, but in any particular case such considerations may well be important.

Still, the obvious does not always occur. Under certain specified conditions the reverse may happen. When a receiver commits himself *voluntarily* to listen to a particular communication, it has been found that a disliked source is more influential than an admired one (Zimbardo, 1960; Brehm and Cohen, 1962). It is as if the receiver cannot justify his behaviour sufficiently by admiration for the source and therefore convinces himself that the message *per se* was worth listening to and hence he is more influenced by it.

Similar counter-intuitive results are sometimes obtained with respect to *reward* or *coercive* power of the source. It is to be expected that the receiver will change at least the public expressions of his attitudes more when positive or negative sanctions following his (non)compliance are stronger. The relevant question is of course whether the receiver has changed his 'real' (latent) attitude more when stronger sanctions are applied. It has been argued by dissonance theorists (cf. Festinger, 1957) that a sanction which is just sufficient to induce a receiver to commit himself publicly to a change of action is most effective in changing his corresponding private attitude. Thus, a person will change his attitude towards a boring task more when he is given only $1 instead of $20 for telling someone else that it is an interesting task (Festinger and Carlsmith, 1959). A great deal of research has been devoted to this question because it appeared to imply contradictory predictions from learning–reinforcement and cognitive–consistency theories. Although the issue has not been settled, it seems reasonable to conclude that experiments like the one just mentioned have specified some conditions under which rewards or punishments have other effects than those commonly expected and usually obtained (Zajonc, 1968). If the acceptance of $20 for attitude change is perceived by the receiver as accepting a bribe and the acceptance of $1 is not, then the effective power of the source over the receiver may well be inversely related to the magnitude of the monetary rewards. Clearly it is too simple to equate power in a communication situation with rewards or punishments.

In general we may conclude that research has more or less shown the obvious to be the case; the greater the expertness, attraction, reward or coercive power of the source over the receiver, the greater the attitude change. It should be realized, however, that the power of the source is not always related in a simple linear way to the various determinants we have discussed. Moreover, it should be clear that an understanding of the power of the source over the receiver in a particular situation requires that one takes into account *all* the relevant determinants. Expertness may be ineffective if it is counteracted by unfamiliarity. Rewards may have the reverse effects when they are perceived as coming from an unattractive source who tries to bribe the receiver.

The structure of the message

The second major determinant of our attitude change model is the *message* communicated by the source to the receiver. In our model this component is mainly represented in the form of a discrepancy between the attitude advocated by the source and the attitude initially held by the receiver. The central thesis of the model is that a larger discrepancy will in general produce more change and this is indeed what has usually been found (McGuire, 1969). Research in this area has, however, largely concentrated on the *form* in which the message is communicated to the receiver. Is an emotionally worded communication more effective than a rational appeal? Does the induction of fear increase or decrease the effectiveness of the communication? Should the source present only arguments in favour of his own position in order to obtain attitude change? Is it better to present arguments in favour of one's position at the beginning or at the end of the communication if one wants to convince someone else?

Before we engage in a discussion of the numerous rhetorical variables which have been studied in relation to attitude change, it is important to realize that research of this kind represents in a sense no more than variations on a basic theme. The main message determinant of attitude change appears to be *what* is communicated (the position advocated by the source) and not the form in which it is communicated. Of course a communication always has to take a certain form, but the question is how important are variations in form (structure, style, media) compared to the fact that a communication with a certain content takes place. If one compares in attitude change studies the differences between various forms of communicating the message with the (control) condition in which no message is transmitted, one finds very often a large difference between the control situation and the conditions in which a message is communicated, but only small differences between the various rhetorical forms. It is these marginal differences that we shall discuss because most message research has dealt with such factors. In our model the effects of these variables can be conceived of as changes in the receiver's perception of positions on the attitude continuum, or as changes in the weights of the source and the receiver. Because such variables have been studied usually in direct relationship to attitude change without taking into account the other components of the attitude process, it is not surprising to find that these studies have produced a good number of apparently contradictory results.

A summary of the findings of such studies would read approximately as follows (McGuire, 1969; Fishbein and Ajzen, 1972; Kiesler and Munson, 1975):

1. Emotional appeals sometimes have more effect on attitudes than logical appeals, but more often there appears to be no difference.

2. In general, higher fear arousal accompanying a persuasive communication produces more attitude change, but some studies have found the opposite result.

3. A skilled or dynamic style of message delivery does not make much of a difference in general.

4. Explicitly drawing conclusions in communicating a message is usually more effective than leaving the conclusions to the receiver.

5. Refuting counter-arguments inoculates the receiver against later attempts to change his attitude again.

6. Repetition of the message by the same source or by different

sources increases the effect, but the increase quickly reaches an asymptote or upper limit.

7. Varying the order of presentation for parts of messages or for messages as a whole shows that sometimes the first parts or the first message have more impact (primacy effect) and sometimes the parts or messages presented at the end have more impact.

It seems reasonable to assume that the effects of most of the so-called message variables can be conceived of as changes in the weight to be assigned to the source of the message. Fear, emotion, repetition more often than not appear to increase the power of the source over the receiver. In a single case – refuting counter-arguments – it seems likely that the weight of the receiver is changed by the communication.

The most disturbing aspect of those results is their inconsistency. It is apparently difficult to make general statements about the influence of message variables. Other factors also seem to determine the effect of these variables on attitude change, but it is not always clear which other factors should be taken into account in each case. We have argued before that these inconsistencies could arise because research has not been guided by a clear conception of the process of attitude change. This seems also to be the opinion of McGuire (1969) and Fishbein and Ajzen (1972) upon whom we have relied heavily for a summary of results. These authors stress the fact that in many cases attitude change has been studied in direct relation to these variables without paying attention to other (intermediate) aspects of the change process. If a message is presented to the receiver, it requires at least that the receiver pays attention to the message and subsequently understands it, if any attitude change is to occur at all. In our model, lack of attention or lack of comprehension would mean that no clear position of the source on the attitude continuum exists and that therefore no discrepancy is perceived by the receiver and hence no attitude change occurs. To state it differently, the message variables discussed above can affect also the perceived discrepancy between source and receiver and in this way have an influence on the receiver's attitude.

A good illustration of the problems which can arise in this respect is the research concerning the effect of the drawing of explicit conclusions by the source. Clinical and educational psychologists have argued for a long time that psychotherapy or teaching are more effective if the patient or pupil discovers for himself the problem or the solution to a problem. A non-directive approach is favoured over a directive one. But in attitude change studies we find that a directive approach which points out the conclusions to the receiver is more effective than an approach which leaves the conclusions to the listener. A likely explanation for this discrepancy has been presented by McGuire (1969). 'It may well be', he writes,

that if the person draws the conclusions for himself, he is more persuaded than if the source draws it for him; the problem is that in the usual communication situation, the subject is either insufficiently intelligent or insufficiently motivated to draw the conclusion for himself, and therefore misses the point of the message to a serious extent unless the source draws the moral for him. In communication, it appears, it is not sufficient to lead the horse to the water; one must also push his head under water to get him to drink (p. 209).

Most of the results reported so far are based upon experimental studies of attitude change in the laboratory. The chief aim of these studies has been or should have been to gain a better understanding of the process of attitude change. To the extent that experimental studies have succeeded in this respect, the results may not have been of direct interest to practitioners who want to influence people's attitudes. Experiments of the kind reported here have primarily theoretical relevance. They show that a certain change is, or is probably, brought about by such and such a factor. They do not show in a straightforward way what one should do in a practical situation. The relevance for the problems of society is only indirect; the experimental road to practice goes via theory. This does not mean, however, that one cannot and should not do any applied work before the theoretical edifice is finished. In many cases it may be sufficient to know simply what works, without having an adequate understanding of why it works. A good deal of field research in the area of attitude change is of this type. The questions society asks are questions like: What are the effects of the mass media? What is the most effective way to eliminate prejudice? What is the best way to introduce innovations? Here we can do no more than point out some of the most important problems studied in field research because each of the questions mentioned would at least require a textbook to itself. Fortunately these do exist. (See, respectively: Klapper, 1960; Allport, 1954; Rogers and Shoemaker, 1971.)

Perhaps the study of the mass media comes closest to laboratory studies of message variables in attitude change research, because television, radio and newspapers are in a way nothing but various ways of conveying messages to a receiver. So, ever since the emergence of the mass media, two questions have been raised again and again: How effective (or dangerous) are these media, and what is the most effective medium? The outcome of a tremendous amount of research into these questions has been, according to McGuire (1969), 'quite embarrassing for proponents of the mass media, since there is little evidence of attitude change, much less change in gross behaviour such as buying or voting'. Similar although somewhat less negative opinions are expressed by other authors in this field (Klapper, 1960; Schramm, 1963; Weiss, 1969; Nan Lin, 1973).

Perhaps the most important issue in mass media research is the rediscovery of the importance of face-to-face communication in changing attitudes. Originally Lazarsfeld, Berelson and Gaudet (1948) proposed a *two-step flow hypothesis* to explain the results of a panel study of voting behaviour, carried out by the authors during the 1940 presidential election campaign in the USA. It was found that very few people changed their minds during the election campaign and that those who did said that they were not affected by the mass media but by their families, friends or co-workers. Because Lazarsfeld, Berelson and Gaudet also found (i) that certain people – later to be called *opinion leaders* – had tried to influence others or had been asked for advice on political questions and (ii) that these people were considerably more exposed to the mass media, they suggested that 'ideas often flow from radio and print to the opinion leaders and from there to the less active sections of the population'. Although this hypothesis has acquired some fame because it is repeated again and again in textbooks, it has received neither direct nor indirect confirmation by subsequent research (Nan Lin, 1973). A much more complex process in which a distinction is made between the 'flow of information' and 'the flow of influence' is necessary to describe adequately the results obtained in mass media research. The mass media appear to be important for the information flow, whereas interpersonal relations are important for the flow of influence. Since interpersonal relations are so important with respect to influence, a good deal of attention has been paid in field research to characteristics of opinion leaders and 'adopters'. We will discuss the results of these studies in the next section.

The characteristics of the receiver

A question which comes to mind immediately when one looks for an interpretation of the weight to be assigned to the receiver in our attitude change model is whether or not this weight represents a general personality characteristic. Are some people easier to influence than others regardless of the nature of the source or the message? If this were the case, it would of course greatly facilitate research on attitude change, because we would not have to search for the specific determinants in each communication situation. Unfortunately the situation is not so simple. Although there is a limited consistency in the extent to which people are susceptible to various forms of social influence in different situations, the correlations between various measures of susceptibility are rather low. We will have to look for a more complex interpretation of the weight to be assigned to the receiver.

The complexity of the relationship between receiver characteristics and attitude change can be nicely illustrated by the apparently contradictory results obtained in studies of the effect of self-esteem. It may seem fairly obvious that people who have a low degree of self-esteem are more susceptible to social influence than people with a high level of self-esteem. Nevertheless one can find some evidence for practically every conceivable type of relationship between attitude change and level of self-esteem of the receiver; positive, negative, curvilinear with maximum influence for people with an average degree of self-esteem, and curvilinear with a minimal influence for people with an average level of self-esteem. McGuire (1969) deserves the credit for bringing some clarity to this, at first sight, incomprehensible collection of research findings. McGuire points out, as we have mentioned before, that the receiver must attend to a message and comprehend it if there is to be any attitude change at all. One must realize that in our attitude change model the position of the source on the attitude continuum is the position of the source *as perceived by the receiver*. If the perceiver does not perceive anything at all or perceives the message in a highly personal way, the position of the source will be unclear or differ from person to person. McGuire argues that many receiver variables such as self-esteem are related in opposite ways to the perception and comprehension of the message on the one hand and, once the message is correctly perceived and understood, to the yielding to the advocated position on the other. Thus high self-esteem may be positively related to understanding the message but negatively related to yielding once the message is understood. If this hypothesis of McGuire is correct, one would expect that self-esteem is negatively related to attitude change when the message is fairly simple and easy to understand, whereas complex messages would lead to a non-linear or positive relationship between self-esteem and attitude change. This is indeed what was found in various studies. In general, McGuire's theory about personality and susceptibility to social influence (McGuire, 1969) appears to be able to explain the diverse results obtained in attitude change studies very well.

It is interesting to compare McGuire's theory, which is largely based upon experimental laboratory studies and is intended to create order in the results obtained by those studies, with the findings of field research on the diffusion of innovations (Rogers and Shoemaker, 1971). Since the adoption of new ideas and new practices is, almost by definition, a complicated affair one expects that comprehension plays an important role in the adoption of innovations and that hence, apart from material conditions, receiver variables such as education, experience, intelligence and flexibility are positively related to the early adoption of innovations. Research by Rogers and Shoemaker (1971) largely confirms this expectation. Early adopters tend to be younger than later adopters, but when adoption requires substantial experience and knowledge older persons may become innovative. Earlier adopters tend to have a higher social status and a higher degree of education, especially in developing countries.

Earlier adopters tend to be less dogmatic and to be able to project themselves into the role of another person. Earlier adopters appear to use more information sources and to use them more frequently. They have in general a more external and cosmopolitan orientation and are closer to the original source of the innovation than later adopters. Of course, between accepting new ideas and applying them in practice financial barriers may exist. Rogers and Shoemaker report also that earlier adopters have higher incomes and more land, and are more specialized. They also have the 'right' commercial orientation and a favourable attitude towards borrowing money. Apart from these last factors, the conclusions of Rogers and Shoemaker appear to correspond fairly well with expectations based on Mc-Guire's theory.

Summary

The main determinant of attitudes and attitude change studied in social psychology is social communication. Attitude change in the receiver of the communication can be viewed as the result of a process of integrating the information presented by a source with the initial attitude of the receiver. Interpreted in this way the major parameters of the attitude change process are: the power of the source over the receiver; the resistance of the receiver; and the discrepancy between the positions of source and receiver on the attitude continuum. The process is complicated by the fact that the resistance of the receiver is also influenced by his position on the attitude continuum. A tremendous amount of research has been devoted to studying the determinants of the three parameters just mentioned. Although many studies confirm what one would expect intuitively, one important complicating factor which is often overlooked in research appears to be the extent to which the message is understood by the receiver.

Further Reading

McGuire, W. J. (1969), 'The nature of attitudes and attitude change', in G. Lindzey and E. Aronson, eds., *The Handbook of Social Psychology*, vol. 3, 2nd ed., Reading, Mass., Addison-Wesley. Includes a comprehensive review of attitude change treated within a social communication framework.

Jahoda, M., and Warren, N., eds. (1966, 1973), *Attitudes: Selected readings*, 1st and 2nd eds., Penguin Books. Both editions contain useful and only partially overlapping selections of important studies on attitudes and attitude change.

Festinger, L. (1957), *A Theory of Cognitive Dissonance*, Stanford, Stanford University Press. The original and very influential formulation of the single most productive theory of attitude change.

Abelson, R. P., Aronson, E., McGuire, W. J., Newcomb, T. M., Rosenberg, M. J., and Tannenbaum, P. H., eds. (1968), *Theories of Cognitive Consistency: A sourcebook*, Chicago, Rand-McNally. A vast compendium containing more material than anyone would ever wish to read about alternative theories of attitude change.

Rogers, E. M., and Shoemaker, F. F. (1971), *Communication of Innovations: A cross-cultural approach*, 2nd ed., New York, Free Press. An introduction to field studies of innovations and their diffusion.

Chapter 12
The Structure of our Views about Society

Henri Tajfel

Introduction

The aim of this chapter is to present an account of how human cognition interacts with social life and experience. But our discussion will have to focus only on certain aspects of this interaction so as to avoid the confusion which would be caused if one brief chapter attempted to deal with too great a diversity of problems. For example, there is little doubt that our ideas about what is beautiful and ugly are, to a large extent, determined by the social context in which they developed; so are our religious beliefs or our political and social ideologies. Whether we are in favour of, or against, what is generally accepted, whether we agree or not with others, the ideas and beliefs remain within a *framework* of socially shared meanings and assumptions, as well as within the common and socially established means, modes and principles of social communication.

But as long as we talk about beliefs, ideologies or concepts of beauty as they are shared within a culture or a sub-culture, or as they differ from one cultural setting to another, we are concerned with *content* rather than with process. The difference between the two can perhaps be described by stating that contents are the end-product of the processes. It is the difference between describing what *is there* and how it came to be there. But this difference is not by any means as clear-cut as it may appear, because the contents of our cognitions directly determine our behaviour, and the underlying processes have to be inferred in turn from this behaviour.

For this reason, cross-cultural comparisons of cognitive behaviour can provide one of the means for the understanding of the processes involved in the interactions between society and cognition. The focus of this chapter, however, will not be on a description of this cross-cultural work.* We shall try instead to present a set of principles which seem generally relevant to the relations between human cognition and social interaction.

This relationship is highly complex. Human cognition is partly created by social interaction, and in turn it partly creates it. Man's cognitive functioning is never static. He acts according to the way he understands his environment. But the way he understands his environment, physical and social, is largely determined by the results of his actions upon it as well as by the demands and requirements for action that the environment presents. All this together amounts to continuous shifts and changes, so that the most important cognitive processes can probably be described as adaptation to change and initiation of change. Thus an understanding of the social context of cognition requires an analysis of the relations between the contents of cognition and changes in these cognitions as they interact with changes in man and in his social environment.

Cole and Scribner (1974) in their excellent account of work on *Culture and Thought* divided their subject-matter into chapters concerned with language, perception, conceptual processes, learning and meaning, and problem-solving. One of the major themes which makes its appearance in most of these chapters is the cognitive activity of categorizing or classifying. This activity provides a link between perceptual and conceptual processes, between how we perceive the world and how we think about it. It will therefore serve both as a point of departure and as a general guide-line for this chapter.

All we know about our world originates from two major sources: sensory information, or 'the evidence of our senses', and social information or the information supplied by others. But there are some difficulties raised by a simplistic distinction between the 'sensory' and the 'social' information; very often such a distinction is meant to imply that there exists a fund of 'basic' sensory information which is *subsequently* elaborated and supplemented by information derived from social sources. No doubt, the biological foundations of human perception are largely unaffected by the social setting of our

---

*Several recent general accounts and collections of these studies are available (e.g. Berry and Dasen, 1973; Cole and Scribner, 1974; Dawson, 1973; Lloyd, 1972; Price-Williams, 1969; Segall, Campbell and Herskovits, 1966; Tajfel, 1969a).

lives; and there is no hope at all that we would ever understand cognitive processes without a close analysis of their physiological basis. It is equally true, however, that the end-result of *all* the factors that contribute to our perceptual experience bears little direct relationship to any one of them taken in isolation. As Gregory (1966) wrote:

The sense organs receive patterns of energy, but we seldom see patterns; we see objects. A pattern is a relatively meaningless arrangement of marks, but objects have a host of characteristics beyond their sensory features. They have pasts and futures, they change and influence each other, and have hidden aspects which emerge under different conditions (p. 220).

The social psychologist is interested in these mutual changes, 'pasts and futures' and 'hidden meanings' from two points of view; how are they affected by the social context in which they appear, and how do they, in turn, affect our social experience and behaviour? A paraphrase from a typical work of Piaget (1952) can be used to describe this relationship. Cognitive functioning can be conceived as achieving an equilibrium between 'assimilation' and 'accommodation'. Assimilation is the extent to which each new item of information we receive from our environment can somehow be made to fit in with the background of experience we already possess; if this new information could not be related in one way or another to our past experience, it would remain completely meaningless. Accommodation is the obverse process; it refers to changes in the ways in which we organize our past experience when new information is obtained. Without such changes, we would not be able to deal with new or unexpected aspects of our environment, physical or social. This is a 'dynamic' view of perceptual experience in which stability and change interact to provide the two necessary ingredients of a successful fit between the organism and its environment. Assimilation insures a continuity between the past and the present. Accommodation is the capacity to deal, from the perspective of the present, with future changes and uncertainties.

A useful point of departure for our discussion is provided by two statements of Bruner (1957a): '... all perception is generic in the sense that whatever is perceived is placed in and achieves its "meaning" from a class of percepts with which it is grouped' (p. 124). And:

the question is 'how one could ever communicate or make public the presence of a non-generic or completely unique perceptual experience ... If perceptual experience is ever had raw, i.e. free of categorial identity, it is doomed to be a gem serene, locked in the silence of private experience' (p.126).

We shall adopt this 'categorial identity' point of view. After describing the general functions of categorizing, we shall first discuss the role played by social factors in our selecting and interpreting of cues from the environment. The two major social factors involved here are social consensus and social values. We shall then provide some examples of categorizing activities, both non-social and social. The way in which these activities interact with social values provides a perspective from which an individual views many aspects of his social environment.

The functions of categorization

The role of categorization in perceptual and other cognitive activities has been for many years one of the central issues in psychological theory. We shall provide a brief summary in the form of a few general statements which appear directly relevant to the process of categorizing considered in its social context.

This process consists of organizing in certain ways the information we receive from the environment. Thus, we tend to ignore certain dissimilarities between individual objects if these objects are *equivalent* to one another for certain purposes – for example, stools, armchairs, or chairs, should we wish to sit down. At the same time, we ignore certain similarities if these similarities are irrelevant for our purposes, if they conceal a *lack of equivalence* with regard to our actions, beliefs, attitudes, intentions or feelings; for example, when we wish to distinguish a friend in a crowd, an instrument in an orchestra, a friendly smile from a mocking one. Without these two modes of organization, adequate reaction to whatever happens in the environment, or adequate action upon it, would not be possible. Thus the principal function of categorizing resides in its role as a tool in systematizing the environment for the purposes of action.

But to systematize is to simplify. The enormous amount of information that we receive from our environment and from the effects of our actions upon it cannot be adequately dealt with unless it is made to fit the background of cognitive structures which are already in existence. One particularly relevant aspect of this simplification has been referred to by Bruner (1957b) as 'going beyond the information given'. Just as the system of categories which is used by an individual must be made to fit the environment, so the information received from the environment must be made to fit the existing system of categories. In other words, various characteristics of objects and events in the surrounding world must be modified so as to be made a part, without too much strain, of the structure of experience that an individual already has at his disposal. If this were not the case, the usefulness of categorization as one of the principal systems of guidance for action would cease. The rapid, continuous and innumerable changes in the individual, in his environment and in the interaction between the two must be treated by the individual *as if* some similarities and some differences were more pronounced than they could, in principle, be shown to be (through, for example, closer attention to details, physical measurement, or lack of agreement with others). The two cognitive activities which underlie this process of simplification are very much like the sins of omission and commission. They consist of selecting certain aspects of the information (and thus, by definition, omitting other aspects) or of modifying some aspects so as to achieve a 'better fit' within a category.

These activities of omission and commission are of particular importance in the categorization of the social environment. The information we receive from our social environment is complex, flexible and ambiguous; so are the ways in which we check on the validity of this information. In addition, there is another complicating factor in the relationship between cognition and society; namely, the interaction between an individual's system of values and his structuring of his social environment.

Selecting information in the social environment

Assigning an item to a category which is interlocked with other categories in the structure of an individual's experience implies a number of basic perceptual activities. These are: selecting for closer attention certain aspects of the environment: identifying a stimulus, an object or an event for 'what it is'; accentuating certain of its features so that it 'fits' in some important ways one category or another; neglecting other features which are less important for the 'fit'; recognizing a familiar object or event on the basis of partial information; and discriminating between objects, again on the basis of partial information, so that appropriate distinctions of category membership can be made between them.

These various aspects of categorial assignment are crucial to the general study of perception. They enable us to come to perceptual 'decisions' on the basis of insufficient or partial information. Experimental examples of these decisions are provided in studies by Bruner and Potter (1964) and Hershenson and Haber (1965). In the former study, subjects were shown on a screen familiar objects (such as a heap of cutlery) projected out of focus, and then the clarity of the projection was slowly and progressively increased. It was found that the *mis*identification of the objects occurring in the earlier and unclear stages of presentation prevented correct identification in the later and clearer stages during which normally no mistakes would have been made. Hershenson and Haber reported that when English and Turkish words were flashed repeatedly on a screen, the rate of correct identification for Turkish words (unfamiliar to their subjects) was slightly faster than the rate for English words – which were presumably more easily misidentified through guessing in the earlier stages of the task.   In the studies just mentioned, the relatively slow and inefficient achievement of the correct response was presumably due to the 'blocking' of continuing perceptual search for a correct identification by the application and persistence of early guesses about the identity of the stimuli (cf. Bruner, 1957a.) For this reason these studies provide a convenient basis for considering the social context of selectivity in cognition.

Two major social determinants of cognitive selection and organization seem crucial; social values and social consensus. The first of these 'may refer to interests, pleasures, likes, preferences, wants, needs, aversions and attractions, and many other modalities of selective orientation. Values, in other words, are found in the large and diverse universe of selective behaviour' (Williams, 1968, p.283). Social consensus, our second determinant, takes many forms; it is also the most effective channel of social information. We shall first consider the role and scope of social consensus in cognitive activity; and then engage in a similar discussion of the role and scope of social values.

(i) *The role of social consensus*

Social consensus takes many forms, the most basic of which is the wide consensus within a culture about the interpretation of the information provided to our senses by the environment. Various aspects of the environment may become more or less salient as a result of the needs and traditions of a society; thus, different cues may be selected for attention and organized as a coherent pattern. An excellent example, even if somewhat anecdotal, is provided by a transcription the American anthropologist Hallowell (1951) once made of how a hunter from the North American Indian tribe of Ojibwa reported being pursued by a mythical hostile giant called *windigo*. This report was mainly a description of a succession of sounds. As Hallowell wrote:

Auditory stimuli alone appear to have been the chief *physical* source of the subject's interpretation of the initial presence of a *windigo* and all his subsequent overt behaviour ... But in principle a succession of sounds is heard which, although they are physical, become significant to the perceiver because they also convey a conventional meaning (p. 183).

Without this 'conventional meaning', the stimuli would not have been selected for attention or organized in this particular manner. But it is important to stress that, once the belief in the *windigo* exists unquestioned, the logic of the inference from the succession of sounds is no less coherent than my inference from another succession of sounds that an aircraft is passing high above the clouds. One's faith in the existence of a phenomenon may be based on checking, rechecking and coordinating the various sources of sensory evidence; but it may also be related to the degree of awareness (or subjective probability) that there exist alternatives to the judgement one is making. A low (or nil) probability that such alternatives exist may be due to the very high social consensus about the nature of a phenomenon, independently of whether it is thought of as being 'physical', 'natural' or 'social'. There are many examples, both in the history of science in our own culture and in the systems of knowledge of other cultures, when the means of 'physical' testing which are, in principle, available are not used because of the very high (or complete) social consensus about the nature of a phenomenon.

This does not mean, however, that we always act as cognitively blind receivers of our cultural inheritance. The social environment moulds the human individual, but the human individual also creates and changes his social environment. In any complex society (and most societies are complex, even the so-called 'primitive' ones) there is always room for disagreement and reinterpretation of whatever may appear, slowly or suddenly, as less than absolutely certain. Without these disagreements and reinterpretations there would have been no advances in science, no changes in art and also no modifications in the established ways of viewing our social institutions. When new alternatives are created, the different versions of what is 'obvious' begin to clash, and the 'evidence of our senses' can be selected and organized in terms of conflicting versions of a consensus adopted by one or another group in a society. Some experimental examples of this process can be found in the recent work by Moscovici described in chapter 8 (e.g. Moscovici and Faucheux, 1972), on the effects that the views of a minority may have in changing the view of a majority in a small group. Another example is provided by certain cultural changes in modes of social communication.

Of these modes of communication, language is obviously the most important, and it is possible that certain differences between languages have effects on the manner in which different linguistic groups organize some aspects of their cognitive experience, for example, recognition and recall of colours (cf. Cole and Scribner, 1974, for a review of this work). But some of the clearest examples of the role of social consensus in the organization of our perceptual experience can be found in the conventional visual representations of the outside world. There is no doubt that these conventional representations are an important part of the visual environment in our own culture. They include art, advertising, plan and map making, photographic reproduction, and a large variety of other means used to convey information visually. Most often, these messages communicate directly and without hitch the information that they are supposed to convey. Therefore, from our point of view, this is an important phenomenon; it provides an example of the social determination of the *rules* for the interpretation of visual experience.

There have been some experimental studies of the difficulties which members of other cultures may have in interpreting modes of visual representation used in our culture (e.g. Deregowski, 1968a and 1968b; Hudson, 1960, 1967; Mundy-Castle, 1966). There exists, however, a similar problem concerning the changing modes of communication within our own culture. Social psychologists have been slow to take up the challenge presented to them by historians of art such as Gombrich (1960, 1965) or Wittkower (1955), who were interested in the psychological problems of communication between the artist and his public. As Wittkower wrote: '. . . one must know or have learned that the irridescent patches of colour in a picture by Turner denote "sea"'. The acceptance by a wide public of an artist's new ways of transmitting his vision is an excellent example of the social diffusion of changes in the ways in which sensory information can be selected and organized. There are two stages in this process: first, bewilderment of the receiver and conflict with the established consensus of what 'makes sense': and then, if the artist is successful, progressive reinterpretation. It must be remembered that many *successful* innovations in painting or music which led to the creation of new 'styles' or 'schools' are basically social, since they originate in groups of people using new idioms common to them whose acceptance gradually spreads beyond the groups where it started. It is impossible to conceive of this process of reinterpretation outside its context of social interaction. But we still know very little about the social psychology of this kind of cognitive change.

We cannot be concerned here with the enormous amount of experimental work on perceptual processes, except to say that the main goal of this work was to elucidate the fine detail of perceptual processes themselves rather than to analyse their relationship to social behaviour. In order to elucidate these relationships a little, we must turn towards a different tradition of work, namely the experimental studies of 'social influence' in social psychology discussed in chapter 8. Most of this work has been concerned with the ways in which an individual's attitudes, perceptual judgements, preferences, opinions and beliefs can be changed by the views of a majority in a small group. It is, however, very difficult to decide to what extent any of these changes can be attributed to 'genuine' changes in perception rather than to the tendency to provide socially 'desirable' responses (cf. Tajfel, 1969a, for a general review of this problem).

Despite these difficulties we are beginning to have some experimental evidence that information received from others may influence an individual's perceptual experience rather than just his public responses without, as far as one can judge, any clear and explicit awareness on his part that this is so. In many of the studies on conformity, subjects denied in post-experimental interviews that they were influenced by others when they had changed their views in accordance with the majority's opinion; but this is indirect and rather suspect evidence, since these denials may well have been caused by the unwillingness to admit what would clearly seem like sheep-like behaviour during the experiment. More convincing data emerge from studies on 'experimenter bias' (Friedman, 1967; Rosenthal, 1966; Rosenthal and Rosnow, 1969). As was mentioned in chapter 1, this work is concerned with the unintended effects on subjects' behaviour of the experimenter's expectations concerning the results of his study. Several studies have shown that, without necessarily being aware of doing so, the experimenter may provide all kinds of cues and hints to the subjects, and that these subtle forms of social influence may cause them to behave in a way consistent with the experimenter's hypotheses about the outcome of the experiment.

These various distortions in the collection or interpretation of data are usually discussed from the point of view of the methodological difficulties that they present in research on human behaviour. But they may also provide useful information about some perceptual aspects of social influence. The intended or unintended cues provided by the experimenter can affect the subjects' behaviour because the subjects may form an idea about the researcher's expectations concerning their behaviour and may then wish to conform to these expectations (e.g. Orne, 1962; Rosenthal, 1966). In doing so, they are likely to use the experimenter or other subjects as sources of information helping them to interpret what is happening in a situation which is unclear or ambiguous. Their newly gained perspectives sometimes provide an example of changes in perception directly caused by social information. Let us use an experimental study (Tajfel, 1966) as an example to clarify this point.

In a long series of judgements, the subjects were asked to decide whether two blocks of wood presented successively were of the same or of different heights. The first block was of constant height in all the pairs; it was compared with others which were of five different heights: two shorter, one equal to the first and two longer. Some of the subjects were asked to decide whether the second block in each pair was *the same* as the first block; others, whether the second block was *different* from the first. The results were that, for each stimulus value, the frequency of judgements 'same' in the first group of subjects was greater than the frequency of judgements 'not different' in the second group (or conversely, for the judgements 'not same' and 'different'). There was, however, a possibility that these differences in frequency were due to the general preference (cf. Wason, 1959) for 'positive' judgements ('same' or 'different') over 'negative' ones ('not same' or 'not different'). In two further experiments with other subjects, identical conditions were used with one difference only; the subjects were promised a fairly substantial monetary reward (to be given at the end of the experimental session) for each correct response, and informed that a penalty would be deducted from the total prize for each incorrect response. The result of these two experiments yielded results very similar to those of the first one. As subjects who were correct all the time would have earned as much as £2·50 in a session of about twenty minutes (this was well before the present period of galloping inflation), it must be assumed that they tried as best they could to be accurate and that therefore their responses reflected their 'genuine' perceptual judgements.

These findings illustrate some of the more subtle effects of social information. The experimenter provided a hint as to what to look for; 'sameness' in one condition and 'difference' in the other. We know from our everyday experience that, when the information received from the environment is confusing and ambiguous (and even sometimes when it is not), we tend to find what we look for. On the basis of much of the argument in the present section of this chapter, we can therefore say that the major effect of social information is that this information contributes in important ways to *directing* our search for some cues rather than others; or, to put it differently, for selecting cues which happen to fit in with our expectations. These expectations are very often socially determined. In addition, the more powerful the weight of social consensus about the nature of a phenomenon, the more likely it is that we shall select in accordance with the cognitive alternatives supplied to us by our social environment. As we have already seen (e.g. the work of Moscovici and Faucheux, 1972), this does *not* mean that important changes of perspective do not happen. On the contrary, they take place very often; but the preliminary condition for their occurence is the creation and diffusion of convincing alternatives to the prevailing modes of social consensus.

(ii) *The role of social values*

The experiments on misidentification of stimuli previously described (p. 307) reflected a 'blocking' of the search process due to an incorrect categorization, based in turn on insufficient information in the early stages of the task. Social values and expectations related to them exert the same kind of influence on category assignment. But there are some important differences between the misidentification of objects or words in the experiments described earlier and the more permanent effects that social values have on the assignment of an item to one social category or another. We are not dealing here, as was the case in those experiments, with an early misidentification which is subsequently corrected with the help of supplementary information. On the contrary, as long as values do not change, their effects on the search for information will help to insure that what is being sought is found. New information is not used in order to correct previous mistakes. It is being selected and reinterpreted so as to confirm and support the structure of the value-loaded categories.

This is a familiar phenomenon in our everyday experience. The denial or reinterpretation of information which contradicts the established pigeonholes is found at every street corner where long hair, dark skin or a police uniform warrant an immediate assignment to a category from which further inferences can then rapidly be drawn. But it will be useful to discuss, with the help of examples from a few experimental studies, various aspects of these phenomena.

The first concerns the kind of mistake that an individual is prepared, or prefers, to commit in identifying someone as belonging to one category or another. The kind of mistake that is preferred depends on its perceived consequences. In general, two types of mistake in categorizing are possible; placing an item in a category to which it does not in fact belong; and excluding it from a category to which it does belong. The preference for the first or the second type of error can be predicted if we know whether a particular act of inclusion or exclusion is likely to help to preserve a system of values or to threaten it. For example, in the case of strong negative evaluation of a group of people, it is very important that an individual who is a member of it should not be missed, and assigned in error to a positively valued category. The search for 'impure' specimens in racist societies provides one instance, as does the close scrutiny of the characteristics of a candidate for the membership of an 'exclusive' club.

There exist several experimental illustrations of these phenomena of over-inclusion and over-exclusion. Their common feature is a considerable ambiguity in the material that the subjects are requested to categorize. This is necessary, since it is particularly in cases of doubt that the processes underlying the category assignments can be most clearly brought to the surface. In addition, the categories to which the assignments are being made must be associated with a clear value differentiation.

The case of over-inclusion in negatively valued categories is well represented in a group of studies on the recognition of Jews which were conducted some years ago in the United States (cf. Tajfel, 1969a, for a detailed review). In the American social context the task of recognizing Jews is one of considerable ambiguity and uncertainty. The degrees of 'value relevance' of the categorization into Jews and non-Jews were provided in the experiments by using as subjects people who had previously been ascertained as being either strongly anti-semitic or non-anti-semitic. A prediction could be made from our previous discussion that the anti-semitic subjects would include relatively more of the 'items' presented to them (such as sets of facial photographs or of persons) into the category 'Jews' since the categorization had a greater value-loading for them than for the non-anti-semites and since the target category had a strong negative value connotation. This is indeed the conclusion that can be drawn from a survey of the findings:

... a general inference can be drawn from most of the studies, namely, that there are some predictable differences between the responses of the prejudiced and non-prejudiced subjects ... that there is a sharp divergence in the nature of recognition errors committed by the two groups ... The mistakes committed by the (prejudiced) group will tend in the direction of assuming that some non-Jews are Jewish rather than the other way around (Tajfel, 1969a, p. 331).

An experiment conducted in South Africa by Pettigrew *et al.* (1958) shows both the over-inclusion into the negatively valued category and the over-exclusion from the positively valued one. Pettigrew *et al.* used the perceptual phenomenon of binocular rivalry (which is caused by a presentation of a separate stimulus to each eye) and the consequent resolution of the binocular conflict. This resolution consists of perceiving one stimulus which is a 'compromise' between the two separate stimuli; the resulting perception shows various degrees of dominance by one or the other of the original separate stimuli. This procedure introduced considerable uncertainty in the task of recognition of race or ethnic group. The subjects were members of the main population groups in South Africa (Afrikaner and English-speaking whites, Coloureds, Indians and Africans). The pairs of photographs of faces presented as stimuli included all the possible combinations of ethnic and racial membership. The subjects' task was to identify the racial membership of the faces. The Afrikaner subjects tended to assign the pairs of faces of composite racial membership more frequently than did the other groups to the extreme of 'African' with a correspondingly less frequent identification as 'Coloured' or 'Indian'. They needed, however, much clearer evidence to assign a composite face to the category 'European'. Lent (1970) repeated the study in Texas, using whites, Mexicans, light-skinned Negroes and dark-skinned Negroes. He failed to replicate some of the previous findings; but he did report that, in response to pairs of faces representing two population groups, there was a difference between various groups of white subjects. These subjects were divided into three groups according to their attitudes: the 'segregationist', the 'neutral' and the 'integrationist'. The first group dealt with the composite photographs by restricting the number of those which they recognized as 'whites' more than did the other two groups.

Thus we have seen how systems of social categories associated with values are preserved through avoidance of category assignments which are incongruent with the evaluations. This is important both theoretically and socially. Theoretically, because it touches upon one of the basic aspects of the cognitive organization of the social environment; socially, because it reflects the norms and values of a society or of a social group in the kind of information about others that its members seek and in the use that they make of this information.

Values and the preservation of social categories

Much of this chapter has been concerned with the *functions* and *uses* of categorization. It is therefore important to clarify what may appear as a contradiction. Our discussion often laid stress on *mis*identification of stimuli and on *biases* in the judgement of items before or after their assignment to one category or another. It may therefore appear that this discussion was not about the functions of categorization but about its *dysfunctions*; not about the manner in which the process of categorization guides our orientation in the social environment, but about its misguiding properties. The contradiction is, however, more apparent than real. The rapid flux of change in the social environment makes it imperative that our interpretations of what happens do not lag behind the events. Rapid categorizing decisions, even when they are based on insufficient evidence, are therefore essential. The point of the experiments on misidentification was not to show that early identifications lead to mistakes (very often they do not), but to create experimental situations which are capable of showing as clearly as possible the essential role that the activity of rapid categorizing plays in our orientation in the environment.

A similar argument applies to biases in judgement deriving from a *previous* assignment of a person, an object or an event to one category or another. First, with regard to function; it is often more important for purposes of orientation in the environment to establish clear-cut distinctions between (or similarities within) categories than to dwell on the exceptions to the rule. In this way, exaggeration of differences between categories contributes to clear discrimination between them whenever this is necessary or important. Second, it is often important for an individual or a social group that their system of social categories be preserved despite the exception and contradictions that may be inherent in it. In other words, social values play an important role in the preservation of systems of social categories.

The preservation of systems of social categories associated with values aims at the achievement of maximum clarity and distinctiveness. A system of categories which has clarity needs to consist of categories which have internal unity and which are, at the same time, clearly distinct from one another. This tendency towards uniformity within individual categories and distinctiveness between them can also be seen in the categorization of non-social stimuli, as was shown in an experimental study concerned with judgements of length (Tajfel and Wilkes, 1963). Three groups of subjects were presented with a series of eight lines which differed in length from each other by a constant ratio. They were asked to estimate the length of each line in turn. For one group, the four shorter lines were labelled A, the four longer ones, B. For the second group, the labels A and B were attached each to half of the lines, but in a random relation to length. The third group had the lines presented to them without any labels. The series of eight lines was presented a number of times in successive random orders. As a result of these arrangements, the first group, which experienced a fully predictable relation between the labels and the length of lines, exaggerated the differences in length between the categories A and B considerably more than did the two control groups. This exaggeration of differences increased further as a function of accumulated experience of the predictable relationship between length and the labels. There was also some evidence (though much less clear-cut) that lines within each of the two categories were judged as more similar to one another by the experimental group of subjects than was the case in the two control groups. Similar results using different types of stimuli were obtained in several other experiments (e.g. Campbell, 1956; Davidon, 1962); and more recently, in studies (e.g. Lilli, 1975; Marchand, 1970) which were based on a systematic set of hypotheses about the effects of classifications on judgement (for details see Tajfel, 1959).

These effects are consonant with the general functions of categorization – the ordering and simplifying of information received from the environment. But we must go further when we consider values in their relation to social category systems. In the case of experiments on judgements of length of lines, an excessive overlapping of categories would lead to a breakdown of the system and, presumably, to a search for a new basis for categorization. When values are involved, however, the breakdown of a system of categories would imply a breakdown of a system of values, and a search for a new basis for categorization could imply the abandonment of an existing system of values. This represents, of course, much more of a crisis than a change in the criteria that are used for value-free categorizations of objects in the physical environment. It is therefore not surprising that the value-loaded social category systems tend to be more resistant to the effects of contradictory information, and that often this information is transformed so as not to appear contradictory.

The social contexts in which the notion of 'race' is used as a criterion for categorization provide examples of this salience and resistance to change in value differentiations in wider social perspectives. Whatever its other uses may be, the notion of 'race' has become *in its general social usage* a shorthand expression which helps to create, reflect, enhance and perpetuate the presumed differences in 'worth' between human groups or individuals. It contributes to making these differences as clear-cut and inflexible as possible. Its application in a wide range of social contexts (cf. Rex, 1969) witnesses to the introduction, whenever possible, of differentiations in terms of values which *increase* the distinctiveness of social categories, strengthen the existing differentiations, and thus contribute to their function as a guide for social action.

We must, however, qualify this statement immediately, as in its present form it might lead to an oversimplification of the relationships between social values and social categories. A particular set of values associated with a system of social categories does not operate in a vacuum; it operates in the context of other values. For this reason, simple predictions of magnified differences between, or similarities within, categories cannot be made without an analysis of other relevant aspects of this social context of values. Detailed examples of such an analysis and of experimental studies concerning several aspects of social behaviour can be found in the volume by Eiser and Stroebe (1972). We can do no more here than indicate the general conclusions which derive from the argument presented earlier in this chapter as well as from much of the previous experimental work (for details, cf. Eiser and Stroebe). These conclusions are as follows:

(i) Differentiations in terms of values tend to be more widespread, frequent and emphatic in systems of categories applying to social interaction than they are in categorizations of a non-social nature.

(ii) A system of categories which is associated with a system of values tends towards self-preservation. This is achieved in two ways: (a) through the selection and/or modification of information received from the social environment in a manner which is consonant with the existing value differentiations; (b) through achieving an increased clarity of the system of categories associated with values and an increased distinctiveness between these categories.

(iii) When a system of categories is associated with values in such a way that there is *conflict* between the different values which are relevant to the distinctions between the categories, a compromise will be achieved. This compromise will tend to favour those value considerations which are more general, more important or more relevant to social action. It follows that, in some cases, conflicts of values will determine changes in a system of social categories.

Summary

In this chapter, we looked at some of the major principles underlying an individual's structuring of the social world in which he lives. The discussion started from a description of the main features and functions of assigning objects and events in the world at large to separate and discrete categories. In turn, we stressed some of the similarities and differences in the systems of categories used to simplify the physical and the social environment. Amongst the major differences are the ambiguity and fluidity of the information received from the social environment as compared with information about the physical environment, and the fact that our orientation towards the people and events which make up our social environment is rarely free of positive and negative evaluations. These two major differences explain in turn why it is that social consensus and social values play such an important role in our subjective structuring of the social environment, both in determining the stability of these structures and their change under certain conditions.

Further Reading

An integrated theoretical treatment of some of the issues discussed in this chapter, together with an excellent review of many of the relevant experimental studies, can be found in:

Eiser, J. R., and Stroebe, W. (1972), *Categorization and Social Judgement*, London, Academic Press. Several chapters in Parts I and II of a collection of articles by J. S. Bruner, *Beyond the Information Given* (New York, Norton & Co., 1973), give the general background to many of the problems and ideas discussed in this chapter.

Berger, P. L., and Luckmann, T. (1967), *The Social Construction of Reality*, London, Allen Lane. This deals with an individual's assimilation of knowledge about the outside world passed on to him by his society. In particular Part III of the book provides a wider perspective on the cognitive interaction between the individual and his society.

Cole, M., and Scribner, S. (1974), *Culture and Thought*, New York, Wiley. This displays the rare quality of combining a well-presented and articulate general perspective on its subject with a selective review of some of the more interesting relevant studies conducted in a variety of cultures.

A chapter by H. Tajfel on 'Social and cultural factors in perception' in volume 3 of G. Lindzey and E. Aronson eds., *The Handbook of Social Psychology* (Reading, Mass., Addison-Wesley, 1969), includes a general introduction and a review of studies concerned with the effects of motivation on social perception, with the influence of social groups on perception and judgement, and with cultural differences in perceptual functioning.

This last topic is also dealt with in a wider framework in:

Lloyd, Barbara (1972), *Perception and Cognition*, Penguin Books. This is an excellent review of work on perception and cognition, mainly concerned with 'prospects for cross-cultural research' as they relate to the development of general cognitive theories.

The problems of social consensus and social categorization are usefully discussed in a general way in several chapters of:
Kelvin, P. (1970), *The Bases of Social Behaviour*, London, Holt, Rinehart & Winston.

Part Four
Interaction and the Social World

Introduction

Some conceptions of social psychology derive from the view that the subject covers a no man's land between 'individual' psychological functioning and large-scale social processes, the domain of sociology, political science, history, etc. As a result, most of the research in social psychology has been devoted to face-to-face interactions between individuals or in small groups. These interactions are often considered in isolation from the general social settings of which they are a part (cf. Moscovici, 1972; Tajfel, 1972, for further discussions). Recent descriptions of the details of face-to-face interactions in 'natural' conditions, or their analysis as 'games people play' as actors on the social stage of their lives, have undoubtedly advanced our knowledge in some ways. But these new approaches ignore the wider social settings of our lives no less than did the earlier experimental studies.

The 'no man's land' separating individual behaviour from society at large simply does not exist. As we said in the Introduction to Part Three, no man is an island. This old truth applies as much to human beings or to a small group as it does to a single individual. We are all, to some extent, creatures of our direct interactions with others; but these interactions are in turn jointly determined by human biological inheritance and the properties of the social structures inside which we live (see chapters 2 and 3).

Part Three of this book was concerned with the 'pictures in our heads' which guide our actions in the social environment. These 'social representations' range, as we have seen, all the way from our views and ideas about other individuals (chapter 9) through the formation and change of attitudes about social issues and events which concern us (chapters 10 and 11) to 'constructions' about the wider social contexts of our lives (chapter 12). The major themes of the five chapters of Part Four link up directly with these 'constructions' of social reality discussed in the last chapter of Part Three. They represent, as it were, reflections of cognitive functioning in some of the wider concrete settings of actual social behaviour.

The concluding part of this book could have been devoted to a discussion of some of the specific *applications* of social psychology to large-scale social problems, such as, for example, the effects of the mass media, the social psychology of education, the reduction of racial prejudice, or the psychology of industrial relations. It adopted instead an approach which is general rather than directly 'practical'.

First the problem of perspectives: applications of social psychology are usually based on a detailed study of a particular social setting (e.g. a hospital, a community, a factory, a special case of race relations) combined with a theoretical perspective (or at least, a set of general assumptions) which determines or influences the selection and interpretation of data obtained from the specific study. These general perspectives or assumptions, together with methods of research, are the social psychologist's basic tools of trade. Applied studies are concerned with special instances of more general cases. For example, suggestions a social psychologist might make about how to reorganize a factory or a hospital will have a lot to do with his general views about social behaviour in organizations (chapter 13). His advice about dealing with the psychological effects on a community of an earthquake will derive from his theoretical perspectives on the interaction between the physical environment and the psychological aspects of a community's social organization (chapter 14). His views about the implications for primary education of socio-economic differences in the use of language will be related to his theories about 'language and society' (chapter 15). And his attitudes towards, for example, the effectiveness of legislation in reducing racial or sex discrimination will be strongly influenced by what he thinks about the psychological foundations of conflicts between social groups (chapters 16 and 17).

The importance of these 'background' perspectives means that, in a book aiming to introduce social psychology, they must be given priority over discussions of special applications, however important these applications may be. But it is the hope of the authors of this book that the general discussions presented in Part Four will help the reader to assess the effectiveness of applications of social psychology to various concrete issues.

A second important point concerns the reasons for the *choice* of the general themes introduced in Part Four. There is a method in the diversity of themes we adopted, and this method is based on two criteria simultaneously applied. One of them has to do with a progression from chapter 13 to chapter 17 in the sequence of the major psychological problems encountered by human groups and *communities*; and the other consists of providing a selection of issues roughly parallel to the treatment of *individual* interactions discussed in Part Two. Thus, we start in Part Four with a chapter about behaviour in organizations as a parallel to small groups discussed in chapters 7 and 8, but one which is wider and more explicitly structured as a setting for social behaviour. Individuals adapt to, confront and create organizations, which are at the same time a product of large social systems or communities. In turn, human communities, small or large, adapt to, confront and create their physical environments – this interaction is the subject of chapter 14.

It remains true, however, that the environment of a social group consists not only, or perhaps not even mainly, of its physical habitat. It is, above all, constituted by the presence around it of *other* social groups which are crucial in determining its mode of existence. The chapter on language in society deals with the major tool of communication between social groups in contact, and it thus parallels chapter 5 which is concerned with communication between individuals. The two final chapters of the book are concerned with another crucial aspect of relations between groups – the social psychology of conflicts between them. Thus, they provide a parallel to chapter 6 which deals with competition and cooperation between individuals.

As we said earlier, chapter 13 on organizations, written by Geoffrey Stephenson, takes up in a number of new ways the themes dealt with in chapters 7 and 8 about small groups. From a general discussion of organizations as 'total institutions', it goes on to consider the individuals' interaction with organizations in which they work and the relations between the various 'roles' they play, both in their working lives and in other contexts. This is followed by a summary of studies on 'job satisfaction' and on the role of leaders in organizational settings.

The problems of adaptation and creativity confronting individuals in organizations are followed, in chapter 14, by Anne Whyte, by those confronting social groups in their physical habitats, both natural and man-made. The chapter reviews various theoretical models used to study the 'man–environment interaction', looks at the perceptions of the environment shared within groups and communities, relates these perceptions to the judgements underlying environmental decisions and deals, in its final sections, with some of these decisions together with their affective and symbolic significance for the communities.

With chapter 15, by Joshua Fishman and Howard Giles, we move from the physical to the social habitat of human groups. The chapter deals not so much with language as with *languages* (or varieties) which co-exist side by side and sometimes constitute the most important and salient differences between social groups in contact. Most linguistic differences between individuals derive, quite obviously, from linguistic differences between social groups to which the individuals belong. But social groups are not just 'in contact'; the nature of these contacts is largely determined by the nature of the social relations between the groups. The major theme of the chapter is the exploration of the effects of these social relations between co-existing groups on the individuals' linguistic interactions, on the difficulties that these interactions often encounter and on the ways of dealing with these difficulties.

In chapters 16 and 17, by Henri Tajfel, we move to an exploration of the psychological aspects of intergroup conflict. Two general approaches to the understanding of these conflicts are considered: the 'individualistic' and the 'group' approaches. The former, discussed in chapter 16, tends to consider intergroup behaviour as one of the settings which reflect or express the emotional and motivational problems that *individuals* encounter in the course of their life experiences.

In chapter 17 the cognitive aspects of intergroup relations are considered in the light of the general discussion about our ways of 'constructing' social reality which can be found in chapter 12, followed by a review of Sherif's theory. This theory represents a clear example in social psychology of an attempt to derive certain principles of individuals' intergroup behaviour from the nature of the relations between the groups concerned, rather than moving in the opposite direction – from individuals' problems to their intergroup behaviour – as in chapter 16. The final section of the chapter goes beyond cases of *explicit* conflict of interests between social groups. It considers, in the light of recent research, the roles played in intergroup behaviour by the development of social identity, by the nature of intergroup comparisons salient in a social system, and – more generally – by the beliefs about the nature of a social system which predominate in the social groups that constitute the system.

Chapter 13
Social Behaviour in Organizations

Geoffrey Stephenson

Introduction – the nature of organizations

What are 'organizations'? There are few social situations in which
behaviour is not organized along certain conventional lines, in which
people do not follow 'rules' and behave in a standard way. Moreover,
groups of previously unacquainted people brought together in novel
circumstances soon develop their own allocation of roles within the
group. Their interaction is soon regularized, as the work of R. F.
Bales (see chapter 7) shows. To the extent that any group of persons
seeks to coordinate its efforts towards attaining goals, we could say
that the group is an organization. According to this view, a family, a
street-corner gang, and a Bales discussion group are all organizations,
for in each case persons agree to behave in a regularized way in order
to further the group's goals. But in this chapter, emphasis will be on
larger-scale viable units, where the explicitness of their goals and the
planning of the members' activities make the epithet 'organization'
particularly appropriate.

An illustration – total institutions

Any organization has its own peculiar demands and traditions which
elicit distinctive responses from its members and forms of behaviour
not necessarily evident in other settings. Erving Goffman (1961) for
example, has written convincingly of modes of adaptation peculiar to
'total' institutional life – an extreme form of organization in which
detailed aspects of life are externally prescribed – as in prisons,
monastic institutions and mental hospitals. In such cases the planning
and control may produce standard modes of adaptation in the de-
tainees. Goffman details the humiliating, de-personalizing 'morti-

fication' processes and the unyielding 'privilege' system of control characteristic of many total institutions. The situation is sometimes coped with by *situational withdrawal* – a state of social apathy differently named and interpreted as one moves from, say, the psychiatric to the religious setting. The *intransigent* line is frequently taken by a minority in the early stages of adaptation and consists of deliberate flouting of rules and appeals to outside authorities. The prolific writer from prisons and special hospitals is well-known to charities, MPs and others whose professional interest in justice offers just a glimmer of hope for the person who feels he is wrongfully detained. *Colonizers* make the most of the available satisfactions within the institution and minimize the importance of their deprivations, whilst still not taking the official degraded view of themselves. *Converts*, on the other hand, act out the role of the perfect inmate, a condition noted by Bettelheim (1943) in his description of those who, in Nazi concentration camps, adopted the attitudes of their guards towards other prisoners; and this condition is also prevalent enough amongst the 'voluntary' inmates of, for example, military colleges (Dornbusch, 1955). In a provocative experimental study Zimbardo *et al.* (1973) detail the fulfilment of such stereotyped roles in both 'prisoners' and 'guards' in a simulated prison. Other characteristic responses to total institutionalization include an obsessive self-regard, and a concern, naturally enough, with time, which is 'endured', 'killed' and 'done', but never evaded (cf. Cohen and Taylor, 1972).

The social relationships peculiarly engendered by the conditions of life in total institutions dramatically illustrate the role of organizational constraints on social behaviour. It may be that the modes of adaptation noted by observers of total institutions have more than passing relevance to behaviour in other institutions – voluntary, work, business, academic, or whatever. David Hargreaves (1972) talks for example, of 'normal', 'delinquent' and 'indifferent' orientations of schoolchildren to schoolteachers. What is equally certain is that the special characteristics of other organizations – for example the wage contract in the employer–employee relationship – will create their own distinctive modes of behaviour and social organization. Nevertheless, the power of organizations to determine lives should not be exaggerated. A number of the studies cited in this chapter demonstrate that organizations are far from being remote, closed systems, totally disregarding the wider social environment. Organizations are sustained by persons with far-ranging allegiances. Even long-term prisoners may carefully cherish ideas of a future life, though contacts with the outside may be deliberately severed in order that time may be done the 'easy' way, concentrating on present details to avoid realization of the long-term horror. 'What appears to be totally unacceptable', say Cohen and Taylor (1972), 'is the idea that one's life is experienced in prison. One may be serving life, but one is not serving "my life"' (p. 93). Behaviour in organizations must be viewed in the context of lives. 'My life' is a more immediate prospect for say the worker than for the prisoner, and it is important always to assess the extent to which the membership of organizations is of personal importance. This should be kept in mind as we consider studies which demonstrate the power of organizational structure to determine behaviour.

In this chapter we shall consider findings from a variety of organizations – mainly work organizations but also from schools and hospitals. The emphasis on work organizations reflects the fact that social psychologists have more frequently been employed in that setting than in any other. The author has attempted to define the important social psychological questions in organizational studies, and to choose the best documented illustrations. The reader is left to consider the application of particular studies to those organizations with which he is most familiar, or most concerned.

Organizational 'givens' and social behaviour

Relations between groups

George Homans (1951) in his influential book *The Human Group*, asked what effect the precise organizational behavioural requirements (the 'external system') has on the developing social relationships of those involved (the 'internal system'). The demands of the job, for example, may prescribe that one group of workers interact more with each other than is the case for those in a second group.

Other things being equal members of the first group will more likely come to like each other and to develop common ways of responding to their situation than will members of the second group. They are more likely, for example, to arrive at a common view about how hard or fast they should work at their jobs and to impose these standards on other members of the group. The 'internal system' may then impinge directly on the organization (the 'external system') by influencing the workers' attitudes towards the aims of the organization. In brief, the demands of the organization are such as to bring about certain alliances and allegiances within the organization which may serve to change, thwart or encourage its formal aims and structure.

Examples from the field of work are cited by Homans (1951) and by Stephenson (1971), but let us take a concrete example outside the context of work. David Hargreaves (1967) in his study of a secondary boys' school in 'Lumley' described how the organization of the fourth year into academic streams profoundly affected the social organization of the entire school. The form 4A contained the academically successful boys who were due to take public examinations after staying on an additional year; boys in 4B had some slight academic pretensions; it was not anticipated that boys in 4C and 4D would succeed academically to any significant extent. Two major friendship groupings emerged as a response to the imposed teaching and examination structure. Interacting together more, boys in 4A and 4B developed an academic orientation. They were pro-school, pro-staff, in favour of participation in school activities and against messing around in class. This was all reflected in their excellent record of attendance, their 'good' behaviour in and out of school and, importantly, in their choice of academically oriented boys as informal leaders. Boys in 4C and 4D also developed a standard 'culture'. Their much higher truancy rates, delinquency within and outside school, and their admiration of and esteem for 'messers' testified to their 'delinquescent' orientation as opposed to the academic orientation of their 'superior' fellows. The policy of streaming was in itself partly responsible for the bifurcation of attitudes, and was, in addition, a perfect instrument for pulling existing social attitudes into good shape, for in many ways the two groupings admirably served the interests of members of the organization. The school's limited resources could be concentrated where they were readily appreciated. Boys from middle-class backgrounds found themselves, regardless of ability, surging upwards into the streams that reflected their own aspirations. Working-class boys found in the culture of the lower streams ample justification for their suspicion of authority and hostility to the unfamiliar intellectual demands of examination-oriented teachers. The stark cultural opposition in the fourth year was, to a degree, sustained from mutual convenience.

Technology and behaviour

Chaplin's satirical portrayal of assembly-line technology in his film *Modern Times* aptly illustrates the point that the manual and machine operations required to produce something ('technology') may determine the pattern of relationships between individuals. Fullan (1970), following Woodward (1965), compared the social attitudes of workers in oil refineries (continuous process technology) with workers in car assembly and engine plants (mass production technology). He predicted that compared with mass production the *technical* integration in process industries would produce a *social* integration of the worker with the company. Low labour costs and the greater interdependence of work activities are two factors in this. Breakdowns in production are especially costly, so that notions of collective responsibility are more salient. In automated plants, small team operations are also common, and necessitate frequent contact between workers and supervisory staff. In addition, continuous process industries frequently offer a well-defined career structure, which serves to increase the worker's sense of relatedness to the company. By way of contrast, there is usually extreme subdivision of labour in mass production technologies; social contacts between workers and with the supervisor are restricted, the latter consisting largely of directives from the supervisor, and the former serving to prevent the formation of purposeful groups. As Blauner (1964) comments, 'On an assembly line a worker may be able to talk with the men on both sides and those across from his work station, but each man is in contact with a different set of workers' (p. 114).

Comparing workers in oil refineries and chemicals (continuous process) with workers in the car industry (mass production) Fullan found that the general level of satisfaction was very much greater in continuous process industries. For example, only 15 per cent of workers in chemicals and oil refineries said their job was 'mostly or always dull'. In car factories, more than twice that proportion – 34 per cent – expressed that view. Moreover, the technology in oil, compared with mass production technology, is said to facilitate integration. It helps ensure, according to Fullan, that the company's industrial relations policies are benign, that workers and supervisors engage in purposeful interaction, and that there is a range of scaled jobs which provide a career structure within the company. The evidence suggests that workers in oil do, in fact, feel more identified with the organization as measured on a number of scales. Fullan lists a number of significant differences in attitude between workers in contrasting technologies. Workers in the oil refineries are more appreciative of the organization than workers in the automobile industry. Compared with workers in continuous process industries, employees in mass production firms are more likely to feel isolated at work, to think poorly of their foreman and to see him as having no influence over higher management, to have a competitive orientation in industrial relations and to devalue the company and their own prospects within it.

The operations required to produce something – be it pupils who can succeed in formal examinations, refined oil, or motor cars – may engender distinctive relationships, and attitudes peculiar to the technology concerned. It may be, as Miller and Rice (1967), and others of the 'socio-technical' school of thought have suggested, that the more adverse consequences of organizational 'givens' may be minimized by reorganization. They suggest that, given the nature of the 'primary task', organizations may frequently be restructured to cope with the conflicting demands of the technology and its members.

Organizational roles and individual performance

The concept of role

In any organization the occupant of a 'status' or position – say that of schoolteacher – has certain obligations to fulfil and certain expectations of others' duties to him. In Linton's (1945) classic account, the *role* is the required behaviour of someone in a given position and the term 'role performance' refers to the actual behaviour of the incumbent. The concept assumes its importance because it implies that individual behaviour or 'personality' may be socially determined. A man will become what he is obliged to be. As William James put it in 1892:

Already at the age of twenty-five you see the professional mannerism settling down on the young commercial traveller, on the young doctor, on the young minister, on the young counsellor-of-law. You see the little lines of cleavage running through the character, the tricks of thought, the prejudices, the ways of the 'shop', in a word, from which the man can by-and-by no more escape than his coat-sleeve can suddenly fall into a new set of folds. On the whole, it is best he should not escape. It is well for the world that in most of us, by the age of thirty, the character has set like plaster, and will never soften again (James, 1961, pp. 10–11).

Goffman (1969) rightly points out that the term role has come to embrace rather more than the prescribed duties and reciprocal rights attached to positions. Hargreaves' (1972) concept of 'position-role' reflects a transition to a broader concept of role as the expected response of persons occupying a given position. 'Role' now usually refers to the commonly shared expectations about what is appropriate conduct for those in given positions. Its content cannot be rigorously defined, and the manner of its performance even less so. Within limits, persons are able to select and emphasize those aspects which are to their liking, and to fashion their own version. Moreover, as Goffman suggests, the extent to which a person demonstrates his affection for a given role may vary. He may contrive to avoid the attitudinal and personal implications of performing a given role, by making clear that his adoption of the role is not from choice. The concept of role has special importance for us because organizations are customarily defined in terms of interlocking, complementary positions and associated obligations, whose coordinated fulfilment serves to fulfil the goals of the organizations. For example, Katz and Kahn (1966) call the concept of role 'the building block of social systems and the summation of the requirements with which the system confronts the individual member' (p. 171). However, the issues are rarely uncomplicated, as the following discussion of role-conflict indicates.

Varieties of role conflict

Hargreaves (1972) discerns six basic varieties of role conflict or 'strain'.

(i) *Occupancy of two or more positions whose roles are incompatible.* It is self-evident that positions may compete for an individual's time, and that conflict may ensue over the priority to be accorded to one or another role. Industry provides the example of the shop steward, who, whilst remaining a workman, by acceptance of office acquires loyalties both to the union, and, indirectly to management (Goodman and Whittingham, 1969). The expectations of two or more of the three parties to which he owes allegiance frequently contradict one another.

(ii) *Disagreement amongst occupants of a position about the content of a role.* To take an educational example, schoolteachers vary considerably in their understanding of the most important educational goals. Secondary modern teachers, for instance, are much more likely than are grammar school teachers to value social and moral training above 'instruction in subjects'.

(iii) *Disagreement amongst occupants of a complementary position B about the content of position A's role.* It needs no one to tell teachers that parents vary in their expectations about teachers. Working-class parents, like the secondary modern teachers, are more likely to stress the school's responsibility for social, and especially moral, training than are middle-class parents.

(iv) *Disagreement between role partners about the definition of one or other role.* This form of role strain may create particularly acute dilemmas for occupants of a position. In recent years university lecturers have been made uncomfortably aware of many undergraduates' concern that lecturers be primarily occupied in teaching. This frequently conflicts with the lecturer's inclination to respond to professional expectations that give precedence to his obligations as researcher.

(v) *Different role partners have conflicting expectations of a third party*. Industrial relationships offer a good example here. Walton and McKersie (1965) describe the varying demands facing chief negotiators at the bargaining table. On the union side, for example, the convenor of shop stewards attempts to satisfy the demands of his own membership, reconcile the conflicting demands of shop stewards belonging to rival unions on his side of the table, satisfy his opposite number that he is negotiating in good faith, and, for good measure, ensure that the wrath of local union officials will not be incurred by an out-of-line agreement. Inevitably, some aspects of his behaviour will appear obtuse or irresponsible to one party or another.

(vi) *A single role partner has conflicting expectations of another*. The family organization frequently encounters this variety of conflict. Adolescence in particular brings to the fore the parents' contradictory expectations that the child be both conforming and independent. A special form of this is held by Bateson *et al.* (1956) to contribute to the development of certain forms of schizophrenic disorder. What the parent *says* is contradicted by his manner. (See chapter 5.) The child thus faces a 'double-bind', because whichever message he pays attention to will arouse guilt from his neglect of the other.

In all these cases, a clear conflict exists between one set of expectations and another. Occasionally, of course, problems arise just because expectations are not clearly defined, or because an individual is not sure of what behaviour is appropriate, as when the child first goes to school. A further instance of role strain occurs when an individual lacks the skills required for the performance of his role, a painfully embarrassing circumstance at least momentarily familiar to everyone on those occasions when – despite all efforts to the contrary – face is lost and we cannot sustain the accustomed, or desired image of ourselves.

Resolution of role conflict

Types of role strain can be delineated, but little systematic work has explored their management by individuals. An interesting exception is the work of Gross, Mason and McEachern (1958), which shows some slight evidence to suggest that personality is important. Some people tend consistently to resolve conflict by yielding to those who could harm them most. Others, on the other hand, fulfil the expectations of those whose pressures are deemed 'legitimate'. The avoidance of role conflict is a precious skill, neglected at our peril, but some types are easier to avoid than others. Conflict between expectations arising from two different positions may frequently be controlled by separating their performance, physically and in time. By custom certain roles take precedence. Conflicts *within* one role on the other hand – of the kind considered by Gross *et al.* – are more difficult to avoid and are highly characteristic of certain positions in organizations. The chief union negotiator we considered earlier (conflict style (v) above) may adopt a number of stratagems for the avoidance of role conflict (Stephenson, 1971). He may try to ensure that his members have moderate expectations in order to prevent ultimate disappointment, or he may attempt to establish a trusting relationship with his opposite number at other times to ensure that his apparently aggressive tactics during the negotiation itself are not taken amiss. These and other similar tactics are commonplace and point to the exertions necessary for persons whose activities systematically impinge on the lives of others.

The existence of role conflict, and associated tactics to achieve its resolution, points up the inadequacy of attempts to reduce social behaviour to the performance of prescribed roles. It has been suggested aptly enough that roles are *created* rather than performed in everyday life. What our positions oblige us to do, and what others expect us to do are important factors determining the image we have of ourselves and the impressions we convey to others. The skill lies in projecting a consistent version of self that does justice to our roles and satisfies our personal vanities. A part we have to take may not match our self-image. Degrading or unpleasant duties will invariably be performed not in one's own name but in the name of the role. A person may contrive to suggest a certain detachment from his role, to emphasize that it is not he who is performing, but the part. As Goffman (1969) states, 'Explanations, apologies, and joking are all ways in which the individual makes a plea for disqualifying some of the expressive features of the situation as sources of definition of himself.'

The concept of 'role-distance' as developed by Goffman (1969) is important for the understanding of behaviour in work organizations. It is a common belief that people should be strongly attached to their occupational roles. Detachment is reckoned inappropriate or undesirable. This may serve very well for persons in professional, craft and other jobs in which initiative and self-expression are possible. It serves less well for those jobs which self-respecting persons may perform only with 'detachment, shame or resentment' (Goffman, 1969, p. 43). In Etzioni's (1961) terms, many workers can be expected to show little more than 'alienated' or at best, 'calculative' attitudes to authority. Goldthorpe *et al.* (1970), and also Ingham (1970), have suggested that calculative involvement is typical of workers in certain tedious but highly paid occupations. The work is disliked, may be thought of as shameful, although welcomed for its material rewards. But the job is not the man: 'Vauxhall is the place where I work – that's all' was apparently a typical comment by workers in Goldthorpe's study. A perusal of the accounts of working life in Fraser (1968, 1969) makes it clear that, as Roy (1955) indicated, many machine and production line workers derive their primary satisfaction from an almost playful group hostility to management, and consequent attempts to 'make out' to their own advantage. This reversal of organizational priorities most aptly expresses the need for role-distance in monotonous and undignified jobs.

Informal roles in organizations

Actors not only enact positional roles. Special parts get created for them. For example, young executives given 'responsible' positions as a consequence of random allocation were, five years later, earning more in better jobs than were comparably qualified persons assigned to less responsible jobs initially (Berlew and Hall, 1966). Reverting to examples from education, all schoolboys are aware of their form's 'clown', 'swot', 'butt', 'scapegoat' and so forth. Once established such reputations may become self-fulfilling. For example, on one occasion, Lacey (1966) observed a grammar school first form when 'a master asked three boys to stay behind after the lesson to help him with a task calling for a sense of responsibility and co-operation. The master called out "Williams, Mann and Sherring", upon which the class burst into spontaneous laughter, and there were unbelieving cries of, "What, Sherring?". The master corrected himself, "No, not Sherring, Shadwell"', thereby confirming once again Sherring's reputation for irresponsibility (p. 249). A sadder case is quoted by Hargreaves (1967) in the study cited previously, concerning a notoriously disreputable character, one Don of 4D: 'One day in the spring term the youth employment officer visited the school to speak to boys in the fourth. As he left the hall at the end of the speech, someone began to cheer. The deputy headteacher, who was standing on the platform, pointed down to the boys and shouted, "You: Go to my room!" The boy who had cheered was a prefect, but Don of 4D stood up, even though he had not cheered. It was as if he expected to be rebuked even when he had committed no crime' (p. 107.)

Don's right to trouble and Sherring's exclusion from responsibility are perhaps obvious examples. Expectations can, however, operate less blatantly but with equally dramatic results. Their insidious influence has been closely studied by social psychologists in recent years in a variety of situations, including the classroom (see chapter 9 on the self-fulfilling characteristics of interpersonal attributions). The incentive for much of this work came from studies by Robert Rosenthal in the early 1960s on the 'experimenter effect' in psychological experiments (Rosenthal, 1966).* Rosenthal showed that in the absence of stringent precautions an experimenter's expectations will bring about their own confirmation. Orne (1962) emphasized the part played by the organized role relationship between subjects and experimenter in such results – for human subjects at least. The position of 'subject' in an organized scientific experiment induces attitudes of respect and deference towards the experimenter. The subject

* Another implication of this work - its reference to our understanding of the effects of 'social information' - is discussed in chapter 12.

wishes to be a *good* subject, to play his proper role in the scientific enterprise. Hence he responds avidly to the no doubt unintentional and subtle cues conveyed by the experimenter as to how he should behave. Rosnow *et al.* (1973) have suggested that the subject's desire to present a favourable self-image is as important, if not more important, than the perceived role obligation to further science and please the experimenter.

In the classroom situation, Rosenthal and Jacobson (1968), claimed to have shown a striking effect on pupils' intellectual development of experimentally induced teachers' beliefs. This work is described in more detail in chapter 9. A recent naturalistic study in schools confirms the original work in a remarkable way. Seaver (1973) studied the consequences of naturally induced expectations in teachers, with no intervention from an experimenter. Many children have had the discomfiting experience of following their older brothers and sisters through school. Such a child may soon come to feel that the elder's reputation is a yoke he cannot escape. Are teachers' expectations of a younger child indeed affected by his older sibling's previous performance in school? And, if so, does the ensuing teacher–child relationship have the expected effect on the performance of the younger child? Seaver studied the performance of seventy-nine children in their first year at primary school whose older sibling had preceded them one or two years before. Twenty-seven of these had been assigned to the same teacher as the elder, and were designated the experimental group. The remainder – taught by a different teacher who would presumably have no particular beliefs about them based on the performance of the elder – served as the control group. At the end of one year a very consistent pattern was evident. On almost all the objective tests routinely administered, the experimental group did *better* than the control group when the older sibling had done *well* at school, and performed *worse* than the control group when the elder brother or sister had previously done *badly* at school. Favourable and unfavourable teacher expectations were apparently having their predictable effects on the performance of pupils. In educational and other organizations there are, of course, more noticeable attributes that may similarly create unplanned roles. Children and others of a particular race, sex, or social background, may find their role and organizational careers to some extent predetermined as those younger children did, to their advantage or disadvantage.

The question of job satisfaction in work organizations

Some traditional theories

Difficulties and strains involved in fulfilling certain roles and in role-conflicts bring us to a related issue, that of 'job satisfaction'. It is a frequent assumption in management philosophies that workers can and should achieve their principal satisfaction in life at work. This belief underlies the major theories of job satisfaction in textbooks of industrial psychology. For example, Mayo argued that work organizations are places where men can regain security lost in the throes of the industrial and technological revolution:

For all of us the feeling of security and certainty derives always from assured membership of a group. If this is lost, no monetary gain, no job guarantee can be sufficient compensation. Where groups change ceaselessly as jobs and mechanical processes change, the individual inevitably experiences a sense of void, or emptiness, where his fathers knew the joy of comradeship and security.

If we fail to provide the worker with this assured group membership, then 'in such a situation, his anxieties – many no doubt, irrational or ill-founded – increase and he becomes more difficult both to fellow workers and to supervision' (Mayo, 1945 quoted in Pugh, 1971, p. 221). The satisfaction of social needs in a face-to-face cooperative relationship with fellow-workers became a paramount goal for enlightened management. Not only would such a policy be humane, it would likely increase production!

Such optimism was short-lived, because, as we saw in chapter 8, socially satisfied workers were not necessarily hard-working. Later investigators have adopted a more complex theory of the needs of man, with an emphasis on 'psychological growth'. Man is seen to progress from a concern with physiological 'deficit' needs (Maslow, 1954) to a preoccupation with the 'social' needs emphasized by Mayo and his followers, finally to a concern with the 'growth' needs of 'self-actualization'. When needs at one level are adequately satisfied then progress is made to the next level. Argyris (1960) suggested that a concentration on social needs at work may seriously frustrate the individual, and hamper the organization, because informal group loyalties may powerfully frustrate organizational goals. Concern with self-actualization, however, offers the prospect of reconciliation between the needs of the organization and the needs of man. The skill lies in ensuring an appropriate match between individual needs and organizational demands.

McGregor (1960) is more explicit about the neglect of the 'higher' needs of workers. Current managerial philosophy makes certain unwarranted assumptions about the nature of man, he says. These are enshrined in 'Theory X' – the 'traditional view of direction and control'. Theory X assumes that man dislikes work by nature, that he must therefore be compelled to work, and that he prefers to avoid responsibility and seek security above all else. This allegedly depressing theory is contrasted with 'Theory Y', which paints a more optimistic portrait of man. According to this theory, man willingly expends effort in pursuit of (self-actualizing) goals to which he is committed. Work organizations must therefore ensure that members are given the opportunity to achieve psychological growth in the pursuit of organizational goals. This is termed integration, which is 'the creation of conditions such that the members of the organization can achieve their own goals best by directing their efforts towards the success of the enterprise' (Pugh, p. 317).

This happy coincidence is certainly not everyone's lot, a fact not lost on Herzberg *et al.* (1959). What happens when the higher-order growth needs are not satisfied by the work a man does? Not active dissatisfaction, according to Herzberg. Such a man will merely not work for the sake of it – he will not be 'intrinsically' motivated to work, but given adequate wages and conditions he will yield an average performance. On the other hand, if security and good working conditions are absent then, indeed, workers will be dissatisfied and put in a less than satisfactory performance at work. The evidence for this 'two-factor theory' of the independent origins of job satisfaction and job dissatisfaction is based on interviews with workers, who were asked to think of times when they felt (i) 'exceptionally good' and (ii) 'exceptionally bad' about their work, to say what events had caused these feelings, and why. In accounts of 'good' times (job satisfaction), work-related reasons for satisfaction were cited by the respondents – promotion, recognition, the rewarding nature of the work itself, achieving results, etc. The causes of bad feelings, however, were laid at the feet of management and the working environment provided for them – 'extrinsic' factors like poor supervision, low pay, bad facilities, inadequate or unfriendly supervision, and no opportunities for friendship. Unfortunately for the theory, Herzberg's results may well depend on respondents being anxious to make a good impression. In a selection interview, 'Herzbergian' results are obtained much more readily than in a confidential research situation (Wall, Stephenson and Skidmore, 1971). The desire to give a good account of oneself probably accounts for the differences obtained in the interview situation. Satisfaction is attributed to own achievement, whereas dissatisfaction is conveniently attributed to a deficient environment. This interpretation received further support in another study by Wall and Stephenson (1970) which showed a highly significant relationship between the personality characteristic 'need for social approval' and the tendency to give results consistent with Herzberg's theory. The evidence suggested additionally that greater distortion occurred in accounts of job dissatisfaction, the implication being that the importance of work-related factors in accounts of dissatisfaction are seriously underestimated.

Is there any evidence at all that satisfaction of needs at work determines satisfaction with one's job? There have been very many attempts to correlate job satisfaction with factors which it is assumed on common-sense grounds will contribute to an individual's well-being: pay, advancement, security, status, complexity of the job, variety, etc. – with disappointing results. Important factors in one situation fail to impress in another (see Turner and Lawrence, 1965). Indeed, it was such inconsistency that drove Herzberg to develop the two-factor theory. The inconsistency should not, however, surprise psychologists. No doubt all persons 'need' food, as they may 'need' other people or a degree of variety in their pursuits. All persons will not, however, *value* the satisfaction of these needs equally. As Vroom (1964) suggests, it is necessary to discover what people *prefer*, and the ease with which they imagine these preferences may be satisfied, before we can reasonably predict their contentment with a particular outcome. Locke (1969) defines job satisfaction and job dissatisfaction as 'a function of the perceived relationship between what one wants from one's job and what one perceives it is offering or entailing'. The *discrepancy* between what is valued and what the existing state of affairs is seen to offer is said to account for an individual's degree of satisfaction with his job.

Orientation to work – the importance of employees' values

A number of English sociologists have recently developed an approach to the understanding of employee-motivation which advances Locke's viewpoint (see Goldthorpe *et al.*, 1970; Ingham, 1970; and Cotgrove, 1972). Let us imagine that for some people work is primarily a means to ends that lie outside the work situation – they adopt a largely instrumental and *economic* attitude to work. Such people should choose jobs that offer good material benefits in the form of high wages and security, and should be prepared to accept certain deprivations in other directions, e.g. boring work and isolation from fellow-workers and supervisors. Others may be *expressively* oriented. For them the work situation is seen primarily as an opportunity for self-fulfilment, in work itself and in cooperation with fellow-workers. These people would seek out jobs that offered intrinsically satisfying work with opportunities for meaningful acquaintance with fellow members of the organization at all levels. Even if not well-paid, such jobs would still be preferred to better paid but less intrinsically rewarding occupations. If these two types of people exist we might find that in low-paid satisfying jobs the *expressive* type predominates and that in well-paid unsatisfying jobs the *economic* type prevails. Moreover, in both instances workers should be largely content with their lot, a prediction that contradicts the views of other theorists we have considered, who stress the unhappiness arising from failure to meet certain expressive needs at work. How can the worth of these alternatives be estimated? Ingham (1970), in a study of unit and small batch production systems in light engineering, suggests that organizational size – independently of technology – directly determines the availability of rewards sought by the two types. Increased specialization and bureaucracy in large firms means that in small firms (i) jobs are more varied, for the workers will be asked to exercise a variety of skills and to rotate jobs if circumstances dictate such a procedure, and that (ii) social relationships are richer, because procedural rules in the large firm prescribe what interaction is permitted between members of the work force, whereas in the small firm it may frequently be possible for the total organization to realize itself as a single work group. Finally, the worker's relationships to those in authority are very different in the small firm from those prevailing in the large firm. Bureaucratization in the large plant yields more levels of authority, with the worker coming into contact mainly with his immediate superior.

Compared with workers in large plants (5000 plus work-force), workers from small firms (sixty-three or fewer work-force) reported more social and work-related rewards. They talked to supervisors, the works manager and the director more frequently on both work, and non-work topics, rotated jobs more frequently, took more breaks between jobs and talked more to their fellow-workers. But workers in the small firms were paid substantially less – about 20 per cent on

TABLE 3 *Available rewards and orientation to work in small and large firms*

	Small firms	Large firms
Type of reward		
economic	low	high
non-economic	high	low
Orientation	social/the work itself	economic/instrumental

average. The preferences of workers reflected these differences in the availability of rewards in small and large firms (see Table 3). Workers in the small firms stated that it was largely the friendly social relations and the interesting work that attracted them to their present job, whereas economic advantages were stressed by workers in the large firms. Workers prepared to change jobs for higher wages were located primarily in the large firms, and workers in small firms gave predominantly non-economic reasons for leaving their last job. Interestingly, workers in both situations liked their foreman, but for different reasons – in large firms because he kept out of the way, and in small firms because he was considerate and friendly!

Are the contrasting orientations merely a rationalization of the circumstances in which the workers find themselves? It is unlikely that this explanation of the results constitutes the whole truth. For a start, workers in both small and large firms were, strangely, equally satisfied with their wages, yet workers in small firms were paradoxically *less* satisfied than those in large firms with the non-economic aspects of their work! Presumably workers in the large plants had markedly lower expectations in this area, which would be consistent with the notion of distinctive values. Moreover, Ingham, following Goldthorpe, shows that an economistic/instrumental orientation is related systematically to social background. The 'instrumental' workers had moved around the country more, and were more likely to have had experience of white collar occupations. Hence, their particular orientation to work may be seen to reflect a life-style concerned generally with maintaining material status regardless of the social consequences. Some credence is lent to this analysis by an American study (Form and Geschwander, 1962) showing that job satisfaction scores are related to the occupational status of an individual relative to that of his father, brother or peers generally. Satisfaction is greatest in those who are upwardly mobile beyond the average, least in those who fall behind. However, Cotgrove (1972) presents an interesting study and analysis of chemical plants in five different regions which challenges some aspects of both Goldthorpe's and Ingham's approach. He concludes that to value the material rewards of a job does not by any means rule out a concern for the intrinsic rewards a job may offer in work. All these writers confirm that the demand to be treated *equitably* is one value of general importance in social life, and one which, regardless of the predominant orientation to work, will markedly affect satisfaction with one's job. A person's rewards, to be fair, must be commensurate with his 'investments' (social worth, skill, age, etc.) in comparison with others in comparable situations. Many writers (see Stephenson, 1971) testify to the important role that social comparisons play in determining contentment with wages. Falling below the achievement of those who are comparably qualified creates feelings of inequity that will seek expression in attitudes to work.

Accepting direction – some questions of leadership

Introduction – relationship to the organization

Organizations may plan the activities of all their members, but some participants find their activities more subject to direction than others. How do organizations control their members? Etzioni (1961) suggests that an effective organization matches the predominant means of control with the orientations of its membership (see Table 4). In

TABLE 4   *Appropriate types of compliance in organizations (after Etzioni 1961)*

Type of organizational power	*Kind of individual involvement*		
	Alienative	*Calculative*	*Moral*
coercive	coercive		
remunerative		utilitarian	
normative			normative

prisons, some mental hospitals and concentration camps *coercive* relations predominate. Work organizations and peacetime military organizations exemplify *utilitarian* relationships, and religious, political, educational and voluntary organizations depend largely upon *normative* commitment from their members. Of course organizations are not strictly limited to one or other kind of power, and individuals may exhibit more than one kind of involvement in an organization. The coercive power of employers may be limited, but it exists, waxes and wanes with fluctuations in the economic climate, and varies from one city to another, certainly from one country to another. Unskilled, unqualified workers are most vulnerable, and their greater tendency to alienation is unsurprising. Some white-collar and professional workers, on the other hand, can afford the luxury of personal belief in the value of their labours, such as to make the organization's remunerative power of secondary importance.

Does it matter to the organization concerned just how authority is exercised? What is characteristic of leadership in successful, highly productive groups? These are questions to which there are few straightforward answers, despite the large number of publications on the topics of leadership, management and supervision which have appeared in the social science literature in the past thirty years or so. Undoubtedly one reason for the failure to achieve valid generalizations is changing expectations stemming from variations in the moral and political climate. There has also been a tendency on the part of psychologists merely to reflect humane concern for conditions in industry, or business zeal, whilst ignoring important questions of description and explanation. However, we have learned something about the effects of technological and organizational factors on style of leadership, and about the effectiveness of different leadership styles. We shall conclude this chapter with a discussion of these problems. For additional material on leadership in small groups and on productivity and effectiveness see the second halves of chapters 7 and 8 respectively.

Factors determining a leader's style of supervision

Relations between a leader and his subordinates are reciprocal; they respond to him, and he responds to them. It is commonly assumed that the leader's behaviour is the more important component, but some recent experiments make it evident that behaviour itself may be determined by the response of his subordinates. Lowin and Craig's (1968) experimental evidence suggests that in exchange for solid accomplishment, supervisors will behave in a relatively relaxed, considerate manner, consulting more with their subordinates. Crowe, Bochner and Clark (1972) extended these findings to show that regardless of a manager's preference for a generally considerate, or generally demanding, remote style of leadership, his actual behaviour was strongly influenced by that of his subordinates. Subjects trained to act 'democratically' produced democratic managers, and 'autocratic' subjects were rewarded with autocratic behaviour from their superiors. This work throws considerable doubt on general statements about the effectiveness of a particular style of supervision that is based on inferences from correlations between supervisory and subordinate behaviour.

Lowin (1968) argues that 'participative decision making' (PDM) – in which decisions are made by those whose job it will be to execute them – meets the needs of subordinates, managers and organizations better than does 'hierarchical control', in which decision making and action are rigidly separated. However, evidence for the effectiveness of PDM is not convincing. The work of Heller and Yukl (1969) suggests that, in practice, a manager's decision-style is determined by his position in the organization. They examined the location of managers on a continuum of subordinate influence from 'own decision without explanation' to 'delegation', as in Figure 15. Senior managers gave more scope to subordinates than did junior managers and supervisors, perhaps reflecting the complexity of the decisions made.

Figure 15   Decision-styles of managers in terms of permitted degree of subordinate influence

Production and finance managers tended to use more 'centralized' procedures (low subordinate influence) than did the less specialized 'general' and personnel managers, there being perhaps less scope for debate and argument about appropriate conduct in the former than in the latter. Amongst senior managers, those with many subordinates tended to use the least time-consuming procedures, 'own decision without explanation' and 'delegation'.

Dubin (1965) likewise reflected on the fact that there is no straightforward relationship between group productivity and the behaviour of work group leaders. He suggested that appropriate and effective behaviour varies according to technology. Close supervision would be deemed inappropriate when the control of production is directly in the worker's own hands. Supervisory behaviour must be appropriate to the work setting. Argyle *et al.* (1958) suggested that another organizational variable, the incentive payments system, critically determines the effectiveness of different supervisory styles. Hunt and Leibscher (1973), and Mannheim *et al.* (1967) showed that the behaviour of supervisors varies according to the work setting, and that in different organizations subordinates demand different attitudes from their supervisors. For example, clerical and manual workers differ in the extent to which they welcome direction and guidance from the supervisor, manual workers receiving more than they expected, clerical workers rather less.

One theory of leadership in organizations has emerged which pays more than lip service to situational variables. Fiedler's (1967) 'contingency theory' of leadership effectiveness, which was outlined in chapter 7, suggests that the favourability of a situation determines which of two styles of leadership ('low LPC' – least preferred coworker – and 'high LPC') is the more effective. What is there about the behaviour of high and low LPC persons which makes them differentially effective in situations which vary in their favourability to the leader? Evidence is slight indeed, and the picture is by no means as clear as previously supposed. Fishbein *et al.* (1969) suggest that high and low LPC persons have a different kind of undesirable coworker in mind when making their judgements. The high LPC person is irked by the pushing, dogmatic, intelligent type, whereas the low LPC person is irritated more by the unpleasant, unfriendly, unwholesome character. Moreover, Fiedler's (1972) own re-interpretation of the LPC score suggests that the putative employee- or task-centredness of the two types emerges only in unfavourable circumstances. 'Employee-orientation' is not a characteristic trait of leaders; it is a strategy variously employed by different leaders according to the favourability of the situation.

Dimensions of leadership in organizations

Fiedler's conception of task and relationship orientations is a variant of the traditional "democratic *versus* autocratic" juxtaposition popularized in social psychology by Kurt Lewin in the 1930s, but both notions confuse a number of different, contrasting behaviours. In fact, Yukl (1971) proposes that three independent dimensions of leadership in organizations can be distinguished – all of which have been at different times associated with the autocratic/democratic division. *Consideration* refers to the leader's concern and respect for his subordinates, whereas *initiating structure* refers to the leader's direction of others towards the attainment of group goals (see the discussion of leadership functions in chapter 7). Yukl proposes that a third dimension of leadership – *decision centralization* – should also be considered. According to Yukl, these three aspects of leader behaviour may vary independently – in principle if not in practice. A leader may be considerate, but unconcerned about allocating roles, or about sharing the responsibility for making decisions. Similarly, he may be concerned with procedure, but be quite prepared to share responsibility with his subordinates for determining the form that procedure should take.

Yukl's analysis is especially useful in its specification of the variables which directly influence the productivity of work groups (see chapter 8), and the ways in which leadership techniques impinge on them. A leader's consideration for his subordinates may improve

Figure 16   Dimensions of leadership style and their main effects on the factors influencing group performance (after Yukl, 1971)

their motivation (as Figure 16 indicates) but it is most unlikely to influence their *level of skill*, or the *organization of the work*, to complete the list of three variables singled out by Yukl.

Decision centralization – the tendency for the supervisor to take all the decisions off his own bat without involving subordinates – directly affects the organization of the work group, and possibly the motivation of subordinates. Initiating structure represents the leader's tendency to involve himself in implementing decisions once made, and this may affect all three variables, but principally the subordinate's level of skill.

In past research the assumption has been that supervisory style will affect group performance principally via its effect on the motivation of employees. Much work has certainly suggested that a leader's consideration for his employees seriously affects their willingness to cooperate with him. There is less certainty about the effects of 'initiating structure' and 'decision centralization'. We must say, however, that to the extent that a supervisor has control over the allocation of persons, including himself, to different tasks, then his tendency to monopolize decision making and to direct operations closely may critically affect the efficiency of the group.

Conclusion

In this chapter, we have brought to the fore some fundamental questions of the relationship of individuals to organizations. There are two points I wish to make in conclusion. In one respect, the individual has been rated too highly in studies of organizational behaviour. Behavioural scientists in hospitals, schools, prisons and work organizations too frequently assume that organizational ends are best served by directing our efforts towards improving skills and changing individual attitudes. We have repeatedly seen, to the contrary, that an individual's 'predispositions are likely to be less critical than the demands of the social system' (Steiner, 1972, p.170). Against this, it must be pointed out that psychologists have been slow to document the effects of organizations upon individuals. The organizational careers of individuals at all levels within organizations have been sadly neglected. Cohen and Taylor (1972) rightly criticize the paucity of psychological research on the effects of long-term custody on personality. Other organizations have fared little better at our hands. The work described in this chapter is a fair sample, and it reflects repeatedly the concern with the contribution individuals may make, or be made to make, to the realization of organizational goals. This is but one side of the coin, and we may hope that future social psychological research will increasingly redress the balance by exploring equally the impact of organizations upon the lives of those who sustain them.

Further Reading

Beynon, H. (1973), *Working for Ford*, Penguin Books. An engrossing study of the impact of the organization on the car worker, and vice versa.

Goffman, E. (1961), *Asylums*, Penguin Books. Illuminative, and influential, discussions of the impact of 'total' institutional life.

Hargreaves, D. (1972), *Interpersonal Relations and Education*, London, Routledge & Kegan Paul. Touches on a number of aspects of the school as an organization.

Katz, D., and Kahn, R. (1966), *The Social Psychology of Organizations*, New York, Wiley. The standard text in the area.

Argyris, C. (1972), *The Applicability of Organizational Sociology*, Cambridge, Cambridge University Press. A critical treatment of work on organizations, stressing the need for better social psychological analyses.

Chapter 14
The Environment and Social Behaviour

Anne Whyte

Introduction

For much of social psychology, the environment forms the stage and background of human thought and action. In studies of the environment it may also play the part of actor, scriptwriter, and even at times that of critic. In extreme cases of environmental hazards it can close the show. In whichever role the environment is cast, the focus of environmental studies is on the interplay between man and his environment. In this it has something to tell us about social behaviour.

At first glance environmental studies are a heterogeneous collection ranging from blacks' images of their ghettos to the behaviour of patients in open-plan wards; and from landscape aesthetics to engineers' attitudes to water pollution. They include research that might otherwise be designated within architecture, urban and regional planning, geography, anthropology, sociology, political science and environmental management as well as psychology and social psychology. It is a genuinely multi-disciplinary field which has received great impetus from the environmental movement of the last decade. As an area of study it has kept close to the practical needs of architects, planners, engineers and governments and has come to identify many of its research questions with the urgent problems of increasing pollution and depleting resources, and the social and planning crises in our cities.

This has led to a body of research which is characteristically problem-oriented, seeking answers which are capable of implementation in the short-term. Its objectives and applications are thus often better defined than its hypotheses and theoretical models. A major contribution of the study of the environment to our understanding of social behaviour has been its application of social and psychological concepts and methods to real situations. On the other hand it has often failed to ask critical questions of the theories it has tested and it has sometimes narrowed down the definition of environment to an arrangement of furniture or the distance between camp-sites. Thus we are sometimes in danger of seeking reality by stepping out of the controlled experimental laboratory only to enter the designed behavioural setting. This is a sideways shuffle that fails to explore the complexity and uncertainty that are key features of the 'real' environment beyond.

In keeping with the spirit of this book this chapter will consider environmental studies as a *social* science. It will extend it to include theory and research in social anthropology and ethnology which is relevant to an understanding of social behaviour in relation to the environment.

The geographic and architectural environment is not only highly variable and complex in space. It also changes through time. Some of these changes are related to recurring environmental processes such as climatic fluctuation and natural erosion and deposition. Likewise, the environment of buildings and cities is undergoing rapid change towards increasing complexity and attempted control. Thus major questions in environmental studies are how *different* environments are related to different social behaviour; and how both behaviour and environment are interacting and adapting to *changes* they are mutually producing for each other. The linking question is how the *complexity* of the environment is reduced to order by man and society and thus forms a basis for social behaviour.

The *physical environment* is a broad concept which includes the *natural environment* of land, air, water, plants and animals, and the *built environment*. Components of the natural environment have their origin independent of man but they are almost everywhere modified by him. The built environment has been the focus of much work on environmental planning and design. It is largely that of towns, villages and cities although it also includes roads, hedges and quarries as these are all the works of man.

Models of man–environment interaction

In the study of the environment the processes postulated between man and environment are parallel to those operating between man and man. Some are familiar and enter everyday language. The land with which we identify we may call our 'fatherland' or 'mother-country'. We 'struggle with nature' and 'gamble on the weather'. The models of interaction used reflect the social nature of the processes involved. They are models of cooperation, conflict, negotiation and attribution as well as those of learning, adaptation and reinforcement. Thus, for example, social response to hazards like drought, earthquakes or air pollution has been analysed within each of the frameworks of game theory, attribution theory, decision theory and organization theory.

The man–environment interaction can be looked at by:

(i) Controlling for the environment and varying social factors (e.g. individual versus group, personality, culture, socio-economic characteristics, role and organization).

(ii) Controlling for social factors and varying environments (e.g. landscape and architectural characteristics, function, arrangement, complexity, nature of environmental processes, uncertainty, magnitude and frequency of events).

(iii) Controlling and varying some of each (social and environmental variables).

Cognitive models

Cognitive models of the man–environment interaction are principally concerned with the reduction of environmental complexity to cognitive order. Order here means the way man categorizes the environment; the number, sequence, size and flexibility of those categories and what elements he puts in them. It also includes the relation of the categories to one another, and their overall organization. The sorts of categories we are concerned with are the conceptualization of cities into districts, paths and landmarks as a means of getting about them; the verbal associations given to abstract qualities of environments (such as natural–orderly); and the bases for discrimination between categories which provide us with environmental constructs and stereotypes. Cognitive models have thus come to be concerned with 'urban images', neighbourhood perception, and 'mental maps'. They also include aspects of personality in relation to the environment, especially the concepts of different 'cognitive styles' and the development of environmental personality scales.

Some of the major questions to which these cognitive models have been applied are:

(i) How does man cognitively structure large-scale environments and environmental processes which he cannot see at one time but may conceptualize as an entity, e.g. neighbourhoods, towns, pollution hazards, extreme natural events, wilderness areas?

(ii) How are differences in cognitive structuring of the environment between socially and culturally distinct groups related to differences in their social (often spatial) behaviour?

(iii) Are differences in cognitive structuring between groups related to different cognitive styles or developmental levels?

(iv) What environmental stereotypes and attitudes do we have?

(v) How do men come to terms with the inconsistencies between their environmental cognitions and the choices they have made?

(vi) What relationships are there between aspects of personality and types of environment?

Decision-making models

Whereas the key words for cognitive models are 'order out of complexity' (see chapter 12), those for decision-making models are 'choice in uncertainty'. The environment presents us with information which is highly varied and uncertain. The individual may move within a short space of time from room to city street, through suburbia and rural landscape to mountains or the sea. Each environment presents risk, opportunity and choice. Alternatives are likely to be unclear, contradictory and open to misjudgement. Social behaviour in relation to the environment can therefore very readily be conceptualized in terms of decision-making, whether the environment is regarded as an information system or a player against man in an environmental game. If we consider the main questions of classic decision theory, each are relevant problems in the study of the environment:

1. How do men judge the utility (attractiveness, value) of different alternatives?

2. How do men judge the probabilities of different alternatives occurring?

3. How does additional information change judgement?

4. How are utility and probability judgements combined to make choices such that the same combination of alternatives does not always produce the same solution (choice)?

5. How does one measure utility and objective and subjective probability?

Many of the decision models have been applied to natural and man-made environmental hazards. Droughts and hurricanes have magnitude and frequency probabilities which can be ascertained from meteorological records and can be compared with the subjective probabilities judged by local residents. Such hazards provide good field situations for analysing social behaviour within an environmental decision-theory framework. Decision models are also applied to spatial behaviour such as when to travel to the beach for the day when the weather is uncertain. Information models of communication between groups and individuals are being explored in two directions: (i) as a means of explaining the diffusion of ideas and spatial migration of people, and (ii) to model the communication of information about environmental risk between groups involved in environmental policy and management.

The types of questions being asked of environmental decision-making models are:

1. How do men judge the magnitude and frequency (probability) and effects (utility) of (i) uncertain but recurring events, e.g. rainfall, water pollution and (ii) very rare events, e.g. nuclear radiation hazard, earthquakes?

2. How do they make choices in response to environmental hazards (i) before, (ii) during and (iii) after the event?

3. How do men (particularly policy-makers and scientists in

contrast to the general public) compare different environmental risks to determine policy priorities?

4. How does information about environmental risk and opportunity pass between groups and affect their judgements and behaviour?

5. How does additional information and different presentation of information affect judgement and choice?

Environmental cognition

It is the existence of variety in the environment that enables us to conceptualize space in terms of sequence, distance and orientation. Without such markers both time and space would be inaccessible constructs to us. As an example of cognitive organization of the environment, let us take the city.

Urban images

How do we cognitively structure a city in order to live and work in it and find our way about? In a number of studies in Europe and the Americas initiated by the pioneering work of Kevin Lynch in his *The Image of the City* (1960) general agreement has been found in the categories people use to simplify urban diversity. Lynch was concerned with the 'imageability' or 'legibility' of the city.

Some cities have high imageability. Others do not. Despite such differences, people appear to organize their images of cities into the same five categories. These are paths, nodes, edges, districts and landmarks. *Paths* are any routeway for walking or driving and together form the framework for the 'mental map' of the city. Where paths lack continuity or are easily confused with each other the entire city image appears to be in jeopardy. *Nodes* represent points of decision and choice. The mental map is orientated and scaled by means of *landmarks* along paths. We mentally calculate distance and our position by reference to a network of landmarks that can be seen from our route. Landmarks provide reinforcement that we are on the right track and act as signals guiding our decisions. As we become increasingly familiar with an area or road we construct for ourselves a denser and more personal network or series of landmarks. The absence of sufficient landmarks can be a significant factor in people's dissatisfaction and disorientation in an area.

Districts are relatively large city areas which the observer can mentally and physically enter and which he sees as having common characteristics despite a detailed diversity of form and function. They seem to be defined in terms of a core area out from which there is a gradient of decreasing similarity towards the edges. *Edges* thus serve to divide districts, but not to define them. Where paths form a poor structure for organizing the urban image, districts sometimes serve to orient and place us. In Boston respondents pointed out that although the paths were confusing the districts were so clearly different from each other that one could always tell where one was. Even confusion can help to locate us. One respondent always knew she was in the North End of Boston as soon as she felt she was getting lost.

Urban images have been obtained by using trained observers and asking samples of the general public to record verbally their impressions, to draw maps, to direct other people in the street, and to walk or drive along specific routes taking a continuous record (either verbally or by eye camera) or responding to an interview or questionnaire afterwards. The use of maps or verbal records produces some difficulty in comparing the images of different ethnic and social groups for much the same reasons that cross-cultural comparisons of IQ tests founder. The ability to draw maps is very dependent on experience and education.

This is one of the reasons why it is difficult to interpret the results of studies which show marked differences between the urban images of different social and cultural groups within the same city. In Los Angeles, Mexicans living almost in the city centre have a restricted and unintegrated image of the city compared to that of white intellectuals living near the university campus. Black residents near Watts, a former riot area, had highly detailed and integrated images of a very localized area. While these results may conform with our cultural stereotypes of these groups, they do not relate to their spatial behaviour patterns in Los Angeles. Both the Mexican and black groups have to travel farther than the whites through the city to get to work but perhaps both cognitively and socially it is a no-man's land to them.

Neighbourhood perception

Within towns and cities, the most important and familiar districts for most people are their own neighbourhood. Despite increasing social mobility, which means that many people will move to several different neighbourhoods, cities and parts of the country during their lifetime, the Community Attitudes Surveys (1969) for England and Scotland found that between 78 per cent and 85 per cent of respondents felt they had a neighbourhood area in which they lived. The size of the area perceived as one's neighbourhood gets larger the longer one lives there and with higher educational and socio-economic levels of the residents. It also seems to get larger in bigger towns and for densely populated areas. Thus there appear to be close parallels with concepts of territoriality in man and animals.

Territory implies boundaries. Where the sense of territory is strong the boundary between two neighbourhoods is likely to be well-defined by both sides. In Belfast in 1969 Catholic and Protestant residents of the Falls and Springfield area and the Shankill Road area found consensus on exactly where the boundary lay between the two neighbourhoods. Where the neighbourhood has less emotive associations, its boundary is more flexible. Residents of the same street in Boston would regard themselves as living in the upper-class neighbourhood of Beacon Hill if they were of higher socio-economic status themselves. Their poorer neighbours were less concerned with the neighbourhood image presented by their address.

People see themselves as living in neighbourhoods. Estate agents and architects can define them. Planners design neighbourhoods in new towns and urban renewal schemes. All these neighbourhoods may not be the same. In a study of housewives' perception of neighbourhoods in Cambridge, Terence Lee (1968) distinguishes between three types of neighbourhood: the social acquaintance, the homogeneous, and the unit neighbourhoods. The first of these, *social acquaintance*, is the smallest and is defined by social interaction – or at least personal knowledge of who lives where. It is the closest urban equivalent to the face-to-face group of rural societies. The *homo-*

geneous neighbourhood is defined by a relative uniformity of housing and socio-economic status of the residents. The *unit* neighbourhood is a functional unit including amenities like shops, schools and churches, and this is the planners' concept of an urban neighbourhood, even though the housewife may need to structure it cognitively as paths and landmarks to get about it, much as she would for the city as a whole. Social interaction takes place largely within the smallest type of neighbourhood and increases rapidly for a newcomer on arrival and then remains static for about five years before increasing again. But this is now and in England.

Environmental stereotypes and preferences

The way people discriminate between environmental categories and the values they put upon them influences the way unknown environments are conceptualized. We are at the centre of our known world. Ethnocentrism is characteristic of all cultures.

Environmental stereotypes and preferences have been considered at two levels. The more general one is that of cultural *world-view* or cosmology, which tends to be 'pre-Copernican' in that it revolves around the observer and is structured primarily in terms of distance and difference from his own particular environment. The farther away the environment and the more unlike his own, the more the observer will see it in terms of stereotypes. In a study of sixteen-year-old American schoolchildren who had recently studied Africa in their curriculum, of the ninety stimulus words given, less than 25 per cent of the subjects chose 'racial problems', 'Muslim' or 'socialism' as descriptive of Africa. However over 80 per cent of them saw it as a land of 'wild animals' and 'black, native savages' with 'cannibals', 'pygmies' and 'witch doctors' brandishing 'spears', 'poison darts' and 'drums'. The study concludes that Tarzan is a hitherto unrecognized great teacher.

Environmental stereotypes have also been considered at the more restricted level of the ranking of places on a scale of preference. Clearly the stereotypes held for places influence the preferences people have for where they would like to live, work, and go for a visit or to study. These preferences have been obtained for samples of people in the USA, Europe, and Africa on the basis of rankings given in questionnaire responses. The scores from samples are obtained by complex statistical analysis and then mapped. These are known as *mental maps* although neither individuals nor groups have conceptualized the country in the spatial terms that the map describes. In England the highest preferences found for British school-leavers were along the south coast extending northwards through East Anglia and along the Welsh Border country. Overall the preference gradient slopes from south to north, with a hole over London.

Environment as uncertainty

Environmental processes provide temporal uncertainty in space. They range from imperceptible, almost continuous movements in the soil to dramatic events like earthquakes and tornadoes. To man they represent opportunity and risk, resource and hazard. In some areas, environmental uncertainty becomes critical enough to form a hazard rather than a resource. Then judgement, choice, communication and strategy all become important elements in social behaviour in the face of uncertainty.

Judgement and choice in environmental hazards

An environmental hazard is *the* event in a series of environmental fluctuations (such as wet and dry years, river flows, coastal storms or earth movements) which cause death or damage to man and his livelihood. In order to be able to act to minimize the effects of the damaging event, the judgement required is to predict correctly when it will occur. The problem is that we do not usually categorize events in terms of their statistical occurrence in time or space. Classical decision theory is based on the axiom that the decision-maker would be rational if he had complete information. For environmental uncertainty, it is more realistic to consider judgement as resulting from:

(i) heuristic biases in the face of incomplete information

(ii) cognitive and motivational adjustments in favour of opportunity and consistency

(iii) the social context in which the judgement is made.

(i) *Heuristic biases*. Degree of uncertainty really forms a continuum but it is helpful here to think of two contrasting types:

1. *The probability distribution is known but the next event is uncertain.* Environmental hazards with a longer history and higher frequency fall into this class, e.g. droughts, floods, cyclones.

2. *Both the probability distribution and the next event are uncertain.* New hazards and very rare events are included, e.g. radiation hazard from nuclear reactors, mercury pollution, major volcanic eruptions.

In the first case the known probability distribution of, for example, floods provides information for predicting the probability of the next event. This information is judgementally distorted however by at least two heuristic biases. One is the well-known gambler's fallacy in which change is seen as a homeostatic or self-regulating sequence so that if he loses a series of bets, the gambler is sure he will win next time to even things (chance) up. Similarly farmers who have suffered a series of drought years see the next year as being more likely to be a wet one; and those who have just had their homes flooded think it shouldn't happen again for some time. Another heuristic bias is to recall an irregular sequence in terms of a pattern. This is to think of continuous time in terms of cyclic time. It is common among all cultures from New Yorkers to Asian peasants to perceive randomly or irregularly occurring natural hazards as having regular patterns of three-, five- or seven-year cycles.

Where both the probability of the next event and the overall pattern of distribution are uncertain, the short run of information that does exist becomes very important for anchoring judgement. This is especially so where the last event was very recent and serious. After the unprecedented disastrous flooding by tidal wave in Bangladesh in 1971 most respondents expected another such disaster soon. Similarly, an accidental breakdown of one nuclear reactor immediately increases our estimates of a future hazard and anchors our judgement at a higher level even though the probabilities are scientifically judged to remain extremely low.

(ii) *Cognitive and motivational adjustments*. Environmental hazard situations provide two sources of paradox. First, they are areas where people live, and return to, even after having suffered from a hazard. Volcanic islands are classic examples. So also is the rebuilding of Managua or San Francisco on exactly the same fault-line locations after disastrous earthquakes had struck them. The second paradox is that as more effort and cost is expended to protect man from natural hazards, for example in the building of flood prevention works, the more economic damage is inflicted by such hazards upon him. The answer to the first paradox lies in the cognitive and motivational adjustments made and to the second in the type of choice made and its social context.

Hazard areas are also places of opportunity; that is, they have high utility in terms of economic productivity, social desirability or personal satisfaction. Some people have less individual choice about being in a hazardous area than others. Where people live and work is usually more fixed than where they go for a holiday. Social and economic mobility also increases their freedom of choice. It is, however, inconsistent for most people that they place themselves in a risky situation, even though they have motivation for doing so. They achieve consistency by either minimizing the risk (cf. cognitive dissonance processes) or by externalizing it (cf. internal–external locus of control). They are more likely to minimize the hazard where they have most voluntarily put themselves at risk, for example middle-class Americans who have built holiday homes on hurricane-prone beaches. These voluntary residents cognitively reduce the severity and effects of past hurricanes and minimize the probability that their homes will be hit in the future. Permanent residents of tornado or flood-prone areas, especially those who are poor and have low mobility, are more likely to achieve consistency by blaming an outside force for the hazard. Whether they attribute the event to god, fate, chance, nature, or the government, they themselves are not to blame. Thus Mexican peasant cultivators attribute drought to god, tornado-hit Midwesterners call it fate, and the urban poor blame the government for the air pollution they cannot escape.

(iii) *Social context of judgement and choice*. The perception of probability and selection among alternatives generally takes place in a social context of other people's judgements and choices. Often 'other people' means other groups with a higher level of information, organization and authority, such as local and national governments. Thus a national policy constrains the degrees of freedom for local or state decisions, and both affect the range of alternatives open to the individual. His choice may be both constrained (in what he is not permitted to do) and facilitated (e.g. by providing him with financial or other aid to conform to regulations).

The effect of one group's choices constraining another has led to widespread feelings of alienation and powerlessness especially among minority groups and among the urban poor in regard to urban environmental hazards which are largely man-made. The social context of choice is not always a constraining one; it can enable the individual to take *more* risk in search of opportunity and gain. The organization of many tribal and peasant societies is based on a system of reciprocity in which both wealth and loss are redistributed among all the members of the community. This buffers the individual against loss and enables him to accept more risk *as an individual*. The community structure evens out the peaks of both individual success and failure, gain and loss. Private and state insurance schemes in our own society serve much the same function for more restricted aspects of environmental and social risk.

Information models of communication

Information is the reduction of uncertainty. In information theory, one 'bit' of information is the amount required to allow one to choose between two alternatives. Information models of social communication have tended to cast the physical environment into one of two roles; as a source of uncertainty or as a producer of spatial 'drag' or friction. In this second group of models it is usually the effect of *distance* on social communication that is being analysed. Distance may be measured in terms of communication or travel time, its frequency, cost and flexibility, as well as in miles and kilometres. Environmental variability is considered here less a source of uncertainty which man seeks to reduce to order, than a factor which can increase or decrease communication 'distance' and thus the rate of the diffusion of ideas or spatial mobility and social interaction.

These models, many of which have been developed in Sweden, provide powerful explanatory tools for social behaviour in relation to space and distance.

Where environmental uncertainty is very high, for example with some new pollution hazards like mercury and cadmium, it is only by different groups or individuals pooling their own bits of information to piece together an environmental 'jigsaw' that the pattern become clear to any of them; that is, the reduction of uncertainty is dependent on the communication. Thus environmental uncertainty can throw into sharp relief social processes of intergroup communication and provides critical field settings for their analysis. These situations are characterized by:

(i) unknown probability distribution of hazard, unknown next event, and unknown extent of harmful effects;

(ii) a low level of standardized and replicable scientific information;

(iii) high conflict and secrecy because of the involvement of commercial interests and the largely institutionalized channels of communication between them, government and other groups.

From the point of view of each group, the information it receives about the dangers and causes of the hazard can only be evaluated in the light of their own knowledge and beliefs and in terms of the attributes of the informing group – whether that group is considered to have authority and expertise, or is obviously biased. On the other hand, the group with the information will only pass it on to others if they are felt to be sympathetic to the informers' problems and share their viewpoint. This is partly because information shared only by group members is an important means whereby each group identifies itself and feels common internal bonds.

The result is that information about potentially serious environmental risks tends to get passed around a small set of groups who are sympathetic to one another and become a general 'in-group' with everyone else forming a peripheral 'out-group'. This communication pattern is built upon the organizational structure of industry, local and national political and administrative bodies, trades unions, the mass media and the public. However, just because a group is officially supposed to inform another group does not necessarily mean that they do anything more than go through the motions of doing so. Real 'information networks' differ from official communication links. They are more informal, more problem-oriented and flexible, and are commonly based on similarity of professional training or background which cuts across institutional affiliations. These 'information networks' are in some respects the learning process by which established organizational links become modified to adjust to new environmental problems.

Environmental design and management

For many psychologists, the core of environmental studies is the analysis of environmental *influence* on social behaviour. They are most simply constructed where the environment is considered as one or two factors (e.g. distance, angle of light) and behaviour is narrowed down to a particular attitude, interpersonal attribute or act. As the environment becomes more complicated, realistic and larger scale, the methodological problems become severe and the explanatory power of these studies lessens. There is much important and practical work going on in this area and good reviews of the field are available. This section therefore will try to serve instead as an introduction and guide to concepts, methods and problems characteristic of the research.

In the built environment, design is usually focused on architectural *form, function* and *quality*. Form is partly style but it is largely a matter of *space* – its amount, arrangement and density of uses and users.

Space

Space speaks. The way we arrange ourselves in space and move across it is an important component of non-verbal communication (see chapter 5), and has been dubbed 'the language of space'. Everyone has a *personal space* which is a small area of space around them like an envelope which moves with the person and represents his individual territory. If others come within this space, he feels intruded upon. The size of the envelope and the whole way we use space is an expression of both personality and culture. In many Latin American societies, people face each other in conversation at a distance which is uncomfortably small for most Englishmen. On the other hand, a straight queue is a peculiarly English way for a waiting group to organize themselves in space. These ideas and terms have been developed by E. T. Hall in two books, *The Silent Language* (1959) and *The Hidden Dimension* (1966).

What space is speaking about is social interaction and individual territoriality; people coming together and staying apart. To take territoriality first; neighbourhoods have already been described as our home territories. Beyond them, we have what has been called a *home range* which includes frequent visits to other areas such as where we shop or work, and longer, less frequent journeys. Neighbourhoods represent fairly permanent territories. Within any setting people also exhibit temporary territoriality. In libraries, for example, people seek privacy by placing themselves at empty tables or as far away from other occupants as possible. They try to mark their territory with carefully placed books or clothing. In old people's homes, armchairs become the sad focus of aggressive territoriality for people who have no other place. Outdoors, temporary territoriality is common in picnic areas and on beaches. Feelings of territoriality differ with personality. Where personalities are incompatible and people are constrained to be together, for example, in prison, territoriality increases. Dominant people tend to have larger territories and move about more freely.

Territoriality and social interaction are interrelated and both are influenced by environmental variables. The arrangement of furniture and interior divisions has been shown to influence both work productivity and friendship in open-plan offices and learning in school classrooms. At a simpler level, conversation is made most difficult by arranging chairs along a wall and is easier over the corner of a table than directly across it in a facing position. Physical proximity either in work, living accommodation or temporarily in any situation, tends to increase social interaction.

Personal territoriality may negate this at *high densities in space* of either people or objects. In these cases, social distance becomes substituted for physical distance. Patients in open-plan psychiatric wards behave in a more isolated and non-communicative way than those in private rooms. In modern high-rise residential blocks, people live physically close together but remain socially isolated from one another. In beauty spots outside, the number of people sharing the same view (although it may be empty of people) affects one's enjoyment of and satisfaction from the place.

These considerations are all factors in environmental design and management. Poor spatial design can retard social objectives and personal satisfaction, and good design can enhance them. The problem for social behaviour is twofold; how does one disentangle the physical components of the environment from the social ones, and whose behaviour is being determined by whose design?

Behavioural settings

The problem of analysing physical and social components of environments is partly a methodological one. Physical layouts of rooms or buildings interact with differences in personality and roles in affecting memory or influencing behaviour. Often the social components are the most important ones; for example, in groups of small children the amount of interaction is related primarily to the social density (the number of children) and not to the physical density of furniture and objects. Whatever the physical design of a room and its contents, people tend to use it in their own way. For example, they do not randomly allocate themselves within space but with reference to their personalities and roles. Leaders tend to select commanding positions such as the heads of tables, or chairs from which all parts of the room can be seen. Their resulting high activity within the social network is thus *both* a function of their physical position in space (environmental determinism) and *the reasons why they selected that position in the first place*.

Observation, interviewing and recording of spatial movement on *behavioural maps* are all common methods applied to social behaviour in the physical environment. An important approach to the study of physical and social components of the environment acting together to influence social behaviour is that of *ecological* psychology. A particular ecological niche is called a *behavioural setting*; a concept developed by Roger Barker (1968). Behavioural settings vary in scale and complexity but they are defined primarily in terms of *function* although they are made up of physical form and social activity. Thus a shop, church, and busy street are each behavioural settings in which behaviour is a function of physical space, time conditions and people. Often it is the 'fit' between these components that is important; for example, physically small churches tend to be under-manned and in them people show greater support and friendship for each other and assimilate new members more rapidly. The key variable here is not just the physical size of the building but its relative deficit of people.

Architectural determinism

Environmental psychology has also become concerned with environmental management and decision-making. In its analysis of how people assess different environments, feel about buildings and landscapes, and identify contrasting problems for concern and action, important gaps have been shown between the views of professional planners and those of the public. In whatever way social behaviour is related to the physical environment, a common issue is that of architectural determinism – someone is designing the behavioural setting. At the level of designing light and heat in rooms, this seems eminently reasonable. At the level of planning cities and motorways, it is less so and there is growing disquiet at the differences between planners' conceptions of 'better cities' and the public's. The issue is a mounting one. Architectural determinism is being taken outdoors where recreation areas are now being designed for behavioural control. Visitors to some American national parks must go along marked paths which in places are fenced off and moved around to even up heavy wear on the natural environment.

The level of control is also increasing. The room thermostat is a classic example of a homeostatic system for environmental control in *response* to outside changes. But if we lose individual adjustment of that control, our comfort may become discomfort and our periods of working and sleeping regulated. Already behaviour in large modern buildings is institutionalized by heating, air conditioning and even lighting all going on and off at uniform times irrespective of individual timetables. The next step is 'anticipatory environments' which do not merely respond to outside changes to equalize them but set environmental factors independently to encourage desired behaviour.

Social constructions of environment

Architectural determinism as we know it is a modern, technological form of environmental and social control. In a more opportunistic and interpretive (rather than engineered) way, many if not all, societies use the occurrence of natural processes, especially extreme events, to influence human behaviour. The social construction or interpretation put upon a blazing meteorite, volcanic eruption or locust swarm, as an *environmental* sign of approval or disapproval of *social* behaviour has been used to make individuals conform to social norms, encourage groups to undertake great works, and rouse whole societies to rebellion or migration. Two corner stones in these social constructions of environment are the uncertainty that the physical environment presents and the affective bonds between it and man.

Affective bonds

Strong affective bonds link man with specific aspects or places in the physical environment. Particular scenes can repel us or provide the source for inspiration and revelation, beauty and awe. For a group living in a particular environment these personal bonds become partly collective ones, shared by the group and thus defining at once both its territory and social identity. The bonds are sometimes best expressed when threatened; when the tribe is relocated, the peasant community broken up, or the slum-dweller rehoused. To leave is to break the bonds with both the environment and the group. When the Masai tribe were relocated, they tried to preserve their spatial cues to group identity by renaming their new environment with the same assemblage of names as their former territory. For the Australian Aborigine, the whole physical environment is his 'living, age-old family tree'.

Symbols

Affective bonds are strongest for particular environmental components and places. Environmental categories such as mountains, caves, wilderness or suburbia also have valency; that is, they are not neutral but evoke positive and negative feelings. The ways they are valued and the meaning derived from them can be abstracted so that both particular places and general categories of the environment become symbols. Even space is symbolic. Upwards is ascendancy, progress, heaven for the upright man. In many cultures, religious and ceremonial buildings have careful, symbolic orientation. Mountains have been symbols of the gods, majesty and terror; a Mount Olympus or Mount Tabor. Caves are secret places, symbols of conspiracy and prophecy. Colours are symbolic and their meaning becomes attached to plants, animals and rock formations possessing those colours: white for purity and black for evil.

The power of these natural symbols for social behaviour lies in (i) the way they are organized to form a symbolic code or language and (ii) the way they are made operational through the interpretation of environmental 'signs'. The second is perhaps easier to understand than the first. Unusual events are attributed with meaning and when they can be predicted, for example solar eclipses, they give the predictors great social power. The timing of a particular event in relation to a particular person is commonly given significance; parts of sea cliffs are often falling away but when it kills a specific individual who just happened to be there at that moment, one asks, Why *him*? Why *just then*? The notions of chance and random variation are difficult ones for most people and most cultures. Thus when an earthquake flattens a village, or a thunderbolt kills one man, we tend to look for causes and apply a social (often moral) interpretation to a physical event – the villagers had abandoned a ritual; the man had betrayed a friend. A similar search for cause in events we cannot explain is found for economic and social forces such as inflation, poverty and conflict.

Environmental symbols are rarely found singly; they have order and structure. One way to view them is in terms of *order* versus *disorder* and the need to keep the two apart. The actual categories of things that are considered to be ordered or disordered vary between cultures as does the importance attached to their separation. Certain classes of food must be kept apart for many middle-eastern societies; in the Indian caste-system the classes were of people. At a more informal level, the categories of health and disease have been found to be symbolically related to rural and urban environments in France (Herzlich, 1973). Health, goodness, sacredness and cleanliness are all aspects of *order* – they are socially desirable; whereas illness, evil, profanity and dirt are all *disorderly*. Environmental symbols may evolve through time. Since biblical times, wilderness has represented disorder, barrenness and danger in western thought. Cities were once prized for being symbols of order, progress and individual freedom. Today, cities are symbols of corruption, decay and social deprivation, and wilderness areas are places of natural order, beauty and freedom. The one we call a concrete jungle; the other we seek to preserve.

Environment as language

The interpretation of order and symbolism in the environment can be regarded as a necessary cognitive and social device for coping with so much complexity and uncertainty – a means of selecting information and avoiding information overload and cut-out. It can also be argued that the environmental language of categories, signs and symbols is not just a syntax or grammar for giving particular messages but has a deep structure which stems from social structure and the need to organize man in society.

According to this view, environmental categories are derived from human ones and both are expressed in myth and acted out in ritual. The structure of myths in all cultures may therefore similarly have a universal pattern because they are fulfilling a common social function, of expressing order in both the physical environment and social relationships, and pointing out inconsistencies within and between them. Certainly the themes of myths show many common features in different cultures; they are frequently concerned with social inconsistencies and taboos such as incest; and myths are everywhere used as parables for pointing out good and bad social behaviour.

Conclusion

This has been a wide-ranging look at the environment and social behaviour. In it I have tried to show that in our informal, everyday approach to the physical environment and in our scientific theories of man–environment interaction we use *social modes of explanation*. In our search for order and causal explanation in the complexity and uncertainty that the physical environment represents, we accord it social status. We compete and cooperate with it, devise strategies to win against it, blame it for our failures and ask it for success. The physical environment has therefore never been an empty stage for human drama. Its relationship to social behaviour is as varied and as finely modulated as the relationships between two people or two societies.

The problems of explanation in the study of the environment are also general ones in social psychology. Three of the more important ones are (i) the relation of human thought to action; (ii) the selection between alternative choices; and (iii) individual variance.

(i) Environmental studies have tended to over-intellectualize human thought and equate it with attitudes or Kellian *personal constructs*. Even in relation to the physical environment, a behaviour 'act' is sometimes more easily achieved through short-lived but tense feelings of anger or fear than more enduring, but less emotion-stirring attitudes.

(ii) In analysing the selection of alternative choices, the notion of *preferences* has been given more attention than either (a) the idea of minimizing regret or (b) the social context of choice as a means of increasing or decreasing individual freedom of action. Both of these seem promising directions for future research.

(iii) In all environmental settings, people have been shown to modify or change the influence of their physical surroundings. Although the prediction of when, and in what direction, provides explanatory headaches for the social scientist, with the prospect of an increasingly controlled environment before us, individual variance in reacting to normative pressures provides mankind with both problems and hope for the future.

Further Reading

The first good textbook to have appeared in this area is:

Ittelson, W. H., Proshansky, H. M., Rivlin, L. G., and Winkel, G. H. (1974), *An Introduction to Environmental Psychology*, New York, Holt, Rinehart & Winston.

There are two other major reviews of the field, especially of the psychological literature:

Craik, K. H. (1970), 'Environmental psychology' (1970), in K. H. Craik *et al.*, eds., *New Directions in Psychology*, vol. 4, pp. 1–121, New York, Holt, Rinehart & Winston.
Proshansky, H. M., Ittelson, W. H., and Rivlin, L. G., eds. (1970), *Environmental Psychology: Man and his physical setting*, New York, Holt, Rinehart & Winston.

The large amount of field evidence throughout the world, on judgement and choice in relation to uncertainty from natural hazards ranging from tornadoes to tidal waves is brought together in:

White, G. F., ed. (1974), *Natural Hazards: Local, National and Global*, London, Oxford University Press.

Cross-cultural perspectives on social structuring of the physical environment and the role of environmental values and symbols are provided by:

Douglas, M. (1973), *Natural Symbols*, Penguin Books.
Tuan, Yi-Fu (1973), *Topophilia: A Study of Environmental Perception, Attitudes and Values*, New York, Prentice-Hall.

Chapter 15
Language in Society

J. A. Fishman and H. Giles

Introduction

Man is constantly using language – spoken language, written language, printed language – and man is constantly linked to others via shared norms of behaviour. Sociolinguistics examines the interaction between these two aspects of human behaviour: use of language and the social organization of behaviour. Briefly put, sociolinguistics focuses upon the entire gamut of topics related to the social organization of language behaviour, including not only language usage *per se* but also language attitudes, overt behaviour towards language (e.g. language treatment and language planning) and towards language users.

The latter concerns of sociolinguistics – overt behaviour towards language and towards language users – are also shared by political and educational leaders in many parts of the world. These are the aspects of sociolinguistics that frequently make the headlines. Many French-Canadian university students oppose the continuation of public education in English in the province of Quebec. Many Flemings in Belgium protest against anything less than full equality – at the very least – for Dutch in the Brussels area. Some Welsh nationalists daub out English signs along the highways in Wales and many Irish revivalists seek stronger governmental support for the restoration of Erse than that made available during half a century of Irish independence. Jews throughout the world protest against the Soviet government's treatment of Yiddish writers and the forced closing of Yiddish schools, theatres and publications, and some Puerto Rican nationalists strive for less (or no) English in Puerto Rican public and official life.

Swahili, Filipino, Indonesian, Malay and the various provincial languages of India are all being consciously expanded in vocabulary, standardized in spelling and grammar and diversified stylistically so that they can increasingly function as the exclusive languages of government and of higher culture and technology. The successful revival and modernization of Hebrew has encouraged other smaller language communities – the Catalans, the Provençals, the Frisians, the Bretons – to strive to save *their* ethnic mother tongues (or their traditional cultural tongues) from oblivion. New and revised writing systems are being accepted – and, at times, rejected – in many parts of the world by communities that hitherto had little interest in literacy in general or in literacy in their mother tongues in particular.

However, sociolinguistics reaches far beyond interest in case studies and in catalogues of language conflict and language planning in the public arena. It is also concerned with describing the generally accepted social organization of language usage within speech communities (or within speech-and-writing communities, to be more exact). This part of sociolinguistics – descriptive sociolinguistics – seeks to provide an answer to the question 'who speaks (or writes) what language (or what language variety) to whom and when and to what end?' (Fishman, 1972a). Descriptive sociolinguistics tries to disclose the language usage norms – i.e. the generally accepted and implemented social patterns of language use and of behaviour towards language – for particular larger or smaller social networks and communities. Another part of sociolinguistics – dynamic sociolinguistics – seeks to provide an answer to the question 'What accounts for differential changes in the social organization of language use and behaviour toward language?' Dynamic sociolinguistics tries to explain why and how the social organization of language use and behaviour towards language have become selectively different in the *same* social networks or communities on two different occasions. It also seeks to explain why and how two separate but once similar social networks or communities have arrived at a quite different social organization of language use and behaviour towards language over a period of time.

So, we shall look first at the descriptive and then at the dynamic approach to language in society, before considering in some detail the social psychological aspects of accent and speech accommodation in face-to-face interaction. Finally, we shall consider two important areas of application of the study of language in its social context.

Describing language in its social context

Unless we can describe, reliably and perceptively, *existing* patterns of social organization in language use and behaviour towards language it will obviously be impossible to contribute towards the explanation of why or how this pattern changes or remains stable. One of the basic insights of descriptive sociolinguistics is that members of social networks and communities do not always display either the same language usage or the same behaviour towards language (Labov, 1972). Perhaps a few examples will help illustrate this crucial point.

Government functionaries in Brussels who are of Flemish origin do not always speak Dutch *to each other*, even when they all know Dutch *very* well and *equally* well. Not only are there occasions when they speak French to each other instead of Dutch, but there are some occasions when they speak standard Dutch and others when they use a regional variety of Dutch with each other. Indeed, some of them also use different varieties of French with each other as well, one variety being particularly loaded with government officialese, another corresponding to the non-technical conversational French of highly educated circles in Belgium, and still another being not only a 'more colloquial French' but the colloquial French of those who are Flemings. All in all, these several varieties of Dutch and of French constitute the *linguistic repertoire* of certain social networks in Brussels. The task of descriptive sociolinguistics is to describe the general or normative patterns of language use within a speech network or speech community so as to show the systematic nature of the alternations between one variety and another among individuals who share a repertoire of varieties (Fishman, 1970; Fishman, Cooper, Ma, *et al.*, 1971).

However it is not only multilingual speech networks or communities (such as those of most Puerto Ricans in the continental United States and very many on the island as well) who utilize a repertoire of language varieties. In monolingual speech communities the linguistic repertoire of particular social networks may consist of several social class varieties, or of social class and regional varieties of the *same language*. Thus, monolingual native-born New Yorkers speak differently to each other on different occasions – and these differences can be pinpointed phonologically (i.e. in the way words are pronounced), lexically (i.e. in the words that are used) and grammatically (i.e. in the systematic relationship between words). The same young man who sometimes says 'I sure hope yuz guys'll shut the lights before leavin'' also is quite likely to say, or at least to write, 'Kindly extinguish all illumination prior to vacating the premises.' It's all a question of when to say the one and when the other, when interacting with individuals who could understand both equally well but who would consider use of the one when the other is called for as a serious *faux pas*. Certainly the varieties of Puerto Rican Spanish utilized by a middle-class network in various urban centres constitute such repertoires and are put to an array of very appropriate and delimited functions.

Situational shifting

The description of societal patterns of language variety use – a variety being either a different language or a different social, occupational, regional or stylistic cluster of phonological, lexical and grammatical co-occurrences, whenever any two or more varieties are present in the linguistic repertoire of a social network – commonly utilizes the concept of *situation*. A situation is defined by the co-occurrence of two (or more) interlocutors related to each other in a particular way, communicating about a particular topic, in a particular setting. Thus, a social network or community may view a beer-party between university people as a quite different situation from a lecture involving the same people. The topics of talk in the two situations are likely to be different; their locations and times are likely to be different; and the relationships or roles of the interlocutors *vis-à-vis* each other are likely to be different. Any one of these differences may determine the use of a different language variety in each case.

Members of social networks sharing a linguistic repertoire must (and do) know when to shift from one variety to another. One category of such shifts is that known as situational shifts. A shift in situation *may* require a shift in language variety. A shift in language variety *may* signal a shift in the relationship between members of a social network or a shift in the topic and purpose of their interaction, or a shift in the privacy or location of their interaction (Blom and Gumperz, 1972).

The reader will note that we have written '*may* require' and '*may* signal'. Does this mean that a shift in situation does not always and invariably require a shift in language variety, or that a change in language variety does not always.and invariably signal a change in situation? Yes, precisely. At times, members of the same speech network or community go from what strikes the outside observer as being one situation to another without changing from one variety to another. Thus, interaction with one's friends and with one's younger siblings may still be acceptably conducted in the same variety. Obviously, what is or is not a different situation with respect to language variety use is a matter of the internal social organization of particular speech networks or communities. Native members of such networks or communities slowly and unconsciously acquire sociolinguistic communicative competence with respect to appropriate language usage. (Other facets of communicative competence were discussed in chapters 4 and 5.) They are not necessarily aware of the norms that guide their sociolinguistic behaviour. Newcomers to such networks or communities – including sociolinguistic researchers – must discover these norms more rapidly, more painfully and, therefore, more consciously (Hymes, 1967).

No speech network has a linguistic repertoire which is as differentiated as the complete list of apparently different role relations, topics and locations in which its members are involved. In each speech network or community, therefore, there are situations which can be clearly differentiated but which are nevertheless classed as requiring the same language variety. Just where the boundaries come between these classes of situations must be empirically determined by the investigator, and constitutes one of the major tasks of descriptive sociolinguistics. Such classes of situations are referred to as *domains*. The derivation of domains and of domain-appropriate usage from the data of numerous discrete situations and the variety shifting or non-shifting which they reveal is done through participant observation, survey methods, experimental designs and depth interviews (Fishman, 1971).

Metaphorical switching

The fact that members of the same speech networks or speech communities may also change from one variety to another without signalling any change in situation is indicative of the social categorizing in which native members so frequently and effortlessly engage (see chapter 12). When variety switching is fleeting and non-reciprocal it is commonly *metaphorical* in nature. This means that it is utilized for purposes of emphasis or contrast. A switch to Cockney where received pronunciation (and grammar) is called for may well elicit a brief raising of eyebrows or a pause in the conversation – until it is clear from the speaker's demeanour and from the fact that he has reverted to RP that only a humorous interlude rather than a change in situation was intended. However, such metaphorical switching can be risky. Metaphorical switching is a luxury that can be afforded only by those that comfortably share not only the same *set* of situational norms but also the same view as to their inviolability. Since most of us are members of several speech networks, each with somewhat different sociolinguistic norms, the chances that situational shifting and metaphorical switching will be misunderstood and in conflict are obviously considerable (Blom and Gumperz, 1972; Kimple, Cooper and Fishman, 1969).

A speech community maintains its sociolinguistic pattern as long as the functional differentiation of the varieties in its linguistic repertoire is systematically and widely maintained. As long as each variety is associated with a separate class of situations there is good reason and established means for retaining them all, each in its place, notwithstanding the modicum of metaphorical switching that may occur. However, two or more varieties with the same societal function become difficult to maintain and, in the end, one must either displace the other or a new functional differentiation must be arrived at between them. Let us look quickly at how such changes in linguistic repertoire or in functional allocation occur.

Language in use: the bases of repertoire change

At the same time that a linguistic repertoire with its particular societal functional allocation of varieties exists in a particular speech community or network, certain of these same or similar varieties may be found in other or neighbouring speech communities or networks in association with other functions. If the members of these differing speech communities or networks are brought into greater interaction with each other, or if their relative power to influence or control over one another changes sufficiently, then the societal functional allocation or linguistic repertoire of one or another or both is likely to undergo change. Thus, most immigrants to the United States have experienced sufficient interaction with English-speaking Americans, particularly at work and in education, to learn English. This has also long been true for French Canadians in large industrial centres such as Montreal. Yet, how differently these two processes of linguistic repertoire change have worked out. In the United States the immigrants largely lost their mother tongues within one, two, or at most three generations. In Montreal each new French Canadian generation starts off monolingual in French and then acquires English later in life without, however, handing on this second language to the next generation as its initial language. How can we best describe and account for this difference in outcome between two populations each of which was *forced* to acquire English for its educational and economic improvement? The difference seems to be related to the ability of one population to maintain a certain societal functional differentiation within its linguistic repertoire while the other was unable to do so.

Unstable bilingualism

American immigrants needed English both as a *lingua franca*, because they came from so many different speech communities, and as a passport to social and economic advancement within Anglo-American society. Because of the severe dislocation of their 'old-country' rural or small town ways of life (as a result of rapid exposure to American urban, industrial contexts) it quickly became impossible for them to maintain the original home and family patterns upon which their only chance for domain separation depended. Those whose English was better progressed more rapidly on the American scene and became models within the immigrant home and within the immigrant organization and neighbourhood. Thus, the home and immigrant life itself became domains of English – particularly under the additional onslaughts of the American school and the Americanizing and amalgamating efforts of American churches. As a result, children of immigrants also became bilingual in the family and immigrant contexts. Only in these contexts could the non-English mother-tongue have been preserved, and then only if they had been able to maintain themselves as separate, self-contained domains.

This the immigrant speech networks could do only in those few cases where immigrants of a single background clearly predominated (as they had for a long time in the case of German-and-Scandinavian-language islands in the Mid-West) or where their social mobility via English was sharply restricted (as in the case of Spanish speakers in the south-west). Almost everywhere else, economic advancement and the dislocation of traditional home, neighbourhood and organizational practices went hand in hand. There was ultimately no domain in which the non-English ethnic language alone was absolutely required for 'membership' and as a result, there was no domain in which it was retained. The non-English ethnic languages continued somewhat longer to serve fleeting metaphorical purposes but there were soon no situational shifts in which they were required. As a result, children who had been bilingual in their family and in the immigrant neighbourhood became increasingly monolingual English speakers as they passed to and through their English-speaking schools, their English-speaking careers and their English-speaking neighbourhoods. Their own children would be raised in English (Haugen, 1953; Fishman *et al.*, 1966).

Stable bilingualism

In Montreal the situation was and still is very different. French speakers were initially exposed to English instruction and to English jobs only slowly over a long period of time. Their elementary schools for long taught entirely French (as did their churches) and even their secondary schools (in which English instruction *was* offered to those few who attended) were under French auspices. The result was that the monolingual French-speaking child remained such as long as his life was restricted to home, neighbourhood and church. He became increasingly bilingual if he passed through more advanced levels of the school and work domains, but he then reverted to increasing French monolingualism when he passed beyond their reach. As a result, the domains of English and of French were kept functionally quite separate. Not only did the English domains reach proportionally fewer French Canadians, they reached them more superficially. In addition, the youngest and oldest members of the community were basically French-speaking (except for metaphorical purposes); thus assuring that the next generation would be basically French-speaking as well (Lieberson, 1965, 1970).

However, something new has recently been added to the Montreal picture. French Canadian education expanded to the point that it produced more well-qualified or highly qualified individuals than could be assimilated into the various English-managed industrial, commercial and cultural enterprises, which traditionally reserved most of their leading positions for English Canadians. As a result, French-speaking élites have increasingly claimed and formed their own enterprises in these domains. For them English has become increasingly superfluous in view of the lack of domain separation and situational need. In addition, of course, it has become symbolic of their not being masters in their own home, and, as such, is opposed both for general symbolic as well as for specifically functional reasons (Lieberson, 1970; Hughes, 1971).

These two sociolinguistic patterns, the American immigrant and the French Canadian nationalist, have been repeated many times in the past century. The Russification of Soviet minorities – particularly the smaller ones – whether they be immigrants to large urban centres in other regions or inundated by Russian and various other immigrants in their own regions (Lewis, 1972), has followed the same path as that of the anglicizing of immigrants to the United States, the Hispanization of indigenous populations moving to urban centres throughout Latin America, or the Wolofization of diverse Senegalese populations in Dakar. Similarly, the 'indigenization' of the domains of education, industry and government (which had previously 'belonged' to English, so to speak), that has increasingly typified French Canada, is not at all unlike the growing displacement of English in Puerto Rico, Tanzania, India, Malaysia and the Philippines (Epstein, 1970; Das Gupta, 1970; Ramos *et al.*, 1967; Whiteley, 1969). The case of the returning Newyoricans in Puerto Rico can follow either of these two patterns, depending largely on whether it will appear to be to their greater benefit in Puerto Rican society to preserve English as a second language (if at all) or as the mother tongue among their children.

The social psychology of speech accommodation

Thus far, we have discussed some of the ways in which people can alter their speech depending on the situation in which they find themselves, and also some of the ways in which the sociolinguistic norms themselves can be modified in response to societal changes. Social psychological formulations can be of considerable value in extending such analyses to handle details of language shifts in face-to-face interaction, particularly in describing and explaining an important aspect of sociolinguistic behaviour, *speech accommodation*. The following section will be concerned with a discussion of this process in terms of notions derived from similarity-attraction, social exchange and causal attribution theories.

Communication in monolingual contexts

One important feature of social interaction is that individuals adapt to each other's speech patterns on a number of linguistic levels and in a manner that is not fully explicable in terms of situational or metaphorical shifting alone. When two people meet there is a tendency, often unconscious, for them to modify their speech in such a way that they become more alike in accent, speech rate, pitch, loudness and so forth. This *convergent* behaviour can be called 'interpersonal accommodation'. Indeed, many speech shifts that we might label 'situational' can also be included within an accommodation framework, as when an adult uses less complex grammatical structures with children and when people use more prestigious pronunciations with others of higher status or speak more slowly to foreigners. In all these cases, people are accommodating their speech to how they believe others in the situation would like to receive it.

In an attempt to deal with such phenomena, Giles, Taylor and Bourhis (1973) proposed a model which considers accommodation to be a means of facilitating social attraction. It has, as its basis, research on similarity-attraction (Byrne, 1969) which suggests that as A becomes more similar to B, this increases the likelihood that B will favourably evaluate A. Interpersonal accommodation through speech is then one of the many devices that an individual may adopt in order to become more similar to another. Specifically, accommodation involves the reduction of *linguistic* dissimilarities between members of a dyad, as when A matches B's dialect, utterance length, or the like. Since increasing similarity between two people along an important dimension such as communication is likely to increase interpersonal attraction as well as mutual intelligibility (Triandis, 1960), accommodation probably reflects a speaker's desire for social approval. It follows that the greater the speaker's need to gain another's approval or attraction, the greater the magnitude of accommodation that will occur.

However, a person will only accommodate to another on given linguistic features if he has the repertoire which will enable him to do this realistically. For example, a person reared in a private school where high prestige pronunciations were enforced may not have enough verbal and vocal flexibility to allow him to accommodate linguistically to a working-class speaker. If, however, he desires the latter's approval, he may well accommodate to him in some *non*-linguistic respect, and this is an issue which will be discussed later.

The model also relies upon notions of social exchange theory (Homans, 1961) in that an accommodative act should incur more potential rewards than costs for the speaker. Such rewards can include a gain in the listener's approval, while the potential costs may include such factors as expended effort and a loss of personal (and sometimes, cultural) identity. However, the specific rewards that can be obtained may depend on the particular linguistic feature, or features, on which the convergence takes place.

Let us consider accent usage and imagine the context of a job interview in which a candidate has a less prestigious accent than his interviewer. One would predict that the prospective employee in this situation would shift his accent more in the direction of his interviewer than vice versa, in proportion to their relative needs for each other's approval. Studies in Britain and elsewhere have shown that the more prestigious the accent you possess the more favourably you will be perceived on a number of personality-related traits (e.g. intelligence, self-confidence). In addition, what you actually have to say will be considered to be of better quality than the same content spoken in a less prestigious accent. Hence the rewards for our applicant accommodating to the interviewer (a process termed 'upward convergence') would include not only his being more comprehensible to the interviewer, and more sympathetic to him, but also his being viewed more favourably on these personality and content dimensions.

Similarly, one could imagine situations (such as an industrial dispute in a small firm) where there might be a greater need on the part of the employer to gain his workers' social acceptance than vice versa. In this case, the employer would be more prone to shift his accent in the direction of the workers than would the workers to him (downward convergence). On the other hand, situations can arise when a speaker wishes to dissociate himself from his listener, perhaps because of his undesirable attitudes, habits or appearance, and so he may modify his speech away from the other, that is, diverge (Giles, 1973).

Support for these notions comes from studies which have shown that some cultural groups are more favourably disposed towards assisting foreigners who accommodate to their language than those who do not (Harris and Baudin, 1973), and from the more general finding that accommodating individuals induce their recipients to evaluate them more favourably (Dabbs, 1969). Naturally, many more empirical questions need to be posed. For example, are there optimally effective strategies of accommodation through speech in different social contexts, and if so, what are they? Are the strategies meaningfully related to individual differences in personality or cognitive style? In what situations and on what linguistic features is a speaker aware that he is accommodating to another?

Intergroup communication in bilingual contexts

Many regions in the world are characterized by the existence of several ethnolinguistic groups who share the same physical and social space. Most countries in Asia, Africa and South America are multilingual, and other obvious examples, such as Canada, Switzerland and Belgium readily come to mind. Even the American melting-pot includes a variety of ethnolinguistic groups whose identity and language are being maintained. Moreover, many American linguists would even include the black community as having a language distinct from that of the whites.

Little work, however, has been conducted on how different ethnic groups communicate with each other, although an interesting series of experiments on cross-cultural interaction has been conducted by Donald Taylor and his associates in Quebec and the Philippines (Simard and Taylor, 1973). They found that on very structured communication tasks, members of between-group dyads (e.g. a French Canadian with an English Canadian) were just as efficient at communicating with each other as members of within-group dyads (e.g. a French Canadian with a French Canadian). Likewise, in the unstructured situation of a free interaction, mixed-ethnic pairs showed the same pattern of conversational topics, did not take longer to begin communicating and did not talk less than same-ethnic pairs. Yet despite this evidence that communication *between* groups can be objectively as successful as within a group, it has been found that not only do subjects enter these intergroup encounters with negative expectations but they also leave them with an unfavourable impression of what has been achieved. Such negative expectations no doubt serve as an important deterrent to intergroup interaction, as does the fact that each group brings to this situation a system of non-verbal message forms which the other is often likely to misinterpret (see chapter 5).

A useful tactic for alleviating intergroup tension and facilitating positive attitudes in between-group situations may be the adoption of accommodative strategies. Giles, Taylor and Bourhis (1973) have shown that the more effort in speech accommodation a bilingual speaker of one ethnic group was perceived to put into his message, the more favourably he would be perceived by listeners from another ethnic group, and also the more effort they would put into accommodating in turn to him. In a follow-up study, however, it was found that the mere *perception* of accommodation was not in itself sufficient to engender positive feelings in the perceivers; the attribution of *intent* behind this accommodation was found to be of crucial importance. And so in causal attribution terms (see chapter 9), listeners of one group who attributed the intention behind another group's accommodation *internally*, such as to a desire to break down cultural barriers, would perceive the other group's behaviour very positively. However, when this same accommodative act was attributed *externally* to pressures in the situation forcing the other group to converge, such positive feelings were not so readily evoked. Similarly, when *non*-accommodation was externally attributed to situational pressures which demanded own-group language, negative attitudes were not as pronounced as when the act was attributed to a lack of effort on the part of the other group. Furthermore, non-accommodative language can be used by a group as a symbolic tactic for maintaining (or even emphasizing) its ethnic identity (see chapter 17), cultural pride and distinctiveness (Bourhis, Giles and Lambert, 1975). This was exemplified recently, when, for the first time, the Arab nations issued an oil communiqué to the world, not in English, but in Arabic.

The situation may become even more complex in a context of severe intergroup tension when valid and reliable information about another group's true intentions is often lacking, and attribution errors may arise due to negative stereotypes that are held about that group (see chapter 17). For instance, we may be more prepared to attribute accommodation by an outgroup member to unknown pressures in the situation or to deviousness than to a sincere desire to reduce tension. In the same way, we may be more ready to attribute his non-accommodation to a lack of effort rather than to consider that he did not have the appropriate language ability or that there were strong pressures in the situation forcing him to use his native language.

Accommodation through language then, is likely to facilitate positive feelings between members of different ethnic groups if it is attributed positively by recipients. This can take on greater significance when the outgroup is conceding to the ingroup on a dimension that is a highly salient aspect of their ethnic identity. Taylor, Bassili and Aboud (1973), using a multi-dimensional scaling procedure found, in Quebec, that language, as compared to ethnic background and geographical residence, appeared to be the most important determinant of French and English Canadian identity. For example, a French Canadian considered himself more similar to an English Canadian who spoke mainly French than to a French Canadian who spoke mainly English. Similar identity patterns have been found recently among Anglo- and Franco-Americans in Maine, and bilingual and monolingual speakers in Wales. On the other hand, one might expect that language may perform a minor role with respect to ethnic identity in some African, Indian and Middle Eastern groups compared to religion and skin colour. If such situations were found to occur, then one would predict that accommodation through *language* would not in these cultural contexts be so effective a device for reducing intergroup tension; perhaps other behavioural concessions would be more appropriate.

One value of considering certain speech shifts in terms of convergence–divergence is that they are likely to have parallels in other *non*-linguistic phenomena. For example, we can find ourselves laughing at another's humour, dressing according to his values and even agreeing with his attitudes. Indeed, the extent to which people adopt these strategies can be gauged from a knowledge of their value system and the degree to which they find others significant enough to desire their approval. A famous Welsh politician, whenever visiting his constituents, used to change from his Rolls Royce to a Mini car before entering the community. This was a convergent tactic deliberately employed in an attempt to reduce the perceived dissimilarities between himself and the electorate. An analogue of the divergent paradigm would be the case of a man returning in his Rolls Royce to the working-class district where he spent his youth. Sociolinguistic behaviour then can have many parallels in everyday, non-linguistic life. The links between the linguistic and non-linguistic patterns need to be further explored and their relationships to general social psychological principles investigated.

Some applications of sociolinguistics

Sociolinguistics has significance for all the topics normally considered as applications of language studies: native language teaching, second language teaching, translation, the creation and revision of writing systems, language policy decisions, and language planning as a whole. In connection with each of these topics successful 'application' depends not only on competent linguistic analysis of the languages being taught, used or developed but also (perhaps even primarily) upon the social circumstances surrounding all applied efforts in connection with these languages. Similarly, many branches of applied social science, including applied social psychology, stand to benefit from sociolinguistics, since numerous questions in education, medicine, planning, industry, etc., deal with group boundaries, role networks, role repertoires, role compartmentalization, social situations, institutional domains, and the like. The confluence between applied linguistics and applied social science is most dramatically illustrated, first in the context of social and national modernization, a context in which applied sociolinguistics has been most actively pursued (Fishman, Ferguson, Das Gupta, 1968), and secondly with regard to recent controversies regarding the nature of the language of black Americans. Let us look at some examples of work in both these areas.

Language planning

The progress of social and national modernization depends to a large extent upon sufficiently widespread as well as sufficiently advanced literacy. However, such literacy is often impossible because writing systems have not yet been devised for the native languages of various larger and smaller speech communities throughout the world. But it is one thing to devise a simple and technically exact system of representing spoken sounds via written symbols, and quite another to get it accepted by its intended users.

To begin with there must be some felt need for reading and writing, some actual or implied gain, and, not infrequently, an absence of major status loss to those who have hitherto been the status and power élites of the society (Garvin, 1959).

Furthermore, the purely visual aspect of writing systems is also a factor in their acceptance or rejection. Many speech communities have insisted on indigenous writing systems unlike those of other written languages, in order to stress their separateness from their neighbours and their independence from 'big brothers' at a greater geographical distance. Others, on the other hand, have demonstrated positive modelling (rather than anti-modelling), or have had such modelling foisted upon them. It is hardly accidental that the new writing systems of many North American Indian groups 'look like English', that those of Latin American Indians 'look like Spanish', and that those of Siberian peoples 'look like Russian'. The determining factors of such modelling and anti-modelling are all social and political rather than merely linguistic and pedagogical (Fishman, 1972b).

Even more complicated socially than the creation of new writing systems is the revision of old ones. Attempts to simplify spelling or writing systems *per se* have been singularly ineffective in modern times although an inordinate amount of time and effort has gone into such attempts (Smalley, 1964). While the writing systems for Czech, Ukrainian, and Romanian were changed from Cyrillic to Roman alphabets during the nineteenth century, and while the Soviets have changed the writing systems of many Asian nationalities (sometimes more than once within a decade or two), others have experienced far greater difficulty. Communist Chinese plans to phoneticize the writing of Mandarin seem to have been postponed for the indefinite future and Soviet efforts to 'declericalize' Yiddish spelling by abandoning the four 'end of word' letters of the traditional Hebrew alphabet have also been abandoned.

In more widely participatory decision-making settings, spelling reform has proved to be, if anything, even more difficult to execute. Thus, while many developing nations of an earlier period were able to push through spelling reforms before literacy became much more than an élitist preoccupation (e.g. nineteenth-century Germany, post-Revolutionary USSR) neither Israel nor Indonesia–Malaysia nor India nor any other developing nation of today has been able to push through the spelling or writing reforms that would make literacy more accessible to all its citizens. Nevertheless, Norway has been able to revise the spelling of both of its standard national languages in modern times, albeit in an atmosphere of considerable conflict (Haugen, 1966).

It is thus exceedingly difficult to come to conclusions of general significance when entire countries or national entities are taken as units of analysis, particularly when these units are at vastly different stages of social, economic and political development. As a result, applied sociolinguistics has tended more and more towards a detailed study of localized cases of language planning. Focusing increasingly upon different reactions to centrally authorized and controlled language innovations (whether these be orthographic or lexical, on the one hand, or the functional reallocation of codes within a speech-and-writing community, on the other hand), such studies do not speak of success or failure as a nationwide phenomenon but rather, of differential rates of acceptance or rejection (cognitively, affectively and/or overtly) in various population segments.

As a result of recent studies it is becoming increasingly possible for language planning agencies (e.g. for those seeking to foster the use of recently established national languages for purposes of higher education, government or technology) to pinpoint the particular programmes, projects or products that are successful with particular target populations and those that are not. It is becoming increasingly clear that the study of role relationships, role networks, role compartmentalization and role access in speech communities and speech networks is a very *practical* matter indeed.

The language of black Americans

Practical implications of sociolinguistic studies are not confined to developing countries alone. The language of blacks in the United States raises many pressing issues. For long, Negro speech was appraised in extremely negative terms, as can be seen from a description of its origin, written in 1722:

Slovenly and careless of speech, these Gullahs seized upon the peasant English used by some of the early settlers . . . wrapped their clumsy tongues about it as well as they could, and, enriched with certain expressive African words, it issued through their flat noses and thick lips as so workable a form of speech that it was gradually adopted by the other slaves . . . (cited in Turner, 1949).

Indeed, even some black scholars in the early sixties were known to downgrade Negro speech as 'abnormal' and 'lazy', considering it grammatically defective and full of mispronunciations. The view that black speech was a *sub*standard form of American English led to what has been termed the 'deprivation' or 'deficit' argument (see Wrightsman, 1972), which proposes that blacks' non-accommodation to white linguistic norms is due to the fact that they have *failed* to learn to speak 'properly'. Some workers attributed this to under-developed cognitive abilities and poor motivation, while the more liberal attributed it to social and cultural deficits of the blacks.

Because of this situation, many educators felt the need to use second language teaching techniques to provide black children with an alternative (or additional) language variety, namely standard white English. But these innovations were not received enthusiastically by all educators, and many have criticized the programmes as being blatantly racist and ethnocentric in that they presume a white linguistic norm is appropriate for everyone in the country.

Today, however, a distinct shift can be detected away from this argument and towards what has been termed the 'difference' position. Indeed, the pendulum has swung so far that some writers have argued that Negro speech is only superficially related to the varieties of American English spoken by whites. They postulate a different basis for black English, derived from an African-based pidgin. Hence, it is more in vogue nowadays to consider black English to be a *different*, not a substandard, variety of English, having its own equally complex rule systems (Labov, 1973). The educational implications of such linguistic theory have been, to all intents and purposes, to initiate a reversal in previous policies. The emphasis now seems to be more on advocating early instruction for black children in their native tongue by means of black English texts. In causal attribution terms, the supporters of the deficit position attributed the lack of black scholastic success internally to the group's inability to cope with complex linguistic and conceptual activities. The difference theorists on the other hand, would externally attribute lack of success to a communication gap between pupil and teacher who are using entirely different linguistic systems. The perceived locus of causality of the problem is of course fundamentally related to the 'therapy' used.

This change in theoretical stance has converged with a more positive view towards the language variety by blacks themselves. McDavid and Raven (1972) state that

> the new militancy of rising expectations following the recent civil rights legislation and court decisions has led to feelings of group identity and pride in all forms of social experience including language, so that the patronizing depreciation of non-standard forms of speech . . . is deservedly rejected.

Nevertheless, the revised educational policies have not escaped criticism either, as blacks as a whole are ambivalent in their attitudes towards their speech. Many black community leaders have denounced language programmes which emphasize black English for they claim it is insulting to black people to suggest that they cannot acquire the language that everybody else uses, and that continued use of black English will ultimately hold their children back. Taylor (1971) has argued that Black communities themselves, not educators or sociolinguists, should now decide whether they wish to accommodate linguistically towards the white majority. Currently, the deficit–difference controversy still rages, leaving the educational and social situation in a state of considerable flux.

Much more study both of black speech and of language modernization remains to be done. It is important to bear in mind that only such study can demonstrate where language planning *per se* must leave off and where wider social planning, including the expansion of opportunity as well as of participation in decision making and decision evaluation, must begin (Rubin and Jernudd, 1971; Fishman, 1973). In such further study, as in future work in sociolinguistics generally, it is to be hoped that social psychology will make even more of a significant contribution than it has so far.

Further Reading

Fishman, J. A. (1972), *The Sociology of Language*, Rowley, Mass., Newbury House. A general introduction to a number of topics in sociolinguistics.

400 Interaction and the Social World

Trudgill, P. (1974), *Sociolinguistics*, Penguin Books. A clear though somewhat restricted introduction which stresses 'linguistics' rather than 'socio'.

Gumperz, J. J., and Hymes, D., eds. (1972), *Directions in Sociolinguistics*, New York, Holt, Rinehart & Winston. A good collection of papers on the topic of language and its social context.

Giglioli, P. P., ed. (1972), *Language and Social Context*, Penguin Books. Another good set of papers in sociolinguistics.

Giles, H., and Powesland, P. F. (1975), *Speech Style and Social Evaluation*, London, Academic Press. A primarily social psychological account of speech accommodation, accent, and other topics touched on in this chapter.

Fishman, J. A. (1972), *Language in Sociocultural Change*, Stanford, Stanford University Press. Discusses issues related to language planning and language problems in developing countries.

Chapter 16
Intergroup Behaviour
I. Individualistic Perspectives

Henri Tajfel

Introduction

The study of intergroup behaviour is often concerned with relations
between members of two or more small groups; but it also encompasses the attitudes and behaviour that men and women display towards
each other because they happen to belong to different nations, races,
social classes, religions or ethnic groups. We hope, in the following
two chapters, to come to some general conclusions which are, at least
in part, independent of the size of the groups that are involved; but
a bias of interest might as well be stated at the outset. This bias will
be towards the 'large-scale' problems of the psychological relationships between human social categories – such as nations, races, ethnic
groups, etc. This is not because the small-group problems are unimportant; but rather because there is at present a greater sense of
urgency – both theoretically and practically – about an individual's
behaviour towards another individual who happens to be of a different 'kind', whatever may be the nature of the assignment into one's
'own kind' and others. The humorist George Mikes once pointed
out the similarity between the major European languages in their
choice of terms for describing someone from another country: e.g.
alien, *l'étranger, der Fremde*. The psychological determinants and
effects of this alienness or 'strangeness' of people who bear different
labels – be they national, ethnic, religious, racial or social – are the
main theme of this and the next chapter.

Following Sherif (1966), we shall refer to intergroup relations as
'relations between two or more groups and their respective members.
Whenever individuals belonging to one group interact, collectively
or individually, with another group or its members *in terms of their*

group identification, we have an instance of intergroup behaviour' (p. 12). And, in endeavouring to avoid a definition of 'group' which would be too narrow for our purposes, we shall follow the historian Emerson (1960) who, confronted with another but not dissimilar problem of definition, wrote: 'The simplest statement that can be made about a nation is that it is a body of people who feel that they are a nation; and it may be that when all the fine-spun analysis is concluded this will be the ultimate statement as well' (p. 102). 'Group' will be used in this chapter very much in the sense in which Emerson used 'nation' in the above quotation.

There is a convergence in the wide sweep of Sherif's and Emerson's definitions, and it is expressed in the italicized part of Sherif's statement. This singles out interaction with members of other groups in terms of group identifications; and it therefore implies that other forms of interaction with people from outgroups are also possible. Indeed, one can think of a theoretical continuum applying to interaction between two or more people which would go from one extreme when an individual acts entirely in terms of 'self' to the other extreme of an individual acting entirely in terms of his group. Neither of these extremes can probably be found in real life, but there is no doubt that approaching the one or the other is crucial to the form that one's social behaviour will take. If I go to see a dentist, I certainly do not act very much in terms of my identification with one group or another; but just the same, much of the behaviour that the dentist and I display towards each other is determined by the criss-crossing of social categories of various kinds to which we both belong and to which we perceive each other as belonging. At the other extreme, if I take part in a race riot or strenuously and vocally support my local team during a football match, or demonstrate against the oppression of my group by another group, I interact with another group – as Sherif wrote – fully in terms of my group identification. However, the truism that marked individual differences will persist even in these situations is still valid.

The two major problems to which an adequate social psychology of intergroup behaviour must address itself are as follows: (i) what are the *determinants* of acting in terms of one's group rather than in terms of self? And (ii) what are the principal *attributes* of acting in terms of one's group rather than in terms of self? These problems have been approached in a number of theories which were concerned with various psychological processes and their effects on various aspects of intergroup behaviour.

Many of these theoretical accounts are concerned with the hostile and aggressive aspects of intergroup behaviour and of the attitudes related to it. In a brief review, we shall follow in this chapter a progression which might be described as moving from an 'individual' to a 'social' psychology of intergroup behaviour (cf. Tajfel, 1972). This distinction is not always clear-cut, but on the whole it is useful because it enables one to locate the assumptions, often implicit, of the theorist, and to identify his main focus of interest.

Many of the 'individual' theories start from general descriptions of psychological processes which are assumed to operate in individuals in a way which is independent of the effects of social interaction and social context. The social context and interaction are assumed to affect these processes, but only in the sense that society provides a variety of settings in which the 'basic' individual laws of motivation or cognition are uniformly displayed. In contrast, 'social psychological' theories tend to start from individuals in groups rather than from individuals *tout court*. They do not necessarily contradict the 'preliminary' individual laws such as those, for example, applying to frustration and aggression or to cognitive dissonance. But they stress the need to take into account the fact that group behaviour – and even more so intergroup behaviour – is displayed in situations in which we are not dealing with random collections of individuals who somehow come to act in unison because they all happen to be in a similar psychological state. To the extent that our task is to explain certain uniformities in the behaviour of masses of individuals who confront each other in certain social situations, the principal question that arises is: Can we explain these uniformities starting from laws of individual behaviour? Or is it necessary for our purpose to take these laws for granted and then apply ourselves to an analysis of the interaction between the individual processes and the social and psychological interdependence within and between human groups which together determine social behaviour?

It would be misleading to claim that the individual theories always ignore the social settings of intergroup behaviour. They do not; when one considers, for example, the views of Freud about the psychology of intergroup behaviour, which also formed the basis of some important subsequent developments, it is clear that for him the motivation of this behaviour originated in the entanglements of emotional relationships within the family, i.e. in the early social relationships of an individual. But this Freudian stress on early social interaction is much less clearly discernible in some of the later derivations from his ideas – such as the frustration–aggression hypothesis. It remains true, however, that for Freud, as for those who modified his ideas later, the group and intergroup settings of social behaviour are like a stage on which a plot laid down elsewhere and in advance is predictably played out. The social psychological theories (e.g. Sherif, 1966) describe a causal process which goes in the opposite direction: they start from certain attributes of the relations between and within human groups, such as the existence of an intergroup conflict, and look at the psychological consequences for the individuals concerned.

In the following pages, we shall first outline some of the influential individual theories concerned with the basic motivations of intergroup behaviour. Starting from Freud, we shall proceed to some of the relevant personality theories and then to the frustration–aggression theory. In the following chapter, we shall discuss some of the individual *cognitive* approaches to intergroup behaviour. The subsequent discussion of 'social' theories will start from an example of the 'social conflict' theory represented by the work of Sherif and conclude with a discussion of the role that the concept of social identity plays in the social psychology of intergroup behaviour.

Two further points need to be briefly made to complete this introduction. The first is that, in our review of the social psychological theories and research on intergroup behaviour, we shall omit some recent widely popularized views about the role of an 'aggressive instinct' in the determination of hostility to people in other groups. Whether these views represent a grossly over-simplified version of Freudian ideas (Storr, 1968) or a variety of speculations about the presumed links between the evolutionary past of our species and the complexities of its contemporary social behaviour (e.g. Lorenz, 1967,

1974; Ardrey, 1966; Morris, 1967), they share two characteristics. The first is their cautious avoidance of any form of confrontation with relevant research on *human* social behaviour; and the other their equally cautious resistance to normally acceptable forms of empirical proof or disproof (cf. Crook, 1971, and chapter 2 of this book for a discussion of some of these speculations from the point of view of recent developments in ethology). We shall not therefore take up our limited space to discuss these views. The second point relates to the first; our review of theories and research aims not at completeness but at the presentation of a framework for considering the social psychology of intergroup behaviour at large; it will therefore have to remain fairly selective.

Freud's theory of intergroup behaviour

'It is always possible to bind together a considerable number of people in love, so long as there are other people left over to receive the manifestations of their aggressiveness' (Freud, 1930, p. 114). This quotation includes two of the crucial ideas in Freud's psychology of intergroup behaviour. One concerns the *inevitability* of outgroup hostility, and the other its *function* in holding a group together. We cannot, in this brief review, do justice to Freud's derivation of his ideas about the sources of intergroup behaviour from his general theory of personality functioning, particularly as some of his conceptions changed from his earlier to his later writings. It is, however, important to place Freud's theory of intergroup behaviour in relation to subsequent developments, some of which owe a great deal to his formulations.

The notions of displacement of aggression on to the outgroup and of its function in maintaining a group's identity and cohesion were firmly based on Freud's serious attempt to encompass social relationships in his 'group psychology'. This psychology was for him 'concerned with the individual man as a member of a race, of a nation, of a caste, of a profession, of an institution, or as a component part of a crowd of people who have been organized into a group at some particular time for some definite purpose' (Freud, 1922, p. 3). Although in his later writings he postulated a separate and independent instinct of aggression (as a manifestation of the universal principle of Thanatos, the death instinct), the mechanisms of out-group aggression were seen in his earlier work as a derivation from more basic principles. These he found in the ambivalence of early emotional relationships within the family. These relationships create, according to Freud, simultaneous love and hatred for the father-figure which must somehow be coped with and resolved.

Here we have the basis for Freud's inferences from his individual psychology to his psychology of intergroup relations. The ambivalence of the emotional family ties is transposed on to group ties, in the form of identifications with a leader and of partial identification with those who share the same leader and therefore the same group identity. The ever-present hostility, which is part and parcel of these emotional ties, must be dealt with in one way or another. As the personal and social controls of guilt prevent the expression of aggression towards its 'direct' objects, outgroups provide the outlet. And thus, as Lasswell (1935) wrote: 'Nations, classes, tribes and churches have been treated as collective symbols in the name of which the individual may indulge his elementary urges for supreme power, for omniscience, for amorality, for security'.

Freud's views about intergroup behaviour can be discussed from two points of view: (i) the nature of the theoretical links between his individual psychology and his 'group psychology'; and (ii) the validity of the hypotheses resulting from these links and extrapolations. Let us refer to these respectively as Freud's postulated 'mechanisms' and his hypotheses. We cannot consider here in any detail the 'mechanisms', as this would lead us to a discussion of many aspects of Freud's personality theories and of their modifications and criticisms. To Freud, a group was essentially '. . . a number of individuals who have put one and the same object in the place of their ego ideal and have consequently identified themselves with one another in their ego' (1922, p. 116). If we consider his intergroup hypotheses as related to the 'mechanisms' on which they are based, it appears that the 'object' which takes the place of the ego ideal must be the leader of a group; and that, in addition, it must be a leader who has charismatic qualities, as without them he would not be able to take the place of the ego ideal. This would appear to limit the scope of Freud's analysis of intergroup behaviour to those groups which do have such leaders; and we know from history, politics and our own experience that intense manifestations of ingroup identification and intergroup hostility are by no means confined to such groups. It might, however, be possible to argue that a group which is emotionally important to us might symbolically stand for an 'object' even in the absence of charismatic leadership, and that therefore Freud's hypotheses about the *necessary* character of intergroup hostility might also apply to such groups.

However this may be, the crucial hypothesis is still that outgroup hostility is unavoidable and that it is a necessary condition for ingroup cohesion. The idea fits in well enough with much of the generally accepted common-sense 'wisdom' (some of it based on the cultural diffusion of Freud's ideas); with a great deal of historical, social and everyday experience; and with some research findings. It would be pleasant to be able to write that there exists equally widespread evidence to *disprove* the hypothesis. This is not so; it is true, however, that most of the evidence points to the conclusion that *increased* outgroup hostility is related to *increased* ingroup cohesion (e.g., the work of Sherif), and not that the former is a *necessary* condition of the latter, or that a group cannot be cohesive unless it finds an object of hatred or dislike outside of its boundaries. We shall come back to these problems in discussing other approaches to the psychology of intergroup behaviour.

Before, however, going further we must briefly return to the relationship between Freud's theory of intergroup behaviour and the social context of this behaviour. The social aspects of the primary and basic emotional urges, as seen by Freud, are undoubtedly part and parcel of his theory. The Oedipus complex, on which the love–hate relationship with the father-figure is based; the guilt and the functioning of the superego which cannot be conceived outside of the setting of human social relations; the displacement of hostility toward outgroups which is inconceivable without the development of *concepts* of ingroup and outgroup – all these features of the theory add up to a good case for classifying it as a 'social' rather than an 'individual' psychology of intergroup behaviour. They also, however, add up to its uncompromising stance of general inevitability. The underlying unconscious processes are supposed to do their work unmodified by all subsequent forms of social interaction. It is, as we said earlier, a drama which is all set and played out before the actors ever enter the scene.

The idea of inevitability is based on at least three assumptions none of which are supported by satisfactory evidence. The first is that early emotional relationships are faithfully reflected in the subsequent adult social behaviour beyond the primary focus of the family; the second – that the nature of these early relationships is 'basic' and unchangeable, unaffected by social or cultural variations; and the third, following from the previous two, that the emotional basis of intergroup behaviour remains constant, whatever may be the nature of the social economic, ideological, historical and cultural relations between human groups.

The authoritarian personality

The problem of *individual* variations in the patterns of ingroup affiliation and outgroup hostility was examined in the famous study on *The Authoritarian Personality* by Adorno *et al.* (1950). The initial preoccupation of the authors with anti-semitism led them to further studies of its more general correlates, including attitudes towards minority groups other than Jews and towards the 'ingroup' of the United States and the 'outgroup' of foreign nations. Significant correlations were found between negative attitudes towards all outgroups. This led to the emergence of an 'authoritarian' and 'ethnocentric' personality syndrome, characterized not only by a generalized attitude towards outgroups but also by a cluster of other social and political attitudes. The relation of this syndrome to the manner of coping with emotional problems rooted in the socialization process was for the authors 'the most crucial result' of their studies. As they wrote, 'there is a close correspondence in the type of approach and outlook a subject is likely to have in a great variety of areas, ranging from the most intimate features of a family and sex adjustments, through relationships to other people in general, to religion and to social and political philosophy.'

The concept of ethnocentric personality links the development of ethnic identity to the processes responsible for intense outgroup hostility in a certain type of individual. Frenkel-Brunswik (1949, 1954) was able to show that this link exists not only in adults but also in children. It is possible that different frequencies of the authoritarian and ethnocentric pattern are encountered in different cultural habitats, and that outgroup hostility related to national affiliation would vary as a result. Thus, the following sequence of statements may help us to assess the contribution that can be made by this body of work to the problem of development of ingroup identification: *some* people will be intensely ethnocentric in a large variety of situations; the form that their ethnocentrism will take is outgroup hostility; their number is likely to vary from one cultural milieu to another.

The long history of jingoism and chauvinism in many countries (of which the post-war American forms stimulated the authoritarian personality study by Adarno *et al.*) provides evidence for the existence of such a category of people, though it does not prove the assumed causal nature of a certain kind of personality dynamics. But there are other reasons why the theory of authoritarian personality cannot provide us with more than a segment of a general theory of ingroup identification. One is that under *some* conditions strong ingroup affiliation coupled with intense outgroup hostility becomes widely shared in large populations whose members cannot all be assigned to the authoritarian and ethnocentric type; the second, that there exist ingroup affiliations which are not intimately linked to strong outgroup hostility; the third, that variations over time in the mass manifestations of outgroup hostility can be related more parsimoniously to the social, economic, and political conditions of the moment.

These limitations have been documented in empirical studies. The relations between personality and socio-cultural factors in outgroup hostility have been discussed by Pettigrew (1958) in conjunction with his work on racial prejudice in South Africa and in the United States. He characterized two extreme positions concerning this problem; one emphasizes 'the personality of the bigot' and neglects his cultural milieu; the other neglects individual differences and views intolerance as 'a mere reflection of cultural norms'. The possibility of a compromise is provided by an analysis of attitudes suggested by Smith, Bruner and White (1956) in which they distinguish between the cognitive, the social and the emotional aspects of the adjustment that an attitude may represent for an individual. The first consists of the individual's appraisal of social reality; the second finds its roots in the network of an individual's reference groups and in his need to adjust his *Weltanschauung* to his identifications with some groups and differentiations from others; and the third is the adoption of attitudes which represent 'a transformed version of (an individual's) way of dealing with his inner difficulty'.

When the development and the incidence of outgroup hostility are seen in this perspective, it becomes evident that neither the socio-cultural factors reflected in the first two functions of attitudes nor the personality factors reflected in the third can provide by themselves a master key to the understanding of this hostility as a shared norm and as a mass phenomenon. Pettigrew summarized a good deal of previous research, but perhaps the clearest examples come from his own data. In South Africa, he applied three attitude scales to his white subjects: an F-scale (measuring ethnocentrism), a C (conformity) scale and an A (anti-African) scale. The C-scale was nearly as predictive of the attitudes towards the Africans as was the F-scale; students born in Africa were found to be more prejudiced, but not more authoritarian, than those not born in Africa; the same was true of students belonging to the Nationalist party as compared with others; the Afrikaaners 'are both more anti-African and more authoritarian, and, when the F-scale differences are corrected for, they remain significantly more hostile to the Africans' (p. 35). Similar results were obtained in a comparison of four small towns in Georgia and North Carolina with four similar locations in New England; and, in comparisons made between various southern communities, those with 'high Negro population ratios (38 and 45 per cent) have significantly higher N (anti-Negro) scale means than the other communities sampled in the South with low Negro ratios (10 and 18 per cent) though they are *not* different in authoritarianism and anti-semitism' (p. 39). Pettigrew concluded that 'in areas with historically embedded traditions of racial intolerance, externalizing personality factors underlying prejudice remain important, but socio-cultural factors are unusually crucial and account for the heightened racial hostility' (p. 40).

Pettigrew's study has clear implications for the role played by out-group hostility in ingroup affiliation. If we follow the general assumption that acute outgroup hostility intensifies ingroup identification, then it could be inferred that this identification is more intense among those of Pettigrew's subjects who were characterized by stronger prejudice. The possibility that this may be due exclusively to authoritarianism is ruled out by Pettigrew's data. There is, how-ever, a possibility of an indirect link which must not be overlooked: in his data from South Africa, Pettigrew found that the authoritarian pattern was relatively more prevalent amongst the Afrikaaners. It is possible that this higher incidence affects the socio-cultural milieu by creating stronger pressures towards conformity of hostile attitudes, and thus that the socio-cultural factors serve as an intermediary link in a causal chain ranging from a certain 'modal' personality pattern to outgroup hostility. But it seems that a direct attribution of pres-sures to conform to the social, economic and political conditions is a much simpler explanation in view of the variation within the life-span of one generation in the intensity of the hostility against various outgroups. A prediction could still be made that a society including a high proportion of 'authoritarians' would produce strong norms (affecting all its members) of intense outgroup hostility and in-group affiliation. It is possibilities of this nature which point to the need for an interdisciplinary approach to the study of ingroup identification. The relative importance of various causal factors can hardly be assessed from the perspective of one discipline alone.

Frustration and aggression

The mass murders of the Second World War, many of them com-mitted by people who did not appear particularly 'pathological', seemed to require *some* kind of explanation in terms of individual differences, and this led to several studies, the first of which was *The Authoritarian Personality*. In considering the frustration–aggression hypothesis (Dollard *et al.*, 1939) and its various derivations, we return to the Freudian tradition of search for explanations in terms of *general* laws of human motivation. Like Freud, the authors of the theory assumed that direct extrapolations from it could be made to social phenomena at large; and like him, they found in displaced aggression one of the pivots of their ambitious attempt to provide a unified explanation.

The original version of the main hypothesis was uncompromising: frustration was seen as a sufficient *and* necessary condition for aggression; and so, aggression was assumed always to follow upon frustration.

This study takes as its point of departure the assumption that *aggression is always a consequence of frustration*. More specifically the proposition is that the occurrence of aggressive behaviour always presupposes the existence of frustration and, contrariwise, that the existence of frustration always leads to some form of aggression (Dollard *et al.*, 1939, p. 1).

This initial version did not stand up to the weight of experimental evidence, and major qualifications were introduced. But common to the initial formulation and to the subsequent developments of the theory were its direct implications, as seen by various authors, for the understanding of intergroup behaviour. Already in 1937, Dollard incorporated an early version of some of these ideas into his analysis of the race and class relations in the American South. In the full statement in 1939 Dollard *et al.* used the concept of displacement of aggression, inherent to the theory, to explain the German attitudes towards Jews after the long-drawn-out frustrations of the treaty of Versailles. More generally, and closely following Freud, the authors linked the individual frustrations, inescapable in an organized society with its rules and inhibitions, to the ingroup-preserving functions of displaced aggression. From his modified version of the theory, Berkowitz (1962, 1965, 1969) drew direct consequences for intergroup behaviour and applied them (1972) to black riots in American cities. Using the concept of relative deprivation to widen the scope of 'frustration', Gurr (1970) wrote that 'the frustration–aggression and the related threat–aggression mechanisms provide the basic motivational link between relative deprivation and the potential for collective violence' (p. 36).

In discussing the theory and its modifications, we shall mainly consider these clearly stated implications for intergroup behaviour; although, since much of the evidence comes from experiments which were not directly concerned with intergroup behaviour, these experiments will have to be included in this brief review.

In view of the difficulties of retaining the initial version of the theory stating the sufficient and necessary relationship between frustration and aggression (cf. Himmelweit, 1950, for a review of the early evidence), Miller produced in 1941 a major qualification of the theory, the core of which was his statement that: 'frustration produces instigations to a number of different types of response, *one* of which is an instigation to some form of aggression'. But this qualification, sensible as it seems, considerably increased the difficulties of testing the theory. As Lange (1971) wrote:

According to one part of the theory frustration will always lead to aggression-instigation, which is a non-observable phenomenon. It does not have to lead to acts of aggression. So if we do not find aggression after frustration we can always explain this by pointing out that there were possibly other competing response-instigations which were stronger than the aggression-instigation (p. 61).

These difficulties of verification, of which Miller was not unaware, become even more acute when one considers the extensions of the theory from inter-individual to intergroup behaviour. In order to attack this problem, we must first consider (in a form necessarily schematic) the sequence of events as it is presented in Miller's revision of the frustration–aggression hypothesis and in Berkowitz's important re-formulation of the hypothesis. We must then look at these sequences in the light of experimental evidence, and finally reconsider them in relation to intergroup behaviour.

The Miller sequence can be presented as follows: frustration (interference with 'instigated goal behaviour') leads to an instigation to aggression. This will express itself in *overt* aggressive behaviour only if there are no competing responses strong enough to inhibit this behaviour. If there are such responses, aggression will not be shown, or it may be displaced from its original target (the frustrating agent) on to some other target which happens to be available. Berkowitz's modification had two principal aims: to widen the concept of frustration, and to provide an explanation for the choice of the target of aggression. Berkowitz's sequence looks schematically as follows:

frustration (including disappointment due to unfulfilled expectations) → arousal of anger → overt aggression *only* if a target is available in the environment which offers cues, acquired through previous learning, which had been associated in the past with aggressive behaviour. Gurr's (1970) important analysis of group violence based on the concept of relative deprivation follows Berkowitz's use of this wider concept of frustration. Gurr's emphasis is '... on the perception of deprivation; people may be subjectively deprived with reference to their expectations even though an objective observer might not judge them to be in want' (p. 24).

The large number of experiments on various determinants of aggression cannot be summarized here. But in order to pursue our argument about the importance of a *social* psychological analysis of intergroup behaviour, some of the social and cognitive factors involved in this behaviour must be mentioned. We have already referred to Berkowitz's extension of the concept of frustration to the perceived failure of expectancies. His theory, however, still stressed the importance of the state of arousal (anger), its association in overt aggressive behaviour with previously learned cues, and the direct transposition of this sequence of events to intergroup behaviour. The sequence does not, however, cause Berkowitz to deny the importance, in other situations, of the *instrumentality* of aggression, i.e. of aggression undertaken in order to achieve certain desired ends. Not surprisingly, there are many studies which show this kind of aggression. Some of them arose out of a theory formulated by Bandura and Walters (1963). It is their view that, as aggression often has instrumental value, it is a response which is widely learned in the course of a child's socialization. Bandura and Walters (and others) have been able to show in several experiments that, without previous frustrations, children become aggressive when they have been exposed (e.g. by watching a film) to a 'model' whose aggression goes unpunished. Kuhn *et al.* (1967) have shown that children who were subjected to frustration (they were not given 'candy' which they had been promised) were *less* aggressive than those who had just been shown an aggressive model. Lange and van de Nes (1973) found instrumentality to be a more powerful determinant of aggression for their adolescent subjects than was previous frustration.

These findings are, however, less important from our point of view than a variety of experimental results which are concerned with the role played by perceived legitimacy in responding to a situation, frustrating or not, with a display of overt aggression. The concept of the *legitimacy* of aggression is crucial to the understanding of inter-group behaviour for at least two reasons: first, because legitimacy has been shown to determine the elicitation or inhibition of aggression independently of such variables as previous frustrations or internal states of arousal; and second, because it can safely be assumed that, in many social situations, the perception of legitimacy of aggression enjoys a substantial social consensus which is usually based on widely shared social norms. Perception of legitimacy is therefore one of the links which enable us to make a transition from the large *diversity* of individual motivational states, which is quite obviously characteristic of most social situations, to the observed *common* features of many individuals' behaviour in intergroup settings.

There is a great deal of experimental research which leads one to conclude that the elicitation or inhibition of aggression are power-fully determined by the perception of its legitimacy in a social situation. One convenient way to classify these experimental results is to consider them from the points of view of: (i) responses to frustra-tion; (ii) elicitation of aggression in situations in which it is not possible to identify immediate previous frustrations.

Amongst examples in the first category is an experiment by Epstein and Taylor (1967) who found that whether aggression did or did not occur after frustration depended upon the subjects' percep-tion of the frustrating agent's intention to attack. In several experi-ments aggression was shown to be inhibited because of the implica-tions of the social relationship between the agent and the victim of frustration. Thus, Taylor and Epstein (1967) found that male subjects did not respond aggressively when the frustrator was a female. Burnstein and Worchel (1962) reported that a colleague who simu-lated deafness for an experiment in frustration was not himself a target of retaliation; instead, aggression centred upon the experi-menter. Lange (1971) found that, amongst the young boys who were his subjects, aggression was *lower* in a frustrating than in a non-frustrating situation when the frustration consisted of an attack upon the subjects' competence to perform a certain task by an older man who was perceived by the subjects as having legitimate reasons for harbouring such doubts.

There have been several experiments in our second category: namely, situations in which aggression was elicited from the subjects without the intervention of previous frustrations. The work of Bandura and Walters was already mentioned. But probably the best-known is a study by Milgram (1974), which led to several other similar experiments. Milgram found that adult subjects, coming from a variety of social backgrounds, were willing to inflict astonishingly intense 'punishments' (in the form of electric shocks) on accomplices of the experimenter who pretended to be slow at learning a task without any other reason than the experimenter's insistence that this was appropriate for the purposes of this 'scientific' study. (Although the subjects believed the shocks to be genuine, this was not the case; the accomplices acted as though they were in pain.) One of the most important features of this study is the social relationship between the experimenter and the subjects. The experimenter was supposed to be a scientist engaged in an investigation about the effects of punishment on learning; acting in this role, he 'legitimized' for the subjects the delivering of highly painful shocks in response to another person's fumbling.

Many of these findings could be explained with varying success on the basis of hypotheses about the individuals' states of arousal, about external cues bringing out aggressive behaviour, or about the instigation to aggress being inhibited by fear of punishment or by the lack of appropriate cues. The point is, however, that there would have to be a variety of *ad hoc* hypotheses to explain the variety of findings, and that each of these hypotheses would have to make un-supported assumptions about the similarity in the 'internal' states of many people. It seems simpler to assume that the display or absence of overt aggressive behaviour by people who find themselves in a similar social situation is powerfully regulated by their socially determined and socially *shared* perception of the legitimacy of aggression in that situation. The advantage of this view is that it does not require us to assume that a variety of individuals find themselves, at certain points of time, in an identical motivational state. This advantage becomes crucially important when we wish to consider the behaviour displayed by great masses of people in many large-scale settings of intergroup behaviour. The legitimacy hypothesis is easily testable; there has been no special difficulty in finding out before, during or after an experiment or a field study what, if any, kinds of aggression were commonly perceived as legitimate in the particular situation and how these social prescriptions related to actual behaviour.

Our aim in this discussion is to review the evidence in order to decide what are the most useful concepts and variables to explain and predict the forms taken by intergroup behaviour in a large variety of social settings. Therefore, it must be stressed again that our concern is *not* to deny the validity of certain motivational hypotheses when they apply to individual or inter-individual behaviour; but rather to consider their usefulness in wider intergroup settings. Some of the important theorists, such as Berkowitz, have by now come to accept the importance of cognitive factors in the earlier part of the causal sequence which they assume to operate. Thus for Berkowitz the state of anger is the intervening 'arousal' variable which, under certain conditions, leads to a display of overt aggression. This state of anger is, in turn, caused by a variety of previous conditions which include such cognitive components as disappointed expectations and relative deprivations. But in the second part of the sequence – the link between arousal and the overt aggressive behaviour – the theory still remains at the level of the individual 'pre-social' functioning. A characteristic example of this theoretical dissymmetry can be found in a paper contributed by Berkowitz (1972) to a collection of articles about the outbreak, a few years ago, of urban riots in the United States. His main argument is that, whatever may have been the background factors which created the state of arousal, the explosive outbreaks of urban intergroup violence were often governed by 'general excitation', and that 'as long as responses are not evoked which interfere with aggression, this general excitation should facilitate the aggression reactions elicited by the aggressive stimuli in the environment' (pp. 88–9). He quotes, as an example, the anti-Soviet riot in Prague in March 1969 which occurred after the

Czech hockey team had defeated the Russians in the world champion-ship tournament. It was 'an event seen on television all over the country' which created the 'excitement of victory that powered the aggressive reactions to stimuli associated with aggression and frustration' (p. 89).

This interpretation of the causes of the Prague riot provides a good example of the theoretical dissymmetry still evident in the 'arousal' view of large-scale intergroup activities. Berkowitz would certainly not deny that the Czechs' continuing 'frustration' dated from several months earlier, when the Soviet troops had occupied Prague. To judge from televised news programmes which were being shown at the time and later, the 'aggressive stimuli' in 1968 – Soviet tanks in the streets of Prague – were being reacted to emotionally and spontaneously, sometimes at great personal risk. At the same time, as it quickly became obvious that the *fait accompli* of military occupation could not be reversed and that head-on resistance was doomed to failure, indirect and often very subtle strategies were developed to show, both inside the country and to the outside world, that the population did not approve of what had happened. These strategies were undoubtedly implemented by small and active groups which were supported and/or joined by the man in the street when-ever this could be done without too great a risk of direct reprisals. In turn, the more 'a-political' a demonstration appeared to be, the more difficult it was for the new regime to react to it swiftly and effectively. The hockey victory was an excellent opportunity for exactly this kind of demonstration at a time when the memories of the summer of 1968 were still very fresh. The jubilant shouting of anti-Soviet slogans was not, at the time, an isolated event due to 'the excitement of victory that powered the aggressive reactions to stimuli associated with aggression and frustration'. It was part of a pattern in which opportunities to show the mood of the country were exploited by some and taken up by many. A social psychologist who attempts to provide an analysis of intergroup behaviour must not confine himself to *ad hoc* assumptions about separate social events, each seen in isolation. The understanding of the *pattern* of intergroup events in Czechoslovakia in 1968, and soon afterwards, does not gain much from assumptions about sudden states of 'arousal' or 'excitation' alleged to be shared by large numbers of people. Undoubtedly, there have been powerful arousals, frustrations and excitations in the course of this sequence of political and social events, and many other such sequences. Their translation into *group* behaviour is only possible when there is a social sharing of an interpretation of the events, a common popular 'theory' about their social causation and a wide consensus about the appropriateness of certain consequent actions.

Thus, according to the theory formulated by Berkowitz, and other similar views, there exists some kind of an 'automatic' behavioural effect when arousal is linked with a haphazard presence of 'stimuli' associated with aggression and frustrations. The 'exuberant Czechoslovaks' who 'ransacked the offices of the Soviet airline, and burned the furniture' (Berkowitz, 1972, p. 89) did not happen to have these offices – the allegedly appropriate stimuli for triggering-off aggression – crossing their line of vision just at the right moment by chance; it is much more likely that they went to find them. The crowds in Paris in 1789 did not riot because they happened to see the Bastille, the 'aggression-producing stimulus'; they converged on the Bastille. Groups of vigilantes touring the streets to pick up their victims often follow the policy of '*search* and destroy' rather than a random sequence of 'see and destroy'. The 'see and destroy' phenomena also undoubtedly exist; but four points need to be made about them. The first is that the consequent aggressions often tend to be selective, as has been shown, for example, in several studies of the recent urban riots in the United States; the second – that this selectivity is powerfully determined by social consensus as to who should be attacked, rather than by random individual cues associated with previous aggressions; the third, that it seems simpler to explain this consensus as based on a socially shared notion (or 'ideology') pointing to certain targets of aggression rather than on a wide sharing of identical aggression-facilitating or aggression-eliciting cues. The final point is more general: even if the previous three points (the first of which is not contradictory to Berkowitz's theory) were not valid, there is still no reason why a social psychological theory of intergroup behaviour should single out for its paradigm examples of random violence rather than the more common examples of intergroup activities which, even when they happen to be violent at times, still show some degree of direction and structuring over time.

The dichotomy in the explanations of mass intergroup phenomena is not, as Berkowitz (1972) wrote, between the irrational and the rational, but between the irrational and the social–cognitive. The social–cognitive causation need not be 'rational' as seen by an outside observer; as a matter of fact, it often may, and does, appear to be highly irrational. But this kind of 'irrationality' is fundamentally different from the irrationality assumed in an approach to intergroup behaviour which extrapolates from a collection of individual motivational states. The latter posits a direct causal link between 'excitement' or 'arousal' shared by many people, and its collective but essentially random 'spilling over' into action at the sight of red rags perceived simultaneously by a large number of bulls. It also needs to assume that what is a red rag to one bull must be as much of a red rag to another; otherwise there is no way to explain why so many people do the same thing at the same time; or – an even more difficult problem – why they act similarly and consistently over long periods of time.

This 'spilling over' assumption of the individual motivational theories is common both to their more recent versions and to the earlier tradition of the original frustration–aggression theorists. In the latter case, perhaps the clearest and still the most influential aspect of the ideas about the 'hydraulics system', in which pent up aggressive drives must 'come out' in one way or another, is in the explanation of displaced aggression. This phenomenon of displacement provided the theory with an explanation of wide-scale social aggressions, such as those against Jews in Nazi Germany, which were assumed to be caused by the inhibition of aggression towards the proper targets, the initial and true agents of frustrations. An early experiment by Miller and Bugelski (1948) provided some evidence of increased hostility towards disliked minority groups after an experimentally induced frustration. Subsequent experiments were, in the main, concerned with the inter-individual rather than intergroup displacement of aggression. But their results were, on the whole, ambiguous, since it is often difficult to decide whether attacks against 'improper targets' were due to a displacement of aggression or to a generalization of aggression; or again, whether the inhibition of aggression against certain targets was due to its displacement towards other targets, or to a generalization of the inhibition.

No doubt, the various ambiguities in the interpretation of the experimental data might be resolved in the future by carefully designed further experiments on interpersonal aggression. These ambiguities are not, however, the most important difficulty encountered in the attempts to extrapolate from individual displaced aggression to large-scale social aggressions. At least in the case of the original Freudian theories, an explicit mechanism for displacement was provided: the repression of hostility towards the father-figure is generalized to the leader of a group, and this in turn creates a displacement of aggression towards the outgroup. In the case of hypotheses based on learning theories, such as the frustration–aggression hypothesis in its various versions, this mechanism has disappeared, and nothing much has been put in its place to help us understand the large-scale 'displaced' social aggression. The notion of *displacement* of aggression inescapably implies in these theories that there is *some* kind of identification by the aggressor of the original frustrating agent – and that the difficulty, internally or externally caused, of retaliating directly against this frustrating agent causes the aggression to be directed at another target. This supposed sequence of causes and effects makes certain assumptions about social events which seem quite untenable. For the sequence to work, we would have to assume that, in very complex social situations, people *know* that their difficulties are caused by a certain social group and that in turn this social group is immune from aggressive retaliation because of internal conflicts or external sanctions; and therefore another group is chosen as a target. No doubt, in some cases such an identification of the original frustrating agent is easily achieved as, for example, in the case of a foreign occupation of a country. But these are special cases. Much more frequent are the social situations in which there is neither an easy identification of, nor consensus about, those who are supposed to be responsible for the frustrations. Who is causing inflation? The direction of retaliating hostility (against private industry, management, the trade unions or the government) will depend upon the underlying and consensual 'theory' of social causation predominant in a particular social group. The hostility (or overt aggression, whenever this is possible) need not be displaced from another target which is, somehow, *really* believed to be the cause of trouble. Its direction is more easily accounted for by the 'ideologizing' of discontent than by a hydraulic mechanism of accumulated tensions which break the inhibiting dams at the point of their greatest weakness. Thus, it cannot be said that the Germans acted against the Jews in the Nazi period in spite of having identified the *real* causes of their troubles. Many Germans believed that Jews *were* a major cause of these troubles, however irrational this belief may now appear, and whatever may have been the social, political and historical factors which led to its widespread diffusion.

Conclusion

In this chapter, we have reviewed some of the major theories attempting to explain human intergroup behaviour on the basis of individual motivation. The principal argument of the chapter was that, although such theories may be able to account for aggression as it occurs between individuals, they are confronted with serious difficulties when direct extrapolations are made from them to problems of *social* aggression, i.e. to the large-scale instances of intergroup conflict and hostility. The intellectual roots of some of these theories are to be found in Freud's views about the functions and the inevitability of outgroup hostility and aggression. These views have strongly influenced theories about individual patterns of intergroup attitudes and behaviour, such as the theory of authoritarian personality; and they have also appeared in modified forms in various theories which have been put forward to account for the relationship between frustration and aggression as it affects intergroup behaviour. Experimental evidence pointing to the importance of shared norms and of perceived legitimacy in intergroup aggressive behaviour was briefly reviewed. It was concluded that an analysis of social variables of this kind contributes to a simple and consistent explanation of social aggression and of its presumed displacement on to selected outgroups, while the exclusive reliance on 'basic' motivational laws leaves the phenomena of social aggression largely unexplained.

NOTE. Suggested reading will be found at the end of the next chapter.

Chapter 17
Intergroup Behaviour
II. Group Perspectives

Henri Tajfel

Introduction

In the previous chapter, we referred to one common element in the various 'individual' approaches to intergroup behaviour: namely, that they are like scenarios of which the plot is laid down before the actors ever step on the stage. This, we tried to show, is as true of Freud's theories of group psychology as of the theories which came later. In all these approaches, the attitudes and behaviour of people towards outgroups are seen as a way of working out individual emotional problems in an intergroup setting. The existence of outgroups is seen as providing an opportunity to release various tensions – one might almost say an opportunity which would have to be invented if it did not exist. This is precisely what was expressed in the well-known saying that if Jews had not existed, Hitler would have had to invent them – and in a sense, he did just that. This 'invention' is the common element underlying terms such as projection, scapegoating, or displacement when they apply to intergroup attitudes and behaviour.

There is no doubt that the causal sequences described in the preceding chapter are of some help in explaining why and how *some* people behave on *some* occasions towards *certain* outgroups. It is also true, however, that too much emphasis on these motivational factors leads to a narrow 'psychologistic' view of what is and always has been an important feature of all societies: recurring social conflict. Certain kinds of relations between national, racial, ethnic or social groups amount to what is the substance of social conflict, since conflict becomes 'social' when it involves relations between large-scale social groups or 'categories' rather than between small groups or individuals. Although social conflicts cannot be analysed primarily in psychological terms, and even less in psychological terms alone, they do have their important psychological correlates or counterparts. These correlates or counterparts of behaviour and attitudes towards people's own and other social groups must be considered against the background of social life and social change rather than being seen as a mere by-product of a collection of individual emotional difficulties, frustrations or projection mechanisms.

We are only now beginning to develop a unified social psychological theory of intergroup behaviour and attitudes pertaining to social conflict, i.e. to the relations between large-scale human groups. We can consider the issues involved by taking into account three approaches to them which, in many ways, complement each other. These are: the cognitive aspects of intergroup relations; the social psychological effects of intergroup conflict; and the relationships between intergroup conflict and social identity.

Cognitive aspects of intergroup relations

We live in a social environment which is in constant flux. Much of what happens to us is related to the activities of groups to which we do or do not belong; and the changing relations between these groups require constant readjustments of our understanding of what happens and constant causal attributions about the why and the how of the changing conditions of our life (Tajfel, 1969b, p. 81).

Causal attributions concerning behaviour of other people with whom we interact have been one of the major areas of theory and research in social psychology; they are discussed in chapter 9 of this book. Here, we are concerned with the individual's understanding of causality in his social world as it relates to his attitudes and behaviour towards his own social group (or groups) and to other groups. Much of this discussion takes up issues which were discussed previously in chapters 9 and 12.

The development and functioning of social categories, as they were discussed in chapter 12 of this book, must be seen as a process which is at the same time cognitive and social. (See Billig, 1976, for a detailed discussion of this issue.) In order to clarify this a little, we must go back to Emerson's definition of 'nation' quoted at the beginning of the preceding chapter. Having tried to isolate various 'objective' criteria for determining what a nation is, and finding exceptions to each of them, Emerson finally settled upon the 'felt' common identity of members of a national group as his ultimate criterion. The implications of this are twofold. In the first place, it is highly unlikely that a national group can be defined through certain similarities (whatever they are) between its members which would at the same time imply that, in the particular respects chosen, most members of that national group are different from most members of other nations. Secondly, the early Lewinian criterion of 'interdependence of fate' for defining a group would probably not work in the case of nations, for the same reason. Therefore, the most important 'similarity' left is that the individuals concerned are consensually referred to by a common label, both by other people and by themselves, and that this common label defines at the same time their national group membership *and* circumscribes the variety of social situations in which they feel or behave as a function of that membership.

It is undoubtedly true that there are social groups which can be defined more easily than a nation in terms of certain objective criteria, e.g. employees of *a* bank, or bank employees generally, or people who share a religion, a political party affiliation, and so on. However, the transition from such an 'objective' group membership to a social psychological one is by no means straightforward. Whether such a transition does or does not take place depends upon social consensus about the significance of people's division into certain categories. For example, people with blue eyes do not generally form a social group in distinction from those with brown eyes, tall people do not form one in distinction from short ones; but people with dark skins (even if their birthplace, language and culture do not distinguish them from others around them) do form a 'group' in a variety of social situations. Bank employees or students may or may not be a 'group' in the same sense. It is the psychological and social significance (which may emerge or disappear as a function of changing social conditions) of the criteria by which they are defined which determines the 'togetherness' of groups. It is important to stress that we are not necessarily concerned here with attributes which are constant and permanent features of an individual's life: one is a member of a particular group only in those situations which are relevant to that group membership. 'Relevance' can be defined in terms of those situations in an individual's life which are characterized for him by the presence – concrete or imagined – of members of outgroups which are significant to him through his membership of his own group. 'Significance' of outgroups can be defined in turn as referring to those groups with which an individual compares his own group. The more these comparisons are made in terms of intergroup differences which have a value connotation for the individual, the more 'significant' they are for him. This would include, for example, the perception of an intergroup conflict of interests; of an intergroup competition in some form of achievement, past, present, or expected in the future; of a dominating and dominated intergroup relationship; and more generally, of a difference between groups with a connotation of superiority and inferiority.

An interesting experiment conducted in Geneva by Doise (1976) exemplifies the importance of this 'situational relevance' in intergroup comparisons. Doise conducted his study with two groups of boys: apprentices who were learning a variety of trades, and pupils from a *lycée* (the equivalent of a grammar school). There were four experimental conditions, only two of which we shall describe here. Different boys took part in each of the conditions. In one of them, boys from each of the groups were asked to rate their own group on a number of attributes which had been ascertained, through previous interviews with other *apprentis* and *lycéens*, to have a strong positive or negative value connotation for them; afterwards they rated on the same attributes the other group. In the second condition, the same ratings were requested, but this time the boys knew, while they were rating their own group first, that they would have to rate the other group immediately afterwards. A comparison of the ratings of own group given in the two conditions showed that there was a significant tendency in the second condition (in which the outgroup became salient in the evaluation of the boy's own group) to stress the positively valued differences in favour of the ingroup or to underplay the characteristics of the ingroup which were negatively valued.

Once a group becomes a socially defined entity, the effects of social categorization discussed in chapter 12 will apply to it. In the case of large-scale social groups (e.g. national, racial, religious, etc.) the resulting social 'images' are referred to as 'stereotypes', i.e. sets of fixed ideas and beliefs held by members of one or more groups about members of another group. We cannot review here the vast literature about stereotypes (cf. e.g., Duijker and Frijda, 1960) but some generalizations emerge quite clearly. They are as follows:

1. People show an easy readiness to characterize vast human groups in terms of a few fairly crude 'traits' or common attributes.

2. These characterizations tend to remain fairly stable for fairly long periods of time.

3. They tend to change to some extent, slowly, as a function of social, political or economic changes.

4. They become much more pronounced and hostile when social tensions between the groups arise.

5. They are learned early and used by children before the emergence of clear ideas defining the groups to which they apply.

6. They do not present much of a problem when little hostility is involved, but are extremely difficult to modify in a social climate of tension and conflict.

The establishment of a theoretical connection between the processes of categorizing and the development of stereotypes owes a great deal to the work of Gordon Allport (1954). His book still remains one of the best written and most lucid accounts of the problems involved. Although many other summaries or 'inventories' have appeared since (e.g. Ehrlich, 1973) it cannot be said that they contain important advances beyond Allport's earlier synthesis. But it is true that his insistence that the functioning of stereotypes needs to be understood as a special instance of the process of categorizing was not accompanied in his writings by a detailed articulation of the way categorizing is reflected in the structure of stereotypes. In order to consider briefly the cognitive 'mechanics' involved, we need to return to the discussion of social categorization in chapter 12 of this book.

Three aspects of this discussion are directly relevant here: the general effects of 'labelling' or categorizing on certain biases in the judgements of an array of stimuli; a distinction between what we shall call the 'inductive' and the 'deductive' aspects of the process of categorizing; and the interaction of values with systems of social categories.

A label attached to a human being, i.e. the assignment of an individual to one or another category, whether racial, ethnic, social class, religious or regional, has some degree of meaning. This meaning consists of the assumed possession by the person of certain characteristics which go with the label; the inference is from the label to these characteristics. It is immaterial whether these relationships have been learned through personal experience of the user of the stereotype or through hearsay, literature, mass media, history books or linguistic habits. In cases of uncertainty and of little knowledge of the individual to whom they apply they determine the direction of search for 'telling signs', a search which is likely to be successful. They determine what will be noticed or ignored, what will become the centre of attention or remain at its periphery.

The subjective definition of a category of human beings will thus direct the search for features which are expected to be found when a specimen of the category is encountered. It will help to focus attention on some things and to deflect it from others. This does not, however, tell us very much about the *direction* of bias, and bias is the essential feature of many stereotyped judgements.

All such judgements are implicitly comparative. A man is not 'tall' in an absolute sense. He is taller than other people. Whether physical or personal characteristics are concerned, stereotypes lead us to minimize certain differences between people who are members of the same group, and to exaggerate the same differences between those people and others who belong to another group.

The point is, however, that not *all* these differences are minimized within a group and exaggerated between groups. Even a person strongly prejudiced against 'coloured immigrants' will not necessarily maintain that West Indian women are bad cooks, although good cooking may be to him an important quality – one of the shining signs of perfection in a good woman. Good or bad cooking is not a relevant aspect of the West Indian stereotype, of the differentiations between West Indians and other people. The content of a stereotype, however acquired, determines the dimensions along which the bias in judgement takes place, and these dimensions are not necessarily a crude duplication of a division into 'good' and 'bad' characteristics. This is an important point; it is possible to predict the nature and the direction of bias from a detailed knowledge of the composition of a stereotype, of the features which are subjectively associated with the label. It is not possible to predict the sort of bias that will occur only from the knowledge that someone has a hostile or a 'tolerant' attitude towards a given group of people.

Stereotyping can be considered as an inescapable adjunct to the human activity of categorizing. As such, it is neither 'bad' nor 'good'; it is there, and it serves some purpose in our continuous efforts to simplify the world around us. But it is hardly necessary to say that there are some important differences between the innocent laboratory games concerned with judgements of lengths of lines, as in the Tajfel and Wilkes and other similar experiments (see chapter 12), and the grimly serious matter of persistent unfairness of which we are all capable in one way or another, when we assume our favourite posture as self-appointed judges of other people's 'nature', 'character' or 'personality'. The two principal psychological differences between the 'neutral' categorizing and the prejudiced stereotyping are in the pronounced sharpening of those differences between human groups which happen to fit the stereotype, and in the resilience of these clear-cut differentiations. Both these phenomena warrant a little more discussion.

First, the sharpening of differences. There is one obvious distinction between 'neutral' categorizations and those which are associated with hostility: in the latter case the classification is not a matter of indifference to the individual. He has a vested emotional interest in preserving the comfortable and comforting segregation of people into sheep and goats. It seems, therefore, that two conditions must be fulfilled for this exaggeration of differences to take place: (i) the characteristic which is judged must stand in a direct and meaningful relation to the intergroup classification which the individual is using: and (ii) the classification itself must be of some emotional relevance to the individual.

To all of us some personal attributes are more important than

others. To one person 'intelligence' may be a more important characteristic of other people than 'honesty'; to another, 'kindness' more
important than 'strength of character'. It has been shown (Tajfel and
Wilkes, 1964) that there is a tendency to judge other people in more
extreme terms with regard to the attributes which are of more importance to those who are making the judgements. (More evidence
is summarized in the books of Sherif and Hovland (1961) and of Eiser
and Stroebe (1972).) Sherif and Hovland were primarily concerned
with attitude formation and attitude change. They described studies
in which their subjects were asked to rate in prescribed terms a number of statements concerning a specific social issue, such as, for
example, that of desegregation. The results showed that people who
were strongly involved in the issue (whether for or against desegregation) tended to assign the statements to more extreme positions
on the prescribed 'scale' than people who were less involved. Similar
findings exist with regard to less inflammatory problems, such as the
existence of fraternities in American colleges. Eiser and Stroebe have
been able to generalize these judgement phenomena beyond problems of attitude scales.

But one may well ask whether the judgements obtained in these
experimental studies have anything in common with judgements made
of members of human groups, who talk, laugh, are happy or sad,
kind or unkind and altogether display the infinite variety of human
behaviour so destructive of any attempt to formulate predictive laws
which imply uniformity.

This question can be rephrased. What are the effects on these judgements of the balance of the amount of specific information we have
(or think we have) about an individual and general information (valid
or not) about the group to which he belongs?

This question is best answered by a few related statements:

1. The less specific information one has about an individual, the
greater will be the tendency to assign to him the characteristics which
are assumed to be those of his group. This means that, on the one
hand, the prejudiced judgements obtained in experiments using a
minimum of information about individuals are of low predictive
value with regard to judgements made of 'real people'. On the other
hand, these artificially extorted judgements are fairly useful as a reflection of sets of stereotypes embedded in a culture.

2. It follows that when there is no emotional involvement in the use of the stereotype, when it represents no more than a moderately useful classifying device for lack of anything better to rely on, it is flexible and capable of change if information is received which flatly contradicts it or generally does not fit in.

3. All this does not apply to stereotypes which are associated with a high emotional charge. In such cases, information is selectively filtered through the focusing of attention on one or another aspect of the situation, and even more selectively remembered. A classic example of this was provided a long time ago by Allport and Postman (1947). In some of their experiments on the spreading of rumour they used a drawing which was presented to the first in a chain of subjects; the drawing was then removed and the first subject described it to a second, who in turn described it to a third, etc. The drawing represented a carriage in the New York subway in the middle of which stand two men, one white and one black, who seem to be quarrelling. The white man has an open razor tucked in at his belt. 'Here is' write Allport and Postman 'a typical terminal report' (the last in a chain of reproductions):

This is a subway train in New York headed for Portland Street. There is a Jewish woman and a Negro who has a razor in his hand. The woman has a baby and a dog. The train is going to Dyer Street and nothing much happened.

It is this selectivity and self-reinforcing nature of stereotypes which go with hostility that present the main difficulty in the attempts to change the 'image' through various educational techniques. Most of these techniques do not present the public to which they are primarily addressed – people who harbour intense prejudices – with effective reasons for selecting and retaining the intended message. Any form of propaganda must remain fairly ineffective as long as it is unrelated to an emotional climate which makes its aims desirable and rewarding, or at least acceptable. The advertisers have learned this simple principle a long time ago, and have been using it only too efficiently in their blend of 'giving the public what it wants' and helping it to want what they wish it to want.

Nevertheless, it is possible that educational programmes may be of some limited use even when they are not associated with long-term social changes. But in order to be useful such programmes would have to conform to certain specific criteria. Heart-breaking stories about 'good' members of groups which are the objects of prejudice are not likely to produce sizeable or permanent changes. If the problem can be defined, as it was above, in terms of abandoning perceptual habits which consist of selection, accentuation and omission of some features of events relevant to a prejudice, communication concerning this problem must attempt a series of specific tasks rather than consist of a sequence of general messages about such-and-such people being 'nice' despite the general opinion to the contrary. This is not impossible. Most studies on stereotypes show that their content is fairly stable within a culture, that there is general consensus about the characteristics distinguishing the group which is an object of discrimination from the group which does the discriminating. It is, therefore, quite feasible to undertake a content analysis which would aim at a specification of the most relevant aspects of this differentiating bias. There is no shortage of sources of material on which such an analysis could be made. It seems that educational programmes, carefully constructed so as to counteract specific aspects of bias known to be particularly widespread or particularly intense, may well have a better chance of success than those based on the idea of a more general frontal attack.

Educational programmes directed at children present their own special problems. Many studies have shown that evaluation of groups other than their own exists in children at a very early age (cf. Milner, 1975, for a recent review). This has some important consequences. Whatever the stage of development at which these value judgements begin to appear, it is clear that they can be observed well before the time when the child is capable of forming abstract concepts and categories relating to the human groups to which his evaluations apply. It is, therefore, obvious that if a child is not ready to use a category such as 'West Indians' or 'Jews' or 'French' or 'Italians', though any or each concrete Jew or West Indian may already be a 'good thing' or a 'bad thing', then no amount of nice and nicely read stories about nice children belonging to one or another of these groups will help. The child will not be capable of generalizing to a category which in his mind exists only in a very rudimentary form. Negative evaluations are learned and over-learned in a variety of concrete everyday contexts. Counter-evaluations must act with the same simplicity and within similar contexts, and apply to people who are real to the child.

At later stages, as more abstract conceptual schemes develop, so can the procedures of counter-evaluation be changed. The ultimate aim is not to prevent the categorization of human beings into distinct groups – this would be impossible and not even desirable – but to help to create categories within which each human being is evaluated as much as possible in terms of specific information about him, and not in terms of a powerful and socially shared evaluation applying to the human category of which he happens to be a member.

'Group' approaches to the psychology of intergroup relations

We argued in chapter 16 that one of the weaknesses of the 'motivational' approaches to intergroup behaviour is that an individual's behaviour and attitudes towards his own and other groups are seen as providing no more than yet another of the many settings in which each of us expresses his internal drives, tensions, needs, etc. As a result, the psychological aspects of group membership and of the society's multi-group organization are neglected in these approaches, and the analysis of intergroup behaviour is unnecessarily restricted to an 'individualistic' view of a human being's social psychological functioning. On the other hand, the cognitive analysis just presented can be considered as providing a description of one aspect of the end-stage of a long process. This long process is a history of certain kinds of relations between human groups. The question then arises: how does the *development* of these intergroup relations affect the behaviour and attitudes of people who compose the groups?

It was this question which provided the starting point to Sherif's classic studies on intergroup conflict and cooperation (cf. Sherif, 1966; Sherif *et al.*, 1961; Sherif & Sherif, 1953, 1969). His field experiments are well known. They were conducted in 'ordinary' boys' holiday camps and although there were some variations amongst the studies, their general design was similar. In all the studies the camp authorities were, unknowingly to the boys, the experimenters who organized and supervised the camp activities in such a way that the effects of intergroup conflict and cooperation could be studied. There were altogether four phases in the experiments. In the first, after the boys had arrived at the camp, general camp activities were organized and the boys were left to themselves to form acquaintances and friendships. In the second stage, they were divided into two groups, care being taken that those who had become friends earlier should find themselves in different groups; the activities were organized separately for each of the groups. The third stage consisted mainly of a number of competitions between the two groups organized by the camp authorities. The feature of all the competitions was that one group had to be unambiguously the winner and the other the loser. In the fourth stage, the two groups came up against problems or difficulties (pre-arranged by the experimenters) which could only be dealt with by their joint cooperative action. This fourth stage was introduced only in the third and last experiment which differed from the first two also in another important respect: it did not have a 'proper' first stage, as the boys arrived at the camp already divided into two separate groups.

The general results are simply described: the intergroup competitions of the second stage easily led to the social psychological effects that we intuitively and commonsensically associate with intergroup conflict. The objective conflict of interest between the groups (the conflict was 'objective' in the sense that one only of the two groups could win, at the expense of the other) led to manifestations of hostility, aggression and denigrating stereotypes between members of the two groups, and created at the same time a variety of symbols of ingroup identity and affiliation which acquired a strong emotional significance for the subjects. The 'superordinate goals' of the fourth stage, defined by Sherif (1966, p. 89) as 'those that have a compelling appeal for members of each group, but that neither group can achieve without the participation of the other', resulted in a lowering of intergroup tensions together with renewal or creation of friendships across group membership; although it remains true that all traces of previous intergroup hostility were by no means removed.

These results are by no means startling or even unexpected. Sherif's studies are important not because he discovered new facts about intergroup attitudes and behaviour; it cannot even be said that Sherif's theory of intergroup behaviour provided important *new* insights about the psychological effects of intergroup conflict. The general implications of his studies are, however, far reaching; they are of two kinds, one which can be described as methodological and the other as metatheoretical.

The methodological contribution consists of devising a series of controlled studies in which the psychological effects of an intergroup conflict of interests are viewed in the context of the *development* of the relations between the conflicting groups, i.e. of the history of these relations. In this sense, Sherif's experiments constitute a new departure. As Billig (1976) wrote, they were a *tour de force*: Sherif managed to create groups with a history which he has been able to control in order to look at the psychological effects of the developing intergroup relations. The fact that, under these simplified and controlled conditions, he has been able to recreate many phenomena which are usually associated with long-term complex social and historical developments greatly adds to the significance of his work.

The meta-theoretical contribution is equally important. We refer to it as *meta*-theoretical because its significance is due not so much to the details of the theory as to the *kind* of theory it is or the approach to the problem that it represents. The subjects who took part in Sherif's studies were 'normal', healthy American boys with no special personality or emotional problems which would distinguish them from the population at large. They behaved as they did as a *consequence* of a certain kind of intergroup relations which were imposed upon them, rather than creating a certain kind of intergroup relations as a result of their emotional or motivational problems. Group membership and intergroup conflict created their own uniformities of predictable social behaviour. This does not enable us to say anything very much about the behaviour of the boys in situations *other* than those involving the relations between the groups. But at the same time, the special features of their intergroup behaviour cannot be understood unless they are considered in their intergroup settings rather than as being secondary to individual emotional problems or to relations between individuals which exist outside of the social settings of group membership. This is what Sherif meant when he wrote that we 'must consider both the properties of the groups themselves and the consequences of membership on individuals. Otherwise, whatever we are studying, we are not studying groups' (1966, p. 62).

In continuing our discussion of the effects of group membership on social behaviour, we must now consider the validity of Sherif's assumption that the kind of intergroup behaviour which was elicited in his studies was fully determined by the existence of an explicit conflict of interests between the groups. In other words, we must ask whether there exist some features of group membership which will lead to similar forms of social behaviour even in the absence of an explicit intergroup conflict of interest. The conflict in Sherif's studies was clearly explicit to the subjects. This was so because it was institutionalized by the camp authorities, and thus it formed a highly 'visible' and legitimized aspect of the social situation. Is such an intergroup conflict of interests a *necessary* condition for the appearance of intergroup behaviour and the formation of the kind of intergroup attitudes that were found by Sherif, or is it possible that there are other determinants of such behaviour? The question is important not only for theoretical reasons. In his recent book, Sherif (1966) used the results of his studies to extrapolate to large-scale social and international conflicts and to draw on this basis some tentative conclusions about how the intensity of such conflicts could be reduced.

In one of Sherif's field experiments, the boys arrived at the camp already divided into two groups, each in separate locations in the camp. In this study some intergroup hostility and stereotyping appeared as soon as the groups became aware of each other's presence, and before the introduction by the camp authorities of any explicit intergroup conflict. Similar results were obtained in an experiment by Ferguson and Kelley (1964) in which the groups were engaged in various tasks, such as making models, drawing up city plans or making up a story. Despite the experimenters' emphasis that no competition of any kind was intended, the members of the groups whose task was to judge the products of their own group and of the outgroup tended to over-value the former and under-value the latter, even when they themselves had not taken part in the work. Rabbie and Horwitz (1969) also found various kinds of intergroup biases when, in a situation involving two groups, only one of the two received rewards, which had been assigned to it through a procedure which was explicitly random and seen as such by the subjects.

Results such as these seem to point towards other processes, additional to those associated with conflicts of interests, which play a role in determining hostility or tension between groups. The groups involved in the various studies just mentioned behaved *as if* their interests were in conflict, as if they considered themselves in some kind of competition, or at least expected some competition to occur in the future (cf. Rabbie and Wilkens, 1971) even when such a view of their relationship was not warranted by the situation. Intuitively or commonsensically this is easily explained: there exists in our culture a widespread tendency for groups (and also for individuals) to compete with no other aim than winning the competition. In other words, no *other* interests may be involved than those of winning; this is, for example, often the case in competitive sports events.

These 'intuitive' or 'commonsensical' notions do not provide, however, much of an insight into the social psychological processes operating in intergroup relations. To begin with, explanations of this kind tend to be circular: e.g., groups compete because, in our culture, groups are 'competitive'. More important is the fact that explanations of intergroup behaviour in terms of the subjects' perception of an experimental situation as a competitive 'game' miss the wider generality of the phenomena of intergroup bias and discrimination. The 'game' perception is no more than an instance of something much more general. Following Turner (1975), we can imagine a theoretical continuum at one extreme of which groups are in conflict entirely for 'objective' reasons, i.e. they are in competition for 'real' benefits and gains in a situation of scarcity. This would be the case of a conflict between nations for territory or economic outlets; or between social groups for distribution of goods and benefits. At the other extreme are situations in which the *only* outcome of intergroup competition can be a change in the *relative* positions of the groups; i.e. it is a competition for outcomes which have no value in and by themselves outside of the intergroup situations.

This second kind of competition is referred to by Turner as 'social competition' to distinguish it from conflicts the aims of which are to obtain or defend 'objective' benefits. It must be remembered that these are two 'theoretical' extremes; that is, they probably cannot be found in their 'pure' forms in real social situations, which are usually characterized by a mixture of the two types of competition and very often reflect a progressive transition from one type to the other. But many social situations can be clearly described as being relatively nearer to the 'objective conflict' variety or to the 'social competition' variety. A familiar example of a mixture of the two is any social or industrial conflict primarily concerned with the creation, preservation or erosion of 'differentials'. One could hardly describe such conflicts as caused by the participants perceiving the situation as a 'game' or generalizing to an industrial conflict the team game norms habitual to our culture. Competitive games are one special example of situations in which groups or individuals create or erode 'differentials' rather than some kind of a basic instance providing us with general explanatory principles.

The two major conditions which form the background of conflicts between groups emerge clearly from the preceding discussion. In one of them, the aim of the group is to obtain 'objective' benefits or advantages for its members at the expense of another group, or in competition with it; in the other, the aim is to do 'better' than another group, even if no *other* benefits than doing better are clearly discernible. Sherif's field studies can be seen as a fairly pure example of the second kind. On the face of it, the major determinant of the hostile intergroup behaviour in these studies was the legitimized and institutionalized conflict between the groups in which the only possible outcome was one group winning at the expense of the other. But as we have already seen, tension between the groups developed in one of the studies before competition between them was made in any way explicit. This observation raises an important theoretical issue: is it possible that intergroup bias and discrimination can be shown to exist in the absence of: (i) any 'objective' advantages that may accrue to the individual members of a group as a result of their actions favouring their own group; (ii) any form of explicit competition between the groups; and (iii) any previously existing hostility between the groups which might otherwise explain discriminatory behaviour in the absence of the first two conditions?

On the basis of data obtained from experiments designed to deal with these questions (Tajfel, 1970; Tajfel *et al.*, 1971) the answers are that intergroup discrimination (or behaviour favouring one's own group at the expense of the outgroup) is clearly present without any explicit competition between the groups, without any link between the subjects' discriminatory responses and their own individual interest, and without previous hostility between the groups. In these experiments, the results of which have been replicated since in a number of subsequent studies, the subjects were divided into two groups on the basis of unimportant criteria (such as preference for the reproductions of one or another of two painters, both unknown to them) and sometimes even explicitly assigned at random to two groups (Billig and Tajfel, 1973). Arrangements were made for group membership to remain anonymous, and in the second part of the experiments each subject was requested to make a number of decisions through which he awarded amounts of 'real' money (which were paid out at the end of the experimental session) to two *other* anonymous subjects designated by code numbers. These two other subjects were identified either as (i) one of them belonging to the 'decider's' own group and one to the outgroup; or as (ii) both belonging to the decider's own group; or as (iii) both belonging to the outgroup. Decisions relating to (i), as compared with (ii) and (iii), showed a highly consistent and significant tendency to favour anonymous members of the ingroup over those of the outgroup.

However, the most interesting data concerned the intergroup 'differentiation' discussed above. The decisions awarding money to two other anonymous subjects consisted of choices made on specially constructed 'matrices', one choice per matrix. These matrices allowed an assessment of the relative 'pull' of several variables affecting the subjects' decisions, since they were so arranged that the different kinds of 'benefits' were in direct conflict with one another on each matrix. For example, in some of the matrices the nearer a subject chose to the term which represented the 'maximum joint profit' in the total amount of money jointly awarded to two others, the further away the choice was from awarding a possible maximum of money to a member of his own group. In other matrices, *maximum difference* in favour of a member of the ingroup was set against both the maximum profit in absolute amounts for a member of the ingroup and the maximum joint profit for the two recipients. To put it differently, a member of the ingroup could get *more* than a member of the outgroup only at the expense of getting less money than he might have got if the subject had decided that it was worthwhile giving a larger amount to a member of the ingroup but an even larger one to a member of the outgroup. The results showed that very often the establishment of a *difference* in favour of the ingroup was more important to the subjects than obtaining the possible maximum of money for their own group.

Another finding pointing in the same direction emerged from decisions concerning two members of the ingroup as compared with those concerning two members of the outgroup. The awards given to two members of the ingroup tended to be jointly higher than those given to two members of the outgroup. The important aspect of this finding, as well as of the previous one about the importance of differences, is that we are dealing here with cases of gratuitous intergroup discrimination. In one case, *both* ingroup and outgroup members are given less than they might be given so that a difference in favour of the ingroup can be established. In the other, the two sets of choices are independent since they are made on different matrices; in other words, the subjects would not need to give any less to the ingroup by giving more to the outgroup. The only possible interest they may have therefore is, once again, to establish a difference in favour of the ingroup.

It appears from these findings that intergroup discrimination persists even when the individual's own interest is not involved in favouring his own group, when there is no explicit competition between the groups, and when there is no trace of a history of previous hostility between the groups. It also appears that the aim of this discrimination is to establish a difference between the groups in favour of one's own, sometimes even when this conflicts with simply defined 'utilitarian' interests of the ingroup.

Further research on these issues is now in progress in several countries, and therefore in this chapter we can attempt no more than a brief summary of the general ideas on which this research is based. It is nearly impossible in most natural social situations to distinguish between discriminatory intergroup behaviour based on a conflict of 'objective' interests between the groups and discrimination based on attempts to establish a positively valued 'distinctiveness' for one's own group. However, as has already been mentioned, the two can be distinguished to some extent theoretically since the goals of actions aimed exclusively at the achievement of a positively valued ingroup distinctiveness retain no value outside of the context of intergroup comparisons. An example would be a group which does not necessarily wish to increase the level of their salaries but are acting to prevent other groups from getting nearer to this level so that differentials can be preserved. But the difficulty with this example – as with many other similar examples – is that, in this case, the preservation of salary differentials is probably associated with all kinds of other 'objective' advantages accruing to the group which cannot be defined in terms of money alone. In turn, *some* of these other advantages will again make sense only in the comparative framework of intergroup competition.

Despite this confusing network of interactions, the distinction is important because it helps us to understand some usually neglected aspects of intergroup behaviour. Belonging to a social group (or defining oneself as a member of a social category) may be roughly considered as placed somewhere along two interdependent dimensions. One of these dimensions is the importance of the membership to an individual; the other – its positive or negative value connotations. We must now return to a distinction made at the beginning of the previous chapter between 'acting in terms of self' and 'acting in terms of one's group'. In many social situations, behaviour approaching one or the other of these extremes is likely to occur depending upon the individual's beliefs about the social system within which this behaviour takes place. If he believes that this social system is a flexible one, i.e. that it is relatively easy to move in it from one group to another, it is likely that in many intergroup situations he will act primarily in terms of 'self'. If, however, the beliefs – whether they do or do not correspond to social reality – are based on the assumption that the only way for an individual to improve his position in the system, or to preserve a satisfactory *status quo* is with his group as a whole and as a member of it, intergroup behaviour is likely to take on some very special characteristics. These beliefs will then be associated with: (i) a certain uniformity of action amongst members of the group in the *relevant intergroup social situations*; and (ii) certain attitudes towards members of the outgroup and forms of behaviour towards them. Individual differences in the outgroup will be of little account and its members will be treated as undifferentiated items in a subjectively unified social category. Theories of intergroup behaviour which stress individual motivation and inter-individual relationships are often based on assumptions about beliefs in the flexibility and individual mobility within the social system. The 'group' theories, represented in the work of Sherif and in the present discussion, take into account a wider range of systems of perceived social causality. The historical and social assumptions and myths about individual mobility and flexibility have undoubtedly found their way into much social psychological theorizing on intergroup behaviour. As Hirschman (1970) put it:

The traditional American idea of success confirms the hold which exit has had on the national imagination. Success – or, what amounts to the same thing, upward social mobility – has long been conceived in terms of evolutionary individualism. The successful individual who starts out at a low rung of the social ladder necessarily leaves his own group as he rises; he 'passes' into, or is 'accepted' by, the next higher group. He takes his immediate family along, but hardly anyone else (pp. 108–9).

This discussion about the psychological conditions leading to group actions has still been mainly concerned with 'utilitarian' aims of behaviour; i.e. this behaviour was seen as furthering or defending the 'objective' interests of an individual perceived by him as impossible to further or to defend on his own, outside the context of actions 'in terms of a group'. This is not, however, the whole story. Experimental evidence which was previously described leads to the conclusion that the establishment of positively valued *differences* between one's own group and others has its own autonomous functions in intergroup behaviour. These attempts to create positively valued intergroup differentiations must be seen as related to the requirements of an individual's image of himself. 'Social identity' of an individual can be conceived as consisting of those aspects of his self-image, positively or negatively valued, which derive from his membership of various social groups to which he belongs. In social systems which are and/or are believed to be strongly stratified and inflexible (i.e., in which passage from one group to another is difficult or impossible), behaviour relating to social identity will be in some ways parallel to actions 'in terms of a group' aimed at preserving or defending one's own interests through those of a group, since individual actions have very little chance of success. In these stratified situations an individual can change a *psychologically* unsatisfying group situation, or preserve a psychologically satisfying one, only with his group as a whole, only if he acts as a member of it. There are many examples of selfless actions or even extreme sacrifice for the sake of a group which show the intensity of social attitudes and conduct to which these 'non-utilitarian' affiliations can lead. At the other extreme they can also result in gruesome instances of discrimination against an outgroup (as in some inter-racial or inter-ethnic conflicts), for which very often no clear reasons can be found if one considers only the more 'utilitarian' aspects of an individual's social behaviour.

It is, however, not possible to understand the forms taken by this behaviour unless one considers them from the outset as being inherently of an *intergroup* nature. A group and its membership can be positively or negatively evaluated only through intergroup comparisons; there is no meaning or significance to such evaluations outside a multi-group context. Even the physical characteristics of a group – such as the colour of its skin, the amount of territory it owns, the wealth it possesses – derive most of their value connotations from comparisons with other relevant groups. The concept of relative deprivation, extensively used by sociologists and political scientists, and in a modified form by economists (e.g. Gurr, 1970; Hirschman, 1970; Runciman, 1972), reflects well this primordial role of social comparisons. A distinction must be made, however, between inter-individual and intergroup social comparisons. The theory about the former was brilliantly formulated by Festinger (1954); it applied, however, in his own explicit statements, mainly to individuals within a group who can effectively engage in these comparisons because they are similar to each other. Intergroup social comparison can have a much wider range. The groups with which comparisons are made must be seen as *relevant* in one way or another to the position and circumstances of one's own group – be it in terms of distribution of power, status, resources, signs of superiority and inferiority, etc. This reaching beyond 'similarity' will operate when there is no escape for an individual, as long as he acts on his own, from the psychological as well as the 'objective' consequences of his group membership.

Thus, in inter-individual behaviour, the basis for social comparison is provided by a certain similarity between the individuals concerned (see chapter 9). In intergroup behaviour this will often be replaced by the perceived *legitimacy* of the perceived relationship between the groups which are involved. Inferiority of a group which is perceived as 'legitimate' by its members will not necessarily lead to attempts at changing the situation. When such inferiority is perceived as illegitimate, *or* when superiority perceived as legitimate is under threat, the attempts to achieve, restore or preserve positively valued intergroup differentiations will appear in the guise of many forms of outgroup discrimination.

Conclusion

In the present chapter, we summarized some of the 'group' approaches to the problems of intergroup behaviour. We came to the conclusion that the requirements of social identity, related to the nature of the objective and subjective relations between groups, to the functioning of intergroup social comparison, and to the significance of perceived legitimacy in this functioning, enables us to consider intergroup behaviour in genuinely social contexts, above and beyond its determination by individual needs or motives which are assumed to operate somehow prior to, or independently of, the social systems in which all human beings live. It is in this sense that these considerations, together with Sherif's group conflict theories, represent a *social* psychology of intergroup behaviour. Much remains to be done: we need to understand better the way in which cognitive processes involved in this behaviour reflect social change and the diffusion of new group ideas and ideologies; what are the social conditions in which *psychological* processes start to operate which help to transform an acquiescent group that accepted its previous 'comparative' fate, whatever it was, into a militant part of a society; in what psychological conditions intergroup discrimination intensifies, and – most of all – what are the psychological conditions in which it can be reduced. There are, of course, strict limits to the effectiveness of these 'psychological' conditions. However important they may be, and however autonomously they may function in certain situations, the historical, social and economic aspects of intergroup hostility and discrimination are prior in their causality to the psychological ones. This does not minimize the crucial importance of an adequate social psychological analysis; rather, it places it in a perspective which includes other kinds of analysis that must be related to it.

Further Reading (Chapters 16 and 17)

Many of the books in social psychology concerned with intergroup behaviour focus too exclusively on problems of prejudice rather than on the wider issues of social conflict; but some of them also discuss these more general issues. The widest critical survey to date of theories and empirical work on intergroup behaviour and social conflict can be found in:

Billig, M. (1976), *Social Psychology and Intergroup Relations*, London, Academic Press.

G. W. Allport's classic on *The Nature of Prejudice* (1954) is certainly worth reading for its intelligent and literate approach to many of the earlier theories. A more recent theoretical survey can be found in:

LeVine, R. A., and Campbell, D. T. (1972), *Ethnocentrism: Theories of conflict, ethnic attitudes and group behaviour*, New York, Wiley.

The chapter by J. Harding *et al* on 'Prejudice and ethnic relations' in volume 5 of G. Lindzey and E. Aronson, eds., *The Handbook of Social Psychology*, Reading, Mass., Addison-Wesley, (1969) provides a useful summary of much of the empirical work in the area.

Watson, P. (1973), *Psychology and Race*, Penguin Books. This contains a number of general chapters about intergroup behaviour which represent well the diverse theoretical perspectives in this field.

The following would be useful for some of the special problems discussed in the two chapters:

Berkowitz, L. (1962), *Aggression: A social psychological analysis*, New York, McGraw-Hill. On theories of aggression, particularly chapters 6 and 7 on applications to intergroup behaviour. More recent views of Berkowitz can be found in his chapter on 'The frustration-aggression hypothesis revisited' in a book, *Roots of Aggression*, which he edited (New York, Atherton Press, 1969). Sherif provides a general summary of his experimental work and theoretical position in his book on *Group Conflict and Co-operation* (London, Routledge and Kegan Paul, 1966).

Good discussions of relative deprivation can be found in:

Runciman, W. (1972), *Relative Deprivation and Social Justice*, Penguin Books (chapters 2 and 3).

Gurr, T. R. (1970), *Why Men Rebel*, Princeton University Press.

Theory and current research relating to the views discussed in the last section of chapter 17 are described in:

Tajfel, H., ed. (1978), *Differentiation between Social Groups: Studies in the social psychology of intergroup relations*, London, Academic Press (European Monographs in Social Psychology).

References

ABELSON, R. P. (1964), 'Mathematical models of the distribution of attitudes under controversy', in N. Frederiksen and H. Gulliksen, eds., *Contributions to Mathematical Psychology*, New York, Holt, Rinehart & Winston.

ABELSON, R. P. (1972), 'Are attitudes necessary?', in B. T. King and E. Mc-Ginnies, eds., *Attitudes, Conflict and Social Change*, New York, Academic Press.

ABERCROMBIE, D. (1968), 'Paralanguage', *British Journal of Disorders of Communication*, 3, 55–9.

ADAMS, J. S. (1963), 'Towards an understanding of inequity', *Journal of Abnormal and Social Psychology*, 67, 422–36.

ADORNO, T. W., FRENKEL-BRUNSWIK, E., LEVINSON, D. J., and SANFORD, R. N. (1950), *The Authoritarian Personality*, New York, Harper & Row.

AHRENS, R. (1954), 'Beitrag zur Entwicklung der Physiognomie und Mimiker-kennes', *Zeitschrift der experimentelle und angewandte Psychologie*, 2, 412–54.

AJZEN, I., and FISHBEIN, M. (1972), 'Attitudes and normative beliefs as factors influencing behavioural intentions', *Journal of Personality and Social Psychology*, 21, 1–9.

ALEXANDER, C. N., JR, ZUCKER, L. G., and BRADY, C. L. (1970), 'Experimental expectations and autokinetic experiences: consistency theories and judgmental convergence', *Sociometry*, 33, 108–22.

ALEXANDER, R. D. (1974), 'The evolution of social behaviour', *Annual Review of Ecology and Systematics*, 5, 325–83.

ALLPORT, F. H. (1924), *Social Psychology*, Boston, Houghton Mifflin.

ALLPORT, F. H. (1962), 'A structuronomic conception of behaviour: individual and collective. I. Structural theory and the master problem of social psychology', *Journal of Abnormal and Social Psychology*, 64, 3–30.

ALLPORT, G. W. (1935), 'Attitudes', in C. M. Murchison, ed., *Handbook of Social Psychology*, Worcester, Mass., Clark University Press.

ALLPORT, G. W. (1937), *Personality: A Psychological Interpretation*, New York, Holt, Rinehart & Winston.

ALLPORT, G. W. (1954), *The Nature of Prejudice*, Cambridge, Mass., Addison-Wesley.

ALLPORT, G. W., and ODBERT, H. S. (1936), 'Trait-names: a psycho-lexical study', *Psychological Monographs*, 47 (whole no. 211).

ALLPORT, G. W., and POSTMAN, L. (1947), *The Psychology of Rumour*, New York, Holt, Rinehart & Winston.

ANDERSON, N. H., and HOVLAND, C. I. (1957), 'The representation of order in communication research' (Appendix A), in C. I. Hovland, ed., *The Order of Presentation in Persuasion*, New Haven, Yale University Press.

ANDREW, R. J. (1963), 'The origin and evolution of the calls and facial expression of the primates', *Behaviour*, 20, 1–107.

ANSCOMBE, G. E. M. (1963), *Intention*, 2nd ed., Oxford, Blackwell.

ARCHER, J. (1970), 'Effects of population density on behaviour in rodents', in J. H. Crook, ed., *Social Behaviour in Birds and Mammals*, London, Academic Press.

ARDREY, R. (1966), *The Territorial Imperative*, New York, Atheneum; London, Collins (1967).

ARGYLE, M. (1967), *The Psychology of Interpersonal Behaviour*, Penguin Books.

ARGYLE, M. (1969), *Social Interaction*, London, Methuen.

ARGYLE, M., ALKEMA, F., and GILMOUR, R. (1971), 'The communication of friendly and hostile attitudes by verbal and non-verbal signals', *European Journal of Social Psychology*, 1, 385–402.

ARGYLE, M., and COOK, M. (1976), *Eye and Mutual Gaze*, Cambridge, Cambridge University Press.

ARGYLE, M., GARDNER, G., and CIOFFI, F. (1958), 'Supervisory methods related to productivity, absenteeism and labour turnover', *Human Relations*, 11, 23–45.

ARGYLE, M., and KENDON, A. (1967), 'The experimental analysis of social performance', in L. Berkowitz, ed., *Advances in Experimental Social Psychology*, vol. 3, New York, Academic Press.

ARGYLE, M., LALLJEE, M. C., and COOK, M. (1968), 'The effects of visibility on interaction in a dyad', *Human Relations*, 21, 3–17.

ARGYLE, M., SALTER, V., NICHOLSON, H., WILLIAMS, M., and BURGESS, P. (1970), 'The communication of inferior and superior attitudes by verbal and non-verbal signals', *British Journal of Social and Clinical Psychology*, 9, 222–31.

ARGYRIS, C. (1960), *Integrating the Individual and the Organization*, New York, Wiley.

ASCH, S. E. (1948), 'The doctrine of suggestion, prestige and imitation in social psychology', *Psychological Review*, 55, 250–76.

ASCH, S. E. (1951), 'Effects of group pressure upon the modification and distortion of judgments', in H. Guetzkow, ed., *Groups, Leadership and Men*, Pittsburgh, Carnegie Press.

ASCH, S. E. (1952), *Social Psychology*, Englewood Cliffs, New York, Prentice Hall.

BABCHUK, N., and GOODE, W. F. (1951), 'Work incentives in a self-determined group', *American Sociological Review*, 16, 679–87.

BACK, K. W. (1973), *Beyond Words: The story of sensitivity training and the encounter movement*, Baltimore, Md., Penguin Books.

BALES, R. F. (1950), *Interaction Process Analysis: A method for the study of small groups*, Cambridge, Mass., Addison-Wesley.

BALES, R. F. (1970), *Personality and Interpersonal Behavior*, New York, Holt, Rinehart & Winston.

BALES, R. F., and BORGATTA, E. F. (1955), 'Size of group as a factor in the interaction profile', in A. P. Hare *et al.*, eds., *Small Groups: Studies in social interaction*, New York, Knopf.

BALES, R. F., and SLATER, P. E. (1955), 'Role differentiation in small decision-making groups', in T. Parsons *et al.*, eds., *Family, Socialization and Interaction Process*, New York, Free Press.

BANDURA, A., and WALTERS, R. H. (1963), *Social Learning and Personality Development*, New York, Holt, Rinehart & Winston.

BARKER, J. D. (1966), *Power in Committees: An experiment in the governmental process*, Chicago, Rand McNally.

BARKER, R. G. (1968), *Ecological Psychology: Concepts and methods for studying the environment of human behaviour*, Stanford, Calif., Stanford University Press.

BARKER, R. G., and WRIGHT, H. F. (1955), *Midwest and its Children*, Evanston, Ill., Row, Peterson.

BARKER, R. G., and WRIGHT, H. F. (1963), *One Boy's Day*, New York, Harper & Row.

BARRY, H., CHILD, I. L., and BACON, M. K. (1959), 'Relation of child training to subsistence economy', *American Anthropologist*, 61, 51–63.

BARTLETT, F. C. (1932), *Remembering*, Cambridge, Cambridge University Press.

BATESON, G., *et al.* (1956), 'Toward a theory of schizophrenia', *Behavioural Science*, 1, 251–65.

BAUER, R. A. (1965), 'A revised model of source effect', Presidential address of the Division of Consumer Psychology, American Psychological Association, Annual Convention, Chicago.

BAVELAS, A. (1950), 'Communication patterns in task-oriented groups', *Journal of the Acoustical Society of America*, 22, 725–30.

BEM, D. J. (1965), 'An experimental analysis of self persuasion', *Journal of Experimental Social Psychology*, 1, 199–218.

BEM, D. J. (1967), 'Self-perception: an alternative interpretation of cognitive dissonance phenomena', *Psychological Review*, 74, 183–200.

BEM, D. J. (1968), 'Attitudes and self descriptions: another look at the attitude-behaviour link', in A. G. Greenwald, T. C. Brock and T. M. Ostrom, eds., *Psychological Foundations of Attitudes*, New York, Academic Press.

BERGER, P. L., and LUCKMANN, T. (1967), *The Social Construction of Reality*, London, Allen Lane.

BERKOWITZ, L. (1962), *Aggression: A social psychological analysis*, New York, McGraw-Hill.

BERKOWITZ, L. (1965), 'The concept of aggressive drive: some additional considerations', in L. Berkowitz, ed., *Advances in Experimental Social Psychology*, vol. 2, New York, Academic Press.

BERKOWITZ, L. (1969), 'The frustration-aggression hypothesis revisited', in L. Berkowitz, ed., *Roots of Aggression*, New York, Atherton Press.

BERKOWITZ, L. (1972), 'Frustrations, comparison and other sources of emotion arousal as contributors to social unrest', *Journal of Social Issues*, 28, 77–91.

BERLEW, D., and HALL, D. (1966), 'The socialization of managers: the effects of expectations on performance', *Administrative Science Quarterly*, 11, no. 2, 207–23.

BERRY, J. W., and DASEN, P. R. (1973), *Culture and Cognition: Readings in cross-cultural psychology*, New York, Harper & Row; London, Methuen.

BERSCHEID, E., and WALSTER, E. (1969), *Interpersonal Attraction*, Reading, Mass., Addison-Wesley.

BETTELHEIM, B. (1943), 'Individual and mass behaviour in extreme situations', *Journal of Abnormal and Social Psychology*, 38, 417–52.

BETTELHEIM, B. (1969), *Children of the Dream*, London, Thames & Hudson.

BEYNON, H. (1973), *Working for Ford*, Penguin Books.

BICKMAN, L. (1972), 'Social influence and diffusion of responsibility in an emergency', *Journal of Experimental Social Psychology*, 8, 438–45.

BILLIG, M. (1976), *Social Psychology and Intergroup Relations*, London, Academic Press (European Monographs in Social Psychology).

BILLIG, M., and TAJFEL, H. (1973), 'Social categorization and similarity in intergroup behaviour', *European Journal of Social Psychology*, 3, 37–52.

BIRD, C. (1940), *Social Psychology*, New York, Appleton-Century.

BIRDWHISTELL, R. L. (1952), *Introduction to Kinesics*, Louisville, Kentucky, University of Louisville Press.

BIRDWHISTELL, R. L. (1961), 'Paralanguage twenty-five years after Sapir', in H. C. Brosin, ed., *Lectures in Experimental Psychiatry*, Pittsburgh, Pittsburgh University Press.

BIRDWHISTELL, R. L. (1963), 'The kinesic level in the investigation of emotions', in P. H. Knapp, ed., *Expression of the Emotions in Man*, New York, International Universities Press.

BIRDWHISTELL, R. L. (1968), 'Kinesics', *International Encyclopedia of the Social Sciences*, 8, 370–85.

BIXENSTINE, E. V., LEVITT, C. A., and WILSON, K. V. (1966), 'Collaboration among six persons in a Prisoner's Dilemma game', *Journal of Conflict Resolution*, 10, 488–96.

BLAU, P. M., and SCOTT, W. R. (1963), *Formal Organizations: A comparative approach*, London, Routledge & Kegan Paul.

BLAUNER, R. (1964), *Alienation and Freedom*, Chicago, University of Chicago Press.

BLAUVELT, H., and MCKENNA, J. (1961), 'Mother–neonate interaction: capacity of the human newborn for orientation', in B. M. Foss, ed., *Determinants of Infant Behaviour*, London, Methuen.

BLOM, J. P., and GUMPERZ, J. (1972), 'Social meaning in linguistic structures', in J. Gumperz and D. Hymes, eds., *Directions in Sociolinguistics*, New York, Holt, Rinehart & Winston.

BLURTON-JONES, N., ed. (1972), *Ethological Studies of Child Behaviour*, Cambridge, Cambridge University Press.

BOLINGER, D. (1975), *Aspects of Language*, 2nd ed., New York, Harcourt Brace Jovanovich.

BOURHIS, R. Y., GILES, H., and LAMBERT, W. E. (1975), 'Social consequences of accommodating one's style of speech: a cross-national investigation', *International Journal of the Sociology of Language*, 6, 55–71.

BOWERS, K. S. (1973), 'Situationism in psychology: an analysis and a critique', *Psychological Review*, 80, 307–36.

BOWLBY, J. (1969), *Attachment and Loss: 1. Attachment*, London, Hogarth Press.

BREHM, J., and COHEN, A. R. (1962), *Explorations in Cognitive Dissonance*, New York, Wiley.

BREWER, M. B. (1968), 'Determinants of social distance among East African tribal groups', *Journal of Personality and Social Psychology*, 10, 279–89.

BRONFENBRENNER, U. (1971), *Two Worlds of Childhood*, London, Allen & Unwin.

BROWN, N. (1959), *Life against Death*, London, Sphere Books.

BROWN, R. (1965), *Social Psychology*, Glencoe, Ill., Free Press.

BROWN, R. and FORD, M. (1961), 'Address in American English', *Journal of Abnormal and Social Psychology*, 62, 375–85.

BRUNER, J. S. (1957a), 'On perceptual readiness', *Psychological Review*, 64, 123–52.

BRUNER, J. S. (1957b), 'Going beyond the information given', in H. Gruber *et al.*, eds., *Contemporary Approaches to Cognition*, Cambridge, Mass., Harvard University Press.

BRUNER, J. S., OLVER, R. R., and GREENFIELD, P. M. (1966), *Studies in Cognitive Growth*, New York, Wiley.

BRUNER, J. S., and POTTER, M. C. (1964), 'Interference in visual recognition', *Science*, 144, 424–5.

BUGENTAL, D. E., KASWAN, J. M., and LOVE, L. R. (1970), 'Perception of contradictory meanings conveyed by verbal and non-verbal channels', *Journal of Personality and Social Psychology*, 16, 647–55.

BURKE, P. J. (1972), 'Leadership role differentiation', in C. G. McClintock, ed., *Experimental Social Psychology*, New York, Holt, Rinehart & Winston.

BURNSTEIN, E., VINOKUR, A., and TROPE, Y. (1973), 'Interpersonal comparison versus persuasive argumentation: a more direct test of alternative explanations for group-induced shifts in individual choices', *Journal of Experimental Social Psychology*, 9, 236–45.

BURNSTEIN, E., and WORCHEL, P. (1962), 'Arbitrariness of frustration and its consequences for aggression in a social situation', *Journal of Personality*, 30, 528–41.

BYRNE, D. (1969), 'Attitudes and attraction', in L. Berkowitz, ed., *Advances in Experimental Social Psychology*, vol. 4, New York, Academic Press.

CAMPBELL, B., ed. (1972), *Sexual Selection and the Descent of Man, 1871–1971*, Chicago, Aldine.

CAMPBELL, D. T. (1956), 'Enhancement of contrast as a composite habit', *Journal of Abnormal and Social Psychology*, 53, 350–55.

CAMPBELL, D. T. (1958), 'Common fate, similarity, and other indices of the status of aggregates of persons as social entities', *Behavioral Science*, 3, 14–25.

CAMPBELL, D. T. (1963), 'Social attitudes and other acquired behavioural dispositions', in S. Koch, ed., *Psychology: A study of a science*, vol. 6, New York, McGraw-Hill.

CAMPBELL, D. T. (1967), 'Stereotypes and the perception of group differences', *American Psychologist*, 22, 817–29.

CAMPBELL, D. T., and FISKE, D. W. (1959), 'Convergent and discriminant validation by the multitrait–multimethod matrix', *Psychological Bulletin*, 56, 81–105.

CAMPBELL, D. T., and STANLEY, J. C. (1966), *Experimental and Quasi-experimental Designs for Research*, Chicago, Rand McNally.

CAMPBELL, J. P., and DUNNETTE, M. D. (1968), 'Effectiveness of T-group experiences in managerial training and development', *Psychological Bulletin*, 70, 73–104.

CARTWRIGHT, D., and ZANDER, A., eds. (1968), *Group Dynamics: Research and Theory*, 3rd ed., New York, Harper & Row.

CATTELL, R. B. (1963), 'Patterns of change: measurement in relation to state-dimension, trait change, lability and process concepts', in R. B. Cattell, *Handbook of Multivariate Experimental Psychology*, Chicago, Rand McNally.

CHANDLER, S., and RABOW, J. (1969), 'Ethnicity and acquaintance as variables in risk-taking', *Journal of Social Psychology*, 77, 221–9.

CHEIN, I. (1948), 'Behaviour theory and the behaviour of attitudes', *Psychological Review*, 55, 175–88.

CICOUREL, A. V. (1973), *Cognitive Sociology*, Penguin Books.

CLARK, R. D., and WORD, L. E. (1972), 'Why don't bystanders help? Because of ambiguity?', *Journal of Personality and Social Psychology*, 24, 392–400.

CLEMENT, D. E., and SULLIVAN, D. W. (1970), 'No risky shift effect with real groups and real risks', *Psychonomic Science*, 18, 243–5.

COHEN, S., and TAYLOR, L. (1972), *Psychological Survival*, Penguin Books.

COLE, M., and SCRIBNER, S. (1974), *Culture and Thought: A psychological introduction*, New York, Wiley.

COLLINS, B. E., and RAVEN, B. H. (1969), 'Group structure: attraction, coalitions, communication and power', in G. Lindzey and E. Aronson, eds., *The Handbook of Social Psychology*, vol. 4, 2nd ed., Reading, Mass., Addison-Wesley.

COLLIS, G. M., and SCHAFFER, H. R. (1975), 'Synchronization of visual attention in mother–infant pairs', *Journal of Child Psychology and Psychiatry*, 16, 315–20.

CONKLIN, H. C. (1954), 'The relation of Hanunóo culture to the plant world', unpublished doctoral dissertation, Yale University.

COOK, M. (1971), 'An anatomy of um and er', *New Society*, 17, no. 455, 577–9.

COOPER, C. L., ed. (1975), *Theories of Group Processes*, London, Wiley.

COTGROVE, S. (1972), 'Alienation and automation', *British Journal of Sociology*, 23, 437–51.

CRANO, W. D., and BREWER, M. B. (1973), *Principles of Research in Social Psychology*, New York, McGraw-Hill.

CROOK, J. H. (1966), 'Gelada baboon herd structure and movement: a comparative report', *Symposia of the Zoological Society of London*, 18, 237–58.

CROOK, J. H. (1970a), 'The socio-ecology of primates', in J. H. Crook, ed., *Social Behaviour in Birds and Mammals*, London, Academic Press.

CROOK, J. H., ed. (1970b), *Social Behaviour in Birds and Mammals*, London, Academic Press.

CROOK, J. H. (1971), 'Sources of cooperation in animals and Man', in *Man and Beast – comparative social behaviour*, Smithsonian Institution, Washington, D.C. (Smithsonian Annual, III).

CROOK, J. H. (1973), 'Darwinism and the sexual politics of primates', *Social Science Information*, 12, 7–28.

CROOK, J. H. (1975), 'Problems of inference in the comparison of animal and human social organizations', *Social Science Information*, 14, 89–112.

CROOK, J. H. (1977), 'On the integration of gender strategies in mammalian social systems', in J. Rosenblatt and B. Komisaruk, eds., *Reproductive behaviour and evolution*, New York, Plenum Press.

CROOK, J. H., and ALDRICH-BLAKE, P. (1968), 'Ecological and behavioural contrasts between sympatric ground dwelling primates in Ethiopia', *Folia Primatologica*, 8, 192–227.

CROOK, J. H., and GARTLAN, J. S. (1966), 'The evolution of primate societies', *Nature*, 210, 1200–1203.

CROOK, J. H., and GOSS-CUSTARD, J. (1972), 'Social ethology', *Annual Review of Psychology*, 23, 277–312.

CROWE, B. J., BOCHNER, S., and CLARK, A. W. (1972), 'The effects of subordinates' behaviour on managerial style', *Human Relations*, 25, 215–37.

CRUTCHFIELD, R. S. (1955), 'Conformity and character', *American Psychologist*, 10, 191–8.

CRYSTAL, D. (1971), *Linguistics*, Penguin Books.

DABBS, J. M. (1969), 'Similarity of gestures and interpersonal influence', *Proceedings of the 77th Annual Convention*, American Psychological Association, 4, 337–8.

DANZIGER, K. (1976), *Interpersonal Communication*, New York, Academic Press.

DARLEY, J. M., and LATANÉ, B. (1968), 'Bystander intervention in emergencies: diffusion of responsibility', *Journal of Personality and Social Psychology*, 8, 377–83.

DARLEY, J. M., and LATANÉ, B. (1970), 'Norms and normative behavior: field studies of social interdependence', in J. Macaulay and L. Berkowitz, eds., *Altruism and Helping Behavior*, New York, Academic Press.

DARWIN, C. (1859), *On the Origin of Species by Means of Natural Selection, or the preservation of favoured races in the struggle for life*, London, J. Murray.

DARWIN, C. (1871), *The Descent of Man and Selection in Relation to Sex*, London, J. Murray.

DARWIN, C. (1872), *The Expression of the Emotions in Man and Animals*, London, J. Murray.

DAS GUPTA, J. (1970), *Language Conflict and National Development*, Berkeley, University of California Press.

DAVIDON, R. S. (1962), 'Relevance and category scales of judgement', *British Journal of Psychology*, 53, 373–80.

DAVIS, J. (1969), *Group Performance*, Reading, Mass., Addison-Wesley.

DAWES, R. M. (1971), *Fundamentals of Attitude Measurements*, New York, Wiley.

DAWSON, J. L. M. (1969a), 'Traditional versus Western attitudes in West Africa', *British Journal of Social and Clinical Psychology*, 6, 81–96.

DAWSON, J. L. M. (1969b), 'Attitude change and conflict among Australian Aborigines', *Australian Journal of Psychology*, 21, 101–16.

DAWSON, J. L. M. (1971), 'Scaling Chinese traditional–modern attitudes and the GSR measurement of "important" versus "unimportant" Chinese concepts', *Journal of Cross-Cultural Psychology*, 2, 1–27.

DAWSON, J. L. M. (1973), *Culture and Perception*, New York, Wiley.

DECI, E. L. (1971), 'Effects of externally mediated rewards on intrinsic motivation', *Journal of Personality and Social Psychology*, 18, 105–15.

DEFLEUR, M. L., and WESTIE, F. R. (1963), 'Attitude as a scientific concept', *Social Forces*, 42, 17–31.

DEREGOWSKI, J. B. (1968a), 'Difficulties in pictorial depth perception in Africa', *British Journal of Psychology*, 59, 195–204.

DEREGOWSKI, J. B. (1968b), 'On perception of depicted orientation', *International Journal of Psychology*, 3, 149–56.

DEUTSCH, M. (1958), 'Trust and suspicion', *Journal of Conflict Resolution*, 2, 265–79.

DEUTSCH, M., and GERARD, H. B. (1955), 'A study of normative and informational influence upon individual judgement', *Journal of Abnormal and Social Psychology*, 51, 629–36.

DEUTSCH, M., and KRAUSS, R. M. (1960), 'The effect of threat on interpersonal bargaining', *Journal of Abnormal and Social Psychology*, 61, 181–9.

DEUTSCH, M., and KRAUSS, R. M. (1962), 'Studies of interpersonal bargaining', *Journal of Conflict Resolution*, 6, 52–76.

DION, K. L., BARON, R. S., and MILLER, N. (1970), 'Why do groups make riskier decisions than individuals?', in L. Berkowitz, ed., *Advances in Experimental Social Psychology*, vol. 5, New York, Academic Press.

DOISE, W. (1969), 'Intergroup relations and polarization of individual and collective judgments', *Journal of Personality and Social Psychology*, 12, 136–43.

DOISE, W. (1971), 'An apparent exception to the extremization of collective judgments', *European Journal of Social Psychology*, 1, 511–18.

Doise, W. (1976), *L'Articulation psychosociologique et relations entre groupes*, Brussels, De Boeck.

Dollard, J. (1937), *Caste and Class in a Southern Town*, New Haven, Yale University Press.

Dollard, J., Doob, L. W., Miller, N. E., Mowrer, O. H., and Sears, R. R. (1939), *Frustration and Aggression*, New Haven, Yale University Press.

Doob, L. W. (1947), 'The behaviour of attitudes', *Psychological Review*, 54, 135–56.

Dornbusch, S. M. (1955), 'The military academy as an assimilating institution', *Social Forces*, 33, 316–21.

Dorris, J. W. (1972), 'Reactions to unconditional cooperation: a field study emphasizing variables neglected in laboratory research', *Journal of Personality and Social Psychology*, 22, 387–97.

Douglas, J. D., ed. (1970), *Understanding Everyday Life*, New York, Aldine.

Douglas, M. (1973), *Natural Symbols*, Penguin Books.

Dubin, R. (1965), 'Supervision and productivity: empirical findings and theoretical considerations', in R. Dubin, G. Homans, F. C. Mann and R. Miller, *Leadership in Productivity: Some facts of industrial life*, New York, Chandler.

Duijker, H. C. J., and Frijda, N. H. (1960), *National Character and National Stereotypes*, Amsterdam, North Holland Publishing.

Dunbar, R. (1975), 'Social dynamics of the Gelada baboon', *Contributions to Primatology*, 6, Basle, S. Karger.

Duncan, S., Jr (1972), 'Some signals and rules for taking speaking turns in conversations', *Journal of Personality and Social Psychology*, 23, 283–92.

Edwards, A. L. (1957), *Techniques of Attitude Scale Construction*, New York, Appleton-Century-Crofts.

Efron, D. (1941), *Gesture and Environment*, New York, King's Crown.

Ehrlich, H. J. (1973), *The Social Psychology of Prejudice*, New York, Wiley.

Eibl-Eibesfeldt, I. (1970), *Ethology, the Biology of Behaviour*, New York, Holt, Rinehart & Winston.

Eisenberg, J. (1966), 'The social organization of mammals', *Handbuch der Zoologie*, 10, 1–92.

Eiser, J. R., and Bhavnani, K.-K. (1974), 'The effect of situational meaning on the behaviour of subjects in the Prisoner's Dilemma game', *European Journal of Social Psychology*, 4, 93–7.

Eiser, J. R., and Stroebe, W. (1972), *Categorization and Social Judgement*, London, Academic Press (European Monographs in Social Psychology).

Eiser, J. R., and Tajfel, H. (1972), 'Acquisition of information in dyadic interaction', *Journal of Personality and Social Psychology*, 23, 340–45.

Ekman, P. (1972), 'Universals and cultural differences in facial expression of emotion', in *Nebraska Symposium of Motivation*, Lincoln, University of Nebraska Press.

Ellis, H. G., Spencer, C. S., and Oldfield-Box, H. (1969), 'Matched groups and the risky shift phenomenon: a defence of the extreme member hypothesis', *British Journal of Social and Clinical Psychology*, 8, 333–9.

EMERSON, R. (1960), *From Empire to Nation*, Cambridge, Mass., Harvard University Press.

EPSTEIN, E. H., ed. (1970), *Politics and Education in Puerto Rico: A documentary survey of the language issue*, Metuchen, Scarecrow.

EPSTEIN, S., and TAYLOR, S. P. (1967), 'Instigation to aggression as a function of degree of defeat and perceived aggressive intent of the opponent', *Journal of Personality*, 35, 265–85.

ESPINAS, A. (1878), *Des Sociétés animales*, Paris, Baillière.

ESTES, R. D. (1966), 'Behaviour and life history of the wildebeeste (*Connochaetes taurinus*. Burchell)', *Nature*, 212, 799–1000.

ETZIONI, A. (1961), *A Comparative Analysis of Complex Organizations*, London, Collier-Macmillan.

EVANS, G., and CRUMBAUGH, C. (1966), 'Effects of Prisoner's Dilemma format on cooperative behaviour', *Journal of Personality and Social Psychology*, 3, 486–8.

EXLINE, R., and ZILLER, R. C. (1959), 'Status congruency and interpersonal conflict in decision-making groups', *Human Relations*, 12, 147–61.

FANTZ, R. L. (1961), 'The origin of form perception', *Scientific American*, 204, 66–72.

FELDMAN, R. E. (1968), 'Honesty toward compatriot and foreigner', *Proceedings of 76th Annual Convention*, APA, 375–6.

FERGUSON, C. K., and KELLEY, H. H. (1964), 'Significant factors in the overevaluation of one's own group product', *Journal of Abnormal and Social Psychology*, 66, 223–8.

FESTINGER, L. (1954), 'A theory of social comparison processes', *Human Relations*, 7, 117–40.

FESTINGER, L. (1957), *A Theory of Cognitive Dissonance*, Stanford, Stanford University Press.

FESTINGER, L., and CARLSMITH, J. M. (1959), 'Cognitive consequences of forced compliance', *Journal of Abnormal and Social Psychology*, 58, 203–10.

FESTINGER, L., RIECKEN, H., and SCHACHTER, S. (1956), *When Prophecy Fails*, Minneapolis, University of Minnesota Press.

FIEDLER, F. E. (1964), 'A contingency model of leadership effectiveness', in L. Berkowitz, ed., *Advances in Experimental Social Psychology*, vol. 1, New York, Academic Press.

FIEDLER, F. E. (1967), *A Theory of Leadership Effectiveness*, New York, McGraw-Hill.

FIEDLER, F. E. (1972), 'Personality, motivational systems, and behaviour of high and low LPC persons', *Human Relations*, 25, 391–412.

FILLMORE, C. J. (1968), 'The case for case', in E. Bach and R. T. Harms, eds., *Universals in Linguistic Theory*, New York, Holt, Rinehart & Winston.

FISHBEIN, M. (1963), 'An investigation of the relationships between beliefs about an object and attitude towards that object', *Human Relations*, 16, 233–9.

FISHBEIN, M. (1967a), 'Attitude and the prediction of behaviour', in M. Fishbein, ed., *Readings in Attitude Theory and Measurement*, New York, Wiley.

FISHBEIN, M. (1967b), 'A behaviour theory approach to the relations between beliefs about an object and the attitude toward the object', in M. Fishbein, ed., *Readings in Attitude Theory and Measurement*, New York, Wiley.

FISHBEIN, M., and AJZEN, I. (1972), 'Attitudes and opinions', in *Annual Review of Psychology*, 23, 487–544.

FISHBEIN, M., and AJZEN, I. (1973), 'Attribution of responsibility: a theoretical note', *Journal of Experimental Social Psychology*, 9, 148–53.

FISHBEIN, M., LANDY, E., and HATCH, G. (1969), 'Some determinants of an individual's esteem for his least preferred co-worker', *Human Relations*, 22, 172–288.

FISHMAN, J. A. (1970), *Sociolinguistics: A brief introduction*, Rowley, Newbury House.

FISHMAN, J. A. (1971), 'The sociology of language: an interdisciplinary social science approach to sociolinguistics', in J. A. Fishman, ed., *Advances in the Sociology of Language 1*, The Hague, Mouton; also published as a separate monograph by Newbury House, 1972.

FISHMAN, J. A. (1972a), 'The link between macro- and micro-sociology in the study of who speaks what to whom and when', in J. Gumperz and D. Hymes, eds., *Directions in Sociolinguistics*, New York, Holt, Rinehart & Winston.

FISHMAN, J. A. (1972b), 'The uses of sociolinguistics', *Proceedings of the Second International Congress of Applied Linguistics*, Cambridge, Cambridge University Press.

FISHMAN, J. A. (1973), 'Language modernization and planning in comparison to other types of national modernization and planning', *Language in Society*, 2, 23–43.

FISHMAN, J. A., et al. (1966), *Language Loyalty in the United States*, The Hague, Mouton.

FISHMAN, J. A., COOPER, R. L., MA, R., et al. (1971), *Bilingualism in the Barrio*, Bloomington, Language Sciences, Monograph Series, Indian University.

FISHMAN, J. A., FERGUSON, C. A., and DAS GUPTA, J., eds. (1968), *Language Problems of Developing Nations*, New York, Wiley.

FLAVELL, J. H. (1968), *The Development of Role-taking and Communication Skills in Children*, New York, Wiley.

FLAVELL, J. H. (1970), 'Concept development', in P. H. Mussen, ed., *Manual of Child Psychology*, New York, Wiley.

FORM, W. H., and GESCHWANDER, J. A. (1962), 'Social reference basis of job satisfaction: the case of manual workers', *American Sociological Review*, 27, 228–37.

FOX, R. (1967), 'In the beginning: aspects of hominid behavioural evolution', *Man*, 2, 415–33.

FOX, R. (1972), 'Alliance and constraint: sexual selection in the evolution of human kinship system', in B. Campbell, ed., *Sexual Selection and the Descent of Man, 1871–1971*, Chicago, Aldine.

FRASER, C. (1971), 'Group risk-taking and group polarization', *European Journal of Social Psychology*, 1, 493–510.

FRASER, C. (1973), 'Determinants of individual and group decisions involving risk', Final Report on SSRC project HR 542, available from British Library Lending Division.

FRASER, C., GOUGE, C., and BILLIG, M. (1971), 'Risky shifts, cautious shifts and group polarization', *European Journal of Social Psychology*, 1, 7–30.

FRASER, R., ed. (1968, 1969), *Work*, vols. 1 and 2, Penguin Books.

FRENCH, J. R. P. (1956), 'A formal theory of social power', *Psychological Review*, 63, 181–94.

FRENCH, J. R. P., and RAVEN, B. H. (1959), 'The bases of social power', in D. Cartwright, ed., *Studies in Social Power*, Ann Arbor, Mich., University of Michigan Press.

FRENKEL-BRUNSWIK, E. (1949), 'A study of prejudice in children', *Human Relations*, 1, 295–306.

FRENKEL-BRUNSWIK, E. (1954), 'Further explorations by a contributor to *The Authoritarian Personality*', in R. Christie and M. Jahoda, eds., *Studies in the Scope and Method of* The Authoritarian Personality, Glencoe, Ill., Free Press.

FREUD, A., and DANN, S. (1951), 'An experiment in group upbringing', *Psychoanalytic Study of the Child*, 6, 127–68.

FREUD, S. (1922), *Group Psychology and the Analysis of the Ego*, London, Hogarth.

FREUD, S. (1930), *Civilization and its Discontents*, London, Hogarth.

FRIEDMAN, N. (1967), *The Social Nature of Psychological Research*, New York, Basic Books.

FRIEDRICH, P. (1972), 'Social context and semantic feature: the Russian pronominal usage', in J. J. Gumperz and D. Hymes, eds., *Directions in Sociolinguistics: The ethnography of communication*, New York, Holt, Rinehart & Winston.

FROMM, E. (1973), *The Anatomy of Human Destructiveness*, London, Jonathan Cape.

FULLAN, M. (1970), 'Industrial technology and worker integration in the organization', *American Sociological Review*, 35, 1028–39.

FURTH, H. G. (1969), *Piaget and Knowledge: Theoretical foundations*, New York, Prentice Hall.

GALLO, P. S. (1966), 'Effects of increased incentives upon the use of threat in bargaining', *Journal of Personality and Social Psychology*, 4, 14–20.

GALLO, P. S. (1972), 'Prisoners of our own dilemma?' Paper presented at the Western Psychological Association convention, San Diego, 1968; also in L. S. Wrightsman, Jr, J. O'Connor, N. J. Baker, eds., *Cooperation and Competition: Readings on mixed-motive games*, Belmont, Wadsworth.

GARDNER, B. T., and GARDNER, A. A. (1971), 'Two-way communication with an infant chimpanzee', in A. Schrier and F. Stollnitz, eds., *Behavior of Non-Human Primates*, vol. 4, New York, Academic Press.

GARFINKEL, H. (1967), *Studies in Ethnomethodology*, Englewood Cliffs, New York, Prentice Hall.

GARFINKEL, H. (1972), 'Remarks on ethnomethodology', in J. J. Gumperz and D. Hymes, eds., *Directions in Sociolinguistics: The ethnography of communication*, New York, Holt, Rinehart & Winston.

GARVIN, P. (1959), 'The standard language problem: concepts and methods', *Anthropological Linguistics*, 2, 28–31.

GEERTZ, D. (1960), *The Religion of Java*, Glencoe, Ill., Free Press.

GERGEN, K. J. (1971), *The Concept of Self*, New York, Holt, Rinehart & Winston.

GESCHWIND, N. (1970), 'The organization of language and the brain', *Science*, 170, 940–44.

GIBB, J. R. (1970), 'The effects of human relations training', in A. E. Bergin and S. L. Garfield, eds., *Handbook of Psychotherapy and Behaviour Change*, New York, Wiley.

GIGLIOLI, P. P., ed. (1972), *Language and Social Context*, Penguin Books.

GILES, H. (1973), 'Accent mobility: a model and some data', *Anthropological Linguistics*, 15, 87–105.

GILES, H., TAYLOR, D. M., and BOURHIS, R. Y. (1973), 'Towards a theory of interpersonal accommodation through language: some Canadian data', *Language in Society*, 2, 177–92.

GOFFMAN, E. (1961), *Asylums*, Penguin Books.

GOFFMAN, E. (1969), *Where the Action is*, London, Allen Lane.

GOLDTHORPE, J. H., LOCKWOOD, D., BECHOFER, F., and PLATT, J. (1970), *The Affluent Worker: Industrial attitudes and behaviour*, Cambridge, Cambridge University Press.

GOMBRICH, E. H. (1960), *Art and Illusion*, London, Phaidon.

GOMBRICH, E. H. (1965), 'The use of art for the study of symbols', *American Psychologist*, 20, 34–50.

GOODMAN, J. F. B., and WHITTINGHAM, T. G. (1969), *Shop Stewards in British Industry*, London, McGraw-Hill.

GOULDNER, A. W., ed. (1950), *Studies in Leadership*, New York, Harper.

GRAEN, G., ALVARES, K., ORRIS, J. B., and MARTELLA, J. A. (1970), 'Contingency model of leadership effectiveness: antecedent and evidential results', *Psychological Bulletin*, 74, 285–96.

GRAHAM, D. (1972), *Moral Learning and Development: Theory and research*, London, Batsford.

GREGORY, R. L. (1966), *Eye and Brain: The psychology of seeing*, London, Weidenfeld & Nicolson.

GROSS, N., MASON, W. S., and McEACHERN, A. W. (1958), *Explanations in Role Analysis*, New York, Wiley.

GRUSKY, O. (1957), 'A case for the theory of familiar role differentiation in small groups', *Social Forces*, 35, 209–17.

GUMPERZ, J. J., and HYMES, D., eds. (1972), *Directions in Sociolinguistics: The ethnography of communication*, New York, Holt, Rinehart & Winston.

GURR, T. R. (1970), *Why Men Rebel*, Princeton, Princeton University Press.

GUTHRIE, G. M. (1970), *The Psychology of Modernization in the Rural Philippines*, Quezon City, Manila University Press.

HALL, E. T. (1966), *The Hidden Dimension*, New York, Doubleday.

HALLIDAY M. A. K. 1970), 'Language structure and language function', in J. Lyons, ed., *New Horizons in Linguistics*, Penguin Books.

HALLIDAY, M. A. K. (1973), *Explorations in the Functions of Language*, London, Arnold.

HALLOWELL, A. I. (1951), 'Cultural factors in the structuralization of perception', in J. H. Rohrer and M. Sherif, eds., *Social Psychology at the Crossroads*, New York, Harper.

HAMILTON, W. J., and WATT, K. E. F. (1970), 'Refuging', *Annual Review of Ecology and Systematics*, 1, 263–86.

HARARY, F. (1959), 'A criterion for unanimity in French's theory of social power', in D. Cartwright, ed., *Studies in Social Power*, Ann Arbor, Institute for Social Research.

HARDIN, G. (1968), 'The tragedy of the commons', *Science*, 162, 1243–8.

HARE, A. P. (1960), *Handbook of Small Group Research*, New York, Free Press.

HARGREAVES, D. (1967), *Social Relations in a Secondary School*, London, Routledge & Kegan Paul.

HARGREAVES, D. (1972), *Interpersonal Relations and Education*, London, Routledge & Kegan Paul.

HARLOW, H. F. (1958), 'The nature of love', *American Psychologist*, 13, 673–85.

HARRÉ, R., and SECORD, P. F. (1972), *The Explanation of Social Behaviour*, Oxford, Blackwell.

HARRIS, M. B., and BAUDIN, H. (1973), 'The language of altruism: the effects of language, dress and ethnic group', *Journal of Social Psychology*, 91, 37–41.

HARTLEY, J., and HOLT, J. (1971), 'Teacher expectations and programmed learning', unpublished ms., University of Keele.

HAUGEN, E. (1953), *The Norwegian Language in America*, 2 vols., Philadelphia, University of Pennsylvania Press.

HAUGEN, E. (1966), *Language Planning and Language Conflict: The case of modern Norwegian*, Cambridge, Mass., Harvard University Press.

HEIDER, F. (1944), 'Social perception and phenomenal causality', *Psychological Review*, 51, 358–74.

HEIDER, F. (1946), 'Attitudes and cognitive organization', *Journal of Psychology*, 21, 107–12.

HEIDER, F. (1958), *The Psychology of Interpersonal Relations*, New York, Wiley.

HELLER, F. A., and YUKL, G. (1969), 'Participation, managerial decision-making and situational variables', *Organizational Behaviour and Human Performance*, 4, 227–41.

HERSHENSON, M., and HABER, R. N. (1965), 'The role of meaning in the perception of briefly exposed words', *Canadian Journal of Psychology*, 19, 42–6.

HERZBERG, F., MAUSNER, B., and SNYDERMAN, B. B. (1959), *The Motivation to Work*, New York, Wiley.

HERZLICH, C. (1973), *Health and Illness: A social psychological analysis*, London, Academic Press (European Monographs in Social Psychology).

HIMMELWEIT, H. T. (1950), 'Frustration and aggression: a review of recent experimental work', in T. H. Pear, *Psychological Factors of Peace and War*, New York, Philosophical Library.

HINDE, R. A. (1959), 'Unitary drives', *Animal Behaviour*, 7, 130–41.

HINDE, R. A., ed. (1972), *Non-verbal Communication*, Cambridge, Cambridge University Press.

HIRSCHMAN, A. (1970), *Exit, Voice and Loyalty: Responses to decline in firms, organizations and states*, Cambridge, Mass., Harvard University Press.

HOLLANDER, E. P., and JULIAN, J. W. (1969), 'Contemporary trends in the analysis of leadership processes', *Psychological Bulletin*, 71, 387–97.

HOMANS, G. C. (1951), *The Human Group*, London, Routledge & Kegan Paul.

HOMANS, G. C. (1961), *Social Behaviour: Its elementary forms*, New York, Harcourt Brace Jovanovitch.

VAN HOOF, J. (1962), 'Facial expressions in higher primates', *Symposia of the Zoological Society of London*, 8, 97–125.

HOVLAND, C. I., JANIS, L. L., and KELLEY, N. H. (1953), *Communication and Persuasion*, New Haven, Yale University Press.

HUDSON, W. (1960), 'Pictorial depth perception in sub-cultural groups in Africa', *Journal of Social Psychology*, 52, 183–208.

HUDSON, W. (1967), 'The study of the problem of pictorial perception among unacculturated groups', *International Journal of Psychology*, 2, 89–107.

HUGHES, E. (1971), 'The linguistic division of labour in Montreal', *Monograph Series on Languages and Linguistics*, Georgetown University Press; also in J. A. Fishman, ed., *Advances in the Sociology of Language II*, The Hague, Mouton.

HUNT, J. G., and LIEBSCHER, V. K. C. (1973), 'Leadership preference, leadership behaviour, and employee satisfaction', *Organizational Behaviour and Human Performance*, 9, 59–77.

HUSTON, T. L., ed. (1974), *Foundations of Interpersonal Attraction*, New York, Academic Press.

HUXLEY, J. S. (1959), 'Clades and grades', *Publications of the Systematics Association*, 3, 21.

HYMAN, R. (1964), *The Nature of Psychological Inquiry*, Englewood Cliffs, N.Y., Prentice Hall.

HYMES, D. (1967), 'Models of the interaction of language and social setting', *Journal of Social Issues*, 23, 2, 8–28.

HYMES, D. (1972), 'Models of the interaction of language and social life', in J. J. Gumperz and D. Hymes, eds., *Directions in Sociolinguistics: The ethnography of communication*, New York, Holt, Rinehart & Winston.

INGHAM, G. K. (1970), *Size of Industrial Organization and Worker Behaviour*, Cambridge, Cambridge University Press.

462 References

ISRAEL, J., and TAJFEL, H., eds. (1972), *The Context of Social Psychology: A critical assessment*, London, Academic Press (European Monographs in Social Psychology).

JAFFE, J., STERN, D. N., and PERRY, J. C. (1973), 'Conversational' coupling of gaze behaviour in pre-linguistic human development, *Journal of Psycholinguistic Research*, 2, 3.

JAMES, W. (1961), *Psychology, the Briefer Course*, New York, Harper (originally published in 1892).

JANIS, I. (1972), *Victims of Groupthink: A psychological study of foreign-policy decisions and fiascoes*, Boston, Houghton Mifflin.

JARMAN, P. (1974), 'The social organization of antelope in relation to their ecology', *Behaviour*, 48, 215–67.

JASPARS, J. M. F. (1973), 'The case against attitudes', Opening address presented at the annual conference of the social psychology section of the British Psychological Association (mimeo.).

JAYNES, J. (1969), 'The historical origins of "Ethology" and "Comparative Psychology"', *Animal Behaviour*, 4, 601–6.

JENNINGS, H. H. (1950), *Leadership and Isolation*, 2nd ed., New York, David McKay.

JOLLY, C. (1970), 'The seed-eaters. A new model of hominid differentiation based on a baboon analogy', *Man*, 5, 5–26.

JONES, C., and ARONSON, E. (1973), 'Attribution of fault to a rape victim as a function of respectability of the victim', *Journal of Personality and Social Psychology*, 26, 415–19.

JONES, E. E., and DAVIS, K. E. (1965), 'From acts to dispositions: the attribution process in person perception', in L. Berkowitz, ed., *Advances in Experimental Social Psychology*, vol. 2, New York, Academic Press.

JONES, E. E., DAVIS, K. E., and GERGEN, K. L. (1961), 'Role playing variations and their informational value for person perception', *Journal of Abnormal and Social Psychology*, 63, 302–10.

JONES, E. E., and GERARD, H. B. (1967), *Foundations of Social Psychology*, New York, Wiley.

JONES, E. E., and GOETHALS, G. R. (1971), 'Order effects in impression formation: attribution context and the nature of the entity', in E. E. Jones, D. E. Kanouse, H. H. Kelley, R. E. Nisbett, S. Valins and B. Weiner, *Attribution: Perceiving the causes of behaviour*, Morristown, General Learning Press.

JONES, E. E., and HARRIS, V. A. (1967), 'The attribution of attitudes', *Journal of Experimental Social Psychology*, 3, 1–24.

JONES, E. E., and NISBETT, R. E. (1971), 'The actor and observer: divergent perceptions of the causes of behaviour', in E. E. Jones, D. E. Kanouse, H. H. Kelley, R. E. Nisbett, S. Valins and B. Weiner, *Attribution: Perceiving the causes of behavior*, Morristown, General Learning Press.

JONES, E. E., WORCHEL, S., GOETHALS, G. R., and GRUMET, J. F. (1971),

'Prior expectancy and behavioural extremity as determinants of attitude attribution', *Journal of Experimental Social Psychology*, 7, 59–80.

JOURARD, S. M. (1966), 'An exploratory study of body accessibility', *British Journal of Social and Clinical Psychology*, 5, 221–31.

KARDINER, A. (1945), *Psychological Frontiers of Society*, New York, Columbia University Press.

KATZ, D. (1960), 'The functional approach to the study of attitude', *Public Opinion Quarterly*, 24, 163–204.

KATZ, D., and KAHN, R. (1966), *The Social Psychology of Organizations*, New York, Wiley.

KATZ, D., and STOTLAND, E. (1969), 'A preliminary statement of a theory of attitude structure and change', in S. Koch, ed., *Psychology: A study of a science*, vol. 3, New York, McGraw-Hill.

KELLEY, H. H. (1967), 'Attribution theory in social psychology', in D. Levine, ed., *Nebraska Symposium on Motivation*, 15, 192–238.

KELLEY, H. H. (1971), 'Causal schemata and the attribution process', in E. E. Jones, D. E. Kanouse, H. H. Kelley, R. E. Nisbett, S. Valins and B. Weiner, *Attribution: Perceiving the causes of behavior*, Morristown, General Learning Press.

KELLEY, H. H., and STAHELSKI, A. J. (1970a), 'Errors in perception of intentions in a mixed-motive game', *Journal of Experimental Social Psychology*, 6, 379–400.

KELLEY, H. H., and STAHELSKI, A. J. (1970b), 'Social interaction basis of cooperators' and competitors' beliefs about others', *Journal of Personality and Social Psychology*, 16, 66–91.

KELLEY, H. H., THIBAUT, J. W., RADLOFF, R., and MUNDY, D. (1962), 'The development of cooperation in the "minimal social situation"', *Psychological Monographs*, 76 (19, whole no. 538).

KELMAN, H. C., and HOVLAND, C. I. (1953), 'Reinstatement of the communicator in delayed measurement of opinion change', *Journal of Abnormal and Social Psychology*, 48, 327–35.

KENDON, A., and FERBER, A. (1973), 'A description of some human greetings', in R. Michael and J. H. Crook, eds., *Comparative Ecology and Behaviour in Primates*, London, Academic Press.

KIESLER, C. A., and MUNSON, P. A. (1975), 'Attitudes and opinions', *Annual Review of Psychology*, 26, 415–57.

KIESLER, C. A., NISBETT, R. E., and ZANNA, M. P. (1969), 'On inferring one's beliefs from one's behaviour', *Journal of Personality and Social Psychology*, 11, 321–7.

KIMPLE, J., JR, COOPER, R. L., and FISHMAN, J. A. (1969), 'Language switching in the interpretation of conversations', *Lingua*, 23, 127–34.

KLAPPER, J. T. (1960), *Effects of Mass Communications*, Glencoe, Ill., Free Press.

KLAUS, M. H., KENNELL, J. H., PLUMB, N., and ZUEHLBE, S. (1970), 'Human maternal behaviour at the first contact with her young', *Paediatrics*, 46, 187–92.

KLINEBERG, O. (1935), *Race Differences*, New York, Harper.

KLOPFER, P., and HAILMAN, J. (1967), *An Introduction to Animal Behaviour*, New York, Prentice Hall.

KOGAN, N., and WALLACH, M. A. (1967), 'Risk-taking as a function of the situation, the person and the group', in G. Mandler *et al.*, eds., *New Directions in Psychology, II*, New York, Holt, Rinehart & Winston.

KOHLBERG, L. (1964), 'The development of moral character', in M. L. Hoffman and L. W. Hoffman, eds., *Review of Child Development and Research*, vol. 1, New York, Russell Sage Foundation.

KOHLBERG, L. (1969), 'Stage and sequence: the cognitive-developmental approach to socialization', in D. Goslin, ed., *Handbook of Socialization Theory and Research*, Chicago, Rand McNally.

KORN, N. ed. (1973), *Human Evolution: Readings in physical anthropology*, 3rd ed., New York, Holt, Rinehart & Winston.

KRAUSS, R. M., and GLUCKSBERG, S. (1969), 'The development of communication: competence as a function of age', *Child Development*, 40, 255–66.

KREBS, D. L. (1970), 'Altruism – an examination of the concept and a review of the literature', *Psychological Bulletin*, 73, 258–302.

KRECH, D., CRUTCHFIELD, R. S., and BALLACHEY, E. L. (1962), *Individual in Society*, New York, McGraw-Hill.

KRUGLANSKI, A. W., and COHEN, M. (1973), 'Attributed freedom and personal causation', *Journal of Personality and Social Psychology*, 26, 245–50.

KUHN, D. Z., MADSEN, C. H., and BECKER, W. C. (1967), 'Effects of exposure to an aggressive model and "frustration" on children's aggressive behaviour', *Child Development*, 38, 739–46.

KUMMER, H. (1968), 'Social organization of Hamadryas baboons', *Bibliotheca Primatologica*, 6, Karger, Basle.

LABARRE, W. (1947), 'The cultural basis of emotions and gestures', *Journal of Personality*, 16, 49–68.

LABOV, W. (1972), 'Language in society', in J. A. Fishman, ed., *Advances in the Sociology of Language I*, The Hague, Mouton.

LABOV, W. (1973), 'The logic of nonstandard English', in J. S. DeStefano, ed., *Language, Society and Education: A profile of Black English*, Worthington, Charles A. Jones.

LACEY, C. (1966), 'Some sociological concomitants of academic streaming in a grammar school', *British Journal of Sociology*, 17, 245–62.

LACK, D. (1966), *Population Studies of Birds*, Oxford, Oxford University Press.

LANGE, A. (1971), 'Frustration-aggression: a reconsideration', *European Journal of Social Psychology*, 1, 59–84.

LANGE, A., and VAN DE NES, A. (1973), 'Frustration and instrumentality of aggression', *European Journal of Social Psychology*, 3, 159–77.

LANGER, E. J., and ABELSON, R. P. (1972), 'The semantics of asking a favour:

how to succeed in getting help without really dying', *Journal of Personality and Social Psychology*, 24, 26–32.

LA PIERE, R. T. (1934), 'Attitudes versus actions', *Social Forces*, 13, 230–37.

LASSWELL, H. D. (1935), *World Politics and Personal Insecurity*, New York, McGraw-Hill.

LAVER, J. (1968), 'Voice quality and indexical information', *British Journal of Disorders of Communication*, 3, 43–54.

LAVER, J., and HUTCHESON, S., eds. (1972), *Communication in Face-to-Face Interaction*, Penguin Books.

VAN LAWICK, J., and H. (1970), *Innocent Killers*, London, Collins.

LAZARSFELD, P. F., BERELSON, B., and GAUDET, H. (1948), *The People's Choice*, New York, Columbia University Press.

LEACH, E. (1972), 'The influence of cultural context on non-verbal communication in Man', in R. A. Hinde, ed., *Non-verbal Communication*, Cambridge, Cambridge University Press.

LEAVITT, H. J. (1951), 'Some effects of certain communication patterns on group performance', *Journal of Abnormal and Social Psychology*, 46, 38–50.

LEE, T. R. (1968), 'Urban neighbourhood as a socio-spatial scheme', *Human Relations*, 21, 241–67.

LEFCOURT, H. M. (1972), 'Recent developments in the study of locus of control', in B. Maher, ed., *Progress in Experimental Personality Research*, vol. 6, New York, Academic Press.

LENNEBERG, E. H. (1969), 'On explaining language', *Science*, 164, 635–43.

LENT, R. H. (1970), 'Binocular resolution and perception of race in the United States', *British Journal of Psychology*, 61, 521–33.

LEPPER, M. R., GREENE, D., and NISBETT, R. E. (1973), 'Undermining children's intrinsic interest with extrinsic reward: A test of the "over-justification" hypothesis', *Journal of Personality and Social Psychology*, 28, 129–37.

LERNER, M. J. (1970), 'The desire for justice and reactions to victims', in J. Macaulay and L. Berkowitz, eds., *Altruism and Helping Behavior*, New York, Academic Press.

LERNER, M. J. (1971), 'Justified self-interest and the responsibility for suffering', *Journal of Human Relations*, 19, 550–59.

LERNER, M. J., and LICHTMAN, R. R. (1968), 'Effects of perceived norms on attitudes and altruistic behavior toward a dependent other', *Journal of Personality and Social Psychology*, 9, 226–32.

LERNER, M. J., and SIMMONS, C. H. (1966), 'The observer's reaction to the innocent victim: compassion or rejection?' *Journal of Personality and Social Psychology*, 4, 203–10.

LEVINE, R. A. (1966), *Dreams and Deeds: Achievement motivation in Nigeria*, Illinois, Chicago University Press.

LEVINE, R. A. (1973), *Culture, behaviour and personality*, London, Hutchinson.

LEVINE, R. A., and CAMPBELL, D. T. (1972), *Ethnocentrism: Theories of conflict, ethnic attitudes and group behaviour*, New York, Wiley.

LEWIN, K. (1951), *Field Theory in Social Science*, New York, Harper & Row.

LEWIN, K., LIPPIT, R., and WHITE, R. K. (1939), 'Patterns of aggressive behaviour in experimentally created "social climates"', *Journal of Social Psychology*, 10, 271–99.

LEWIS, G. (1971), 'Language maintenance and language shift in the Soviet Union', *International Migration Review*, 5.

LIEBERMAN, M. A., YALOM, I. D., and MILES, M. B. (1973), *Encounter Groups: First facts*, New York, Basic Books.

LIEBERSON, S. (1965), 'Bilingualism in Montreal: a demographic analysis', *American Journal of Sociology*, 71, 10–25; also in J. A. Fishman, ed., *Advances in the Sociology of Language II*, The Hague, Mouton.

LIEBERSON, S. (1970), *Language and Ethnic Relations in Canada*, New York, Wiley.

LIKERT, R. A. (1932), 'A technique for the measurement of attitudes', *Archives of Psychology*, 140.

LILLI, W. (1975), *Soziale Akzentuierung*, Stuttgart, Verlag W. Kohlhammer.

LINTON, R. (1945), *The Cultural Background of Personality*, New York, Appleton-Century.

LLOYD, B. (1972), *Perception and Cognition: A cross-cultural perspective*, Penguin Books.

LOCKE, E. A. (1969), 'What is job satisfaction?' *Organizational Behaviour and Human Performance*, 4, 309–36.

LOOFT, W. R. (1972), 'Egocentrism and social interaction across the life span', *Psychological Bulletin*, 78, 73–92.

LORENZ, K. (1967), *On Aggression*, New York, Harcourt, Brace & World.

LORENZ, K. (1974), *Civilized Man's Eight Deadly Sins*, London, Methuen.

LOTT, A. J., and LOTT, B. E. (1965), 'Group cohesiveness as interpersonal attraction: a review of relationships with antecedent and consequent variables', *Psychological Bulletin*, 64, 259–309.

LOTT, B. E. (1955), 'Attitude formation: the development of a colour-preference response through mediated generalization', *Journal of Abnormal and Social Psychology*, 50, 321–6.

LOWIN, A. (1968), 'Participative decision making: a model, literature critique, and prescription for research', *Organizational Behaviour and Human Performance*, 3, 68–106.

LOWIN, A., and CRAIG, J. R. (1968), 'The influence of level of performance on managerial style: an experimental object lesson in the ambiguity of correlational data', *Organizational Behaviour and Human Performance*, 3, 440–58.

LUKES, S. (1973), *Emile Durkheim: His life and work*, London, Allen Lane.

LURIA, A. R. (1961), 'The genesis of voluntary movements', in N. O'Connor, ed., *Recent Soviet Psychology*, New York, Liveright.

LYNCH, K. (1960), *The Image of the City*, Cambridge, Mass., M.I.T. Press.

LYONS, J. (1968), *Introduction to Theoretical Linguistics*, Cambridge, Cambridge University Press.

LYONS, J. (1972), 'Human language', in R. A. Hinde, ed., *Non-verbal Communication*, Cambridge, Cambridge University Press.

McArthur, L. A. (1972), 'The how and what of why: some determinants and consequences of causal attribution', *Journal of Personality and Social Psychology*, 22, 171–193.

Macaulay, J. R., and Berkowitz, L., eds. (1970), *Altruism and Helping Behavior*, New York, Academic Press.

McClelland, D. C. (1961), *The Achieving Society*, Princeton, Van Nostrand.

McClelland, D. C., and Winter, D. G. (1969), *Motivating Economic Achievement*, New York, Free Press.

McClintock, C. G., and McNeel, S. P. (1966), 'Reward level and game playing behavior', *Journal of Conflict Resolution*, 10, 98–102.

McDavid, R., and Davis, L. (1972), 'The dialects of Negro Americans', in M. E. Smith, ed., *Studies in Linguistics in Honor of George L. Trager*, The Hague, Mouton.

McDougall, W. (1908), *Social Psychology*, London, Methuen.

McDougall, W. (1933), *The Energies of Men*, New York, Scribners.

McGrath, J. E., and Altman, I. (1966), *Small Group Research*, New York Holt, Rinehart & Winston.

McGregor, D. (1960), *The Human Side of Enterprise*, New York, McGraw-Hill.

McGuire, W. J. (1969), 'The nature of attitudes and attitude change', in G. Lindzey and E. Aronson, eds., *Handbook of Social Psychology*, vol. 3, 2nd. ed., New York, Addison-Wesley.

McGuire, W. J. (1973), 'The yin and yang of progress in social psychology: seven koan', *Journal of Personality and Social Psychology*, 26, 446–56.

Madsen, C. M., and Shapira, A. (1970), 'Cooperative and competitive behaviour of urban Afro-American, Anglo-American, Mexican-American, and Mexican village children', *Developmental Psychology*, 3, 16–20.

Maitland Bradfield, R. (1973), *The Natural History of Associations*, London, Duckworth.

Malinowski, S. (1923), 'The problem of meaning in primitive languages. Supplement to C. K. Ogden and I. A. Richards: *The Meaning of Meaning*', London, Routledge & Kegan Paul.

Mannheim, B. F., Rim, Y., and Grinberg, R. (1967), 'Instrumental status of supervisors as related to worker's perceptions and expectations', *Human Relations*, 29, 387–97.

Marchand, B. (1970), 'Auswirkung einer emotional wertvollen und einer emotional neutralen Klassifikation auf die Schatzung einer Stimulusserie', *Zeitschrift fur Sozialpsychologie*, 1, 264–74.

Maslow, A. H. (1954), *Motivation and Personality*, New York, Harper.

Mayo, E. (1945), *The Social Problems of an Industrial Civilization*, Cambridge, Mass., Harvard University Press.

Mead, G. H. (1925), 'The genesis of self and social control', *International Journal of Ethics*, 35, 251–73.

Mehrabian, A., and Ferris, S. R. (1967), 'Inference of attitudes from non-verbal communication', *Journal of Consulting Psychology*, 31, 248–52.

MEHRABIAN, A., and REED, H. (1968), 'Some determinants of communication accuracy', *Psychological Bulletin*, 70, 365–81.

MEICHENBAUM, D. H., BOWERS, K. S., and ROSS, R. R. (1969), 'A behavioural analysis of teacher expectancy effect', *Journal of Personality and Social Psychology*, 13, 306–16.

MEICHENBAUM, D. H., and SMART, I. (1971), 'Use of direct expectancy to modify academic performance and attitudes of college students', *Journal of Counselling Psychology*, 18, 531–5.

MESSÉ, L. A., DAWSON, J. E., and LANE, I. M. (1973), 'Equity as a mediator of the effect of reward level on behavior in the Prisoner's Dilemma game', *Journal of Personality and Social Psychology*, 26, 60–65.

MICHENER, J. (1971), *Kent State: What happened and why*, New York, Random House.

MILGRAM, S. (1961), 'Nationality and conformity', *Scientific American*, 205, December, 45–51.

MILGRAM, S. (1974), *Obedience to Authority*, New York, Harper & Row; London, Tavistock.

MILLER, A. G. (1972), *The Social Psychology of Psychological Research*, New York, Free Press.

MILLER, D. T., and HOLMES, J. G. (1975), 'The role of situational restrictiveness on self-fulfilling prophecies: A theoretical and empirical extension of Kelley and Stahelsky's triangle hypothesis', *Journal of Personality and Social Psychology*, 31, 661–73.

MILLER, E. J., and RICE, A. K. (1967), *Systems of Organization: The control of task and sentient boundaries*, London, Tavistock.

MILLER, N. E. (1941), 'The frustration-aggression hypothesis', *Psychological Review*, 48, 337–442.

MILLER, N. E., and BUGELSKI, R. (1948), 'Minor studies in aggression: the influence of frustrations imposed by the ingroup on attitudes towards outgroups', *Journal of Psychology*, 25, 437–42.

MILLET, K. (1971), *Sexual Politics*, London, Hart-Davis.

MILNER, D. (1975), *Children and Race*, Penguin Books.

MINTZ, A. (1951), 'Nonadaptive group behavior', *Journal of Abnormal and Social Psychology*, 46, 150–59.

MISCHEL, W. (1968), *Personality and Assessment*, New York, Wiley.

MISCHEL, W. (1973), 'Toward a cognitive social learning reconceptualization of personality', *Psychological Review*, 80, 252–83.

MONTAGU, M. ASHLEY, ed. (1973), *The Origin and Evolution of Man*, New York, Crowell.

MORENO, J. L. (1934), *Who Shall Survive? A new approach to the problems of human interrelations*, Washington, D.C., Nervous and Mental Diseases Publishing Co.

MORRIS, D. (1967), *The Naked Ape*, London, Jonathan Cape.

MOSCOVICI, S. (1967), 'Communication processes and the properties of language', in L. Berkowitz, ed., *Advances in Experimental Social Psychology*, vol. 3, New York, Academic Press.

MOSCOVICI, S. (1972), 'Society and theory in social psychology', in J. Israel and H. Tajfel, eds., *The Context of Social Psychology: A critical assessment*, London, Academic Press.

MOSCOVICI, S., and FAUCHEUX, C. (1972), 'Social influence, conformity bias, and the study of active minorities', in L. Berkowitz, ed., *Advances in Experimental Social Psychology*, vol. 6, New York, Academic Press.

MOSCOVICI, S., and PLON, M. (1966), 'Les Situations colloques: observations théoriques et experimentales', *Bulletin de Psychologie*, 19, 702–22.

MOSCOVICI, S., and ZAVALLONI, M. (1969), 'The group as a polarizer of attitudes', *Journal of Personality and Social Psychology*, 12, 125–35.

MOYER, K. E. (1971), 'The physiology of aggression and the implications for aggression control', in J. L. Singer, ed., *The Control of Aggression and Violence*, New York, Academic Press.

MULDER, M. (1960), 'Communication structure, decision structure and group performance', *Sociometry*, 23, 1–14.

MUNDY-CASTLE, A. C. (1966), 'Pictorial depth perception in Ghanaian children', *International Journal of Psychology*, 1, 289–300.

MURCHISON, C., ed. (1935), *Handbook of Social Psychology*, Worcester, Mass., Clark University Press.

MYERS, D. G., BACH, P. J., and SCHREIBER, F. B. (1974), 'Normative and informational effects of group interaction', *Sociometry*, 37, 275–86.

MYERS, D. G., and BISHOP, G. D. (1971), 'Enhancement of dominant attitudes in group discussion', *Journal of Personality and Social Psychology*, 20, 386–91.

MYERS, D. G., and LAMM, H. (1976), 'The group polarization phenomenon', *Psychological Bulletin*, 83, 602–27.

NAN LIN (1973), *The Study of Human Communication*, Indianapolis, Bobbs-Merrill.

NAROLL, R. (1970), 'Galton's problem', in R. Naroll and R. Cohen, eds., *A Handbook of Method in Cultural Anthropology*, New York, Natural History Press.

NEMETH, C. (1970), 'Bargaining and reciprocity', *Psychological Bulletin*, 74, 297–308.

NEMETH, C. (1972), 'A critical analysis of research utilizing the Prisoner's Dilemma paradigm for the study of bargaining', in L. Berkowitz, ed., *Advances in Experimental Social Psychology*, vol. 6, New York, Academic Press.

NEWCOMB, T. M. (1961), *The Acquaintance Process*, New York, Holt, Rinehart & Winston.

NEWMAN, R. W. (1970), 'Why Man is such a sweaty and thirsty naked animal – a speculative review', *Human Biology*, 42, 12–27.

NISBETT, R. E., CAPUTO, C., LEGANT, P., and MARACEK, J. (1973), 'Behaviour as seen by the actor and as seen by the observer', *Journal of Personality and Social Psychology*, 27, 154–64.

470 References

NISBETT, R. E., and SCHACHTER, S. (1966), 'Cognitive manipulation of pain', *Journal of Experimental Social Psychology*, 2, 227–36.

O'DELL, J. W. (1968), 'Group size and emotional interaction', *Journal of Personality and Social Psychology*, 8, 75–8.

ORIANS, G. (1969), 'On the evolution of mating systems in birds and mammals', *American Naturalist*, 103, 589–603.

ORNE, M. T. (1962), 'On the social psychology of the psychological experiment with particular reference to the demand characteristics and their implications', *American Psychologist*, 17, 776–83.

OSGOOD, C. D. (1971), 'Where do sentences come from?', in D. D. Steinberg, and L. A. Jakobovits, eds., *Semantics: An interdisciplinary reader*, Cambridge, Cambridge University Press.

OSGOOD, C. E., SUCI, G. J., and TANNENBAUM, P. H. (1957), *The Measurement of Meaning*, Urbana, University of Illinois Press.

OSGOOD, C. E., and TANNENBAUM, P. H. (1955), 'The principle of congruity in the prediction of attitude change', *Psychological Review*, 62, 42–55.

OSKAMP, S. (1971), 'Effects of programmed strategies on cooperation in the Prisoner's Dilemma and other mixed-motive games', *Journal of Conflict Resolution*, 15, 225–59.

OSKAMP, S., and KLEINKE, C. (1970), 'Amount of reward as a variable in the Prisoner's Dilemma game', *Journal of Personality and Social Psychology*, 16, 133–40.

PATRICK, J. (1973), *A Glasgow Gang Observed*, London, Eyre Methuen.

PETTIGREW, T. F. (1958), 'Personality and sociocultural factors in intergroup attitudes: a cross-cultural comparison', *Journal of Conflict Resolution*, 2, 29–42.

PETTIGREW, T. F., ALLPORT, G. W., and BARNETT, E. O. (1958), 'Binocular resolution and perception of race in South Africa', *British Journal of Psychology*, 49, 265–78.

PIAGET, J. (1926), *The Language and Thought of the Child*, London, Routledge & Kegan Paul.

PIAGET, J. (1928), *Judgment and Reasoning in the Child*, London, Routledge & Kegan Paul.

PIAGET, J. (1932), *The Moral Judgement of the Child*, London, Routledge & Kegan Paul.

PIAGET, J. (1952), *The Origins of Intelligence in Children*, New York, International University Press.

PIAGET, J. (1953), *The Origins of Intelligence in the Child*, London, Routledge & Kegan Paul.

PIAGET, J. (1955), *The Child's Construction of Reality*, London, Routledge & Kegan Paul.

PIAGET, J. (1965), *Études sociologiques*, Geneva, Librairie Droz.

PIAGET, J., and INHELDER, B. (1956), *The Child's Conception of Space*, London, Routledge & Kegan Paul.

PIAGET, J., and INHELDER, B. (1964), *The Early Growth of Logic in the Child*, London, Routledge & Kegan Paul.

PLATT, J. (1973), 'Social traps', *American Psychologist*, 28, 641–51.

PLON, M. (1974), 'On the meaning of the notion of conflict and its study in social psychology', *European Journal of Social Psychology*, 4, 389–436.

PREMACK, D. (1970), 'The education of Sarah', *Psychology Today*, 4, 55–8.

PRICE-WILLIAMS, D. R., ed. (1969), *Cross-cultural Studies*, Penguin Books.

PRUITT, D. G. (1967), 'Reward structure and cooperation: the decomposed Prisoner's Dilemma game', *Journal of Personality and Social Psychology*, 7, 21–7.

PRUITT, D. G. (1970), 'Motivational processes in the decomposed Prisoner's Dilemma game', *Journal of Social Psychology*, 14, 227–38.

PRUITT, D. G. (1971), 'Choice shifts in group discussion: an introductory review', *Journal of Personality and Social Psychology*, 20, 339–60.

PUGH, D. S. (1971), *Organization Theory*, Penguin Books.

RABBIE, J. M., and HORWITZ, M. (1969), 'Arousal of ingroup–outgroup bias by a chance win or loss', *Journal of Personality and Social Psychology*, 13, 269–77.

RABBIE, J. M., and WILKENS, G. (1971), 'Intergroup competition and its effect on intragroup and intergroup relationships', *European Journal of Social Psychology*, 1, 215–34.

RADLOW, R., WEIDNER, M. F., and HURST, P. M. (1968), 'Effect of incentive magnitude and motivational orientation upon choice behavior in a two-person, non-zero-sum game', *Journal of Social Psychology*, 74, 199–208.

RAMOS, M., *et al.* (1967), *The Determination and Implementation of Language Policy*, Quezon City, Alemar-Phoenix.

RAPOPORT, A., and CHAMMAH, A. (1965), *Prisoner's Dilemma*, Ann Arbor, University of Michigan Press.

RAPOPORT, A., and CHAMMAH, A. (1966), 'The game of chicken', *American Behavioral Scientist*, 10, 10–14 and 23–8.

REX, J. (1969), 'Race as a social category', *Journal of Biosocial Science*, Suppl. 1, 145–52.

RHEINGOLD, H. L., and ECKERMAN, C. O. (1971), 'Departures from the mother', in H. R. Schaffer, ed., *The Origins of Human Social Relations*, London, Academic Press.

RHINE, R. J. (1958), 'A concept-formation approach to attitude acquisition', *Psychological Review*, 65, 362–70.

RICHARDS, M. P. M. (1974), 'The first steps in becoming social', in M. P. M. Richards, ed., *The Integration of a Child into a Social World*, Cambridge, Cambridge University Press.

RICHARDS, M. P. M., and BERNAL, J. F. (1972), 'An observational study of mother-infant interaction', in N. J. Blurton-Jones, ed., *Ethological Studies of Child Behaviour*, Cambridge, Cambridge University Press.

472 References

ROBINSON, W. P. (1972), *Language and Social Behaviour*, Penguin Books.

ROBSON, K. S. (1967), 'The role of eye-to-eye contact in maternal–infant attachment', *Journal of Child Psychology and Psychiatry*, 8, 13–25.

ROETHLISBERGER, F. J., and DICKSON, W. J. (1939), *Management and the Worker*, Cambridge, Mass., Harvard University Press.

ROGERS, C. R. (1973), *Encounter Groups*, Penguin Books.

ROGERS, E. M., and SHOEMAKER, F. (1971), *Communication of Innovations*, New York, Free Press.

ROHNER, P. R. (1974), 'Parental acceptance-rejection and personality development', in W. Brislin, S. Bochner, and W. J. Lonner, eds., *Cross-cultural Perspectives on Learning*, Beverley Hills, Sage.

ROKEACH, M. (1960), *Open and Closed Mind*, New York, Basic Books.

ROMMETVEIT, R. (1972a), 'Deep structure of sentences versus message structure', *Norwegian Journal of Linguistics*, 26, 3–22.

ROMMETVEIT, R. (1972b), 'Language games, deep syntactic structures and hermeneutic circles', in J. Israel and H. Tajfel, eds., *The Context of Social Psychology: A critical assessment*, London, Academic Press.

ROSENBERG, M. J. (1956), 'Cognitive structure and attitudinal effect', *Journal of Abnormal and Social Psychology*, 53, 367–72.

ROSENBERG, M. J. (1960), 'Cognitive reorganization of response to the hypnotic reversal of attitudinal effect', *Journal of Personality*, 28, 39–63.

ROSENBERG, S. (1968), 'Mathematical models of social behaviour', in G. Lindzey and E. Aronson, eds., *The Handbook of Social Psychology*, vol. 1, Reading, Mass., Addison-Wesley.

ROSENTHAL, A. M. (1964), *Thirty-eight Witnesses*, New York, McGraw-Hill.

ROSENTHAL, R. (1966), *Experimenter Effects in Behavioural Research*, New York, Appleton-Century-Crofts.

ROSENTHAL, R., and JACOBSON, L. (1968), *Pygmalion in the Classroom: Teacher expectations and pupils' intellectual development*, New York, Holt, Rinehart & Winston.

ROSENTHAL, R., and ROSNOW, R. L., eds. (1969), *Artifact in Behavioural Research*, New York, Academic Press.

ROSNOW, R. L., GOODSTADT, B. E., SULS, J. M., and GITTER, A. G. (1973), 'More on the social psychology of the experiment: when compliance turns to self-defence', *Journal of Personality and Social Psychology*, 27, 337–43.

ROSS, A. S., and BRABAND, J. (1973), 'Effect of increased responsibility on bystander intervention: II, The cue value of a blind person', *Journal of Personality and Social Psychology*, 25, 254–58.

ROTTER, J. B. (1966), 'Generalized expectancies for internal versus external control of reinforcement', *Psychological Monographs*, 80 (1 whole no. 609).

ROY, D. (1955), 'Efficiency and "the fix": informal intergroup relations in a piece-work machine shop', *American Journal of Sociology*, 60, 255–66.

RUBIN, J., and JERNUDD, B., eds. (1971), *Can Language be Planned?*, Honolulu, University Press of Hawaii.

RUBOVITS, P. C., and MAEHR, M. L. (1971), 'Pygmalion analyzed: toward an explanation of the Rosenthal–Jacobson findings', *Journal of Personality and Social Psychology*, 19, 197–203.

RUBOVITS, P. C., and MAEHR, M. L. (1973), 'Pygmalion black and white', *Journal of Personality and Social Psychology*, 25, 210–11.

RUNCIMAN, W. G. (1972), *Relative Deprivation and Social Justice*, Penguin Books.

RYLE, G. (1949), *The Concept of Mind*, London, Hutchinson.

SANDER, L. W., STECHLER, G., BURNS, P., and JULIA, H. (1970), 'Early mother–infant interaction and 24-hour patterns of activity and sleep', *Journal of the American Academy of Child Psychiatry*, 9, 103–23.

SARTRE, J. P. (1946), 'Portrait of the antisemite', *Partisan Review*, 13, 163–78.

SCHACHTER, S. (1971), *Emotion, Obesity and Crime*, New York, Academic Press.

SCHACHTER, S., and SINGER, J. E. (1962), 'Cognitive, social and physiological determinants of emotional state', *Psychological Review*, 69, 379–99.

SCHAFFER, H. R. (1958), 'Objective observations of personality development in early infancy', *British Journal of Medical Psychology*, 31, 174–83.

SCHAFFER, H. R. (1971), *The Growth of Sociability*, Penguin Books.

SCHAFFER, H. R. (1977), *Mothering*, London, Open Books.

SCHAFFER, H. R., and EMERSON, P. E. (1964), 'The development of social attachments in infancy', *Monographs of the Society for Research in Child Development*, 29, no. 3 (whole no. 94).

SCHRAMM, W., ed. (1963), *The Science of Human Communication*, New York, Basic Books.

SCHULMAN, G. I. (1967), 'Asch conformity studies: conformity to the experimenter and/or to the group?', *Sociometry*, 30, 26–40.

SCODEL, A., MINAS, J. S., RATOOSH, P., and LIPETZ, M. (1959), 'Some descriptive aspects of two-person non-zero-sum games, I', *Journal of Conflict Resolution*, 3, 114–19.

SCOTT, W. A. (1968), 'Attitude measurement', in G. Lindzey and E. Aronson, eds., *Handbook of Social Psychology*, vol. 2, Reading, Mass., Addison-Wesley.

SEAVER, W. B. (1973), 'Effects of naturally induced teacher expectancies', *Journal of Personality and Social Psychology*, 28, 333–42.

SEGALL, M., CAMPBELL, D. T., and HERSKOVITS, M. (1966), *The Influence of Culture on Visual Perception*, Indianapolis, Bobbs-Merrill.

SEMIN, G. R., and GLENDON, A. I. (1972), 'Polarization and the established group', *British Journal of Social and Clinical Psychology*, 11, 213–21.

SERMAT, V. (1967), 'The possibility of influencing the other's behavior and cooperation: Chicken vs. Prisoner's Dilemma', *Canadian Journal of Psychology*, 27, 204–19.

SERMAT, V. (1970), 'Is game behavior related to behavior in other interpersonal situations?' *Journal of Personality and Social Psychology*, 16, 92–109.

SHATZ, M., and GELMAN, R. (1973), 'The development of communication skills: modifications in the speech of young children as a function of listener',

Monographs of the Society for Research in Child Development, 38, no. 5 (whole no. 152).

SHAVER, K. G. (1970a), 'Redress and conscientiousness in the attribution of responsibility for accidents', *Journal of Experimental Social Psychology*, 6, 100–110.

SHAVER, K. G. (1970b), 'Defensive attribution: effects of severity and relevance on the responsibility assigned for an accident', *Journal of Personality and Social Psychology*, 14, 101–13.

SHAW, J. I., and SKOLNICK, P. (1971), 'Attribution of responsibility for a happy accident', *Journal of Personality and Social Psychology*, 18, 380–83.

SHAW, M. E. (1954), 'Some effects of problem complexity upon problem solution efficiency in different communication nets', *Journal of Experimental Psychology*, 48, 211–17.

SHAW, M. E. (1964), 'Communication networks', in L. Berkowitz, ed., *Advances in Experimental Social Psychology*, vol. 1, New York, Academic Press.

SHAW, M. E. (1976), *Group Dynamics* 2nd. edi., New York, McGraw Hill.

SHAW, M. E. and SULZER, J. L. (1964), 'An empirical test of Heider's levels in attribution of responsibility', *Journal of Abnormal and Social Psychology*, 69, 39–46.

SHEFLEN, A. E. (1964), 'The significance of posture in communication systems', *Psychiatry*, 27, 316–31.

SHERIF, M. (1935), 'A study of some social factors in perception', *Archives of Psychology*, 27, no. 187.

SHERIF, M. (1936), *The Psychology of Social Norms*, New York, Harper & Row.

SHERIF, M. (1966), *Group Conflict and Cooperation: their social psychology*, London, Routledge & Kegan Paul.

SHERIF, M., HARVEY, O. J., WHITE, B. J., HOOD, W. R., and SHERIF, C. (1961), *Intergroup Conflict and Cooperation: the Robbers' Cave experiment*, Norman, Oklahoma, University of Oklahoma Press.

SHERIF, M. and HOVLAND, C. I. (1961), *Social Judgment: Assimilation and contrast effects in communication and attitude change*, New Haven, Conn., Yale University Press.

SHERIF, M., and SHERIF, C. W. (1953), *Groups in Harmony and Tension*, New York, Harper & Row.

SHERIF, M., and SHERIF, C. W. (1969), *Social Psychology*, New York, Harper & Row.

SIDOWSKI, J. B. (1957), 'Reward and punishment in a minimal social situation', *Journal of Experimental Psychology*, 54, 119–26.

SIEGEL, S., and ZAJONC, R. B. (1967), 'Group risk-taking in professional decisions', *Sociometry*, 30, 339–49.

SIMARD, L., and TAYLOR, D. M. (1973), 'The potential for bicultural communication in a dyadic situation', *Canadian Journal of Behavioural Science*, 5, 211–25.

SIMMEL, G. (1950), *The Sociology of Georg Simmel*, translated and edited by K. H. Wolff, Glencoe, Ill., Free Press.

SINCLAIR, J. M., and COULTHARD, R. M. (1975), *Towards an Analysis of Discourse*, London, Oxford University Press.

SINHA, D. (1969), *Motivation of Rural Population in a Developing Country*, Bombay, Allied Publishers.

SLOVIC, P., and LICHTENSTEIN, S. (1971), 'Comparison of Bayesian and regression approaches to the study of information processing in judgement', *Organizational Behaviour and Human Performance*, 6, 649–744.

SMALLEY, W. A. (1964), *Orthography Studies: Articles on new writing systems*, London, United Bible Societies.

SMITH, D. H., and INKELES, A. (1966), 'The OM scale', *Sociometry*, 39, 353–77.

SMITH, M. B., BRUNER, J. S., and WHITE, R. W. (1956), *Opinions and Personality*, New York, Wiley.

SNOW, R. E. (1969), 'Unfinished Pygmalion', *Contemporary Psychology*, 14, 197–9.

SPECTOR, P., TORRES, A., LICHTENSTEIN, S., PRESTON, H. O., CLARK, J. B., and SILVERMAN, S. B. (1971), 'Communication media and motivation in the adoption of new practices: an experiment in rural Ecuador', *Human Organization*, 30, 39–46.

SPITZ, R. A., and WOLF, K. M. (1946), 'The smiling response', *Genetic Psychology Monographs*, 34, 57–125.

STAATS, A. W., and STAATS, C. K. (1958), 'Attitudes established by classical conditioning', *Journal of Abnormal and Social Psychology*, 57, 37–40.

STEINER, I. D. (1972), *Group Process and Productivity*, New York, Academic Press.

STEPHENSON, G. M. (1971), 'Intergroup relations and negotiating behaviour', in P. B. Warr, ed., *Psychology at Work*, Penguin Books.

STERN, D. N. (1971), 'A micro-analysis of mother–infant interaction', *Journal of the American Academy of Child Psychiatry*, 10, 501–17.

STERN, D. N. (1974), 'Mother and infant at play: the dyadic interaction involving facial, vocal and gaze behaviours', in M. Lewis and L. Rosenblum, eds., *The Origins of Behaviour, I*, New York, Wiley.

STERN, W. (1950), *Allgemeine Psychologie auf personalischer Grundlage*, 2nd ed., The Hague, Nijhoff. (First published 1934.)

STONE, G. P., and FARBERMAN, H. A., eds. (1970), *Social Psychology through Symbolic Interaction*, Waltham, Mass., Ginn-Blaisdell.

STONER, J. A. F. (1961), 'A comparison of individual and group decisions involving risk', unpublished Masters's thesis, School of Industrial Management, Massachusetts Institute of Technology.

STONER, J. A. F. (1968), 'Risky and cautious shifts in group decisions: the influence of widely held values', *Journal of Experimental Social Psychology*, 4, 442–59.

STORMS, M. D. (1973), 'Videotape and the attribution process: reversing actors' and observers' points of view', *Journal of Personality and Social Psychology*, 27, 165–75.

476 References

STORMS, M. D., and NISBETT, R. E. (1970), 'Insomnia and the attribution process', *Journal of Personality and Social Psychology*, 16, 319–28.

STORR, A. (1968), *Human Aggression*, London, Allen Lane.

SWINGLE, P. G. (1970), 'Exploitative behavior in non-zero-sum games', *Journal of Personality and Social Psychology*, 16, 121–32.

SWINGLE, P. G. (1973), *Social Psychology in Everyday Life*, Penguin Books.

TAJFEL, H. (1959), 'Quantitative judgement in social perception', *British Journal of Psychology*, 50, 16–29.

TAJFEL, H. (1966), 'The nature of information in social influence: an unexplored methodological problem', Proceedings of the XVIIIth International Congress of Psychology, Moscow, Symposium 34, *Methodological Problems in Social Psychology*.

TAJFEL, H. (1969a), 'Social and cultural factors in perception', in G. Lindzey and E. Aronson, eds., *The Handbook of Social Psychology*, vol. 3, 2nd ed. Reading, Mass., Addison-Wesley.

TAJFEL, H. (1969b), 'Cognitive aspects of prejudice', *Journal of Social Issues*, 25, 79–97; also in *Journal of Biosocial Sciences*, 1, suppl. no. 1.

TAJFEL, H. (1970), 'Experiments in intergroup discrimination', *Scientific American*, 223, 5, 96–102.

TAJFEL, H. (1972), 'Experiments in a vacuum', in J. Israel and H. Tajfel, eds., *The Context of Social Psychology: A critical assessment*, London, Academic Press (European Monographs in Social Psychology).

TAJFEL, H., ed., (1978), *Differentiation between Social Groups: Studies in the social psychology of intergroup relations*, London, Academic Press (European Monographs in Social Psychology).

TAJFEL, H., FLAMENT, C., BILLIG, M., and BUNDY, R. (1971), 'Social categorization and intergroup behaviour', *European Journal of Social Psychology*, 1, 149–78.

TAJFEL, H., and WILKES, A. L. (1963), 'Classification and quantitative judgement', *British Journal of Psychology*, 54, 101–14.

TAJFEL, H., and WILKES, A. L. (1964), 'Salience of attributes and commitment to extreme judgements in the perception of people', *British Journal of Social and Clinical Psychology*, 2, 40–49.

TANAKA, J. (1973), 'Social structure of the bushmen', in C. R. Carpenter, ed., *Behavioral Regulations of Behavior in Primates*, Lewisburg, Buckwell Press.

TAYLOR, D. M., BASSILI, J. N., and ABOUD, F. E. (1973), 'Dimensions of ethnic identity: an example from Quebec', *Journal of Social Psychology*, 89, 185–92.

TAYLOR, O. (1971), 'Some sociolinguistic concepts of Black language', *Today's Speech*, Spring, 19–26.

TAYLOR, S. P., and EPSTEIN, S. (1967), 'Aggression as a function of the interaction of the sex of the aggressor and the sex of the victim', *Journal of Personality*, 35, 474–86.

TELEKI, G. (1973), *The Predatory Behavior of Wild Chimpanzees*, Lewisburg, Buckwell Press.

TERHUNE, K. W. (1968), 'Motives, situation, and interpersonal conflict within the Prisoner's Dilemma', *Journal of Personality and Social Psychology*, Monograph Supplement, 8, 1–24.

TERMAN, L. M. (1904), 'A preliminary study of the psychology and pedagogy of leadership', *Journal of Genetic Psychology*, 11, 413–51.

THURSTONE, L. L., and CHAVE, E. J. (1929), *The Measurement of Attitudes*, University of Chicago Press.

TIGER, L. (1969), *Men in Groups*, London, Nelson.

TIGER, L., and FOX, R. (1966), 'The zoological perspective in social science', *Man*, 1, 75–81.

TINBERGEN, N. (1953), *Social Behaviour of Animals*, London, Methuen.

TINBERGEN, N. (1972a), *The Animal in its World*, London, Allen & Unwin.

TINBERGEN, N. (1972b), 'Functional ethology and the human sciences', *Proceedings of the Royal Society*, London, 182, 385–410.

TORGERSON, W. S. (1958), *Theory and Methods of Scaling*, New York, Wiley.

TRIANDIS, H. C. (1960), 'Cognitive similarity and communication in a dyad', *Human Relations*, 13, 175–83.

TRIANDIS, H. C. (1961), 'A note on Rokeach's theory of prejudice', *Journal of Abnormal and Social Psychology*, 6, 184–6.

TRIANDIS, H. C. (1972), *The Analysis of Subjective Culture*, New York, Wiley.

TRIPLETT, N. (1898), 'The dynamogenic factors in pace-making and competition', *American Journal of Psychology*, 9, 507–33.

TUAN, YI FU (1968), *The Hydrologic Cycle and the Wisdom of God*, Toronto, University of Toronto Press.

TUCKMAN, B. W. (1965), 'Developmental sequence in small groups', *Psychological Bulletin*, 63, 384–99.

TURNER, A. N., and LAWRENCE, P. R. (1965), *Industrial Jobs and the Worker*, Cambridge, Mass., Harvard University Press.

TURNER, C. E. (1933), 'Test room studies in employee effectiveness', *American Journal of Public Health*, 23, 577–84.

TURNER, J. (1975), 'Social comparison and social identity: some prospects for intergroup behaviour', *European Journal of Social Psychology*, 5, 1–31.

TURNER, L. D. (1949), *Africanisms in the Gulla Dialect*, Chicago, University of Chicago Press.

TURNER, R. (1974), *Ethnomethodology: Selected readings*, Penguin Books.

VALINS, S., and NISBETT, R. E. (1971), 'Attribution processes in the development and treatment of emotional disorders', in E. E. Jones, D. E. Kanouse, H. H. Kelley, R. E. Nisbett, S. Valins and B. Weiner, *Attribution: Perceiving the causes of behavior*, Morristown, General Learning Press.

VERBA, S. (1961), *Small Groups and Political Behavior*, Princeton, Princeton University Press.

VIDMAR, N. (1970), 'Group composition and the risky shift', *Journal of Experimental Social Psychology*, 6, 153–66.

VIDULICH, R. N., and KREVANICK, F. W. (1966), 'Racial attitudes and emotional response to visual representations of the negro', *Journal of Social Psychology*, 68, 85–93.

VINE, I. (1970), 'Communication by facial-visual signals', in J. H. Crook, ed., *Social Behaviour in Birds and Mammals*, London, Academic Press.

VINOKUR, A. (1969), 'Distribution of initial risk levels and group decisions involving risk', *Journal of Personality and Social Psychology*, 13, 207–14.

VINOKUR, A., and BURNSTEIN, E. (1974), 'Effects of partially shared persuasive arguments on group-induced shifts: a group-problem-solving approach', *Journal of Personality and Social Psychology*, 29, 305–15.

VOISSEM, N. H., and SISTRUNK, F. (1971), 'Communication schedule and cooperative game behaviour' *Journal of Personality and Social Psychology*, 19, 160–67.

VROOM, V. H. (1964) *Work and Motivation*, New York, Wiley,

WALKER, T. G., and MAIN, E. C. (1973), 'Choice shifts in political decision-making: federal judges and civil liberties cases', *Journal of Applied Social Psychology*, 3, 39–48.

WALL, T. D., and STEPHENSON, G. M. (1970), 'Herzberg's two-factor theory of job attitudes: a critical evaluation and some fresh evidence', *Industrial Relations Journal*, vol. 1, 41–65.

WALL, T. D., STEPHENSON, G. M., and SKIDMORE, C. (1971), 'Ego involvement and Herzberg's two-factor theory of job satisfaction: an experimental field study', *British Journal of Social and Clinical Psychology*, 10, 123–31.

WALLACH, M. A., KOGAN, N., and BEM, D. J. (1964), 'Diffusion of responsibility and level of risk taking in groups', *Journal of Abnormal and Social Psychology*, 68, 263–74.

WALSTER, E. (1966), 'Assignment of responsibility for an accident', *Journal of Personality and Social Psychology*, 3, 73–9.

WALSTER, E. (1967), '"Second guessing" important events', *Human Relations*, 20, 239–50.

WALTERS, R. H., and PARKE, R. D. (1965), 'The role of the distance receptors in the development of social responsiveness', in L. P. Lipsitt and C. C. Spiker, eds., *Advances in Child Development and Behaviour*, 2, New York, Academic Press.

WALTON, R. E., and MCKERSIE, R. B. (1965), *A Behavioural Theory of Labour Negotiations*, New York, McGraw-Hill.

WASHBURN, S. L., and LANCASTER, C. S. (1968), 'The evolution of hunting', in R. B. Lee and I. DeVore, eds., *Man the Hunter*, Chicago, Aldine.

WASON, P. C. (1959), 'Processing of positive and negative information', *Journal of Experimental Psychology*, 11, 92–107.

WATSON, A., and MOSS, R. (1970), 'Dominance, spacing behaviour and aggression in relation to population limitation in vertebrates', *Symposia of the British Ecological Society*, 10.

WAXWEILER, E. (1906), 'Esquisse d'une sociologie', in *Travaux de l'Institut de Sociologie* (Institut Solvay, Notes et memoires, part 2), Brussels, Mischet Thon.

WEISS, R. F. (1962), 'Persuasion and acquisition of attitudes: models from conditioning and selective learning', *Psychological Reports*, 11, 709–32.

WEISS, W. (1969), 'Effects of the mass media of communication', in G. Lindzey and E. Aronson, eds,. *The Handbook of Social Psychology*, vol. 5. 2nd ed., Reading, Mass., Addison-Wesley.

WHEELER, L. (1970), *Interpersonal Influence*, Boston, Allyn & Bacon.

WHITELEY, W. (1969), *Swahili: The rise of a national language*, London, Methuen.

WHITING, B. B. (1963), *Six Cultures*, New York, Wiley.

WHITING, J. W. M. (1959), 'Sorcery, sin and the superego', in *Nebraska Symposium on Motivation*, Lincoln, University of Nebraska Press.

WHYTE, W. F. (1955), *Street Corner Society*, Chicago, University of Chicago Press.

WICHMAN, H. (1970), 'Effects of isolation and communication on cooperating in a two-person game', *Journal of Personality and Social Psychology*, 16, 114–20.

WICKER, A. W. (1969), 'Attitudes versus actions: the relationship of verbal and overt behavioural responses to attitude objects, *Journal of Social Issues*, 25, 41–78.

WICKLER, W. (1967), 'Socio-sexual signals and their intra-specific imitation among primates', in D. Morris, ed., *Primate Ethology*, London, Weidenfeld & Nicolson.

WIENER, M., and MEHRABIAN, A. (1968), *Language within Language: Immediacy, a channel in verbal communication*, New York, Appleton-Century-Crofts.

WIENER, M., *et al.* (1972), 'Non-verbal behaviour and non-verbal communication', *Psychological Review*, 79, 185–214.

WILLIAMS, R. M. (1968), 'The concept of values', in *International Encyclopedia of the Social Sciences*, vol. 16, New York, Macmillan and The Free Press.

WILSON, E. O. (1975), *Sociobiology, the New Synthesis*, Harvard, Belknap.

WITKIN, H. A., *et al.* (1962), *Psychological Differentiation: Studies of development*, New York, Wiley.

WITTKOWER, R. (1955), 'Interpretation of visual symbols in the arts', in *Studies in Communication* (Communication Research Centre, University College, London), London, Secker & Warburg.

WOLFF, P. H. (1963), 'Observations on the early development of smiling', in B. M. Foss, ed., *Determinants of Infant Behaviour, II*, London, Methuen.

WOLFF, P. H. (1969), 'The natural history of crying and other vocalizations in early infancy', in B. M. Foss, ed., *Determinants of Infant Behaviour, IV*, London, Methuen.

WOODWARD, J. (1965), *Industrial Organization: Theory and practice*, London, Oxford University Press.

WORTMAN, C. B., and LINDER, D. E. (1973), 'Attribution of responsibility for an outcome as a function of its likelihood', *American Psychological Association, 81st Annual Convention*, Montreal, 1973.

WRIGHTSMAN, L. S. (1972), *Social Psychology in the Seventies*, Monterey, Brooks/Cole.

WRIGHTSMAN, L. S., and BRIGHAM, J. C., eds. (1973), *Contemporary Issues in Social Psychology*, 2nd ed., Monterey, Brooks/Cole.

YUKL, G. (1971), 'Toward a behavioural theory of leadership', *Organizational Behaviour and Human Performance*, 6, 414–40.

ZAJONC, R. B. (1960), 'The process of cognitive tuning in communication', *Journal of Abnormal and Social Psychology*, 61, 159–67.

ZAJONC, R. B. (1968), 'Cognitive theories in social psychology', in G. Lindzey and E. Aronson, eds., *The Handbook of Social Psychology*, vol. 1, Reading, Mass., Addison-Wesley.

ZELAZO, P. R., and KOMER, M. J. (1971), 'Infant smiling to non-social stimuli and the recognition hypothesis', *Child Development*, 42, 1327–39.

ZIMBARDO, P. G. (1960), 'Involvement and communication discrepancy as determinants of opinion conformity', *Journal of Abnormal and Social Psychology*, 60, 86–94.

ZIMBARDO, P. G., HANEY, C., BANKS, W. C., and JAFFE, D. (1973), 'The mind is a formidable jailor: A Pirandellian prison', *The New York Times Magazine*, 18 April, Section 6, 38–60.

List of contributors

John Hurrell Crook, Reader in Psychology, University of Bristol.

J. Richard Eiser, Senior Lecturer in Social Psychology, Institute of Psychiatry, University of London.

Joshua Fishman, Research Professor of Social Linguistics, Yeshiva University, New York.

Colin Fraser, University Lecturer in Social Psychology and Fellow of Churchill College, Cambridge.

Howard Giles, Lecturer in Social Psychology, University of Bristol.

Gustav Jahoda, Professor of Psychology, University of Strathclyde.

J. M. F. Jaspars, University Lecturer in Social Psychology and Fellow of St Edmund's Hall, Oxford.

H. R. Schaffer, Professor of Psychology, University of Strathclyde.

Geoffrey Stephenson, Professor of Social Psychology, University of Kent.

Henri Tajfel, Professor of Social Psychology, University of Bristol.

Anne Whyte, Research Associate in Environmental Studies, University of Toronto.

Index

More About Penguins and Pelicans

Penguinews, which appears every month, contains details of all the new books issued by Penguins as they are published. It is supplemented by our stocklist, which includes around 5,000 titles.

A specimen copy of *Penguinews* will be sent to you free on request. Please write to Dept EP, Penguin Books Ltd, Harmondsworth, Middlesex, for your copy.

In the U.S.A.: For a complete list of books available from Penguins in the United States write to Dept CS, Penguin Books, 625 Madison Avenue, New York, New York 10022.

In Canada: For a complete list of books available from Penguins in Canada write to Penguin Books Canada Ltd, 2801 John Street, Markham, Ontario LR3 1B4.

Penguin Education
Some recent and forthcoming titles

THE DEFERENTIAL WORKER

Howard Newby

In recent years the changes in rural life wrought by the mechanization of agriculture and the consequent 'drift from the land' have been both subtle and far-reaching. Yet the views of agricultural workers – the group most directly affected – are seldom heard. This book is the first systematic study of the social situation of the agricultural worker since these changes became widespread.

FACING UP TO MODERNITY

Peter L. Berger

These trenchant and stimulating essays illustrate five features of modernity and its dilemmas. One, the undermining of cohesive communities where humans found security. Two, the obsession with time and bureaucratic programming. Three, the counterpoising of the individual and society, which causes identity crises and alienation. Four, the process of 'liberation' which undercuts the basic human desire for a structure of generally shared assumptions. And five, increasing secularization which frustrates our deep need to believe in a meaningful cosmos.

COLLEGES IN CRISIS

David Hencke

The upheaval in teacher training over the last few years has entailed the closure of some fifty institutions, mergers among many others, and has created a new group of institutions, the colleges of higher education. What was the purpose of this reorganization? Why did the predicted expansion in teaching posts fail to materialize?

David Hencke discussed these events with teachers, college principals, lecturers and members of the James Committee. His account of the government reports, the arguments between policy-makers and educationalists, and the ways in which colleges reacted to the reorganization call is clear, well-documented and essential reading for anyone concerned with teacher training.

Penguin Education
Some recent and forthcoming titles

ENDLESS PRESSURE

Ken Pryce

Ken Pryce, himself a West Indian, is a sociologist who spent four years living and working with the immigrant community in Bristol. Spotlighting the Jamaican community, he describes the different ways in which immigrants react to the strains and frustrations of life in an alien culture in this outstanding work of empirical sociology. His description of their way of life is often humorous, always lively and compelling: but it is also a story of grim reality, with little to tell about integration, and his conclusions are deeply disturbing. Above all, however, Ken Pryce helps us towards an understanding of what is going on and offers an essential opportunity to improve race relations in this country.

GEOGRAPHY OF ELECTIONS

P. J. Taylor and R. J. Johnston

With the help of charts, maps and diagrams, the authors range from Newfoundland to New South Wales in a lucid, international study of the complex relationships between society, geography and electoral systems. They examine single transferable vote, proportional representation, first-past-the-post and many other systems in the context of different countries and particular campaigns, and analyse every scale of election from British Trade Union practice to the Presidential elections in America. There are also chapters on electoral abuse and electoral reform, and a section on the European Parliament to round off an invaluable reference book.

and a reprint:

INTRODUCING SOCIOLOGY

Edited by Peter Worsley

This exciting and wholly original text is, first and foremost, an introduction to sociological ideas and practice, rather than an exhaustive summary. Avoiding jargon but retaining scientific rigour, the contributors draw their subject matter from the common life-experiences of most people born into the mid-twentieth century. The examples used have been deliberately chosen from a wide range of cultures and societies to underline the international roots and relevance of modern sociology. The book is divided into three main sections and includes an extensive further reading list and author and subject indexes.

Some recent and forthcoming Pelicans

BIOLOGICAL IDEAS IN POLITICS

W. J. M. Mackenzie

Professor Mackenzie pulls into context the various biological and sociological ideas about the human function and place in the larger schemes of nature. This book explores the current debate between science and 'non-science', reporting the dialogue between scientists, philosophers, sociologists and politicians, and offering a fascinating exposition of how man now sees himself and his future.

THE FOUNDATIONS

An Anatomy of Philanthropy and Society

Ben Whitaker

Ben Whitaker makes a penetrating analysis of trusts and the 'philanthropoids' who run them in a critical, but generous, study. He reveals an alarming gap between their stated intentions and their cost-effectiveness, and, in some cases, an equally alarming interchangeability between foundation and government personnel. In view of his revelations, it is hardly surprising that such powerful bodies, however well-intentioned, should arouse suspicion.

'An extremely readable and commendably brief yet comprehensive account of life in the circumscribed world of the philanthropoids' – *Economist*

THE GROWTH OF CRIME

The International Experience

Sir Leon Radzinowicz and Joan King

Crime is growing, both in industrialized and underdeveloped countries; among the traditionally crime-prone and among the hitherto law-abiding. Traditional offences are increasing, but so are new forms of crime made possible by more sophisticated technology.

This is the first authoritative attempt to take a comparative look at every aspect of crime and law enforcement from an international perspective, to assess what reforms have been tried, what has failed and what has been effective. The authors' conclusions make depressing reading; for the problems of modern crime may ultimately be beyond the scope of criminal justice systems anywhere.

Some recent and forthcoming Pelicans

ORDER AND DISPUTE
An Introduction to Legal Anthropology
Simon Roberts

Simon Roberts contends that legal theory has become too closely identified with arrangements in western societies to be of much help in cross-cultural studies of order. After all, there are many societies which survive in a remarkably orderly way without the help of judges, law-courts and policemen. But conversely, by looking at ways in which these other societies keep order and solve disputes, he shows that they can give us valuable guidance in the contemporary debate about order in our own society.

POWER POLITICS
Martin Wight

Power Politics provides a historical introduction to the cardinal principles of international politics. Concentrating not on the ephemera of current events but on the features of international politics that are fundamental and enduring, Martin Wight has written a classical account of the international system that arose in Europe at the start of the modern era, spread itself over other continents, and still provides the political framework of the world.

WHITE MAN, WE WANT TO TALK TO YOU
Denis Herbstein

The Soweto uprising marked the emergence of a generation of black students who have assimilated the new confidence inspired by the Black Consciousness philosophy. The enforced use of Afrikaans as a medium of school instruction was for them a challenge to be met initially by peaceful protest, but, in the face of vicious reaction from white authorities, in a fury of retribution.

Denis Herbstein offers first-hand, factual reporting of the events in the townships, police stations, courts and in parliament. Together with the incorporated texts of conversations that he held with both black and white, he builds up a portrait of a troubled country which is neither pretty nor reassuring.

'Beautifully written and atmospheric'
The Sun

Readers love
Daniela
SACERDOTI

'Beautifully written.
A great book'
Lesley Pearse

'Emotional. Mysterious.
It made me think and I couldn't
put it down' Daily Mail

'Heartwarming and intriguing' Dani Atkins

'I fell in love with this book' *Prima* magazine

'Beautifully written. A great book' Lesley Pearse

'I was hooked from the beginning' Alice Peterson

'Emotional. Mysterious. It made me think and I couldn't put it down' *Daily Mail*

'Heartwarming and mysterious with great atmosphere' Katie Fforde

'Beautifully written and atmospheric' *The Sun*

'Will satisfy even the most hopeless romantics. Her descriptions of the idyllic, wild isle are evocative and vivid' *Daily Express*

'Sacerdoti writes beautiful fiction that feeds the soul' Shari Low, *Daily Record*

'Such a beautifully written book. Fills you with hope' *Rea's Book Reviews*

Daniela Sacerdoti is a phenomenon.

Over one million copies of her novels have been sold in ebook, her debut novel *Watch Over Me* was the eighth bestselling Kindle book of all time in 2015 and she was also ranked as the eleventh top-selling Kindle author. Daniela writes fiction for adults (the Glen Avich series), young adults (the Sarah Midnight trilogy) and children. Her novels have been translated into twelve languages.

Daniela was born and raised in Italy. She studied Classics, then lived in Scotland for fourteen years, where she married and taught in a primary school. Daniela's children's book *Really Weird Removals.com* was shortlisted for the Scottish Children's Book Awards. She has also written for the BBC. Daniela, her husband and their two sons make their home in a tiny village in the Alps.

To discover more about Daniela and her world, visit www.danielasacerdoti.com or find her on Twitter @danisacerdoti.

Daniela
SACERDOTI
I Will Find You

REVIEW

Copyright © 2018 Daniela Sacerdoti

The right of Daniela Sacerdoti to be identified as the Author of
the Work has been asserted by her in accordance with the
Copyright, Designs and Patents Act 1988.

First published in Great Britain in 2018
by HEADLINE REVIEW
An imprint of HEADLINE PUBLISHING GROUP

First published in paperback in 2018
by HEADLINE REVIEW
An imprint of HEADLINE PUBLISHING GROUP

1

Cataloguing in Publication Data is available from the British Library

ISBN 978 1 4722 3507 7

Map illustration by Laura Hall

Key motif © biancardi/Shutterstock

Typeset in Baskerville Std by Jouve (UK), Milton Keynes

Printed and bound in Great Britain by Clays Ltd, Elcograf S.p.A.

MIX
Paper from
responsible sources
FSC® C104740

Headline's policy is to use papers that are natural, renewable and recyclable
products and made from wood grown in well-managed forests and other
controlled sources. The logging and manufacturing processes are expected to
conform to the environmental regulations of the country of origin.

HEADLINE PUBLISHING GROUP
An Hachette UK Company
Carmelite House
50 Victoria Embankment
London EC4Y 0DZ

www.headline.co.uk
www.hachette.co.uk

To Simona, the little light

Seal Island

E

N

S

W

MAINLAND
this way →

Sorren's Cottage

Sea Rescue

ROAN

Stella Maris

Catriona's Cottage

Seal Distillery

OLLABERRY

CORRYWRECKAN
Whirlpool

INIS ROAN
Island of the Seals

CONTENTS

Ane thing I'll gie ye, ane thing an more
Ane thing awash upon the shore
A silver comb for your hair of gowd
A silver comb for a love unbowed

Twa things I'll gie you, twa things an more
Twa things awash upon the shore
A gowden coin, a shining sun
Twa spirits dance as one

Three things I'll gie you, three things an more
Three things awash upon the shore
A spring-green apple, crisp and cold
The taste o' a life as yet untold

Fower things I'll gie ye, fower things an more
Fower things awash upon the shore
A bonny bluebell, tho sma' an peerie
Its scent, like you, is sweet an dearie

Five things I'll gie ye, five things an more
Five things awash upon the shore
An egg in a nest of a bird that flies
Two bright white wings in stormy skies

PROLOGUE

Last night he came to me; my love came back to me.

The sky was rumbling and the sea was wild; no boat could have sailed to the island. Only a dead man would make it here on such a night, a man who could walk on water and breathe lightning. It meant my love was dead; it meant the days spent looking out to sea, waiting for him to return, had come to an end.

Wave after wave the sea broke on the shore; memory after memory my heart broke inside me. The sea was so close it was nearly on my doorstep. I opened my eyes after falling asleep at the fire, and Duncan was there, standing between me and the embers. At that moment, as he stood silent and bleeding before me, the glow of the burning peat shining through him, I knew that he would never stop bleeding, and I knew my life was finished too.

My love extended his arm, slowly, slowly, and I reached out to touch him. My fingers touched his cold hand; his blue lips opened to speak and warn me, warn me of the fire, the fire that was rolling and rolling towards me, sweeping the land, roaring all the way to the island. He stood cold and white, his fingers touching mine, and told me he had sent help but had been betrayed — and that not help but harm would come to me. He told me to run. Then slowly,

slowly, as frozen, silent tears fell down my cheeks, slowly, slowly, my love faded away. Oh, the pain to see the face I loved so much become gossamer and disappear – colder and colder his fingers, his hands dissolving and leaving nothing behind.

And then a voice rose from inside me, a voice that was Duncan's but came from my heart. It was the voice of the waves and the rain and the flashing sky.

I will find you.

LOW TIDE

Cora

I'd run out of tears, and so had Stephen. It'd been strange seeing my six-foot-tall brother, who always had a way of making light of everything, sobbing like a child at our mother's funeral. Now he looked young and vulnerable standing behind Mum's armchair, his arms on the back-rest, surrounded by boxes and black bin liners, his hair sticking up as it always did, making him look like an eternal little boy. I went to him: an irresistible desire to look after my baby brother, to make it all better for him like I did when we were children.

We were at the Holy Heart, the assisted accommodation where my mum had lived her last year; they'd kindly allowed us to keep her room for a little longer, until we were ready to sort through her things. And now it was nearly done. But Mum had been gone a long time, longer than the three weeks since she'd passed away. Her mind had been failing her, slowly at first, then faster and faster, until she didn't know who we were any more; she didn't know who *she* was any more. All that was left of my cheerful, vibrant, always-on-her-feet mother was a fragile shell, lost in a world of her own making. That was when my brother and I began wishing she would be freed of this life, and at the same time began to really face the possibility of *our* life without her.

Us without *her*.

The impossible, becoming real.

Every day as she fell into nothing, slowly forgetting who she was, my mum asked me the same thing: 'Will you open the curtains, please, Cora?' Except the curtains were already open. She couldn't see the light any more; she didn't know it was there. She didn't know if it was night or day. But still she was hungry for light and life and air – *open the curtains* meant let the light in, deliver me from this darkness.

Even if looking after her was heartbreaking – the times she became confused and upset, and even angry, were terrible to navigate – my mind was full of happy memories as I did so. She'd given my brother and me the gift of a happy childhood, and she'd been there for us as we became teenagers and young adults. Always there, always smiling, like all her thoughts were in colour in a black and white world, and her love seeped from everything she did.

Funny, the things you remember, but right at that moment, standing among the boxes that had been my mother's life, what came back to me was the time the house was flooded. It was my thirteenth birthday and I was beside myself with excitement – all my friends were coming, and I was wearing my best outfit: a miniskirt, and a green T-shirt from BHS that I thought was the height of glamour. It wasn't long since my father's death, and both Stephen and I were raw and vulnerable. That was also why Mum wanted to make my birthday special. She had the place decorated from top to bottom with balloons and home-made bunting and signs, and sandwiches and cakes and sweets were laid out beautifully on the tables we had carried up from my dad's workshop.

Twenty minutes before the party was due to start, all hell broke loose. A few days earlier, we'd had some pipes repaired – I think the plumber must have used Sellotape, because now, suddenly, they all exploded, leaving us ankle deep in water, water dripping from the ceilings, water rising as if we were on the *Titanic*. I started screaming, while Stephen tried to protect the food with his chubby little hands.

My mum stood, eyes wide, immobile.

For a moment.

Then she sprang into action. She instructed one of my uncles to call the plumber and hold the fort; to tell all the guests that turned up that we would be in the park. She distributed trays and cakes and plates among all of us and instructed my other uncle to carry the tables, and off we went, to the modest little urban park two streets away. In ten minutes, my mum had ribbons and bunting on the trees, the tables up again and blankets on the grass. The *Happy Birthday Cora* sign hung between a tree and a lamp post. Just as the guests began to arrive, an ice cream van drove by, and my mum opened a tab for everyone. It was the best birthday of my life.

When we came home after the party to find every floor and wall and ceiling soaked, my mum simply crossed her arms with a smile and said, 'I'm so glad you had a good time. That's all that matters to me.'

This woman, widowed at forty, with two kids to bring up, was our strength; she was the reason we knew how to keep going when everything seemed lost, when everything seemed to be working against us. I couldn't fall into a black hole now, even if she was gone and I felt so alone; it would have been against everything she had taught me.

As we packed her things, sweetness mixed with sorrow. My mum had lived a long and happy life. Happiness was her knack, actually. I can count on my fingers the times I saw her sad. She'd gentle ways and a soft voice – people thought she was a kindly, mild-mannered woman, and she was, but underneath her sweetness, there was a steely will, an unwavering loyalty to her heart.

In my hands, I cradled a framed photograph of my parents, looking impossibly young. My dad's hair was combed to one side and he wore, awkwardly, a Sunday shirt – he'd been a shy working-class man who had, people said, punched well above his weight in falling for my mother: beautiful, educated, talented. Mum wore a gorgeous full-skirted dress and her usual smile, her hair curled and framing her face. She looked like a fifties beauty queen. In marrying my father, she'd gone against her family – her love for him had been stronger than the rules she was supposed to abide by. She had given up on an easy life and her art studies to struggle beside him; and, it seemed to me, she'd never regretted it, because they'd loved each other until the day he died.

He was young, he suffered much. Mum was broken herself, but she sheltered us from the pain.

My mum loved intensely.

My mum lived in bright colours.

And me?

Where were my bright colours, I wondered, looking at my parents' fingers lightly entwined, if at thirty-one I'd never even fallen in love?

'I'm going to do the chest of drawers,' my brother said, breaking the flow of my thoughts. His voice had a strange note, and I realised how rarely through the years I'd heard sadness in his tone, or even just tiredness; he was always cheerful, just like Mum, and full of energy. Funny how my parents had brought up two children the same way and we'd turned out so different. I was quiet, solitary, allergic to change, just like my father, while my brother had inherited my mum's taste for adventure and carefree optimism. He'd been in Malawi, working in an animal sanctuary, when Mum had fallen ill. I was a homebody; the only way I ever wanted to see Malawi was through David Attenborough's eyes.

'Hey. Have you been sleeping enough?' I said, lifting myself on my toes and ruffling his straw-blond hair. Stephen was born when I was seven, and because both our parents worked, I took care of him a lot of the time. Maybe that was why I'd never really felt a longing

11

to become a mother; I'd already helped to bring up a little boy.

'Depends on your definition of enough,' he replied, attempting a smile.

'Mmmm. Listen, when we're finished here, come back to the house and I'll cook you something.'

'Can't. I'm on call from six.' Stephen had just started working at a veterinary clinic. Not that his shifts ever stopped him from partying or changing girlfriends every few months; that was all part of his zest for life. I still couldn't keep up with the latest Martha-Iona-Alison . . .

The thought made me smile, even if everything around me and inside me was sad. My brother had that effect on me. I stepped slowly, carefully through life, evaluating and weighing every move; Stephen glided, assuming everything would go well. And even when it didn't, he shrugged it off and kept going. Just imagine the scene: a studious, shy red-haired schoolgirl, sitting at the kitchen table bent over books she had to work hard to understand; and a little blond boy finishing his homework in a moment, easily, his bright mind deciphering everything his sister couldn't, then running out to play with his friends and coming home dirty, happy and without a care in the world. That was me and my brother.

'Cora . . . what's this?' While I was lost in thought, Stephen had unearthed a little wooden box with a lovely geometric pattern on the lid.

I peered at it. 'I thought I was sort of familiar with

everything my mum owned, but I've never seen this before. Have you?'

He shook his head. I lifted the lid carefully – the box looked very old and the wood seemed worn. Inside, resting on a bed of yellowed paper, was a key, slight and unadorned, and a bit rusty.

There are moments in life that become etched in your memory: the summer day you first swim in the sea; the moment you're handed a book you'll grow to adore; your first kiss. Good or bad, such moments make up the jigsaw of your life, the essence of who you are.

Opening the mysterious little box was one of these.

Stephen picked up the key and handed it to me. There was a thin, yellowed label hanging from it, and I turned it over gently, as if it might crumble under my fingers. *Gealach, Seal*, it said in an old-fashioned slanted cursive. For some reason, I couldn't tear my eyes away from the writing. My fingers curled around the key harder than they needed to.

I was aware that Stephen was speaking, but I didn't hear the words. I held the cold, rusty key until it became warm in my hand, warmer and warmer – and then suddenly cold again, so cold it was nearly painful. A strange feeling took hold of me, something I couldn't put into words, something I didn't understand. Sadness? No, not exactly. Homesickness . . . desire . . . longing? Yes, longing. *Yearning.* The feeling you get when you look at something very, very beautiful – an untouched forest, a misty landscape, a stormy sky, the vast grey expanse of the sea. Yearning, though you're not exactly sure for what.

'Earth to Cora?'

'Sorry, did you say something?' I forced myself back to the here and now.

'What does the label say?'

'I'm not really sure. Ge . . . Gealach? I don't know how to pronounce this. What language is it? *Ge-a-lach, Seal* . . . No idea.'

Stephen shrugged and took the key from me. 'No idea either. I think Gealach is Gaelic. Sounds like it. Remember Iona?'

'Yes, I remember Iona.' I sighed and smiled. Another girlfriend, one Mum and I had particularly liked and were quite gutted to see joining the well-frequented club of Stephen's ex-girlfriends.

'She spoke Gaelic. This looks like the stuff she read.' He shrugged.

'There's something else in there,' I said. Flattened against the bottom of the box was a photograph, slightly curled at the edges, with that seventies brown look to the paper. I unpeeled it carefully. It was a picture of my mum and a young woman whose face I couldn't quite place, though she looked familiar and recalled in me a vague feeling of sweetness. My mum's smile was broad and unclouded as ever, but in that picture even more so, as if all the happiness in the world was gathered in her face. The two women had their arms linked, their hair and skirts blown by the wind.

'Hey . . . that's Aunt Toffee!' Stephen said, and gently took the picture from me.

'Who?'

Stephen touched the slender, smiling figure. 'Do you not remember Aunt Toffee and Uncle Skirt?'

I laughed. 'Toffee and Skirt? Are you sure you're not imagining these people?'

'Absolutely not! Those weren't their real names, of course . . . I called her that because she always gave me toffee. And Uncle Skirt came to a Christmas dinner in our house wearing a kilt. I think I was four and I ended up under the table laughing because I'd never seen a man in a skirt before. Mum and Dad were mortified.'

I shrugged and shook my head. 'No. Doesn't ring a bell.'

'Honestly, you have the memory span of a goldfish, Cora.'

'Probably that Christmas I was too busy making stamps with potatoes – you know, to decorate wrapping paper.'

'You were always making something. Remember that year you glued your fingers together? We spent four and a half hours in A and E. A nurse gave me a chocolate Santa.'

I took the photo from him. 'And you have a freaky memory. The things you remember!' I turned it over, hoping to find out more, and froze. The words *Seal Island* were written on the back, in Mum's careful handwriting. 'Look, Stephen. Seal Island. *Seal* . . . You said Uncle Skirt was wearing a kilt that Christmas?'

15

'Yes. I can't believe you don't remember.'

'So he was Scottish?'

'He must have been. And look . . . look at the wall behind Mum and Aunt Toffee. It looks like one of those places you see in the Highlands. And the wind . . . Look at their hair blowing . . .'

Yes. For a moment I could almost feel the wind; I could almost hear it blowing. It was like a jigsaw, the pieces whirling in front of my eyes and refusing to fall into place. All these pieces made a picture – but I had no idea what.

'Cora, you okay? You look a bit pale. Shall I make you a cup of tea?'

'No, it's fine. Don't worry. Just . . . it's been quite a day,' I said, and nearly without noticing, out of a sudden, primeval need for solace, I leaned my head against his chest and wrapped my arms around his waist. He'd been much taller than me since the age of thirteen, sprouting up while I remained small, just like Mum. He held me tight, and the comfort was immeasurable. My brother was a part of me. He returned my hug, then gently pulled away.

'I need to go. I'm so sorry I have to leave you here alone . . .'

'It's work, you can't help it,' I said, and carefully placed the box, with the key and the photograph inside, in a bag by the door. Stephen looked around, and I with him. The room was bare, everything packed up. All trace of Mum was about to be gone. Everything had been loaded onto the van, clothes and books and knick-knacks, some to be thrown out, some to be donated, and some – the things she loved the most, our family memories – to come home with me.

Stephen seemed to fold his broad shoulders into himself, leaning towards me as if he wanted to shelter me from the painful reality.

'So . . . it's done,' he said softly.

'It's done,' I repeated, looking around the empty room again, and I could feel my eyes welling up. The day had been slow and painful, but even what seems to stretch for ever sooner or later comes to an end – and finally the sky was darkening outside, night was falling at last. Relief mixed with pain as this terrible chore was finally finished.

And life without my mother began.

'Will you be okay?' Stephen asked.

I tucked a strand of hair behind my ear. 'Of course. Of course. I'll be fine.'

'Yes, I know. I mean, I know you'll be fine. You're never not fine. Even when something like this happens, you seem to be able to navigate things.'

Did I? Because it didn't feel that way. I looked out of the window beside me, so that he couldn't see my face. My reflection shone vivid in the darkened glass, but the tears on my cheeks were hidden from sight. I stood there for a moment, my eyes moving to the anodyne prints on the wall – freesias, roses, a basket of fruit – looking at them but not seeing them. My right hand felt warm again from the key, my fingers burning. I flexed them, lost in thought.

The wooden box.

The key.

Gealach, Seal.

Something has called me were the words that exploded through my mind, unexpected, only partly understood.

That evening I sat in my living room, exhausted in body and soul. My dog, Sasha, lay at my feet, all silky fur and soft snoring. I had wrapped myself in an oversize cardigan, and the scent of melissa, orange and cinnamon wafted from a mug of herbal tea. I curled up in my armchair, too tired to do anything else, and undid the knot at the top of my head. My hair fell about my shoulders, like a curtain between me and the world. Every bone hurt from moving all those boxes – and from the grief of doing it.

I looked around me with tired eyes. I'd switched the lamps on, and a lovely fire was burning in my pellet stove – a rare thing in my neighbourhood – against the chill of early spring. With the bright, colourful tapestries I'd woven hanging on the walls, the bunches of herbs drying in the kitchen, every single surface covered with some work in progress – candles, soaps, the home-made skincare I sent all over the world – the warmth of the stove slowly filling the air, I should have felt so at home, so peaceful. I always did at 16 Pennington Road, not too far from Brick Lane, and still my haven from the world, the place where I'd lived all my life.

I seemed not to have noticed that the day had turned into night. I sat immobile, in silence. One by one the lights of the city went on: in the block of flats in front of my house, in the Sindhus' curry shop across the way, in the launderette beside it, in the little Spar with the office workers flocking in after their shifts. I knew that two streets down, the vendors of the East End markets were packing up their stalls to go home, the remains of a day's trading on the ground – bits of fruit and vegetables, leaflets and papers, empty boxes and food wrappers, all to be swept up early in the morning. Black and white and brown faces, jeans and saris and tunics, braided hair and headscarves, short skirts, suits and uniforms, the people of London were ending the working day. The familiar city constellations, made of artificial lights and lamp posts, were lighting up, and a new crowd, those who would populate the pubs and restaurants and work the night shift, was coming out. The chaotic, dirty, exciting hustle and bustle of an east London evening. The landscape of home.

Usually I enjoyed feeling the city all around me, contemplating from my window the crowds coming and going, looking at the silhouettes of people cooking and watching TV in the houses across the road; but tonight I was empty – there was no joy in my heart, and home just didn't feel like home.

Once, when we were children, my mum went to visit a sick friend up north. She'd never left Stephen before, and at the age of three, he was very upset. At dinner time, he crouched on the lino beside the fridge and burst into tears of grief and protest. 'This is not my house,' he said between sobs. Mum wasn't there, therefore this wasn't his house.

I felt like that now.

A lump formed in my throat again. In spite of the heat from the stove, I shivered. I'd been sitting here for nearly two hours, I realised, in a sort of haze of grief – what to do next? I just wanted to not exist, to stop feeling so empty, so full of grief. I was in a fog of tiredness and pain. Enough. It was time to move, to stop this terrible sadness seeping into my veins and making me sink deeper, deeper.

I gathered what was left of my strength and filled Sasha's bowls with food and water, then leaned against the kitchen table and surveyed the place. Mum's things sat in the middle of the room, the boxes and bags carefully, lovingly lined up. My eye fell on her treasured statue of the Virgin Mary, Star of the Sea, sticking out of one of the boxes. I remembered her saying the rosary in front of the statue every night and wondering why she was so devoted to it when none of our London-born-and-bred family had anything to do with the sea. Funny, Stephen had just told me I could navigate things. *Will you show me the way through this storm, Star of the Sea?*

I took the statue out and placed it on the coffee table, then sat cross-legged on the floor. I knew it was a bad idea, because I couldn't take any more emotion, but I decided to go through an old photo album. Images of my childhood – holidays, birthdays, Christmases – passed before my eyes, a tapestry made of many threads woven into each other to tell our story: my mum's, my dad's, my brother's and mine. Tears fell down my cheeks – I'd thought I had no more, but I was wrong – and small sobs shook my chest.

Mum. Mum. What will I do without you?
This is the time I won't make it, this is the time I won't be fine.
Where are you, Mum?

Was she really in heaven, as she'd firmly believed in life? Was she really in the arms of the Star of the Sea?

I once saw a movie in which the earth had spun off its axis – a tiny movement, nearly imperceptible, that still brought on a near-apocalypse. People were running around trying to avoid falling ice blocks and lightning storms, migrating birds got lost and died in the streets, the sea swallowed whole cities. And all this for a movement as small as the hundredth part of a degree. My mum's death had been like that – a tiny event in the big picture of things, no more than a minute shift of the axis, and yet it had brought a monumental change in my life, a change to everything I was, everything I loved, everything I'd built up to then. The axis had moved, the magnetic field had been disrupted – birds were flying aimlessly, the sky was sporting strange auroras, the sun was suddenly rising and setting in a different place. I existed in a world that had changed all its rules.

Sasha's nose rested against my bare leg, trying to give me comfort, but I kept sobbing, trying to dry my tears with my hand as they fell.

'Right, Sasha. Time to sleep,' I whispered. As I moved the cardboard boxes from the floor to the table one by one, just in case Sasha decided that something in them looked tasty, an object slipped out of a box and fell on the floor with a clatter. It was the box, the box with the key.

I knelt on the floor, tucked my hair behind my ears and placed the box on the palm of my hand.

And it called me, again.

I *had* to open it once more; and so I did, slowly, as if I were performing a ritual. My fingers curled around the key, and again I was flooded with strange emotion, as if all the colours around me were suddenly sharper, the noises louder. The words *Gealach, Seal* danced in front of my eyes and in my mind. I could feel my heart beating and my blood running in my veins, while thoughts exploded in my mind like fireworks.

I needed to remember.

There was something I needed to remember.

And then it was finished, and the key lay inert and cold on my skin. All of a sudden, my lids were so heavy I thought I might fall to my knees, curl up on the carpet and sleep there among my mother's belongings, like a baby falling asleep in its highchair. All the strength was gone from me.

I barely made it upstairs, where I threw myself on the bed, still holding the key. I just wanted to close my eyes in the darkness.

Sleep came so fast, so heavy, that it felt like anaesthetic. More than falling asleep, I tumbled into it, not even bothering to get undressed or pull the duvet over me. As I slipped away, still feeling the metal of the key on my palm, listening to Sasha softly snoring in her armchair, a strange scent reached my nostrils – a scent I couldn't recognise – and I was somewhere else, somewhere else entirely.

A dream came to me, playing itself in still images with sudden vivid scenes, like a black-and-white picture with brightly coloured details. I was on a grass-covered sand dune, the wind blowing strong on my face, in my ears, in my hair, red strands dancing in front of my eyes. Half hidden by a grassy mound in front of me was a grey stone cottage with a thatched roof, right on the beach. I made my way down the dune and stepped through what felt like a passageway – a stream in between two lips of land, with only a few inches of water running in it and broad, slippery grey stones as its pavement. I stood in front of the house, the sea behind me and at the same time in front of me, enveloping the cottage and me like we had both sailed away. Everything was drenched in golden light; the sun was setting over the horizon.

It was then that I saw her.

Her face shone white from the narrow window, her eyes gazing out to sea; the glare blurred her features, but I could see that her dress was a deep, dark vermilion, a splash of colour behind the grey glass, and that her hair was long and bright red, a shade lighter than mine, a hue I'd never seen before. She didn't look at me, though I was standing right in her eyeline; she was too busy scanning the sea to notice I was there. I shielded my eyes and tried to see, tried to make out her face to no avail – and then I glimpsed someone else out of the corner of my eye. It was a man, walking up the beach, the setting sun in his eyes, his face a golden blur. The moment I saw him, a warm, all-encompassing feeling washed over me. I *knew* him, and I hadn't seen him in a long time; but now, finally, he was back. I could have cried with joy and relief. Although the sun was in front of him, his face was still in shadow. I wanted to keep looking at him; it seemed to me that I was starving for him, and I'd been starved for a long time.

Suddenly the sky darkened and the glare disappeared, and I could see the window clearly. At that moment, the woman turned her eyes towards me, and a name resounded in my ears: *Margaret*. I trembled and blinked, trying again to make out her features . . .

I woke in the darkness, and for a moment I didn't know where I was. I was still full of my dream – or vision, should I say, because it had been so vivid, so real, and coming from such a strange, unnaturally deep sleep.

Margaret.

I'd nearly seen her face, but I'd woken an instant too soon. Sasha was on top of me, her nose against mine and a question in her soft dark eyes. The light of the street lamps, seeping through the window onto my wall, the silhouettes of my furniture, the weight of the dog; everything real mixed in my consciousness with the vastness of the sea, the golden light, the grass and the flowers swaying gently to and fro, to and fro. I could still feel the wind around me, and the long, deep shivers that had run through my body when the woman had looked at me from the dark window. A moment more, just a moment more, and I would have seen her face, and the man's too, but the dream had vanished and I'd been called back.

My hand met something cold and hard pressing against my side, under the duvet. The key. I must have brought it to bed with me and then forgotten.

The house was still and silent, and even the street outside, hardly ever completely empty of movement and sound, seemed to be suspended in stillness. Slowly reality seeped back and chased the dream away. I touched Sasha's silky fur, taking comfort in her loving presence, and hugged my knees. What had just happened? Was I the kind of person who had *visions*? Was I going crazy?

Yes, it was the most likely explanation. I was losing my mind.

It had felt good. For a moment, lost in the dream, I had forgotten how much strife there was in my life right now. How much pain. And the intense, heartbreaking, almost painful joy I'd felt when I saw the man had left me liquid inside.

Blinking sleep from my eyes, I wondered whether I had gone mad with grief. How else could I explain what I'd seen?

Cora

'Cora?'

'Yes. Yes, sorry. Didn't get much sleep last night,' I said.

Lorraine, my agent, raised her mint mojito and smiled. We'd had lunch at Sea Containers, and now we sat across each other in the adjacent bar, which apparently was a haven for celebrities – and no wonder: the view across the Thames was incredible.

The Thames was a restless river, I thought as I watched it. Like a motorway made of water, boats and barges forging up and down, endless bridges as far as the eye could see, standing arched like whalebones on a beach. It had no peace. Still, only yesterday I had loved just that about my city, about my river: that it never stood still, it always moved, it *created*. It made new things happen and old things finish, or simply built upon them, layer over layer. I was such a London girl; now, though, the Tube made me breathless and the sheer number of people made me feel as if I was alone in the world. I'd begun to feel overwhelmed by the noise and the smells of the city. Another consequence of the shifting axis, I supposed.

'You look so cute. As usual,' Lorraine said, interrupting my musings. I was wearing a shirt I'd made myself from a vintage flowery fabric, and a simple pair of jeans. I liked wearing home-made outfits with a retro twist – it was part of my work, making clothes with vintage and recycled cloth.

'Thank you, so do you,' I replied, and she certainly did look lovely in a stylish black leather skirt, her dark hair up in a ponytail. Her almond-shaped eyes were black and velvety, and she turned heads wherever she went.

'So. How is the writing going?' She took a sip of her cocktail and sat back on the chair, crossing her black-stockinged legs. And there they were, the words I'd feared and yet known she would say. My new book, *Lovemade* – the follow-up to *Heartmade*, my TV series and tie-in book – had been stalling since my mum's health had started to go downhill. Lorraine had been very supportive – she was one of my best friends and, after my mum, my most enthusiastic cheerleader. Had it not been for her, I would have kept weaving small tapestries in my studio, making my crafts in my kitchen and selling at markets. She'd made my career, and I was grateful. But as understanding as she might be, sooner or later I had to face my publishers and the ever-sliding deadline.

'Do you want me to tell you what you want to hear, or the truth?' I said tentatively.

Lorraine smiled, her dark eyes warm. 'Hey. With all you've been through recently . . . Don't worry. If we don't make the deadline again, they'll have to understand. What happened with your mum . . .'

'It's not . . . it's not *just* what happened with Mum.' I struggled to find the words. It was difficult for me to open up even to the closest of friends. I listened well but spoke little; that was just my way. 'It's that . . .'

'You're not inspired?' She tried to finish the sentence for me.

I shook my head and sighed. Give me some threads to weave into a design; a plant to tend, something to bake, something to knit – I'm in my element. Turning silence into words, restraining my thoughts into rigid structures . . . not so much.

'I *am* inspired. My work inspires me . . .' There was no doubt about that. I loved what I did. I'd created a job from nothing – blogging when nobody else did yet, holding workshops all over London, selling my products at farmers' markets, giving up evenings and nights and weekends, slowly making a name for myself. 'Just . . .'

Lorraine nodded. 'I get it. It's grief,' she said, and took another sip of her cocktail, leaving a trace of red lipstick on the glass.

A heartbeat, in which I debated trying to explain the way I felt and decided against it. I'd let Lorraine believe in her own explanation. I took a sip of my Campari and looked resolutely down. As long as she could renegotiate my deadline, I didn't need to tell her that I'd been feeling like a stranger in a strange land.

And maybe she was right, maybe it was grief. Or maybe grief was just the catalyst for something that had been long coming.

Anyway, *I just can't write* is not something an agent likes to hear.

'So, what's the plan now? Recover, rest and get to work refreshed?' she said.

I opened my mouth to try and explain. 'I suppose so. Things are changing so fast. It's hard to decide what to do next.'

'You always know what to do next.'

'Do I?' *You always seem to be able to navigate things . . .* Stephen's words echoed in my mind. And now Lorraine was saying the same thing. There seemed to be two Coras: the strong, balanced, resilient one that other people saw, and the vulnerable one who nobody knew. Not even myself, maybe.

'Yes,' Lorraine continued. 'The next project, the next skill you're going to learn. You know, I always envied you those qualities . . . your strength, your level-headedness . . .'

The having weird dreams and hearing voices.

The feeling lost and alone in your own home.

The unique sensation of trying to walk when your legs have been cut off.

'Mmmm. I don't know about that. I just keep going, like everybody else.'

'Well, you know I'm here, if there's anything I can do.'

'I know,' I said, and the kindness in her face made me look away, overwhelmed. But then I decided to seize the moment. 'Thank you. I just need more time to write *Lovemade*.'

'I'll discuss a revised deadline, don't worry. Just have a think about when you can hand in the book, and we can take it from there. But if you feel this project is not for you, we need to tell them sooner rather than later . . .'

'No, no. Of course not. I *want* to write *Lovemade*. I just need . . . I just need a bit longer. And some headspace.'

'And you'll have it. Promise. Look, my next meeting . . .' She shot a glance at her watch and then lifted her bag onto her lap, taking out her phone. 'I'll just call them and say I'll be late. So we can chat a little more.'

I put my hands up. 'No, it's fine. Go. Honestly.'

She looked at me, phone in hand. 'Will you be okay?'

'Of course. Of course I will be.' I smiled, a smile I didn't really feel and that Lorraine, knowing me well and being a perceptive woman by trade and personal inclination, didn't buy.

'Right, then. I'll call you tomorrow,' she said, and held me close to her. She smelled of expensive perfume – she always appeared sophisticated and yet unfussed, like a model on a day off. 'I want to see you again soon . . . and I mean as a friend, not your agent.'

'Yes. We'll speak tomorrow,' I said, and returned her hug.

'Remember, I'm in your corner, Cora.'

'I know.'

Lorraine left with one last wave, making her way

through the punters who stood between our table and the door, clustered round the bar. The crowd kept swelling, and I knew I wouldn't be allowed to sit at a table on my own for long. Suited young men, just out of work, ordered drinks and chatted, an imperceptible touch of brashness in their voices, a hint of competition. The girls and women looked lovely with their carefully put-together outfits and made-up faces: a tall woman in a tight yellow dress, whose black skin contrasted beautifully with the vibrant colour; a tiny brown-haired girl wearing a gossamer-thin pink top and a plaited silk skirt, a fairy in disguise. I looked at them as if we came from two different planets.

I stepped out of the restaurant, nearly having to elbow my way out. I'd hoped to be able to breathe outside, but it was rush hour, and the streets were full of people going home after work. I braced myself to face the bus, overflowing with people and travelling an inch an hour, and then the Tube, where, being so short, I always ended up unhappily nestled into somebody's armpit. All my life I'd loved the crowds, the hundreds of skin colours, the babble of different languages. I'd loved the shops, the voices, the noises, the dirty pavements where people walked and talked and lived their lives; London was my home, all those people were my home.

But not today.

Tilting axis.

I thought of Lorraine's words: that I always knew what to do next. Maybe once, but not any more. Maybe my mother had been the hidden compass inside me, and now that she was gone, I was lost.

Darkness was gathering in the corners of the sky, the shop windows lighting up one by one. In the dusky light, I saw that there was someone sitting on my doorstep – Stephen, hair sticking up, his work bag beside him. My heart soared on seeing him. 'Hey, silly. Why did you not wait for me inside?'

Stephen got up, six feet of energy and wrinkled clothes. 'Hey. I didn't have my key with me. You insist on not having a phone, so I just waited,' he said quite cheerfully, without reproach. Not having a phone was just another consequence of my obsession with living simply, and he accepted it – most of the time.

Sasha began to bark and scratch beyond the door. 'Did she go crazy when she heard you?' I said, pushing the key in.

'She didn't hear . . .' but he couldn't finish the sentence, because a hairy copper-coloured tornado leapt on him, her tail wagging so hard her whole body was wagging too. Sasha loved my brother, and she was even ready to forgive the fact that he was her vet. Stephen stood unsteadily, trying to keep her in his arms by propping her up with a knee. They were both unwilling to accept that she wasn't a puppy any more, and too heavy to be picked up. Where Sasha was concerned, Stephen was like an indulgent father – he couldn't say no.

I laughed as he placed a hand on Sasha's bottom,

trying to hold her up. 'I thought a vet would know how to discipline a spoiled dog!'

'She's my *girl*. God, Sasha. Either you go on a diet or I start weightlifting. Down you go . . . there. Are you feeling okay, Cora? You're so pale again . . . These days you look like the Bride of Dracula.'

'Charming! I'm fine, thanks. The Tube was packed, and I didn't sleep much last night. I'll make us tea. Come on,' I said, leading him to the kitchen.

'So what was it today? Weaving baby blankets from kelp?'

I laughed. Stephen had a gentle way of teasing me and my passions. 'I met Lorraine in town, and, you know, I tried to write . . .'

'Tried?'

'Yes. The book that doesn't want to be written,' I said, and I must have looked particularly despondent, because Stephen gazed at me with concern.

'Forget the tea. Let me cook something for you and we can chat, okay?'

I smiled. 'You, cook?'

He shrugged. 'As in, let me go across the road and grab some fish and chips.'

'That's more realistic,' I laughed, while Sasha's tail wagged like crazy at the mention of the familiar but forbidden treat.

Half an hour later, we were sitting at my kitchen table in front of a greasy, delicious dinner still in its wrapping. Fish and chips makes no sense on plates, I always think.

'You know, I've been thinking a lot about that little box we found yesterday,' Stephen said. He wasn't the only one. 'I don't know why. It's just . . . well, Mum made quite a stringent choice of things to bring into Holy Heart. She wasn't always lucid at that time, but she knew what mattered: Granny's jewellery, her prayer books, the statuette of Our Lady' – he waved towards it, sitting on my chest of drawers – 'and the box. It must have meant a lot to her. And the weird thing is, we knew nothing about it. Neither of us had seen it before.'

'But we helped her sort her stuff. So if we didn't see it . . .'

'She must have slipped it in secretly,' Stephen said, and a strange prickling spread through my chest, my hands.

'But why?'

Stephen opened his hands, as if to say, *Who knows?* 'Anyway, this is for you.' He rummaged in his work case and took out a Waterstones bag. Inside was a small book: *A Travel Guide to the Hebrides.*

'Is that a hint?' I laughed. 'Are you saying I need a holiday?'

'We both do. But that's not why I bought it. Look, go to page . . . thirty-two, I think . . .'

I thumbed through until I got to the page he'd said – and nearly dropped the book. There was a breathtaking picture of a dark, dramatic sky, and the title at the top of the page simply said: *Seal.*

'So that's where it is,' I whispered, unable to unglue my eyes from the dark sky, beneath it what looked like a giant eye made of water: Corrywreckan, the caption said, the biggest whirlpool in Europe. It was easy to imagine a sea monster under there, scaly head and fins, mouth open to swallow boats and men. For a moment, I couldn't look away.

'Yes. Seal is in Scotland, like we thought. So that's the Scottish connection, Uncle Skirt's kilt and all that. That other word, Gealach . . . it *is* Gaelic, like we thought. I googled it, and it means "moon". Where's the key, by the way?'

'Oh, I put it away,' I said quickly. The last thing I wanted was something strange to happen in front of my brother, some preternatural tiredness, or voices, or a dream. 'But here's the photo.' It was propped against the statue of Our Lady.

He took it from my hand and looked at it thoughtfully. 'Isn't it weird, the way we found that box? Very *Twilight Zone*-y . . .'

You don't know the half of it, I thought. Should I tell him about the dream? I wasn't worried about him judging me, thinking I was crazy – I just feared he would worry about me. But I was desperate to confide in someone. It would have been reassuring to share these visions I'd been having, somehow banishing them from the realm of the crazy to everyday life.

'When was Mum in Scotland?' Stephen asked, shaking me out of my thoughts.

'What?'

'If that picture was taken on the island of Seal, *when*

was it taken? I don't remember her leaving us for any long periods.'

'It must have been before we were born or when we were very small, because I can't recall her going away without us either. Except . . .' That time when Stephen had sat on the floor crying. 'Remember when she went to see a sick friend, somewhere up north . . .'

'Yes, I was distraught,' he said.

'You were. Funny, that memory came into my mind just yesterday. That's the only time I remember Mum going away. They seem so close in that picture, she and Aunt Toffee . . . But I can't remember Aunt Toffee being around at all.'

'I can, mainly because of the toffee, as you can guess. But at some point, she just vanished.'

'Maybe they had a falling-out.'

'Mum, falling out with a friend? Unlikely.'

'True,' I said, and I felt the revelations gathering on my tongue; I was desperate to confide in Stephen.

'We'll probably never know what happened,' Stephen continued. 'Especially if we can't remember her real name. I suppose what I'd really like to know is what the key is for—'

'Stephen. Something happened,' I blurted out, getting up. The words were out of my mouth before I could rein them in. And maybe it was right that way; maybe it was right for my brother to know, as crazy as it all seemed. 'It's difficult to explain . . .'

36

'Try me.'

'I . . . I had a dream. When I touched the key. You know, Mum's key.' Stephen raised his eyebrows. Clearly he didn't know where I was heading with this. I stood up and began making coffee, just to have something to do with my hands. 'Okay, the thing is . . . I dreamed of this place. There was sea all around . . . and a house with grey walls, and a woman at the window . . .'

'Did it upset you?'

'Not as such. It's just that I think it has something to do with the key.'

'Listen. I'll tell you where all this is coming from. Mum is always on our minds, and then we found the box . . . You mixed it all up in your head, and it came out a bit like a film.'

I opened my mouth to argue. *There's something more about all this. Please listen to the things I can't explain and the words I can't find.* 'Yes. Yes, of course,' I said instead, deflated.

Stephen smiled, and I mirrored his smile – strange how sometimes a smile is like tears, really, like a way of crying that doesn't show as much. 'I just want you to be happy,' he said. 'And I know you haven't been happy in a long time.'

'Same here,' I said, and I took in his face, so similar to mine with its light green eyes and pale skin, the scattered freckles and the way he had to look down when he was saying something important. I knew my brother so well, I could detect his most imperceptible mannerisms, and now I knew he was trying to tell me something.

'You know what I've been wondering?' he said. And somehow, I was sure of what was coming next.

'What?'

'Whether Mark got in touch. I mean, after the funeral.' There we go. Of course.

Mark was my ex-boyfriend. We'd been together since I was seventeen, until he'd asked me to move in with him and I'd said no, much to my family's chagrin. That was nearly three years ago now.

'Stephen . . .'

'I know, I know. But has he?'

'He sent a card.'

'Right.' A beat. 'I like the guy, Cora. I can't help it. He was good for you.'

'Mark wants to settle down and I don't. That's why we broke up. Things haven't changed. And anyway, he signed the card "Mark and Rose".'

'They've split up.'

'How do you know?'

'Mark's mum told me.'

'You speak to Mark's mum?'

'I met her in the launderette, that's all. Look, I'm the last person to advocate settling down, but then I'm not a thirty-odd-year-old woman . . .'

'Because at thirty-one you might as well hurry or you'll be left on the shelf, I suppose!' I snapped, my eyes wide.

'Ah, stop it, Cora, you know I just want the best for you.'

'I know. I know.' I turned away, suddenly feeling as if I

was suffocating. In this city, in this house, in this life. 'I can't fabricate something I don't feel. I just can't. It's as simple as that.'

Stephen nodded. 'No. You can't fabricate a feeling. I know exactly what you mean, because . . . well, you know my thing with girls . . .'

'Yes, I do. I have one word for you: Iona. Ah, no, wait. I have quite a few more!'

'I know, I know. I just don't seem to be able to . . . Well, I *fall* in love, and then I don't *stay* in love. Oh God, this has got heavy.'

'Mmmm. I can't fall in love at all,' I said, and the weight and intimacy of those words was too much, even with my brother.

'We haven't even got the excuse of a dysfunctional family,' Stephen said.

'You'd be hard pressed to call our family dysfunctional.' I smiled, recalling the loving looks and hugs between my parents, the cuddles they gave us, the peaceful atmosphere of our home.

'Maybe that's it. We were so happy, the four of us, and then the three of us when Dad passed away, that nothing quite compares. Or maybe . . .' He shrugged.

'Maybe?' I said, a lump in my throat.

'Maybe our hearts are just asleep.'

'Yeah.' I nodded, keeping a frown resolutely on my brow, trying not to cry, busying myself with pouring the coffee. 'That's it. Our hearts are asleep.'

And then I remembered the dream. Maybe my heart

was beginning to awaken. But it was awakening to an empty landscape, and solitude.

After Stephen left, I stood in front of my bedroom mirror. I tilted my head to one side, meeting my eyes in the glass. A cascade of wavy red hair. Thin pale hands, half hidden by red velvet – no, that wasn't me. That was the girl in my dream ... But those images had been so intense, they'd felt as corporeal, as *alive* as my reality. I ran my hands over my hair, my waist, my hips. I was myself, and yet I'd been *her*. I'd felt her feelings.

My hand encountered a little hard bump on my side – the key, sleeping in my jeans pocket. I slid my fingers inside and touched it . . .

And for a moment, a single, magical moment, I thought I heard a voice softly calling.

Cora.

Cora.

Many times in that house my name had been called. The voices were still there, trapped in the corners of the ceilings, in the fissures of the wooden floor, in the walls themselves, along with the layers of voices and conversations that had taken place there year after year. The house was full of *Cora, Cora*, memories of people coming and going and looking for me – today, yesterday, ten years ago.

And now, woven into the fabric of all these voices, there was another voice, another call, different from the others. A voice coming from far away, another frequency entirely. And then another word, one I didn't understand. Not my name any more, but someone else's; a whisper so low, so imperceptible, you could easily believe it had never happened. Strange, but it seemed to me that with the whisper came a soft draught, like a gentle gust of wind, but so delicate that it was more like the ghost of a wind that had once blown somewhere else, at some other time.

I closed my eyes, hoping it would happen again, and that maybe this time I could make out the whispered word, but there was only silence. There was just me and the darkness of the room; the street lights outside, Sasha's quiet snoring. The tap-tap-tap of rain on the windows, the distant rumble of a bus somewhere, car headlights tracing a yellow arc on the wall. One by one the sights and noises around me returned to my consciousness.

Mum? Was it you?

Was it you?

But there was no answer.

I'd brought the Star of the Sea upstairs, together with the photo of my mum and Aunt Toffee. Their smiling faces watched over me from my bedside table. I picked it up and studied the image. Mum and her friend stood in front of what appeared to be a whitewashed wall; behind them, barely visible, was a door – a red door, it seemed, though only the outer frame was visible. I narrowed my eyes, peering, and made out a square tile just beside the door, peeking out from behind Aunt Toffee's skirt. Maybe that could tell me more. I ran downstairs, taking the steps two at a time, and grabbed the magnifying glass I used for textiles.

There. The tile said *LACH*.

Was this Gealach?

My heart was beating in double time; something told me I was on the right path. A sleepy Sasha followed me as I went to switch on the laptop. After some searching, I found what I was looking for – someone who could help me find out what and where Gealach was, if it still existed at all.

> *To: Alistair McDaid, Islay, Eilean and Seal Homes*
> *Dear Mr McDaid,*
>
> *My name is Cora Gale and I'm writing from London. I wonder if you can help me. My mother, Beatrice Lamb Gale, passed away recently, and while going through her things I found a box with a key in it. There's a label on the key that says 'Gealach, Seal'. I'm wondering if it's the key to a property on Seal, maybe somewhere called Gealach? I would be very grateful if you could help solve this little mystery, though I understand it's a long shot. Below is my phone number. Feel free to call me if it's not too much trouble.*
>
> *Best regards,*
> *Cora Gale*

Pressing send felt like stepping onto a rope bridge over an abyss, hoping it would hold. Hoping what awaited as I took the first step was safe passage.

All I had to do now was wait.

The first thing I did when I awoke, still sleepy from a night spent thinking about Seal, was to check my email:

no reply from the Hebridean estate agent. I sighed and fell back on the pillow.

The city woke too, and my house with it. As Lucy, my employee, arrived and settled down to work, a courier came to collect two small tapestries I'd been commissioned for a boutique, and cup after cup of coffee was made. I ignored the siren song of my loom, where I was working on some beautiful, earthy-smelling Shetland wool, and instead sat at the computer, determined to get the writing going, while half of my brain listened out for the phone or the pinging of my inbox.

The phone rang several times: the beekeeper I bought beeswax for my candles from; someone trying to sell me a mattress; a girlfriend inviting me to a baby shower. Each time my heart leapt into my throat and then sank again. How busy could Mr McDaid be? How much buying and selling happened on those little islands? Surely he'd find the time to write or call. Unless he thought it was some weird email not worth following up.

The evening shadows were beginning to fall as I stood in front of the living-room window, more despondent than I had any right to be. My reflection shone in the darkening glass – no tears, this time, just eyes that seemed so far away, it felt like they belonged to someone else.

And then the phone rang again.

Weird – the ring was always the same, of course, but to my ears, this time it sounded different. It *had* to be the call I was waiting for.

'Miss Gale?' The Scottish accent hurried my heart.

'It's Alistair McDaid here, from Islay. I received your email.'

A beat, as I breathed in. 'Yes, yes, like I said in my message—' I took another breath, longer, preparing myself to explain, but he interrupted me.

'I took the liberty of doing some research for you. The property is indeed on Seal. Gealach Cottage.' He pronounced Gealach in such a beautiful way, it was like hearing a miniature song. 'The owner is a Beatrice Lamb, of 16 Pennington Road, London, E1 8GP. You said in your email that Mrs Lamb is your late mother?'

'Yes,' I said in a thin voice.

'Well, as your mother has passed away, I suppose the owner of Gealach might now be yourself.'

I remember every word of that conversation, every single word. The man at the other end of the line had no idea, but he had just set me on a journey, an inevitable one – one I felt was written in the stars.

In the gathering shadows, I stood looking at the picture of the cottage, so far from here it might as well be on another planet. I had to go there. I needed to go. I had no idea what awaited for me, but can we really plan every step of our way? Life throws up unexpected twists, and now it was taking me to an aqua-coloured world under huge, windswept skies, where maybe I would find a part of my mother I had never known existed.

Or, said a voice in my head, a long-lost part of me.

Margaret

Glen Avich, 1744

'My feet are about to fall off,' my cousin Mairi whined, her face flushed, her dark hair shiny with moisture. I stayed quiet. I had no strength for complaints or consolation – I had to save it all for the long march. 'Easy for you!' she continued. 'You're strong as an ox. To think my aunt fretted so much over you, small and sickly as you were . . .' I refrained from saying that I was *not* as strong as an ox, I just didn't complain. Ever. There was no point. It didn't help anyone and only brought your spirits down. 'And it's going to rain,' she said, adding to our list of woes, kicking her long skirts sulkily with every step.

'Oh well, it'll refresh us!' Ally said, forever cheerful. He was only twelve, and I was sure the long journey had taken a lot out of him, but he was too sunny-natured to let it show.

'It'll chill us to the bone!' Mairi said, and I had to agree with her.

The dark sky was reflected in the expanse of Loch

Avich, the wind slowly rising and rippling the surface. I gazed into the water as I walked along the shore. My feet were hurting terribly and I was starving, but if I stopped I would never start again. We'd been travelling for over three days with not much food and hardly any sleep, eastwards through moors and forests towards Castle Innes. I was impatient to arrive. Impatient and just a little bit frightened, though I would not have admitted that to anyone.

I lifted the hood of my homespun cape over my head, waiting for the downpour. My mother was right: Loch Avich *was* black, darker than my beloved Loch Awe. She'd told me as much as she lay dying, and described the island right in the middle, the one I was looking at now, black against the grey sky, all rocks and wind-bent trees. I could easily have cried again, remembering my darling mother and her white fingers through my hair, her soft kiss and the way she held me so dear. But I would not. I was not to cry; I was to survive.

In her agony, my mother was afraid not for herself but for me, afraid to leave me with my father and his family, who'd used up all the love they had on my dark-haired, docile brothers and sisters and had none left for me, red-haired and not exactly malleable. Mairi and Ally too were rejects – children of a poor branch of the family and orphaned young. It was telling that even in these troubled times, nobody could be found to escort us to Castle Innes – we were to go as servants, on foot and alone, and if we needed help, we would have to find it ourselves. My thoughts went to the dagger hidden in the folds of my skirts, and the other one, the small, near-invisible one, that they would not find unless they stripped me naked.

Our family had fallen on hard times, had fallen far and fast; my father had lost most of his power and influence after breaking the alliance with the Inneses, for a reason I was not to know, in circumstances I was not to talk about. I wasn't concerned about wealth or power – I was at my happiest in the herb garden I'd set up, or in the woods looking for medicine plants, away from my brothers and sisters, who couldn't conceal their hostility towards me, and from my father, who could not hide his silent scheming. My mother was always in her room, slowly fading – trouble in her lungs, the white death that claimed more people than any other ailment, more even than the sword. But now that she was gone, and with Father planning to use me as a bargaining chip, to marry me off in exchange for some petty political alliance that would never restore him to his old power anyway, there was nothing left for me to do but leave.

Before I left, my father gave me one last chance to change my mind, and offered marriage to Robert Moffat, a fifty-year-old merchant who looked like he'd just survived a bad case of scurvy, with thin limbs and a curved back. My father said I could not hope for more – at twenty years old I was already second-rate goods, not to mention that people said I was a changeling because I liked herbs and plants, and because of this hair of mine, so red you could see it at night, my mother used to say.

She said it sweetly – she loved my hair – whereas when my father declared that nobody would want to see my face first thing in the morning and last thing at night because I had eyes that burned, it wasn't meant as a compliment. If I stayed in Lochawe, the best I could hope for was marriage to a man whose legs were the size of my arms. No thank you.

There was another reason why I'd agreed to go to Castle Innes: my aunt, Helen Beaton, was known as a healer and an apothecary, and I wanted to learn from her. She was my father's sister, but I hoped she'd not inherited his peevishness and temper. I wanted to master the art of healing, to do more than get married and have children or help Lady Innes do her hair. I wanted to be useful.

And now here I was, walking along Loch Avich, nearly there. It had started to rain, and neither Mairi nor Ally was talking any more, both their faces invisible under their hoods. Our feet splashed and slipped in the muddy grass. I remembered every step of that long, long walk, the rain dripping from my soaked hair, how ruined my feet were when we lay in the heather at night and I finally took off my rough leather boots. Dark, confused dreams of ravens with pointed beaks and oily wings twirled in my mind all night, until I woke my cousins, and, after a small meal of oatcakes and water, we started again. But now the journey was almost finished at last. When the grey stones of Castle Innes appeared in the distance, my heart soared and my stomach churned at the same time. There lay my future, whatever it might be.

Innes

I woke with a splitting headache and a dry mouth. Something was buzzing somewhere. For a moment, I didn't know where I was – I didn't recognise the white walls, or the smell of summer and gasoline mixed together, wafting off the streets and seeping through the window. Then, slowly, it came back to me. I was home, if you could call this anonymous three-room flat in a strange city *home*. The dry mouth and the pounding headache weren't a hangover, likely as that might be, but jet lag. I'd been to Colombia – two weeks in the thick, humid air of the Pantanal, powered by coffee as strong as a punch in the face, had drained me. Summoning the little energy I had left, I rummaged in the mound of clothes I'd left on the floor when I'd come in, until my hand curled around the buzzing phone.

'Innes.'

'Just the man.' In spite of my fuzzy head, I recognised my agent's voice at once. After ten years of working as a wildlife cameraman, I was never short of jobs – I had no family or ties, the kind of guy who could leave for the other side of the world with four hours' notice and was fine not to come home for months at a time. The kind who didn't *have* a home. Perfect for this job. 'How are you?'

'Absolutely great, as usual,' I rasped.

'Yes, I can hear that from your voice.'

'You're phoning me in the middle of the night because . . .'

'It's two in the afternoon, Innes.'

'In London, maybe.'

'No. In San Francisco. Where you are now.'

'Oh.'

I opened the curtains and realised that the blackout blind was down. When I rolled it up, the blinding light of the Californian spring afternoon filled the room. I blinked and shielded my eyes. Born and bred in Scotland, a place of gentle silver light, I could never get used to strong sunlight, even if I'd been away from Scotland since I was seventeen years old.

'The main guy is looking for you.'

'Who's the main guy?'

'Crispin White.'

Oh. Crispin White was a director and producer with a huge reputation in the business. He worked on low-budget, small-distribution documentaries that brought in hardly any money but were jewels of beauty and integrity.

'Good. Is it Land and Sea Productions, then?'

'It is indeed. This one's on Seal Island; you heard of the place?'

No words came to me. Only a vision of waves, grey waves, and an empty space where a little boy's trust used to be. Oh yes, I'd heard of Seal Island.

'Innes?'

'Not happening.'

'You crazy?'

'Look, I can't, okay?'

'You don't even know when it is!'

'It's not a matter of schedule. I just can't.'

'Alan . . .'

'It's *Innes*.'

'Sorry. I don't understand. You've coveted this for ages . . . to work for Crispin White—'

'Well I don't any more,' I said, and I didn't care if I sounded childish. This wouldn't happen; it was as simple as that. I would not go back to Seal Island.

'Crispin wants you. Of all the people he could have, he asked for you.'

'Well he can't have me.'

'Why? You're Scottish, aren't you? Do you not want to go home for a bit?'

A pause. 'Goodnight, Mike.'

'It's two in the aft—'

I put the phone down.

It was impossible to go back to sleep, though my limbs felt like lead and my head was full of cotton wool. Just hearing those words – Seal Island, and Alan, my own name, the name my father had given me and that I'd tried to leave behind for ever – had been enough to send adrenaline coursing through my veins. Exhausted and wired, the worst combination.

I could think of something that would make it all better, of course, and it was only two flights of stairs and a hundred yards away. Twenty dollars would get me enough to relax me, then forget, then pass out again.

And then I would wake up with empty bottles on the floor and the smell of alcohol seeping through my skin, knowing that I had failed once again. But this would happen much, much later, in a time and place that seemed far away, the consequences out of focus, while the relief that alcohol would bring me was right in front of me, tantalising, calling me, offering me respite, promising to make me forget.

Forget, forget, forget, Alan. Alan is not your name. Those memories are not there. It never happened.

You never heard your name screamed in anger; your skin never broke under the blows.

You were never on Seal Island. In fact, the place didn't even exist.

Then why was I walking slowly, almost blindly, towards the kitchen; why was I crouching down and opening a cupboard I never went into, and reaching for a box I never opened? What was I doing with a crumpled, yellowed card – a birthday card – the writing inside faded and stained? A simple birthday wish, and then three letters; three letters that made me sick with anger and resentment and longing, and a homesickness that twisted my guts.

Three letters, a signature: *Mum*.

I dozed off, and then . . . was it dawn already? The sun was blinding, even if it was still low on the horizon. I blinked, feeling my eyes dry and raw, swallowing sip after sip of strong, bitter coffee.

Jet lag, difficult decisions and ghosts from the past don't mix well. I was a mess.

A good way to shut down your brain and stop thinking is to ingest some alcohol, anything going. Amazing how it works. A dram of whisky and your muscles loosen; another one and everything looks rosy; yet another and you don't care if you live or die. All the world is gone, all the memories are gone and you are free. It doesn't last long. One glass after another, and then the bottle, and it doesn't even matter what you're drinking as long as you're blotting it all out. And then you get angry. Your voice is superimposed on the voice from the past, until they're one.

Until you're *him*. The Guy.

I'd learned, though. I knew how to drink without anyone noticing. I knew how to drink in between, so I'd keep functioning.

Maybe running water would help me think, help me decide. I stepped into the shower and closed my eyes.

Decide?

Really? Had the island not given me enough strife,

enough pain? Did I really need to *decide* whether I was going back for more?

Sometimes you need to walk away and not look back. Doesn't matter if what you leave behind is a mess, if memories haunt you, if the child inside you, the child you used to be, never stopped screaming. You just have to go.

Then why could I not stop thinking of the Seal proposal, the sound of the sea in my ears, the memory of the wind in my hair, the sweet roll of the hills behind my closed eyelids?

Seal, Seal . . .

Some things are better left alone, because once they're awake, they won't leave *you* alone. When I left that living hell on my island home, I left someone behind. Someone I couldn't help loving, because my love for her was written in my very cells. The water ran, the faces of the people I'd lost danced in my mind. The reasons why I was alone, a whole ocean between me and the place I was born, burned me and would never stop.

I rubbed my eyes and slowly walked to the wardrobe, hunting for clean clothes. I grabbed a pair of jeans and a T-shirt from among all my outdoor gear – and that was when I saw it: Letty's shirt, white with the tiniest pink flowers, buried under mounds of my own clothes. When I'd broken up with her, I'd put all her belongings in cardboard boxes and driven them over to her house, but I'd forgotten that shirt, accidentally on purpose. I could have put it in an envelope and sent it to her, but I couldn't bear to get rid of it. Her white, white face when I told her it was over was etched in my memory. The hurt in her eyes, her broken voice. The pain, the anger.

She didn't understand I was doing it for her. That I was doing her a favour, saving her from the life my mum had, and my sister-in-law too, though only for a short time.

The warm water helped clear my thoughts a little. I turned the tap all the way to the blue and gasped under the sudden freezing cascade, my skin puckering up all over. It hurt, and that was good. And then it came to me.

A memory, stronger than everything else.

A strong hand keeping my head underwater as I struggled to breathe . . .

I swallowed.

Anger kills you. Anger eats you up inside and spits you out, changed, cruel, ready to put other people through what you've been through.

Forget, forget.

Forget Seal Island.

I'd run away years ago and would never go back. I would keep on running, from the island, from myself.

Running.

And running.

Empty and alone and exhausted, a demon at my heels, a demon that was my father, or maybe myself. A demon that would never leave me alone, because it was inside me.

There was no escape.

But instead of just leaving it, putting it all away in the

corner of my mind that guarded everything to do with Seal, I found myself dialing my agent's number.

'It's Innes . . . Yeah, I'll do it. He can phone me for details.'

It was time to face the demon, to drag it into the light, and either kill it or die trying.

Cora

I stood on the ferry deck, the coldest wind I'd ever felt on
my face, in my hair. It had all seemed spectacular enough
as I sat on my sofa watching the documentary *Hebrides*,
wanting to see what was ahead of me, but being here was
something else entirely. I could not have foreseen the
beauty, the peace, the sense of harmony that exuded from
the sea, mirroring the sky in shades of grey and sweet light
blue; and the way the coast in turn mirrored the sea in its
waves, its hills and mounds and valleys, up and down like
a song. Nothing here was man-made, unlike London,
where nothing was left that had not been shaped by man.

Being here was like a dream. I closed my eyes, my
hands on the iron rail around the deck, and let the wind
seep into me, laden with salt and spiced by the hint of
pine and juniper and smoke that wafted from somewhere
on land. I thought I heard a distant sound – a low, elem-
ental noise of water whirling, whirling: Corrywreckan,
or my imagination? Beside me, Sasha sat still and calm,
her long ears blowing in the breeze, occasionally lifting
her head, her black nose quivering to smell the world

around her. She seemed to like the water. Seagulls screamed overhead; a crewman dropped some heavy ropes; a father called his son to join him below deck.

And then silence fell.

Sasha and I were alone on the deck. I think I held my breath as we slowly sailed inside a fog bank, and all the world turned white and soft and secret. The horizon was invisible, and the mounds and shapes of the nearby islands had dissolved into nothing. With the mist and the silence came a strange feeling – heat burning me up all of a sudden, and then cold filling my bones and making me shiver. Like the moment I'd touched the key for the first time . . .

I rubbed my forehead and held the collar of my jacket tighter around my neck as the ferry slowly advanced. As I shivered and peered into the thick white mist, I noticed something to the left of me – a splash of colour – together with the uncomfortable feeling of being observed in a moment when you know that your face and body are revealing your innermost thoughts. Standing at the far corner of the deck was a man with blond hair and a short red beard, something in his face made him look like he came from another time. But then everything in this fog, moving slowly on a dreaming sea, seemed from another time or another world. He wore a camouflage jacket, and a huge backpack sat at his feet next to a square black box. Maybe it was a musical instrument. As soon as he saw me looking back at him, he turned away to gaze out to sea, but before he'd managed to do that, our eyes met, and I knew I'd seen him somewhere before.

It was just a moment – a moment where I saw black, then felt a cold, wet, steely surface against my cheek – and suddenly I wasn't there any more, but with someone else. I could see my own hand – it was very white and thin, I remember thinking – pressing something against damp, hard stone. And then another hand – this one large, with long, strong fingers – coming to cover mine, hold my fingers and squeeze them until my small hand disappeared in his.

And then I was back, I was myself again. The first face I saw was that of the blond man, his ice-blue eyes. I was lying on the deck, my head in his lap, and he was holding my hands and saying things I couldn't make out. 'I'm going to call someone,' I heard all of a sudden, and he was disentangling his fingers from mine. Was he leaving me? Was he going to let go of my hands?

'No. No. Stay,' someone said, and a part of me recognised my own voice.

'Okay. Okay. Don't worry. I'll stay,' he replied, but by then I was back to full consciousness, and I knew who I was and where I was. I cringed at what I'd just said and pulled my hands away in embarrassment and sat up, then started to get back to my feet. The man with the ice-blue eyes tried to help, but I refused with a mumbled 'I'm fine.' I quickly looked for Sasha's leash – thankfully she'd stayed beside me all the while – and held it tight again. Instinctively I brought my hands up to my eyes and studied them – still thin and small, but not as white, and wearing my little enamel owl ring. Definitely my own hands.

'I'm so sorry. I must have had a dizzy spell . . .'

But I had no time to think, no time to examine the vision in my mind, because all of a sudden the grey silhouette of Seal was emerging out of the mist. I turned to thank the stranger – had I really been lying with my head in his lap, had he really been holding my hands? – but he was gone. I caught a glimpse of his jacket as he moved among the other passengers getting ready to step off the ferry, a sudden strange regret seizing my heart, and then he disappeared. I lifted myself on my toes to look over the heads of the few bystanders, searching for him. But he really wasn't there any more; I would have seen him, because there wasn't exactly a crowd.

And anyway, what would I have said to him? *Hi, please don't go?* The key-related dreams and visions were strange enough, but to add a sudden faint, leaning my head on a stranger's lap and growing convinced I'd seen him before . . . Clearly it had been a trick of the mind, the excitement of coming to Seal, and of all that was ahead of me. I put it out of my mind.

I drove off the ferry, parked as close to the pier as I could and stepped out to take a good look at the beauty of this place. As I stood next to the car and gazed around me, my heart soared. It just *soared*, for no other reason than that everything was breathtakingly beautiful and pure, and it made me feel like I was in some windswept northern Eden.

Salt in my hair, sea spray on my face; the black, black

eyes of a seal, and another, and another, peeking out of the water; the yellow flowers – what were they? Broom? And beyond the flowers . . . As I lifted my gaze, for a moment I forgot where I was. A row of multicoloured houses where trees and stone cottages should be . . . No, that was not what I'd thought I would see. I blinked. The landscape I should have been contemplating was clear in my mind for a moment – dark trees, and brown and purple hills dotted with stone houses and thatched roofs – but where would I have seen that?

Why was I expecting something different from what was there?

Maybe I'd seen a picture in the book Stephen had given me, or maybe it was a scene from the documentary I'd watched.

I took a deep breath, letting the cold, pure air fill my lungs, then started walking, clutching the Gealach key in my pocket. I was looking for the Seal Inn, where I would ask for . . . what was it, a strange name? I took out my scribbled note from my pocket, Alistair's instructions: *Seal Inn – ask for Sorren.* Right.

Oh well. The only way was ahead. The old Cora would have scurried straight back home to her safe, familiar environment, the nest she'd built for herself, but the new Cora walked on. Sasha trotted at my side, so excited, she could barely keep in a straight line. A million new scents were making her little black nose quiver, and her eyes were shining, much like the seals' eyes, I thought.

I was quite sure I'd stepped back in time, as I walked

towards the coloured houses and onto the main street, following Alistair's directions. I was still a bit shocked after what had happened with the blond stranger, and passing out that way. Thankfully nobody else had seen me fainting, or they would have insisted on taking me to a doctor, and I was fine, just a bit . . . overwhelmed. As I walked, I suddenly caught sight of a tall blond man wearing a camouflage jacket a few hundred yards in front of me. My heart barely had time to skip a beat before he disappeared into a side street. Looking at him from afar, I realised that his hair reminded me of something or someone – but there was no time to wonder who.

The street was half empty and cobbled, and the shops were quiet. A sweet scent I didn't recognise filled my nostrils, and I sensed the light beginning to change ever so slightly, ever so slowly, the milky air turning lilac, the first sign of the long Scottish dusk. My eye was caught by a small alcove dug into a stone wall and covered in glass; inside was a tiny statue of Our Lady, Star of the Sea, holding the baby Jesus, who in turn was holding the North Star. At her feet were crudely carved boats.

I stopped in my tracks. I couldn't believe it. To find the Star of the Sea here! Mum's statuette was in the car, carefully wrapped – I'd brought it so that I could have a piece of her there with me. It was just a moment, but I suddenly saw her – wrapped in a dressing gown, sitting on the bed that had been hers and Dad's and where now she was sleeping alone; she was saying the rosary, her eyes fixed on the statue as if it could help her keep her course, slowly fingering the beads and then letting them go ... Of course, I had read that Seal was a Catholic island, while others had a Protestant majority. Maybe finding the Star of the Sea was an omen. A good omen, like coming home.

Finally, the sign I was looking for came into view: Seal Inn. A narrow alley led me into an inner courtyard, on the far side of which was a whitewashed building, its windows shining golden, music seeping out of them. When I opened the door, the sound of fiddles and a delicious warmth washed over me, and I longed to step in; but I wasn't sure what to do with Sasha, so I just stood there for a moment, looking around me.

The music was in full flow and I desperately wanted to tap my foot – the cascade of rippling notes, the fiddle and the accordion and something else, a kind of pipes but lighter, sweeter, was irresistible. I couldn't see the musicians, though, as the tune was coming from somewhere off the main room. There was a lovely sweet scent in the air – I recognised the same scent I'd smelled outside, and now I knew what it was: peat, slowly burning in the fireplaces, mixed with a subtly malty, honey aroma. The ceiling was low and criss-crossed with dark wooden beams, and every free space on the walls was filled with framed pictures, horseshoes, musical instruments and photographs. This place seemed to have come out of a novel or a film.

A dark-haired man waved at me from the counter. 'Come in! Bowl of water for the wee fella?'

'Girl, actually. Sorren?' I stepped closer to make myself

heard. He had the soft accent I'd come to recognise from the people I'd heard on the ferry.

'Yes. You must be Cora. Alistair said you were coming and that you had a cocker spaniel with you.'

'That's me! She's my business card, I suppose. I'm the girl with the cocker!' I laughed. 'Thanks for doing this for me; it's so kind of you to offer to take me to Gealach. I hope I'm pronouncing it right, Alistair told me on the phone . . .'

Sorren laughed too. 'Gaelic is not the easiest language to pronounce. You're very welcome, it's no bother taking you there. And you're welcome to Seal Island too. Oh, wow,' he said, tilting his head a little.

'What? Something on my face?'

'No, no, sorry. Just . . . Now that you're under the spotlight, I can see you properly.' I raised my eyebrows. 'You look a lot like a friend of mine.'

'Oh. Okay.' And then it was my turn to do a double-take. A man appeared at my side, looking at me with a smile on his face. I knew him. But how could that be? How could he be here, in this castaway place?

'Cora?'

'Neal Monahan? Is that you?'

'The very man! Can you believe this?'

I felt my colour rising. I'd met Neal two years ago while shooting the TV series of *Heartmade,* and he seemed to have taken a shine to me. Okay, I know I sound like my gran when I say that, but how else can I describe it? A *fascination*? Whatever it was, I had to turn him down.

Yes, the usual reason: Neal was funny, intelligent and sweet – and he was also good-looking, which was a lovely bonus – but something was missing. There always was, with Mark, and also with the couple of guys that came after him. One or two dates and that was it – *Shall we be friends?* I would say, hiding my freezing heart behind a smile.

'I . . . What are you doing here?' I said, returning his hug.

'Shooting a documentary. I don't usually do wildlife, but the director is a friend, and this place . . .' He opened his arms wide, gesturing to the surroundings. 'Well, I couldn't miss out. And then I found out you were coming to the island! Sorren was on a call with the estate agent, I was having a drink, he mentioned your name . . .'

Sorren smiled. 'Sorry, conversations have a terrible habit of being overheard in this place.'

'As you just proved,' Neal said drily. 'Anyway, I thought it must be fate.' He had soft brown eyes, with a perpetual smile in them, and big square hands he used to underline what he was saying. When we were shooting *Heartmade*, the word on the street – or on set – was that quite a few girls there had a weakness for him.

'What a coincidence!' I laughed, but I was actually quite astonished. What were the chances?

'I know! Anyway, if it's okay with you, I'll take you to the cottage. Sorren explained where it is, and I drove by yesterday to have a look at it. I have some peat in my car for your fire.'

'That's so kind of you,' I said, my head spinning a little with all that was happening. The strange spell on the ferry, seeing Seal for the first time, the sense of déjà vu and the feeling that the island should look different, that I'd seen it at some point in time and that was not how it looked. And now, a face from my past. It was like the wheels of destiny had started turning in my life, all together, all of a sudden.

Sorren glanced at his watch. 'I'd love to offer you a bite to eat and something to drink, but you need to hurry . . . Just a moment,' he said, and disappeared into the back, only to reappear a moment later with a large box that he handed to me. 'Here's a wee hamper with bread, milk, tea, you know, the lot . . . also some bridies – you can warm them in the stove – and a bit of cake. Oh, and some tablet.'

'You shouldn't have. Thank you so much . . . Me and my twenty-five guests will love this!' I laughed.

Sorren looked at me intensely. 'My God. Even the way you laugh . . .'

'What? Your friend?'

'Yes. Catriona is her name. Wait till you meet her.'

'Does she have red hair?' I asked, running a hand through my long wavy tresses. 'Because a lot of people seem to find I look like their red-haired friends and family. They seem to forget the face.'

'No, actually, she doesn't. It's more . . . your eyes.'

Neal was looking at his watch. 'Sorry to interrupt, but we do have to run, or we won't get there. Let's go.'

What was all this watch-checking? 'What? Why would we not get there?' I asked, following him out of the pub, with a wave to Sorren. Sasha and I nearly had to run to keep up with his long legs.

'Because the tide will come in soon, of course. Is your car down at the harbour?'

'Yes. What do you mean? About the tide?'

He stopped for a moment and stood in front of me. 'Have you forgotten?' And then, seeing my face: 'You don't *know*, do you?'

I was beginning to feel quite alarmed. 'What do I not know?'

'I can't believe they didn't say . . . Well, I suppose instead of telling you, I'll *show* you.'

The evening shadows were beginning to fall as we made our way back through the silent streets. Everything was beginning to feel a bit eerie, hills and houses melting into the lilac light, the sky darkening slowly and the first stars starting to appear. The bright squares of the lit-up windows made every home look so welcoming and safe, and the outside so very wild. I couldn't wait to get to the cottage.

When we arrived at the harbour, I noticed that the waves breaking on the shore had become higher, that the tide was coming in. When you think about it, it's not easy to get your head around that – that land we stand on is regularly covered by millions of cubic miles of water. Part of me was pondering the philosophical implications of that – how tiny human beings are, and the forces of nature and all that – and part of me kept thinking of tea and cake. I was tired and cold and I wanted home, even if it was an unknown, strange home. And I was sure Sasha felt the same; I could see it in her downward tail.

'Do you want to come with me? You can get your car tomorrow,' Neal said. I smiled inwardly. Men always assume you'll feel safer if it's them driving you on unknown or difficult routes. They are wrong.

'I'll be fine.' I smiled. 'I'll follow you.'

'Cora. You have a Fiat 500,' he said, resting a hand on my tiny car.

'Yeah.'

'That's a city car. You need a four-wheel drive here. Honestly.'

'I believe that a car is only as strong as the willpower of she who drives it,' I said, laughing.

'I cannot believe you got yourself, a dog and all your stuff in this . . . this Smurfs' car!'

'Well, I have a van coming up, it will probably get here tomorrow. With all my work stuff. Come on,' I said, opening the door for Sasha.

'It's okay, the road is tricky. I'll come with you. There's no room in the boot for the peat. I'll have to carry it on my lap,' he said, good-naturedly enough, and lifted an enormous sack of peat from the back of his Jeep.

The three of us set off, a woman, a man and a dog, plus a sack of peat, a large hamper and my luggage, in my little cream-coloured pod of a car. We drove in the pitch dark, headlights breaking a sea of black. It all seemed surreal, being here so far from home, and with someone from my past, someone I'd thought I'd never see again.

He was right about the road being tricky – parts of the way seemed to be right on the beach, or across heathery moors. I must admit that had it not been for Neal guiding me in the blackness, I would have struggled. I began to understand what he meant about a Fiat 500 not being the best car for this terrain, but I was determined to pretend the noise of the wheels screaming *Where's the asphalt?* was completely normal. About twenty minutes in, he pointed somewhere out of the window on the left-hand side.

'Turn here.'

'Left?' It looked to me as though where he was pointing there was nothing but sea.

'Yes.'

'You sure?'

'Yes.'

'As in, into the sea?' I was a bit alarmed.

'I know, it does look like it. But trust me, there's a tiny road there . . . Here we are. That's it. From now on, it's on foot.'

As I slipped out of the car, I swayed a little, the darkness taking my balance away. For a moment, I was suspended above land, breathless and blind – as if I was falling into the sky and into another world, another time. Sky and land and sea, everything was black, except for the lights of the village on the other side of the bay, hanging off the darkness like jewels.

'You okay?' Neal came round the car to stand beside me.

'Yes. Yes,' I said with a smile, unable and unwilling to tell him how disoriented I felt. I pulled myself together and took my torch out of the boot, together with the heavy backpack in which I had placed my immediate necessities. The beam of light from the torch illuminated grass and heather, and then wide, flat stones, wet and slippery with seaweed.

'Careful now,' Neal said and offered me his arm. I would have loved to refuse and manage on my own, but in the darkness, balancing the backpack and the torch, I didn't feel so steady, unlike Sasha, who was bouncing on her soft paws with the sureness of a wolf – a small, auburn, floppy-eared wolf. The sea was dreadfully close on both sides of the narrow pathway, so close that I could feel its spray as the waves broke against the rocks. I took Neal's arm gratefully as we stepped onto the slippery stones. In the light of the torch, I could see little shells clinging to their surface.

Like they'd just been *underwater*.

Oh.

It was beginning to dawn on me, and I was about to ask Neal the question on my mind, when he stopped. I'd been walking with my head down, quite focused on not slipping and, possibly, drowning, but now I looked up, and in the light of my torch, I finally saw Gealach.

The place I'd dreamed of before I was even sure of its existence, the place where the red-haired, red-clad woman scanned the sea and waited. I was sure of it: it was the same place.

'And that's your very own bit of Seal real estate,' Neal said, breaking my breathless silence. Beside the door, a small stone plaque with the cottage's name. The plaque I'd seen in the photo of my mother and Aunt Toffee. She'd stood right here, my mum, in her summer dress, her hair in the wind, her arm in Aunt Toffee's. Smiling together like they'd missed each other much, like they'd missed Gealach so much . . .

'Cora?'

'Yes. Yes, sorry. The path we've just been on . . . it gets covered with water, doesn't it? That's why you and Sorren said to hurry.'

'Exactly. Low tide, you can get in . . . or out. High tide, you're cut off. For about six hours. Did they not tell you when you bought the place?'

Speechless, I shook my head as this piece of information sank in. And then I could only say, 'I didn't buy it. It was my mum's.'

'Oh well, there you go. Was she Scottish?'

'No, but Aunt Toffee was,' I said, still in a haze. I raised my head. The woman at the window . . .

'You had an aunt called Toffee?'

'Long story.'

A cottage on a little island . . . on a bigger island. Cut off from everything for half the time, floating on the sea, unreachable, untouchable. Elation began to course through me, a sense of happiness and enthusiasm I hadn't felt in a long time. Here I was, in the pitch dark, on a tiny island in the west of Scotland. Everything was new, everything felt like an adventure, and my soul was *singing*.

In spite of the tantalising smells, Sasha remained firmly at my side, unsure of the new environment. She was a strange mixture of courage and shyness, I often thought, as though two dogs inhabited her brain. A lot like her owner, I supposed. And then we heard a thump, and another, and water splashing.

Neal took the torch and pointed it to the far side of the half-moon beach, where grey rocks gathered to make a tiny mound. 'It's the seals. There's a whole pod here, ten or so. Living on your private beach.'

'Seriously?' I said, following the beam of light. And there they were, round black eyes and shiny bodies, whiskers like little dogs. It was magical. Instinctively I looked at Sasha, but she was gazing at the seals and didn't stir. 'Do they actually live here?'

'Oh yes. You'll get to know them. Where I come from, in Kerry, there was a pod living right in front of my grandmother's house. She swears they recognised her.'

'Amazing!' I breathed, and Neal laughed. 'What?'

'Nothing. Just, you're so enthusiastic. It's refreshing. Okay, I've got the key. The honour is yours.' He pulled it from the pocket of his jacket: a key to Gealach, all shiny and new.

'I'm going to try my mother's key first,' I said. My heart was pounding as I unzipped my own pocket and my fingers touched the cold, rusty metal.

Slowly I opened the door.

As I stepped inside, I closed my eyes – I wanted to breathe in the scent of the place, the damp, the salt water, the faint aftertaste of seaweed and peat. It was a mixture I'd never smelled before, and it opened unknown paths in my brain. A story that had never been told – mine – over the many stories that the cottage must have seen . . .

I heard a click behind me and opened my eyes at once. 'It looks like there's no electricity,' Neal said.

'Yes,' I said in a small voice. I didn't want to break the spell. I walked in, illuminating the place with my torch. There was only one room downstairs, with a corner kitchenette – a stove with an ancient kettle on it, and a sort of credenza – and a beautiful stone fireplace in the far corner with a sofa and an armchair in front of it, covered by dusty sheets. Beside the fireplace, stairs led to the second floor – which, Alistair had explained to me, was a rarity for a cottage so ancient. Apparently the original structure dated from the eighteenth century. And judging from the cover, the magazine in the fireplace dated from the eighteenth century too – *The Sheep Farmer*, featuring a ruddy-faced man with an Aran sweater beside a thoughtful-looking sheep. A piece of a lost life, I thought, fascinated.

'Did you *know* there was no electricity?' Neal asked.

'Oh yes,' I said, and unzipped a pocket of my backpack, taking out a box of candles and some matches. Sasha didn't move from my side – she was so close to me, her nose nearly touched my shin. I lit a handful of candles and secured them on the kitchen table with a few drops of wax. I would look for candle holders later.

'Good thinking. It doesn't look half bad, actually,' Neal said.

It didn't look bad at all, I thought happily. The warm light of the candles danced on the whitewashed walls and the slate floor, and outside, the waves ebbed and flowed. It was chilly – actually, the air was colder inside the cottage than out, and even Sasha seemed pale, if that's possible of a dog – but with the fire going, and a few blankets, we would be just fine.

'Look, are you sure you want to stay here tonight?' Neal looked around.

Did my mum sleep here?

If I looked with his eyes, it *was* cold, dark and, I had to admit, a little bit scary. The wind was howling outside and the sea roared so close, it felt like it wanted to swallow Gealach and me.

'I'm sure they have room at the Seal Inn . . .'

'Room at the inn.' I laughed, just a tad hysterically.

'. . . or I can put you up,' Neal continued. 'I'm only a bit further down, near the beach. I'm renting a fantastic place, glass all over, designed by an architect, you know . . .'

'Fancy. But no, that's okay. I'll stay here and brush up on sheep farming.' I picked up the magazine and waved it.

Neal laughed. 'I'm not hitting on you or anything, I promise.' He put his hands up. 'I learned my lesson first time round.'

'No, of course not.' I looked down, confused. 'It's just that I'll be here for a while.' I shrugged. 'I might as well get used to it. Both of us, eh, Sasha?' From the backpack,

I pulled out her favourite blanket, a small Totoro one that a friend had brought us from Japan, and she took it in her mouth and curled up with it in front of the fireplace.

'Someone wants that fire lit.' Neal smiled and began piling peat in the hearth. 'Fair enough. The days will be getting longer anyway; night falls very late here in the summer. I'm a bit jealous, actually.'

'Why?'

'The view. Like living on a boat in the middle of the sea. Like you're about to float away any moment.'

'Not literally, I hope. That was so kind of you, to get the peat for me.'

'No worries,' he said in his easy way as he bent over the fire.

'No, really. And bringing me here . . . Will you be okay to walk home?'

'Oh yes. It's only twenty minutes down the beach. I'm sorry I couldn't get the house ready for you – I was working all day. Anyway, why don't you give me your number? I'll have a bit more time now the other cameraman has arrived . . . Not that he got in touch or anything . . . apparently he's a bit difficult.'

I ignored his reference to having free time. 'No, it's okay, I wanted to see the place the way it was, you know.'

I turned around to look out at the sea. The window seemed such a flimsy barrier – I was aware I was sitting in front of a little fire on a stone floor, and the floor had been laid on rock, and the rock was an island emerged from the ocean.

Seal, Seal, Seal.

It made so much sense. Me, being here, in this house, on this island – a moment in time that was meant to be. Another déjà vu.

'Cora?'

'Yes, sorry. My number.' I gave it to him.

'Thanks. I'll just give you a few pointers for lighting a peat fire. Make sure you get the old ashes out . . .'

Why did it feel like I was always meant to be here?

'Firelighters are great; I got a few for you . . .'

Like all my life I'd waited to be on this island at the edge of everything.

'You build a kind of castle with the turf . . .'

Like all my life I'd been waiting for Gealach.

I knelt on the black slate floor, watching my little fire come to life. I hadn't listened to a thing Neal had told me, I realised. Oh well, I was pretty sure I could do it myself: I'd practised in London, with the keeper of all human knowledge, YouTube. I had to learn anyway, if I didn't want to freeze to death.

'Thank you, Neal. For everything.'

'No problem. Someone's made herself comfortable!' He laughed. Sasha had formed a perfect circle, her tail nearly inside her mouth, snuggled up against the Totoro blanket, and was out cold. Her breathing sounded a bit like the waves. 'I'll see you tomorrow.'

You will? I hesitated for a moment, then thought, well, why not?

'Sure.'

'I'll call you later, if that's okay. Just to make sure you're all right.'

'No need, I'll be fine. I've put you out enough already . . .'

'Now that's the Cora I know! But why not accept a hand if you're offered one?' he said jokingly.

'Never!' I laughed. 'And anyway, maybe it won't work. The phone, I mean. I didn't really want one, you know, it's because of my brother, he would go out of his mind with worry if I didn't have one up here. Maybe there's no signal . . .'

'Happy with no electricity, hoping for no signal . . . What is it with you and technology?'

I shrugged my shoulders. 'I just don't like it.'

'Well, you came to the right place,' he said with a laugh, and I couldn't help but smile a smile of pure happiness.

The fire was relatively warm – if you sat nearly *in* it. Actually, it wasn't the fire not being warm enough; it was the place having stored season after season of dampness in its walls. Thankfully I had my jumper, and a cup of tea made from a perfectly functioning stove. After Neal left, I realised that I hadn't invited him to share Sorren's hamper, and I was embarrassed about that. I'd have to invite him over again. Sorren's provisions had been like a banquet, in a place where the nearest shop was six miles away. Six miles of blackness and a causeway across the sea. I'd warmed and devoured the bridies, which turned out to be pastry parcels full of meat, and the chocolate cake was one of the best I'd ever eaten – I wouldn't have been surprised to find out the guy was a chef. Now that I was something close to human again, I could phone Stephen and pretend that everything was under control.

After half an hour trying to find a place where my phone would work, finally I located a spot where a straggly signal from somewhere could be found.

'Cora!' Stephen's voice was a mixture of relief and distress.

'The very one!'

'I tried to call you like twenty times!'

'I can only get a signal in the bedroom, standing left of the window, turned westwards. It took me ages to figure out.'

'Oh God. Anyway, you won't believe what I found out. I mean, are you okay?'

'I am,' I said, laughing. 'What did you find out?'

'That the road to the cottage goes *underwater*! I phoned the estate agent guy because you weren't replying, and he said yes, she must be in because the tide just changed and she couldn't have got out again . . . so I said, *What?* And he explained. Please tell me I misunderstood.'

'No, you didn't. I'm breathing through a snorkel right now. Oh look, a squid just swam in front of me!'

'Very funny. Seriously, Cora, are you okay?'

'Of course I am. The tide thing is fine; it just comes and goes every six hours, so you sort of have to synchronise with that. It's no bother.'

'Oh God.'

'Relax! It's beautiful here. There are seals living right

on the beach, pretty much in what passes for the cottage garden.' I paused, looking around me. 'You know, I'm wondering if I'm retracing Mum's steps; if she slept here, if she fell asleep looking at this ceiling. It's like there's a whole piece of her life we know nothing about.' I don't seem to know much about my own life right now, I thought. I was quiet for a moment.

'Cora?'

'I'm here.'

'Eat. And sleep. And cover up – it's cold up there.'

'I have my wetsuit, don't worry.'

'Ha ha.'

'Anyway, yes, Mum, I'll look after myself,' I said, and the joke was bittersweet.

After I'd ended the call, the chill air made me look for the fire, where Sasha was dozing. I joined her and I was so sleepy all of a sudden that I could have nodded off there and then. I contemplated making a sort of nest on the sofa and sleeping there, close to Sasha's warm fur, but then I thought of the soft goose duvet I'd brought, and made my way back upstairs, hot-water bottle in one hand, candle in the other, dog at my heels. I could have used the torch, but candlelight was so beautiful, project-ing magical shadows on the walls.

The bedroom was austere, to say the least – a double bed with an iron frame, a lopsided wardrobe and a small bookcase with more sheep-themed magazines. Its simpli-city appealed to me, though; it rested my senses and my mind. I walked to the small window, from where I could see that the pathway to the cottage had been completely replaced by black waters. For a moment, the image reminded me of something – the dream? The candle flame flickered and danced with the soft draught inside the cottage, making warm golden shadows on the walls. My image was reflected in the glass – a red-haired woman with a candle in her hand – yes, it was just like the dream. I swallowed. Suddenly I felt the need to turn around quickly, as if someone was at my shoulder . . .

But the room was empty, and Sasha was placid and sleepy on the floor, not alarmed at all.

I rested the candle on the bookcase, and changed into my nightie as quickly as I could to avoid being frozen where I stood. I considered slipping my jumper back on afterwards, and heavy socks, but I decided to see if the duvet was enough. Usually Sasha didn't sleep with me, but that night she jumped on the bed and burrowed under the covers, a warm silky cocoon. I could feel her wet nose against my arm, and I kissed her soft furry head. 'Night, my friend. Thanks for following me all the way here,' I whispered. I'd like to say that her shiny brown eyes told me, 'I'll follow you to the ends of the earth,' but actually they said, 'When are we going home?' Poor Sasha.

'Night, cottage,' I whispered, then I snuffed out the candle and closed my eyes. I suppose it was strange saying goodnight to a house, but it just came out.

I was so tired after all the excitement, and the soft sound of the sea and the darkness were so beautiful and complete, that sleep came to hold me in its arms, to lull me away from everything. But that night it brought no rest – instead it brought a story, a story I'd seen before: a woman standing at an open window, her hair flowing, and a man coming up the beach, walking towards the setting sun. Again the woman's face was hidden, and the man was so far away, it was hard to distinguish his features . . .

I woke up suddenly, still full of the dream, and became aware that I wasn't in bed but standing at the window in the darkness, my bare feet on the cold stone floor. Had I sleepwalked? I leaned my forehead against the glass. I was shaking all over. All of a sudden, a soft thud made me jump. Sasha was on her feet in a heartbeat, her nose up in the air, sniffing. We both stood frozen, listening to the darkness around us, but there was only silence again now, except for the soft noise of the sea.

I threw myself back into bed and curled up, burying myself in the duvet and trying not to leave even the smallest patch of skin exposed to the freezing air; but Sasha didn't follow. Suddenly she yelped. Another thump had come from downstairs. I sat up, goosebumps covering my arms and my heart pounding. There was no doubt: someone was in the cottage with me.

Margaret

'We are McCrimmons! We come from Lochawe to serve Lord Innes!' I shouted.

The wind brought the horse's scent to me first, in spite of the rain, and then I saw him. A man on a bay stallion, a sword at his side. It had to be an Innes man, for sure – we were too close to the castle for him to be a stray, a highwayman, a thief. But my hands were shaking anyway. I stopped dead in my tracks and signalled to Mairi and Ally to stop too. Mairi's face grew white under her hood. Two girls and a child, away from the protection of their own clan or village – what threat could we pose? No, not a threat. Loot. Human loot. Once again I cursed my father for sending us alone through a land at war.

The man said nothing and came no closer. I could hear the blood in my ears.

'Let's just go,' Mairi said in a small voice. I began walking again, Mairi and Ally trailing behind me with an anxious gait that begged to break into a run. The silent man kept following us but came no closer.

If that was the Innes welcome, it wasn't a very warm one.

The rain had started again, a freezing drizzle, and the world was a sea of grey, muted green and brown. Finally, the whole of Castle Innes, a squat, robust structure with thatched cottages all around, was revealed. Hooded figures watched us from the turrets, though I knew we must have been such a sorry sight, exhausted and soaked, that they wouldn't deem us worthy of an arrow. The man on the bay horse galloped away, probably back to his patrol.

The huge wooden gate with its steel bolts was opened without us needing to call out, and we were stopped on the threshold and told to go no further. We were all searched, and our daggers taken – the ones they could find, of course. Someone was sent for – a man called William, who could vouch for our identity having seen us in Lochawe. But William was out hunting, and it was a long time before we were let in. And then it was straight to service, without food or drink, our clothes having dried on our backs without a fire, leaving us cold and sore. I wondered why all this caution – was it like this in all big castles, all powerful families? It felt as if the Inneses were under siege.

Ally was sent to the stables, while Mairi and I were given enormous aprons and dispatched to the kitchen. My future had seemed much grander as I'd gazed at the castle from far away, but now here I was, wearing an apron like a servant girl, a grumpy bonneted woman shouting orders at us before we could even get a cup of water. 'Follow me, and be quick!' I thought I'd seen a shadow of a moustache on the woman – yes, I was right. Definitely a moustache. 'You, with the fairy hair! Oh, my people would say you are a changeling,' she said, tilting her head to one side. Yes, thanks, like I haven't heard that before. 'Don't stand there gawping! Come!'

I hurried on, wondering how foolish my father must have been to have lost our position this way, from the velvet and silk of my childhood to an apron. But better being a servant than married to a man who looked like he had scurvy and a nose like a bird of prey – and not in a good way. Oh, I forgot – he was bald, too. He had no hair except two wispy bushes above his ears. *No hair, no hair, no hair,* I repeated to myself with every step as I ran after the woman. Anything was better than sleeping with him. Or with anyone I hadn't chosen myself . . .

'There's a banquet in the castle tonight; you're to help in the kitchen and then run upstairs to see to Lady Innes. When she calls you, you *go*!' The woman stopped suddenly to wave a finger in front of our faces, and we nearly ended up with our noses in her ample bosom. 'Undo those braids and put your hair up, changeling! What possessed you to do your hair like that? And take your apron off before you go and see to her; she hates kitchen smells. Hurry!'

I would take my apron off, but I would not redo my hair, loose on my shoulders with braids on the sides, gathered up in a knot in the back. My wet nurse, Magnild, had taught me how to braid my hair intricately – that was how women did their hair in her homeland in the north. Often my father, and my mother too, had told me that those braids made me look like a wild woman, but I would never change.

Mairi and I scurried about, lifting our skirts up over our ankles. The kitchen was enormous, at least compared to ours. A small hill made of pheasants and rabbits lay on the table, and I immediately had the feeling that it was destined for us. And I was right: we were to pluck the pheasants and skin the rabbits, and then we were to gather the feathers and skins to be kept and used, and throw the bones and unusable bits to the pigs.

I was never one to complain about work, but my feet hurt terribly and I was parched with thirst and light-headed with hunger. Mairi worried me more, though: she looked terribly pale and at times I thought she was swaying a little. When a small moan escaped her lips, I'd had enough.

'We need water and food,' I said to the bonneted woman, who went by the name of Morag. She was stirring an enormous pot over an open fire, and snapped her head around, apparently incredulous that I'd dared to speak. 'We've been walking for nearly three days and have barely eaten or slept.' Mairi looked at me and then at Morag, frightened, but my voice didn't waver. I wanted to keep the goodwill of the Inneses, but I was a McCrimmon and nobody's slave.

Morag turned back to the fire. 'You'll have water and food when you finish.'

'We'll have water and food now, before we faint, and then we'll finish our work. We'll only take a short while.'

'How dare you speak to me like that?'

'We've given our loyalty to the Inneses,' I said, feeling vaguely ridiculous as I made my speech with feathers in my hair and blood on my fingers, 'but we're McCrimmons and no servants. We'll eat and drink after our long journey, and then we'll do whatever you need of us.'

Morag opened her mouth to speak, and she seemed so furious that for a moment I was sure we would get a thrashing, McCrimmons or not. And so, although I hated to attract attention that way, I *looked* at her. I'll say no more, except that my look could do quite a few things, like curdling milk, or stopping hens from laying eggs, or making things fall off shelves. This time, the fire flickered high and sparks exploded, making everyone jump. I was triumphant and frightened at the same time – it wasn't wise to show what I could do, but I had no choice.

We were given water, and bowls of cold porridge with cream. I stayed true to my word and didn't take long before returning to work. I laboured as quickly as I could, all the while wondering where my aunt Helen, the herbal healer, could be – I couldn't wait to meet her. Her reputation had spread throughout Scotland, and even further if rumour was correct. And to visit her herb garden, that would be a dream come true . . .

Finally the birds and the rabbits were ready, and I prepared a bucket of offal and other parts that would not be eaten. They seemed to be a lot pickier than we were in

Lochawe, where the offal would be mixed with oat and spices and boiled. The Innes family was wealthy – I could see that from the rich rugs on the walls, the roaring fires, the neatly dressed servants. Yet still men carried swords inside and sentries stood on the grey towers, as though we weren't in a time of peace.

I made my way outside with the bucket; it was a relief to get out of the smells and grease of the kitchen, into the fresh air and wind. Morag barked after me, but there was a slight tremor to her voice. She was just trying to assert her authority over me, to save face in front of the other servants. 'Don't you dare be dilly-dallying outside!'

I ignored her and stepped through the kitchen garden, not particularly impressed by the thin, water-soaked cabbages and thinking the place could do with a spruce-up. A few dogs gathered around me, attracted by the smell of the bucket, but they stopped jumping up and yelping as soon as they met my eyes, and instead followed me in a silent, panting procession. Every step was agony on my raw feet, and I could feel the wetness of blood in my boots. Suddenly I didn't know what was left and what was right; dizzy and drained with exhaustion, in spite of the creamy porridge, I lost my bearings entirely.

The wind changed, and all I could smell was the beautiful, pure scent of rosemary coming from somewhere west of me. I looked around: the pigsty was nowhere to be found, but this had to be Helen's herb garden! Wild plants tamed and ready for the taking, some familiar and some I'd never seen before . . . juniper and foxgloves and lavender, meadow sweet and borage and marigolds. I could see, I could *feel*, that someone had put their loving hand to those plants. For a moment I thought maybe Helen was there, and I scoured the place; but there was only me.

I rested the bucket on the grass, much to the dogs' joy, and wandered around, enchanted. An idea came into my mind, and I searched for – there! – burdock. I could pulp it and put it on my sore feet that night. The burdock tucked safely in my apron pocket, I closed my eyes for a moment, breathing in the sweet scents of the medicinal herbs. Helen had built a real apothecary. What wealth for Clan Innes, certainly worthier than tapestries and banquets. I wondered if they were aware of it, if they valued Helen and her garden as much as they should, or if they treated her like they treated their pledge clans – like us. After the welcome we'd had, I saw Lord Innes and his family in an even darker light than before.

Remember, Margaret: wife of a man with legs thinner than your arms. Bald head. And when he laughed, he sounded like a woman . . .

Yes. Yes. I was lucky to be here. And if Helen agreed to teach me what she knew . . .

The sound of running water came to my ears – I'd been too taken by the garden to notice it before – and I followed it. It was a small stream, winding its way through the hazel copse bordering the gardens. I knelt down, a little smile on my lips, and drank thirstily. And although I knew I was in for a scolding from Morag when I got back, I couldn't resist taking my boots and stockings off.

All of a sudden everything seemed better, brighter, with the scent of herbs and the cool water and the chance for a moment alone.

I shuddered a little at the sight of my bleeding feet, nearly flayed at the sides where the boots had scraped the skin away. The relief was immense as I immersed them in water so cold it took my breath away. A hint of red coloured the stream for a moment.

'Your feet look terrible,' a male voice said, making me jump. I turned around to see a tall young man, soaked from head to toe. How had he come so close without me hearing him? A pair of bright, clear blue eyes shone out of his muddy face, and in his hands he was holding a heap of fat salmon. Someone was going to have a supremely tasty meal tonight. My heart was beating hard at his sudden appearance, but he didn't seem dangerous.

'They're fine,' I told him. I'd been brought up not to complain, ever. 'I'll put some burdock on them; they'll be better in no time.'

'Like a young Helen Beaton. What's your name?'

'Margaret McCrimmon.'

'Oh. You're one of the McCrimmons from Lochawe. That's why your feet are in a state, because you walked all the way here.'

'Aye.'

'Do you have shoes?'

I laughed. 'Yes, of course. What do you take me for? We're not entirely destitute, you know!' I was dreading the moment I would have to put the boots back on. I'd walk in my stockings for a few days, I resolved. Anyway, why was this stranger so interested in my feet? 'Do you not have something to do?'

'Yes, I'm sorry. Just . . . I wanted to help.'

I grimaced a little as I stepped out of the water and onto the grass. 'That's kind of you, but I don't need help.'

'Sure. Sorry. I never knew the McCrimmons had such . . . *bright* hair.'

'Not all of them. Just me.'

'Ah. A changeling,' the man said, and his eyes glimmered. Second time since I'd arrived. I hated being called a changeling, not to mention people commenting on my hair. It happened often enough back home, having this hair and grey eyes in a family of dark-haired, blue-eyed people.

'I'm my parents' daughter,' I said curtly, and walked away, holding my boots and stockings, trying in vain to look dignified but hobbling a little on my painful feet.

As predicted, I was given a scolding for having been away too long. My heart sank when I realised I'd left the bucket of entrails in the herb garden – the dogs must have had a banquet, for sure – but I had no time to retrieve it, because Lady Innes needed me. I'd already made her wait, which, thinking back, wasn't exactly a smart move, but the garden and the flowing water had been such a balm for my tired body and soul.

As I made my way through the castle, looking for Lady Innes's rooms, my thoughts went to Mairi and Ally and how they were faring. Suddenly a low, hard voice behind me stopped me and made my heart pound. I jerked around.

'You are Margaret.' A woman with a tanned, deeply lined face grabbed my arm. I thought of the forgotten bucket and wondered if my comeuppance had arrived. The woman's black eyes reminded me of something, of someone . . .

'Yes.'

'Of course,' she said, eyeing my hair and tilting her head to one side, as if she somehow approved of what she saw. 'I hear you'd like to learn from me.'

Helen! Helen Beaton, the aunt I'd never met. Of course: she had my father's eyes. How did she know I dreamed of learning from her?

'Yes. Yes please. I would be so happy—'

'I don't have time to teach foolish girls, or anyone for that matter.' I bit my lip. 'And one more thing. If you think you have a friend and ally in me just because I'm your aunt, think again.'

The words hit me like a kick in the stomach, and I felt myself paling in anger, but I remained quiet. Of course. My father's sister. What did I expect? I didn't need that haughty, selfish, presumptuous woman to help me. I would do it all myself.

But the thought of that beautiful garden . . . so much goodness in it, all those remedies to give relief to human ailments and grief. I was dying to learn my way around it. Oh, the woman wanted a slap! But there was nothing I could do. I followed her with my eyes as she disappeared down the stone stairs, and resisted the temptation to make her trip.

'Where are you going? I've never seen you before.' A girl with pale eyes and straw-blonde hair stopped me.

'I'm Margaret. I've been called to help Lady Innes. I'm looking for her rooms.'

'This way,' she said briefly, and led me to a wooden door, leaving me there. I knocked, and an older woman with a sweet, fair face appeared. I opened my mouth, but before I could speak, a melodious voice coming from somewhere in the belly of the room interrupted me.

'Is that Margaret McCrimmon?'

'Go!' the old woman whispered, and pushed me gently forward.

I crossed the room to another chamber, where a huge four-poster bed with deep-blue hangings dominated the space. Sitting at the window, beautifully dressed in velvet and lace, sat Lady Innes. Her companions were scattered around the room, folding dresses, embroidering; one of them sat opposite Lady Innes with a book – the Bible, I thought.

'My lady,' I greeted her, curtseying.

'You are just like I imagined you,' she said with a smile. Only then did I notice how hollow her face was, how her cheekbones jutted out as if her skull was only covered with a thin layer of skin. Her cheeks were flushed in a way that made her look fevered.

'You . . . *imagined* me, Lady Innes?'

'Lady Dolina. Please call me by my own name. And

yes, I imagined you. Helen told me so much about you. About your intelligence. Your courage. And about your hair!' She smiled mischievously.

Helen? Helen Beaton? Why would that old hag take an interest in my arrival? How did she know anything about me? She had seemed simply inconvenienced by my presence. I had no explanation for this, but no time to think about it either, because Lady Dolina stood up and put her arms around my waist. She smelled of lavender, and something else . . . pine . . . rosemary . . . calming herbs, herbs to heal a variety of ailments. Helen's concoction, probably. But as she stood close to me, I sensed that there was only one ailment that tormented her, and that would not leave her a way out – the same that had taken my mother.

'Small and slender, like me! That's good . . . none of my ladies would fit this,' she said, and stooped to open a dark, heavy chest. Immediately one of the women hurried to hold the lid, and another bent beside her to help. 'No, not this . . . that one beneath, the red one,' Lady Dolina said, and even just that small effort had given a breathless sound to her voice.

Her companion, a stout lady of middle age and sparse hair, lifted up the most beautiful dress I'd ever seen. I'd never been one for fancy gowns when I was a little girl, because they were a hindrance while climbing trees and running, and then when I became a young woman they brought me too much attention. I was afraid that people would notice I didn't look like my siblings; and that I would look beautiful and be asked for in marriage, when I had no intention of getting married. But secretly I'd always admired beautiful frocks.

This dress, this creation that Lady Dolina had taken out of her trunk, was a sight to behold: a deep vermilion, soft as rain, but thick and warm. She ran a hand over it as her companion held it up; the fabric changed colour as it moved, with the velvet yielding one way or the other. The neckline was low and the sleeves ended in a ruffle. There was no lace, no silk, no ribbons; it was beautiful and yet austere, almost pure.

'This will fit you perfectly,' Lady Dolina said.

I was speechless for a moment. I'd barely arrived, we'd hardly spoken, and she was giving me a dress? 'Lady Dolina, I can't . . .'

'It's too big for me now,' she said, and for an instant she looked afraid. The sickness was consuming her. 'As soon as I saw you coming in, I thought, oh, I can give her the red dress! I love it, you know? I wore it when I came to the castle. Lord Innes said that only whores wore red,' she added in a soft voice, as if she were in a dream.

The contrast between her lovely gesture and the cruelty of her reminiscence, the vulgarity of the word, hit me. How could Lord Innes have spoken to such a sweet, beautiful woman like that? To his wife?

But then so many husbands said worse – did worse.

'Please take it. But don't wear it here. I don't want my lord husband to scold you.'

'Lady Dolina . . . thank you . . .' I began to curtsey again, but she stopped me. 'No need. Now help me dress, sweet girl . . .'

At that moment, there was a commotion at the door of the main chamber. The women seemed to gasp all at once, and a deep, manly voice resounded in the otherwise quiet rooms.

'My lady wife, I thought I told you to be ready early!'

As her husband strode in, Lady Dolina paled even more, and her cheeks became redder. Yet her eyes hardened, and she looked at him without fear.

'I shall be ready on time, my lord husband.'

'Yes. You will,' he said, and the threat in his voice was unmistakable.

Lord Innes turned towards me and I hastened to curtsey, albeit reluctantly. It was then that I noticed his eyes – cold, full of a fury so deep that it had no fire in it, only ice. Blue ice. I was sure that those eyes were the last thing many men and many creatures had seen, in battle or in the hunt.

'Who are you?' he asked me.

'Margaret McCrimmon, my lord.'

To my surprise, he laughed. It was a scornful sound, and my stomach clenched. 'Of course! I should have known. Hamish's daughter. Oh yes, I did say you could come and serve me, I remember now. We all owe charity to those in need.'

He knew very well who I was. This little pantomime was just to humiliate me. My heart quickened with rage.

Lord Innes gazed at me, still with a smile on his face, and I realised that my anger amused him.

'Thank your father for this, wench. You could have married one of my sons. You could have been a lady too. And instead you'll be skinning rabbits and scrubbing floors.'

I remained silent.

'Haste, woman,' Lord Innes said to Lady Dolina, and turned around to leave. As he was on his way out, the fire hissed and danced as if a strong breeze had come in all of a sudden. He stopped and gazed at it for a moment, then walked away without any further words. I knew I had to control my anger, or it could spell disaster for me.

Lady Dolina felt hot under my fingers, as if she were running a fever. After Lord Innes's visit, all strength seemed to have left her, and we dressed her as if she were a rag doll. My heart broke to see that her life force, flashing so strong and proud in her eyes when Lord Innes had addressed her with such disrespect, had ebbed away so quickly.

We left the chamber and descended the stone steps, towards the banqueting hall. As Lady Dolina and her companions walked ahead, the portly lady who had shown me the way to the inner chamber stopped me and signalled towards the tables at the bottom of the hall, where the small nobility and traders sat. Oh well, at least I wasn't going to eat porridge in the kitchen and pick the bones that were left. That was something.

'What happened, where have you been?' Mairi whispered.

'Helping Lady Innes. She's a kind spirit. You?'

'I was in the kitchen the whole time. Ugh. Better than being in Lochawe begging food off your father, though. Ally?'

'I was in the stables,' he whispered, leaning towards us. 'You should see the horses they have! This is the best thing that has ever happened to me!' I couldn't help but smile at seeing the normally quiet Ally so animated, his freckled face a picture of delight.

I was about to reply when a man with an enormous blond beard sitting across from me hissed something about Lord Innes and his sons being about to join us for dinner. With the long feud between our two families, I'd never seen the Innes offspring before, but having met the father, I wasn't exactly looking forward to meeting the sons.

A hush came over everyone. I turned towards the arched entryway, and there they were, leather and steel, walking as if they were stepping among enemy clans rather than in their own hall. I was hoping to get a better look at them, but my silly cousin managed to spill ale all over my dress, and I was trying to dry myself as they passed our table. When I looked up again, I could only see their backs. The grey-haired laird, carrying a heavy sword by his side – was he always armed at dinner? – had an agile gait, as though he could fend off an adversary at any moment and still keep walking. All of a sudden, in his place, I saw a wildcat pacing, muscles dancing in its back, in its legs – and then Lord Innes, bellowing to bring in the food, was back. The man following him had to be Duncan, the elder son – a strong, tall man like his father, with hair so dark it was nearly blue. He seemed to have inherited his father's proud way of carrying himself. The younger son, Cameron, was lagging behind, and when he turned his head, I saw his face. He seemed angry – mutinous – with features all scrunched up. He looked like a turnip, my mother would have said. All in all, I wasn't that impressed. Two angry bulls and a dried-up tuber.

They sat at the high table, with a flurry of servants rushing to make sure they had everything they wanted. I'd decided they weren't worth my attention, so I was ready to help myself to what was on the table for us – some mutton (not much) and oatcakes (many) – but just as I was lowering my eyes, I did a double-take, choking on my watered ale, making my dress even wetter than it was already, prompting Mairi to bang not-so-gently on my back. I spluttered some more ale and then took a gur-gly breath.

Duncan Innes was the man with the salmon.

The man I'd met by the stream, who had asked if I had shoes.

And I'd spoken to him like he was a peasant. I felt my cheeks burning and I was sure I'd turned scarlet. The shame was killing me. If he had taken offence, he'd send me away . . . I downed a mug of ale and tried to forget about it, but I couldn't. I had to apologise to Duncan and tell him I'd had no idea who he was. I couldn't believe I'd spoken to a laird like that! But what was he doing, so wet and dirty and looking like a beggar or worse? Yes, he'd been fishing, but there was no need to cover himself in mud. And he could have told me who he was. Maybe he was already planning to watch me squirming afterwards – now that would be a truly Innes thing to do. I kept my head low and my eyes resolutely on my plate. I thought I saw him smirking, but it might have been my imagination.

Night fell at last. I didn't think I could stay awake one more instant; I thought my legs would buckle beneath me. And judging from her face, Mairi was feeling the same. Without much ceremony, we were shown the little room where we'd sleep, together with a blonde girl who didn't offer her name. I washed my face, took my torturous boots off and laid my head down. I wanted to say a prayer, but I was too tired to even formulate the words in my mind . . . and then the whole sorry scene came back into my mind. The young laird carrying salmon, and me laughing in his face. Tomorrow I'd probably be sent away. If not worse. At once, I was wide awake and fretting.

I got up, every bone hurting, and stepped out of the room on stockinged feet – I couldn't face those boots again. The castle seemed quiet, until I got downstairs and realised that many men were still up and, I noticed, armed. Servants were passing around pints of ale and trays of bread. It was as if the place wouldn't rest, couldn't rest. There was a considerable group of men in a corner, still draped in plaids and capes, hair wet with moisture – they must have just arrived. The whole atmosphere made me feel on edge, as though cold blue sparks were running across my skin. Something was happening at Castle Innes; something was happening to the clan.

I tiptoed around, trying to pass for one of the girls who were serving ale and bread, looking meek enough not to alarm anyone, searching for Duncan Innes. I was directed to what they called the lord's hall, a small room just off the main hall where meals were taken. A thin man with a ridiculous bonnet and a long fur-lined tunic stood in front of the door, on either side of him a burly guard, hand on sword. These people really seemed to see enemies everywhere. Maybe for a reason.

'They are very busy. They certainly don't have time to speak to *you*,' the man in the fur tunic said, looking me up and down scornfully.

I felt my cheeks burning with rage and humiliation.

Fine. Thinking about it, Duncan didn't even deserve an apology. If he chose to walk around his estate looking like he had just crawled out of a muddy hole, he had to expect to be mistaken for a servant!

At that moment, I heard a deep voice shouting a name – MacGregor – and then a thump, like a fist on a table.

The MacGregors. The Inneses' traditional enemies, and because of our alliance, the McCrimmons' enemies too. I knew too little to decipher the game of alliances taking shape, as the exiled prince gathered support for his cause from France. I knew enough to know that in such a complicated game, you would need the gift of divination to understand where to align yourself so you wouldn't be ruined. Or, considering the number of armed men I saw around, destroyed. I was more disquieted than I could say; like a cat before a storm, feeling with every bit of my mind and body that something was brewing.

Back in our room, the blonde girl was sleeping, while Mairi lay on her bed, her head resting on her hand, with a strange smile on her face. Without saying a word, she lifted her chin towards my bed.

On the rabbit-fur blanket was a pair of beautiful soft leather boots, exquisitely decorated with an intricate embroidered pattern. I was so surprised that I couldn't even find an answer for my cousin, who was teasing me about having found a suitor, and one with money, and how she was certainly going to find out who it was.

'Who brought these?' I asked eventually, cutting her jibes short.

'Morag herself. She wasn't too pleased.'

'Did she say who they were from?'

Mairi shook her head. 'But I bet you know.'

And I did. There was no other explanation – nobody else knew how mangled my feet were, except for Ally, and he certainly wouldn't have access to something like this. I sat on my cot cradling the boots, and as soon as Mairi turned over to sleep, unexpected tears gathered in my eyes. I wasn't one to cry much – actually, I wasn't one to cry at all – but it was such a kind gesture. I was so used to being strong and fighting for every little thing, I'd forgotten how it felt to be looked after. I stroked the soft velvet of the dress, and then rested a hand on the leather of my boots. Lady Dolina was a kind woman, but it was the young laird's thoughtfulness that left me speechless, because I would never have expected it. Not from Lord Innes's son.

I dried my tears and slipped my strong mask back on before anyone could see. And at that moment, our tiny room was filled with sound. It was a faraway kind of sound – it *felt* far away even when it was close – one that overwhelms you with emotion and pride and dread and desire for you don't even know what: the sound of the pipes. Mairi and the blonde girl awoke, dazed, and I ran to the window. The whole castle was waking up. Instead of a dark, quiet courtyard, I saw bonfires, and men, and a circle of pipers. The tune the pipes were playing disquieted me deeply. It wasn't a celebration, and it wasn't mourning. I closed my eyes and listened for a few seconds – and then I knew.

It was war.

FLOOD TIDE

Innes

I wish I could say I stepped onto Seal a new man, strong, too strong to ever be hurt again, and free of all demons. But in truth, I was so petrified I couldn't even speak, and for a long moment I contemplated turning back and running away, back to Oban and to Glasgow and to San Francisco, away, away from here.

And then I saw my mother, standing on the pier, waiting for me.

I was horrified, and angry, and happy, and melting with seeing her again. My mother. It was like wild animals fighting each other inside me, each trying to win – the love, the fury, the guilt at having left. The anger.

The *anger*.

'Hi,' I said. She was wearing a pink cardigan and blue trousers, her hair in a halo of curls around her face, looking younger than she did when I was a teenager. I was frozen and uncertain about what to do, my whole body fighting with itself. I wanted to hold her, I didn't want to, and I just stood there like the little boy I used to be; but my mother ignored my coldness and confusion, and simply threw her arms around me. When we disentangled, I saw tears in her eyes. Well, nothing different there. That was the way I remembered her from my childhood – crying, defeated. Helpless.

'Alan . . .'

'Innes,' I said simply. My father had named me, and I couldn't bear it. I'd renamed myself.

'Innes. Of course, I always forget.'

But I noticed at once that something in her was different, and it wasn't just the clothes and the haircut – I don't think I'd ever seen my mother with short hair. It was . . . something else. An aura of cheerfulness, in spite of the tears of emotion in her eyes. And then I noticed the woman standing beside her, a human explosion of colour in a flowery dress, with a fabric flower in her brown hair.

'You remember Sylvia, don't you?' my mother said, gesturing to the woman. Of course I did – my brother's wife, someone else caught in the wreck that was our family. Was she living on Seal? Was she back in our loving family fold?

'Innes,' Sylvia said, and her eyes were wide, as if she saw through me – as if, in me, she saw someone else. And I knew who: my brother. We looked nearly identical, so much so that when we were young, we were often mistaken for twins. Unexpectedly, she hugged me. An awkward embrace – I didn't like physical contact at the best of times – and then we stood, even more awkwardly. She was small, smaller than I'd remembered, with long, straight hair and a bright smile. Her colourful clothes and the way her eyes became half-moons when she smiled made me think of a pixie. I could almost imagine pointed ears peeping out of her hair. And then, as always when I was near my family, a thought came to stab me: this delicate woman . . . had my brother ever . . . ? But I didn't want to finish the thought. I had to get it out of my mind.

There was a young girl standing with them, but she couldn't be . . . she couldn't be . . . Pamela was a baby, surely?

'And this is Pamela?' I managed to say, half choked. My niece. She, too, with a ready smile, came to hug me. She was dressed in her blue school uniform, one sock up and one down, her almond eyes full of life. She seemed to vibrate with energy and zest – maybe it was her personality, or maybe all children are like that, new and joyful and full of expectations. Letty's son had been the same. But that was another thought I didn't want to entertain. I held Pamela's tiny frame, and the impulse to protect her, and the guilt for not having been there, filled me to the brim.

The daughter my brother had refused to even acknowledge; the child my father wanted dead before she was born.

We made our way towards my old house – that place I knew so well, the place I'd so wanted to forget. As I lifted my camera onto my shoulder, I saw out of the corner of my eye a flash of copper – it was the woman who'd fallen on the ferry deck, standing alone and contemplating the machair, the blue air of dusk giving a cold hue to her hair. I forced myself to look away – there was something magnetic in that vision, something that made me want to keep looking.

Pamela held my hand as we walked. I'd been ambushed. My mum had said nothing about Sylvia and Pamela being here on the island. The debris of my brother's life.

We never stood a chance, my brother and I, did we?

We were both bound to go the same way as our father. To be like him.

Not only had my mum changed; the house had changed too. It wasn't so much that the dark furniture and the old wallpaper had been replaced with new things and vibrant colours; it was that the atmosphere was so different from what I remembered. There was no other explanation but my father's death, and maybe Sylvia's presence. Yet still the place was so full of memories – bad memories – that I couldn't quite relax, not even sitting on the sofa with a cup of tea in my hand.

Nice touch, not to offer me a drink. Wise.

'So, Morag tells me that you're here to shoot a documentary,' Sylvia said with a smile. Her voice was soft and high, like a bird's.

'Yes. All through the summer.' I watched her watching me, intensely. I wondered if she missed my brother. We were so alike, after all.

In many ways, I thought, and my stomach clenched for a moment.

Pamela perched herself on the armrest of the sofa I

was sitting on, a piece of paper in her hands. 'I drew this for you!'

It was surprisingly accurate for a ten-year-old: an enormous dolphin filling most of the space with blue, and a tiny man with a camera to one side.

'This is you.' She pointed at the figure. It had bright yellow hair.

'I love the colour of my hair in this picture.' I smiled, and Sylvia and my mother laughed. Mum was standing in front of the fireplace – she never sat down.

My mother's laughter. A rare, rare sound as I was growing up.

'Mum said you take pictures of dolphins,' Pamela said, and tilted her head in a way that squeezed my heart. For a second, she'd looked just like my brother. Weird, that she had grown up away from him, and still had his mannerisms.

'That's right. That's what I do for a living,' I said. But it was only partly true. I couldn't film underwater. Some things The Guy had done to me . . . but no, I would not think of that now.

'I like dolphins and horses,' she said, brushing her straight fair hair away from her forehead.

I'll never forget when we learned that there was a high chance of Pamela having Down's syndrome. I was seventeen and still living at home, in a crazy, masochistic, ever-failing attempt to protect my mother. I remember my father's ranting. I remember him calling Pamela a word that I can't even repeat in my thoughts. She was a mistake, he'd said, like a cake that doesn't come out well – you throw it in the bin and start again. My brother, after the test they'd done on the growing baby, came home to receive guidance from the ultimate authority, from the makeshift God our father was to him. He bought everything The Guy said. The ranting and shouting became cold, low voices – a decision – and then the call to Sylvia, a call I didn't witness but could imagine.

But Sylvia stood up to them; she kept her baby and she was out of our lives. Good for her, I'd thought at the time: this family brought nothing but grief to anyone who came near. My brother came back to live on Seal and started acting like a watered-down copy of my father – two bullies, the old one soaked with alcohol and the younger soaked with fear and an endless sense of inadequacy and rage.

And then the accident happened. The one that saw both my parents end up with knife wounds. Inflicted by me, apparently. After that, it was time for me to go. At last. I left the island as a pariah. Well, every story needs a villain, I suppose. And my father was good at playing the wolf in sheep's clothing, so that the villain had to be me.

Many times over the years I tried to call Sylvia – I tried to write her a card, a letter. But I couldn't bring myself to do it. I didn't want to, maybe. I wanted her away from them, away from me, away from the cursed Innes blood. It was the right decision, and I should have been consistent – I should never have got another woman, another child, involved in the mess. Sylvia's heart had been broken, Letty's heart had been broken . . .

If I didn't know better, I would have thought the Inneses were cursed.

My mum took Pammy's picture from me, interrupting my thoughts. 'I'll put this on the fridge . . . Oh, it means the world to have you back, son,' she said softly. I knew that there was much more she would have liked to say, but couldn't. In our family, nobody really *spoke*. Because we all had too much to say, too many painful things. Things that we pretended not to feel, not to know.

Her words, though meant to be loving, angered me. *I bet it means the world to you that my father didn't kill me*, I might have said, maybe, if I'd replied – and so I didn't, I just looked down. Sylvia must have sensed my tension, because she began to chat about my job, asking me questions about what a wildlife cameraman actually did, and making jokes about hiding in bushes with bits of tree on my head – quite accurate, actually.

'What's for dinner, Granny?' Pamela threw her arms around my mum, who responded with a sweet, immediate affection she'd never had for us boys. I knew it wasn't because she didn't feel it, or because she wouldn't have wanted to; but because she was always afraid that any tenderness towards us would rouse The Guy's rage. To see her and Pammy embracing was a bittersweet joy. Pammy was a physical child, I'd noticed, and I could see that my mum loved the freedom to show such pure, unbridled affection. Pamela was unique, and by that I didn't mean her extra chromosome; I meant the way she seemed to have brought sunshine inside our home at last.

'A special dinner for your uncle. Steak pie, like we make it in Scotland. Because he must have missed it out there in California.'

In spite of my confused feelings about being home, I couldn't help but smile. All these years had gone by, but she remembered my favourite dish. It was a little thing, a silly thing maybe – this woman who'd never stood between her son and a six-foot man with heavy fists, this woman who'd cried in the night and still never left, who'd made her life with a bully whose blood and influence made my brother and me tainted, corrupted, sick – she'd remembered my favourite dish.

She was my mother, and I loved her; but I knew I could never forgive her.

My old room was now Sylvia's, but she'd moved in with Pamela for the duration of my stay. The walls were painted bright green – I could guess at Sylvia's influence in the choice of colour – and the furniture was all changed, but the gaudy, faded flowers in the old carpet still watched me like spiteful eyes. I stayed up late, reading; once upon a time this would have been a night to drink, and then drink some more. But I was three years sober, and I would not fall, not tonight.

Everyone else was asleep; I decided I would have a quick, quiet shower and try to sleep. Insomnia is the worst thing, when you're exhausted by plane journeys and time zones, and yet you still can't let yourself go. Dazed with exhaustion, I stood in the bathtub and closed my eyes under the chilly spray. Slowly the water became warmer and warmer, and I stretched out my arm to pick up the shower gel . . .

And there they were, the green tiles bordering the bathtub, green with an orange flower in the middle.

Many times those tiles had been at my eye level, their pattern imprinted on my retina as I desperately tried to breathe, water coming out of my mouth, my nose, dripping from my hair. And then I would be pushed down again, my lungs exploding, my terrified tears mixing with the water. Behind me, my mum didn't even scream any more; she simply stood in silence, shaking. As if she herself was being drowned.

'Did you learn your lesson, Alan?'

'Yes! Yes!'

'I don't think so,' he'd say, and he'd keep playing his little game until I lay on the bathroom floor, half unconscious from the lack of air, and vomiting water.

It was like it happened yesterday. Like it was happening all over again.

I can't remember exactly what happened after my flashback. I know I got dressed slowly, trying to control the trembling of my hands, making my movements careful, deliberate. I stepped back into my room in silence, an abyss of pain and terror where my heart used to be. A grown man, having reverted to a child.

That smell. That smell was everywhere. The aniseed

sweets my father used to mask the smell of alcohol – how could I not have been aware of it when I arrived? Nausea overcame me as the scent filled my nostrils, making me want to run and run, and keep on running. All of a sudden, I couldn't take it any more. I stepped out of my room and started down the stairs, silent and sweating and shaking.

'Innes?' A voice came from the shadows. Someone was standing on the landing – Sylvia. Panic made everything sway. I struggled to get my voice out, and when I did, it sounded hoarse.

'I woke you up. I'm sorry.'

'No problem. Are you feeling okay?'

There were flowers on her belly, on her breasts. A flowery dress. Flowers and colours dancing in my delirium, hiding within the shadows; kind eyes, kind hands. But I still had to go.

'Tell my mother I'll be back tomorrow,' I said, and then there was the night and cold air and relief, and running towards the only safe place I'd known as a child.

Good God, free me from all this.

Good God, make me forget.

When I came to the beach, I could think again. Things had stopped whirling and I was steady on my feet, the black sky over me and the black earth under me. And in front of me, wide and powerful and pure, the expanse of the sea.

I wiped the sweat off my forehead and breathed deeply, inhaling wind and salt and minuscule particles of seawater. A white sliver of moon peeked from the clouds; a feeble light, but still a light. My island, the place I'd missed desperately. The place I loved and hated with all my might.

Was this where I belonged? Was this the right time to come back?

Would there ever be a right time? I asked the waves over and over again.

I made my way towards the beach and climbed a grassy dune I knew like the back of my hand – and there it was, my childhood shelter, the abandoned cottage on the shore where I slept when things got too much at home. There I would be safe.

I could almost see my child's feet stepping on the slippery stones, my small hands on the door – when my name was still Alan – but it was a grown-up who walked towards the cottage now, seeking safety, running away from ghosts and memories.

Silently I opened the door, the familiar scent of sea and damp and mould hitting me. I tiptoed inside – even if the place was abandoned, making a lot of noise just didn't seem right. Like disturbing the ghosts.

And there it was, my nook by the fireplace where I would curl up in a nest of blankets and sleep like a stone without fear of my father. The blankets weren't there any more, of course, nor was the stash of sweets, oatcakes and Ribena I'd kept for emergency dinners; but even in the cold, with nothing but my clothes to sleep in, it felt like a refuge.

I looked around me, trying to see in the feeble light of the moon – there had been no time to grab a torch, not when suddenly you feel ten years old again, and full of anger and terror, and you just want out before you get grabbed and half drowned. The ancient green velvet armchair, the little makeshift kitchen, the crucifix on the wall. My hand brushed the windowsill – and yes, tiny bird bones mixed with sand were still there, like the sea had come inside somehow, through the glass and the wooden frame. The sheep-farming magazine was still on the table, and the rusty kettle on the stove, as if the owners had just walked out. There were many cottages and houses in the Hebrides left like that: simply abandoned, like time inside them had ceased to flow.

That was when I registered something strange, something not quite right. It took me a moment to realise what it was. I could smell burning peat. It was an almost omnipresent smell on the island, but at Gealach we were away from everything, and the nearest cottages were too far for me to be able to smell their fires. I negotiated my way in the gloom and knelt in front of the fireplace. Beneath the burnt black turf, there was an orange glow.

Somebody had been here. Somebody must have discovered my childhood refuge – maybe kids looking for somewhere to party, or some lost soul like I had been. Oh well. It didn't matter – actually, I was quite grateful, because it meant I wouldn't freeze to death. I'd spend a few hours here, on the dusty armchair, and watch the embers glow until morning.

As I turned the turf carefully with my fingers, it occurred to me that maybe the tongs I used to keep here were still around. I stood up quickly and moved towards the wall to feel for the fire tools, and as I did so, I tripped on something and hit my head on the fireplace. Pain exploded behind my eyes, together with the metallic smell of blood. Great. My hand clutched to my forehead, cursing under my breath, I checked to see what I had fallen over. It was a bag. A backpack.

Somebody was here.

Before I even had time to think, an apparition floated above the stairs in the silver light of the moon: long hair, white nightgown, black pools for eyes. I thought my heart would give out there and then. Cold sweat mixed with the blood on my face, and I opened my mouth, but no sound came out. The White Woman, I thought. The banshee.

'Who *are* you? Get out!' she screamed.

I froze. The apparition had an English accent and a soft alto voice.

'Get out, I said!' She was holding something, her arm shaking badly. I blinked in the gloom – it was a Swiss army knife. 'I'm not afraid to use this.'

I found my voice. 'Actually, it looks like you are. Your hand is shaking. Ouch,' I added, as a fresh wave of pain hit me.

'Oh my God! You're bleeding!' the woman said, still holding the little knife in front of her.

'I fell. Look, please put that knife down. It's . . . disquieting me.'

'Finding a man in my house in the middle of the night is disquieting *me*!'

'*Your* house?'

'Yes, my house.'

'Look, this place is empty . . . was empty. I used to come here years ago. I didn't know there was anyone here . . .'

'Did you not see my car outside? Did you not see my things?'

'How could I? It's pitch dark! I tripped over your bloody backpack!'

'It's not pitch dark. There's moonlight. Anyway, I want you to go. Now.'

'I can't go *now*, unless you want me to drown.'

'What do you mean?'

'The tide just turned. There's no way off the island. I barely made it in.' *You crazy woman*, I wanted to add, but didn't.

'Oh. Yes.'

'Do you want me to sit outside for the next six hours?'

'Well . . . yes?' She sounded shaky.

'Sorry, but I'm not going anywhere.'

Her eyes widened in the gloom – I suppose I could be intimidating. I was a six-foot bearded man, and she was tiny and pretty much helpless, apart from the little knife. Now she was scared, and I felt terrible.

'Honestly, I mean you no harm,' I said. 'I would have never come in had I known you were here. If you let me stay for the next six hours, I'll be gone as soon as the tide turns.'

'Really?'

'Really.'

'You'll be gone?' She began to lower the arm holding the knife.

'I'll be gone. And anyway, the most you can do with that is pluck my eyebrows.'

'What? Oh. Shit,' she said, realising she was actually brandishing the tweezers part of the Swiss army knife. She tried and failed to find the blade.

'Look, you don't need a knife.'

'True. I have a guard dog.' She moved sideways, her elbow brushing the wall, to reveal a beautiful dog with dangling ears – maybe a cocker, but I couldn't see properly – sitting on the stairs behind her. The dog didn't seem very dangerous, its little black nose and big frightened eyes peeking from behind the woman's nightie.

'It does a great job keeping you safe.' I smiled. 'Oh, it's gorgeous! Come here . . . good dog . . .' The cocker was immediately reassured and bounced towards me, seeming keener on having its head rubbed than tearing me to shreds.

'Sasha!' the woman whispered, in the same tone as if she'd been saying *Et tu, Brute!*

And then I realised that the name rang a bell. Sasha. A dog called Sasha.

I took a step forward and studied the woman's face,

her hair shining copper in the moonlight. It was the woman from the ferry, the woman I'd held in my arms.

Our meeting had been surreal, and yet, it seemed, inevitable. Fateful, I suppose.

I was on the ferry, on the deserted deck – everyone else was inside, out of the icy wind and drizzle. Behind me, the rugged coastline; in front of me, the islands: those were the shapes of my own landscape, the shapes of my memories. I'd taken that ferry a million times, to and from Oban, when I lived on Seal. The little boy I was and the man I'd become stood side by side, holding the metal rail and breathing in the wind. That was when I saw a shiny copper beacon against the backdrop of blue and grey. A woman with a mane of wavy hair so lovely that for a moment I couldn't look away. She saw me staring – great, she probably thought I was a creep – and I was about to turn away from her when something happened.

It was all very fast – in a moment, the woman had fallen to the ground, on her knees. Her face was white as ice, her eyes open but, it seemed, unseeing. I ran to her, feeling the ferry sway under me and nearly losing my balance as it cut through the waves, and threw myself on the deck beside her, drawing her head onto my lap. I could see her chest heaving and her pulse was strong under my fingers, so I knew she was breathing, I knew her heart was beating. Even in my fear and alarm I couldn't help noticing how soft her hair felt through my fingers. It was just a moment, a surreal moment where it seemed to me that this had all happened once before – kneeling over that strange woman, her unseeing grey eyes, the way she trembled in my arms.

And then I was back in the here and now, and she was getting up, murmuring words of apology and reassurance.

'I'm okay . . . I must have been dizzy for a moment . . . I'm fine now,' she said, and her voice was soft and low, with a hint of a London accent. Earthy.

When she disentangled herself from me, letting go of my hand, my body didn't like it – I had to fight the impulse to take her hand again, to try to be close to her once more. And so, although I kept an eye on her to make sure she really was fine, I turned away from her and left as quickly as I could to resume my place on the other side of the deck, next to my backpack and my camera. I saw her stepping inside, still looking a bit dazed, and disappear.

And now here we were.

'It's *you*!' she exclaimed, and with a snap that made her jump, something sprang up from the knife. Tweezers again. 'Shit! You followed me from the ferry!'

'Will you put down that . . . that weapon, you maniac!'

'Oh, I'm the maniac? You follow me here and jump on me in the middle of the night, and I'm—'

Suddenly I was fed up with trying to convince her I wasn't an axe murderer. 'I didn't follow you here. And I didn't jump on you. Look, I'm exhausted, I haven't slept in three days . . .'

'Three days? Are you on drugs?'

'No, I flew through a few time zones. I'll just sit here and wait for the tide. You go back to bed, okay?' At that moment, Sasha rolled over on the floor, tummy up, waiting to be stroked. I had to laugh.

'I'm not going back to bed with you here,' the woman said, but her voice sounded softer. 'Also, you're bleeding.'

'Yeah. It doesn't matter.' I shrugged, and all of a sudden, my limbs felt like lead. With the jet lag and the nerves about coming to Seal, I'd forgotten the last time I'd slept, and my eyes were closing. I crouched and rubbed Sasha's tummy – animals seem to like me, for some reason. They don't realise, I suppose, who I am inside.

'I have a first-aid kit,' the woman said, and made it sound like a question.

'Good for you,' I said quietly. I was drained.

'I mean, I can see to your head.'

'It's okay. Don't worry, I won't bother you. I'll just sit here . . .' I let myself fall into the armchair.

'Oh, enough nonsense. I'll patch you up. It won't take a second,' the woman said, and placed the knife on the table. Against the moonlit window, the shape of her body was visible for a moment through the nightgown. It would have been polite to look away. I didn't. 'By the way, the knife is there if you make a sudden move.'

'You'll tweeze me into submission?' I suggested.

I saw the shadow of a smile on her face, and her hair fell like a lustrous curtain as she rummaged in the backpack I'd tripped on and took out a flowery bag.

'You're going to do my make-up?' I said.

'What? Oh, you mean the bag. No, that's just where I keep my first-aid stuff.' She produced a candle and a box of matches, and a tiny, trembling flame bloomed in the darkness. In the candlelight, her face was beautiful, with high cheekbones and lips like the queen on a playing card. 'Now, lie back a bit . . . Right. Ouch. You took quite a knock. Is your head okay? Feel sick, dizzy?'

'I'm fine. Bit . . . surreal, but fine. Your feet must be freezing,' I said, noticing her little white feet, the toenails delicately painted mother-of-pearl.

'They would be freezing if I could actually feel them,' she agreed.

'By the way, my name is Innes.'

'Cora,' she said, zipping the first-aid bag closed.

Cora, I repeated in my mind. Cora, the woman with the soft, earthy voice and the hair like autumn leaves . . . the woman I'd found in my haven, my place of safety. Gealach and Cora . . .

The adrenaline of the strange encounter was ebbing away and my eyes were threatening to close. 'So . . . I'll just sit here for a while,' I said. I stretched my legs and crossed my arms, trying to get comfortable on the chair, just like I'd done years before when I was small enough to curl up in it.

'Okay,' she said simply. She stood looking at me for a moment, and then she must have decided I was no threat, because she disappeared upstairs, followed by the dog. I thought she'd gone to bed, but after a minute she re-appeared with a pile blanket. Sweet-scented hair brushed my face for a second as she bent to tuck it round me. I was too tired to consider how strange the whole situation was, but to my sore body and sore heart this was enough: that there was someone laying a blanket over me and making sure I was warm.

She revived the fire and sat on the sofa opposite me, covering herself in a duvet and curling her legs beneath her so that her delicate feet disappeared under the folds. Then she closed her eyes.

The sun was beginning to rise, impossibly early as it does on Scottish summer nights, and in the half-light everything seemed other-worldly. I was half asleep and had no control over my thoughts. For just a moment I allowed myself to imagine that I could hold that body close to mine, that her hair would brush my chest again . . . and then I let myself slip away, warm in Cora's blanket, and fell asleep in minutes.

Cora

I woke with a jolt, full of the terrible dream I'd had. People huddling together, the sound of screams and the bright flash of blood. Even in the dream, even asleep, I looked for the red-haired woman, but she wasn't there. All of a sudden I became aware of a man's presence nearby, and I jumped up, the cold slate of the floor under my feet. Had I really slept beside a total stranger? He could be anybody!

I looked into his peaceful face – the blue shadows under his eyes and the golden five o'clock shadow on his jaw – and I felt vaguely guilty. He didn't seem dangerous at all. At the same time, though, as I contemplated his build under the blanket, I decided I'd better keep my guard up.

'Hey . . . hey . . . wake up. The tide is out,' I said, shaking his shoulder.

'What? Oh yes. Yes, sorry,' he said, and jumped up from the chair, the blanket falling to the floor. 'I'll be going. Sorry about this.'

'Well . . . what about a cup of tea? Coffee?'

He rubbed his face with his hands. 'Okay, then. A cup of extra-strong coffee would be great. And then I need to rush back; they'll wonder where I am.'

'Yeah,' I said, and waited. Surely he'd offer an explanation as to what he was doing in my cottage in the middle of the night. Or what he was doing in an abandoned cottage, anyway, because that was what he had believed it to be. And *who* was going to miss him and wonder where he was?

He was silent.

'Coffee coming,' I said finally, and busied myself with the tiny camping stove I'd brought. It had been a great challenge to pack everything I needed into my little car, but I'd managed. The kettle I'd found in the kitchen was more rust than anything. 'Surreal, isn't it?'

'What?' he said, rubbing his forehead.

'What?' My eyes were wide. 'That we're here at all! I mean, it's weird enough that I actually own a cottage on a Scottish island, but then the tide thing, and being on an island on an island, if you know what I mean . . . and then you sneaking in in the middle of the night . . .'

'I didn't sneak in. I told you, I didn't know there was anyone here. This place has been empty for ever. I used to come here all the time as a child.'

'Still surreal. There. Sugar and milk?'

'Black. I've been drinking Colombian espressos for the last three weeks, my stomach has a hole in it as it is.'

'Colombia? For work?' I handed him the cup. For a second our fingers brushed, and I felt the warmth of his

126

skin. He probably hadn't noticed that light touch, but I had.

'Yeah.'

'What do you do?'

'I'm a cameraman.' Oh. Like Neal. Maybe he was the second cameraman whose call Neal was waiting for.

'Okay, cameraman. Want to join me on the *patio*?' I smiled, and opened the door. Beautiful, scented, chilly sea air filled the place, and I closed my eyes for a moment, the hot cup in my hand, the wind lapping my bare feet.

We stepped outside and sat on the rocks, the stone cold on my skin, covered only by my nightie. The feeling of the hard, smooth pebbles under my feet was wonderful, as if I'd plugged myself into the earth and was recharging. In front of us, sea and sky. Wasn't the Scottish sky supposed to be constantly overcast? Because now it reflected the sea, dark blue and glass green, fluffy white clouds pushed westwards by the wind. You know when something is so beautiful, you could just cry? This was one of those moments. It was weird to share it with a stranger.

'And what a patio . . .' Innes said.

I stole a look at him, and was surprised at the way my breath caught a little. I'm not easy to impress, and my indifference towards men has always been a difficult, unresolved part of my life. But there was something in the shape of his face, in the colour of his eyes – the lightest blue I'd ever seen – that made my heart skip a beat. I was aware of his proximity and wasn't sure whether I wanted to get even closer or if I wanted to stand up and step away. I hugged my knees and crossed my arms, balancing my mug as best I could.

'What are you doing up here all on your own, then?' he said, and rubbed one of his eyebrows with his knuckles. I noticed the tattoos covering his arms; on some men, tattoos look out of place, like camouflage on a bank clerk, but on Innes they looked a bit like battle scars. They suited him in a way, like they had a story to tell.

'Well, it's a little hard to explain. I inherited this cottage from my mum.'

'Was she from the island?'

'No. We have no idea how she came to own it.'

'Family secrets, then,' he said. His eyes were fixed on the sea.

'Maybe. I don't know. Her name was Beatrice Lamb,' I said. Maybe he'd heard of her somehow.

'A wee holiday, then?'

I was disappointed for a moment. The name obviously hadn't rung any bells.

'Not exactly . . . I'm a crafter. I make things. My speciality is textiles. Tapestries,' I explained. 'But I'm here to write a book, really.'

'Oh, that's why you travel light. A laptop and you're good to go.' He'd noticed quite a few details about me, but he wasn't saying much about himself, I realised.

'Actually, there's no power in the cottage, still. I'll use notebooks. The bulk of my stuff should arrive later. I need quite a lot of things to try out the recipes for the book, some more obscure than others . . . beeswax, oil, borax, white vinegar, royal jelly . . .

'Cool.'

'And a loom. A small one.'

'Like the Lady of Shalott.'

'Who?'

'Tennyson. The Lady of Shalott, a dame who lives in a tower and weaves a tapestry of the world outside. She looks at things through a mirror, because if she looks directly towards Camelot, she'll die.'

I smiled. You wouldn't have thought that a man who looked like Innes – how can I put it? *fierce* – would quote Tennyson.

'Very romantic. What happens in the end?'

'She dies of a broken heart,' he said cheerily.

'Oh. Shouldn't have asked. So, are you from around here?'

He ignored the question. 'Come on, I want to show you something.' He got up and took me by the hand. His touch was strange and yet familiar, like when you're about to fall and the impact with the ground is a shock, but an expected one. I let him hold my hand – I didn't take it away.

We stood on the pebbled beach, Sasha beside us, wagging her tail. Innes looked at her. 'Wait, maybe we should shut her in the house. Sorry, Sasha, nothing personal.'

I managed to cobble an answer together – the touch of his hand made it quite difficult to think. 'No need. Sasha doesn't run after anything. She's a very philosophical dog, you know? She sits and watches, and—'

'Shh,' he said gently, his hand moving up my arm. He could have circled the whole thing with his fingers. Maybe I should have felt vaguely threatened by that, but for some reason, I didn't. 'Listen . . .'

There was a sound above the ever-present swooshing of the waves – a bit like frogs croaking, but higher and softer.

'Corncrakes,' he whispered, and his fingers slipped down my arm again. He held my hand and led me along the little white half-moon beach. And there they were, two . . . three little birds, a light brown colour with a hint of warm caramel, their backs speckled. They were exquisite, singing their croaky song.

We were silent. I was aware of his breathing as the corncrakes sang and the seagulls cried. I felt his hand squeezing mine, and when I stole a glance at him, I saw that he was gazing out to sea. There was a shadow of a smile on his lips, but it wasn't reflected in his eyes. In fact, he seemed somehow sad, as if he was contemplating something he'd lost, though he had it just in front of him.

I wondered what his story was, and I wanted to ask, but he clearly wasn't a man who invited questions.

Now that's *surreal*,' he said. I turned towards him, openly this time, waiting to hear what he meant. He looked into the distance, his eyes half closed, as if he was appraising a camera shot. But he didn't elaborate. 'Well, thanks for not stabbing me. Or tweezing my eyebrows,' he said instead, handing me his half-empty mug. Again the smile, contradicted by the sorrowful eyes. 'And for the coffee.'

'You're welcome.'

'Bye then,' he said simply, and began to make his way towards the causeway, leaving me cold and quite bereft. *What?* All I knew was his name and that he was a cameraman. Way not enough. He'd turned up at the cottage believing it was abandoned, to spend the night. Why had he left wherever he was staying? To be alone? To ... escape?

'Bye,' I said, ignoring the tiniest little squeeze to my stomach. I needed to be alone, I needed to get on with things, to set up the cottage, to start work. I needed him to go.

So why exactly did a part of me want to ask him to stay a little longer?

Like when he'd let go of my hands on the ferry.

'See you,' he called over his shoulder as I watched him go, standing with the wind's caress on my body.

See you? Was that hope, creeping into my heart? And why should I hope to see him again? To see him again, let him hold my hand again. And unravel his secrets: because I knew that the way he'd arrived at the cottage in the middle of the night was too strange for the man not to have a story.

'Sorry, one last thing,' I had to ask, calling to be heard over the sound of the waves.

He turned around, standing against the sky.

'Sure.'

'Are you an escaped criminal? Wait! You've been in a Russian prison,' I said, pointing to the tattoos on his arms.

He smiled, and this time it reached his eyes. 'How did you guess?' he said, and turned and walked away, jumping across the stones with the sea on both sides as if he'd done it a million times before. I followed him with my eyes until he disappeared.

I finished my coffee slowly, taking in the beauty around me and trying to digest the strangeness of the past night. Seagulls flew in the blue sky; the sea whispered and sang, nearly smooth under the gentle wind.

Innes. It must be a Scottish name, because I'd never heard it before. It was a white-blue name, the colour of water and ice, I thought – I always associated names and people with colours. His eyes were icy too, a shade of blue so clear it seemed white.

Now that he was gone, I was alone – alone in the place I would call home for the next three months. This place was truly mine.

Here I could breathe, I could expand.

I could have peace.

I could learn to feel whole again, even if my mum was gone.

Outside, sea and sky; inside, the stories of all those who had lived here before me. And now, my story too.

I had a lot to do. A book to finish, and Mum's mystery

to unravel. Not to mention the dreams I'd had about the cottage, even before seeing it. Maybe researching the history of the place would give me an answer to those too.

Shivering, I got dressed in jeans and a jumper, and pondered the most bizarre night of my life. I unearthed my phone: a missed call from Neal – oh yes, I'd forgotten he was going to call me – and a couple of texts from a very anxious Stephen and Lorraine. Honestly, they fussed over me like two mother hens. I was just texting to reassure them that I was still alive and in pretty good form when the phone rang. The removals company.

'We're nearly here, love.'

'Oh brilliant! Thankfully the tide is out.' *Love*, I wanted to add, but resisted.

'The what, sweetheart?' I wondered how many more pet names he could come up with.

'The tide. I'll explain when you're here.'

'That's perfect, pet.'

'No problem, *darling.*'

'What?'

'Sorry, the signal is funny up here. See you in a minute,' I said quickly.

I made my way across the tiny causeway gingerly, Sasha following me with her tail upright, nose in the air. As I stood on the machair at the end of my strange watery driveway, I took in the landscape in daylight. I could see nothing but heathery moors and sea. The hamlet of Roan, as well as the tiny village of Ollaberry that I'd read about in the guide, were invisible from this angle.

The only sign of the presence of humans was some ruins towards the east – a church, I thought. No houses, no boats; just land and sea and sky. It was absolute solitude, loneliness even – and absolute freedom.

After a few minutes of standing in the wind, I was glad to see the van arrive. A burly man in a T-shirt – probably trying to be manly by braving the cold, but looking a bit like a gannet with ruffled feathers – stepped down from the driver's cabin. An older man with puffy cheeks sat in the passenger seat.

'I'm telling you, it's a miracle we're here,' the driver said. 'They've never heard of road signs in this place. We went around the island twice.'

'Sorry . . .'

'Not your fault, love. And you're staying here all alone?'

'Looks like it.' I shrugged. 'So, the house is just down that way . . .'

'Okay, jump up, I'll drive down there.'

'No, you can't drive to the cottage, you see . . .'

'What do you mean, doll?'

Call me doll again and I'll thump you, I thought. 'I mean, we need to carry the boxes over that causeway there.'

'What? You must be joking! I'm not paid for that.'

A few seconds of deep breathing.

'You are paid to carry all my stuff inside my house.'

'I'm not paid to go swimming, doll!'

'Right. Okay. Fine. Leave the boxes here, I'll carry

them.' I was a bit apprehensive about balancing them across the causeway, but I refused to admit it.

'You?' he snorted, looking down at my five foot two of not exactly pure muscle. People often underestimate how strong I am. 'You can't carry them! Come on!'

'Well, I have no choice. You're not doing it, and there's nobody else for miles around. Please open the van,' I said.

'Suit yourself, do—'

'And don't call me doll,' I said calmly. Enough was enough.

'Fine. Fine. Jesus, they've opened the mental hospital and the crazies are all out,' he said, circling his finger against his temple.

I was in the middle of a little fantasy where I threw the moron in the sea and watched him struggling against a strong undertow when a voice resounded over the noise of the waves. A man was coming over the small mound that led to the causeway, a man with an intense stare, long hair and a step that made it clear his intentions weren't friendly.

A *big* man, may I add.

Innes was back.

'What do you think you're doing?' he thundered.

'My job?' The removals guy looked positively scared for a moment, then puffed his chest out like a gorilla and squared up to Innes.

'You can't drive on the machair, you idiot!'

'The what? Speak English, mate.'

'This place is *alive* and they just drove over it!' Innes murmured, and the sudden quietness of his voice made him all the more menacing.

'Look,' said the driver. 'You're all crazy. Take your stuff and I'm going back to the real world, okay?'

I couldn't believe what happened next. In a moment, Innes had pushed the removals man against the side of the van. The guy was beefy – no wonder, with the job he did – but Innes was stronger. He lifted him off the ground and slammed him against the metal. I was too astonished to say anything; I just clamped my hand to my mouth.

'Listen to me now,' he said calmly. 'You're going to unload those boxes, then drive away. And be thankful I don't break your fucking nose.'

The removals man swayed a little as Innes let him go. He shook his head, trying to act outraged but actually looking frightened. 'You're a madman,' he said, without conviction.

'He didn't know he couldn't drive here! And I didn't either!' I shouted at Innes while the removals guy unloaded my boxes as fast as he could.

Innes ignored me completely, and instead crouched down, feeling the soil and grass with his hands. I had no idea what he was up to. He didn't lift his head even when the van left, a good deal faster than it had arrived.

'What are you doing?' I asked, but he didn't reply. He stood and crouched again a couple of times, then looked up and closed his eyes, and a great sigh came from him.

'It's intact. Oh. It's intact.' The relief on his face was immense. He looked so different from the Innes who'd threatened the guy just a minute before.

I knelt beside him. In a delicate gesture, he reached out and gently stroked the grass open, and there it was – one of the prettiest things I'd ever seen. A little nest with three . . . no, four eggs inside, white with a blue tinge, and speckled. The nest itself was a tiny miracle, a circular tapestry woven with incredible care and skill.

'I'm sorry. I really didn't know,' I said, softly this time.

'Corncrakes' nest. Please be careful around here,' he whispered. 'Like I said, this place is alive.' His fingertips touched the eggs one by one, soft as a feather, as if he were blessing them. It was surprising to me how this man could be savage one moment and sweet the next, so rough and yet so tender. 'I'm sorry too. I saw the van from a distance and ran back.' His stare turned steely, and once again he was his other self, the man capable of a fury that terrified me.

I frowned. 'He needed to be told off, yes, but not slammed against his van like that. You could have done serious damage.'

Innes looked down and said nothing. Then, in one swift movement, he rose and walked away. Again that feeling of abandonment – but then I recalled his cold rage of a few minutes before, and I was afraid, and relieved that he'd gone.

Margaret

The next morning, while the other servants were eating porridge in the kitchen, their breath condensing in white puffs in the early-morning chill, I went looking for Duncan. I had to be quick, because soon Lady Dolina would call me, and I didn't want to leave her waiting. I was wearing the red dress she'd given me, and Duncan's boots, the signs of their kindness towards me. I didn't care if I was at the receiving end of many a strange look, wondering where I could have found such beautiful things when I'd arrived in homespun, and boots so thin and rough they'd flayed my feet.

As I stepped out into the cold grey light, a small figure bumped into me. Ally. 'Have you seen Lord Duncan?' I whispered. 'I have an errand . . .'

'At the stables. If you want to catch him, you need to run. He's leaving . . .'

Without waiting for him to finish, I set off. I wanted to apologise to Duncan for speaking to him like I'd done; I wanted to thank him for the boots, so soft at every step. Now my wounds would heal . . .

I ran. And there they were, Lord Innes and Cameron, with his sour, dried-up face, intent on hitting a stable lad with a vicious fist before climbing onto his white horse. But where was Duncan? And then he emerged from behind another rider, on a horse whose mantle was the colour of autumn leaves, the blond mane and tail blowing in the early-morning breeze. He sat tall and proud, his wavy black hair moist and his purple-blue plaid on his shoulder; unafraid, but with a frown of worry on his face.

The strangest feeling hit me, sudden and sure – that I'd seen him somewhere before, that it wasn't the first time we'd met, or the second, or the third, or the tenth; it was like I'd known him for ever. As I stood there, unable to call him, rendered mute by the presence of his men, he turned around on his horse. Our eyes met for a moment, and his frown dissolved. I simply looked at him, his eyes the same blue ice as his father's, and yet so different. Then he smiled, a smile that wanted to be cocky, almost teasing, but all of a sudden turned sweet, as if with his eyes he was asking me a question. But I didn't know what that question was . . . He raised his hand and squeezed his horse's sides with his legs, and they were off.

'It's perfect on you. And that colour . . . with your hair, and the red of the dress, you truly look like a little flame,' Lady Dolina said, sitting at the loom, her hands idle in her lap. Weaving seemed too hard a task for her today, weak and empty as she was – empty as if her spirit itself was slowly leaving. It was a shame, because she was very skilled; the place was full of the tapestries she'd woven, hanging on the walls and from the windows to keep out the draughts. The hangings made her room look like a small church with stained-glass windows.

Lady Dolina had taken me under her wing – she said I reminded her of herself before she'd married Lord Innes. She wanted me at her side almost all the time, as she declined in both body and mind, sick with the vexations her husband put her through every day. After his first wife's death, Lord Innes had wanted someone who could provide him with more sons – daughters were not much use, except to make alliances. But Lady Dolina had been unable to give him what he wanted, through no fault of her own; although she'd given birth to three children, all had died in infancy. She was a sad figure who seemed to have been drained of all life, and enjoyed having me near because I had so much of it inside me.

'Thank you, my lady,' I said as I finished changing the bed. I'd been told I would have to change it every morning, because at night Lady Dolina coughed badly, and the linen would stain. The sheets would take days to dry, even in front of the fire, so we needed an endless amount of linen.

Suddenly I jerked my head up – it wasn't like me to be so jumpy, but after the pipe playing, the gathering of men I'd seen last night at the castle and Lord Duncan's sudden departure this morning, I was impregnated with a sense of doom. The pipes, sometimes far, sometimes near and more deafening than ever, had gone on all morning. It was an almost constant sound, from here and from everywhere around, every other castle and tower and hall. Or maybe it was just me, hearing them all the time: when a cow bellowed in the distance, when thunder rolled low over the hills, even when hooves sounded on the cobbles, coming closer and closer.

My family had been torn apart by the animosity with the Inneses, caused by my father's foolish pride, so I was used to things changing suddenly, to life falling apart in a day. But this was different, I knew it. Only the highborn, only the men made decisions – but paupers and servants and women would listen and learn and talk. News spread like wildfire, news of trouble that was not just about us, not just about the whole of Scotland, but further – England and France and even America, places so far and strange to us they might as well be on the moon. And it all seemed to centre on a young man by the name of Charles Stuart, whom they called the true king of Scotland.

Loyalties were being decided in rooms and halls where women had no access, let alone a young woman like me, not much more than a servant. In a country divided like Scotland, where clan was the first bond and allied clans the second, unity was pretty much impossible. Yes, everybody knew what was happening, from the lairds to the humblest scullery maids and stable lads. Scotland was rising, Scotland was being divided in two. A low rumble had begun to shake the earth and fill the sky. Part of me was full of natural joy, because I was young and in a new place and I wanted to see everything and learn everything and do everything; but another part, the part that listened to the quiet whispers of my blood, was very afraid.

'I saw Lord Innes and his sons leaving early this morning . . . It didn't look like they were going hunting,' I said in a tone that I hoped was casual. The plump woman with thin hair who was helping me change the linen looked at me as if I'd just thrown Lady Dolina's loom out of the window. Apparently I was too *new* to be talking in the lady's presence – or to be talking about such matters at all.

'Yes,' Lady Dolina said, looking out of the window.

I contrived a laugh that wanted to be unconcerned. 'Men's matters! There's always something . . . My father too, back home—' But Lady Dolina interrupted me.

'The MacGregors always gave my own father, Lord McAlpine, such grief. I think my lord is trying to bring them on our side . . . Ach, not even the Bonnie Prince himself could do that. But my lord thinks he's smarter.' She looked down, but, I noticed, she didn't look around. She didn't care if someone heard. A dying woman is not afraid. I swallowed at the mention of the MacGregors. It was the second time I'd heard them spoken of since I'd arrived. They were known for their fieriness, for how easily they took to their swords. And for the rivalry that went back three generations. I was afraid for Duncan . . .

Afraid for Duncan?

Yes. To my shame, I had to admit he'd been in my thoughts.

Never before had any boy or man caught my attention. But his eyes looked at me – those weren't the eyes of a predator, eyes like his father had. And the kindness in giving me those soft boots I was wearing right now, the sweetness of that thought – I had never before met a man who would do such a thing. Then there was the way he'd looked at me when he was about to leave. The way his face seemed as familiar to me as that of my own mother.

Like I'd met him many, many times before. Like we'd never parted.

I folded the dirty linen to carry it downstairs, and when I looked up, I realised that Lady Dolina's gaze was on me. Our eyes met for a moment, but I could not read what she was thinking.

Underneath the high stone ceiling, women were coming and going with trays and cloths, cleaning tables, tending to fires. As I stood and watched them, suddenly the fires in the stone hearths became flames; flames that would soon engulf my life and that of Castle Innes, until the Scotland we used to know was changed in ways so deep, so painful, that nothing would be the same again, and a new Scotland, wounded and weak and mourning, would be born . . .

'Doing nothing, I see. Stealing food and lodging.'

A voice made me turn. It was Helen. Before I could stop myself, my eyes narrowed, and I frowned.

'Get that look off your face, witch.' I startled at her words and looked around, hoping nobody had heard. 'And come with me. You're going to help me in the garden. But you'll have to keep your mouth shut. I hate people talking to me when I work.'

My heart soared. 'Seriously?'

'Oh yes. Just because your father is my hapless oaf of a brother, it doesn't mean you have no sense about you. So I'll give you a chance. Also, you don't look anything like my brother.'

I ignored that remark. Like my mother always did too.

Innes

As if seeing my mother and being back on the island again wasn't enough to throw me, Cora had to come into the mix, to make me sway and falter with one look of her clear eyes. Well, at least she'd already seen me for who I was. There would be no surprises, then, when we met again – because we would, I knew. After the ferry, and the way I'd found her again in darkness and silence, owner of the place that had been my shelter, there was no doubt we'd meet again.

It was time to stop thinking about Cora now. I had to call Neal Monahan and get to work, and somehow face Mother after having left the house in the middle of the night.

She pretended nothing had happened, greeting me as if I'd slept in my own bed, as if nothing was amiss. She'd always been good at that. I had the decency to feel vaguely guilty about having disappeared that way. She'd probably guessed where I was – years ago, she'd asked me where I spent all those nights, and apparently my answer – in an abandoned cottage, all by myself, at the ripe old age of ten years – pacified her. Better there than home, she probably thought.

I had a shower – no memories allowed, no thinking – got changed, and treated myself to a chat with Pamela, who was in great form and eager to go to school. Pamela seemed to know a lot more about life than I ever would, sitting in front of her cornflakes, chatting about how her teacher was planning to make a big picture with lots of pink spring flowers on it – 'fawers', she called them.

'She's a good girl,' I said to Sylvia softly, surprising even myself.

'She is. I'm very lucky.' Her words hung between us, full of meaning. The girl who was not wanted, the girl who was born anyway.

Never again would I forget I was her uncle.

My mum left the room, and Sylvia placed her small hand on my arm. 'I just wanted to say . . .'

'I know. Look, I'm sorry about last night.'

'No, no. I . . . I understand. I just wanted to say I'm so happy you're here. And I hope you'll stay a while. A long while. Oh, sorry, I'm putting you under pressure.' She blushed, her generous lips curving into a smile. I could certainly see why my brother fell for her.

'No, not at all. I don't really have plans at the moment.'

'You know, you always looked like Douglas, even when you were younger, but now . . . it's uncanny.'

'I haven't spoken to him in years. And I don't want to.'

She nodded. 'Do you want to know something funny?'

I lifted my chin. She bent towards me, until we were very close. Her flowery breath was on my cheek.

'I love him still,' she murmured, so that Pammy wouldn't hear her.

I was speechless. Her words had made me hollow with pain: for her, for Douglas, for Pamela; for the family they could have been.

Sensing how lost I was for a reply, she smiled and looked down. 'Are you happy to be back? I mean . . . I know this place wasn't always good to you, but . . .'

'Happy is not the right word. But I suppose in a way it's good to be back, yes.'

'It's great for us. To have you back, I mean,' she said, and her cheeks turned a soft pink. I couldn't find the words to reply to that, and for a moment the silence stretched between us. Maybe she wanted me to say things I couldn't say; there was a hidden meaning to her words, her expression, that I didn't want to acknowledge. It was my mother who broke the silence, stepping back into the room and interrupting our whispers. Sylvia pulled back. 'So, what will you do today?'

'I'm filming assorted wildlife. I have a brief as long as my arm. What, exactly, is to be decided today with the other cameraman.'

'You know, since I've been living here, I can't get enough of the dolphins. They're so beautiful!' Sylvia said with a bright smile. I wondered what this luminous woman might have seen in my stormy brother in the first place. Did she think she could save him, heal him? 'Will you be filming them?'

'Oh, I don't film anything to do with water. Me and water aren't exactly friends.' A clatter. Mother had dropped a ladle.

'Seriously? For someone who was born on an island . . .'

'I know, I know. Phobias are weird, I suppose,' I said. Mother's hands were shaking as she lowered some dishes into the sink. Obviously I would never tell anyone why water freaked me out. Why I couldn't even have baths. Some things can never be put into words.

'Will you be shooting just on Seal, or on other islands too?'

'This documentary is all about Seal. This place is like a universe in itself . . . I could do a whole series on it. You find everything here. The mountains and the cliffs and the fields, you know, so gentle, and Corrywreckan, all the power of the sea right there, in one place . . .'

'It must have been hard to be away for so long,' Sylvia said, and her eyes seemed to say much more than her words. I'd got carried away. Time to change the subject.

'Yes. Well. So what will *you* do today?'

'I'm helping out at St Fintan, you know, just a nursing assistant, but I love it. I also do art courses there, for the patients . . .'

'St Fintan?'

'The new clinic and rehabilitation centre they've opened in Ollaberry. Did you not know?'

I shook my head. It felt like change never came to

Seal – yet sometimes it did. After all, I'd been away a long time.

'They do great things there. I only work part time, rest of the time I'm a mum . . .'

'Will you be home for dinner, Innes?' my mother intervened.

Home? Was Sylvia part of the family who lived in this *home*, Sylvia and Pamela, come to sweep away the curse that weighed on us?

Out of the corner of my eye, I saw my mum standing in front of the sink, tea towel in hand, waiting to hear what I'd say.

'I . . . Yes. Of course. I'll be home for dinner.'

'I'll make you a fish-finger sandwich,' Pamela said, the tenderness of a five-year-old in a body that looked older but really wasn't.

I want to be there for you, I thought in the blink of an eye.

'That sounds amazing. Thank you,' I said, and my eyes met Sylvia's and saw something I didn't expect, I didn't expect at all.

And now Neal and I were sitting in the Design Gallery – a coffee shop that had been opened recently and I'd never been in – discussing shoots. I usually worked on my own – I wasn't keen on teamwork – but I would have to make an exception this time.

'Quite a list,' Neal said, looking at my laptop in front of us, Crispin's brief on the screen. He was incredibly detailed in what he wanted, and I was surprised he didn't plan to sit on our shoulders all summer as we shot. The plan was that he'd come over at the end of the month to review what we'd done.

'There's a little pod down the west side, you know where the ruined church is?' Neal said, attacking his bacon sandwich.

'I thought we said you'd do the boat shoots?' For a moment, my stomach churned. I was fine taking ferries or ships, but a little boat, close to the water, terrified me. *Thanks, Dad.*

'Yeah, no, I was talking about a beach,' he continued. 'There's a little house there, but the seals treat it like just another rock.'

It sounded exactly like Gealach.

'This old friend of mine, Cora, she's just arrived on the island and she's staying there. The seals didn't even notice. She has a dog that sits and stares at them and doesn't bark . . .'

I had to interrupt Neal's stream of consciousness. 'An old friend of yours?'

'Yes, she's pretty amazing, to be honest. Gorgeous. Anyway . . .' He laughed, and a liquid anger made its way down my throat and into my stomach. 'I kind of had a thing for her when we worked together a few years back, but hey, she turned me down. Maybe this time around she won't!'

I swallowed. What could I say? *Stay away, she's mine?* I barely knew her; I'd only met her twice, and the first time she was passed out with that strange episode on the ferry.

'Oh, yes. Cora. I know her.' My voice sounded gelid. Good.

Neal let his sandwich fall and looked up at me, his smile suddenly quite cold, quite fixed. 'Do you?'

Our eyes locked, and an image flashed in my mind: two stags crashing horns.

'She's pretty unusual, you know,' Neal said, shaking his head a little. 'She's the kind of woman you respect.'

Right. Are there any kinds of women you *don't* respect?

Anyway. For him to tell me something like that, to remind me that Cora deserved respect, my reputation must have come onto his radar. And maybe he was right; maybe my thoughts about her weren't exactly pure, my plans not exactly uninterested.

Was that a sin?

Was it a sin that I already dreamed of holding her, even when I knew well I couldn't offer her anything but a collection of moments?

I didn't want any ties, and after the Letty experience, I knew I never would. One of the reasons why I'd done so well in my job was because I'd go anywhere, at any time. Still . . . to forget everything for a night or two, to let myself hold someone and be held – *that* I did allow myself. Occasionally. It had to be brief, it had to finish before the woman involved could get hurt or disappointed, as she inevitably would. She could give me her body, but she was not allowed to give me her heart, because I could not hold anybody's heart in my hands. The girls I'd left behind had been with me for too short a time to realise I was not a good man, I was not a man to love. And who knows, maybe it would happen with Cora too: maybe I could take what I needed and leave what I could not be trusted with. Leave too quickly for her to be sad, to regret, maybe even to remember . . .

It was hard not to think about the softness of her skin as our fingers met over the cup of coffee, the way her hair caught the rays of the early sun. She was beautiful, with those sweet curves I could guess at underneath her night-gown, with the white skin of her neck . . . I could take those thoughts and carry them with me, like talismans, as I faced the memories of the past. Because I knew those memories would come back – and that was why I'd pan-icked in the middle of the night and run away. The Guy was rotting in his grave, but everything he'd done to us was still there, in our bodies, in our hearts, in our minds.

'Yes. She *is* the kind of woman you'd respect,' I said.

I would respect her enough to take her, and to not be there when she woke up the morning after.

So much of my job meant being still and quiet. Once all the equipment was set up, that was what we aimed for: silence and stillness and pretending we didn't exist, we weren't there at all. Let the world around us go on with-out us, and take it all in without being a part of it.

That had been my plan when I returned to Seal. Not really get involved, do my job, see my mother, maybe look the ghost of the child I used to be in the eye and say, *He can't hurt you any more.* But something quite unexpected had happened. The truth was, in spite of all the strife, being back on Seal was so good, I could have cried.

I hadn't cried since the day I left, not once, not even when the Letty thing fell apart; but the scent of the machair, and the greeny-blue colour of the sea, and the shape of that coast, the shape I knew as well as I would have known the shape of my wife – all that could have brought me to tears. Oh, it was incredible to be back on Seal. My island.

You are back, you are back, the wind was saying. *Son of Seal, you are back.*

Of all the things that had been taken away from me – my childhood, my faith in the world, the chance to love and be loved – losing the island had been the worst. I'd done my best to try and forget how much I loved Seal, but she kept coming back to me. In my dreams, I walked on the soft white beaches, and looked into the seals' lucid black eyes.

When my family abandoned me, the island had been all I had left. I was the four-year-old who went to the beach alone, who sat among rock pools and little seaweed mounds and felt safe. And when I discovered the cottage, I was more at home in that cold, sandy, deserted place than in my own home.

There's this story I'd always felt was mine. Four hundred years ago, the Clan MacGregor was outlawed after killing some members of the Clan Colquhoun. The Colquhouns laid their relatives' bloody shirts in front of King James, and from then on, the MacGregors weren't allowed to carry their own name. They had to hide – they became Clann a'Cheo, children of the mist, or children of the smoke.

That was me, a child of the mist, a child who hid. The boy who slipped out of the house without making a noise, who managed to move around invisibly, trying not to be noticed. Trying not to catch his father's eye. The boy who couldn't keep his own name, because too many times the sound of that name was followed by beatings that left him bloodied and half deaf. Alan had become Innes.

My father too had been stripped of his name. In my mind, he was never my father; I didn't know the word Dad. He was only ever The Guy.

Dr Innes. Pillar of the community. Yes, the man who beat my mother and me – who raped her on the stairs when he was so intoxicated he'd even forgotten his own name, let alone the fact that his children were in their rooms, hands over their ears, waiting for it to stop – was an esteemed, respected member of society. Corduroy jacket, impeccable shoes – no mean feat on an island with just a few roads – his children's drawings and pictures of his family all around his study. Pats on the back for his friends, smiles and a sympathetic ear for the women, a warm but firm father figure to the children. Someone who had a comforting word for those in pain, a thought for the lonely, a joke for children scared of a needle or refusing medicine. He would drive out in a storm if somebody needed him; he would come out at night to discuss a matter that wasn't letting you sleep; he was the man who oversaw island life as if he was everybody's dad, grand-father, brother. When he was Dr Jekyll, he had a heart – for real. What nobody knew was that when he was full of drink and turned into Mr Hyde, he was a monster. No, nobody knew. The whole island looked up to him until the day he died, falling down the stairs, too drunk to see where he was going. Seal mourned their hearts out.

Which is why I hated them all, the islanders.

My people.

Because how could they not have noticed anything? How could they not have seen? He was careful, yes – no visible bruises, and we children were never to change for sports in front of other people. Our legs being black and blue was easily explained by shinty, or fooling around the way kids do. But they must have seen the way my brother and I flinched if somebody made a sudden gesture, the way my mother smiled but her eyes were dead.

The way she did her hair that night at the ceilidh for the Sea Rescue, so that her bald patch didn't show after he'd torn out a fifty-pence-sized piece of her scalp.

Nobody said a thing.

He said that if I spoke out, nobody would believe me, and he was probably right. But if they did, if I spoke out and anyone believed me, he'd kill my mother, he said. He terrified me. I thought I would come home and find her dead. Sometimes he even said it was all in my imagin-ation. That I was crazy. There was this terrible illness called *schizophrenia*, he explained carefully, pronouncing the difficult word slowly – I was so young, I couldn't even say it – that made you imagine things that weren't true, and probably that was what I had, because he'd never filled the bathtub and then pushed my head underwater, I had dreamed that all up. But he couldn't convince me of being mentally ill, however hard he tried. I knew what was real, I knew what was happening. So he said that if I told anyone, he'd kill my mother.

I never told.

The closest I ever got to coming clean was with Mrs McLean, the school's head teacher. I was friends with her son, Sorren, and I often went to their house. She sensed something was wrong, and unlike everybody else, she questioned my brother and me. Once, twice. Three times. Gently, without probing.

I told her everything was fine.

Maybe she believed me, maybe not, but she couldn't have come out with accusations without us backing her. She said she was there if I needed her, and when she said that, she looked at me for a long time. I remember that moment well, because her eyes were a startling blue, and I looked into them like you would look at a buoy when you were drowning.

My brother told The Guy about Mrs McLean asking questions. My father said she was a fucking meddling bitch. My brother repeated it to me: she was a *fucking meddin bitch*. He was seven at the time.

We weren't allowed to go to Sorren's house any more, but Sorren and I remained close friends. He was the only one who stood by me as I grew angrier and angrier, as my fame as a dangerous young man spread through the island. When Isla, his sister, drowned, I remember looking at Sorren and thinking, *Now you know pain. Now you are one of us.* At the funeral, I held Mrs McLean in my arms, surprising everyone and alarming a few. This brotherhood and sisterhood of pain I had been born into – I'd wished the McLeans, the family I'd always wanted, might never be part of it.

Nobody else saw what was happening behind closed doors – or *wanted* to see it. Like that time The Guy burned my mother with an iron; she said she'd had an accident while she was doing his shirts. Being a doctor gives you the freedom and ability to patch up your family after you've torn them to shreds. And apparently nobody will ask questions. The solicitor, the priest, the Presbyterian minister, the owner of the golf course – through prestige or money they were the good and the great of the island. I can't be *sure* they knew, and both my mum and The Guy were very, very good actors. But over and over again I asked myself: did anybody even suspect that my mother was a little too accident-prone?

And us. We were good actors too; we were their children, for sure. Douglas learned to smile the way he always had done yet be a bully behind closed doors. As for me, I went from being a timid, chronically frightened child to being bad. *A bad one, the Innes boy.*

It started with bashing my fists on the desk in school – the first time I did it, red in the face and breathing hard, I scared myself. The noise made me jump and I burst into tears. The shock on Mrs McLean's face was worse. I had no words to explain that I didn't mean it, I didn't know how all that rage had come out of me.

And then I couldn't stop. I hit, I shattered, I shouted. My mother cried and The Guy shook his head, while people wondered how two good people like my parents, upstanding members of the community, could possibly have such a troublesome son.

I had my first drink at twelve. It seemed the solution to all my problems. Oh, how clever I'd been to find the remedy to all ailments, and so handy, with bottles everywhere around the house – hidden only if company came. It made me brave enough to hit my father back, though I was so small, still, that I stood no chance of stopping him; but at least it made me forget.

I wasn't as good as my parents at hiding things. The whole island knew I was a tearaway, one to keep away from their own sons and daughters. I was desperate to leave Seal, but I was terrified that if I did, The Guy would kill my mother. I earned a living working in the fish factory in Ollaberry and drinking all night. Douglas lived by himself – wise decision, I suppose. Survival. So it was just my mother, The Guy and me.

How cosy.

I believed I was a bodyguard to my mother. I was her guardian and her protector now that I was as big as The Guy, and as angry. Until the day came when I realised the truth: she didn't want to be protected from him. She was playing his game, dancing this horrific dance with him. She would never stand up to him, no matter what.

Because she didn't want to get rid of him, she didn't want him out of her life – she needed him. It dawned on me suddenly, one day when he came out of his study smelling of aniseed and alcohol – the sweets weren't enough to hide his reek – and for no reason, no reason at all, hit her repeatedly over the head. I wasn't in the room, but I heard him; when I walked in, she had her hands on her temples and was bent over like she was about to be sick.

Nothing new there. I was used to it. We would fight and I would make him leave her alone. She would smooth down her hair, the white scar showing below her three-quarter-length sleeve, and keep on with what she was doing as if nothing had happened.

Despair is resilient.

But this time it didn't work that way. Something had happened in the sick, sadistic workings of his mind to make him decide that beating and burning and drowning weren't enough. This time he grabbed a knife from the drawer – the knife block had been discreetly put away by my mother; the normality of madness, I suppose: are you scared that someone in your household is going to try and kill you sooner or later? Easy, hide the knives and it'll be all right – and pushed her against the fridge. There was a moment, a heartbeat, before I realised what was happening – before my brain could interpret what was being impressed on my retina: my mother with a knife at her belly, pressed against a fridge with a Sunny Majorca magnet on its door, pinning down a Chinese takeaway menu, and a tiny stain of tomato sauce down in the lower left corner.

Again, the normality of madness, all these little details of daily life: a souvenir from a friend who'd gone on holiday; the way we always had Chinese on a Wednesday from the tiny place owned by silent people who never smiled but always gave sweets to us kids; a smudge of tomato left on the fridge after you've made beans on toast for your husband, before he holds a knife to your belly and threatens to spill your guts.

'Please don't,' I remember saying in a quiet voice.

'Get out, Alan,' my mother said, equally quietly. In her voice there was terror and resignation in equal parts. Neither of us was asking how my father had come to this, what could possibly have happened, what we had done to cause it. He didn't need a reason, we both knew that.

With her eyes my mum was saying: *My time has come.*

And in those weird lucid moments that happen sometimes, I realised she was relieved.

It's nearly over, I'm nearly free.

At that moment, I hated her.

The Guy turned around and placed the knife on the table. His hand was steady, even if he was drunk. Maybe he was the devil. My mother swayed, holding on to the kitchen counter to keep standing. Her eyes were wide; they fixed on the knife. The Guy ran a hand through his hair and straightened his shirtsleeves.

'Any chance of some toast and butter, Morag?' he said calmly. 'I'm famished.'

My mother's eyes moved slowly towards him. She nodded.

If he wasn't the devil, he was crazy.

'Mum. Come. Come with me.'

'Just a minute, Alan. Your father wants toast. You go, I'll catch you later.'

I was used to my mother's compliancy, but this was too much. Maybe she was in shock. 'Mum. Please. Come with me.'

'She's not going anywhere, Alan,' my father said.

I grabbed the knife from the table. 'Mum. Can you see this knife? *Can you see it?*'

'Morag, get behind me,' my father said.

'What?'

'You are bad, Alan. Bad since the day you were born.'

'What?' I repeated.

'You pull a knife on your own mother? What kind of man are you?'

'I didn't—'

'You *did*. You pulled a knife on your mother and me. You fucking bastard of a son!' And then he grabbed the knife from me, so fast that I didn't even realise what was happening. He held my mother's arm in a vicious grip and ran the blade over her skin, leaving a red trail. She grimaced but didn't scream, as if she was thinking, *If I endure it, it will be over faster.* And then he let her go and slashed his own arm, deep and savage, like he hated himself.

'It was you!' I said unnecessarily, pathetically. 'It was you, not me.'

'Who will believe you, son?' he said, and placed the bloodied knife on the table. 'You did this.'

'I'm calling the police . . .'

'Yes. Call Mike. Go ahead, Alan. Call him.' He was calm, though the blood was gushing down his arm, though my mum was leaning against the counter, tears on her cheeks, her eyes those of a broken woman. I swallowed. Mike. Officer Mike Duff. He was a friend of The Guy, like everyone who mattered on the island, and he hated me. In a small place where nothing ever happened, he'd had to break up fights I'd started, stopped me because I was driving too fast, too drunk.

The Guy was looking at me with no expression on his face. His eyes were empty. Many years later, I filmed alligators in the Florida swamps. One of them came close to me and I looked into its eyes, and I saw my father's eyes that day – the day of the knife.

'Go on. Call him. Call Mike,' he goaded me. 'You'll end up in prison on the mainland.' I knew he was right.

'Mum will tell him the truth,' I said. 'Won't you, Mum?' I implored.

'Of course she will,' The Guy said. 'We both will. That you went crazy and slashed us with a knife. That's the truth, isn't it? Is that what you want? To end up in prison?'

I cried. I was a six-foot-tall seventeen-year-old, and I cried.

For a moment, I pictured myself grabbing the blade and sinking it into his flesh, his life flowing away together with his blood.

But I was no killer.

I hung my head, and a sickly smile appeared on his

lips. 'It's time for you to go, Alan,' he said, almost gently. 'All boys sooner or later must find their own way in life. You won't need to pack. All you have belongs to me anyway. Just go.'

My head spun. I couldn't possibly leave my mother. 'Mum, please. Come with me,' I said once more, like many times before.

'It's time for you to go,' he repeated. 'And before you leave, I'm going to have to make you pay for what you did to us today. Come here,' he said, the knife in his hand. 'I'm sorry. It hurts me more than you.'

I shook my head. 'No.'

'It's you or your mother.'

'I'll kill you.'

He shrugged. 'No you won't. You want a future. Be a good boy: come here and roll up your sleeve.'

I don't remember much about what happened next. I have a vague memory of the blade down my arm, but I can't remember the pain. There was a lot of blood. I didn't fall, I didn't cry out. I thought I would die of humiliation. But it was exactly how he'd said: it was me or my mother, who was already white and trembling and holding her injured arm. And so it had to be me. I shook with anger and dreamed of taking the knife and plunging it into his heart, over and over again. Someone was crying, long sobs and wails. It was my mother.

'He's crazy. Can you not see it?' I whispered, my eyes on hers. And then I said it one last time. 'Please come with me.'

She just looked at me. She looked at me, and didn't move.

I walked out into the cold and the wind, and bled all the way to the cottage on the beach. The next day I went to Sorren and asked for a loan of the fare to London. He looked at me, at my bleeding arm and dead eyes; he didn't suggest calling my father to see to the cut, and instead went to do it himself, but I shook my head. I didn't want anyone to touch me. He said I could stay with him as long as I wanted to, that he didn't care what trouble I was in, he would stand by me.

Sorren gave me some money and I went to London with nothing but the clothes on my back. At the moment of leaving, I made him promise not to tell anyone. I was sure The Guy would kill my mother; that she would stay there and let it happen. I made him promise on his own mother's life.

In London, I survived. And then I went from surviving to making a living. I wasn't Alan any more; I was Innes. Alan was dead.

I spoke to my mother on the phone sometimes.

Every once in a while, something in me exploded, and then I punched the wall. I broke my knuckles a couple of times. If the wall wasn't enough, I went looking for fights. I came home bloodied and kept drinking until I passed out.

And then I met Letty, and there was some relief; until I managed to destroy that too.

Margaret

I was in heaven.

I was in heaven because Lady Dolina had agreed to let me work in Helen's garden whenever she didn't need me, and so my time was shared between my beloved lady and my beloved garden. Yes, I'd grown to like Lady Dolina – maybe even love her, though such a short while had passed since I'd arrived. She was vulnerable and fragile, and yet she was like a flaming sword that had been plunged in cold water over and over again, made strong, resilient. Even if her body was slowly letting her down, her soul burned bright and her mind was so sharp, though people didn't seem to notice. She knew everything that was going on in the castle, and she'd chosen me as her confidante.

A week had passed since Duncan left, and to my shame, I was dreaming of him. I kept waking up thinking he was in the room, bent over my bed. Touching my skin and stroking my hair . . .

I awoke red-faced and full of confusion, for once unable to see rhyme or reason for these dreams. Maybe because this wasn't a matter of foresight or vision, but a matter of love.

For someone I'd seen three times, and spoken to once?

I was glad that Lord Innes was away – I was frightened of him, and at the same time I was frightened of my deep dislike for him, which might cause my temper to flare and make things very difficult for me. I had to be wise. I had to be calm. And most of all, I had to be *humble*, which was hard for me. But if it meant I would see Duncan again, I could face Lord Innes's vicious, angry figure stalking the castle and occasionally coming to harass Lady Dolina for no reason at all.

The moment I'd been waiting for so long came at last; the men returned. I was in the garden with Helen, and I sensed them riding towards us well before they were close enough to be heard. As I saw them coming inside the castle walls, Duncan and his bay mare among them, I began to tremble. When would I see him? And when I did, would he speak to me? Or would he ignore me, my dreams having been some form of pathetic desire I should have been strong enough to squash at the very beginning? He disappeared into the belly of the castle with the other men, all of them walking urgently, like the devil was at their heels.

I waited and hoped, hoped and waited, all day, the hours trickling by too slowly to bear. Until finally he came looking for me. I was doing Lady Dolina's hair, braiding it with a white ribbon to make it look thicker, when he came in. I tried to hide my confusion as the man who'd often materialised in my dreams walked into my reality, covered in mud, lines of worry on his face, yet his eyes burning blue and clear and truthful. I kept my own eyes down, for fear he'd see what was inside my heart.

'Mother,' he said. 'I would come close, but . . .' He opened his arms to display the mud on his clothes.

Lady Dolina stood up, gently freeing herself from my hands entwined in her hair. I noticed he called her Mother though there were no blood ties between them, but instead a deep bond of affection.

'I wish to be alone,' she said, and everyone dropped what they were doing, abandoning embroideries on stools and straightening skirts to leave. I did the same, still not daring to look at Duncan though desperately wanting to, but Lady Dolina gently stopped me, a hand on my arm. I stood still. When the room was empty, she threw her arms around Duncan and held him tight.

'I find you well, and beautiful as ever,' he said.

'Liar,' she replied, her eyes big in her hollow face. 'Soon I will be gone, and I won't miss much of this world. But I'll miss you.'

A cloud of genuine pain shadowed his eyes. 'Mother, don't . . .'

'And now tell me the truth. What is happening?'

'My lord father's poisonous pride, that's what's happening.' His words strangely echoed what I'd so often heard said about my own father: that his pride had ruined us. I'd always been told that he'd slighted the Innes clan, but the short confrontation with Lord Innes made me want to know exactly what happened. 'He thinks he has everyone at his feet,' Duncan continued, 'but it's not so. Not any more. We're outnumbered, and the MacGregors—'

'Gold always spoke loudly enough for them.'

'Gold we don't have much left of.' I was surprised at this statement – the castle seemed to be a forbidding place, like a fortress, but not without resources. By my standards, they were living in luxury.

Lady Dolina glanced towards the window. 'I just want you to be safe. For the people of this castle to be safe . . .'

'And we will be. Mother, please do not fret.'

'No. No.' She smiled a brittle smile, and there was a moment of silence. My heart was beating so hard, I thought they would hear it from Lochawe. 'Margaret, today the sun is shining so brightly, I wish I could go out myself. But I feel so weak and the cough was so bad last night. Would you go and pick some flowers for me, so that I may feel like I'm part of this beautiful spring?'

'Of course, my lady.'

'Son, would you accompany her? You know what colours I like. You can show her the flowers I love best.'

Lady Dolina glanced at me, a look that was neither cheerful nor sad, but knowing, and I felt the blood rise to my cheeks.

As I followed Duncan through the corridors of the castle and into the sun, I could feel people falling silent, girls giggling, heads turning. It was like everything had slowed down, and all voices had been muted, and part of me felt as though I was walking towards my destiny. And still, as the sun dissolved the shadows of the castle and blinded me, for a moment I wanted to run.

Part of me was happy; part of me knew better than to let my head be turned. The young laird of the castle. I would not be the first girl he'd pursue, nor would I be the last.

We walked in silence, and when I mustered the courage to glance across at him, I saw that his cheeks were burning. I couldn't believe it. Was he as nervous as I was? Because I *was* nervous. And not just because of the dreams I'd had, and the feelings that curled up inside my heart like little green blossoms; but also because he, his brother and most of all his father held my life in their hands. I couldn't afford to be defiant.

'You came to say goodbye when we left,' he said in a voice that nearly made my thoughts melt away, though a small part of me remained aware, concentrated on survival.

'I wanted to apologise,' I said.

He laughed. 'For what?'

'For speaking to you like a . . . you know . . . like a servant. You were carrying salmon! You were covered in . . .' I opened my arms. He was *still* covered in mud.

'That's a bit of a habit,' he agreed. 'But there's nothing to apologise for. My father decided that you should be a servant in the kitchen, but the McCrimmons used to be our peers. My lady mother tried to help. It's a cruel game my father is playing.'

'It was *my* father's foolishness.'

'That too, yes. But let's just say that my own lord father would have been quick to take advantage.'

'Do you know exactly what happened?'

'No. Whatever it was, it took place behind closed doors.' And then, after a small pause: 'Are they comfortable?' For a moment, I was confused by the change of topic. 'The boots?'

'They are. So much. Thank you.'

'Your feet were in a bad way.'

'They were fine.'

'I see you've been brought up like me – absolutely never complain!' he said, and ran his hand over a rosemary bush.

'I think so, yes,' I laughed. 'For Lady Dolina . . . I'd like to pick some iris, I think. They grow so plentifully along the stream.'

'That's where we first met, remember?'

I blushed. The memory of how I'd spoken to him was very vivid. Had it been Cameron, I would have been in for a thrashing. 'I remember.'

All of a sudden, Duncan's fingers brushed mine. 'You know, I've been thinking about you . . . pretty much all the time.'

I kept walking, pretending that nothing had happened, that he hadn't touched me. I was sure I looked like a fool, but I couldn't help it. I just couldn't believe he had come out with something like that. I was twenty years old and nothing like this had ever happened to me. Nobody had come near me – I suspect it was because they were scared of the strange things happening around me, or because of the rumours that I was a changeling. Men were for me as remote as a distant land, as remote as America would be.

'Since you arrived, I have had . . . dreams,' he continued. Dreams? Dreams like mine? 'Have you?'

'Have *I* had dreams? No, of course not! What you're saying is quite absurd . . .'

'Sorry. But surely you've sent them to me.' Had I? Could I do that? I didn't know. Sometimes I did things that surprised myself. '*And* you've been thinking about me,' he said, with a certainty that annoyed me.

'Now wait a minute,' I began, even as a voice in my head said, *Stop, don't say too much, don't let your temper take over; this will end very badly.* 'Do you expect me to fall into your arms like all the other girls do, just because you're the laird?'

'No. I don't expect that.' He looked hurt, and my heart sank. 'And *all the other girls* don't do that. Because I don't ask them; I don't look for them.'

'Well, then.' A pause, laden with annoyance on my part, hurt on his, which in turn made me even angrier, trying to save face.

'So what do we do?' he asked, his eyes alight.

'We forget about all this and you go looking for some maid you can have fun with until you marry a lady.'

To my amazement, his face fell, and my heart sank further. What was I doing?

'Fine. If that's what you want, fine,' he said, and walked away. Just like that.

I bit my lip. I was too proud to call him back . . .

'Duncan!'

. . . but I did. I called him back.

He turned around and looked at me, a question in his eyes. And the question was, *Do you trust me?*

'Don't go.'

He was back in two long strides, and before I could do anything about it, his arm cinched my waist and he placed his lips on mine, soft as a feather.

I was left swimming in a sea of sweetness. I walked back to Lady Dolina alone, my arms full of irises, feeling like I'd begun to fall, making my head spin and my heart beat a strange, uncontrollable rhythm.

Later that night I lay in my bed, dreaming of what had happened, dreaming of his arms around me and of how blue, how clear his eyes had been as he kissed me. Silent crying awoke me. Fiona, the blonde girl Mairi and I were sharing a room with, was quietly sobbing.

'Fiona? What's wrong?' I sat on her bed in the darkness, only guessing the features of her face in the light of the moon. To my embarrassment, she threw her arms around me and I felt her body, breathed in her scent. 'You are with child!' I said surely, whispering in the darkness.

She dried her face with the palm of her hand, eyes big in the gloom. 'How do you know?'

'I just do.' I didn't tell her that I could smell it. I never wanted to bring attention to my gifts. 'What are you going to do?'

'I don't know. I'm afraid Lord Innes will send me away. Me and my baby will starve!' Another fit of tears.

'You and your son will not starve; you have to keep hope!'

'My son? How do you know it's a boy?'

'I . . . I don't know. I just guessed, that's all. Can the father of the baby not do anything for you? Who is he?'

Fiona seemed to think for a while. Her face worked as if a million contrasting thoughts fought in her mind. Finally, she spoke. 'The father of my son is the young laird, Duncan.'

Cora

Innes left, this time for good. After the incident with the removals man, our goodbyes were awkward, distant – all of a sudden, I had a measure of how tightly this tall, strong man was wound. He looked into my eyes and I know he saw a vague sense of trepidation – he seemed embarrassed by it, nearly ashamed. This time I didn't want to say 'don't go yet' – and still, when he left, I couldn't stop thinking about him.

But I had a lot to do. I needed to get the cottage in shape, and get to work on *Lovemade*. Not to mention the strangest, vaguest side of my Seal mission: discovering my mum's story. I couldn't stop thinking about her, every step I took – would she have seen this landscape, would she have stepped on these stones, would she have stood on this beach and watched the seals sunbathing? I kept recalling memories of my childhood, looking for a Scottish connection, but I couldn't find one.

For every hour I spent working – a handkerchief in my hair, my hands in Marigolds, like a fifties housewife – I spent another hour looking at the sea, in quiet bliss. How come the water was aqua? Light aqua, like a Caribbean beach. And how many times a day could the sky change, how many different ways did it have to enchant me? Was the sky in London so magical, only I never noticed because the horizon was cluttered with buildings? To the left of me, the pod of seals sunbathed, swam, looked around with eyes that seemed so innocent, so dog-like – and yet they had something human about them too. Who knows, maybe one day one of those seals would shed her skin and come ashore to have a chat with me, long black hair down her back, asking for raw fish with her tea . . . A selkie, now that would be a lovely idea for a tapestry! Maybe I could include it in *Lovemade* . . .

Oh.

My inspiration was coming back.

A sigh came up from the depths of me.

Maybe that little part of me that had been buried with my mum, lost in the cold and dark with the withered roses on her coffin, had risen again – and slowly, translucent and gossamer-thin, the Cora I had lost was making her way from London to Seal to find me and be whole again.

Maybe it was a fleeting moment, but I was happy.

I was happy in a place where if I opened a cupboard too hard it would come loose in my hand, a place I couldn't leave in any other way but boat or swimming for half the day and half the night, a place where the only company for miles was a pod of seals, a shelf of sheep-farming magazines, and of course my darling Sasha.

Anyway. I had to reintroduce myself to the concept of

earning a living. Any moment now I would get that message from Lorraine – *So, how is the writing going?* And I was desperate, after months of struggling, to reply, *Very well, thank you.*

An intrusive, unwelcome thought forced its way into my mind.

I would not think of him.

Who was Innes, anyway? I asked myself while scrubbing the uneven stone floor. A stranger who had come into my life and just as quietly left it. I would not think of him.

No. What I would think of instead was the way he'd slammed the removals guy against the side of the van – yes, the man was odious, but he didn't deserve to be manhandled that way. Innes was a bit of a psychopath, clearly.

But he was defending the nest . . .

Enough.

One last wipe, and I removed the Marigolds. Cleaning the place had been quite a feat, especially because I'd inherited my mum's cavalier attitude to housework – a messy house is a happy house, she always said when the kitchen was strewn with my crafting experiments and Stephen's toys. Also, the cottage had been abandoned for so long, it was no wonder that I had found sand on the floor and on every surface, and even tiny bird bones on the windowsills downstairs. I had no idea how the birds could have got inside, but it felt like the place belonged to the sea and the land and their creatures as well as me, so I wiped underneath and left the delicate bones there on the sill, a bird graveyard in miniature. At least these birds had flown, and they had done so in what I thought was simply the most beautiful place on earth.

Mum's last gift, bringing me here.

I took a breath and surveyed my materials, now unpacked and strewn about the downstairs room – strange powders in plastic bags, threads and wool, sweet-scented oils in bottles, fragrant bags of herbs and dried flowers, fabric-bound notebooks with white pages on which I would write my book, because I couldn't plug in the computer, of course. And most important of all, my beloved loom – not the one that took up half my studio back home, but a smaller one I'd used at school, before I went on to study textiles. With the loom in the corner and the air full of scents, even if the smell of the sea was so strong, the place already felt a little bit like home. I wondered if people would be able to guess my job simply by looking at my things. Not even I had a definition, which was why I'd come up with *Heartmade*, a kind of umbrella word, meaning simply that everything I made came from the heart.

Gealach was cosy now, like a little universe, self-contained and happy to be inside itself, but the wind blew around it and sang an enticing song, and the scents of the machair, dancing in the sunshine, were calling. When everything was sorted, when my loom and the bright threads were set up near the fire and all my materials were lined up and waiting for me to start, I felt free to go outside at last.

The sun had come out, after a grey start to the day,

and the beauty was too absolute to do it justice with words. The sea was as green as if a million gems hid at the bottom of it, and the grass and the wild flowers danced as though they were happy to be alive to see such a day. The wind was blowing strong and chilly, but I didn't step back in to get my jacket – I wanted to feel the fresh air on my skin, I wanted it to blow away all the strife and suffering of the last few months.

Mum, how you'd have loved this place . . .

But you did see it. And you never told us.

Why?

In the middle of the causeway, I stopped and closed my eyes, letting the sea air caress my hair and my body. It was as if I was standing in the sea itself, with water on both sides of me. As if I could just give the sea all my sorrow, all my past joys, everything that was no more – let it all go and start again afresh.

When I finally opened my eyes, I felt like something had shifted inside me, as if the communion of sea and sky had soothed the hole that my mother's death had opened in my soul.

I ran along the rest of the causeway, followed by Sasha, and at the end, we stood for a moment deciding what to do. I wanted to go to the hamlet of Roan, down along the coast, to get some groceries in and stave off scurvy, given that I only had canned food on my shelves – handy in case of zombie apocalypse, I supposed. But first, something else beckoned me – a place that had been calling to me since I'd arrived: the ruined building that I'd thought might be a church, its broken spire and half-eaten arch rising towards the sky. It was simply the most romantic thing I'd ever seen, something out of a gothic novel or an old-fashioned postcard.

Sasha and I walked towards it along the beach, treasures appearing in front of my feet with every step – shells and seaweed and sea glass, a wealth of small, magical things that I could use in my projects. I resolved to go treasure-collecting as soon as I could. On my left was the sea; on my right, the brightly coloured meadow of the machair. Having seen the little nest, so precious and fragile with its speckled eggs, I knew that the dancing grass hid untold life. It seemed incredible to me that such fertile ground could be so close to the salty sea.

The ruins came closer and closer. I climbed a sand dune to reach them, and as I stepped down the slope, I realised that the waves ebbed and flowed almost as far as the church ground itself. Without noticing, I began to slow my pace, as if I was arriving for a service. The wind must have kept blowing and the waves breaking on the shore, but it seemed to me that silence had fallen. Slowly I walked the perimeter, stones crumbling and eaten away, covered in moss, two walls miraculously standing. Against the furthest wall, two ... three pews, the wood rotten and crumbling. I turned towards the sea, and then back again to the pews.

And all of a sudden, I *knew*.

The sea had destroyed this church; a huge wave had come and swallowed half of it. While the lower part was now in pieces, its stones scattered on the seabed, its pews slowly dissolved in the water, the other half still stood, as a reminder that the sea gives and the sea can take away. And now a question rose into my mind – a question so terrifying, it brought tears to my eyes: when the sea took the church away, was it already abandoned? Was it empty? Or were these people sitting in those pews when the wave came?

A low buzz started in my ears, and my head began to spin. The sound in my ears was a bit like when your blood pressure plummets, but not quite – it was softer than that, and like it came from far away – and at that moment I knew I'd heard it before. But I had no time to wonder when, because suddenly everything changed in front of my eyes. The empty, rotten pews and the ruined church disappeared, and I saw a handbag floating in the water, hymn books black against the white foam. A walking stick, a coat, a candle, washed up on the shore . . . The little statue of the Star of the Sea. I stood knee deep in the freezing water, feeling the currents pulling me, spotting a white hand, a face, a shoeless foot, a blonde bun come undone and floating . . .

And then it was all over.

I shivered, deeply. What had just happened to me?

It hadn't been a dream, but a *vision*. And stronger than the one on the ferry, the white hand on the stone . . .

What was Seal doing to me?

Like a flash, I remembered the day of my thirteenth birthday, when the pipes burst and my house flooded. As I saw my mum standing ankle deep in water, I'd felt a low buzz in my ears, and for a moment, I'd seen the same scene that had appeared to me now, the white hand and the blonde hair floating, the hymn books and the walking stick, yes, I'd seen all this before . . .

As I hurried to step out of the church, I saw that just at the back of it lay an ancient graveyard. I stood there for a moment, calming my galloping heart. Maybe I wasn't remembering right. Maybe I was superimposing a new memory onto an old one. Yes, that had to be it. I breathed in deeply, Sasha gazing up at me, sensing my distress.

The tombstones stood mossy and eaten by lichen: people long gone, people who had been loved and cherished, or maybe lost and alone – it made no difference now. I walked among the graves; each told a story. And then I saw them, row after row of identical stones, all arched, all grey, and all with the same date: 14 August 1946. Hugh John, Fiona and Mary McDonald. Elizabeth McNeil. Laurie and Mary Anne McCrimmon, Malcolm McLean, Kenneth and Hannah MacLean . . . *Taken by sea*, said the McLean grave.

Yes. I must have been right – the wave did happen, the people did die.

I spotted a group of tombstones that stood like crooked teeth, so eaten up by lichen that the writing on some of them wasn't even visible. And beyond them, some flat ones, the stone weathered and softened by age. They seemed a lot older than any of the others, and I crouched to make out a date: 1756. These people had lived and died over two hundred and fifty years ago. I couldn't help touching the stone lightly. *Hello*, I said in my heart, with a tenderness I couldn't explain. *Hello, people of long ago.*

It seemed to me that they answered, because a gust of wind blew through the trees and then the tombstones, lifting my hair and passing over me. I turned towards the church, as if I could hear singing and whispering through its stones, whirling around them and blowing out to sea. When I turned back, the letters engraved on one of the tombs seemed to rise and become tangled in my hair, dancing in front of my face.

Something made me kneel on the stone and trace the words slowly with my finger: *Margaret McCrimmon*. All of a sudden, the strange humming noise began building up in my ears again and my head started spinning. What would I see now? I wondered.

Margaret. Margaret McCrimmon.

The woman from my dream? Surely Scotland must have been full of Margarets . . . but I *knew*, I knew it was her. I tried to get up but couldn't – everything was dancing and swaying too much. I rested my head in my hands; it wasn't sore, I just needed to steady it. The humming noise grew louder and louder, and the whispers clearer and clearer, until finally I lifted my face and saw her, strawberry-blonde hair blowing in the wind, long and lustrous, a face of perfect loveliness. She seemed to be hovering a little above the ground; coming from the woods like a visitation. Margaret!

My mouth hung open, my heart ran away like a wild horse, and I thought I would die of fright there and then.

But the tall, impossibly beautiful girl stepped towards

me with a smile. 'Are you okay?' she said. For a visitation, it was quite a mundane thing to say.

'I'm fine . . . just a bit dizzy, that's all.' As I raised my eyes to her face, I couldn't help sucking in my breath. It was like looking in a mirror. 'Oh my goodness! Are you my long-lost sister?' She *had* to be the lookalike friend Sorren had talked about that first day in the pub. Yes, her hair was a different colour, and her eyes were bright blue while mine were somewhere between pale green and grey; but our features were identical.

'Oh . . . that's crazy. We do look alike. Separated at birth!' She smiled again.

I struggled to find my voice. When I opened my mouth, for a moment it felt as if I could speak with the voice of the sea, ebbing and flowing in the background. 'Someone at the Seal Inn . . . Sorren . . . told me that I looked like a friend of his, Catriona. But this is uncanny.'

'That's me. I'm Catriona,' she said and offered her hand. Her skin was warm and dry.

'Cora. I'm staying at Gealach, down along the beach,' I said cheerfully, and took a breath to compose myself. The mystical moment was over, the real world was back; I was glad to meet someone local.

'Are you feeling better now, or still dizzy?'

I looked away. I didn't really want her to ask why I was kneeling on that tombstone – I wouldn't have known how to answer. 'I'm fine. I don't know what happened.'

'It happens, sometimes. I mean, it happens here, at the

church. To some people,' she said, and looked straight at me, her bright blue eyes so clear, so intense. What did she mean? But she didn't elaborate, and the conversation turned mundane. 'You out sightseeing?'

'Yes. With my dog,' I said, pointing at Sasha happily digging holes in the sand. Her black nose had turned light brown. 'I thought I would have a wander before going to get some groceries in the village.'

'Oh, look at her, she's lovely! I didn't see her there. What's her name?'

'Alexandra Romanova, known as Sasha,' I replied, and Catriona laughed.

'You know,' she said, pointing at the grave I'd been kneeling on, 'that's an ancestor of mine. Margaret McCrimmon.'

'She's an ancestor of yours?' I didn't want to tell her how I'd heard the name Margaret in my dream, and how strange I'd felt when I saw the tombstone . . . It would have been impossible to explain anyway.

'Oh yes. They say there's quite a story about your cottage, and Margaret is a part of it.'

I was stunned for a moment. Would that involve my mum, and how she'd come to own the cottage? But it couldn't, because Margaret had lived three hundred years ago. 'Oh . . . I'd love to know more. Maybe you knew my mother . . . Beatrice Lamb? She owned Gealach.'

'She owned it? Lamb . . . Let me see. No, sorry. I've never heard of any Lamb on the island. Gealach has been empty for a long time. The last tenant was a Hugh Lyons; he passed away when I was a girl. Listen, why don't you come with me? I'm going to the Seal Inn for a drink. You said you knew Sorren, didn't you?'

'Sure!' I said, trying to silence the little voice that said, *You're supposed to be working, you've got a deadline.* 'Is it okay to bring the dog? Sorren let her in when I arrived, but the place was deserted then.'

'Ach, he will. Nobody will mind, believe me.'

'So, what were you doing out here yourself?' I asked. The church was miles from anywhere.

'Just getting a bit of fresh air,' Catriona said casually.

Seriously? Was there anywhere on Seal that didn't have fresh air? Oh well. Maybe the islanders just liked walking, that was all.

Once we were on top of the sand dune, I turned back one last time to look at Margaret's grave, and at the church half taken by the sea – 14 August 1946, the day the sea came on land.

Roan was so pretty on that sunny day, it looked like it had come out of a postcard. The row of brightly coloured houses stood along the bay, red and yellow and blue and green and orange, side by side like a rainbow. The fishing boats swayed on the blue, blue waves, and the sun shone on the machair. Perfect.

'This is breathtaking,' I said, as we stood on the pier for a moment before turning into the high street.

'Nothing compares to Seal.' Catriona smiled. 'It's perfect on a sunny day like this, and it's equally pretty on a rainy, dark day. Just in a different way.'

'So true,' I said. I'd been there only a short time, but already I felt as if Seal was a little bit mine. I was proud of it, as if it belonged not just to its people, but to me too. Which was weird for a girl who had lived among asphalted roads and buses that made everything tremble and people occupying every square metre of space available. And liked it.

Catriona smiled and waved to a lady coming out of the hairdresser's, all blue rinse, woollen skirt and thick flesh-coloured tights. Catriona couldn't take two steps without waving to someone or exchanging a few words in that enchanted, musical English that was the Seal language, or in Gaelic. I'd noticed that there were a lot of sweet island grannies, always ready for a chat or just a simple greeting. They queued at the post office and sat in the coffee shop, waited at the hairdresser's and came out of the church in little clusters, talking about their children and grandchildren on the mainland or further away, about the weather, about who had died and who'd got married and who had left the island to look for their fortune.

'That was Babs. She watched my sister and me when we were wee.'

'Were you born here?' I asked.

'Oh yes. And here I'll stay. I wouldn't live anywhere else. I came close to leaving once, but now I ask myself how I could have ever even considered it.'

'Well, I never thought I would leave London,' I said, shrugging.

'And then you did? I mean, do you not live there any more?'

'Yes, yes. I meant, I came up here. Temporarily.' We walked leisurely down the high street, while I took mental notes of postcards and souvenirs I wanted to send home to Stephen, Lorraine and Lucy. They would enjoy a Scottish-themed parcel.

'A holiday? Or something more long term? If I may ask . . .'

'Well . . . longer than a holiday, shorter than long term. It's hard to explain. What happened was . . . Well . . . my mum died.' I swallowed.

There. I'd put the words 'mum' and 'died' in the same sentence without bursting into tears. That was something. Once again, like many times before, I pondered how easily women share, and by sharing words share grief and love and stories, in an unsaid *you're not alone.* 'And you, Catriona? I mean, what made you nearly leave?'

'Me . . . I got my heart broken. I'm sorry about your mum.'

'Thanks. And I'm sorry about your heart.'

'Oh, it's okay. Hearts are highly mendable, have you noticed? Someone stitched it back together again,' she said, and her lovely face broke into a smile.

For some reason, I found myself thinking of Innes.

*

'See? I met my long-lost twin!' Catriona said to Sorren as we made our way into the inn. Sorren was drying a pint glass, looking quite dishevelled. In spite of that, I couldn't help noticing how attractive he was, in a gentle, cheerful way – with those chiselled features and thick, wavy dark hair. He and Catriona would have made a perfect couple.

Sorren stifled a yawn. A five o'clock shadow made him look like he hadn't slept much. 'Oh, hello! Crazy, isn't it?'

'I suppose they say that we all have a double, some-where in the world,' Catriona replied with a smile, but I was a bit disquieted. There was a link between my mum and Seal, a link I knew nothing about – and now I'd met a girl who had my eyes, my features, though she was tall and slender and I was small and curvy. 'You're always here! Are you skiving from the restaurant?'

'Restaurant?' I asked.

'My real job,' Sorren said. 'I'm a chef. I own a place called Stella Maris.'

I remembered the chocolate cake; so I'd been right! Maybe I could barter some home-made candles for another hamper or two; it would be better than cooking on a two-ring stove that looked like it hadn't been used for years. And then I realised – the name of his restau-rant, Stella Maris: Star of the Sea. I thought of Mum's little statue, and the coincidence made me smile.

'Actually, I'm both here and there, at the same time, or so it feels. Helping Dad out for a bit,' he told Catriona. 'Mum has gone to Eilean to stay with Theresa. She had her gall bladder out. Bowl of water for the lady? And maybe a little treat?' He looked at Sasha, who was wagging her tail irresistibly.

'Yes please,' I said.

Catriona sat at a table near the counter and I joined her. 'Is there anything Theresa hasn't had taken out? I'm surprised she's still whole. Sort of.'

'Oh, I know. Appendix, tonsils, kidney stones, an ulcer, two hip replacements . . .' Sorren's voice trailed away as he disappeared for a second into the back. He reappeared with a dog bowl and two bone-shaped biscuits.

'Thank you so much,' I said, trying to hold a super-excited Sasha.

'Is she recovering okay?'

'Oh, yes. Sheer willpower. You know the way she gets over operations by circumnavigating the island on her Zimmer frame. So, what shall I get you?'

'Coffee and cake for me, if there's any cake going. Cora?'

'Same. It took me forty-five minutes to scramble eggs on the stove this morning – I'm not joking – so I'd better eat before I go back to my time-warp cottage and exist on custard creams.'

'So, your cottage. Gealach,' Catriona said once Sorren had brought our coffee. 'My teacher, Mr Campbell, who knows everything about this island, told me that there are only two truly ancient sites here on Seal: the standing stone over near Ollaberry – St Fintan's Staff, they call it – and the ruins of an ancient watch-tower where Gealach is now. I think he even tried to involve Historic Scotland or something to try and see and what's underneath the cottage, but nothing came of it.'

'Oh!'

'Yes. Legend goes that some Jacobites hid there during the rising, but they were all killed.'

'Was Margaret McCrimmon one of them?' I asked.

Catriona poured sugar into her cappuccino. 'Yes, apparently.'

'If you're looking for tragedy, assorted deaths and lost loves, come to the Highlands and Islands; we have one at every corner,' Sorren said, placing our cake in front of us. 'Someone wrote a song about it, I think . . .'

'She died there? I'm not sure I'll sleep at night now,' I said, and it was no joke. The red-haired woman at the window flashed before my eyes. 'Who killed her?'

Margaret, Margaret. Who came to Gealach looking for you?
Who drew your blood?

'I suppose in a classic song it would be her jealous lover,' Catriona said. 'But no, apparently it was her lover's father, Lord Innes. And she cast a curse on his family . . .'

Sorren's eyes lit up. 'Innes? I never knew they had such a history . . . We have Inneses on the island,' he explained to me.

'I know. I met one. Well, Innes is his *first* name . . .'

'There are quite a few men called Innes around here, I think . . . Oh, wait a minute. Is he tall, tattooed, a bit . . . a bit . . .'

'Scary?' I said.

'Yes!' Sorren's eyes lit up. 'That's Alan! He hasn't called here yet. Oh, that's so good he's back . . .'

'Alan? I'm confused.'

'Alan Innes. He doesn't like being called by his first name.'

'Oh. Why?'

'I suppose you're better asking him yourself,' Sorren said, and frowned a little.

'Oh, sorry, I didn't mean to . . .'

'No, no, not at all. Only . . . well, he can be funny with these things, you know, family things, so I tend not to talk about it.'

I knew it. I knew the man had a past . . .

'There's another sad story connected to your cottage,' Catriona said, tucking a strand of golden hair behind her ear and rocking the leg she'd crossed over the other. On her lovely white neck, just below her ear, was a heart-shaped birthmark, light brown, no bigger than a five-pence coin. Her beauty was so perfect that even a birthmark seemed to add to it.

'Told you,' Sorren called, walking back behind the counter.

'In 1946, a storm . . .' Catriona began.

'. . . destroyed the church when the congregation was in, and many people died . . . they floated away to sea and drowned.' I'd finished her sentence without thinking. Just as the last of my voice vanished in the air, almost echoing in the sudden silence, a long shiver travelled through me like cold fingers down my spine.

Catriona's eyes were huge and very blue. She looked surprised. 'Oh, you *read* about it?'

I shook my head. 'I kind of . . .' I knew it. I *saw* it. 'Well, I guessed. Half the church was missing, and now it opens straight onto the sea. And then I saw the graves, all with the same date . . .'

'You guessed?'

'I guessed,' I repeated, and blushed. I thought Catriona narrowed her eyes and studied me for a moment, but I might have been wrong.

'Two of the people who died that day lived in your cottage, you know,' she said. 'Two McCrimmons, cousins of mine.'

'Everybody is related to you guys.' I smiled, remembering the mysterious Margaret again. The memory of the dizziness I had experienced in the churchyard, the humming in my ears, was disquieting, and my smile turned wistful.

'I know!' Catriona said. 'Everywhere I turn there's a cousin five times removed or something. But it's nice. I like it. I suppose that's what's sad about people scattering all over the world: you lose your connections, a bit of your history . . . Oh, the Campbells!' she said as a cold draught hit my back and I turned around to see who'd come in. A small group of people holding various musical instruments made their way to the minuscule stage against the far wall. 'Have you heard them before?'

'I think so,' I said, as the musicians settled and took out their instruments. A few tentative notes rose in the air. 'I heard the fiddle player the day I arrived,' I said, gesturing towards the black-haired young man holding the violin. 'But they were in the other room . . .'

'Yes. This is new,' Sorren said. 'Our mini stage! They're so good that people come from Glasgow and Edinburgh to see them; the least we could do was give them a nice space to play in, rather than off in that side room.'

'That's Rosalind,' Catriona said, pointing to a tall, slender woman with long dark hair who had come to stand beside the Campbells. 'She has a voice to die for, and guess what, she's my cousin!'

As soon as Rosalind began to sing, I was silenced, and so enchanted I couldn't even swallow. I sat there, hypnotised, listening to her siren's voice, pure and natural – she had no microphone. After a couple of lines, my hands and feet were suddenly cold, and my heart started to pound. I wasn't sure when or where, but I'd heard that song before, and for some reason it seemed to awaken a wave of emotion that threatened to overwhelm me.

> Ane thing I'll gie ye, ane thing an more
> Ane thing awash upon the shore
> A silver comb for your hair of gowd
> A silver comb for a love unbowed
>
> Twa things I'll gie you, twa things an more
> Twa things awash upon the shore
> A gowden coin, a shining sun,
> Twa spirits dance as one

Three things I'll gie you, three things an more
Three things awash upon the shore
A spring-green apple, crisp and cold
The taste o' a life as yet untold

Fower things I'll gie ye, fower things an more
Fower things awash upon the shore
A bonny bluebell, tho sma' an peerie
Its scent, like you, is sweet an dearie

Five things I'll gie ye, five things an more
Five things awash upon the shore
An egg in a nest of a bird that flies
Two bright white wings in stormy skies

It was like an incantation; the tune lively, accompanied by a dancing fiddle, yet still terribly sad, like the bitter-sweet memory of things once loved and now lost, and never found again . . . like a story of chances not taken. I didn't understand the words, but the tale the song told me was the story of a safe life, without the perils of love. In Rosalind's voice, I heard myself. I heard all that could be and wasn't, because I had tucked myself away.

I was safe with my friends, my crafts, my books, while love was something far away, unknown, too dangerous to get near to. People said I was picky, I was looking for something that didn't exist, but the truth was, I didn't want to wake up my heart. My life was perfect the way it was. Sometimes, though, on moonlit nights, or when sweet music played, or when I saw two people looking into each other's eyes with that kind of rapture you only see when someone is in love – at those moments I felt there was something missing, something with no name and someone with no face . . .

This was one of those moments, when music spoke of something different, something *more*, and just out of reach. I lost myself in it for a while; then I raised my eyes and I saw him, looking at me from across the room.

Innes was there.

For an instant, just for an instant, he seemed vulnerable, full of a sadness I couldn't even begin to know. He was a mystery to me. He seemed to have the body of a strong man and the eyes of a child. And then, all of a sudden, his expression hardened, and his look chilled me to the bone. It was as if I'd caught him in an unguarded moment, and he hated me for it. I looked away, stung. To think I was dying to tell him what I'd found out about the cottage, and ask if he knew anything more about the Gealach stories Catriona had mentioned. But with the way he'd looked at me, I was frozen.

Catriona looked over and waved to him – without much enthusiasm, it seemed to me – and he replied with an almost imperceptible nod.

'Hey, girls.' A cheerful Irish voice interrupted my thoughts, taken up by the song and, to my shame, by Innes's face.

'Neal, hi . . .'

'How are you? You never replied to my text,' he said

with a smile. His words were a bit possessive, but his tone wasn't, so I smiled back.

'Sorry, things have been a bit crazy at the cottage, you know. I had to set it all up . . . Actually, I'd better head back before it gets dark.'

'No problem. Hey, I'll walk you home.'

'It's okay, I'll take her. I'm going that way.' Innes had come to stand beside Neal, and he didn't *ask*. He *told* us. And when I saw his expression – serious, intense – as much as I didn't particularly like being contended for that way, as if I had no will of my own, I had no choice but to accept.

I got up, holding my jacket, as the Campbells threw themselves into a crazy reel. *Doing what I'm told. Now that's not like me . . .*

There was more than a hint of annoyance in Neal's voice. 'You're going that way? But there's nothing else that way.' Innes simply ignored him.

I desperately wanted to suggest we all went together, because that was the polite, the diplomatic thing to do. But I simply looked at Innes and felt myself blushing. Silence fell over the table – the voices would have been drowned out by the music anyway – and everyone looked at me. It was as if a choice had been made, a road had been taken, and it was too late to reconsider, too late to turn back.

Rosalind began to sing again, a Gaelic song whose meaning I didn't understand but that made me feel homesick for I didn't even know what.

I mouthed goodbye to Neal and our eyes met for a moment, but it was like I didn't even see him, as if for me he wasn't really there. I waved to the other punters of the Seal Inn – I couldn't help noticing Catriona's raised eyebrows, a look that I could only decipher as concern. Her worry followed me briefly as we emerged into the wind and the just-fallen darkness, clinging to me like a spider web, and then faded away as Innes and I began to walk in perfect rhythm, as if we'd known each other for ever.

Margaret

I dug into the earth, harder than I had to. I dug into the earth like I wanted to destroy instead of plant. Helen's eyes were on me, but I ignored them. I refused to cry.

I'd been taken for a fool, I had to admit it. Me, wise, cautious, the girl who never lets herself be carried away. The girl who looked at love like a yoke. Everything I'd tried to avoid, I'd ended up falling into – so much for not letting myself go! I'd been a fool. Every time I saw Fiona's pale face, the rounding of her belly, I felt sick.

I would put it all behind me, never think of it again. But it hurt, because in such a short time, Duncan had seeped into my heart and taken up residence there. It would be hard to rip him out of me. I would do it, though.

Oh, my thoughts were like blades, cutting me inside, one after the other!

'I think you're going to stab me with that fork,' Helen said, her hands clutching some torn weeds.

'Sorry,' I said curtly.

'Things aren't always what they seem, you know.'

I looked at her. Helen had never really spoken to me before – apart from barking orders or imparting her knowledge, in short, dry sentences. And I liked it that way. I didn't want her to elaborate. Especially if it was about something she'd heard; something between Duncan and me, something between Fiona and me.

'When I first came here, the lairds were little boys,' she continued. 'It was a shame to see how their father treated them. And I have a strong stomach.'

Why would I want to hear about the Inneses' childhood? I wanted to say. What do I care? But I kept my counsel. I had to remain on Helen's good side, or she would not let me work with her, just as I was beginning to learn. And in my heart of hearts, I hoped that learning how to be a healer would be my way out of there – not just Castle Innes, but any castle, any place governed by a man, anywhere I would have to do what I was told and follow orders instead of being my own mistress.

'Take your own father, for example.' What? What did my father have to do with the Innes boys and how they were brought up? Had she inhaled one of those concoctions she kept for pain? They could addle the mind.

'What about my father?' I said, and I couldn't keep the irritation out of my voice. 'What does he have to do with anything?'

'Your father, my brother, is a fool. But a proud, honourable fool. And Duncan is an honourable fool too. Your father was destroyed. He's a finished man, has been for ten years' – she laughed a bitter laugh – 'stumbling through his days in fury because of the evil of one man. And Duncan—'

'My father was never proud or honourable. And I am not interested in hearing what you have to say about Duncan.'

Helen stopped weeding for a moment and looked at me. 'My brother sheltered you. He never told you what really happened. Now think about it. The men who love you, they will shelter you. Whether it's good for you or not, whether you need it or not.' She tucked a tendril of coarse hair behind her ear, and in doing so, left a trace of mud on her cheek.

'I don't care about any man. Father or brother or . . . lover. I want to be like you. I want to be my own person, not somebody else's property. Being lied to, used, bartered like a thing . . .'

'You want to be like me?' she said softly, sweetly. Yes, softly and sweetly. I thought it was another woman in front of me, so quick was her change, so strange her tone. 'I have nothing. All this can be burned down in the space of a few heartbeats. I can be thrown out, I can be killed, I can be . . .' a hesitation, 'accused. Of anything. If a remedy works, if a remedy doesn't work. We can be *accused*, Margaret.' She lowered her tone. I swallowed. How much did she know?

'Why are you telling me this?'

'When you find an ally, don't let him go. And Duncan is an ally to you. Do you understand me?'

A gust of wind blew rain onto us, and water on my

eyelashes made me blink. When I could see again, Helen was bent in two over the hard soil, and I knew there would be no more words.

I would not listen anyway. She knew nothing. My father was not honourable, Duncan was not an ally but a spoiled young laird in lust, and sometimes things were exactly what they seemed.

Duncan went away again for a few days – he tried to say goodbye, but I took great care that he wouldn't have the chance. And then, when he came back, I avoided him in every way I could. If he had lied to me, if he was an entirely different person from the one I'd thought, who knew what he could do to me? I'd been reminded that I couldn't trust anyone at the castle. The apple never falls far from the tree, I thought bitterly, and Duncan was just like his father and his brother.

But I also feared I would break down and cry tears of betrayal and loneliness. And that I couldn't allow myself to do, ever.

I was bent over a row of mint plants, their sweet scent comforting me, when he finally found me alone. It was a blustery day, and grey clouds galloped above our heads, the air full of moisture and smelling of rain soon to come. I tried to ignore him, but I knew it was impossible. He took my arm and made me get up, gently but firmly, and when I tried to walk away, he kept hold of my arm and wouldn't let me go.

'Margaret?' There was no anger in his voice, in spite

of his grip on me; more of a pleading question. But I was far from being softened. I never would be. 'You're avoiding me . . .'

'Go away, Duncan.'

'What . . . Margaret, what happened?' His face looked sincere. It couldn't be. He was lying, of course.

'You want to know what has happened? I *know*. That's what's happened. I know.'

'What do you know?' He seemed genuinely bewildered.

'About the baby.'

'About . . . Oh. Of course. Of course, I should have known she was going to tell you,' he said, but he didn't look cross with Fiona. He didn't look as though she'd revealed a secret she was supposed to keep. All my anger came out. Let him be furious with me, let the Inneses do their worst. They were a bunch of wild dogs, for all the gold and the titles.

Duncan let go of my arm, but I would not walk away. I wanted to stay and tell him how deceitful he was, how much pain he'd caused me. 'You should have told me you were going to have a son, don't you think?'

'How do you know it's going to be a boy?' he had the courage to say. He talked about it as if it was some minor incident, like twisting an ankle, or losing game to an unruly hunting dog. I would not answer that question.

'Stay away from me, Duncan. Do you understand me?' I said, echoing Helen's words.

For a moment, anger passed across his face like a black cloud. Was I really talking to the young laird like that? I didn't care, I was too humiliated. He was just like all those other high-born men, thinking only about themselves, using and discarding women as though we were worth less than horses. And we *were*.

'I do. I do understand. But you don't.'

'I knew I was right about you. Taking your pleasure wherever you wanted . . .'

'My *pleasure*? You know nothing! *Nothing!*'

'I know that your son will be born in less than five months, and Fiona will be sent away. Who knows what will happen to them, all because you had to have your way.' I was panting.

'They won't be sent away. They'll stay and be looked after. My father won't let an Innes child go.'

'So you admit it! You admit it's your child!' I took a breath. 'You deceived me. But that's fine, Duncan, it's fine. I'll nurse my heart back to health.' Would I? 'I never really believed you anyway,' I lied, 'but Fiona, and the baby . . .'

'I told you, they will be fine. And no, I do not admit it, because the baby is not mine.'

Our eyes locked, and he took my arm again, fingers burrowing into my flesh, nearly hurting me. It felt like the truth. But he'd just admitted that Fiona's baby was an Innes child . . .

'Duncan, there was no covenant between us,' I said. 'No promise. You don't owe me anything. You can tell me the truth.'

'It is the truth, Margaret, do you hear me? I never

touched Fiona. I can't deny that I . . . yes, I did know women before you. But since I met you, everything has changed. Can you see, can you see, Margaret? Everything has changed.'

'Are you saying that Fiona lied?'

Duncan shook his head. 'She said what I told her to say. Because if my father knows the baby is an Innes, he will keep it here at the castle. I told you, he won't let an Innes child go.'

My mouth was open. I was still reeling from all that had happened, too shocked to let relief wash over me. 'You told her to lie? You are . . . you are going to be the father of a baby not yours? Let him carry your name?'

'The baby is entitled to our name. He's Cameron's son. My brother.'

'Cameron?' I thought of his thick lips, his dried-up face, his careless ways. The way he'd punched that stable lad . . .

'I've been cleaning up his messes all our lives,' Duncan added.

I studied his face. The whole of my being was telling me it was the truth. But still I couldn't let myself believe him.

'I don't understand. Would your father not keep the baby if he knew it was Cameron's?'

Duncan shrugged. 'Oh, he would. But Cameron denied it's his. He told Fiona there's no way to prove it – and he's right. He was just going to tell our father that it was nobody's child, and Fiona would be sent away with nothing.'

'But why? I mean . . . it's an illegitimate child, but still an Innes. Does Cameron not want—'

'For my brother, Fiona is less than a mare. An animal. You don't think she wanted him, do you?' His face was full of disgust. I understood what he meant at once. Fiona had not given herself willingly. She had been raped.

It took me a moment to recover my voice. She was so young, so innocent . . .

'Margaret, I would never, ever . . . You must believe me. I'm telling you the truth.'

'I believe you,' I whispered, and gazed into his eyes. Tentatively he put his arms around my shoulders and held me to him – chastely, lovingly, although both our hearts were beating hard with the closeness of the other's body.

It was just like Helen had said: he was honourable.

'If it wasn't for you, Fiona . . .'

Duncan smiled a bitter smile. 'My father will not keep anyone who's not useful. He throws out servants when they are sick. My mother died alone, because he would not assist her. For him, she was done. She could never give him any more children, so he might as well let her die. As for Lady Dolina . . . My father married her hoping for more sons. When she lost one baby after another, he would have loved to send her back to her father. But he didn't dare. The McAlpines are not to be messed with.'

'Poor Lady Dolina.'

'Yes. She has a kind heart. And that doesn't serve you well, in my clan.' He entangled his fingers in my hair and undid the leather straps that kept my braids together. My hair fell loose, and as it caught the blue light, for a moment it seemed to move by itself, to snake down my back as though it had a life of its own. 'And you, Margaret? Do you have a kind heart? Or will you break mine?'

My throat seized. *Do I have a kind heart? With the things I can do, the things I have to hide from everyone? Do I have a kind heart, or a black one?*

Thankfully, before I could answer, he kissed me, and then again, and again, and he did so in a way that made me feel sure I would never be able to speak again. Finally, cradled in his arms and safe, I studied his face once more. He was not handsome like some prince from a fairy tale would be, but he was strong, and his touch dissolved me; and most important of all, his eyes told me he would not entrap me, he would not dominate me.

'You are different,' I said, matter-of-factly. Yes, I was sure now.

'Different from whom?'

'Your father. And your brother.'

'Cameron was different from my father too. Had you known him years ago, you wouldn't have recognised him. He was always sick, he cried easily, he was scared of his own shadow. He wasn't made for war, but for books. My father moulded him to his own image. I'll let you imagine how he did that. Cameron is his favourite son now, but he wasn't when we were growing up. He was always the one to get the beatings, the shouting. He adapted. He became who my father wanted him to be.'

'And so you're helping Cameron with this . . .'

'I'm not helping him. I'm helping Fiona. We were brought up together, Margaret. When I was a child and my mother was alive, things were very different here. We were less wealthy, less powerful. Fewer than fifty people lived at Castle Innes. Fiona came with her mother when she was barely old enough to work. I've always been fond of her – no, not that way, don't worry,' he added, seeing the consternation on my face. 'I will not let her down now.'

'I understand.' The scent of mint was strong in my nostrils. Something rose between us – with my relief about Fiona's baby and him opening his heart – like an invisible hue that had coloured the air mother-of-pearl and gold. He lifted his hand and ever so gently traced the contours of my face; tucked a bright tendril behind my ear.

'Margaret, I . . .'

Something happened then. Something I wasn't expecting.

On a hot summer day many years ago, my brothers and I were playing on the moors. We came to Loch Awe and the boys took their clothes off to go swimming. I knew I was not supposed to do that. I knew that if I swam in my underwear like a peasant girl, my mother would give me a good thrashing and keep me indoors for the rest of the summer. I stood on a rock and watched my brothers swim and splash and jump. And then I crouched down, holding my skirts, and looked into the water.

It was blue.

Not black, not grey; blue and green, glittering in the sunshine, little fishes darting and seaweed dancing. And below, below, the shadows of the ancient houses built into the loch.

I jumped in. I knew about the consequences, and I was frightened of them, but I jumped in anyway, because the delight promised by those waters was too much to resist. And just as I'd jumped into Loch Awe that day, today I fell into his lips, into his chest, into his hands. I was someone who'd never been touched by a man before, and yet I knew what to do. I knew it was desire, but the way he looked at me was so intense, so loving – I believed him, yes, I chose to believe him. And when he said, *I think I love you*, I thought someone else, someone more worldly-wise than me, would have calculated in her mind what she could get from the young laird, would have known how to use her body, the secret knowledge that all women have, to make him do her bidding; but I couldn't. As he touched me, I couldn't speak; I could only look into his eyes and wonder how this man had stolen my heart so fast, my jealously guarded heart.

And when it was finished, he held me and whispered in my ear, 'It's like I met you somewhere before. Like you were the first face I saw when I was born.'

I didn't have the words to say that while we were making love, I'd remembered Magnild, my wet nurse, making me close my eyes and lay my fingers on my eyelids, telling me in her strong northern accent that spoke of barren lands and fire-filled earth that the face I'd see would be the face of my one true love. And I'd seen Duncan's.

Innes

I'd been to so many places, I travelled so often, sometimes I forgot where I was. Once I was in Brazil, and I
tried to buy a bus ticket to Lisbon. At Tokyo airport, I
was due to fly home – let's call it that – to San Francisco,
and instead I boarded a plane to Istanbul. I was due in
Turkey, yes, but a week later. My pockets were full of
loose change in at least three different currencies, and I
was usually in the wrong time zone, waking up at two in
the morning and falling asleep when normal people were
going to work.

But since I'd been back on Seal, all confusion was
gone.

I knew where I was, and what time it was, and I was
aware of everything, everything. Because I was home.

Yes, I would leave as soon as we finished shooting, and
might never be back. But for now, all my scattered
thoughts and memories had been gathered up, and the
way I was usually there in body and somewhere else in
mind just didn't apply tonight.

I was walking with Cora through the island dusk as it

slowly turned into another wild and windswept night – this woman who only a few days ago I hadn't known, in this place I'd known for ever, but somehow they seemed to be equally familiar. Yes, Cora and I were walking together, side by side, and it was strange and sweet, and at the same time, it felt so normal.

Like the first cup of coffee in the morning, like warmth coming from a fire, like standing at the window and watching the moon move through the sky. You had coffee in the morning a million times, a million times the fire warmed you up, of course the moon would be walking in the sky, whether you saw it or not. All of this was normal and miraculous. And being with Cora was normal and miraculous at the same time.

She was someone I'd spent only a little time with, someone I'd never really spoken to, never really touched. I knew nothing about her. But since I'd seen her on the ferry, I couldn't get her out of my mind. Even as I saw my mother again, with all the turmoil it caused, the joy, the heartbreak, the memories, Cora was in my thoughts, even then. And when I'd recognised her, pure in her white nightgown and bare feet, a part of me had thought it couldn't possibly be a coincidence. Life didn't work like that. It didn't write a script for us, a tidy sequence of scenes to follow. Life was messy and unfair, and as a rule, it did not give you a chance. And still, there she was.

She walked beside me, simple in her jeans and sweater, her dog by her side and that incredible hair down over her shoulders.

Would I be very shallow if I said that what had made me look at her for the first time was the colour of her hair? I'm not sure why. Sure, her hair was beautiful. But it wasn't just that. It was like . . . a beacon. Or a call. It was her way of telling me, 'It's me.' It was like I'd met her somewhere before.

There had been many girls. Girls for a night or two. My only antidote to loneliness.

Because before them, there had been Letty. Letty and little Hank, her son. And never again would I allow myself to hurt anyone the way I'd hurt them. Letty's face when my hand rose to hit her, one night when there was more alcohol than blood in my veins. The way I hit the wall instead, my knuckles bleeding. Letty shaking and crying. Hank appearing in the doorway. *Are you hurting my mum?*

I left the next day. Letty tried to stop me; she said I just needed help with my drinking, that I hadn't meant to hit her – which was why I'd hit the wall instead, with such force that I walked around with broken bones in my hand for weeks, until I decided to go to the doctor. I deserved the punishment, I thought.

But I couldn't risk hurting Letty; I couldn't risk being to Hank what The Guy had been to me. So I left anyway, in spite of her pleas. And since then I hadn't touched a drop.

'Can I ask you a question?' Cora's voice resounded in the purple light. She turned to look at me, and I could see her face slowly blurring before my eyes, losing its contours in the magic of dusk. The sky was changing slowly from light blue to dark lilac, and a hint of orange lit the sea in the west.

'Mmm?' Maybe if I opened my mouth she would know what I was thinking. She would know I was dying to run my hands through those silky strands . . . she would know I had a plan. A plan for tonight. A plan that was rapidly dissolving as she looked into my eyes with a strange trust, a strange innocence.

'When you broke into my house . . .' She looked at me with a mocking smile.

'Ha ha.'

'Well, when you were about to leave, this morning, you looked out to sea and you said, *Now* that's *surreal*. I'm curious. What did you see?'

'Oh. Nothing really. It wasn't anything surreal as such. It was more a kind of . . . déjà vu. Like I'd stood there before. I mean, of course I'd stood there before a million times, but it was like . . . like I'd lived that moment already.' That was more words than I'd said to anyone in a long time.

'Oh. That's funny.'

'Yeah?'

'When I arrived on Seal, I had a similar thing. I thought I'd seen this place before,' she said, and all of a sudden she was so close, I could smell her scent, warm, spiced, like something growing in the dark, waiting to reveal its beauty.

'Maybe in a book, or on TV?' I said, trying to keep my tone steady.

'Maybe. But . . . well, the way I remembered it was different from the way it looks now.'

'How different?'

'Only a few houses, and none of them painted or whitewashed. They were made of dark stone . . . And hardly any boats.'

'That's the other side of the island. The north-west. It's nearly empty. So that's what you probably recognised.' She didn't reply. 'Your cottage is right in the middle of it, all that emptiness. I know it well.'

'You grew up on Seal, didn't you?'

Another waft of cinnamon and ginger and secret warmth – and oh, that again: her fingers brushing mine. And me pretending nothing happened.

'Uh-huh. And I was always wandering there, you know, to Gealach. It was so peaceful, compared to my house.' I stopped. I didn't want to tell Cora anything about that time, so why were those words coming out? 'Anyway, I'm filming at the cliffs on the north side now. Puffins. And then I'll move closer to you, come and meet your seals.'

'Oh, I love those seals! Their eyes are so human – honestly, Innes, it's like having *sea people* living there with me.'

'Selkies,' I said, and felt a smile opening up my face. It was impossible not to share her enthusiasm, almost child-like. Yes, there was something childlike about her, something endearing. Pure.

'Exactly! So, you're filming with Neal?'

Hearing his name made me bristle. I tried to read her face, but her features were in shadow.

'With Neal, yes. So, you're interested in knowing what Neal is doing,' I said with a hint of pettiness.

'I worked with him once.'

'You did? On a documentary?'

'A TV programme. *Heartmade.* You know, about my crafts. Neal was a cameraman.'

Okay, so they had history. Now even more I wanted to take him by the scruff of the neck and growl at him to stay away from her. But then it would be a lot better for Cora if I stepped back and let Neal, cheerful, even-tempered, funny Neal, do his thing . . .

I knew I was no good, and that would not change.

Yes, I should step back.

Silence fell inside me, and suddenly the moon didn't seem as white, the night as scented, the sound of the sea as magical.

'Hey,' she said sweetly. She seemed unaware of my tone when I'd asked about her interest in Neal. 'Tell me about yourself. Why did you leave Seal?'

Tell me about yourself. The words that turned my muscles into granite.

'I wanted to see the world,' I replied quickly – too quickly. It was my standard reply. But I knew the Seal grapevine would let something slip sooner or later. About why I left, about me. Most people on the island pretty much despised me. They even feared me, in a way, and I suppose that made sense.

When she learned the truth, surely she would want nothing to do with me.

'You don't want to talk about it,' she said, and I smiled in the darkness. There was no fooling her, no keeping the conversation formal, drenched with truths untold. 'It's okay. I understand. Sasha! Stay close,' she called to her dog, to defuse the moment, I thought.

'What about you? Why did you come up here, all on your own?'

'I'll tell you, but you might not believe me. It's crazy, it sounds like a film.'

'Try me.'

'So, my mum died,' she said, and I could hear her voice catching a little. I found her in the darkness and rested my hand on her back, just for a moment. The play of her muscles as she walked, her warmth . . . 'And we found out she owned Gealach, and she'd never told us.'

'Was she from the island?'

'No way, no. Mum was a real cockney. We – as in my brother and I – found a picture of my mum and a friend together up here. But we never knew she'd even been to Scotland.'

'It does sound like a film, actually.'

'I know. And there's more. But it's all very weird, so maybe I'll leave it for another time. Oh, Innes, look! That bit of sea! Look!' She pointed to a small whirlpool in between the rocks, the waves breaking onto it with such violence that they rose into the sky. Wild, untamed. 'You know, for me, going home normally means taking the Tube or walking past rows of houses and shops. With lamp posts and car headlights. And noise.'

'And how is this for you? The dark and the silence?'

'It's strange. But it's also natural. It's hard to explain. Oh, I'm not very good with words, never have been. To think that I'm writing a book!' she laughed. 'It's like when you think something is going to be completely weird and alien, and when it actually happens it's like . . . you know, it's like drinking your coffee in the morning. The most routine of routine mornings.' I smiled in the darkness, again. We'd had the same thought, we'd painted the same image. 'I'm not saying that it's not incredible,' she continued, and she was nearly dancing, gliding light and graceful over grass and stones. 'It is. I feel like I'm in a film or a novel. *Rob Roy* or *Braveheart* or something . . . I need to get some blue paint.' She laughed, an earthy laugh, warm, joyful. The laugh of someone who had never known bitterness or anger.

And then it happened again – our fingers brushed. By chance, by design. But this time, I found her hand in the darkness and held it, guiding her across the causeway to Gealach, the small silhouette of her dog running in front of us. We stood at her door on the half-moon beach, the pod of seals sleeping under the moonlight, and I pulled her to me, and she didn't resist. I cupped the back of her neck, underneath all that soft, heavy hair, and she closed her eyes. She was the wind, and the sand under my feet, and every star that shone beyond the clouds . . .

Her hands were clasped around my back. She looked up at me – she only came to my chest – and her eyes glimmered in the moonlight, the seals' eyes on the rocks strangely mirroring hers.

In them, I saw innocence.

The words came from somewhere inside me, somewhere that had been shut and bolted for a long, long time. 'It's like you were the first face I saw when I was born,' I whispered, and the strange power of those words shattered me.

My plan had been to be with her for a little while; to spend a short time together without a past and without a future. I'd done it before, after all, and it had worked out fine – if by fine you mean sleeping with someone you don't care about and who doesn't care about you, and going back to your lonely life afterwards. The lonely life that nobody sees or considers, because you're one of them, the ones unconnected to a family, to friends or neighbours; the ones who wander around the world alone. I looked into her eyes – they were grey now in the gloom, but I remembered that they were green, and speckled like the corncrakes' eggs – and I knew she couldn't be one of those women. She was delicate and . . . untouched.

And my plan dissolved, just like those waves breaking against the rock.

Even if my instinct, my body, my heart told me to kiss her long and hard, to take her inside and not leave her until dawn broke . . . even if I had to force my hands to let go of her, to stop feeling the softness of her under my fingertips . . . I did what was best for her. Ignoring how she was tilting her chin slightly, her lips looking for mine, I left a single slow, lingering kiss on her forehead, and nothing more.

I knew that Cora wasn't a little girl. She was capable, determined and strong, strong enough to come to Seal alone, all the way in the middle of nowhere.

But she was *pure*.

And I was tainted.

I let her go and walked across the causeway without looking back.

Cora

He kissed me.

And then he left.

I stood there, eyes closed, waiting for more, wanting more. But he had gone, stepping onto the causeway in between the two wings of rising sea, swallowed by darkness. Inside the cottage, I leaned against the door, trembling with cold and with desire. What was happening to me? Be careful what you wish for, I suppose. Half my life I'd wished I could feel this way for someone, I'd wished my heart would finally wake up. The music I'd heard in the Seal Inn had been like a spell, allowing me to soften and open. And now that my heart was awake, I was afraid.

Could I not have fallen for Mark, my first and only boyfriend and my safe haven, the man I knew everything about: his history, his family, every corner of his heart and soul? No. It had to be a stranger. A stranger who'd rescued me from a fainting fit as if I was in a Jane Austen novel; who'd appeared in my house in the middle of night and ended up sleeping in the dusty armchair beside me, his breathing soundtracking my dreams; who'd decided it would be a terrible idea to actually kiss my lips and hold me in his arms, and had instead given me the kiss of a guardian angel, on the forehead, and then disappeared.

'Oh, for heaven's sake, Cora!' I said aloud. Sasha looked up at me and tilted her head slightly, her long ears dangling, and then went to sit beside her bowl. Dogs have no specific views on romantic matters, I suppose; they're more focused on practicalities. I revived the fire to make sure it would still burn – turf is really low-maintenance, I was discovering – gave Sasha food and water and then stood, my hands on my hips and a million thoughts in my mind. I contemplated going to sleep. Impossible. I thought it would be wise to write a little, given that my work on *Lovemade* had finally taken off, but as my eyes fell on the loom in the corner, I felt it calling to me.

I lit a few candles, then sat and arranged the threads. I began to weave without a plan, without direction. I never do this usually, I don't weave blind – it would be like trying to write a book without having any idea of the plot. But this time my hands kept going by themselves. I only stopped to slip on a jumper and fetch Sasha's blanket from upstairs, so she wouldn't get cold, before returning to my slow, peaceful, near-hypnotic work.

After a while, I could see what I was actually weaving, though the work had only just begun and there was a long way to go before I'd finish. The image had flown out of my mind naturally, taking shape under my fingers, revealing itself without me having much say in it: a red-headed woman with a baby in her arms, standing against a red and yellow sun. In the background, the sea, a graveyard, a ruined church . . .

I leaned back in my chair and rubbed my forehead. Really, it was time to get some sleep. I stood up, followed by a subdued Sasha – it was one in the morning, after all. Catriona came into my thoughts. It had been strange to find her out there, in the middle of nowhere . . . She'd said Margaret was her ancestor; the woman whose grave had called to me. And what she'd told me about the people who'd lived at Gealach and drowned in the church . . . I still hadn't found any trace of my mum's presence at Gealach, any reason for us owning the cottage – maybe the family who'd drowned in the church was, somehow, the missing link?

I was pondering all these stories hanging unfinished and incomplete, just like the threads of my tapestry, when my phone beeped. For a second my heart jumped, thinking it might be Innes, but then I realised I hadn't given him my number. Who'd be texting me so late?

Lunch tomorrow?

Neal. Oh.

Sorry, I can't, I typed instinctively.

But then I remembered.

I remembered how I had felt when Innes had left me standing there alone, how my lips had tingled with desire; the way he had tormented me by holding me close just for a moment and then letting me go. Leaving me alone when I was on fire. Leaving me alone when I didn't know what was going on, I didn't know if I'd imagined it all; if I was some kind of sad individual having ideas about a man who had simply wanted to kiss me *on the forehead*.

Honestly.

Sure, I typed, with a kind of mean satisfaction. *12 at the Seal Inn?*

But when it came to pressing send . . . I couldn't.

I didn't want to go to lunch with Neal. Certainly not out of revenge on Innes.

Sorry, Neal, too much on, really trying to get this book done x

The moment I sent it, I felt I had recovered my self-respect. Good on you, Cora.

Oh well, I'll drop by at some point, he replied after a few seconds.

I didn't have time to think about an answer, because all of a sudden, I heard a tiny noise behind me – a rasping, a squeak – and then Sasha went crazy, running and pouncing on the hard stone floor, just as a little brown mouse, no bigger than my thumb, sprinted for its life and seemed to vanish into thin air, probably slipping into a crack in the wall. Sasha tripped up on her own paws and yelped loudly.

'Oh, baby, come here,' I soothed. 'What's wrong? Did you hurt yourself? Good girl . . .' I checked her over gently – there was nothing wrong with her except a bit of a tender spot on her hip – but as I knelt on the ground, I felt something sharp under my knee where only the smoothness of the floor should be. A raw, raised edge. I traced it with my fingers in the flickering light of the candle – it was a square tile cut into the stone floor. So much to do, so many repairs, I thought, planning to ask Sorren if he knew of a workman who could fix that quickly. I didn't want to trip and fall on such a hard floor. But how could such a square be accidental? I traced it with my fingers once again. It had to be deliberate. Maybe there was something underneath . . . but whatever it was would have to wait till daylight.

I was about to get up when something cold brushed my hand, and then my cheek. A draught. A draught coming from the floor.

How could that be? This place had no basement, and it was built on rock. I rested the candle on the floor and dug around the edge of the tile with my fingernails. Eventually the stone came loose. I lifted it, revealing wooden planks underneath and a semicircular metal handle covered in rust. I took hold of the handle and pulled, and to my shock, a little wooden hatch lifted, just big enough to fit one person. One small person, that is. Cold air, and the scent and noise of the sea hit my face, my nose, my ears, lifting my hair.

What was under there? Some sort of secret passage to the beach? All I could make out in the flickering candle-light was a kind of floor made of rocks cobbled together unevenly over compacted sand. I remembered what Catriona had said about the ancient watchtower under the cottage. Had I found its remains?

I retrieved my torch from the kitchen cupboard and shone it downwards. Now I could see that below the hatch was a space large enough to fit a person and that if I lowered myself down slowly, I wouldn't twist an ankle, or worse. *Probably.* I sat on the floor and let my legs dangle, then lowered myself down under Sasha's bemused eyes. As I landed, I lost my balance and fell onto my knees. The torch rolled away and switched itself off, and for a moment I panicked – I was alone in the dark, and the sea was so close, the waves in my ears like they were about to swallow me at any second. Sasha was barking from somewhere above me, and the sea hissed and howled like a banshee . . .

Finally, my blind fingers curled around the torch and found the switch – and everything was illuminated. There were walls on three sides, but the fourth, the one to the left of me, opened to some kind of tunnel. That was where the noise was coming from. I was vaguely aware that Sasha was still up there in the cottage, her long ears dangling above the hatch, looking down at me; I prayed she would not jump after me. Only then did I realise that it would be extremely hard to climb back up, therefore I had to either find a way out – maybe swimming – or wait for someone to come looking for me. Clearly I hadn't thought that through.

'Stay!' I shouted to Sasha, without much hope that if she wanted to jump, my command would make her desist. Sasha was a dog with a mind of her own.

Holding the torch in front of me, I walked slowly in the only direction I could go: towards the sound of the waves. I realised I was crouching a little, my back rounded, though the ceiling was high enough for me – it felt like the whole cottage was weighing on me. The sound and smell of the waves became stronger and stronger with every step. From my living room, straight to the sea – it was a bit like in *Where the Wild Things Are*, where the little boy goes to sleep and floats away on a boat. The gloom was making me dizzy – the blackness seemed to swallow the light of my torch – and my legs weren't too steady; but for some reason, I felt compelled to keep going towards the sound of the sea, even if I didn't know what was ahead, even if I was afraid I would, somehow, walk straight into the water.

I heard Sasha's distant barking, and turned around suddenly – too suddenly, because I slipped on the wet, clammy floor and fell heavily on my side. I lay there for a moment, breathless, feeling nothing; and then the pain in the arm and hip that had taken the brunt of the fall exploded, and I groaned quietly. Was I whole? Was something broken?

I was gathering my strength to get up when the light of the torch still in my hand illuminated something on the wall. Graffiti, carved into the stone. My fingers followed the thin furrows as I made out the word:

Margaret.

A tide of emotion overwhelmed me.

Margaret, Margaret. Who are you?

The flash of a face, white in the gloom, too quick for me to really see her – and in the distance the sound of bagpipes, yearning and sorrowful.

Sasha barked again, and her call brought me back to reality. I got up slowly, bruised and sore – I could just imagine the black and blue patterns I would have on my skin tomorrow. There was no way back, and the sound of the sea kept beckoning me, and so on I went.

I must have been walking for a few minutes, no longer, but because of the gloom and the disorientation I couldn't be sure. I seemed to be on a slight incline, a downward slope. The semi-darkness lifted slowly, and with every step the song of the waves was louder – until I came out of the tunnel carved in the stone, and without warning the gloom turned into moonlight. Fresh, salty wind enveloped me as I stepped onto a tiny beach that opened among the stones. Two paces on the sand and the waves were licking my feet already, drenching them through my trainers.

I blinked. The sea was immense. Ebbing and flowing like the breath of the earth itself – inhale, exhale, inhale, exhale, the rhythm of the planet's heartbeat.

After a lifetime in London, I'd never had the chance to experience something like this; in the city there is no heartbeat, just constant drumming, and no breathing, just panting to keep up with the breakneck speed. Time-lines are decided by the opening and closing of shops and offices, by traffic lights, by human, artificial rhythms that go against our bodies and offer us no rest.

Here, my heart was beating in time with the earth and my breath flowed with the waves and the tides. Lost in the immensity of the night, I felt like all the reasons in the world were there within me, all the answers to all the questions ever asked, there in the beauty and power of the black, black sea.

After a moment, I looked around me, the light of my torch illuminating my surroundings. There was a wall of rock behind me, and no way off the beach except by swimming. Now I could see clearly why the cottage was cut off at high tide – it had been built in a cove guarded by low but steep cliffs, and the only other access would have entailed climbing the sheer rocks, wet with sea spray. I could go back into the tunnel, but I knew it would be near impossible for me to lift myself back up into the house.

I allowed myself to panic for just a moment, and then my pragmatic nature took over. I inspected the rocks, a mixture of boulders and smaller stones. They were packed closely together, with few footholds, but I had to try. I pushed the torch into my pocket and began to climb. There were only a few stars in the sky – it was a cloudy night – and the light of the moon was weak. Slowly, though, I made my way up, my arms hurting from the effort. I was strong, but climbing such a rock face was way beyond my comfort zone.

I could feel my heart thumping in my ears, and I was panting with effort and fear. If I slipped, I'd either break all my bones on the tiny beach, or I'd fall into the water and the black sea would take me . . .

But I didn't slip. I pulled myself onto the final boulder and was still for a moment, first on all fours and then kneeling among rock pools that reflected the light of the moon. Carefully, slowly, I stood and looked around. I was just above the cottage, on the other side from the causeway. I glanced down; all I could see was the foamy black water, the little beach hidden from view somewhere below the rocks. I would walk along the cliffs and get back to the cottage over the causeway – thankfully, the tide was out.

Had my mum known about the tunnel; had Aunt Toffee known, when they came to Gealach? A secret tunnel to the sea. For a quick escape, or a hiding place. Who would have need of such a thing?

I made my way back to the cottage, walking slowly in the blustery night. *Margaret, Margaret,* said the wind on my face.

Margaret

Had I known how little time Duncan and I had left to spend together, I would have treasured every moment, slowed down time, tried harder to steal him from his duties and hide myself from mine. But I couldn't have imagined what was coming next, I couldn't have guessed that time for us was running out when it hadn't even begun. Maybe I was a fool, because I knew that a storm was coming and I knew it would break Scotland in two. But I was young and I had hope, hope against hope; and also, I couldn't see the hidden dagger, the unexpected place the blow would come from. Duncan and I were together, somewhere beyond time and consequences; nothing else mattered. We made love by the water and whispered secrets in the high grass; we let the Scottish wind caress our skin and lay wrapped in his plaid. We made each other laugh and hummed old songs together, looking at the lilac-grey clouds above us. We exchanged promises we meant to be true, and we thought life together was just starting.

Days followed one another, and they were enchanted.

We were under Lady Dolina and Helen's safeguard; they protected us and sheltered us from curious eyes. I was so full of love, I thought I could face anything: I could face Duncan's family's anger, I could face shame, wagging tongues – anything, as long as we were together.

And then the summer came to an end, and the seed that had been planted by my father years ago finally took, and produced a black, black blossom.

I woke to a dark, drizzly day feeling sick to my stomach. There was a black cloud over the castle, sullen faces and silent men and women going about their work a little faster, a little more anxiously.

I managed to grab Ally outside the stables. 'Is Shabana being prepared?' Shabana was Duncan's beloved mare. Ally nodded and ran, not wanting to be seen chatting when he had to work. I prayed Duncan and I would snatch a minute alone to say goodbye – and finally we did, behind the stables, getting slowly drenched by a fine but freezing drizzle.

'I need to go, Margaret. I've been called away,' he told me in the low, soft voice I loved so much.

I know, my love. I saw the horses being readied, I wanted to say, but there was a knot in my belly that didn't let me speak.

'The MacGregors . . . they aren't happy with us. My father has tried to serve too many masters. He has relinquished his honour, Margaret. And my honour too. But I think we can sort it. If I manage to keep my father and

Cameron on the leash, at least.' I was shocked to hear him talking like that.

'Will you be in danger?' I whispered. There was no sense in asking that question. I knew he would be, and I knew he would deny it.

'No, not yet anyway. And you really have no reason to worry. My father and Cameron will be here.'

'Lord Innes and your brother aren't going?' I asked, my stomach knotting even further.

'It's better I take care of this.' His reasoning made sense, but I didn't like it. I didn't trust Duncan's brother, and his father least of all.

'But—'

'Shh.' He put his finger to my lips, and in his eyes, I read his message: *It's my duty.*

I knew I had to be silent, because words would not help. I kissed him, and felt myself melt all the way down to the deepest parts of me. I knew then that falling in love could be as painful as it was sweet – heart-wrenchingly painful. I didn't want to let his hands go, and I held them with both of mine – and it wasn't right, I knew it wasn't right; I was a clanswoman, and our men would not live long, peaceful, sheltered lives, but be called to fight in an ever-changing game of supremacies and loyalties. Clanswomen must be ready to let their men go, and go themselves.

And so I relinquished his hands, relinquished them to the Innes family, to do what he needed to do.

I watched him leaving, and I trembled. I felt Fiona

take hold of my hand, and there were tears in her eyes too. 'It's all his father's doing, you know,' she said.

'And you seem to have become his good friend.' I was unable to keep the anger out of my voice. Fiona had become Lord Innes's pet, following him around like a faithful dog. 'You should choose better, you know, Fiona. You should choose better who to give your loyalty to.'

She let go of my hand. 'Whether I choose wisely or not, Margaret, we might still end up crying together,' she said quietly, and the hair on the back of my neck stood up.

Lady Dolina was more flushed than ever, and once again, like many times before, I changed linen that was spotted with blood where she'd coughed.

'I am afraid, Margaret.'

'I know. So am I.'

'You are afraid for Duncan. I am also frightened for you.'

'For me? Why?'

'Because my lord husband doesn't like anyone fulfilling their heart's desire. He enjoys destroying. And I worry that your love for Duncan will enrage him just because it is a good thing, a joyful thing. And because he won't marry Anne MacGregor.'

'Anne . . . Anne MacGregor?' Was he betrothed? It couldn't be! He would have told me . . .

'Yes,' she said. 'That is my husband's plan anyway. Duncan and Anne. It would put an end to the feud. But Duncan won't hear of it, and she will not accept Cameron . . .'

'Is she allowed to choose?' There was bile in the back of my throat, thinking of my Duncan with someone else.

'His father keeps her in great consideration, yes.'

'Unusual,' I said, and I couldn't keep the bitterness out of my voice.

'And still I hope this is the time . . . Oh, how I hope this is the time . . .'

'What time? What time, Lady Dolina?' She couldn't answer for a while, racked by coughing. My heart broke for her and a terrible thought crossed my mind – that she might die before Duncan came back.

'When they come for my lord husband, and finally he leaves me alone,' she managed finally.

I was chilled to the bone by the distress in her voice, and relieved when I was finally free of the stuffy air in her room and the sweet, sickly smell of illness. I went to Helen's garden, but all there was to do there was gather what was left and save it from the disaster that was coming. Duncan was there every moment – in my mind, in my heart, in my working hands. And something else: I was afraid not only for his safety, but for ours too. The black cloud I'd felt over the castle was still there, even heavier and more suffocating.

That was when I saw them: three ravens perched on the stone wall, enormous, sharp-beaked, feathers black and oily and little eyes darting everywhere. I was sure then that something terrible was about to happen, and there was nothing I could do.

I just want to see you again, Duncan, I said to myself

over and over again, my mind too fraught for proper prayers. I stood and looked over to the hills, and the sound of ghostly hooves filled my ears. I knew it wasn't possible to hear horses without seeing them, when they galloped on the soft heather; but I did, and I smelled their sweat, and the rage of those who rode them. The words I'd heard whispered for weeks came back to me – *MacGregor*, and *betrayal*, and the forbidden name of our true king.

I braced myself for the storm.

That night, we all gathered in the hall as usual. There were a few people missing, I noticed, and not just the men who'd gone with Duncan; there was a nasty fever around, and Helen was looking after the sick. I now sat with Lady Dolina's companions, closer to the high table, and Fiona, her belly rounder by the day, sat among us. Everybody thought she was carrying Duncan's child.

That night, the air was still – there was no wind, which was rare in this land of ours. The moon shone bright in a cloudless sky, and it felt like everything was waiting. All of a sudden, there was a buzzing sound in my ears, and the din of the hall was replaced by silence, as if I were underwater. I turned my head slowly. Emerging out of the darkness on the threshold of the great hall was an apparition. A tall, thin woman with red hair.

Hair as red as mine.

She was naked, eyes enormous, arms wrapped around herself and smudges of ash on her cheeks. She was looking at me. And then I saw that she was burning feebly, thin, transparent flames visible at the tips of her hair, on her hovering feet, her shoulders. She was on fire, and I knew who she was. I didn't move or make a sound as I felt goosebumps slowly rise on my arms, and invisible fingers touch my forehead.

'Margaret McCrimmon!' Lord Innes's drunken voice rose from the silence, and I knew the ghost had come to warn me. I looked over to the high table. He was red in the face, his eyes shining with a mixture of whisky, anger and nasty amusement.

He knew.

All eyes turned towards me. Lady Dolina was white, with two dots of sickly high colour on her cheeks.

'You have very good friends here in the castle, don't you, Margaret?' he said.

My mouth opened, but no words came out. I was speared in place by fear and shame. And something else: a slow-burning fury that was beginning to snake through my being. My anger terrified me, because I knew that if I let it loose, it could cost me my life. I kept my eyes down.

Lord Innes spoke again. 'You have two very good friends. Fiona here. And my son, of course.'

'Yes, my lord.'

'Come. Come, daughter. Come here and let me look at you properly – let me look at the woman my son has chosen.'

We'd been given away. It could have been anyone, but I knew it had been Fiona – from Lord Innes's mention of her name, from her eyes lowered to the table, from her shaking hands.

I stood and made my way between the tables. And then I looked at him, and he smiled, a smile that chilled me and burned me up at the same time. The apparition was still hovering in the doorway – I could see her orange-red light out of the corner of my eye.

'Shame Duncan is not here. I would love to hear from him what he sees in you. Apart from a young body, of course.' His words repulsed me, but there was no desire, no perverted yearning in his eyes. I was reminded of what Duncan had said about how Cameron viewed Fiona – like a mare. An animal. Same with me, I suppose. 'So, Margaret. What do you think's going to happen now?'

What to say, in order to survive? 'I am going to serve the Innes clan like my ancestors before me,' I said in the steadiest voice I could muster.

'Your ancestors?' Lord Innes repeated in the deadly silence. The apparition floated in the gloom, and I wondered if it had come to take me away. Was it my time to die? 'Your ancestors weren't much good. Your father brought ruin on you all.'

Anger smouldered inside me. I didn't have much care for my father, but I wasn't going to shame him in front of Lord Innes, in front of all these people. After all, I bore his name. 'I won't repeat his mistakes.'

'No, you won't. You'll do for me what he wouldn't.'

The burning woman lowered her arms slowly, slowly.

I had no idea what Lord Innes meant; I had no idea what the apparition was trying to tell me.

'Although you are not his seed . . .' I felt my knees buckle. Nobody had ever said that aloud. Did he know? Did he know where I was from, who I really was? '. . . you seem to have his pride. Oh yes. Your father is a very proud man. Proud, and foolish.'

I never would have called my father proud. Foolish, yes. But not proud. Lord Innes seemed to know my family in ways nobody else did, not even me. I remained quiet. I wanted him to keep speaking. I needed him to reveal what he knew, because I had no idea what to say, what to do.

'And now, Margaret McCrimmon, *kneel*.'

I blinked. Did he mean me to curtsey, to pay homage to him in the middle of our exchange? I was so ashamed, I was trembling, but I did what he asked. The whole hall was looking at me.

'No, no, dear,' he laughed, a parody of the benevolent uncle. 'On your knees.'

As his request sank in, it was as if somebody had lit a fire at my feet, and the flames were rising, licking my flesh, setting my whole being on fire. I was burning like the apparition was burning.

'*That* is what your father refused to do. He would not kneel. But I'm not a vindictive man. I destroyed him, but I didn't kill him. And now you will pay his debt. You will bend your knee in front of me.'

So that had been my father's so-called foolishness. His

refusal to humiliate himself in front of this cruel, deluded monster. All those years I had despised him, and all he'd done was refuse to kneel?

Then nor would I.

'I will not kneel in front of you, Lord Innes,' I said, and I was too angry to wonder if those words would cost me my life.

I wish I could forget what happened after – hands that pushed me down, my face pressed against the floor, and then the rip of fabric, the bite of the whip. Blood running down my back. The apparition brought her hands to her face in silent tears –burning, burning – and then disappeared. There was silence except for a few muffled cries from among the women.

They didn't kill me, although not a word of remorse came out of my mouth.

They let me go; they let me flee from the castle, shivering with pain and cold, the smell of my own blood in my nostrils. I was alone in the windless, moonlit night.

But I didn't cry.

Cora

When I opened my eyes to silvery white light and wind
song around my window, the world was a blur. My night
had been heavy with dreams, and my sleep dense and
restless at the same time. I blinked, and a pair of soft
brown eyes came into focus. Dog breath completed the
job of waking me up. My mind was agitated, but for a
moment I couldn't remember why. Something had happened the day before, something sweet and strange,
something momentous . . . *the kiss*. Of course, Innes's kiss,
and I stretched my limbs in sweet recollection . . . And
then he'd left me standing there in the dark and the wind,
alone. I hated him, he was just a—

Good God! I thought suddenly, jolting up. The tunnel!
There was a tunnel underneath my house – and Margaret's name carved in the stone. And then the dream I'd had
came back to me, the dream that had made rest impossible, even in sleep . . . I was sitting in a church, a handbag
on my lap, black shoes, heavy woollen stockings. A beautiful song was in the air, a black-clad woman singing a
hymn – was it Rosalind? And then, without noise and in

slow motion, as happens in dreams, the sea came in, wave after wave, too fast for us even to scream. Roaring, relentless, it swallowed everyone sitting in the church that day.

But when the sea was done, I wasn't drowned; I was still standing, salty water coming up to my shins, the debris left over from the drowned congregation all around me – a hymn book, a walking stick, something knotted up that looked like tangled seaweed but was a shawl, the shawl of the woman I'd seen sitting in front of me. The church was gone, and with the building everyone who'd been inside it. And then the scene changed, and it was my mum who was standing in the water in our home, and a wave came to take her away, sweeping her off her feet. I tried to grab her hand, but I wasn't quick enough, and she disappeared as I was calling her name . . .

Overcome by anguish, I got up. I wanted to forget all about the dream, and I did so with a freezing shower that shook me out of my melancholy. After that, I went downstairs, looking forward to a cup of strong coffee and some experimenting with lip balms – home-made cosmetics were a big, and extremely fun, part of my new book. Coffee in hand, I walked over towards the loom to have a look at last night's work, throwing a glance at the now-closed hatch, covered by the slate tile. What was the tunnel for? Why had Margaret carved her name there? Who *was* Margaret, the woman in red, the woman killed in this house, and what was she trying to say to me?

Clearly I couldn't be distracted by Innes. I had to find out more about how I'd come to own the cottage, and about Mum's story, and Margaret's story, and why the mysterious woman kept coming into my dreams. Not to mention the fact that I had a book to finish, that I had—

The next thing I knew, there was scalding coffee on my feet, and the cup was in pieces on the stony floor. Sasha yelped in alarm. My heart felt like it was about to leap out of my chest, and I couldn't catch my breath.

The tapestry was finished.

The round yellow sun and the church ruins, and in the foreground two red-haired women, each holding a baby, their fingers entwined; both women looked like me, with their blue eyes and long locks. I took a breath so deep, it felt like I was trying to suck all the air out of the room.

I must have sleepwalked again – like when I'd woken up standing at the window. There was no other explanation, unless the tapestry had woven itself. Or Sasha had done it. I giggled nervously, and then clasped my hands over my mouth. Really, I'd woven the tapestry while I was sleeping? It was too weird for words.

Suddenly I felt an overwhelming desire to phone home, to speak to my brother, to hear a familiar voice, without mystery, without complications. But first I had to sweep away all signs of upset from my voice, or Stephen would notice and worry.

I cleaned up the mess on the floor and made myself another coffee, then positioned myself at the window upstairs, the only place where reception was good enough for a proper call. Everywhere else it fluctuated so much that I could only send texts.

'Hey. It's me.'

'Hey. You're lucky, I was just about to leave for work. How are you?'

Well, I'm still having visions and dreams, and I finished a tapestry in my sleep, and I kissed a man who's the poster child for messed up. But all is great, really. 'Yes, fine. Absolutely fine. All normal.'

He sounded suspicious. 'Yes?'

'Totally.'

'Cora?'

'Mmm? You know that pod of seals I told you about, just by the house? Well, I swear one of them looks just like Mrs Sidhu's father-in-law.'

'I think you're trying to distract me.'

'Look, it's nothing really. I kind of—'

'You met someone?' he said excitedly. I laughed. Who needs female friends when you have Stephen?

'Kind of. It's not very straightforward.'

'Go for it, sis.'

'You don't even know him!'

'*Go for it.*'

'Fine. Fine. Well, I'll do my best. Also, I found a tunnel underneath the house.'

'Smugglers? It's all so adventurous. It's like you ended up in the Famous Five! Anyway. I want to know everything about the guy. Everything. What's his name?'

Clearly, there was no distracting him.

'Innes.'

'Nice name. God, I wish I could come up and check him out.'

'Oh, Stephen, please do.'

'Things aren't great here, Cora. The other partner – remember Niamh? She caught hepatitis eating seafood in Newcastle . . .'

'As you do . . .'

'So I have even less time.'

'Well, soon.'

'Soon, I promise. And keep me posted on the man, okay?'

I rolled my eyes, but he'd made me laugh. 'Bye, Stephen.'

The phone call with my brother had calmed me a little, and I was in the middle of a chapter that required a lot of work, but I needed out. I felt like I was suffocating, the four walls of the cottage, laden with history and memories, closing in on me. I had to clear my mind and heart of what the place was doing to me: all the new stuff in my life I didn't know how to handle, all the strange things that were happening and that belonged in films and books, not in reality. For a moment, I thought I'd go back to the tunnel and rest my hand against Margaret's name once more, to see if some answers came to me – like when I touched the key – but just thinking of lowering myself into the gloom made me feel slightly ill. So much for the woman who always knew what to do next.

I resolved to go to the village, bringing my notebook with me. That way I could do some work, and if I bumped into Catriona, I could tell her about the tunnel and ask her if she knew any more about Margaret. I wrapped my jacket around me quickly and stepped out into the wind, Sasha following me readily. The sky was greyish-purple, so low I thought I could raise a hand and touch the clouds. The wind blew from sea to land, bringing salt and moisture and making the island shiver. I walked along the beach and through the machair, onto the grit road and across moors dotted with sheep and the occasional cow, seagulls overhead, the glimmer of the sea never far away. Maybe I was hoping to see Innes; maybe he would take me away from my thoughts and worries for some time alone together, some more talking and . . .

Another kiss.

God, I was reverting to a sixteen-year-old, hoping to hold hands and kiss at the cinema or at the park after school. But everything was strange and confused. Gealach was a place full of ghosts and untold stories, and I wanted to lean my head on Innes's chest and let him hold me. With his arms around me, I would feel safe.

And that would be the first time in my life that I'd looked for safety in a man. The first time in my thirty-one years that I'd been hungry and thirsty for someone. It was a visceral thing, something I didn't understand and couldn't rationalise. It was like another woman was living through me, feeling through me. And all this for a man I was better off staying away from, I thought, remembering how he'd handled the removals man, his arms shaking with fury, as if he was stopping himself from doing more damage. I couldn't deny, not even to myself, that he was dangerous – I could see it in his eyes.

On and on I walked, along a road that had become familiar but today felt eerie. For some reason, I kept having the feeling that there was someone else walking with me. I couldn't see anyone's shadow, or hear any footsteps but my own, yet still the feeling was unmistakable. It was as though if I turned fast enough, I would see them – if I stopped, they would bump into me . . . And then, as I contemplated the heather flowering purple on both sides of the road, all of a sudden I remembered my mum's handbag falling one day, and dried heather wrapped in tissue peeping out of her wallet. She'd hurried to put it back, but not before gazing at it for a long moment. I was already in my twenties when that had happened, and I'd noticed my mum's strange expression. I remembered wondering for a moment where the heather had come from, but then forgetting all about it.

Had it been heather from Seal?

I stopped briefly and picked up a twig, and once again I felt someone, something, looking over my shoulder. I resumed my walk, faster than before. Finally Roan appeared in the distance, and Sasha and I increased our pace even further. I could feel little beads of sweat on my temples. I needed a drink. A hot toddy, something to warm my bones and calm my nerves. And I needed a dose of reality.

I stood outside the Seal Inn and called Lucy to check in on the business. It wasn't concern that made me call – I knew Lucy, I knew how smoothly she would run things. The call was for me – to remind myself of who I was and what I did and everything I'd worked for. Lucy, as predicted, sounded cheery and in charge. She was just walking down Pennington Road, she said, nearly at the house.

I could picture every step she was taking on the road I knew so well: the asphalt while I'd walked on grit; the shop windows while my walk had been bordered by fields and moors; the voices and sounds of people and cars and buses while I'd had silence.

No wonder I'd been imagining things. Here the mind could go wild, the heart could cast back through time . . .

'And how's the book going, Cora?'

'Surprisingly well. Different. I think Lorraine will be surprised. In a good way, I hope!'

'Well, here I am. Call any time, but don't worry. It's all in hand.'

'I'm sure,' I replied, and a wave of homesickness washed over me. But it was just a moment. Seal was where I needed to be, even if for a moment I'd been gasping for the smell of traffic and chip shops and the voices of my London.

Big drops of water began to splash onto my phone, and I hurried out of the rain and inside the inn. As I'd hoped, Catriona was there, having her breakfast. She was sitting at the counter, stunning with her strawberry-blonde hair and her eyes that seemed to shine from the inside. Yes, she looked like me, but I was a more homely, more ordinary version of her beauty.

'Come in, come in,' Sorren called when he saw me hesitating at the door, waiting for a seal of approval on Sasha's presence. 'What can I get you?'

'A hot toddy, please, Sorren.'

'For breakfast?'

'Yes. Let's just say my night was eventful.'

'I don't want to know,' Sorren laughed, and I felt myself blushing up to my ears. I couldn't summon a reply.

'Come,' Catriona said.

We sat near the fire, Sasha on the floor beside us. I let myself fall into the red velvet chair with a sigh.

'Are you okay? You look a bit pale.'

'Yes, fine.' I smiled a brittle smile. 'The walk was quite cold, that's all.' But in the warmth of the fire, I began to relax.

Once again, I considered the strangeness and yet the beauty of the situation. I thought of the day I'd met Lorraine at Sea Containers – so many people, and not even the river had any peace. It was an amazing spot, yes – the heart of London, the Thames – but . . . unquiet. Everything was hard work, even walking, dribbling through the crowds. But here on Seal, there were just a handful of people. The sea, the sky and a few brightly coloured houses. The fire smouldering, and a soft fiddle music that seemed to be always there.

'This music just melts me. It's beautiful. Where is it coming from?' I looked around me.

'The Campbells live next door. I don't think that family ever does anything but play.'

'Mmm. I wish Innes was here today.'

'Do you? Innes?' Her eyes were wide.

'Rosalind! Rosalind, I meant Rosalind!' Oh God, stupid subconscious. 'I can't wait to hear her singing again.'

Catriona smiled, the living picture of what you'd call a knowing smile. 'You're a bit strange this morning, Cora. Are you sure you're all right?'

'Totally fine.'

'You're falling in love, aren't you?'

'What? Me? I . . .'

'Everyone does. Well, nearly everyone. The island does that to you.'

I started breathing again. 'Oh, yes . . . the island. Actually, you're right. I am very much in love. Sorren placed a steaming hot toddy in front of me, the sweet scent of lemon and cloves wafting from the glass.

'Thank you, Sorren.'

'No problem. If anyone asks, there's no alcohol in that, not at this time of the morning. But I know someone in need of a drink when I see one.'

'And then winter comes . . .' continued Catriona, rolling her eyes.

'What happens in winter?'

'The weather gets bad, the island empties and people see the harsher side of it. Only when winter comes will you know if you really love Seal. Sorry to sound a bit like a preacher.' She laughed.

'Well, I won't be here. I'll leave when summer finishes.'

Catriona smiled again, but it wasn't an open smile. It was a little enigmatic, like she was thinking something she wasn't saying.

'You know, I only found out I owned Gealach about a month ago. My brother and I inherited it from my mum.'

'Beatrice Lamb. Was she Scottish at all?'

'No, London born and bred. But she's been here. I'm not sure when. Her friend left her the cottage, and we think she was Scottish. Aunt Toffee.' I smiled. 'We called her that because she always gave us toffee. We can't remember her real name. Maybe she got the cottage from the McCrimmons you told me about, the ones who died in the storm? But that can't be right, because you said that someone lived there before me, Hugh . . .'

'Hugh Lyons. He was a tenant, if anything. Probably he just squatted. There are so many empty places around here.'

'But he had been gone for a long time, judging from how I found the place.'

'Yes. Well, about Beatrice Lamb . . .'

'Everyone called her Bea,' I said, and a hand clasped at my heart.

'Bea Lamb. I'll ask my sister and my mum; they know everyone, even more than me. I more of . . . guess things about people, really. Like I was reading a book . . . a "book of souls". Usually I guess right.'

'A sixth sense,' I said, smiling, but the memory of the visions I'd had was raw in my mind, and my smile was accompanied by a chill feeling.

Catriona looked down. 'Well . . . that might be. It's just the way I am.'

For a moment, I was embarrassed. Had I said something controversial? It was meant as a joke.

'I'm sorry, did I . . . did I offend you?'

She smiled. 'No, not at all. Just some people can be funny with the way I am.'

'What do you mean . . . the way you are?'

'Oh, never mind. It's difficult to explain. So, how are you getting on at the cottage?'

'Good.' I smiled. 'It's an amazing place. Only . . .'

'Only?'

'Well, strange things are happening to me.' I laughed, but I was nervous. I took a little sip of my hot toddy, for Dutch courage.

'I know what you mean. Believe me, I know.'

'You do?'

She took a breath. 'If I told you I had a dream about you? And that's why I came looking for you at the old church?'

'I wouldn't be surprised,' I said calmly, but my heart was beating fast. 'I started dreaming when we found the key to the cottage. I dreamed of Margaret.' Catriona nodded, as if she wasn't surprised either. 'I think she's trying to tell me something.'

'The dead often need to speak to the living. To guide us, to make things right, to remember things. To heal us and help us. In rare cases, to lead us astray. But not in

Margaret's case, because she's a McCrimmon, and the McCrimmon women stay in the light.'

I was speechless. I sat with my hand in the air, holding the glass, and my mouth slightly ajar.

Okay. Witches central.

At least I wasn't the only one experiencing all these weird phenomena. Not least the overwhelming feeling that someone had followed me all the way from the cottage. *The dead often need to speak to the living . . .*

'But what she wants to say to you, I cannot know. Or why she chose you and called you all the way here.'

'Why she chose me. I see,' I said, and took another sip, more of a glug, really. 'I found a tunnel underneath the house. It leads to the cave just below the cottage, straight to the sea. Margaret's name is carved in the stone of the wall.'

'Really?' Catriona's eyes widened.

'You said she was killed there?'

'Yes. But that's all I know. All that anybody knows, really. I have this feeling there is no way to find out more . . . unless she tells you.'

'Catriona, you're freaking me out.'

'Well, it's a bit scary at the beginning, but you get used to it.'

'To the dead talking?' I asked, in a voice that was too calm.

'Yes,' she said.

I took another glug of whisky, and it went down the wrong way. I coughed and spluttered until I thought I would be one of those dead talking, while Catriona went to the bar for a glass of water. When I was breathing again, she decided it was time to change the subject.

'Is something happening between you and Innes? If I can ask?'

'How do you know? Is this one of your "guesses"?'

Catriona laughed. 'No, not at all. Anyone could see! Not to mention your Freudian slip . . .'

'I don't know. I don't know what's going on. Anyway, I'm not here for romance. I'm here to write my book.' I lifted my notebook.

'Life has a habit of ignoring our plans, as I'm sure you've noticed.'

'True.'

'You know, there are things about Innes . . . I'll tell you what, Cora. Ask him—'

'He pulled a knife on his parents!'

Catriona and I jumped out of our skins, and Sasha jerked up too. The pub had seemed to be empty, and our conversation had been so intense it had blocked everything else out, but now I turned round to see a clean-cut man sitting on the other side of the counter, beside a woman with hair curled so tightly she seemed to have used some precision instrument.

'Everybody knows it. That poor man, his father,' the man continued, as if it were normal to jump in on a private conversation, 'he was the best. Oh, the best. We all looked up to him, you know. Alan gave him hell. Absolute hell. And then he tried to kill them . . .'

'That was just gossip, Sandy. Stop talking rubbish.' Sorren was very pale.

'You would say that. You were always his friend. You're misguided. And Innes is bad. Rotten to the core.'

'Oh, aye. Rotten to the core,' the woman with the perm echoed.

I wasn't expecting to be so upset by their words, but surprisingly, tears sprouted in my eyes.

I wanted them to stop talking.

I wanted them to stop saying those things about Innes.

I barely knew him, but pulling a knife on his parents? The man who'd kissed my forehead so tenderly?

The man who'd slammed someone against the side of a van and threatened to break his nose.

'He's a bad boy who grew up to be a bad man,' Sandy insisted.

Sorren shook his head. I could see his effort to keep calm. 'No. He's one of the best people I know.'

'Then how do you explain what he did to his parents?'

Sorren was quiet for a moment. 'By what his parents did to him.'

'You bought into all that vicious gossip? They brought him up in an upright household, gave him an education . . . You disappoint me, Sorren. You really do. Well, I won't be sitting here listening to lies about Doctor Innes. I will not.'

The man called Sandy strode out of the pub, followed by the woman with the perm, her lips pursed.

'What was that about?' I asked, shocked. 'What did Innes do?'

Sorren raised his hands, a tea towel over his shoulder, as if to say he didn't want to talk about it, and stepped into the back room, his cheeks flushed.

'Some people are judge and jury,' Catriona said. 'Innes never got on with his father. I didn't like him much either. After Innes left the island, his father told anyone who'd listen that his son was deranged, an alcoholic; that he'd threatened them with a knife . . .'

'And is it true?' I said in a small voice. I thought of Innes's eyes when he'd threatened the removals man, of the fury in them, so much more than that man deserved.

Catriona looked at me. 'His father had a gash on his arm; he said that Innes did it. That's all I know.'

A cold shiver travelled down my spine, in spite of the warmth of the fire and my hot toddy. Could that be true?

Should I close my heart?

Did I still have time to do that?

A part of me knew that I'd looked into the fire, and that it would be impossible for me now to ever look away.

HIGH TIDE

Margaret

I woke, still sore with shame and humiliation, to the sound of thundering horses and shouts, and the smell of fire in my nostrils. The black waters of Loch Avich were as calm as ever; dawn had barely broken. In the distance, I could see flames licking Castle Innes, little black figures running out through the gates, being speared by men on horses. The MacGregors had struck before dawn, when everyone was asleep. Whatever game Lord Innes and his allies had played, whatever dangerous tapestry they'd woven, his clan, those left behind, would be the ones to pay.

I should have run away, but I went in the opposite direction – I ran towards the castle. I had to find Mairi and Ally and Helen, and Lady Dolina. I ran blindly until I saw a band of galloping men coming towards me – and then Lord Innes's cold, cold eyes met mine. He and his men were running away, saving themselves and leaving their people to die.

Inside the castle, the noise stopped at once, and I felt like I was underwater, moving slowly, slowly in the deadly silence. Men and women covered in blood, some of them lying still, some of them begging for help, some still trying to run. And the thatched roofs and the stables burning, burning.

I walked on as if I were untouchable.

And maybe I was, because blades came for me, and then stopped.

I felt a terrible heat beside me, and I saw the burning woman advancing with me, her long red hair trailing behind her. We walked side by side through the hall, through rooms and corridors, through the destruction of Castle Innes. And then I heard screams – Lady Dolina's screams – and reality came back. I saw them taking her, white and unable to stand, her front spattered with blood, and spiriting her away, while her women were slain one by one. Fiona begged for mercy, hoping her pregnant belly would save her; it didn't. Many others were skewered or set alight.

I found Mairi huddling in her room; I held her hand and we ran and hid. There was no trace of Ally – I didn't know then that I would never see him again. They didn't find us, Mairi and me, because I knew how to hide, I knew how to disappear. Helen was nowhere to be seen.

When silence fell at last, Mairi tried to drag me out of our hiding place; she wanted to walk back to Lochawe and hope the fall of Clan Innes wouldn't follow us there. But I couldn't leave; I had to wait there for Duncan to come back and find me. Because I knew he would. I was covered in sweat, even with the wind blowing, and burning up with a fever. I hoped it was just the shock and the fear, but two women and a bairn had fallen ill in the days before the MacGregors came for us, and I knew the sickness had taken me too.

I stood and gazed at what was left of Castle Innes, a wreck of smouldering stones, the ground littered with corpses and crying women. It was all gone, all gone. I walked among the ruins, disbelieving, my hair blowing in the wind and my skin burning, burning. The stench was unbearable. I had no tears; it was all too terrible even to cry. I thought I was delirious, because I heard my name being called, but I wasn't. Helen lay on the ground, seemingly unharmed, but somehow I knew at once that she was not for living.

'Margaret ... my garden ...' she rasped, and it sounded like she was breathing blood.

'Your garden is safe. It's all safe. I saw it on the way here. It was as lovely as ever and all in bloom; they haven't even touched a flower,' I said, and I realised I was struggling to get the words out, as if my mouth couldn't quite obey my brain. I was falling fast, I could feel it. Helen didn't smile; she didn't believe me. Her eyes closed, mercifully, and she drew her last breath.

There was nothing left for me there, nothing alive, nothing whole; nothing that hadn't been violated and burned. But Duncan was coming to get me; he was coming back. I couldn't go back to Lochawe, I had to wait for him. The pain in my bones was such that I could barely walk, and the whole world was swimming in front of my eyes.

I made it to the stream, walking through what remained of Helen's garden, among mangled bushes and flowers flattened and shredded by heavy boots. I was burning up, and the running stream seemed the only way to cool me down a little. I tried to take my dress off, but my fingers couldn't manage the hooks and buttons, so I clawed at it until I ripped it. Standing in my underclothes, shivering in the freezing water, I saw the swelling under my arm and burst into tears at last.

I sat down in the water, and now my skin was burning with the cold. Long, violent shivers shook me, and my teeth were chattering. I knew that if I stayed there, I would end up drowning, and even if a part of me knew that the plague would kill me anyway, and that maybe it would be easier to die this way than struggle in a long agony, I clung to life. I tried to get up and reach the other bank, but although it was just a few steps, I collapsed. I was too weak to lift myself out of the water. *Duncan, Duncan,* I called in my heart. *Please, let me see you one last time.*

I was too far gone to hear the horse's hooves, or his beloved voice calling my name; all I knew was that two strong arms picked me up, and in a far region of my mind I understood that my prayer had been answered. He lifted me onto Shabana and we took off, but I had already passed out, lost somewhere that was not sleep, but something deeper and deadlier, that wanted to claim me for itself.

Innes

I was barely through the door, laden with equipment, when Pamela jumped on me – literally.

'Welcome back,' Sylvia smiled, while Pamela squeezed me tight.

It was the weirdest feeling in the world, to be welcomed with such warmth, such love. Usually when I came home, all that awaited me was silence. Not even a cat. Hell, not even a goldfish. But there she was, this girl who shared my blood, holding me like I was actually good, good and kind. Like I deserved to be held.

And Sylvia, looking at me in a way that made me wonder if she wasn't searching for traces of her lost love, for a way to give me what she would have been so desperate to give to Douglas.

'Uncle Innes! Do you want to see my dressy-up costume?'

'Uncle Innes is tired,' Sylvia said, caressing her daughter's arm with the palm of her hand. 'In a wee while, Pammy . . .'

'No, it's okay, I'd love to see it.'

My mother stepped out of the kitchen. 'Hi, sweet-heart . . . It's on my bed, darling – do you mind?' she said to Sylvia.

'It's okay, I'll get it. I'm going to get cleaned up any-way,' I said, and made my way upstairs.

Almost immediately, I had second thoughts.

My parents' room.

I wasn't supposed to go in there. I wasn't allowed. One time my father had found me playing cars on their win-dowsill; I'm not going to say what happened afterwards.

But the old man was dead. I could go wherever I wanted within this house – I didn't have to sneak any more, hoping he wouldn't see me, hoping he didn't decide I needed punishing. Just so he could have a bit of fun doing it. I stepped into the room, my heart beating faster than I liked to admit, and smiled inside as I saw the cos-tume, a pink thing of ruffles and ribbons, thinking how proud Pammy was going to feel with this on. I lifted up the silky dress – and saw my father's face staring at me from my mother's bedside table.

My mouth fell open – just like in a stupid cartoon where surprise means your eyeballs fall out. All these years, my mother had kept a picture of him beside her, in his king-of-the-world pose, arms folded, legs apart, the big smile of the predator. And above it, on the wall, a crucifix, a tiny picture of Padre Pio, and another photograph of my father, framed in pride of place above her bed.

A sanctuary to the monster.

I ran downstairs and gave Sylvia the dress with shaking hands. I had to get out of there. I was choking; the reek of aniseed was everywhere, his hands were on me, his presence filled my mind . . .

'Innes, are you going?' My mother's voice.

For a moment I thought I could swallow it once again, the bitter pill.

Stay quiet.

Don't hurt her feelings.

But I couldn't. It was like acid, burning me from the inside.

I walked slowly to the kitchen and stopped in the doorway. She was mending something. 'I saw the pictures in your room, Mother.'

The colour drained from her face and she looked up, needle poised. Sylvia stood there, holding the dress, looking from one of us to the other.

'Why?' I said. 'Why are his photographs there, in the place of honour? You really can't live without him, can you?'

'He was my husband. And your father. I owe him this, to keep his photograph in the house, to go to the graveyard and see him.'

'You *owe* it to him? You didn't learn anything, did you? You don't regret anything. That man ruined my life . . . and Douglas's too.'

'He hurt you, I know, but I think you turned out quite well . . .'

I couldn't quite believe what I was hearing.

263

'Innes,' Sylvia said, 'she means you're a good person, a successful man. That's what she was trying to say . . .'

'Please, Sylvia, stay out of it. Nothing has changed, has it, Mother?' I struggled to keep my voice down, because I didn't want to upset Pamela.

'He's not here,' Mother replied. 'He's not here to hurt us any more; is that not enough? He died just there, at the bottom of the stairs.'

'How can you look at his face every day, every night? Your loyalty is still with him, isn't it?' All my rage was coming out. I knew that soon I would start shouting, and I hated myself for it. I had to get out, I had to go, before I said too much.

'My loyalty? My loyalty is with him? You have no idea . . .'

'Innes . . .' Sylvia tried to intervene again.

'You were distraught when he died, Mother. And now I find a bloody shrine to him!'

'I was distraught, yes, but not because he'd died!' she shouted. For a moment, I was shocked. My mother never raised her voice. Sylvia rested a hand on her arm, and they exchanged a look I couldn't decipher.

'Alan,' she said, and rubbed her forehead, then smoothed her hair back in her old, familiar gesture. 'I love you so much; I love you and your brother more than anyone . . .'

'Really?' I said, and now my voice was low and cold. 'When you let *that man* hit me over the head with what-ever came to hand? I was six years old. I had so many blows to the head I couldn't see right. I couldn't see the

264

fucking blackboard at school. Where were you when I was screaming, Mother?'

'I was trying to keep you and your brother alive!'

'You did what he wanted! All the time. All the time you appeased him.'

'Oh, Alan. Of course I appeased him. I had ways to calm him so he wouldn't kill me. How do you think you and your brother were conceived?'

I couldn't say any more; I didn't want to be there. There was no end, there was no sorting it out, no healing. No hope. The pain would repeat itself over and over and over again.

There was no hope for me.

I didn't run out, I walked, dazed by pain and disappointment. Slowly, deliberately, deaf and blind to everything around me, until the sea was there in front of me, and I was alone with my island. Or I thought I was, because I heard footsteps behind me, and when I turned around, there she was, Sylvia, with those enormous brown eyes, her arms extended to me.

'I'm sorry. So sorry,' she said, and before I knew it, her head was against my chest and I was holding her, and her lips looked for mine and found them – the sweet taste of kindness, the balm to my broken soul. For a moment it seemed that this way, everything would fall into place. I would fix what my brother had broken, I would look after Pamela, I would bring everybody back together. Keep them all around me, this shattered family. Forgive. Live again.

Let the wounds heal, turn into scar tissue.

Her kiss was soft and slow; her body enveloped mine, though she was so small . . .

'Sylvia, no.'

I couldn't. I couldn't let myself take comfort from this beautiful, loving woman, because I could give nothing back – because it wasn't her in my heart. Maybe it would have been perfect, but how could I ever build a life on a lie, how could I heal the past if it meant denying *her* – denying Cora?

'Innes . . . why?' she whispered, and the pain and dis-appointment in her voice broke my heart.

'I don't think I'm the one you want,' I said. 'I'm not Douglas. I can't make things right for you, and you can't make things right for me.'

Her voice was so low, I nearly couldn't hear her. 'It *felt* so right. You can't say it didn't . . .'

'I can't take this from you, Sylvia. I can't . . . lose myself in you. Do you understand? It wouldn't be fair.'

'Innes, since you came back, I . . .'

I held her to me, and her words were muffled against my chest. 'Please, don't say it,' I begged her, and cradled her like a little girl. 'You're better off without me. I can promise you that.'

She pushed away from me, and dried her tears. 'I'm sorry. It was a mistake.'

'I'm sorry too – please, there's no need to explain or apologise. It was a moment, just a moment.'

'There's something you need to know,' she said, her voice still full of tears, but her usual poise back.

'Tell me. If it's about Pammy, you can count on me. I know I haven't been there . . .'

'It's not about Pammy. It's about your mother.'

I stood in silence, my stomach clenched. I was furious with my mother, and disappointed . . . but was she ill? Was she okay? A mixture of feelings churned inside me and I was speechless.

'Remember she said she was distraught, but not because your father had died?'

'I understand she was relieved, but she still keeps—'

'No. She didn't mean that. She didn't mean she was just relieved. Your mother told me something,' Sylvia said, and took a breath like she was readying herself to tell me a story. 'You know she doesn't drink much. Actually, she doesn't drink at all. But we had a party for her birthday a few months ago, and there was this sweet wine, and people over at the house, and she was so happy. Then everyone left, and she was really tired more than anything, so I helped her upstairs to make sure she was all right. Believe me, this never happens; you don't need to worry about that. With what she went through . . .'

'She loathes alcohol. I know,' I said, more and more agitated. What was she getting to?

'She stood at the top of the stairs, holding my arm. Then she looked down and just said, "He was terrified." I asked her what she meant, who was terrified. And she said, "My husband." I remember it word for word, Innes. She said, "He slipped down the stairs. I didn't push him, though I might have wanted to. He lay down there on the carpet, he was still alive. He was look-ing at me. He was terrified. He told me to call for help, and blood came out of his mouth. I sat on the stairs and watched him die." '

For a moment, I didn't understand what she had said. Then the words sank in, slowly, slowly. My mother had killed The Guy. By letting him die.

Yes, she *had* escaped, in the end.

'She keeps all those pictures of him, yes. But it's guilt, or maybe keeping up appearances. Whatever it is, I can assure you it's not love.'

'Did you tell anyone?'

'No. And I never will. But I couldn't let you believe she loved him. I just couldn't let you think she was ever on his side. Innes, she was brainwashed! I swear, when she speaks about your father, it's like she's talking about some pagan god who had the power to kill you all with a look, a thought. She married him at seventeen; she was a child! He had terrified her to such an extent, she couldn't even think for herself. It's a miracle she found the strength she did. You must forgive her,' she said, and there was a hint of steel in her eyes. 'Because in the end, she came good for you and your brother; she risked all she had. She let your father bleed out on the floor, and I call that a good thing.'

I looked into her eyes, and she held my gaze.

'You must forgive her,' she said again.

I felt my heart, like you feel a bone to see if it's broken. There, I found the words: *How do you think you and your brother were conceived?*

268

And I hardened up. I thought of The Guy dying at the bottom of the stairs, and my mother not moving to call for help, waiting for him to die, and I thanked her for that – but loud and impossible to ignore, the child in me shouted, *Too late, too late!*

It was too late for all of us.

'I'm sorry, Sylvia,' I said. 'I can't be the man you need. But most of all, I can never, ever forgive my mother.'

I took it for granted that my feet would take me to the off-licence, to the Seal Inn, to anywhere with alcohol in it; but I was desperate and poisoned and trying hopelessly to swim against the current of shame and betrayal, The Guy's final moments playing over and over in my mind – the blood coming out of his mouth, my mother sitting there silent, unmoving, waiting for him to die. Finally the punishment had come to him, and still it wasn't enough, and still it didn't fix anything – and so I went to look for innocence. I went looking for Cora.

Cora

I was walking back from the Seal Inn after a few hours' work there, making my way along the narrow causeway. The water was so high already, it nearly lapped my feet. Another hour and I wouldn't be able to get home. The afternoon light was opaque and milky, and everything looked like a dream. I was reeling with what I'd heard. What should I believe? Those people's accusations, or Sorren's defence? Even Catriona seemed strange about Innes, like she didn't trust him. It was as though he was two people: one capable of terrible things, and the one I'd glimpsed when he kissed me. And for some reason, I couldn't get him out of my mind. I was furious with myself for that, but I couldn't help it.

What I needed was a good working session, to focus my thoughts. In my mind, I imagined sitting at the table with my notebook full of ideas and glued-on thread samples and shells, sand between the pages, ready to start a whole new chapter. My work had always been there, through the ups and downs of life – a place where I could express myself, where I could escape from the world or feel I could master it.

I'd barely stepped onto my little half-moon beach when out of the corner of my eye I saw someone coming onto the causeway after me – a tall man, wearing a shirt open to the waist, his arms covered in tattoos.

My heart skipped a beat, and I blinked. The light was so treacherous . . . There was something about the man – he looked like Innes, but I wasn't sure . . . He was walking so fast, he was almost running – running from something, running to something? But when he stepped onto the sand, when he stood still and looked at me in the muted light, the milky sky behind him, his hair blowing in the wind, there was no doubt.

I saw his eyes, so clear, so full of pain.

His hands, tight into fists.

His chest heaving.

Innes, as if he'd walked out of my thoughts and into reality.

Our hearts spoke to each other and I knew what to do – I opened my arms, and he threw himself into them. He was tall and strong, and I was small – but I was strong too, and I could hold him. I could hold the weight of his body, the weight of his cares. He said nothing, but held on to me, his arms around my waist, his face buried in my neck. Maybe he was dangerous – I *knew* he was dangerous – but right now he was lost, and I had to be there for him.

At last he freed me from his embrace, and I took his hand. It was so big, my own looked childlike in comparison.

'Please tell me. Tell me what's wrong. What's happened

to upset you like this?' Maybe I wanted to go back into his arms. Maybe I, too, needed to be held. 'Innes, please . . . I know about your family. I mean, people have told me things, but I need to know the truth. You've suffered, I can see that. Let me help you . . .' I was terrified of saying too much or too little – terrified that he would go because I was getting too close, too soon, or because he felt I didn't care. But something had happened, and it was me he'd come looking for.

'I'm sorry. I don't know why I came here . . .' He was whispering, but somehow I heard him over the noise of the waves, as though my ears were attuned to his frequency. I took a step towards him, and our arms looked for each other, our hands touching bare skin – and then he had taken me by the waist, and my breath caught as his face came close. His eyes were closed as he drank me in, and finally his mouth looked for mine. I was ready and waiting for him, my lips slightly open to receive his kiss . . .

'Hey, Cora!'

Innes froze at the sound of a man's voice. I stood flushed, my knees weak, my lips tingling, full of a tenderness I couldn't contain. Neal was coming across the causeway with a bottle in his hand.

'Hello, Innes. Fancy seeing you here,' he said, and there was a cold edge to his voice.

'I see you had other plans,' Innes said softly in my ear.

'No, I—'

'Yeah, we had half an arrangement, didn't we?'

'Actually, I said I was busy, Neal.'

Innes looked me straight in the eye, and smiled a sad smile. 'I think it's better if I leave.'

I didn't return his smile – I was too upset that our moment had been interrupted. 'Better for who?' I asked, and the emotion in my voice must have surprised Neal, but I didn't care.

'Not for me, for sure,' Innes said.

'For me, though! We can't drink this if you're around, can we?' Neal lifted the wine bottle.

I couldn't believe my ears. He had never been so crass before. What had possessed him?

'And anyway, you were busy somewhere else, weren't you? Was that your girlfriend, you know, the small one with the short hair?'

What?

'That was my brother's wife. Ex-wife. And there is nothing between us,' Innes whispered to me.

'It didn't look like it. You seemed pretty close to me.' Neal shook his head. He'd been drinking already, I realised.

Innes tried to ignore him. 'Cora, I—'

'It's okay. I don't need to know. You don't have to tell me . . .'

'There's nothing to tell!' he exclaimed.

'You seemed quite ready to get a room,' Neal goaded him.

Innes stood, cheeks flushed and fists flexed, but he didn't move. 'I shouldn't have come looking for you,' he said to me. 'I'm sorry.'

'Oh well. You kept my place warm, anyway.'

Okay, Neal had gone too far. I turned to him, ready to put him in his place, but I wasn't quick enough. It was a moment, a blur: Innes launched himself at him like a predator, and punched him so hard that Neal fell to the ground, with a sickening sound of bone on rock. Innes didn't wait for him to get up; he punched him again and again, his rage coming from somewhere I didn't know, I didn't understand, but that terrified me.

I think I must have screamed, and the sound broke the evil spell. Innes stood, his knuckles red and a look of consternation on his face. Neal was wailing softly, and it was such an eerie sound, I thought he was about to die.

Innes stepped onto the semi-flooded causeway behind him, and I trembled, because with one wrong step he could have fallen in the sea. But he kept himself steady, and for a moment it looked like he was about to walk on water.

'Innes, the tide! Please come back!'

I knelt beside Neal – he was holding his face, blood trickling through his fingers – but it was Innes's name I called, over and over again.

'I'm sorry. I'm sorry. I . . . I'm so sorry,' he called to me, and then he was gone, running not from us but from himself, towards a place where there was no land, only sea.

Cora

Neal's nose was broken, but he didn't seem to have any head trauma. Not that I'd know much about that, but he was conscious, and apart from spouting venom, he wasn't delirious. I could hear a nauseating crunching sound when I touched his nose – small bones were broken, cartilage pushed out of place. But it wasn't his nose that worried me; he was holding his left arm with his right hand, and couldn't straighten it. I was worried that the horrible sound I'd heard when he'd fallen against the rocks had been his arm fracturing.

We were stuck in the cottage for the next six hours, so I did my best with my small first-aid kit, disinfecting his nose and splinting the arm to keep it steady, but I knew that in spite of Neal's protests, we had to get him seen. What tortured me most, though, was that I didn't know where Innes was and I couldn't look for him. I was afraid for him, so afraid. In his state of mind, I was worried he'd do something stupid.

'I hate doctors.'

'Neal, you're not a child. Get over it. And please stop

moaning, I can't take any more. My brother broke his leg when he was seven, on a slide, of all places, and he didn't moan half as much as you.'

'They probably gave him proper painkillers, not bloody paracetamol.'

'Well, excuse me if this is not a hospital.'

'You act like it's my fault. Like I was asking for it.'

'You were. Oh, pick up!' I said into the phone. 'Please, pick up!' Neither Sorren nor Catriona was answering. I couldn't find anyone to go looking for Innes. I could only pace up and down in front of the window and will the tide to recede.

After six long hours of moaning and trying to manage Neal's considerable pain on paracetamol, we were finally able to leave the cottage. It was nearly midnight, and the island surgery must be long closed. I decided to drive straight to the Seal Inn and look for Sorren. We made quite an impression staggering into the pub, Neal holding a bloodied handkerchief – the blood kept trickling from his nose, thin but constant – and as white as a sheet.

'What happened?' Sorren said, and took him by the arm, leading him to sit in the back.

'Innes happened. That bloody son of a bitch.' Well, I couldn't blame Neal for not being the forgiving type.

'Where is he now?'

'Oh, okay, thanks. I'm a mess, but let's all worry about the guy who beat me up.'

'I don't know. He ran off just as the tide was turning. I was so scared he'd drown,' I said, and immediately realised that the intensity of my tone left no doubt about my feelings. 'I tried to phone you, and Catriona . . .'

'I was working, and Caty is at her sister's; no signal there. Did you see him reach the other side?'

I shook my head. 'I lost sight of him,' I said, and hated myself for it, though I knew I wasn't to blame.

'Okay. I'll get someone to hold the fort here, and I'll drive around and—'

'Er, excuse me?' Neal said. 'What about me?'

'It's a broken nose, Neal, you'll survive,' Sorren said. I could see he didn't like Neal much for some reason, and I wondered what had happened in the last few years to turn that cheerful, easy-going man into someone so unpleasant.

'He needs to be seen,' I said. 'He hit his head quite hard. And his nose is . . . well, it's in pieces actually. I can feel them crunching.'

Neal looked like he was about to pass out. 'I think my arm is broken too.'

'Good God, what did Innes do, run you over? Take him to St Fintan, you know, the clinic? I'm sure there'll be someone on duty . . . Do you know where it is?'

I shook my head, images of Innes walking on water – and falling – dancing in front of my eyes. Sorren gave me directions, and I loaded Neal carefully into the passenger seat of my tiny car and set off.

Although the island roads were dark and winding, we reached St Fintan in less than half an hour. The clinic was housed in a period red-brick house; inside, though, it was shiny, brand new and chemical-smelling. It reminded me of my mum's sheltered accommodation. We found a young Chinese nurse, who explained that they were a rehabilitation clinic for long-term patients and not an A & E, but after taking one look at Neal's face and the way he held his arm, she led us to a treatment room. She palpated his arm, and Neal screamed so loudly I was worried he'd wake the whole clinic up. Just when I thought he couldn't get any whiter, his colour drained even further and he was sick beside the treatment bed.

'Wait for me here. I'm calling Dr Woerner.'

We watched her go in silence. I wondered if Dr Woerner was on shift already, and if not, how long it would take him to arrive; in the meantime, I cleaned up the mess and threw the paper in the bin. Neal had lain down on the bed, his colouring now more green than white.

'He's mental.' His voice was hoarse; there was blood on his teeth and the skin around his eyes had a weird yellowish tint. Soon it would turn purple.

'He shouldn't have done this, I know,' I said. 'But you shouldn't have poked him.'

'I can't believe you're defending him!'

'I'm not. But the way you spoke to him . . .'

'So I said something he didn't like. Do you beat people up who say things you don't like?'

'There's no point in talking about this now, Neal.'

'But he's mental. Actually crazy, asylum crazy. They told me.'

'Who told you?'

'Everyone. Only Sorren had anything good to say about him. Everyone else on Seal told me to stay away from him. I'm supposed to work with the guy!'

I looked down. I thought of the wounded man in my arms, the pain in his heart as he'd held on to me. As if I could save him . . .

'Cora?' A soft soprano voice called my name from the doorway. I looked up and saw a small, short-haired woman with lively eyes.

'Yes?'

'I'm Sylvia, Innes's sister-in-law. I'm working a night shift tonight.'

Great. Just what I needed. After what Neal had said, Sylvia was just about the last person I wanted to see that night.

'I know who you are,' I said. There was a pause. She must have read my tone.

'Oh. Good . . . I recognised you from your hair,' she said quite sweetly. 'Are you okay?'

Fancy you asking, I thought, but then I felt so bad about it that I found it in myself to smile. 'Yes, yes. Don't worry. I'm fine. It's Neal, Innes's colleague, who needs attention.'

Tell me, is there something going on between you and Innes? How do you know who I am? And who the hell told you about my hair?

Should I be afraid of you?

'What happened?' she asked.

'Oh, nothing. It's all fine.'

'Innes?'

I looked down. 'Yes. And now I don't know where he is.'

Her eyes found mine. 'You go and look for him. I'll stay here.' We both glanced over at Neal, looking even worse under the neon lights, then Sylvia beckoned me out into the corridor. 'Look, Cora, I know there's something going on between you and Innes . . . it's the Seal grapevine. And, well, I won't stand in your way. I thought . . . I thought Innes could help me put a patch on something that was ripped. Something I miss. *Someone* I miss. Because you know, my husband, Douglas – Innes's brother – he wasn't a bad man. He hit me and he terrified me, but he wasn't a bad man . . .'

I blinked. 'I'm sorry? He sounds pretty bad to me!'

'My husband was destroyed by one of the people who should have loved him the most: his own father. *He* was the real monster.'

'Innes's father?'

She nodded. 'If I told you the things he did to them, you would not believe me. Morag, their mother, she said that Douglas adapted faster, better. He became his father's ally. He became like him so he could survive. Innes never could. Out of the house he went crazy – he drank and started fights – but at home he was his mother's protector. Nobody knew what was going on with the family; my father-in-law was a doctor, a respected man in the community. Nobody knew . . .'

Oh, Innes . . .

'Innes has been drinking for many years, but he has

turned the corner now. I was hoping I could help him . . . I got this notion in my head that we could make things right. But he doesn't feel that way towards me, and tonight I understood that I don't either. It was an illusion. I was just looking for another Douglas.' Her eyes were truthful, transparent. 'I care for Innes very much, Cora . . . I know he can be saved, he can be different from his father and his brother . . . Oh, here's Dr Woerner. You go and look for Innes.'

'Thank you,' I said. Sylvia just looked at me, an indefinable sorrow in her eyes. She'd loved a lost man – she loved him still.

And Innes? Would he be lost too?

I stepped back into my little car, exhausted. Everything was so dark – a sea of black where both land and water dissolved. My thoughts went to Sasha; she was inside the house, thankfully, so she couldn't be caught unawares by the rising tide. At least I wouldn't have to worry about that. But where was Innes? I checked my phone – a message from Sorren, saying there was no trace of him. All I could do was drive around looking for him, and pray. I called to my mother to keep him safe, to keep me safe. I missed her so much now that she wasn't here to listen, to give advice, to stroke my back the way she used to when something, big or small, was worrying me.

I drove and drove, the headlights illuminating the road in front of me – the bright eyes of sheep and deer and rabbits, the silent moors and fields, blowing wind and black, black water, ebbing and flowing, ebbing and flowing.

The ruined church rose in the distance, and I stopped the car. I was drained, and so frightened, my legs were trembling. As I walked towards the graveyard, I saw that a corner of the sky was turning grey. Dawn was on its way. Maybe this night would end – though it seemed impossible.

I knelt in front of Margaret's grave. The words came by themselves, together with hot, helpless tears.

'Where is Innes, Margaret? Where is he?' My voice seemed to echo in the silence, as if a hundred women were calling with me. 'I heard your name when all this started. I heard your name in my house. And now here we are. You carved your name in Gealach. Who are you? What are you trying to say to me?'

It happened slowly. The light changed, the world became very cold and very strange, and the figures took shape in front of me, as though they were on a black canvas. I saw them again – the woman at the window, the man coming up the beach. But this time something was different, because I could see the woman's face.

The woman was me.

I felt as though I was falling, falling – and then my fall was broken when I saw the man walking towards the setting sun. His ice-water eyes, his blond hair – Innes. All of a sudden, although I was standing at the window and he was on the beach, his whisper seemed very close: *Corrywreckan. Don't let me fall.*

The world came into focus again, and I knew what to do. I knew where Innes was.

I don't think I'd ever driven so fast in my life. I was too worried for Innes to think about the fact that I'd had another vision, or that I was acting on the request of a dream man. All I knew was that Innes had asked me not to let him fall, and I wouldn't. I ran as fast as I could along the shore – my steps should have been heavy with sleeplessness and fatigue, sinking in the sand, but instead I flew. And then I saw him, at last. The way he stood, the way he was looking at the water – his arms opened, like a crucifix. Like someone who'd been marked for sacrifice. The waters of Corrywreckan whirled beneath him, beautiful and terrible, hungry and yet indifferent. *Please don't jump. Please don't jump.*

Maybe I should have walked to him carefully, in case I startled him, but I was too frightened not to shout. 'Innes! Please, don't!' I called, and I knew from the slight movement in his shoulders that he had heard me. I froze. Then he turned around, and for a moment, his face was that of a child. I could see him as a little boy, I could see his eyes, terrified, betrayed by those who should have loved him the most.

Slowly I walked to him, and with every step I contemplated catastrophe. His body, strong and tall, turning insubstantial as a feather against the cliffs as he jumped, as he shattered on the rocks and disappeared in the roaring waves . . .

I walked on, step after step, hoping, praying, hoping,

praying . . . until I took hold of him, and wrapped my arms around him, and leaned my cheek against his back, tying him to me, stopping him from jumping – because if he did, he would carry me with him.

'Come with me,' I whispered. The waves roared below us, black and foaming – I could hear Corrywreckan screaming, ready to swallow us both and take us down into the deep.

'Please, go away,' he pleaded, and I was even more chilled when I realised that he meant it. He wasn't imploring me to stay, not to abandon him – he really wanted me to go. He wanted it all to end.

'No,' I said, as simply as that. 'I won't go away.'

'Cora, I'm damned. Do you hear me? Look what I did to Neal. I've done it a million times. I'm just as bad as my father. I nearly destroyed Letty . . .' I didn't have time to wonder who Letty was. 'I will destroy you, if you let me.'

I could feel his despair like an aura around him, and for a moment I trembled. I knew that I shouldn't get too close to him, that I might be trapped for ever in his shadows. They were part of his core, and sooner or later they might claim him for themselves. I could only guess what steps his father's ferocity might have danced around his heart. I wanted to believe in him – but I couldn't help being afraid.

If I stayed with him, his darkness might take me too.

But he needed me, and I would not let him down. He was shaking, and I saw he was fighting against himself, against the impulse to turn around and hold me, to touch me, to feel my skin.

'There's a way out. I promise you. I promise you,' I said into his back, and I cradled him gently. A step backwards, away from the abyss. Just a little step. Both of us, away from the deep. Maybe I could dare to take his hand and rest it against my heart – hold us both in my embrace, keep him safe, give him a home. A soft drizzle was falling on us, a thin veil over our skin.

'I won't go away,' I repeated. 'I won't leave you.'

I felt him move imperceptibly, step away from me – would he run, would he take flight down the cliff like a seabird? I was about to tighten my hold on him when I realised he was turning around. Slowly, slowly he turned. I took his face in my hands, and I wondered if it was wet with rain, with sea spray or with tears.

'Come. Come.'

I pulled at his hand gently, took a little step away from the cliff, and he followed me. I was so relieved, I could have burst into tears. Away from the abyss, down, down towards the beach, towards salvation. And then relief turned into something else as he wrapped his arms around me and I breathed him in, a scent of salt and warm skin. He held on to me like a drowning man to a raft. And I was not ashamed, I was not hesitant when my lips looked for his and I kissed him, a kiss that was neither sweet nor tender. Passion to forget pain. Passion to feel alive . . .

'No. Cora, no. You are . . . innocent.'

I couldn't help laughing a little, even if I was still reeling from the trauma of seeing him standing on that cliff. 'I'm not that innocent!'

'No, no,' he repeated, shaking his head. 'I know things . . . things I don't want you to know. You have peace. I'm lost.'

'You are not lost, can't you see? I've found you,' I said, and then I didn't speak any more.

Innes

I was burning, torn between what I knew was best for Cora and what I so desperately wanted to do. I welcomed the rain, cool against my skin, as I tried desperately to rein in my thoughts, to make my muscles obey so that my body would walk away from her. I had to make that impossible effort, I had to leave her alone. The sound of the waves, the sound I was so used to, was now as loud as a hurricane in my ears. I could hear the mermaids singing – and one of them was in front of me, silently crooning her innocent, knowing song. Older and stronger sailors had been enchanted by such a song; who was I to resist? I supposed letting her go would be easy: just say something ugly, push her away, and I wouldn't need to leave – she would. But I couldn't do it; my body wouldn't let me. She was so close I could smell her, even over the scent of salt – the warm, milky, secret scent of women. Layer after layer she took her clothes off, keeping her eyes on mine in a way that was vulnerable and infinitely strong at the same time, and I knew she'd be cold and so I held her to me, I folded her into me. And then it was too late to stop.

Oh, I'm flesh and bone. Flesh and bone, and I don't know what tomorrow will bring, and I am so alone.

A strange thought made its way into my mind: if I took her now, maybe then I could let her go for ever. Our bodies together once, and then she would be mine for all the days to come, because nothing could undo what we had done. I could hold her tight inside me, keep the memories of her as I kept the memories of my terrors. Not just scars, but something beautiful . . .

Cora lifted her hand. I thought she would stroke my face, and I closed my eyes in expectation, but instead she touched my forehead with cool fingers, as if she could see the turmoil of my thoughts.

'I know,' she said. 'I know what happened to you.' I hated pity, but she spoke to me with infinite compassion.

'Cora . . .'

Heal me. Save me.

Come and know me, Cora. Not just who I am now, but who I used to be. Before my heart and body were broken and my soul blackened.

Her fingers touched my back and my chest, and felt the landscape that was my life: the trenches and ditches my father had left in my flesh. I heard her gasp, and then she looked for my eyes, and under her gaze, I took my shirt off. And there they were, the worst years of my life, laid bare for her to see. This time she didn't gasp – she just stopped breathing for a moment, frowning, as if her mind refused to believe what her eyes saw. She met my gaze, and in my eyes, she saw the terrible truth, the truth of my days and nights of terror. She saw a child hiding in the cupboard under the stairs, dragged out by a foot, kicked in the side until his bones were broken.

Her face crumpled, and tears fell down her cheeks.

There. Her innocence, gone.

Cora

He shook his head, almost imperceptibly – no words, please, he was saying.

I wrapped my arms around him, stroking his battered back, following the scars with my fingers. How savage it must have been, to leave such marks, strata of cruelty, newer ones over older ones – it must have gone on for years. My tears fell on his chest, and his arms were tight around me; he was cradling me as if *he* wanted to comfort *me*, instead of the other way round. His skin smelled like the sea breezes, and my senses were both numbed and heightened by his closeness. The cruel white pattern of his scars began to disappear in front of my eyes. All I could feel were his hands, strong and assured on my body, following its curves, helping take my clothes off sweetly, slowly, one by one. When only my underwear was left to protect me, he looked for my eyes. My skin puckered up with the cold and with expectation.

And his eyes asked me a question. *Are you sure you want this?*

For a moment, I was frightened – but I knew it was too

late to stop. It was like this moment was meant to be, like it had been planned for a long, long time and we could not stop it, even if we wanted to. I closed my eyes, my breathing now ragged – there was no stopping, no way back. He laid me on the soft grass, and I didn't open my eyes. I trusted him to keep me safe.

Innes

She was all I'd ever dreamed of. And now I lay on her bed, after a night enveloped by a wind that would have been freezing for anyone but an islander, with Cora in my arms – with home in my arms. Yes, she was *home*.

And I would break her.

I would break her, I thought in despair. She lay curled into me, her soft back bare – her skin so silky, I thought even water would slip down and not drench her. I held her closer, infusing the heat of my body into hers. I could protect her from the cold; I could protect her from other people. I could not protect her from me. I hid my face in her hair, breathing in the scent of shampoo, of salt, Cora's scent. She'd looked at me like I was worthy of love, but she was wrong. She didn't know I could drink and drink until I thought that smashing my head against the wall was a good idea. She didn't know I'd spent years shooting wildlife all day and drinking all night, in places where I could find fights to make me bleed and women to help me forget. She didn't know there was a woman before who'd trusted me, and I'd dashed her hopes, and her son's, because I couldn't change.

It was because of the curse, because I was, and always will be, a child of the mist, like the MacGregors. There was no choice for me. I would not take and destroy Cora, my Cora, who never was mine.

Gently I kissed her forehead. I saw that her eyes were open – she was awake. I held her body to mine for a second. She called my name, she called my name with those lips I'd kissed over and over and over again . . .

'Innes?'

'My love . . . listen. Listen, don't be upset. Don't be upset, but I have to go. Just for a bit.'

'What do you mean? Where?'

'To get better,' I said, and I ripped myself from her.

Cora

I would not cry.

'Please don't go . . .'

I would not cry.

'Innes. Stay.'

I would not cry.

He hesitated for a moment, and I thought he was about to hold me in his arms and stay, stay.

But he turned around, and walked out of the room, out of the cottage, out of my life. He left me there, trembling, with the sheet around me and Sasha resting her nose on my shin in silent sympathy.

He was gone, and I was lost.

A hint of thunder resounded far away in the sky. My heart was broken.

I would not cry.

Cora

'*. . . time to wrap up, but before we go, remember that a red weather warning has been issued for the west, with heavy showers and gale-force winds. Stay indoors if you can, and stay safe . . .*'

'That sounds scary,' Gaby from the shop said, looking out of the window, towards the west, as the radio programme reverted to music. I had no idea what she was talking about. I had heard the words but could not decipher the meaning. My head was killing me, and I was hot and cold, taking my jacket on and off. I kept looking around for Innes, and hated myself for it. He'd chosen to go.

I never wanted to see him again.

I wanted to hold him and tell him it was okay, everything was okay – whatever burden he carried, I could help him bear it.

I hated him.

I loved him.

Oh my God, I loved him.

Imagine the irony. I had thought I couldn't fall in love, and now that I had, now that I knew I could, it had ended this way – *I have to go, it's better for you, Cora*. A vague promise to come back that for me was just not enough, nowhere near enough.

'Cora?'

'Oh, sorry, Gaby.'

'Not at all. How can I help you?' she said and tilted her head, studying me.

I was sure I didn't look good. After Innes had left, I'd got up to work, to write, to resolutely busy myself and prove to the world that my life did not depend on him. But then a headache had come over me, and a pain in all my bones, and I'd fallen asleep in front of the fire. I'd dreamed of Margaret again, and the kilted man – but instead of coming up the beach, the man was walking away. I could see Margaret on the half-moon beach, all the pain in the world etched on her face, the face that was also mine. I'd woken up in tears – the tears I hadn't cried when Innes had left – and realised at once that I was burning up. I'd given all my medicine to Neal, so now I'd dragged myself to the village with Sasha to get some more.

'Are you okay?' Gaby asked.

Difficult question.

'I . . . I'm looking for Lemsip, I think. I'm not feeling so good . . .' I touched the back of my head, under the weight of my hair, and it came away wet with cold sweat.

'Cora! There you are!' Catriona stood in the shop doorway. 'I came looking for you at the cottage . . . Did you hear the news? There's going to be a storm. Don't go back to Gealach; come home with me.'

'I need to go back, I . . .'

'Why? You have Sasha with you, there's no need.'

'Thanks, but I'll be all right.'

'Look,' she whispered, so that Gaby wouldn't hear. 'Sorren told me what happened yesterday. If you're with Innes, that's okay, that's good, but if you're alone . . .' She threw a glance towards the car parked outside.

'I'm not with Innes. He's gone.'

'Right.' She looked at me curiously. 'It's really not safe there, Cora. And . . . you're not well, are you?'

I attempted a smile. 'It's just a cold, I'm not dying.'

'Well you look terrible, but apart from that, they say it's going to be the strongest storm of the last hundred years, and—'

'Margaret was there,' I said hazily, 'during many storms.'

'Margaret?'

'Her name is carved in the stone. I have to go,' I said.

'Cora . . .' She took my arm. 'You're burning up. Please come with me.'

'Look, I'll pack an overnight bag and then come, okay?' I conceded impatiently, and pushed past her out of the shop.

'If you're not at my house in an hour, I'm coming to get you!' she called after me, but I didn't look back.

I wanted to be at Gealach, nowhere else. I wanted to be there and I wanted Margaret to tell me whether the kilted man was ever coming back to her. I stood on the beach in the rising wind, waiting – but who was I waiting for? I thought my dress should be red, and I was surprised when I saw jeans. I didn't know who I was. I didn't want to be alone there; I wanted Duncan to come and get me.

No, I wanted Innes. Who was Duncan? My head hurt so much I couldn't even think, and my skin was slick with sweat. The sea was screaming like the souls of all who had drowned in it through the ages, and my legs began to buckle beneath me. I was back to myself, and terrified. The sky was livid and the waves grew higher and higher. I remembered the radio bulletin, and the coming storm. The storm of the century, they'd said.

I'm sorry, Margaret. I have to leave or I'll die here, I thought with a clarity that cut through the fever and the strange delirium. 'We're going, Sasha,' I said, and led her inside to pack a bag. I was shocked to realise how high my fever had got even in the short journey from the village. I was so tired, so sore, and there was black all around the edges of my vision.

'Oh, yes please, Mum,' I said. She was just there, offering me tea, telling me to sit down and rest.

Maybe I could rest for a minute. Just a minute. I curled up in front of the fire, sick with heartache. I felt Mum's hand on my forehead – she was so tall, and she shone, yes, she shone like fire. Was that really my mum? I fell asleep with her name on my lips, a sick, fevered sleep that was a little bit like death.

Margaret

The memory of what happened next is woven not into my brain, but into my body. Fevered heat, ripping my clothes off in delirium; throat so parched I thought it would bleed; pain, days and nights of pain, deep in my bones. I saw Duncan's face near mine, whispering words I couldn't understand, his cool hand on my forehead. I have a vague feeling that it was wrong, that he should not breathe the same air as me, because then he might get sick, and I pushed him away. But then I called his name to bring me water and save me, save me. Until I could speak no more and I thought I was dead.

Yes, that's it, I'm dead. Duncan still spoke in my ear as he took me in his arms and lifted me up, and I didn't feel pain any more. The sky was above me and the sweet scent of greenery around me – I thought it must be heaven. I was so thankful for this; I hadn't thought I would see the world outside ever again. Duncan was walking on, carrying me, and all I could do was wonder where he would bury me. I tried to tell him how grateful I was that he had tried to save me, but only a tiny croak came out. I couldn't speak. A song was in my ears, the singing stream. *That's where he's going to take me; he's going to follow the stream and lay me in the river.* I felt like I was falling, but Duncan was holding me, and the soft grass was beneath me. Oh, to feel grass and the cool ground against my skin again. How lucky I was, luckier dead than I was when I was alive.

But to die at twenty . . . I began to cry, the tears drying up at once on my hot, hot skin. Duncan took my clothes off – at last, those horrible rags that smelled of sickness and despair, no matter how many times he changed me as I lay dying. The smell was on my skin as well. But now he'd throw me in the water and I'd be pure again. Would he kiss me, before he let me go?

And then I realised that I was cold. For the first time in days, I was cold as the wind blew on my naked skin. I'd burned up and I'd finished burning, and now I was gone, all gone. My teeth began to chatter and I shivered once, twice, so deeply that it was painful. But if I was shivering, if my teeth were chattering, how could I be dead? Duncan lifted me up again, his fingers sinking into my flesh as he carried me towards the stream. Step after step, he walked into the water. *Is he killing me? Is he drowning me so I don't suffer any more?*

The water was freezing, and I cried and cried all the tears in the world, because I was only twenty and I didn't want to die. I looked into Duncan's face, and I saw that he was crying too. He held me as the stream flowed over my body and took the sickness away, and the smell, and

300

the sweat and the pain. I heard him calling to God. He must be angry because God had taken me away from him. But he didn't sound angry. He sounded thankful. He was saying *thank you, God, thank you, God*, as he took me back to the bank and laid me down, and wrapped me in his plaid.

He was gone for a little while, and I fell in and out of sleep – and then I felt heat beside me, not the sickly heat of fever, but the lovely heat of fire. He laid my head in his lap and caressed my hair, drying it at the fire, strand by strand.

'Duncan?' I whispered, and my voice sounded strange because my throat was so dry.

'My love. It's a miracle.' His nose against mine, his eyes closed. His tears fell on my cheeks.

'I'm alive?'

'Yes. Yes. Oh darling, I thought I'd lost you.'

'I'm thirsty,' I said, and he stepped away for a moment, and then he made me drink from his hands.

'You'll never lose me,' I said, and my own words echoed in my mind like a prayer, like a promise. Like a spell.

He brought me to a place far away, as far as we could go – but not far enough. The boat rose and fell on the gelid waves as we sailed to the islands, a few of the surviving Innes men with us, looking for a safe place. I didn't know at the time – although I should have guessed – that the safe place was meant for me only.

I remember my white hands holding on to the boat;

Duncan's profile as he looked out towards the green-grey cliffs of Sìle. I didn't think we could possibly come to land there, but a small pebbled beach appeared, and the mossy remains of a watchtower that seemed built by ancient peoples, and there we stopped. A couple came out of the tower, a minister and his wife, Annie. They led us inside, and I was speechless with gratitude as I saw that they'd made a little home for us inside the watchtower, with cots covered in fur, a glowing fire, and a wooden table set with bread, cheese, smoked fish and ale. That night I fell asleep to the sound of the sea, and I let myself believe that maybe we would be safe.

The next day, Duncan insisted we marry. To say those words, for me, wasn't even necessary – we were married already, for all eternity, and God knew it. This was for the world, for our families, so that we could live together like man and wife. And so we wed in a church so close to the sea it was almost on the shore, grey stones covered in moss and lovely spires that called to the sky. We stood side by side, me in a red gown borrowed from Annie – not exactly the colour for weddings – and him with his sword by his side, even in the church. A marriage made in time of war.

And then he told me he would not stay on Sìle. He would leave me there and return to what was left of his clan, his father and his brother. I begged him over and over again not to go, and I was still begging as he walked along the beach towards the boat that would take him away from me. I should have known better than to do so;

as if I didn't know that hiding away with me would have destroyed him as a man, would have shamed him for ever. But maybe he could have withstood the shame for love of me, I thought – maybe the two of us could come first, and the world after.

It was a vain hope – Duncan was and would remain a clansman, a laird, loyal to his family. And nothing could change that. If he didn't have his pride, he had nothing. He kissed my lips, he kissed my belly, and he went. One man, Malcolm, was left on Sìle to protect me.

I wandered on the beach and on the moor, but I could not find peace. Annie came sometimes to keep me company, but my heart was grey. And then, on my long walks, I began to see plants I recognised, herbs I was familiar with; I took to gathering them, and drying them, and making poultices and salves. Soon word spread, and people came to see me with their ailments. Every day I waited, every day I dreamed of him, but life began to have purpose again. A new joy filled me, and I believed that he would return, and everything would be sorted, and we would be a family.

Not long afterwards, word came that Duncan was in Arbroath prison, a place where sickness and starvation would get you long before any sword; but I kept gazing at the sea, and waiting, and I never, ever lost hope.

Cora

I woke up with the sound of the sea smashing against the land, hungry, furious. The world lit up and then fell into darkness again as lightning hit the island and the surrounding sea.

The sea wants to kill me.

It took a few minutes for me to figure out the situation, fevered as I was. The waves were so strong, it sounded like they were coming inside. I staggered onto my little beach – there was no causeway left. The tide had come in, but it was higher than usual, so high that it was lapping my feet. I was stuck. I could never reach Catriona's house now. And even if Catriona came to get me, she wouldn't be able to reach me.

And something told me that the water would not stop.

The rumble of thunder deafened me for a moment – Sasha yelped by my side. I was so scared, I couldn't think, and the fever made me slow and unsteady. Suddenly the sky was lit with lightning, all the way from the sea to the side of the island, crowning the hills with yellow ribbon, and I feared I would be struck down. How could it have been so fast, how could the storm have risen so much? The sea roared once more, and a huge wave broke on the cove, and another, and another, higher and higher, until I grabbed Sasha and ran back inside, and stood in the kitchen, my hand over my mouth. The waves were hitting the cottage, hitting the windows and the door, wanting to come in.

If I had to die, I thought, I would go down fighting.

'Come on, Sasha,' I said, and it came out like a broken cry. I opened the hatch to the tunnel, and the wind and the sound of the waves overwhelmed me. I knew I might be jumping to sure death by drowning, if the water had come as high as that already. But if I didn't try to escape, I would simply be waiting for the sea to come and get me. I held Sasha to me as tightly as I could, my arms aching and the dog squirming, and let myself fall. I was so sore and weak that I couldn't land on my feet, but ended up sprawled almost flat instead, a stone embedding itself in my side and making me scream with pain. I saw black for a second, and then, as I came to myself, I saw that my fingers were covered in blood. Oh well, at least I hadn't drowned. Yet.

Sasha was shaking and squashing herself against my legs. I had to pull at her to come with me, by the ears, the tail, the hind legs. She was yelping with pain, but I couldn't leave her in that dark tunnel on her own. If I could be saved, she had to be saved with me. I whispered reassuring words to her, but they couldn't be heard over the noise. I followed the tunnel, dragging Sasha with me, until a livid grey light told me we were nearly out.

'Come on, Sasha. Come on!' But she had stopped and refused to go any further. I stepped forward and peered out – and then I saw why she didn't want to move. The beach at the back of the cottage was gone, and in its place there was only sea. *Oh, Mum. I'm not ready to come to you yet.*

I crawled back and curled up, Sasha in my arms, my back against the wall. Helpless tears ran down my face. My eyes fell on the word carved in the stone: *Margaret.* I touched it lovingly, desperately.

Please help me, Margaret. Help me.

Margaret

I knew no pain like childbirth, I knew no joy like childbirth. Over and over again I thanked God that Annie was there, holding my hand, whispering words of comfort like my mother should have done. Many times I called my mother's name – the secret name I was not to say, ever, lest they get me like they got her. Annie placed the baby on my chest, and I saw it was a girl. She was perfect, with a silky mop of red hair, now matted with my blood, and a tiny birthmark on her neck – some would have said the mark of a witch.

She was Catriona, like my mother.

I kept Catriona at my breast as much as I could, and even when she wasn't nursing, still I held her. I couldn't let her go. I remembered what Duncan had said about Innes children: how Lord Innes would not let them go. Whenever I thought of Duncan in Arbroath prison, I saw him lying in filth and slowly starved of food and sunlight, and my heart broke time and time again.

Last night he came to me; my love came back to me. A storm had hit the island. The sky was rumbling and the sea was wild; no boat could have made it here. Only a dead man could come here on such a night, a man who could walk on water and breathe lightning. And so, the days spent looking out to sea, waiting for him to return, had come to an end. Wave after wave the sea broke on the shore, memory after memory my heart broke inside me. The sea was so close it was nearly on my doorstep. I opened my eyes after falling asleep, and Duncan was there, standing between me and the fire. At that moment, as he stood silent and bleeding before me, the glow shining through him, I knew that he would never stop bleeding, and I thought my life was finished too.

But then sounds of life came from the bear fur beside me – the cream and honeycomb voice of my daughter. Cream and honeycomb . . . her little beating heart said I had to keep living. My dead love was a ghost at my door, but my daughter was alive and calling for me, warm in the fur her father had given us. *Catriona, my sweet darling, live on and be happy because your father could not; live on and be happy because your mother is broken.*

My love slowly extended his arm, and I reached out to touch him. My fingers touched his cold hand; his blue lips opened to speak and warn me, warn me of the fire, the fire that was rolling and rolling towards me, sweeping the land, killing everything it touched, all the way to the island. He stood cold and white, his fingers touching mine. He told me to run. Then slowly, slowly, as frozen, silent tears fell down my cheeks, my love faded away. Oh, the pain to see the face I loved so much become gossamer and disappear – colder and colder his fingers, his hands dissolving and leaving nothing behind.

And then a voice rose from inside me, a voice that was Duncan's but came from my heart. It was the voice of the waves and the rain and the flashing sky.

I will find you, it said.

When, when, when? asked my anxious heart. *When, when will I see him again, and how? How will he find me?*

My heart asked the waves, and asked and asked until the morning, while hastily I gathered what little I had, but no reply came. By then, the tide was high and there was no way for my sweet child and me to leave by land; the storm was raging, and there was no way for us to leave by sea.

I stood on the shore and waited, until the water drew away and the way was clear.

But it was too late. The fire Duncan had warned me about, the fire had come.

Innes

I wanted to stay so badly, so badly. To be with her, look after her. Heal in her the wound I couldn't heal in myself, wake up beside her every day of my life. Forget about the bottle for good, forget about the rage, be the man I could have been, had I not been shattered and twisted by the one who was supposed to take care of me.

She'd kissed my scars – from the belt, the burns, the blows. The scars that my father had taken great care in keeping hidden, by hitting me and burning me and cutting me where nobody would see. She'd followed them with her fingers, like they were something beautiful instead of repugnant.

But nothing I did or nothing I touched could ever be beautiful. I had to change. Become someone who didn't frighten women and batter men and drink himself to sleep like I used to. Heal myself at last.

I'd chosen to end my life by water, my ultimate fear, but she'd saved me.

Had I dissolved myself in Corrywreckan, in the waters of my island, I would never have felt her body in my arms. I would never have been one flesh with her. I'd lived for a reason. For another chance . . .

I couldn't wait – I packed my bag quickly and left my mother's house when everybody was out. I left a note for Pammy: *I'll be back soon, sweetheart – Uncle Innes.* I would be back and be the uncle she deserved.

The pier was deserted – where was everyone?

'No ferries today?' I asked a fisherman.

'You mad? None. Tomorrow as well. Have you seen the sky?'

Only then did I see it. Stormy skies were normal on Seal, but there was something strange about today. The sky was yellow; the air itself had a livid tinge. How could I not have noticed? I'd been too lost in my own thoughts.

'There's going to be a proper storm. They said not to go on the beach at all, the waves will be so high. I'm off home,' the man said.

Cora.

Cora alone in her cottage, on the sea.

I ran.

The causeway was gone, and Cora's car was there, right at the end of the grit road. I cursed myself over and over and over again for not having got there earlier. I came as close as I could to the house – and then I saw. The beach had disappeared, and water was lapping at the cottage. I stood there for a moment, panting, the rain falling on my face. If I tried to swim across, I would be swept away by the current. I climbed onto the slippery rocks behind the house, all the while calling Cora's name with all my might – but the sea and the wind and the thunder were too loud for her to hear me, I was sure. I stood on the highest boulder, but I couldn't see anything.

The waters whirled dark and foamy – but I, who couldn't even have a bath for terror, was not afraid. Cora was there, and if she drowned, I would drown too. I jumped into the sea.

The water was so cold, it was like being stung by a million needles. I couldn't breathe. Terror overcame me – water in my mouth, my nose, my ears, trying to keep my mouth closed, breathing water anyway; the tiles all around the bathtub, green with an orange flower in the middle; my mother's screams, my mother's silence. The door closing – let us get on with it, Morag . . .

But no – no, this wasn't back then, this was now, and my Cora was in the water. I could stay afloat, I could swim. In spite of the fury of the waves and the lashing rain and the flashing lightning, I swam with all my might towards the cottage. The cove behind the house was gone too, but the dark mouth of the cavern that opened in the rocks was still visible. And inside, bright against the dark, was a flash of red – Cora's hair – and there she was, holding Sasha. I could see from her stance that she was readying herself to jump into the water.

I don't know how I got to her. Somehow I reached what was left of the shore, a thin sliver of land, and crawled inside the cave. I held her in my arms, cradled her and caressed her wet hair. She was shaking and her teeth were chattering. Our eyes met, and I only had one thing to say: *I will never leave you again.*

We had two choices: swim and maybe drown, or lift ourselves up into the flooded cottage and maybe drown. Neither looked good, and I had to think fast. 'Come,' I said to Cora, shaking her out of her state of shock. 'Come!'

We half ran, half crawled along the tunnel to the hatch beneath the cottage, and I took her by the hips and lifted her up so she could climb inside.

'Sasha!' she screamed, and only then did I realise that the little dog was behind me, drenched and terrified. I tried to grab her, but she was too slippery, and she ran away and disappeared into the darkness.

'Sasha! Sasha, no!' Cora was distraught, but there was nothing I could do about it – I had her life in my hands. I tried to lift myself up too, but there was so much water in the cottage that my hands couldn't find a safe grip. Seawater kept falling on my head, on my face – the cottage was flooding. I didn't have time to ask myself if this had been the wrong choice – I had to reach Cora, and with a huge, impossible effort, I eventually made it.

What happened next is not clear in my memory. The waves were eating the cottage, one by one, taking a bite of it with every attack. Cora and I stood hand in hand until the next wave came for us. One moment we were standing beside the fireplace; the next we were in the open sea. Cora's eyes kept closing, and I was whispering in her ear, *please don't sleep, please swim with me, I love you, I love you.* I thought I would freeze, I thought I would suffocate, but I couldn't freeze and I couldn't suffocate because Cora was depending on me.

I swam as best I could with Cora in my arms, and then all of a sudden something took hold of me and pulled at me – was it a current, dragging me to my death? But there were stones under my back, and a face above me: Sorren, lashed by the rain and crouching in the wind. Cora lay white and still beside me – was she dead? I reached for her hand and squeezed, but there was no squeeze back.

If she was gone, I would not breathe either.

Margaret

I knew Lord Innes was coming; I knew it like you know a storm is coming when you see the sky darkening and hear the roll of thunder. I held my dagger close to me, hidden inside my skirt, cold metal against my fingers.

I waited on the small pebbled beach, my hair blowing in the wind and my back straight, until he galloped in.

'Duncan is dead,' was the first thing he said, and although I knew it already, it was as if his horse had galloped right over my chest.

'It was you who killed him,' I said quietly as he dismounted. He stood so much taller than me, so much physically stronger, his eyes cold and his hand on his sword. But I was not afraid. Not for me.

'Be quiet, whore!' I flinched at that insult. I was no whore. I had loved, loved so much and so deeply, and I'd been too young and too foolish to understand that my love would destroy Duncan. 'I didn't kill my son. The clan needed him. The MacGregors slaughtered him in prison.'

The MacGregors. The sickle had fallen from somewhere we didn't expect, from traitorous hands. They'd got inside Arbroath too. 'They'll pay for it,' Lord Innes said, looking me in the eye, and I nodded. For a second he and I, though we loathed each other, were united by hatred and desire for revenge. 'I don't want to kill you, Margaret, but I will if I need to. I'm here for my son's child.'

He knew? For a moment, the shock took my breath away, and I stood panting. A gust of wind hit me in the face, stinging me with sand. Duncan had told him about Catriona, our sweet child, born of us not even a month ago?

'My son begged me to look after him. Give him to me.'

'I don't believe you. He wouldn't have asked you to take her away from me.' No. There was no doubt in my mind: he would never have asked him that. Never would he have wanted to separate my daughter and me.

'*Her?*' Lord Innes turned his head and spat on the ground. 'Of course my son would produce a female! And no, he didn't want me to take the bastard girl away. He wanted me to look after you both. Duncan was a fool. He was bewitched by you.'

Bewitched. That word.

'You don't need her,' I told him. 'You said it yourself, she's just a bastard girl. You don't need her at all.'

'She'll be useful. She has Innes blood. I'll marry her off as soon as possible and she'll give us the new generation. Otherwise, it's all finished. Where is she?'

'She's mine. And Duncan's. You can't have her,' I said, but my heart was full of terror. How could I stop him?

'Where is she?'

He threw me aside, and I nearly fell. I steadied myself and ran inside. He was standing before Catriona's cot.

'Leave her alone!' I cried, and he slapped me so hard that I fell and hit my head on the stone. There was nobody to help me. I watched him take Catriona, and my baby began to cry and cry. I crawled across the floor and clawed at his shins. Everything was spinning and blurred. Something salty trickled into my mouth, and I knew it was blood, my blood. 'Leave her. Leave my daughter. Leave my daughter with me,' I kept saying, but I couldn't scream, I wasn't making sense. My head was throbbing.

He threw me one last glance, as if he were looking at an animal, at a pile of rubbish.

'She's an Innes. She'll be raised an Innes.'

I gazed at him.

I simply gazed.

And there she was, the burning woman, appearing inside the room with her long limbs and her glowing hair. Slowly she nodded towards me.

'There is something you need to know,' I said, and my voice sounded a bit like the wind, like the waves. I'd never done this before, but I suddenly knew how to do it, and I knew why: I'd heard my mother, long ago.

Not the one who'd raised me. The one who'd given birth to me, the one who was killed. The burning woman, burned at the stake as a witch: my mother.

It was why I didn't like people pointing out my hair,

because I didn't want to attract attention to myself. Women like me are better off if they're out of people's minds, out of their thoughts.

Lord Innes was a fool. He didn't hear the threat in my voice. Not yet.

'You will stay quiet,' he said, 'and do what I tell you. You'll stay out of my granddaughter's life.'

'I will, yes, because you'll kill me and I won't be able to stop you. But you must know that the rumours about me are right. I *am* a changeling. My parents found me, and you know where they found me, Lord Innes?'

His face drained of colour all of a sudden. It was strange, and beautiful, to see that powerful man, the man who had just broken my heart and taken my love and my daughter from me, so afraid.

'They found me in the witch's house. My mother was Heather McCrimmon, a clanswoman of my father's who had been kept secret, given her reputation. She'd been burned alive.' As I spoke, my mother's ghost wrapped her arms around herself, her huge eyes full of pain, her skin smudged with ash. 'She could heal or hurt people to her will. I have the same powers, Lord Innes, and I tell you, two things will come to pass: your name will be cursed and your mind will be cursed and your death will be cursed. And Duncan and I will live again and again until we are reunited.'

It was like an incantation, and he was paralysed. Quietly, gently, I took my daughter from him . . . but he came back to his senses.

'Dirty mad witch!' he screamed, and he unsheathed his sword.

For a moment I thought, yes, sweet sword, release me from this life without Duncan – but I had Catriona to think of. I opened the hatch and jumped into the bowels of the tower. The tunnel was black; the sound of the waves seemed sweet in comparison to Lord Innes's steps resounding, it seemed, all around me. I took the dagger I always carried with me, and carved my name into the stone, quickly, barely scraping the word. Maybe someone would remember. Maybe someone would remember me.

He found me, of course.

He took my baby and laid her down gently, so she would not get hurt. There were no more words from me, no curses, no pleading. My destiny was clear now.

He buried his sword deep inside me, and left me there to bleed to death. *Catriona, Duncan*, I said in my heart as life flew out of me. My little family. The family I had had for a moment and then it was gone, beautiful and fleeting like a rainbow. And then I saw my mother burning again, consumed by flames – and Lord Innes finally able to see her, screaming in horror and pain as his own clothes and hair and skin caught fire. He threw himself onto the sand with terrible screams, and each of his screams was sweet music to me. Catriona was crying, and I knew Annie would come for her; I knew my mother would make sure she was found.

I crawled onto the stones, and then onto the sand and into the sea, my blood, my red dress and my red hair floating in the grey waters.

319

I will find you, Duncan had said.

I will find you, my love, I whispered.

Blood flew through my fingers, and I sank into the water. I couldn't feel my limbs, I couldn't feel anything any more – everything was black, swallowed by watery darkness. Yes, death was here to take me. I didn't want to leave my daughter behind, but I wanted to die. Because when I died, that would be the time Duncan would keep his promise and come for me. I longed for the end, so that we would be together. I closed my eyes and fell into the darkness, into the sea, in my heart a silent call: *Duncan, my love* . . .

But then my eyes opened again in a sea of screams – my own screams. I was screaming to fill my lungs with life.

'There, there, my wee bairn,' a soft woman's voice said into my ear. She smelled sweet, warm, milky.

And in a moment, I knew.

I knew the deeper meaning of what Duncan had said: *I will find you*.

And then it all faded, my old life as Margaret swept away by my new life, like a watermark or a half-remembered song.

Innes

We flew to the hospital on the mainland by helicopter, Cora's hand in mine, her faint, ghostly breath steaming the oxygen mask. In between her breaths, I held mine too; together we inhaled and exhaled as I willed her to live.

They took her away. I stood while the doctors took possession of her, and I was grateful to them and hated them at the same time – I wanted them to leave her alone, I wanted them to help her breathe. They insisted on checking me over, pushing something against my heart. If you need to see if my heart is beating, I wanted to say, check Cora's!

Time passed, slow and unbearable, Sorren standing far from me and yet close, waiting. Finally a nurse called me in, and I heard murmured words about her being fine, about making her comfortable. She lay pale on her hospital bed, her hair redder than ever, long and impossibly beautiful, like liquid copper. I was afraid to touch her.

I laid my fingertips on her cheek, on her lips.

I kissed her, a long, sweet kiss. At last our breath was one, as it was supposed to be.

I'll give you everything, Cora.
I'll give you all I have.

In the background, Sorren and Catriona were talking about calling Cora's brother, that maybe some estate agent from Islay would have his number, that surely he'd come and . . .

And then their voices seemed strangely far away, as if I were underwater again. My ears were buzzing, and my left arm seized; I think I moaned, because someone came to me, and her mouth was opening and closing but I didn't know what she was saying. The pain began, slight at first, and then so strong that my face was covered in sweat, and my hands clasped my chest, and then there was no more air coming into my lungs. I saw the floor, the white tiles – and then there was darkness, and I knew I was not breathing, my heart was not beating, and the life I'd often cursed had finally been taken from me, just when I'd found, after so many years, a light.

Mum, I forgive you, was my last conscious thought, and then I fell into darkness. And the darkness had something at its core. A woman at Gealach's window, her hair and her red dress flowing in the wind. The woman was Cora, and I think I cried, because it was then I realised I'd known her for ever, I'd searched for her everywhere, through time and space – and once again I'd lost her.

Cora

I slept, and when I fell into oblivion, all the pain from my battered bones and my flesh skinned by the rocks faded away. I slept and I dreamed, I dreamed the most beautiful dream, more beautiful and sweeter than anything life had given me before. I was on the beach in front of my cottage, my hair and my red dress blowing in the wind – the woman at the window was Margaret, and she was me. And there he was, Innes, coming up the beach with the golden light of sunset setting his hair on fire. He wrapped his arms around my waist and kissed me. His lips were salty – and then I noticed that he was drenched in water, his hair dripping, his clothes sticking to his skin.

'Goodbye, Cora,' he said, and as he said my name, the word Margaret seemed to echo over it. But all I really heard was goodbye.

Goodbye?

No, it couldn't be. He couldn't possibly leave me . . . But he was, turning around and slowly stepping away, and not on the sand but on the water, every step taking him deeper and deeper into the ocean.

I awoke in terror. Something was suffocating me – something over my mouth. I ripped it off; it felt cold and limp on my skin. I tried to call – *Innes, Innes, Innes* – but my voice was weak and hoarse.

I kept calling his name as they touched my every bone to see if it was broken, as they dressed my wounds, throughout murmuring words of comfort and making sounds like you would to a baby to keep them calm. They wrapped something tight around my arm and pumped it, and finally left me alone. After a time that seemed endless, the door opened and Catriona came in.

'Innes?'

'Darling. Darling, it's okay, it's all okay . . .'

'He's gone? He's gone? He said he wouldn't go. He said he'd stay with me . . .'

'Oh, Cora. You're still unwell. Don't think about that now, don't think of anything. You need to rest. You know, Sasha is waiting for you at my house . . .'

'Sasha is safe?'

'You won't believe this, she swam all the way to the shore. I have no idea how she did it. A little dog, and such a storm . . . it was a miracle!'

At that moment, when I knew that my Sasha was safe, tears began to roll down my cheeks.

'When is Innes coming back?'

And then I saw Catriona's face, and I knew he never would.

Cora

I sat at my window nursing a cup of tea and watching the London evening unfold. The lights in the Sidhus' shop, the launderette window all lit up, the office workers buying meals for one in the Spar. Everything normal, like nothing had happened.

Like I never went to Seal.

Like I never knew Innes.

But hanging on the wall, there above the chest of drawers where I first laid the box with Gealach's key, was the tapestry I'd woven on the island – or that someone had woven for me. Two red-haired women, side by side.

They could be Margaret. They could be me. We were interchangeable, both lost in the folds of time, both at the centre of a story of loss, in the same place. Margaret's spirit inside me, and after me . . . after me, I didn't know.

Everything was back to normal, yet my life had changed completely. *I* had changed completely.

'Cora,' Stephen called, and I turned away from the darkening sky to look at him. Since I'd got back nearly ten months before, Stephen had moved back in. To look after me when the loss of Innes and the consequences had left me bereft, numb. He never said he was there to check on me, to make sure I was okay; he knew I wouldn't like it. I preferred to think I relied on myself only, that my little brother was the one to lean on me – but it wasn't so. Only in the last few weeks had I begun to feel myself again, the strong woman I was.

The strong woman I was *before*.

'You know when I went to Glasgow?' I nodded. Stephen had been away for a few days for work. 'Well, while I was up there, I did some research.'

My heart started pounding at once. I knew what he was talking about. From his tone, from the way he frowned and looked down. From the way every word he spoke sounded as if he were tiptoeing.

'Did you? About what?' I turned away again, my eyes fixed on the launderette's bright blue sign. A bus hid it from view for a moment, its low rumble echoing through the glass.

'About the cottage.'

The very word was like a knife in my heart. I dreamed of Gealach so often – pieces of my life floating on the water, the place crumbling stone after stone, falling into ruins and sinking to the bottom of the sea. In an involuntary gesture, I clasped my hands together. I could still feel Innes's hand holding mine, his steadfast hand, the hand that would not let me go. In the dream, we'd be slammed around by the stormy sea, whipped by the lashing water, trying to stay afloat among the debris of my life – then the waves would come and take him away too, and he would look at me one last time, a look that begged me to hold on to him, not to let him go . . .

'Right.'

'Or should I say, about our mum. About why Aunt Toffee . . . Agnes Halton . . . left the cottage to her.'

All of a sudden, I was angry. I'd been in a fog of grief for months, and though it had lifted so that I could see a direction again, that grief would never leave me. I was still walking on a tightrope, petrified that I could fall at any moment – that a word, a memory, a song would plunge me back into despair. And I couldn't let that happen. I had to live my life, for my family.

'Stephen, what's the point?'

'Look, I know you don't want to hear about it. But you need to know this. Honestly. Listen.' He came to sit across from me and leaned towards me, his elbows resting on his knees, his eyes serious. 'Our mum's name wasn't Beatrice Lamb,' he said quietly. 'Her name was Mary McCrimmon.'

'What?' His words swirled in my mind, and then slowly sank in. 'She wasn't . . . Stephen, I don't understand.'

'I know. I was shocked too. She'd been adopted. She only found out later in life, when Agnes contacted her. Mum and Agnes were sisters.'

My head spun. *Mary McCrimmon.*

'How . . . It can't be true.' My chest was rising and falling quickly. 'It can't be.'

'It is. Agnes's brother-in-law told me. Aunt Toffee was originally Agnes McCrimmon. Halton was her married name.'

'Wait, wait. Her brother-in-law? How did you find him?'

'I was lucky. I couldn't find anything about Agnes, so I looked for Uncle Skirt – Martyn Halton, his name was . . .'

'How did you know his name?'

'Well, remember the book he wrote?'

I shook my head slowly. 'As usual,' Stephen smiled. 'Appalling memory. He wrote a book about trams, he even gave me a tiny toy tram . . . So I did some research on that. As you can imagine the bibliography wasn't enormous. I cross-referenced . . . nice word, isn't it? It's like I'm a real detective. Anyway, I cross-referenced the names and the dates and the bios and I found Martyn. I googled his name and there it was, picture and all. His obituary. He'd died in a car accident with his wife, Agnes McCrimmon.'

'That's why we never saw them again . . .'

'Exactly. Martyn had a brother – they mentioned him in the obituary – and I found him in a retirement home. He's like eighty-five, but his kids gave him a tablet and put him on Facebook, so I was able to find him. He was quite close to Agnes, so he knew the whole story.'

Stephen took a breath. I was silent, overwhelmed by the revelations.

'You see, Agnes was three when she was adopted, so

she knew. However, she didn't know she had a sister until she was in her mid forties.'

'Can you imagine?' I managed to say. 'For Mum, to find all this out . . .'

'I know. It's incredible. Our grandparents were from Seal, our mum was from Seal, and Aunt Toffee was our real aunt. They died young . . . that's why their daughters were adopted.'

My heart seized at those words. 'How did they die? Our grandparents?'

'In a storm . . . a freak accident. A church was flooded during Mass.'

Of course. The great wave that swept the church away. My visions. It all made sense . . . The names of the two McCrimmons on the tombstones! I'd been looking at my grandparents' grave without knowing.

'Their two daughters, Agnes and Mary, were adopted. Eventually Agnes tracked Mum down and told her everything. Remember the first time she came to visit? After a little while, Mum sent us over to Mrs Fornero at the launderette . . .'

'I remember now, yes.'

'That must have been when Agnes told Mum what had happened, and told her her real name too. My God, when I think what Mum must have been through . . . She didn't even know her real name. Can you imagine?'

'I . . . I need a glass of water.'

'Are you okay?'

I nodded. 'Yes. Oh, Stephen. There was a family, on the island,' I told him. 'McCrimmons.'

'Relatives of ours?' he said, grabbing a glass of water from the kitchen and bringing it over to me.

I shrugged. 'Almost certainly. And this girl, Catriona. We became friends. We looked like each other. Seriously, it was like we'd been separated at birth. We're probably cousins.'

'It's like . . . like we're not who we thought we were. Why do you think Mum never told us?'

I looked down. 'I think she wanted to protect us. You know, she didn't want us to go through what she'd been through. Finding out she wasn't who she thought she was. That she was never Beatrice; she was Mary.'

'I suppose. She didn't want us to know she'd suffered. I wonder if Dad . . .'

'Probably. He was there when they met Agnes and her husband, wasn't he?' I said.

'Yeah. What were they like?'

'Who?'

'The McCrimmons. On Seal.'

'Quite amazing, actually. Catriona is . . . a special person. She . . .' Could I tell him about Catriona's gift? The gift I'd probably inherited, given the visions I'd had on the island, and the dreams, and just everything that had happened? I would, one day. But not now, not yet. 'She was lovely. It's funny, you know, but on the island, I felt at home. Yes. I felt like I was coming home.'

'And now we know why.'

Yes. That, and the fact that I'd met the love of my life there.

Innes, my Innes.

Yearning of long ago and yearning of now mixed in my heart and made me swim in a state of constant longing. Every night I dreamed of his breath on my skin, his hands on my body. *You must live your life and be happy*, he would say. And I obeyed his words faithfully, as faithfully as I could, though the happiness side of things was hard without him.

There were no tears in my eyes as I made my way towards the cot in the corner – I didn't want Maggie to see me cry, never. I wanted to give her joy and love and hope, not sorrow. She was born after her dad's heart had given way; she'd already had her share of grief. I gently moved the draperies – I'd wanted an old-fashioned cradle for my baby Margaret, one that I could softly swing to send her to sleep – and lifted my daughter up, breathing in her sweet, milky scent. She looked at me, and her eyes were so light, so clear – Innes's eyes. Gently I traced the birthmark on the side of her neck. The tiny heart imprinted on her skin, just like Catriona had. Now it made sense.

I will find you, Innes, I whispered.

I will find you, my love.

BOOK OF SOULS

Sheona

Glen Avich, 1820

Sheona held the comb in her hand, her eyes shining at the sight of something so precious. 'Are you sure this is for me? It's beautiful . . . It must have cost you a month's wages!'

'It's for you. And never mind what it cost me. You know why a silver comb?' Alistair said, a smile in his voice. When he'd arrived in Glen Avich to work as tutor to the Ramsay children, love was the last thing on his mind. He'd never thought he would meet someone like Sheona, never. And still, when he first saw her walking to church on a Sunday morning, that incredible hair twisted up, he knew he had to get close to her.

Sheona broke off a twig of heather and slid it behind her ear. 'Why?'

'Because when I saw it, I imagined it going through your lovely hair,' he said and caressed her silky head, her bright red hair, a shade so rare and beautiful, evoking strange memories in him. Sheona closed her eyes, like a cat being stroked. 'And because of the song. The song you sing to your sisters.'

'Oh, yes,' she said, and took a breath.

> Ane thing I'll gie ye, ane thing an more
> Ane thing awash upon the shore
> A silver comb for your hair of gowd
> A silver comb for a love unbowed . . .

Sheona sang softly, beautifully, with a voice that blended perfectly with the sound of the wind on the moors. A Scottish voice, the spirit of Scotland itself, Alistair thought in awe. What had he done to deserve her? For her to be thrown into his path like a precious shell on a beach. His family would never approve – they didn't have much money, but they certainly had a lot of pretensions. Someone like Sheona would never do. He was working as a tutor for a while to set some money aside, and then he would go to university in Edinburgh and study law, like his uncle – he would go up in the world and, his family hoped, marry money.

Alistair didn't care for his family's plans. He would just tell them all to go away, and in time they'd accept his Sheona. Sweet, kind, cheerful Sheona, with a hard life and no complaints, asking so little and giving so much. She trusted him. And he would never let her down, never.

'There is something I need to tell you . . .' She looked down, and her cheeks were flushed. Half frightened, half happy, the words were spilling from her tongue. He was already smiling before she spoke; he'd guessed what she was about to announce. 'I am carrying your child,' she said, and she couldn't keep the joy out of her voice. Even if she knew that it would all be so difficult, that her father would be furious, she knew Alistair wouldn't disappoint her.

And he didn't, because he held her and over and over again he said, *My child, my child, my child. We'll be together, the three of us.*

There was a sea of flowers in front of them, a sea of waves behind them, and in the middle, two people entwined, his fingers in her bright hair, his lips on her forehead, her cheeks, her hands.

But a cloud darkened her face, and Alistair knew why. They had to decide what to do next, before she began to show. Because of Donald Murdo, Sheona's father, the man everyone in the village was afraid of. And they were afraid for a reason.

'I'll take you away. You don't need to worry about your father, or anything else. We'll go away to Edinburgh, you and me.'

Sheona nodded, her eyes full of trepidation. Yes, they would run away, and her father would never find them. Her fingers felt his face, as though she wanted to study his features. The face she'd seen in her dreams long before they met; the face of the man she knew she was always meant to love.

Alistair stood for a long time, waiting. They were supposed to meet behind the church and leave Glen Avich

for ever, he with all his belongings in a bag and a letter
from his uncle that would guarantee a position; she with
a growing belly. Where was she? A terrible premonition
took him. She would not have changed her mind; something had happened. He ran to her house – if her
father was there, it didn't matter. He was ready to
barge the door open, when he heard her feeble voice
calling him in. He would take her away now, and nobody
could stop them, certainly not that miserable bastard of
a father . . . He blinked in the gloom of the small house.
The first thing he saw was the outline of a woman standing by the fire – rags in her hands – scarlet on white . . .

'Peg?'

'Fancy seeing you here. You, of all people.' She couldn't
hide her contempt.

He thought his heart was going to explode. 'Sheona . . .'
he managed to say between gasps. The sight of the bloody
rags made him unsteady on his feet. *Sheona, my love.*

'You guessed. These are hers,' she said, lifting the rags
soaked with blood.

'What happened? Tell me what happened!'

'She was with child, but I suppose you knew that
already, didn't you, Alistair Gibson? Just as well Donald
was too drunk to notice why his daughter was so sick. He
thought it was his beating. He is still convinced Sheona is
pure. Pure! Like I didn't see her walking over to the loch
every night when her father was passed out from drink.
And to meet you, who else? Where were you when he
was *killing* her?'

He turned his back to the cruel woman and kneeled beside Sheona. 'My love . . .' he whispered. The baby was gone, but Sheona would be safe. She had to be . . . 'He beat you,' he spat.

'All is forgiven,' she murmured in a voice that was almost inaudible.

Forgiven? He could never forgive Donald for what he had done to his sweet, beautiful Sheona. He took her in his arms and cradled her, making soothing noises. She was alive; nothing else mattered. Their child was lost, but they'd been given another chance. He could still take her away – why had he waited so long? He'd been a fool.

'It's all fine, Sheona. All fine. We'll go, we'll . . .' His voice trailed away. She was looking at him – a long, long gaze that felt like hands hanging on to him, begging, *Don't let me go.* He saw the life ebbing from her eyes, and then his Sheona was gone.

Catherine

Glen Avich, 1916

They passed a group of girls playing, ignoring the drizzle
that fell on their hair and their shoulders – little Louisa
was among them, singing and skipping.

> Twa things I'll gie you, twa things an more
> Twa things awash upon the shore
> A gowden coin, a shining sun
> Twa spirits dance as one

'Lulu! Tell Mother I'll be home in an hour!' Fraser
called.

'Don't be late, Mum will be furious. Will you come
too, Cathy?'

Louisa adored Catherine, her brother's fiancée. She
loved the way Cathy curled her copper hair at the sides of
her face, the way she always kept up with the latest fashions even if she couldn't afford to shop in Aberdeen, like
Lady Ramsay did. She was a skilled dressmaker and her

creations could rival the pieces photographed in magazines. When she grew up, Louisa wanted to be exactly like Cathy. Some girls in the village said that her bright red hair was common, but Louisa thought it was beautiful.

'I can't, Lulu, I'm sorry,' Catherine said. 'I must go home, they're waiting for me. Later on, maybe.'

'But first, some kissing!' Louisa teased them, and her companions giggled.

'Be quiet, cheeky!' Fraser pretended to be angry, but he adored his wee sister. As far as Fraser was concerned, Louisa could get away with murder.

They walked on while Louisa and the other girls made kissing sounds and giggled some more. The day brightened up in that sudden, unpredictable way Scottish weather had – and Fraser and Cathy stole some time alone, away from everyone. And kiss they did, on a day so sunny, under a sky so blue, that it felt like nothing could go wrong.

They'd always known it, Fraser and Catherine. They'd always known they were made for each other. In fact, they'd decided they'd get married when they were five and sharing a potato scone on the way home from school. They would live in the house on the loch shore, the one a bit aside from the others, where Jim Isherwood stayed. They told each other so in a matter-of-fact way, as though no other plan could ever shape their lives.

Fifteen years on, here they were, holding hands and kissing on the grass. To Cathy, it was a day like any other. She didn't know he was about to shatter her dreams.

Without looking into her eyes, casually, as if it was just a momentary thing of not much importance, he said, 'Cathy, listen . . . I'm going to enlist. I'm going to fight in Europe.'

She was silent, mouth agape. Yes, there had been noises among his group of friends. John Blakeman, in particular. But she never thought . . . When she found her voice again, she struggled not to show her anger. 'Why, Fraser, why? It was John, wasn't it? He shamed you because he's going and . . . and . . .'

'Cathy. Cathy. Listen to me. John has nothing to do with it. I have to do this.'

'No you don't! It's their fight, not yours! Not ours!'

'That is not true. It's our fight too. We're fighting for freedom. For the common people all over Europe . . .'

'You're parroting other people's ideas. I don't care about people I've never met. I care about you, and your mum, and Louisa. And myself,' she added miserably. Slowly, slowly, the drizzle began again.

'It's the truth. Can you not feel it happening, Cathy? This is a battle of ideals. More than just nations facing each other. We need to be on the right side, on the side of justice, and maybe we can stop it . . .'

'Nothing of what you say makes sense to me. I just want you to stay,' she said, her voice calm, controlled. She wanted to cry, but she wouldn't, not in front of him. Not if it meant going home with red eyes and worrying her mum, who had enough troubles of her own, having been widowed the year before, and with two little ones,

Cathy's brothers, to bring up alone. Cathy felt her hands trembling, and then her whole body, like she was very cold all of a sudden. Dark thoughts began to make their way into her mind.

'I want you to have this,' he said, and took out a little velvet pouch from his jacket. Catherine opened it with fingers that were shaking so much he had to help her. Inside there was a golden coin, shiny like it had just been polished. A coin of gold like a shining sun – just like the song, Catherine thought through the veil of grief that seemed to shroud her. She was more frightened than she could tell him. It wouldn't be the first time she had had a feeling that turned out to be true. Her mother and her grandmother were like that too. And what she felt now was *grief* – the blackest, deepest grief imaginable.

'What is it?' she said in a small voice.

'I was given it when I was born. Keep it with you . . . for luck.'

At the station in Aberdeen, she held him tight, like she would never let him go – but soon she would have to. She would have to let him go far away to Europe, to a place where men mangled each other and ended up buried in the mud. She and Louisa and Fraser's mother kept waving slowly, slowly, until the train was out of sight.

Every day she hoped, every day she waited. She sewed dresses for the local women, helping her mum; she went to church and prayed until her knees were numb; she made her daily pilgrimage to the Pattersons', whose kitchen was the village post office. There she often met Fraser's mother, a lively woman by nature, whose life was being drained by the wait day by day, day by day. She often had Louisa with her – the girl seemed to have grown up all of a sudden, her eyes, once carefree, now shadowed with worry, their innocence lost.

When Fraser's mum and Cathy met, there was always something unspoken between them, something hidden – something that could never be admitted aloud. They missed Fraser, and oh, how much they loved him; but they were also *furious* with him, because he had left them to fight a fight they did not understand – that they understood with their minds only, but still thought absurd.

One afternoon, when the post had finally reached Glen Avich after its long, winding daily journey, Catherine set out to walk to the Pattersons'. There were two letters, one for Fraser's mother, one for her. The sender was not Fraser, but John, the friend who'd gone with him.

She didn't need to open the letter. The moment she touched it, she knew. And when she did open it, with shaking hands, the words she read told her she was right – black on white like spiders on a sheet, they told her Fraser was not coming back. At that moment, his mother and Louisa came in, and their eyes met. They saw Cathy's face, they saw the letter in her hands; they were full of disbelief and grief and despair, mouths mute and yet screaming. Fraser's mother's handbag fell to the floor, its contents scattered. And then she fell too, senseless, Louisa and Cathy kneeling beside her, the horror of it all filling the Pattersons' kitchen and the whole of the village. Fraser McCrimmon would not be coming back to Glen Avich.

They were meant to be together, Fraser and Cathy. They had always known. She had always known. And now she knew that destiny had played with them, it had driven them close then separated them again. She made a promise to his soul, whether it was in peace or restless and lost: nobody else would ever touch her again.

Libby

London, 1943

Kenneth cursed his leg. He cursed the sickness that had taken him at six years old and left him limping and weak. He cursed all that kept him from enlisting, and he cursed the men and women who muttered under their breath when they saw him – why was he not at war? Was he a coward, someone who sent other men to fight and die while he hid at home? Then they'd see his short, twisted leg and understand, but by then he was already burning with shame. He looked strong, with broad shoulders, and taller than most – at first sight, he seemed more than able. He died inside every time.

'Kenneth!' Libby waved to him, a smile on her face, running to him fresh and fragrant as she always was. This horrific war, the fear, the bombs, the sacrifices – little food, a lot of darkness, children gone from the city as if a pied piper had called them away – Libby seemed to glide through everything, keeping her love of life, her serenity intact. Kenneth still wondered what she saw in

346

him – how could such a beautiful, sunny woman have fallen for someone like him? A cripple? 'Don't be stupid,' she'd say. 'You make my heart fly.'

And she sang, she sang like a chaffinch. Every Friday at six, after the news, Libby had her own programme, where she sang and lifted the hearts of men and women all over the country. On Friday nights, Kenneth was with the Home Guard, in a makeshift station set up in a school, waiting to help when the bombs hit. They had a wireless and always listened to Libby's songs.

'How was your day?' She smiled, and held his hand as they walked. As always, he'd gone to collect her from her house and take her to the recording studio. The school where the Home Guard met was only a few hundred yards from there, and he preferred to be with her as night fell and the risk of bombing rose. And not just because of the bombs, but also because no lights were allowed, and walking through the black streets was very dangerous. Bombs had fallen there already, a whole building in pieces just across the road from the school, the rubble making a small artificial hill as a reminder of human folly.

'A blur.' He shrugged. 'I don't think I've slept in a week. I might start to see battalions of elephants making their way through London.'

'Working at the newspaper all day and Home Guard all night, it can't be easy.'

'It's fine. Easier than fighting at the front, for sure.'

'Stop it, Kenneth,' she said, and stood in front of him,

holding both his hands. Lovingly she stroked his cheek, and he knew what she was thinking – that he should stop berating himself for something that was not his fault.

'What's the plan for tonight's show, then?'

'A Scottish evening. To please Mum!' Libby's mother, Elizabeth McNeil, had left the island of Seal in the west of Scotland to marry a Londoner.

'It will please me too,' Kenneth said. He was Scots born, though he'd moved south with his parents when he was very young. 'After the war, we'll get married. And our honeymoon will be in Scotland.'

'I can't wait, my love,' she said.

Kenneth stroked her long red hair. She had chosen not to cut it in spite of the fashion, which wanted it short and curled at the sides. He loved her hair – it was the first thing he'd noticed about her, and the reason why he'd had the overwhelming feeling he'd met her before.

'Good luck with your Scottish evening,' he said, and kissed her on the cheek.

'That's all?' She laughed, and held his face in her hands. As she kissed him long and tenderly, for a moment the war disappeared, London disappeared, and they were alone together on a Scottish island, under a pewter sky.

'Oh, wait,' Kenneth said, and took out a crisp green apple from his pocket. 'Mrs Smythe gave it to me.'

'Thank you so much! Oh, how I'm going to enjoy this!' She contemplated the apple as though it was a gem. Fruit was so hard to get hold of in London these days.

With a smile, Libby turned and began to walk towards

the studio, and Kenneth watched her go – her pale yellow dress, the silky curtain of her hair, her cheerful step as she ran up the steps of the building. It was then that he noticed a tiny bunch of daisies growing out of the rubble. He took it as a good omen, and decided that it must be nature's way of telling them that the war would finish soon, that all the destruction would end. And he and Libby would be free to marry, free to live their lives.

That night, Kenneth sat beside the wireless, listening to Libby sing.

> Three things I'll gie ye, three things an more
> Three things awash upon the shore
> A spring-green apple, crisp and cold
> The taste o' a life as yet untold

'The voice of an angel,' an older man, Jack, said in a cockney accent.

'Not right in the head, to go with Ken!' another elderly man sitting beside Jack said without malice. They were both too old to enlist in the army, and the Home Guard allowed them to make their contribution. Kenneth joined in the laughter, then got up to put the kettle on, moving carefully by the feeble glow of the oil lamp, the windows covered to hide any light. They had a long night ahead of them and needed plenty of tea to keep them going.

Jack tapped his hand on the table, keeping the rhythm of the song. 'Is that her playing the piano?'

'Yes. She plays the violin too, you know . . .'

Kenneth's words were interrupted by the siren that announced imminent bombing – nothing new there, it happened nearly every night. But before they could even move, there was an ear-shattering noise, as if a hundred thundering clouds had gathered in the building. Debris fell over their heads – the bomb had been near. *Very* near. The two older men hurried towards the door – their job was to put themselves in danger on the streets of London, to try and guide as many people as possible to the shelters – but Kenneth hesitated.

The wireless.

Instead of Libby's sweet voice coming from the box, now there was only white noise. Maybe something had happened to the signal. Or maybe . . .

He ran as fast as his leg allowed him. Twice he fell, because of his leg and because of the unbroken darkness. The rumbles and thundering noises continued, and buildings collapsed around him, though he could only hear them and not see them. There was dust in his mouth, in his lungs, and the night was full of screams.

He stepped on what should have been grass, but now the little park was covered in rubble. The chaffinches are gone, he thought, confused. The eggs must be broken, the birds must be dead.

His heart sank. At that moment, he was sure of what he'd find; he was sure that there was no salvation.

He climbed on the rubble covering the park, the tops of the trees sticking out of pulverised bricks and planks and things he couldn't give a name to in the deep darkness – he thought he saw a foot; he thought he saw the top of someone's head. There it was, the place where the recording studio used to be – a mound of ruins.

Somewhere beneath it was Libby; and with her, his heart.

Mary Ann

Skye, 1971

What could be merrier than a wedding? Everyone was dancing, the little band was playing and the rafters of the Campbell house were roaring. Angus, the groom, had not stopped smiling for hours. His family and the bride's family were all tipsy and happy, and for one night oblivious to any strife and toil of daily life. Angus was a good man, and the bride, Mary Ann, a real catch; he could not believe his luck.

Mary Ann wanted to cry, but could not. The tears would show on her face, her eyes would redden, and everyone would get upset; she couldn't have that. Silent and unseen, she slipped outside into the windy night and sat on the stone wall, bringing her hand to her forehead. It was difficult to shake the feeling that she was falling into a deep well, falling into nothingness, instead of taking the first steps into a beautiful new life. Her long, bright auburn hair blew in the breeze.

I'm not in love with Angus McNeil. And I just married him.

To say it, even if just in her thoughts, felt good and terrible at the same time. To admit the truth was healthy; to contemplate the kiss of death on her life, the fact that she would never be allowed to love for real, was more than she could take. Angus was kind, and a hard worker, and handsome, with his fair hair and his honest blue eyes and his strong fisherman's hands. And he loved her. She was lucky.

But then there was Patrick.

Patrick, who'd come and gone from her life; Patrick, who'd had a life of his own; Patrick, who'd shown her love – and passion, though she blushed to remember – and then had drowned on his fishing boat. His family knew nothing about Mary Ann.

His wife knew nothing about her.

She'd never meant for it to happen, but when she'd seen him, she thought she'd known him for ever. 'I'll sort everything out, I promise,' he'd said. 'Please wait for me.' He'd given her a bluebell, and she kept it pressed in her diary.

Would he have kept his promise if he had not been taken by the sea? Mary Ann believed so, desperately. Sarah, her sister, was sure he would not have done. And that Mary Ann was indeed lucky to have Angus.

'Mary Ann!' A voice resounded from inside the house. Light and music came from the windows, while she was alone in the darkness.

She didn't trust herself to answer.

She allowed herself to remember the terrible dream

she'd had the night before. Terrible because it was too sweet, too precious. It made no sense to keep yearning, and it had to be forgotten at once, without delay – now. It awoke things that were lost and that she had to let go, and waking up like that, overflowing with love, to then get ready to marry another man was too heartbreaking for words. And yet she had to recall the dream, she had to recall those moments with Patrick, though they'd only happened in her imagination. Remembering them was painful, but terribly, terribly sweet. They were in the bluebell woods, like he'd promised, holding hands. His hair was golden and his eyes ice-clear – that striking colouring that made him stand out in a crowd. They walked in the sea of purple until they reached an old gnarled oak, then nestled among its roots . . .

Mary Ann felt her cheeks – they were hot, in spite of the cold air. She saw her breath come out in white puffs, in rhythm with her beating heart. Light and music behind her, the dark sea in front of her. And in between, a dream of love lost.

Just a dream. A dream that felt so real, so obvious – of course she and Patrick were together; they *had* to be. Patrick was not married, Patrick had not died at sea. They were man and wife, Patrick and Mary Ann, like it was always meant to be. A part of her was even surprised at having woken up, as if the wedding to Angus, the dancing tonight, the pale blue dress that her mother had sewn her were the dream, and walking through bluebell woods with Patrick was her real life. How tender, how raw her heart felt, and her mind, her body, her whole being; so sweet and hungry for kisses and touch, but from one man only. The dream was more real than reality.

She would never feel like that again. Never would she be so lost in love. Never would her heart be so full again. She was longing to close her eyes, to swim in the dream's warm waters . . .

'Darling?'

She jumped a little in the dark. Angus had come to sit beside her and wrap an arm around her shoulder. Without noticing, she leaned a little into him; he felt warm, and strong.

'Yes. Just getting some fresh air, sorry.'

'It's fine. It's all fine, Mary Ann. I'll make you happy,' he said softly, and it was more words than he, a silent man, would normally say.

Mary Ann took a deep breath. Yes, she thought, surprised, incredulous. She could be happy again.

'Thank you. Will you tell my mum that I'll just be ten minutes, time to cool down a bit?'

'Of course. Want me to stay with you?'

'What about our guests?'

Angus nodded, and stood up, his expression unreadable. He was a quiet man, but not a foolish one; he knew that Mary Ann's mind was somewhere else, though he had no idea of the whole story. He simply hoped that with time, and love, and babies coming, she would settle and love him like he loved her.

As she heard him open the door, for a brief moment

Mary Ann thought she would take his hand and let him lead her inside; she would leave the night and the roaring sea, and walk in among music and family and friends, the distant call of her lost love always with her, like a white pebble in her hand, but a whole life ahead of her to live.

But it was just a moment. No, she would not hold his hand, and no, she would not go back to her family.

But yes, she could be happy again.

She closed her eyes, and she could hear Patrick calling her name. Calling, calling her down the grit road and to the moonlit beach. She could still hear him calling as the waves closed over her head, as his ghostly hands held hers, as she went to be with him. *I will find you*, was her last conscious thought, while her lungs filled with water.

I will find you.

Author's Note

'If you're looking for tragedy, assorted deaths and lost loves, come to the Highlands and Islands; we have one at every corner,' Sorren says to Cora. And he's right: Scottish history is unique in being epic, tragic, heartbreaking and downright romantic. From the Picts to the Vikings to the Jacobites, every era has its heroes. I chose to set Margaret's story in the Jacobite period, when Charles Stuart, known as the Bonnie Prince, tried to regain the throne of Scotland for himself and the Stuarts. But he was doomed to fail. Let down by France and chased by the English armies, the Bonnie Prince lost Scotland. The battle of Culloden, on 16 April 1746, was a massacre; the clans were scattered and many were executed. Scotsmen were forbidden from wearing kilts and playing bagpipes. Today, Culloden is still commemorated as a tragic, terrible moment in Scottish history, where the last chance for independence and freedom was lost.

Although this novel is set against the backdrop of the Jacobite rising, its events only echo the main characters' story. What destroys Clan Innes in the end is not the English armies, but the enmity between clans and the inability to truly come together. The rivalry between the Inneses and the MacGregors is invented, as is the massacre of the Innes clan at the hands of their enemies. However, it has its roots in reality: the story that Innes recalls about the MacGregors killing members of the Clan Colquhoun and being outlawed is true. It's also true that the MacGregors were then known as Clann a'Cheo, children of the mist or children of the smoke – something that is portrayed beautifully in Babs MacGregor's Gaelic poem, 'Children of the Smoke'. The poem has been put into music within the Gaelic language and music project *Struileag*, and it was this song that made me want to use the MacGregors' story in a novel.

If you're looking for romance and adventure set against a Jacobite backdrop, look no further than Diana Gabaldon's wonderful Outlander series, which inspired my mention of the terrible Arbroath prison.

I hope you enjoyed travelling in eighteenth-century Scotland with me – I will be taking further journeys in Scottish history and I'm looking forward to my readers accompanying me there.

Daniela Sacerdoti

Acknowledgements

First and foremost, my gratitude goes to Ross Walker for his beautiful poem at the front of this book, the song-thread that keeps the book together.

My heartfelt thanks go to the following heavenly people: Ariella Feiner, Sherise Hobbs, the team at Headline and United Agents, especially Emily, Becky and Jamie. Thank you to my mum (a classic!) and my sweet girl-friends Romina, Francesca, Irene and Gabriela. Thank you Cinzia Tarditi, accordion player, who helped our family bloom and gave us so much joy with her gift of music. Thank you to Babs MacGregor for the poem 'Children of the smoke'. And always and forever, thank you Ross, Sorley and Luca, for everything.

Read on for an exchanting extract from the
next Seal novel . . .

Come Back to Me

Coming soon from Headline Review

Grace

October wrapped itself around me like a blanket, and I loved every moment of it. Darkness falling earlier and earlier after the long summer nights, the turning leaves and their symphony of reds, yellows and browns, the chill in the air, the sweet wind and rain and mist and how they softened the island, how they made it look like a dream risen out of the sea – autumn was truly my season.

I was in a good mood. The surgery had been full earlier on, but I was nearly finished, as long as nothing else cropped up. I entertained the hope of being able to work on the music Rosalind and I were arranging for the Christmas concert. The sheets were folded in my bag, reminding me how much I wanted this concert to be perfect . . . no, not perfect: happy. I wanted it to be a moment for us islanders to be together in joy, to celebrate our community. Yes, it was only the beginning of October and there was plenty of time for rehearsals, but believe me, with the kind of singers we had – me included – we needed all the practice we could get. Apart from Rosalind, of course, whose truly magical voice kept everything together.

I opened my door and peeked out.

'Who's next? Oh, hello, Kenny. Come in. How can I help you?'

Kenny McFadyen, a sheep farmer who owned a small flock in the southern part of the island, was – how to put this – an old-fashioned man. He could have gone on the cover of *Shepherd* magazine, if such a thing existed. He had it all: the woollen hat, the thick jumper, the ruddy complexion and the big calloused hands. In the ten years I'd been on the island, he'd been to the surgery only once, and that was because he'd broken his arm after falling while repairing a stone wall. Even then, he was so reluctant to see a doctor, it had taken him two weeks before he'd decided to come. Two weeks with a broken arm, medicating with whisky.

'I have a terrible pain in my foot.'

'Okay. Take your shoe and sock off and I'll have a look.' Kenny took off a heavy boot and a sock that had seen better times and I examined his foot. 'Right. It seems fine to me, no broken bones, I don't think. Only a bit red.'

I wondered if maybe it could be his joints acting up, after so many years outside in the damp fields and a house where the only source of heating was a peat fire, but I wanted to make sure. 'Can you show me your other foot? I want to compare, to see if this is one swollen.'

'My other foot?' Kenny looked panicked.

'Yes. You have two, don't you?' I smiled. We'd known each other for a long time, and I knew he wouldn't feel demeaned by my little joke.

'I can't show you my other foot.'

'Why not?'

'It's this one that hurts.'

'Yes, I understand, but I need to see the other one to decide if the one that hurts is actually swollen. Don't worry, it's nothing bad; I think it might be rheumatism or a bit of arthritis. I can give you some anti-inflammatories to get the edge off the pain, and—'

'I can't, Doctor,' Kenny interrupted me. 'I can't.' He spoke in a *that's it, no more discussion* kind of voice and began slipping his sock back on, avoiding my eye.

I couldn't let this go. 'But why? It won't take a second . . .'

'Because I only washed *this* foot! The sore one. I haven't washed this one . . .' he pointed to his shod foot, 'in a … while now. A long while.' He was bright red.

'It doesn't matter, really . . .' I began, but he was already making for the door, hopping with his shoe in his hand like the devil was at his heels – which it probably was, given his allergy to washing them. I ran after him, trying not to laugh.

'Kenny! Come back! I don't mind, honestly.'

Three pairs of eyes – Lorna, our receptionist, Mrs Gibson and Mrs Taggart – followed Kenny as he leapt through the tiny waiting room and outside, and then turned to me as I gave up the chase, my hair in disarray. 'Everything okay, Doctor?' Mrs Gibson said cheerfully. Lorna and I called Mrs Gibson and Mrs Taggart 'G and T'; they came to see me at least once a week, not because there was anything wrong with them usually, just as a recreational activity.

'Everything is fine,' I said with a sigh.

'He's always been allergic to soap, that one,' Mrs Taggart said.

My jaw dropped and my eyes met Lorna's. Yes, we all knew that the wall between my room and the waiting area was so thin that any ailment discussed was everybody's business; not to mention the way our tiny chemist shared premises with the Spar, so you could buy bread and milk while standing side by side with Nuala Hutchison discussing her psoriasis and Malcolm Laird describing the terrible things that eating cheese did to him. But everybody pretended they didn't know, to keep up appearances.

'If he had a bath, there'd be nothing left of him!' said Mrs Gibson, and the pair of them cackled like the witches in *Macbeth*, their knitted berets bobbing in unison.

'Now, now,' Lorna reproached them gently. Lorna was like a human tea cosy, in both looks and personality. She wore her blonde hair in a bun on top of her head and clad herself in pastel-coloured cardigans and woollen skirts. She was the island's soft-spoken, understanding mother. She worried for everyone, including me – fretting over my skipped meals and home visits in the middle of the night. She also helped me with the house a couple of times a week, and with all those errands I struggled to do because of my time-consuming job.

Being a doctor on Seal wasn't like being a doctor in Edinburgh. Now I lived and practised in a place where everyone knew me and I knew everyone, where I got to treat three generations of the same family. I knew who was going out with whom; who was getting drunk in the pub every night and who was doing it secretly at home; who took the ferry to Oban to see someone they weren't supposed to see; who'd started taking the pill though her parents knew nothing about it; who was trying for a baby and who had just conceived; who came to the surgery every week for a chat just to know they were not alone; who was forgetting things a bit too often and was too scared to tell their offspring in case they forced them to move off the island to somewhere they could be looked after; who'd just been given terribly bad news and his family had no idea, and so you met them at the Saturday-night ceilidh and had to smile, pretending you didn't know that their husband and father and grandfather would be gone soon. And then there were the surprises, like when you delivered a baby at home, a little boy who'd decided to come too soon; and then marvelled all over again when the same baby turned into the toddler who launched into *Ba ba back ship, have you any woo* in church, while everyone else was intoning 'Abide with Me'.

I was a newcomer, and yet I was embedded in this community. My predecessor was an American doctor who had lasted only a couple of years, and before her the legendary Dr Innes, whose shoes were incredibly hard to fill – and now here I was, Grace Chatto from Edinburgh, unmarried, no children, choosing to live somewhere remote instead of Roan or Ollaberry, the only two villages on the island. Alone in a cottage in the middle of nowhere.

When I'd first arrived, some were unconvinced,

especially after the infamous Dr Green from Arizona, who had declared that if she had to spend another winter on this island she would jump off a cliff. People were dismayed, as she told all and sundry how much she hated the island and how she could not leave fast enough, and then went away without looking back, carrying with her all the history the community had entrusted to her, as if it didn't matter. I'd never forget our first and only meeting, where she warned me how I would get depressed here for sure; that she'd come looking for wilderness and a life close to nature, and all she'd found were barren hills and black mornings and endless rain. I nearly felt sorry for her. And I admit I did feel a hint of apprehension at the decision I'd made, as it had been so sudden, and not well received by my family. But I was going to make it work. I was going to do right by the people I'd come to look after.

Yet even after the trauma of Dr Green, most people welcomed me with open arms and a lot of useful advice, such as to keep candles and matches in at all times; no, you won't be able to get everywhere by bike; and whatever you do, don't get too close to the edge of the beautiful cliffs behind your home, because bits of them drop into the sea of their own accord. This last being the most useful tip I ever received, because only this month past a small piece of the island had fallen off, and we'd ended up on the national news.

I'd been very happy in Edinburgh. I had my work, I had my family – especially my two beloved nephews. But here on this island I had discovered a new way of life and a new me – no, not a new me: a *freer* me. Seal suited me like a made-to-measure dress – the hills weren't barren to me, they were a symphony of earthy colours; the weather fronts coming in from the Atlantic invigorated me; and the small appointments of island life – the choir, the ceilidhs, the community garden, the travelling library, the fund-raisers for the school and for the Sea Rescue, the yearly celebration of the Blessing of the Boats – were the punctuation of my weeks, my months, my years, setting the rhythm to my existence.

And then there was Fergus, my neighbour.

My friend, my best friend.

More than a friend, really.

Fergus, who'd disappeared almost completely in the last month or so, apart from a few harried texts . . .

Keep in touch with me

Daniela
SACERDOTI

Sign up for my newsletter
www.danielasacerdoti.com

Become a fan on Facebook
f OfficialDanielaSacerdoti

Follow me on Twitter
🐦 DaniSacerdoti

Con amore,
Daniela x

'Will satisfy even the most hopeless romantics. Her descriptions of the idyllic, wild isle are evocative and vivid'
Daily Express

'I was hooked from the beginning'
Alice Peterson

'The supernatural element gives The novel its edge'
Sunday Express S magazine

'I fell in love with this book'
Prima magazine

'Heartwarming and intriguing'
Dani Atkins